THE ROUTLEDGE COMPANION TO ANIMAL–HUMAN HISTORY

The Routledge Companion to Animal–Human History provides an up-to-date guide for the historian working within the growing field of animal–human history. Giving a sense of the diversity and interdisciplinary nature of the field, cutting-edge contributions explore the practices of and challenges posed by historical studies of animals and animal–human relationships.

Divided into three parts, the *Companion* takes both a theoretical and practical approach to a field that is emerging as a prominent area of study. Animals and the Practice of History considers established practices of history, such as political history, public history and cultural memory, and how animal–human history can contribute to them. Problems and Paradigms identifies key historiographical issues to the field with contributors considering the challenges posed by topics such as agency, literature, art and emotional attachment. The final section, Themes and Provocations, looks at larger themes within the history of animal–human relationships in more depth, with contributions covering topics that include breeding, war, hunting and eating.

As it is increasingly recognised that nonhuman actors have contributed to the making of history, *The Routledge Companion to Animal–Human History* provides a timely and important contribution to the scholarship on animal–human history and surrounding debates.

Hilda Kean was Dean of Ruskin College, Oxford. Her many books include *The Great Cat and Dog Massacre: The Real Story of World War II's Unknown Tragedy* (2017); *Animal Rights: Political and Social Change in Britain since 1800* (1998); *The Public History Reader* (with Paul Martin, 2013).

Philip Howell is Reader in Historical Geography in the Department of Geography at the University of Cambridge. He is the author of *Geographies of Regulation: Policing Prostitution in Nineteenth-Century Britain and the Empire* (2009) and *At Home and Astray: The Domestic Dog in Victorian Britain* (2015).

THE ROUTLEDGE COMPANION TO ANIMAL–HUMAN HISTORY

Edited by Hilda Kean and Philip Howell

LONDON AND NEW YORK

First published 2019
by Routledge
2 Park Square, Milton Park, Abingdon, Oxon OX14 4RN

and by Routledge
605 Third Avenue, New York, NY 10017

First issued in paperback 2020

Routledge is an imprint of the Taylor & Francis Group, an informa business

© 2018 selection and editorial matter, Hilda Kean and Philip Howell; individual chapters, the contributors

The right of Hilda Kean and Philip Howell to be identified as the authors of the editorial material, and of the authors for their individual chapters, has been asserted in accordance with sections 77 and 78 of the Copyright, Designs and Patents Act 1988.

All rights reserved. No part of this book may be reprinted or reproduced or utilised in any form or by any electronic, mechanical, or other means, now known or hereafter invented, including photocopying and recording, or in any information storage or retrieval system, without permission in writing from the publishers.

Trademark notice: Product or corporate names may be trademarks or registered trademarks, and are used only for identification and explanation without intent to infringe.

British Library Cataloguing-in-Publication Data
A catalogue record for this book is available from the British Library

Library of Congress Cataloging-in-Publication Data
Names: Kean, Hilda, editor. | Howell, Philip, 1965- editor.
Title: The Routledge companion to animal-human history/edited by Hilda Kean and Philip Howell.
Other titles: Companion to animal-human history
Description: Milton Park, Abingdon, Oxon; New York, NY: Routledge, 2018. | Includes bibliographical references.
Identifiers: LCCN 2018009449 | Subjects: LCSH: Human-animal relationships–History. | Animals–History.
Classification: LCC QL85.R67 2018 | DDC 590–dc23
LC record available at https://lccn.loc.gov/2018009449

ISBN 13: 978-0-367-73365-0 (pbk)
ISBN 13: 978-1-138-19326-0 (hbk)

Typeset in Bembo
by Sunrise Setting Ltd, Brixham, UK

CONTENTS

List of figures   viii
List of contributors   x
Acknowledgements   xiii

Introduction   1

1 Writing in animals in history   3
   Philip Howell and Hilda Kean

PART I
Animals and the practice of history   29

2 The other citizens: nationalism and animals   31
   Sandra Swart

3 New political history and the writing of animal lives   53
   Mieke Roscher

4 Public history and heritage: a fruitful approach for privileging animals?   76
   Hilda Kean

5 Wildlife conservation as cultural memory   100
   Jan-Erik Steinkrüger

6 The experimental animal: in search of a moral ecology of science?   121
   Robert G.W. Kirk

7	Animals in the history of human and veterinary medicine *Abigail Woods*	147
8	Animal matter in museums: exemplifying materiality *Liv Emma Thorsen*	171

PART II
Problems and paradigms   195

9	Animals, agency, and history *Philip Howell*	197
10	Representing animals in the literature of Victorian Britain *Jennifer McDonell*	222
11	'And has not art promoted our work also?' Visual culture in animal–human history *J. Keri Cronin*	251
12	When Adam and Eve were monkeys: anthropomorphism, zoomorphism, and other ways of looking at animals *Boria Sax*	273
13	Exhibiting animals: zoos, menageries and circuses *Helen Cowie*	298
14	Topologies of tenderness and violence: human–animal relations in Georgian England *Carl Griffin*	322
15	The history of emotional attachment to animals *Ingrid H. Tague*	345
16	Surviving twentieth-century modernity: birdsong and emotions in Britain *Michael Guida*	367

PART III
Themes and provocations   391

17	Breeding and breed *Neil Pemberton, Julie-Marie Strange and Michael Worboys*	393

18 Animals in and at war   422
    Gervase Phillips

19 Hunting and animal–human history   446
    Philip Howell

20 Eating animals   474
    Chris Otter

21 Animals and violence: medieval humanism,
    'medieval brutality', and the carnivorous
    vegetarianism of Margery Kempe   499
    Karl Steel

Conclusions   **519**

22 The triumph of animal history?   521
    Philip Howell

    Epilogue   543
    Harriet Ritvo

Index   545

FIGURES

2.1	Bumper sticker, Kimberley, South Africa, January 2014	43
4.1	Steven Mark Holland, *Memorial to Animals in War*, Sculpture Garden, Australian War Memorial, Canberra, Australia, unveiled 2009	81
4.2	Pikeman's Dog Memorial, created by Charles Smith and Joan Walsh-Smith, located on the site of the Museum of Australian Democracy at Eureka in Ballarat, December 2014	86
4.3	Harrie Fasher, *Silent Conversation*, 2014, from *Spirited: Australia's Horse Story*, National Museum Australia, Canberra, exhibition 11 September 2014 to 9 March 2015	90
10.1	Queen Victoria and Sharp, Balmoral Castle, 1866	223
10.2	Jumbo and his keeper Matthew Scott. Barnum poster, c. 1882	224
11.1	Edwin Landseer, *A Distinguished Member of the Humane Society*, exhibited at the Royal Academy Exhibition of 1838	257
11.2	Leonard Nightingale, *Welcome Morsels*, exhibited at the Royal Academy Exhibition of 1887	261
11.3	E. Gilbert Hester after Edmund Caldwell, print of *For the Safety of the Public* (original painting exhibited at the Royal Academy Exhibition of 1887)	264
11.4	J.A. Shepherd, *A Member of the Royal Humane Society*, published in *Moonshine*, 17 August 1889	266
12.1	Ota Benga at the Bronx Zoo, 1906	274
12.2	Postcard showing two pictures of Baldy in his zookeeper uniform, sold by the New York Zoological Park	275
12.3	From the Bible initially published by Antoine Verard, 1510 edition	281
12.4	Erhard Aldorfer, illustration showing Adam and Eve, from the Matthew Bible, first published in 1537	282
12.5	Jan Brueghel the Younger, 'Terrestrial Paradise', c.1620	283

12.6	'The ballot box of the future', cartoon from *The Day's Doings*, a newspaper published in London and sold in the United States, 1870	287
12.7	Illustration to Captain Cook's *Voyages*, 1785	289
12.8	Howler monkeys in the role of Adam and Eve. Illustration to *Geographical Distribution of Animals* by Adam White, 1867	289
13.1	Robertson's Royal Menagerie, 9 The Strand, c.1820	301
13.2	Keeper Sam Morton weighs the young Pipaluk, from *Pipaluk, 'The Little One'*, Amsterdam: Lutterworth Press, 1968	303
13.3	An anteater paces on an unsuitable concrete surface, Audubon Zoo, New Orleans, 1952. *The Times Picayune* 1 October 1952. Photographer O.J. Valeton	307
13.4	'Attempt to remove Jumbo, the great elephant, from the Zoological Gardens', *Illustrated London News*, 25 February 1882, 200	310
13.5	'A tame ocelot', W.S. Berridge, 'The wooing of the wild', *The Animal World* Volume II (New Series), January 1907, 230–232	314
14.1	William Holman Hunt, 'Our English Coasts' ('Strayed Sheep'), 1852, Tate Gallery, London	323
14.2	George Stubbs, 'Hambletonian, Rubbing Down', 1799–1800, Mount Stewart Collection, County Down	329
17.1	Principal points of the dog	404
17.2	Fancy poultry	407
17.3	'The bull-dog'. From W. Youatt, *The Dog*, London: Society for the Diffusion of Useful Knowledge, 1845, 151	410
17.4	'"Top", a pure bulldog'. From Stonehenge [John Henry Walsh], *The Dog*, third edition, London: Longmans, Green, 1879	410
17.5	Captain Holdsworth's Sir Anthony, bulldog	411

CONTRIBUTORS

Helen Cowie is Senior Lecturer in History at the University of York, UK. Her research focuses on the history of animals and the history of natural history. She is author of *Conquering Nature in Spain and its Empire, 1750–1850* (Manchester University Press, 2011), and *Exhibiting Animals in Nineteenth-Century Britain: Empathy, Education, Entertainment* (Palgrave Macmillan, 2014) and *Llama* (Reaktion Books 2017).

J. Keri Cronin is Associate Professor in the Department of Visual Arts at Brock University, Canada, a founding member of the Social Justice Research Institute at Brock, and a fellow of the Oxford Centre for Animal Ethics. Her most recent book, *Art for Animals* (Penn State Press, 2018), explores the central role that art played in late nineteenth- and early twentieth-century animal advocacy campaigns.

Carl Griffin is Reader in Historical Geography at the University of Sussex, UK. Carl is the author of *The Rural War: Captain Swing and the Politics of Protest* (Manchester University Press, 2012) and *Protest, Politics and Work in Rural England, 1700–1850* (Palgrave, 2014). He also co-edits *Rural History* for Cambridge University Press.

Michael Guida is a cultural historian with a particular interest in the place of nature in industrial modernity in Britain. He has a PhD in Media & Cultural Studies from the University of Sussex, UK, where he is a Research Associate and Tutor.

Philip Howell is Reader in Historical Geography in the Department of Geography, University of Cambridge, UK. He is the author of *Geographies of Regulation: Policing Prostitution in Nineteenth-Century Britain and the Empire* (Cambridge University Press, 2009) and *At Home and Astray: The Domestic Dog in Victorian Britain* (University of Virginia Press, 2015).

Hilda Kean was former Dean of Ruskin College, Oxford, UK, and is honorary senior researcher at UCL. Her many books include *Animal Rights* (Reaktion, 1998), *The Public History Reader* (with Paul Martin, Routledge, 2013), and *The Great Cat and Dog Massacre* (University of Chicago Press, 2018).

Contributors

Robert G.W. Kirk is Reader in Medical History and Humanities, Centre for the History of Science, Technology and Medicine (CHSTM) at the University of Manchester, UK. His work examines nonhuman animals in human cultures, particularly nonhuman roles in science, medicine and technology, as well as the place of animals in history and historical writing.

Jennifer McDonell is a Senior Lecturer in English in literature at the University of New England, Australia. She has published on animals in the works of Charles Dickens and Elizabeth Barrett Browning, and on Robert Browning and material culture. Her article 'The animal turn, literary studies, and the academy' is reprinted in Blackwell's *Literary Theory: An Anthology*, 3rd edition (2017).

Chris Otter is Associate Professor of History at Ohio State University, USA. He is the author of *The Victorian Eye: A Political History of Light and Vision in Britain, 1800–1910* (University of Chicago Press, 2008) and is completing a book on food systems and nutritional transition in Britain from 1750 to today.

Neil Pemberton is a Research Fellow in the Centre for the History of Science, Technology and Medicine and Wellcome Unit for the History of Medicine at the University of Manchester, UK. He is the co-author, with Michael Worboys, of *Mad Dogs and Englishmen: Rabies in Britain, 1830–2000* (Palgrave Macmillan, 2007), *Rabies in Britain: Dogs, Disease and Culture, 1830–2000* (Palgrave, 2012), and, with Julie-Marie Strange and Michael Worboys, *The Invention of the Modern Dog: Breed and Blood in Victorian Britain* (Johns Hopkins University Press, 2018).

Gervase Phillips is Principal Lecturer in history in the Department of History, Politics & Philosophy at Manchester Metropolitan University, UK. He is the author of *The Anglo-Scots Wars, 1513–1550* (Boydell, 1999) and numerous articles for academic journals including *The Journal of Military History*, *War & Society*, *The Journal of Historical Sociology* and *The Journal of Interdisciplinary History*.

Harriet Ritvo is the Arthur J. Conner Professor of History at the Massachusetts Institute of Technology, USA. Her books include *The Animal Estate* (Harvard University Press, 1987), *The Platypus and the Mermaid* (Harvard University Press, 1997), *The Dawn of Green* (University of Chicago Press, 2009), and *Noble Cows and Hybrid Zebras* (University of Virginia Press, 2010).

Mieke Roscher is Assistant Professor for Cultural and Social History and the History of Human–Animal Relations at the University of Kassel, Germany. She is author of *Ein Königreich für Tiere: Die Geschichte der britischen Tierrechtsbewegung* (Tectum, 2009).

Boria Sax is the author of many books, including most recently *Lizard* (Reaktion Books, 2017) and *Imaginary Animals: The Monstrous, the Wondrous, and the Human* (Reaktion Books, 2013). He is currently finishing up a cultural history of dinosaurs. He teaches at Sing Sing prison and in the graduate literature program of Mercy College, USA.

Karl Steel is Associate Professor of English literature at Brooklyn College and the Graduate Center, City University of New York, USA. He has published primarily on medieval animals, ecocriticism, and posthumanism, with his first book, *How to Make a Human: Animals and Violence in the Middle Ages* (Ohio State University Press, 2011), concentrating on systematic medieval thought on animals, and his forthcoming book, *Medieval Nonhumanisms: Sympathy, Edibility, and Vulnerability* (University of Minnesota Press, 2019), treating a variety of non-systematised cultural practices.

Jan-Erik Steinkrüger is Postdoctoral Research Assistant at the Department of Geography of the University of Bonn, Germany, and was visiting professor at the University of Graz, Austria, in 2016/2017. He has been working in the fields of historical and cultural geography, leisure and tourism geography, and animal geography.

Julie-Marie Strange is Professor of British History at the University of Manchester, UK. Her books include *Fatherhood and the British Working Class, 1865–1914* (Cambridge University Press, 2015), *Death, Grief and Poverty in Britain, 1870–1914* (Cambridge University Press, 2006) and, with Neil Pemberton and Michael Worboys, *The Invention of the Modern Dog: Breed and Blood in Victorian Britain* (Johns Hopkins University Press, 2018).

Sandra Swart is Professor in the History Department, Stellenbosch University, South Africa. She received her DPhil in Modern History and simultaneously an MSc in Environmental Change and Management, both from Oxford University (2001), UK. She researches the shifting relationship between humans and animals and is the author of *Riding High: Horses, Humans and History in South Africa* (Witwatersrand University Press, 2010).

Ingrid H. Tague is Professor of History and Associate Dean of Arts, Humanities, and Social Sciences at the University of Denver, USA. She is the author of *Women of Quality: Accepting and Contesting Ideals of Femininity in England, 1690–1760* (Boydell Press, 2002) and *Animal Companions: Pets and Social Change in Eighteenth-Century Britain* (Pennsylvania State University Press, 2015).

Liv Emma Thorsen is Professor Emerita in the Department of Cultural History, University of Oslo, Norway. She is the author of *Hund! Fornuft og følelser* (Pax Forlag, 2001) and *Elephants are not Picked from Trees: Animal Biographies in Gothenburg Natural History Museum* (Aarhus University Press, 2014).

Abigail Woods is a qualified veterinary surgeon and Professor of the History of Human and Animal Health at King's College London, UK. She is the lead author of *One Health and its Histories: Animals and the Shaping of Modern Medicine* (Palgrave, 2017).

Michael Worboys is Emeritus Professor in the History of Science, Technology and Medicine in the Centre for the History of Science, Technology and Medicine at the University of Manchester, UK. He is the co-author, with Neil Pemberton, of *Rabies in Britain: Dogs, Disease and Culture, 1830–2000* (Palgrave, 2012) and, with Neil Pemberton and Julie-Marie Strange, *The Invention of the Modern Dog: Breed and Blood in Victorian Britain* (Johns Hopkins University Press, 2018).

ACKNOWLEDGEMENTS

We are extremely grateful to our excellent editorial team at Routledge during the development of this project: Eve Setch, Amy Welmers, and Zoe Thomson. Hilda Kean would also like to thank Russell Burrows and Philip Howell for their support. Philip Howell would similarly like to thank Elizabeth Mozzillo and Hilda Kean, and to acknowledge Garry Marvin for his invaluable advice in writing Chapter 19.

Introduction

1
WRITING IN ANIMALS IN HISTORY

Philip Howell and Hilda Kean

Introduction

This *Routledge Companion* adds to the emerging literature on animal–human history, and aims to be a guide and resource for current and prospective historians. One of its distinctive aims is that of approaching both visual *and* written histories of animals and animal–human relations, to re-present and underscore the role of nonhuman animals as historical actors. Our argument is illustrated on the cover of this book. The image of the traces of an elephant's passing is taken from the work of the leading animal artist Nick Brandt. The relationship between humans and animals is a central part of Brandt's photographic work, rightly identified by Peter Singer as an essay in environmental ethics.[1] Brandt has written that for between ten and twenty years he has driven through countless areas where there had once been abundant animal life, life which 'now has been relentlessly wiped up'.[2] His response has been not only to create new photographic presences but also to contribute to our understanding of *their* place in *our* world. As he comments, 'I took the pictures of the animals in these books in an attempt to capture them as sentient creatures not so different from us. I have sought to photograph them not in action, but simply in a state of *being*'.[3]

He has portrayed the visual impression of animals because 'I wanted to show these animals as individual spirits, sentient creatures equally as worthy as life as us'.[4]

Brandt's discussion of his personal experiences is reflected in several accounts that tend to draw upon both artistic and historical perspectives on animals.[5] Steve Baker has recently concluded that 'The look of the animal, the visual representation of the animal, still matters, still figures, and it's the thing that art ... can handle most persuasively'.[6] This is not just a contemporary project: it is strikingly obvious that written works can be analysed with due regard to the relationship between animals and artists as they have existed in the past. As Diana Donald notes in her perceptive work:

> Landseer's concept of nature was wholly antithetical to that of earlier sporting painters, with their paradisal, verdant landscapes: his concept suggested an

overwhelming pessimism, a loss of belief in the benign governance of the universe. Man, like his animal victims, was condemned to a harsh struggle for survival, and perhaps to a lonely end.[7]

This focus on animal–human relationships in recent approaches to animals in the visual field forms a certain contrast with previous, explicitly *historical* discussions of animals that do not focus on photographic or print material. Often cited is the influential account provided by Keith Thomas, whose magisterial *Man and the Natural World* is tellingly described by the author as a 'mixture of compromise and concealment'.[8] In his introduction Thomas referred to a 'devotion to rural pursuits ... characteristic of the English upper classes', 'common to many members of the first industrial nation' and a more recent 'profoundly anti-urban bias'.[9] Thomas recognises that 'the animal and vegetable world has, after all, been a basic precondition of human history'.[10] Just as significantly, Thomas argued that the subject had much to offer historians but also that 'it is impossible to disentangle what the people of the past thought about plants and animals from what they thought about themselves'.[11] Here we are presented in many ways with an account of a past era of history, now long gone. This strikes out rather differently to the explicit imagery of elephants in Brandt's encounter with the recent past. These animals are currently, as Brandt writes, engaged in 'being', as 'sentient creatures'. We can still *see* them, if we look hard enough. Now it is true that Thomas's pioneering book did draw upon prints of animals (the publisher Allen Lane sourced thirty historic images), but their analysis was minimal compared to the attention given to the written word. To some extent this reflects the historian's method. In a reflective mood in the *London Review of Books*, Thomas has admitted that 'My notes are voluminous because my interests have never been very narrowly focused'.[12] For all that Thomas contributed to the emergence of animal–human history, enlarging the scope of historical concern, this concern with *writing* limits our ability to make animals visible. Thomas accepts that 'diverse topics ... can't be investigated in a single archive or repository of information. Progress depends on building up a picture from a mass of casual and unpredictable references accumulated over a long period'.[13] Despite this, like subsequent historians, Thomas tended overwhelmingly to rely on literary sources and archives, with the result that the animals' presence is often virtual.[14]

This is not the only way forward. As many of the contributions in this volume suggest, there is an explicit relationship between the *physical* presences of cultural animals and the function of historical or heritage works. Take for example, in fairly conventional terms, the recent Berlin-based project of artists and historical commentators articulated in the project entitled *Animal Lovers*, explicitly embarking on a search for emancipated human–animal relationships.[15] From 2010–2011 the Berlin artist Anselmo Fox reimagined the 1873 Victory Column located at the Großer Stern (Great Star) central square in Berlin's Tiergarten by showing bees flying in and out of the damaged parts of the bronze sculpture of Victory herself, revealing the monument as a flawed allegory for war, destruction and nationalistic delusion, but showing as it does so that the animals follow the line and path of a way of seeing despite the obstacle in front of them, penetrating it and revealing its fragility.[16]

Part of the point here is to ask the question to what extent animals are involved as agents in social processes, and to explore the relationship between artistic practice and quasi-historical features. Such an approach has been common to the work of a number of writers today in explaining the specific impact of animals in existing countries. Accounts in this book relate both to the existing presence of current *and* historical animals as well as to the conventional historical analysis of written descriptions. We do not have to choose between them. As we note subsequently, several contributors refer to past and present archival material but at the same time have acknowledged the role of animals themselves in making an animal- and human-history. So we accept the mixture of 'compromise and concealment' but we also construct an explicit exposition of the way in which the 'sentience' of creatures becomes part of an historical method.

The nature of animal–human history

This may be jumping too far ahead for those who cannot find any meaning in the juxtaposition of 'animal' and 'history'. We do not have to look very far, or very far back, even in academia, to find statements as categorical as this, from David and Ann James Premack: 'While a vast number of histories have been written about human beings, one could not write a history of the chimpanzee, nor of any other animal'.[17] Outside of the charmed circle of academia, we can quite easily be reassured that while all animals have an evolutionary past, 'Only humans make history'.[18] Challenging these ideas is never easy, as it depends of course on what we mean by 'history'. The Premacks defined history as 'a sequence of changes through which a species passes while remaining biologically stable'; and since for them 'animals have not undergone significant change while remaining biologically stable', ergo they can have no history as such.[19] This still leaves plenty of room ('perhaps', say the more cautious Premacks) for writing about the history of humans' attitudes to animals, and their treatment of animals – and indeed historians have long since accepted that a history of relationships with the natural world, with the 'environment', and even with a range of nonhuman animals is not only possible but valuable too. There is no real difficulty conceding this point, even if we up the ante to claim that history requires a consciousness of history, and a means of transmitting this on to future generations of a species. This is the familiar idea that 'Man is an historical animal, with a deep sense of his own past'.[20] But Dorothee Brantz observes that 'even if animals live without a sense of the past, is it logical to conclude that they have played no role in the development of human societies?'[21] We would in fact have to search hard for historians who believe that 'only humans make history' in the most restrictive sense – the conceit that other animals do not participate in human history at all – even if 'Too often such animals become written out of the actual processes of history'.[22] Questions of consciousness are for many a bridge too far – taking us into philosophical debates and ethological theories for which historians have no great claim to expertise. But even here, the most categorical statements may be given some nuance. Mahesh Rangajaran, for instance, in a recent discussion of lions in the Gujarat from ancient times to modern, suggests that changing relationships with people reflect not just human practices or beliefs or representations of animals, but something like the 'culture' and the 'memory' of those lions themselves; and while he is tentative on the question of historical consciousness, this need not debar nonhuman animals, as animals, from what we conventionally recognise as history:

> It is surely going too far to endow lions with a sense of history such as humans have or historians imagine, a sense in which the past is re-imagined in multiple, contested ways to debate how the present came to be. Nevertheless, there is a complex tapestry of human–animal relations, and within that, the idea that animals too evolve, not only in simple biological terms but also in terms of patterns of behavior, deserves consideration.[23]

This focus on relationships, and on milieu, is something that animal–human historians have been particularly strong in promoting – even if there are special problems of access and interpretation to be considered. Here, we may remark that an aversion to 'animal history' seems particularly absurd if we consult our cousins in archaeology and anthropology, for whom the idea that people are entangled with animals, and with their environments and all sorts of 'things' is hardly news.[24] History presents specific problems, for sure, which go beyond the discipline's traditional reliance on written sources, or the difficulties in terms of access to archives that are often not part of the public domain of historical memory, and which are often guarded by institutions wary of criticism, scholarly or otherwise.[25] Nor is it only because archives and other records are themselves anthropocentric artefacts ('The current paucity of traces for the hunter-historian to follow is neither accidental nor innocent. It is a product of the history we want to tell').[26] Beyond these issues lies the way in which human history and culture is seen as somehow separate from the natural world. Again, at the very least we need to unsettle the antithesis between nature and culture that animates so much modern, Western thinking, our understanding of history included. Thus David Gary Shaw notes that 'we also want to theorize the animal in history because it helps us think even harder about who, these days, the "we" of history is'.[27] So long as we divide the world into nature on the one hand, all other animals of all shapes and natures rudely herded into this corral, and 'culture' on the other, as the work of humans alone, we are not likely to get very far beyond the history of human attitudes, beliefs, and practices towards animals, useful as this is. To go further, to fully open up history to the animal presence that we invoked earlier, we have to escape the gravitational pull of anthropocentrism. In this regard, the theoretical and methodological insights of scholars who have refused to accept the nature–culture dualism are absolutely vital. A famous example: the sociologist Michel Callon described the ways in which the humble scallop, the Brittany fishermen who harvested them, and a series of scientific researchers, some of them interested in conserving stocks, acted together in relationships that are impossible to capture by labelling some things natural and other things social; instead, it is the process in which some things are included (as identities or actors for instance), and others excluded or silenced, which he found essential.[28] Therefore, instead of starting with a proposition – animals cannot have agency, for example – Callon prefers to follow what happens, notably the power relationships that exist between different types of 'actors' whether they be human or nonhuman. In other words, nonhumans might be considered on the same footing, history-wise, at least at the beginning of our research. It is a matter of what these writers have termed 'generalised symmetry', not privileging one or other 'actor' in a priori reasoning.

Now in summary form, this kind of argument is familiar in many circles, so that more apologies are in order; but the point of raising it here, even so briefly, is merely to place the emphasis on *methodology* rather than on the kinds of a priori and blatantly *parti pris* arguments that one sometimes encounters when the history of animals is raised. The methodological issues should never be confused with those of principle, or ontology. We want in this *Companion* to encourage students and readers of animal–human history to resist the seemingly inarguable 'common sense' exampled above – the ideas, for instance, that animals, other animals, simply *do not* have 'agency', 'consciousness', 'history', and so on. Whether they take the form of wheedling blandishments or categorical imperatives these ideas have been used to dismiss even the possibility that nonhuman animals are worthy of our attention as historians. The question, as ever, is what we *mean* when we argue such things – and whether they indeed stand up to scrutiny. In this volume we try to provide resources for historians, especially those encountering this range of arguments for the first time. Our intention is not to close down debate – our contributors indeed provide different answers from different perspectives, and we are aware that plenty of excellent historical work can be done without swallowing the corpus of critical theory whole. At this juncture in the development of animal–human history – we prefer this formulation to the alternatives of 'animal history' or 'human–animal history' – diversity rather than consistency is more noticeable, and it deserves to be celebrated as much as condemned. We already have something like a canon – the classics of our young field that are required reading and which quite quickly mapped out its contours; and there are also collections that illustrate the kinds of work that historians have accomplished. But we intend this volume to be both survey and sourcebook, something that represents the state of the art, and at the same time can be consulted for up-to-date discussions of the key themes and arguments in the discipline.

The practice of animal–human history

We start by considering the practice of history, thinking of where animal–human history may contribute to established paradigms, such as political history. In our first substantial chapter, Sandra Swart traces the connections between animals and nationalism, and specifically the role of nonhuman animals in the propagation of 'national' histories. It may seem puzzling to begin our survey of animal–human history with the political, and with the Herderian understanding of nationalism, given that the status of man as a 'political animal' (Aristotle's *zoon politikon* or Aquinas's *animal civile*) is one of those qualities that supposedly elevate the human being over his animal counterparts. Yet these presumptions to human exclusiveness, even with the supposed 'naturalness' of the nation-state, generate objections aplenty. To the evolutionary biologist of a certain stripe, it might be supposed that the nature of evolutionary competition, aggression, and territoriality implies a certain continuity between human 'tribalism' and animals' group identities – as in the once influential popular accounts of Robert Ardrey.[29] These views trace a kind of 'animal nationalism' in nature, in basic biological drives and forms of animal association. This is a not quite outdated approach, its dynamism recognisably ahistorical, insofar as it confuses territoriality with territory; as the geographer Stuart Elden notes,

> The problem with this is that while it can tell us something about human behavior in space, it is not at all clear that it can tell us something about "territory". In part this is due to the obvious point that human social organization has changed more rapidly than biological drives.[30]

On the other hand, an 'eco-cosmopolitan' framing might look to nonhuman animals lending their agency to the politics of nationalism, as 'other citizens' who despite their lack of interest in demarcating and respecting human political boundaries, nevertheless form 'nations' of different kinds.[31] As a provocation, this promotion of a multispecies transnational politics serves at the very least to destabilise the 'national' basis of conventional histories. But animals are also conscripted as an element of banal nationalism, and Swart illustrates just how commonly the animal – or rather, specific animals – become proxies for the imagined community of the nation and for its projects of exclusion and othering (in the most extreme cases, Tiago Saraiva has recently reminded us that nonhuman animals were mobilised in the performance of fascist modernities).[32] Here, Swart's observations confirm the fact that anthropocentrism does not always, or even typically, entail speciesism, because the invocation of animal others is a way of avoiding either our common humanity or the supposedly inclusive political citizenship we imagine when we speak of nations. She points us nevertheless towards a political history of a more-than-human kind.

These themes are picked up by Mieke Roscher, who explores in her contribution the opportunities for animal–human historians opened up by the rise of the 'new political history' and a cultural history of politics, while being at the same time cautious about the challenges that lie ahead – challenges that derive from the familiar constraints of traditional political history but also the anthropocentric presumptions of these new approaches. It is as well to leave behind the former, with (at the risk of caricature) its focus on high politics and conventional political actors, on events and 'great men'. A turn to the everyday and the ordinary, as well as to discourses and representations, mentalities and symbolic systems, is far more amenable to animal–human historians interested in a more-than-human political history. Yet here there are further problems. Roscher notes in passing the counterargument to extending our conception of political history, which goes that if politics is now everywhere it is also nowhere, and that more specifically if we include nonhuman animals, or even things, matter, bodies of all sorts, then the basis for defining the 'political' as a separate sphere is lost. Roscher emphasises however the contrast between the symbolic and the real animal, for the interest in culture risks reducing the political history of nonhuman animals to their representation merely – as in Swart's 'national animals'. A pure culturalism of this sort appears to ignore the material reality and presence of the political animal. Roscher argues that we need not be caught upon the horns of this dilemma, having to choose between real and symbolic animals: she turns to a conception of politics based not on political actors, however constituted, but on a relational account of agency, with the focus on practices and performances. Here she insists that we can have our representations of animals as political actors in history (she calls this the political historiography of animals) and at the same time an account of the ways in which real animals (for Roscher, 'political animals') enter into the 'meaning-making' of political action through their encounters with human beings and their cultural/political systems. This sounds forbiddingly abstract – and Roscher draws upon performativity theory, Science and Technology Studies, 'praxiography' and 'body history' to make her points – but she illustrates this with examples from the animal–human history of the Third Reich, a specific, extreme, tragic animal–human constellation that nevertheless serves as a case study of how nonhumans *co-produce* political history.

These contributions lead neatly enough into Hilda Kean's overview of the role of animals in 'public history'. However troublesome that term is to define, we recognise that much of the running in the representation of animal–human histories has taken place outside of the academy, in the kinds of exhibitions and monuments and memorials that Kean examines here. Public history has included animals in these 'more-than-human' histories without the kind of high theory or conceptual jargon regularly to be encountered in academic animal–human history, and which is almost by definition off-limits to non-specialists. Nor do we see replicated an emphasis on the acquisition of knowledge for its own sake – for as museums and other institutions struggle to connect with wider and more diverse audiences, they situate themselves in very different social and political contexts, where buzzwords such as participation and inclusivity are prominent. Of course, we can and should be critical about the turn to public history, especially where 'heritage' and the narration of 'national identity' are concerned – but we might also see opportunities in the collaborative process of *history-making* that is at the heart of public history. Kean shows us both sides of this debate, considering, with a focus on Australia, how animals and their histories have been enrolled in the presentation of national (if not necessarily nationalist) stories – but viewing them as positive starting-off points for an animal–human history that is not confined to the seminar room. Sometimes this has been at the expense of a certain academic rigour, but even so we can still appreciate the presence and agency of nonhuman animals as participants in the process of making history. Kean reminds us that 'animal–human historians' – at least, those of us who are employed in institutions of higher education and evaluated on our academic research – do not *on our own* produce 'history'. If we are to bring nonhuman animals back into history, we need to accept and even celebrate, if never uncritically, the diverse histories that are at work in the world.

Drawing on vital work in memory studies, Jan-Erik Steinkrüger follows the lead of the previous chapter in arguing that history-making is an ongoing, dynamic process, and that animals are an integral part of this form of public history. Steinkrüger takes up Kean's themes of animal memorialisation, but heads in a different direction, considering the ways in which animal conservation might be interpreted as a form of cultural memory, and thus a practice of making history. As he suggests, animal conservation projects of all kinds are not a matter of 'nature' distinct from 'culture'. They typically invoke the latter in the terms of history and heritage, especially in the powerful ideal of preserving (or reintroducing) animals as a living patrimony or collective property, handed down from historical past through threatened present to hoped-for future. The concept and practice of national parks, where the historical existence of animals is often bought at the expense of remembering human histories, exemplifies this kind of animal–human political history. Steinkrüger focuses in this chapter on the business of collective memory, or rather more precisely *cultural memory*, asking which animals (including humans) are remembered, which animals (including humans) forgotten, and why. His examples of animal conservation in Africa demonstrate that historiography is a critical form of cultural memory-work, especially so in a postcolonial frame. The power of media – not academic history – is emphasised throughout, as with Kean's chapter. Steinkrüger aims to show how wildlife conservation is inextricably entangled with animal–human history – and his worked example of efforts to save central Asia's Przewalski's horse bears this out. This is an important lesson for animal–human historians who tend to approach their topics from the direction of cultural history, and with a pronounced focus on the modern, urban West. Steinkrüger demonstrates the narrowness of our optic, and the limitations of our own historiographical habits.

Turning to an historiography that all too quickly sequesters questions of culture from those of 'science', Robert Kirk takes a similarly critical stance. Looking at the transformation of animals and animal bodies into the collective 'experimental animal', Kirk points out the limitations of an historiography that sees controversies about experimentation and vivisection in particular, as somehow *really* about human concerns, not about animals at all. He argues that the history of animal experimentation struggles as a result with the animal as anything more than a symbol. Kirk looks instead at the potential of the history of science as an alternative to an anthropocentric 'social' history where taking animals seriously is concerned, and though he notes the advantages of such approaches in terms of rich descriptive accounts, he identifies a disabling lack of interest in normative questions. That the two concerns, the empirical and the ethical, might at least partially be reconciled is exampled through the development history of animal welfare science – yet here again the full import of animal–human relations, including the nature of emotional and affective attachments, remains unrecognised. Kirk's purpose here is to argue for the integration of moral values and ethical concerns in the production of scientific knowledge and the material practices upon which it depends). This means taking seriously the emotions of nonhuman animals as well as those of humans, and confronting the history of our empathy with other species – not as part of a congratulatory narrative of care and animal welfare within the scientific community, but as part of what Kirk calls here a 'moral ecology of science'.

Abigail Woods' account of the divergence and convergence of animal and human medicine is also placed here because of what it tells us about the disciplinary process by which animal and human histories are quarantined. Woods' theme is medical and veterinary history, but the conclusions are scalable out and up. The disconnect between medical history/veterinary history and animal–human history is puzzling, notes Woods, particularly insofar as nonhuman animals have left far more obvious traces in the historical record here than in other fields. If any subdiscipline should afford opportunities for an integrated history, then the history of medicine and veterinary science should be it, yet historians in this field have for Woods been largely guided by anthropocentric assumptions and concepts, and it is probably fair to say that it has been relatively resistant, until quite recently, to the theoretical insights provided by Science and Technology Studies and allied perspectives. Lest this account seem too carping, we should recognise as Woods does that the problem is not just on that side of the fence: for animal–human historians have typically focused on wild and companion animals, largely neglecting those animals whose lives or bodies have contributed to medical science; by contrast, experimental animals, and the specific topics of vivisection, zoonotic and contagious diseases, have been quite well covered by medical and social historians, as she herself shows in some detail, with a very useful summary of key contributions and an assessment of their significance. The lessons here include an awareness of the limits placed on the biological control of animals, including ourselves: the British BSE/vCJD crisis of the late 1990s is not now a part of students' memories – it has thus become 'historical' – but it and a host of other phenomena form a reminder that animal–human relations are a critical part of contemporary 'risk society'.[33] Woods notes that historians are influenced by the present and its particular concerns, though it is just as important for contemporary scholars to be aware of the historical precedents. But Woods is surely right to look to identify the dominant human-centred perspective as the major barrier to a truly animal history of medicine, and she is right too to fly the flag for the 'One Health' movement and what it portends.

Woods notes in her chapter the privileging of the symbolic over the material in animal–human history. Liv Emma Thorsen's chapter, by contrast, explores the question of why animals' materiality really matters. In its concern for the display of animal remains in museum collections it belongs with the business of public history. But it also forms a bridge between these questions of historical praxis and the issues of theory and methodology that are collected in the following section, under the rubric 'problems and paradigms'. Thorsen sets her sights on the material as well as the animal turn, demonstrating that even after death, animals exhibit agency. She considers the role of animal remains in provoking affective or emotional responses, by attracting various interested parties, actors, or 'friends', and also by constructing meaning for us through particular sets of relations in specific contexts, networks or assemblages. That this means the production of what we understand as history is evident from the fact that animal remains become exhibits in *historical* narratives – and not just in 'natural history' museums. Thorsen shows, through her intriguing examples, how dynamic and contingent are 'nature' and 'culture': a hippopotamus, an exotic exile in Renaissance Florence, travels after death from spectacular individuality to being the representative of the species, as the Medici collections are purified in the Age of Enlightenment into the products of culture and nature respectively (and then only provisionally). In Oslo, by contrast, in the Romantic Age, a poet's dog is gifted to science before being reunited with her owner's *geist* in the modern celebration of genius and *genus loci*, thus reclaimed from 'science' and returned to 'culture'. These histories of taxidermied animals (along with Thorsen's many other examples) show us that the meaning of life and death, persons and things, essences and relations, is far from clear-cut. Animal–human history is inherently material, and inherently messy as well.

Historiographical challenges

We move in the second section of this book to considering key historiographical problems. In the initial chapter in this section Philip Howell tries to lay out as clearly as possible the genealogy of the conception of 'agency', and in particular the problems involved in suggesting that humans have distinctive attributes that gives them an 'agency' or power that all other animals signally lack. We arrogate to ourselves the position of an imperial race, and, as the neglected eighteenth-century English philosopher Abraham Tucker puts it, 'delighting to draw comparisons between ourselves and the irrational tribes, or studying to exaggerate our own nobility and pre-eminence of privileges above them'.[34] Howell also notes the connections to social theory and social history, where the idea of agency has been important in recovering the lives and experiences of the less privileged, the subordinated, and the exploited. Animals as historical subjects are confronted with an unwelcome choice in this regard – waiting to be the beneficiary of this ethical extensionism, but as a distant cousin of the historical family the last cohort to be considered worthy of being included in a 'social' history; or else relegated to evolutionary or environmental history, to the matter of things and Nature. Howell suggests that we might want to replace 'history from below', with its hierarchical presumptions, with the fact that animals are beside us, and that these relationships with other animals are part of what we like to think of as 'our' agency. In this relational conception of agency there is no distinction between now and the historical past, save that there are special issues in research and writing about animals' agency. Howell finishes therefore by considering three paradigms in histories of animal agency: ascribed agency, proactive agency, and (his preference is obvious enough) 'assembled agency'. Being precise as to what we mean when we write about agency is a necessary first step towards writing more convincing more-than-human histories.

This hardly exhausts the issue, of course. Jennifer McDonell's chapter on animals in Victorian literature tackles a number of pertinent themes – that of animals' agency, the possibility of writing a history of emotions that includes other animals, and the problem, above all, of representation itself. We locate her contribution in this second section principally because of this issue of representation: we might feel that in the field of literature, at the heart of the humanities, so to speak, we are about as far away from real animals as we are ever likely to get. Classic debates in animal studies indeed revolve around this question of 'representation', with the early and powerful insistence that animals disappear when they become the matter of culture now matched by more nuanced assessments and indeed increasingly voluble counterarguments.[35] Looking for the traces of animals in texts is sometimes bracingly straightforward, however – we are thinking of the marvellous example of the Deventer cat who one night in or around the year 1420 pissed on a medieval manuscript, much to the annoyance of the monk who came to resume his work the morning later:

> *Hic non defectus est, sed cattus minxit desuper nocte quadam. Confundatur pessimus cattus qui minxit super librum istum in nocte Daventrie, et consimiliter omnes alii propter illum. Et cavendum valde ne permittantur libri aperti per noctem ubi cattie venire possunt.*
>
> (Here is nothing missing, but a cat urinated on this during a certain night. Cursed be the pesty cat that urinated over this book during the night in Deventer and because of it many others [other cats] too. And beware well not to leave open books at night where cats can come.)[36]

We need to think carefully, however, about the ways in which culture is co-produced by human and other animals. In McDonell's examples, for instance, we have a veritable carnival of animals, including the monstrously or whimsically transmogrified chimera, not only in marginal texts – children's literature, say, or genre fiction – but also in the most canonical and popular texts. McDonell argues that Victorian literary texts offer, if not uniquely then certainly in an exemplary form, accounts of relational and situated animal agency that tally very well with contemporary conceptions. In one sense, for sure, we have a discourse of animality that reduces some people, some types of people, to mere animals – particularly in the racial and imperial registers – but we also, in this enlarged sympathy sense not only an acknowledgement too of our shared creatureliness but also (and we raise this tentatively) a recognition of the ways in which oppression of animals intersects with other forms of oppression.[37] We may dismiss this strain as a no more than sentimental surplus, a form of allyship (to borrow the associated term) that oppressed animals might well do without.[38] but the provocation in human beings of anxiety and unease, in the highest expressions of art and culture, surely confirms Philip Armstrong's argument that animals are 'central to the mission of modernity'.[39]

Keri Cronin accomplishes for the visual arts what Jennifer McDonell does for literature. Part of her argument is emphatically methodological, a plea for animal–human historians to be creative and diligent in their use of visual material, and to be equally careful to assess content according to context. Images are no less complex than textual material, and teasing out layers of meaning is far from straightforward, as Cronin shows using images associated with nineteenth-century animal advocacy, and tacking between the reality of animals' lives, the production of artworks, and the subsequent circulation of prints and adaptations. Cronin asks, however, what would *art history* look like if we took animals seriously? Like McDonell, she is not convinced that all we see, all we can see, is our human world. Acknowledging the importance that animal advocacy groups gave to the visual arts in enlarging human sympathy towards nonhuman animals, Cronin addresses the problem of representation by refusing to see this imagery as a kind of anthropocentric cul-de-sac or echo chamber; instead, she asks how representing animals might be a guide not only for how people lived with animals in the past, but also how we might live with animals in the present and the future. So in addition to her methodological guidance, Cronin offers a case for seeing nonhuman animals as a part of the production of visual art, through their material substance and by being embraced by visual technologies, but perhaps more importantly as an inextricably element of visual regimes that are caught up with a variety of animal–human relationships.

Boria Sax tackles the central question of anthropomorphism in his chapter, beginning with the painful but instructive history of the zoological exhibition of 'primitive' humans and 'civilised' apes. The easy interchangeability, for spectators, of pygmy and chimpanzee, as Sax argues, points to the confusion at the heart of the concept of anthropocentrism, its dependence on its shadowy sister, zoomorphism, and the seemingly incessant production of anthropomorphic hybrids. This in general terms is a familiar argument. But Sax notes that the anthropocentrism alternately accepted or critiqued today should be understood as a very selective revival of attitudes both antique and antic, a continuing conversation that is especially dependent on spiritual and theological perspectives on the nature of humans versus other animals. The Judeo-Christian tradition, for instance, is still routinely castigated for its endorsement of anthropocentric reason and lack of environmental awareness, but of course, as in the classical myths, the divinity makes use of animal avatars as well as the man of sorrows. Sax's chapter is essential reading in that he reminds us that zoomorphism not only survived Descartes, Linnaeus, and Darwin but that their ideas prompted and provoked anthropological anxiety. Sax puts forward the monkey or ape as the troublemaker in the Garden of Eden, and sees anthropomorphism reaching an apogee in the late nineteenth and early twentieth centuries. In short, zoomorphism, like the indomitable Lilith, continues to vex the happy family of Adam and Eve, and their children's hegemony over the Earth and all its creatures.

Sax's chapter leads straight into the question of exhibition, a prominent theme in the history and the historiography of animals, and a particularly provocative one given the antipathy towards zoos and the other popular animal entertainments of our own day. All attempts to rebrand zoos and safari parks at the heart of contemporary wildlife conservation have failed to blunt the force of criticism from animal welfarists and animal rights activists.[40] The question of what we are doing when we make a spectacle of nonhuman animals has been on the table at least since the art critic John Berger's influential essay, 'Why look at animals?'[41] Berger's bleak assessment was that the real animal is fated only to disappear with the rise of these exhibitionary complexes built for viewing.[42] Others quickly joined him – too quickly – in asserting that in zoos and their like the animal is already virtual, and has nothing much any more to do with 'nature'. The history of zoos indeed suggests a rather more complex story, something that Helen Cowie takes up in her chapter, looking at the variety of ways in which animals were exhibited in the past, and what this history means for us. For Cowie the exhibition of 'exotic' animals in zoos, menageries, circuses and other animal performances, is certainly about power, but this is not just the familiar business of human dominion over animals or over nature, or even the impress of imperialism and the colonial monopoly of knowledge, though it surely is these things.[43] Exhibiting animals in these widely different ways also takes us into the history of national and civic pride, and also that of class, for the casual visitors and audiences at animal shows have found themselves as much under observation as the animals themselves. Cowie also reminds us that concerns over welfare, the definition and distribution of cruelty and care, and the agency of animals themselves all have a distinctive historical pedigree. Whatever we think now of animal spectacles, whether we stress the 'clownishness' or conservation, we should all attend to this history lesson.[44]

Carl Griffin notes in his chapter that when species meet, the result is not always pretty. 'Being with' other animals means companionship and affection, but also violence and – to use that resonant word – 'brutality'. As with Karl Steel's later contribution, we cannot quarantine such violence to the distant and unreformed past, to the supposedly nasty brutishness of the middle ages, for instance, nor to the world of the countryside or of the working classes – all of these familiar shorthands in the reassuring reasoning of moral improvement, but poor guides in themselves for the animal–human historian save as indexes of ideology. Griffin argues how little consideration the treatment of animals in rural settings has received until recently, either from environmental or animal–human historians. This may sound surprising given the centrality of animals in agrarian capitalism, but those histories have arguably neglected the affective relationships involved in favour of their status as things, as property, as capital. The main theme indeed has been the domination of animals, the invention of Nature with a capital N as something to be mastered, with emotion involved perhaps only as a matter of scientific, national, and human pride in such mastery.[45] Griffin is hardly an apologist for the age, as his studies here and elsewhere of animal maiming and other forms of violence towards animals suggest, all in the context of the rapid proletarianisation of farm labour. But the existence of attitudes that are associated with, but are not exhausted by, the production of fleshy capital is something that Griffin is at pains to emphasise here – and for which the humble pig, the companion of the cottager and slum-dweller alike, is particularly emblematic. Affection for animals, even those destined for slaughter, needs to be recognised as a central part of the fateful process by which animal bodies and human labour became commodities in the modern age. An environmental or a rural history that registers only the blood and the brutality, particularly in the context of cultural self-congratulation, will fail to show how nonhuman animals shaped our past.

These ideas are picked up by Ingrid Tague, who rightly reminds us that emotional attachments to animals are far older than the familiar narrative, of 'pets' filling an absence produced by the development of urban and industrial society, suggests.[46] Tague does not universalise pet-keeping, which would deprive it of anything but the deepest of deep histories, instead insisting that we can and should historicise these feelings for animal companions, and consider nonhuman animals within what is known now as the history of emotions. The problem of 'doing emotions history' *with animals* is raised here very explicitly, however. This constitutes a major methodological problem, which justifies placing Tague's important contribution at this point in the volume, along with her honourable reservations about what animal–human historians can reasonably achieve. Tague argues that imposing a human understanding of 'emotion' upon other species, and a contemporary and provisional understanding at that, risks ignoring the rich experiential world of other animals that is no less important for being effectively beyond the grasp of humankind. Tague's expertise leads her to focus not on animals' emotions themselves as with the contexts and regimes by which emotions are recognised and valorised. As an avowedly 'traditional' cultural historian, whose interest is principally on the cultural construction of 'emotion', Tague is extremely well placed to examine the changing perceptions of animals' emotions and emotions about animals in the early modern period. She revisits a series of savants, not to idly cheer Montaigne or hiss Descartes, but to show that reciprocal emotional bonds were centrally on the agenda for philosophers and scientists concerned with reason, morality, and society itself. Emotional attachments to animals were not dismissed herein as expressions of vulgar 'sentiment', but understood rather as part of a shared culture of *sensibility* that allowed animals to inveigle their way into the human emotional world, and via a concept of natural *sympathy* that explained society's ties as emotional connections with various others, including nonhuman ones.

Tague sees where we are now, with regard to emotions, history, and animals as at an impasse. But 'Rethinking animals as subjects makes us remap human–animal boundaries in emotive as much as ecological terms', and there are plausible ways forward.[47] A vital contribution is made by Michael Guida, for though the subject – birdsong in early twentieth-century Britain – sounds as relatively niche in appeal as twitching, this chapter explores the role of emotion and sentiment in animal–human history. Guida resolutely avoids being bullied out of a consideration of 'sentiment', as mere sentimentality, say, something for poets rather than scientists, or (in a more modern guise) simply a matter of social construction, another version of the idea that animals disappear in modernity. But the role of *birdsong* is a recognition of the continuing presence of birds in humans' lives, and, more importantly, a register of the agency of birds in broadcasting their 'songs' (for whatever reason) and the agency or affect of these 'songs' beyond their bodies. It is both charming and sobering to reflect that these sounds were thought fit for humans to broadcast, over the airwaves, to an avid radio audience, particularly in times of national stress and anxiety: firstly and more generally in the context of worries about the wrong kind of 'signals' being 'received' in people's newly porous homes – here the positive, natural, and transcendent quality of birdsong might drown out the hubbub threatened by technological modernity – and secondly under the specific challenges of the wartime Home Front and the struggles to maintain 'morale'. Singing then of arms and the songbird Guida shows not only that the sound of birds resonated in British national life, but more generally that animals are an inseparable part of the history of emotions, hitherto almost exclusively an anthropocentric enterprise.[48] The birdsong that Guida takes as his focus can be understood, from one angle, as an expression of animal 'emotion', but perhaps more significantly he shows how this was bundled up with humans and machines in distinctive emotional regimes.[49]

Larger themes and big histories

The final set of chapters take on the larger themes in the history of animal–human relations. Neil Pemberton, Julie-Marie Strange and Michael Worboys first take as their theme the practice of animal breeding, and with it the cryptic and troublesome concept of 'breed'. These are obviously connected, but they are far from inseparable: the latter is a latecomer, a relatively recent concept, certainly compared with the long history of human intervention in the sexual reproduction of nonhuman animals. Even where we narrow our focus to the scientific or selective breeding that is such a familiar feature of the late eighteenth/early nineteenth-century 'age of improvement', it is the variety of practices that are wrapped up in the single idea of breeding that we should emphasise, not just the undifferentiated domination of animals by humanity. 'Breeding' is, as the authors point out, an umbrella term, taking in both livestock and 'fancy' animals, breeding for utility or for whimsy – and even this distinction is not as secure as it might seem at first sight. The development of cattle, racehorses, pigeons, poultry, and dogs, covered in this chapter, bear out this complex history of genetic manipulation. We can also note that the abstract scientific understanding of breeding – the idea of 'artificial selection', most famously – derives in part from these practical considerations but also distorts our understanding of what breeders actually did and how they themselves understood what they were doing.[50] Lastly, with the rise of 'pedigree' dog breeding in the later nineteenth century further troublesome complexities are introduced, the notion of dog 'breeds' promoting ideal-type 'standards' while acknowledging the plasticity of canine bodies. Pemberton, Strange and Worboys argue that a 'breed' is an artefact of the imagination rather than a fact of nature, a way of thinking, a word (we might even say, a speech act). A breed is no more, and no less, than a 'brand', a manipulation of consumer tastes as much as of DNA. The invention of breeds is a fateful one: because it acknowledges the entanglement of animals and humans over the longest term, the power of people to alter the very nature of what an animal *is*; but also because it imposes a certain rationalisation of breeding and a vision of nature moreover that threatens to bleed over into the concepts of 'race' and rank ('good stock'), culture and civility ('good breeding'), that are used still to separate the human sheep from the human goats.

In his wide-ranging chapter, running from the grieving horses of Homer's Achaeans to the weaponised animals of contemporary conflicts, Gervase Phillips tackles the history of nonhumans in war. He reminds us of the essentially continuous exploitation of animals as tools of war, on the battlefield as mounted units, and in the supply chains as beasts of burden, and points to the significance of animals not only in specific military struggles but also in the long-run history of empires, cultures and civilisations. The importance of nonhuman animals in the campaigning history that is the meat and drink of military historians has not been wholly neglected – but the fruits of this research are the work of a cadre of specialists typically marginalised from the historical mainstream. The 'big histories' of war and conflict, and of violence have, by contrast, proved less amenable to taking on board the significance of animals.[51] The point is that there is a critical need for joined-up thinking in understanding the history of war, bringing together the insights of military specialists and animal–human historians. For Phillips, there are nevertheless real opportunities to forward an animal–human history through an engagement with a military history that was never as obtuse as its critics make out: there are interesting comparisons to be made, for instance, between the recovery of soldiers' experiences and those of the animals who accompanied them to battle, and fought alongside them in battle. All the same, the clear need is to weigh up an awareness of animals as military materiel with an engaged awareness of their affective or emotional states as combatants and as they were caught up in conflicts. After all, humans and other animals share an evolutionary history; some of the effects of war hardly discriminate between animal and human bodies, including the effects on the mind and the psyche. The pity of war must have something of the animal in it, not least the reduction of people to a creaturely life. But taking the animal standpoint is not merely a guide to human suffering: Phillips reminds us not only of the need to attend to the specifics of animals in and at war, but also of the co-specifics involved, particularly in his sobering concluding discussion of humans and dogs as 'co-belligerents' sharing a history of violence.

In his own chapter on hunting, Philip Howell contrasts the incommensurability of hunting histories deriving from contemporary science and the politics of hunting. To some, hunting is natural, authorised by the violent, carnivorous record of our prehistoric ancestors, and thereby right: the idea that hunting/meat-eating made us, and continues to make us, human. The 'hunting hypothesis' that underwrote these ideas in post-war paleoanthropology has, by now, attained 'mythic' status, but it is no less influential for all that: despite decades of criticism, hunting and humanity are indelibly associated. We cannot deny the prehistoric record out of hand, but neither can we use this to divert attention away from the extremely varied histories of hunting in recorded history, and what it tells us – which is often not about meat per se than about power and privilege, or about very complex social relations rather than some spuriously homogeneous 'humanity', or about the appropriation of nature by a relatively recent capitalist regime. Howell uses this chapter not to survey the entire field of hunting in history but instead to emphasise this diversity, and to undercut competing attempts to sum up what hunting *is*: that it is about pursuing 'wild' animals in 'wild' places, for instance, in a kind of violent enmity or even a 'war' against 'nature'. Few of these broad characterisations hold water, even if they can be readily mobilised for contemporary political purposes. All the same, perhaps as historians we should be most on our guard against the enduring idea of 'Man the hunter', 'the Man-making tale of the hunter on the quest to kill and bring back the terrible bounty'.[52] We might prefer the advice of the writer Ursula K. Le Guin: that 'storytelling might pick up diverse things of meaning and value and gather them together, like a forager rather than a hunter waiting for the big kill'.[53]

Chris Otter considers the theme of meat eating in a similarly wide-ranging and complementary contribution, noting the deep history of eating animals alongside a concern for the transformations ushered in by the modern era of historical capitalism, and the dramatic changes brought in in the space of a human lifetime – along with what this 'Great Acceleration' presages. Otter is concerned here to explore the importance of ancient domestication alongside more recent phenomena such as scientific breeding. He turns specific attention to the 'big three' of contemporary commercial farming – cattle, first, and some way ahead, vying for first place in terms of numbers and biomass, pigs and chickens. Otter's work is a model of an holistic history, taking in changes to animals' bodies together with changes in food preparation and consumption, within a framework that emphasises the role of commodification and appropriation in contemporary capitalism-as-global-ecology. With apologies to the pig, it is the broiler chicken, forty days from cradle to grave, hatchery to butchery, and unlike its competitors wholly unprotected by religious scruples, which is the very icon of our biological control of animals. There are *limits* – in the cultural making of meat the aversion to eating certain animals (horses, say) or indeed to eating meat at all, and in the physical machinery resistance in various forms from the predated – but the most important are the blowbacks of environmental degradation and biosecurity that most obviously threaten the regime of cheap food upon which contemporary capitalism depends. Otter's chapter takes us far away from the self-congratulatory narratives of dominion – domestication of animals as 'a triumph of human wit and will', and puts in their place an awareness of the fragile web of life under late capitalist modernity in which we and the animals we eat are enmeshed.[54]

The substantive chapters in this volume end with Karl Steel's consideration of animals, violence, and the meaning of the 'medieval'. Steel first points out that the middle ages are, to us, 'uncanny', in that we both inherit its ideas, many of them sophisticated and subtle, some of them short and emphatic in their anthropocentrism, but at the same time we rush to praise ourselves by disavowing the age's 'brutality' towards animals. Steel does not wish to replace a familiar portrait of brutish medieval with an unfeasibly benign version of the middle ages. Rather, he asks what cruelty to animals meant, to them, and to us. His icon here is the fourteenth/fifteenth century Christian mystic, Margery Kempe, and in particular her beliefs as to the rights and wrongs of eating animals. Characterising her practice as a 'carnivorous vegetarianism', Steel is at pains to emphasise how difficult it is to pin someone like Kempe down, in the terms of modern theriophily – and by extension how difficult it is to make sweeping statements about attitudinal changes over the long term. Margery's intemperate tears and her dog-like devotional howling, affect us oddly, as they should. Steel's aim then is to restore the *strangeness* of the middle ages, and so to complicate the conventional chronologies of cruelty and violence and compassion. For nonhuman animals – especially, if not exclusively – the politics of time and historical temporality are fraught with their own forms of violence. In animal welfare narratives, time is typically mapped out in space, to accuse others of 'anachronistic' behaviour, 'medieval' brutality, say, so that questioning these practices serves to puncture the self-regard of Western modernity. In its place we might be tempted to give up on history altogether, or take shelter in either the bromide of 'progress' or the perhaps equally pleasurable conviction of declension. But Steel's work suggests the need for closer readings, but beyond that what he calls historical heterogeneity, something that would not mean, for animal–human history, neat archaeological layers or nicely bounded communities, but a new kind of history altogether.

Conclusions

The concluding reflections attempt to sum up where we are, which is certainly sobering when we consider animals' lives. As Daniel Bender has recently put it, 'We exist at a remarkable, if tragic, moment in our human and animal histories'.[55] Matthew Calarco is more forceful still:

> Never before in human history have so many animals been subjected to horrific slaughter, unconscionable abuse, and unthinkable living conditions. The present conditions under which many animals live has a unique history that requires both material and ontological analysis, and it is a history that needs to be attended to in its *specificity* so that we might learn better how to transform it for the present and the future.[56]

Stated as sharply as this we come to the question of what our ethical commitments and political praxis should be, something that defies easy answers. Animal–human history, at least that practised in the academy, may find itself uncomfortably placed here: too 'contemplative' for activists for a start – but also figured by some as too conservative a discipline to take on board the kind of presumptions of, for instance, the 'posthuman' turn in critical theory. Falling between these stools – too 'humanist' for animal studies, too 'academic' for animal advocates – may not in fact be as awkward as it first appears, and there is no necessary match up – quite the opposite – between activists and critical philosophers. We can surely fly a flag for what we can think of as the basic research that animal–human historians accomplish; the animal–human historian Louise Robbins noted some time ago that for all of the benefits of what is now touted as 'big history', such 'wide-angle views smooth over much varied topography'.[57] So there is no inconsiderable virtue in writing by contrast small histories, properly attendant to context and cultural nuance. The conclusions offer up some ideas about how we might connect these small stories and big stories, those of modern capitalism's 'historical nature' in particular.[58] We hope that in this collection we have offered up reflections on animal–human histories that achieve precisely that, contributions that map unexpected connections and reveal unexpected connections:

> As animals migrate from the margins of history to its main stage, they reveal paths hidden beneath the routes blazed previously by historians. Telling stories through and with animals will untangle historiography, showing how ideas, processes, and actors can be pulled apart in new ways – making audible historical subjects long relegated to our silenced wilderness.[59]

This is no longer as controversial as it once seemed. We should be wary of talking of the 'triumph' of animal–human history, but most mainstream historians would now accept that a wider range of 'actors' contribute to the making of history, including (though not only) nonhuman animals.[60] As Frederick Brown argues, 'Nonhuman animals have witnessed the same history humans saw, looked for opportunities to thrive, aided humans in countless ways, and thwarted human plans'.[61] But perhaps we should insist more strongly, more bolshily even, that 'history-making extends beyond what humans do'.[62] The anthropologist Anna Tsing reminds us that storytelling – including writing 'history' – is something that we do *with* other animals, a point that we raised right at the start, and whose purport is so beautifully illustrated by the work of Nick Brandt on the cover of this book:

> 'History' is both a human storytelling practice and that set of remainders from the past that we turn into stories. Conventionally, historians look only at human remainders, such as archives and diaries, but there is no reason not to spread our attention to the tracks and traces of nonhumans, as these contribute to our common landscapes. Such tracks and traces speak to cross-species entanglements in contingency and conjuncture, the components of 'historical' time. To participate in such entanglement, one does not have to make history in just one way. Whether or not other organisms 'tell stories', they contribute to the overlapping tracks and traces that we grasp as history. History, then, is the record of many trajectories of world making, human and not human.[63]

History (with the capital H) is itself a way of being in the world. Saying that we as humans have History, and other animals do not, is one story, one way of making the world. But it isn't the only one. The question we are now concerned with is what happens to 'history' when we recognise that, then as now, we live in the world with animal others? The remaking of history is a task still to be accomplished – but we hope that this collection has suggested some answers to a question that is central not just to animal–human history but to the meaning of history itself.

We leave the final word to Harriet Ritvo, whose pioneering work in animal–human history has long been a personal and professional inspiration. Ritvo's contributions have ranged from the detailed, scholarly investigation of the place of nonhuman animals in Victorian Britain, where animal–human history, natural history, and environmental history mingle and merge, to the methodological and conceptual understanding of what animal–human history is, and what it might be.[64] Ritvo's reflections on this collection return us to the persistent problem of how to make the past and continuing presence of animals visible in our histories. She points to the pros and cons of diversity and interdisciplinarity, noting that opportunities are always accompanied by costs. But in her characteristic generosity Ritvo emphasises the work that remains to be done, and in exactly this spirit we see this *Companion to Animal–Human History* as an invitation to a shared enterprise.

Notes

1 N. Brandt, *Inherit the Dust*, New York: Edwynn Houk Editions, 2016; and also see foreword by P. Singer in N. Brandt, *A Shadow Falls*, New York: Abrams, 2009, available at http://nickbrandt.com/UserImages/11/11129/file/A%20SHADOW%20FALLS%20 FOREWORD%20PETER%20SINGER.pdf, last accessed 24 September 2017.
2 Brandt, *Inherit the Dust*, 7.
3 N. Brandt, *Across the Ravaged Land*, volume 3, New York: Abrams, 2013, 13.
4 Brandt, *Across the Ravaged Land*, 14.
5 See for example S. Nance (ed.) *The Historical Animal*, Syracuse NY: Syracuse University Press, 2015, especially introduction, 1–4, and D. Brantz (ed.), *Beastly Natures: Animals, Humans, and the Study of History*, Charlottesville VA: University of Virginia Press, 2010.
6 S. Baker, *Artist/Animal*, Minneapolis MN: University of Minnesota Press, 2013, 228.
7 D. Donald, *Picturing Animals in Britain 1750–1850*, New Haven CT: Yale University Press, 2007, 305.
8 K. Thomas, *Man and the Natural World: Changing Attitudes in England 1500–1800*, London: Allen Lane, 1983, 303.
9 Thomas, *Man and the Natural World*, 13 and 14.
10 Thomas, *Man and the Natural World*, 16.
11 Thomas, *Man and the Natural World*, 16.
12 K. Thomas, 'Diary', *London Review of Books* 32, 11 (10 June 2010): 36–37, available at www.lrb.co.uk/v32/n11/keith-thomas/diary; last accessed 24 September 2017.
13 Thomas, 'Diary'.
14 Thomas, 'Diary'. Thus the influence in such history-making should apparently relate to those human absences that are referenced in Thomas's statement that 'They may not have much sense of world geography and probably can't even draw a map. But if you want to know how to get somewhere, they are the ones to take you'.
15 Artists in this exhibition 'encourage us to consider non-human animals as our equals': see M. Antlfinger, A. Holck, U. Hormer, M. Maage, F. Schmitcz, *Animal Lovers*, Berlin: nGbK, 2016, 4. See also https://archiv.ngbk.de/en/projekte/animal-lovers/, last accessed 24 September 2017.
16 A. Fox, *Habitats 11*, 2011–2016: see Antlfinger et al., *Animal Lovers*, 20, and http://anselmofox.eu/werk/habitate-ii/, last accessed 24 September 2017. The Victory Column was designed by Heinrich Drake to mark the Prussian defeat of the Danes in 1864, but by the time of its inauguration in 1873 victories over Austria and France were also commemorated.

The German sculptor Friedrich Drake added the bronze sculpture of Victoria, subsequently used by Soviet soldiers for target practice during World War II.
17 D. Premack and A.J. Premack, 'Why animals have neither culture nor history', in T. Ingold (ed.), *Companion Encyclopedia of Anthropology*, London: Routledge, 1994, 350–365, 350.
18 K. Malik, Pandaemonium blog post, 26 October 2011, available at https://kenanmalik.wordpress.com/2011/10/26/all-animals-have-an-evolutionary-past-only-humans-make-history/, last accessed 6 April 2017.
19 Premack and Premack, 'Why animals have neither culture nor history', 350.
20 G. Barraclough, quoted by J. Tosh and S. Lang, *The Pursuit of History: Aims, Methods, and New Directions in the Study of Modern History*, fourth edition, London: Pearson Longman, 2006, 50.
21 D. Brantz, 'Introduction', in D. Brantz (ed.), *Beastly Natures: Animals, Humans, and the Study of History*, Charlottesville VA: University of Virginia Press, 2010, 1–13, 2.
22 H. Kean, *The Great Cat and Dog Massacre: The Real Story of World War II's Unknown Tragedy*, Chicago IL: University of Chicago Press, 2018, 7.
23 M. Rangajaran, 'Animals with rich histories: the case of the lions of Gir Forest, Gujarat, India', *History and Theory* 52, 4 (2013): 109–127, 125.
24 This is not to say that incorporating nonhuman animals has been consistent or wholly uncontroversial. For some contemporary arguments, see C. Watts (ed.), *Relational Archaeologies: Humans, Animals, Things*, Abingdon: Routledge, 2013, and P. Descola, *Beyond Nature and Culture*, Chicago IL: University of Chicago Press, 2013.
25 For some discussion of problems, see D.E. Bender, 'On zoo sources', in *The Animal Game: Searching for Wildness at the American Zoo*, Cambridge MA: Harvard University Press, 2016: 373–375; see also Kean, *Great Cat and Dog Massacre*, 168–169.
26 E. Benson, 'Animal writes: historiography, disciplinarity, and the animal trace', in L. Kalof and G.M. Montgomery (eds.), *Making Animal Meaning*, East Lansing MI: Michigan State University Press, 2011, 3–16, 11.
27 D.G. Shaw, 'A way with animals', *History and Theory* 52, 4 (2013): 1–12, 11.
28 M. Callon, 'Some elements of a sociology of translation: domestication of the scallops and the fishermen of St Brieuc Bay', *The Sociological Review* 32, S1 (1984): 196–233. This can also be found in J. Law (ed.), *Power, Action and Belief: A New Sociology of Knowledge*, London: Routledge & Kegan Paul, 1986, 196–233.
29 See R. Ardrey, *The Territorial Imperative: A Personal Inquiry into the Animal Origins of Property and Nations*, New York: Atheneum, 1966.
30 S. Elden, *The Birth of Territory*, Chicago IL: Chicago University Press, 2013, 4.
31 As in Neels Ahuja's example of 'cetacean nations': see N. Ahuja, 'Species in a planetary frame: eco-cosmopolitanism, nationalism, and "The Cove"', *Tamkang Review* 42, 2 (2012): 13–32. The concept of a cetacean nation or nations has a rather longer history, for which see J. Nottman, 'Interspecies: welcome to the cetacean nation', 1994, available at www.interspecies.com/pages/cet_%20nat.html, last accessed 7 April 2017.
32 T. Saraiva, *Fascist Pigs: Technoscientific Organisms and the History of Fascism*, Cambridge: MIT Press, 2016.
33 See S. Hinchliffe, 'Indeterminacy in-decisions: science, policy and politics in the BSE (Bovine Spongiform Encephalopathy) crisis', *Transactions of the Institute of British Geographers* 26, 2 (2001): 182–204. A wider treatment is provided in S. Hinchliffe, N. Bingham, and S. Carter, *Pathological Lives: Disease, Space, and Biopolitics*, Hoboken NJ: Wiley-Blackwell, 2016, especially Ch. 6, 'Attending to meat'. For the need for historical perspective on such issues, see P. Atkins, 'Fear of animal foods: a century of zoonotics', *Appetite* 51, 1 (2008): 18–21.
34 A. Tucker, *The Light of Nature Pursued, Volume III*, London: W. Oliver, 1777, 5.

35 M. Scholtmeijer, *Animal Victims in Modern Fiction: From Sanctity to Sacrifice*, Toronto: University of Toronto Press, 1993, 5 and 92, invokes the eternal 'quarrel between culture and the animal', arguing that 'Culture knows animals best in their role as victims'. P. Armstrong, *Animals in the Fiction of Modernity*, Abingdon: Routledge, 2008, 2, insists that 'animals mean whatever culture means by them'. But rather than see animals as at best merely good to think with, we might consider the presence of animals in literature, and in the structures of feeling that underwrite it.
36 T. Porck, 'Paws, pee and mice: cats among medieval manuscripts', *Medieval Fragments* blog, 22 February 2013, available at https://medievalfragments.wordpress.com/2013/02/22/paws-pee-and-mice-cats-among-medieval-manuscripts/, last accessed 7 April 2017, translation by Thijs Porck, used with permission. See also M.H. Porck and H.J. Porck, 'Eight guidelines on book preservation from 1527: how one should preserve all books to last eternally', *Journal of Paper Conservation: IADA Reports – Mitteilungen der IADA* 13, 2 (2012): 17–25, 20.
37 Debates over intersectionality are discussed in the conclusion to N. Taylor, *Humans, Animals and Society: An Introduction to Human-Animal Studies*, New York: Lantern Books, 2013. For the difficulties translating the language and politics of intersectionality to animal rights, see Earthling Liberation Kollective, 'Why animal rights fails at intersectionality', available at https://humanrightsareanimalrights.com/blog/oppression/why-animal-rights-fails-at-intersectionality/, last accessed 7 April 2017.
38 Consider Scholtmeijer, *Animal Victims*, 297: 'In their very being, animals repudiate our efforts to subjugate them to cultural purposes'.
39 Armstrong, *Animals in the Fiction of Modernity*, 1.
40 See the film *Blackfish*, directed by G. Cowperthwaite, and produced by CNN Films, released in 2013.
41 The latest edition of this classic essay and its themes is J. Berger, *Why Look at Animals?*, London, Penguin, 2009. A recent and pertinent companion piece is provided by S. O'Brien, 'Why look at dead animals?', *Framework: The Journal of Cinema and Media* 57, 1 (2016): 32–57.
42 Zoos are 'built for viewing': S. Willis, 'Looking at the zoo', *South Atlantic Quarterly* 98, 4 (1999): 669–687, 675.
43 Vinciane Despret makes the point that animals in laboratories should also be regarded as exhibits, on show, and the claims made for pure and precise science judged accordingly: V. Despret, *What Would Animals Say if We Asked Them the Right Questions?*, trans. B. Buchanan, Minneapolis MN: Minnesota University Press, 2016.
44 Willis, 'Looking at the zoo', 680.
45 See for instance Nathaniel Wolloch's plangent thesis on early modern anthropocentrism and the scarcity of pro-animal sentiment to be found: N. Wolloch, *Subjugated Animals: Animals and Anthropocentrism in Early Modern Culture*, Amherst NY: Humanity Books, 2006.
46 Louise Robbins, who like Griffin sees that 'tenderness existed side by side with brutality and indifference', is notably cautious when it comes to these affective questions and comparisons: 'Whether people feel the same range of emotions about animals today as they did in the past is impossible to know' is Robbins' concluding sentiment: L.E. Robbins, *Elephant Slaves and Pampered Parrots: Exotic Animals in Eighteenth-Century Paris*, Baltimore MD: Johns Hopkins University Press, 2002, 232, 234.
47 Rangajaran, 'Animals with rich histories', 110.
48 The field as presently constructed is more aggressively anthropocentric than Guida suggests. A recent survey is J. Plamper, *The History of Emotions: An Introduction*, Oxford: Oxford University Press, 2015.

49 This is an example of 'the hybridisation of animal–human–machine', that Andy Flack has explored in a comparable context. See A.J.P. Flack, 'Lions loose on a gentleman's lawn: animality, authenticity and automobility in the emergence of the English safari park', *Journal of Historical Geography* 54 (2016): 38–49, 40.

50 See P. Howell, *At Home and Astray: The Domestic Dog in Victorian Britain*, Charlottesville VA: University of Virginia Press, 2015, Ch. 4.

51 We are thinking of Steven Pinker's Pollyanna-ish *The Better Angels of Our Nature: A History of Violence and Humanity*, which considers animal welfare as an index of the decline of violence, and would surely account for the decline in numbers of animals dying in state-based armed conflict (if Pinker had thought of it) in the same way; but this decline of violence is as absurd as his statistical illiteracy when it comes to human combatant deaths when we think of the so-called 'war against animals' promoted by the agro-industrial complex. See S. Pinker, *The Better Angels of Our Nature: A History of Violence and Humanity*, London: Penguin, 2012. An obvious exception to the lack of discussion of animality and animals in big picture accounts of war and violence is B. Ehrenreich, *Blood Rites: Origins and History of the Passions of War*, London: Virago, 1997.

52 D.J. Haraway, 'Sowing worlds: a seed bag for terraforming with Earth others', in M. Grebowicz and H. Merrick, with a 'seed bag' by D. Haraway, *Beyond the Cyborg: Adventures with Donna Haraway*, New York: Columbia University Press, 2013, 137–145, 137–138. This essay is reprinted in D.J. Haraway, *Staying with the Trouble: Making Kin in the Chthulucene*, Durham NC: Duke University Press, 2016, 116–125.

53 As cited in A.L. Tsing, *The Mushroom at the End of the World: On the Possibility of Life in Capitalist Ruins*, Princeton NJ: Princeton University Press, 2015, 287.

54 A.J. Toynbee, *A Study of History: Abridgement of Vols 1-VI by D.C. Somervell*, Oxford: Oxford University Press, 1987, 168.

55 Bender, *The Animal Game*, 9.

56 M. Calarco, *Zoographies: The Question of the Animal from Heidegger to Derrida*, New York: Columbia University Press, 2008, 76.

57 Robbins, *Elephant Slaves and Pampered Parrots*, 4.

58 We might consider Donna Haraway's recent suggestion (following James Clifford) that what we need should not be regarded as 'big' or 'small', but stories rather 'just big enough to gather up the complexities and keep the edges open and greedy for surprising new and old connections'. See: D.J. Haraway, 'Anthropocene, capitalocene, plantationocene, chthulucene: making kin', *Environmental Humanities* 6, 1 (2015): 159–165, 160. See also Haraway, *Staying with the Trouble*, 185 n.54.

59 D. Vandersommers, 'Narrating animal history from the crags: a turn-of-the-century tale about mountain sheep, resistance, and a nation', *Journal of American Studies* 1–27 (17 November 2016): 2–3, available at https://doi.org/10.1017/S002187581600133X, last accessed 23 March 2017. Similar sentiments are expressed by E.S. Benson, 'The urban upwelling', *The American Historian* 6 (2015): 40–44.

60 See J. Specht, 'Animal history after its triumph: unexpected animals, evolutionary approaches, and the animal lens', *History Compass* 14, 7 (2016): 326–336.

61 F.L. Brown, *The City is More than Human: An Animal History of Seattle*, Seattle, WA: University of Washington Press, 2016, 244.

62 Tsing, *Mushroom at the End of the World*, 173.

63 Tsing, *Mushroom at the End of the World*, 168.

64 The classic substantive work is: H. Ritvo, *The Animal Estate: The English and Other Creatures in the Victorian Age*, Cambridge MA: Harvard University Press, 1987. But animal–human historians should also turn to her collection *Noble Cows and Hybrid Zebras: Essays on Animals and History*, Charlottesville VA: University of Virginia Press, 2010.

Bibliography

Ahuja, N. 'Species in a planetary frame: eco-cosmopolitanism, nationalism, and "The Cove"', *Tamkang Review* 42, 2 (2012): 13–32.

Antlfinger, M., Holck, A., Hormer, U., Maage, M., and Schmitcz, F. *Animal Lovers*, Berlin: nGbK, 2016.

Ardrey, R. *The Territorial Imperative: A Personal Inquiry into the Animal Origins of Property and Nations*, New York: Atheneum, 1966.

Armstrong, P. *Animals in the Fiction of Modernity*, Abingdon: Routledge, 2008.

Atkins, P. 'Fear of animal foods: a century of zoonotics', *Appetite* 51, 1 (2008): 18–21.

Baker, S. *Artist|Animal*, Minneapolis MN: University of Minnesota Press, 2013.

Bender, D.E. *The Animal Game: Searching for Wildness at the American Zoo*, Cambridge, MA: Harvard University Press, 2016.

Benson, E. 'Animal writes: historiography, disciplinarity, and the animal trace', in L. Kalof and G.M. Montgomery (eds.), *Making Animal Meaning*, East Lansing MI: Michigan State University Press, 2011, 3–16.

Benson, E.S. 'The urban upwelling', *The American Historian* 6 (2015): 40–44.

Berger, J. *Why Look at Animals?* London: Penguin, 2009.

Brandt, N. *A Shadow Falls*, New York: Abrams Books, 2009.

Brandt, N. *Across the Ravaged Land*, volume 3, New York: Abrams, 2013.

Brandt, N. *Inherit the Dust*, New York: Edwynn Houk Editions, 2016.

Brantz, D. 'Introduction', in D. Brantz (ed.), *Beastly Natures: Animals, Humans, and the Study of History*, Charlottesville VA: University of Virginia Press, 2010, 1–13.

Brantz, D. (ed.), *Beastly Natures: Animals, Humans, and the Study of History*, Charlottesville VA: University of Virginia Press, 2010.

Brown, F.L. *The City is More than Human: An Animal History of Seattle*, Seattle, WA: University of Washington Press, 2016.

Calarco, M. *Zoographies: The Question of the Animal from Heidegger to Derrida*, New York: Columbia University Press, 2008.

Callon, M. 'Some elements of a sociology of translation: domestication of the scallops and the fishermen of St Brieuc Bay', *The Sociological Review* 32, S1 (1984): 196–233.

Despret, V. *What Would Animals Say if We Asked Them the Right Questions?*, trans. B. Buchanan, Minneapolis MN: Minnesota University Press, 2016.

Descola, P. *Beyond Nature and Culture*, Chicago IL: University of Chicago Press, 2013.

Donald, D. *Picturing Animals in Britain 1750–1850*, New Haven CT: Yale University Press, 2007.

Earthling Liberation Kollective, 'Why animal rights fails at intersectionality', available at https://humanrightsareanimalrights.com/blog/oppression/why-animal-rights-fails-at-intersectionality/, last accessed 7 April 2017.

Ehrenreich, B. *Blood Rites: Origins and History of the Passions of War*, London: Virago, 1997.

Elden, S. *The Birth of Territory*, Chicago IL: Chicago University Press, 2013.

Flack, A.J.P. 'Lions loose on a gentleman's lawn: animality, authenticity and automobility in the emergence of the English safari park', *Journal of Historical Geography* 54 (2016): 38–49.

Fudge, E. 'Milking other men's beasts', *History and Theory* 52 (2013), 13–28.

Haraway, D.J. 'Sowing worlds: a seed bag for terraforming with Earth others', in M. Grebowicz and H. Merrick, with a 'seed bag' by Donna Haraway, *Beyond the Cyborg: Adventures with Donna Haraway*, New York: Columbia University Press, 2013, 137–145.

Haraway, D.J. 'Anthropocene, capitalocene, plantationocene, chthulucene: making kin', *Environmental Humanities* 6, 1 (2015): 159–165.

Haraway, D.J. *Staying with the Trouble: Making Kin in the Chthulucene*, Durham NC: Duke University Press, 2016, 116–125.

Hinchliffe, S. 'Indeterminacy in decisions: science, policy and politics in the BSE (Bovine Spongiform Encephalopathy) crisis', *Transactions of the Institute of British Geographers* 26, 2 (2001): 182–204.

Hinchliffe, S., Bingham, N., and Carter, S. *Pathological Lives: Disease, Space, and Biopolitics*, Hoboken NJ: Wiley-Blackwell, 2016.

Howell, P. *At Home and Astray: The Domestic Dog in Victorian Britain*, Charlottesville VA: University of Virginia Press, 2015.

Kean, H. *The Great Cat and Dog Massacre: The Real Story of World War II's Unknown Tragedy*, Chicago IL: University of Chicago Press, 2018.

Law, J. (ed.), *Power, Action and Belief: A New Sociology of Knowledge*, London: Routledge & Kegan Paul, 1986.

Nottman, J. 'Interspecies: welcome to the cetacean nation', 1994, available at www.interspecies.com/pages/cet_%20nat.html, last accessed 7 April 2017.

Nance, S. (ed.), *The Historical Animal*, Syracuse NY: Syracuse University Press, 2015.

O'Brien, S. 'Why Look at Dead Animals?', *Framework: The Journal of Cinema and Media* 57, 1 (2016): 32–57.

Pinker, S. *The Better Angels of Our Nature: A History of Violence and Humanity*, London: Penguin, 2012.

Plamper, J. *The History of Emotions: An Introduction*, Oxford: Oxford University Press, 2015.

Porck, M.H. and Porck, H.J. 'Eight guideline on book preservation from 1527: how one should preserve all books to last eternally', *Journal of Paper Conservation: IADA Reports – Mitteilungen der IADA* 13, 2 (2012): 17–25.

Porck, M.H. 'Paws, pee and mice: cats among medieval manuscripts', *Medieval Fragments* blog, 22 February 2013, available at https://medievalfragments.wordpress.com/2013/02/22/paws-pee-and-mice-cats-among-medieval-manuscripts/, last accessed 7 April 2017.

Premack, D. and Premack, A.J. 'Why animals have neither culture nor history', in T. Ingold (ed.), *Companion Encyclopedia of Anthropology*, London: Routledge, 1994, 350–365.

Rangajaran, M. 'Animals with rich histories: the case of the lions of Gir Forest, Gujarat, India', *History and Theory* 52, 4 (2013): 109–127.

Ritvo, H. *The Animal Estate: The English and Other Creatures in the Victorian Age*, Cambridge MA: Harvard University Press, 1987.

Ritvo, H. *Noble Cows and Hybrid Zebras: Essays on Animals and History*, Charlottesville, VA: University of Virginia Press, 2010.

Robbins, L.E. *Elephant Slaves and Pampered Parrots: Exotic Animals in Eighteenth-Century Paris*, Baltimore MD: Johns Hopkins University Press, 2002.

Saraiva, T. *Fascist Pigs: Technoscientific Organisms and the History of Fascism*, Cambridge, MA: MIT Press, 2016.

Scholtmeijer, M. *Animal Victims in Modern Fiction: From Sanctity to Sacrifice*, Toronto: University of Toronto Press, 1993, 5.

Shaw, D.G. 'A way with animals', *History and Theory* 52, 4 (2013): 1–12, 11.

Specht, J. 'Animal history after its triumph: unexpected animals, evolutionary approaches, and the animal lens', *History Compass* 14, 7 (2016): 326–336.

Taylor, N. *Humans, Animals and Society: An Introduction to Human-Animal Studies*, New York: Lantern Books, 2013.

Thomas, K. *Man and the Natural World. Changing Attitudes in England 1500–1800*, London: Allen Lane, 1983.

Thomas, K. 'Diary', *London Review of Books* 32, 11 (10 June 2010): 36–37.

Tosh, J. and Lang, S. *The Pursuit of History: Aims, Methods, and New Directions in the Study of Modern History*, fourth edition, London: Pearson Longman, 2006, 50.

Toynbee, A.J. *A Study of History: Abridgement of Vols 1-VI by D.C. Somervell*, Oxford: Oxford University Press, 1987, 168.

Tsing, A.L. *The Mushroom at the End of the World: On the Possibility of Life in Capitalist Ruins*, Princeton NJ: Princeton University Press, 2015.

Tucker, A. *The Light of Nature Pursued, Volume III*, London: W. Oliver, 1777.

Vandersommers, D. 'Narrating animal history from the crags: a turn-of-the-century tale about mountain sheep, resistance, and a nation', *Journal of American Studies* 1–27 (17 November 2016): 2–3, available at https://doi.org/10.1017/S002187581600133X, last accessed 23 March 2017.

Watts, C. (ed.), *Relational Archaeologies: Humans, Animals, Things*, Abingdon: Routledge, 2013.

Willis, S. 'Looking at the zoo', *South Atlantic Quarterly* 98, 4 (1999): 669–687.

Wolloch, N. *Subjugated Animals: Animals and Anthropocentrism in Early Modern Culture*, Amherst NY: Humanity Books, 2006.

PART I
Animals and the practice of history

2
THE OTHER CITIZENS
Nationalism and animals

Sandra Swart

'Wounded Lions angry and disappointed after Springboks victory', 'Angolan Black Antelopes outrun the Lions of the Atlas', 'Congo's Leopards devour Mali's Eagles', 'Wallabies wallop Los Pumas', 'Vultures off to a flying start against Mauritius': one reads the headlines and one might be forgiven for thinking that there is a global war raging in the animal kingdom. It appears to be an apocalyptic post-human extension of the nation-state; as though governments had wearied of human casualties and decided to appoint animals as their proxies – like knights of olde jousting to represent their kings. Another image is that of the more jaded of the Roman emperors, wearying of his *bestiarii* slaughtering exotic creatures and simply pitting the beasts against each other for the thrill of the crowd. Or perhaps it is rather as if heraldry itself had come to life and suddenly the lion *rampant* confronts a griffin *sergeant* or a springbok *courant*. This muscular menagerie of competitive and athletic beasts struggle to defend their nations' honour. They seem to have taken Darwin's hypothesis to heart and wish to see if really only – literally – the fittest survive. To turn from the sports pages, however, to the political cartoons, we see international disputes between the British bulldog, the Spanish bull, the Russian bear, the New Zealand kiwi, and the South African springbok. Sometimes even real, living animals make the political pages: in 2014, for instance, an endangered Siberian tiger named Kuzya crossed the frozen Amur River into China, prompting an international incident – after consuming some Chinese chickens. Kuzya inspired an even less diplomatic Russian-born tiger named Ustin to cross the border into Chinese territory and go on a sustained goat-killing spree. Ustin and Kuzya were not just any tigers – they were rescued as orphaned cubs, taught to hunt by Russian officials, and released into the wild by President Vladimir Putin himself. Since these tigrine wanderings, there have been outraged calls in Chinese social media for Putin's tigers to be hunted and killed. Others have declared it a Kremlin spying mission through the GPS collars on the beasts. A Chinese official noted worriedly that the Russian tigers clearly had plans to cross the border again – but the sub-text is clearly a fear of the Russian Bear following the tigers' example.

This chapter is intended to introduce the critical theme of animals, nationalism and national histories by offering both a brief overview of the existing historiography (to convey the main arguments and debates) as well as offering an illustrative case-study to understand these approaches at work. In this way it is intended to introduce newcomers to 'animal–human history' to a particularly important topic, as well as act as a reference guide and companion to the existing literature on this topic.

This chapter first discusses our historical understanding of nationalism, and then examines the literature on what we think of as the 'Good Animals' of nationalism. It explores the historical dimensions to the choice of 'national animal', defined as any creature that over time has come to be politically identified with a nation-state. The chapter draws on conventional understandings of nationalism (formal state-directed programmes), but also draws on Billig's influential model of banal nationalism, the quotidian construction of a nation built on a shared (albeit constructed) sense of national belonging among humans, which often deploys non-human animals – both symbolically and materially.[1] The literal clash between animals and the rhetoric attached to it is examined by looking at the research at the intersection of nation and class, race, gender – to which this chapter adds 'species'. As will be demonstrated, such rhetoric over 'Good Animals' is banal but far from benign.

The chapter then explores the 'Bad Animals' of nationalism. Certain animals have been understood as 'bad' by and for the nation-state. The chapter looks at how some key historians have discussed the construction of 'vermin' as a national problem. There has been an all too easy slippage, at some historical junctures, eliding human and animal 'vermin'. The chapter subsequently turns to the clash between 'Good' and 'Bad' animals: specifically, the politics of the alien versus the native animal. The chapter shows how humans can be forced into the category of the Bad animal too. The relationship between the 'Good' and the 'Bad' animal is explored through an analysis of the relationship between the 'native', the 'natural' and the 'nation'. The chapter looks at roles the 'animal-citizens' play in the story a nation tells about itself. A metaphor about methodology taken from ecological sampling is apposite here in explaining the case-studies used: one throws a wired square called a quadrat at random onto the ground and then one scrutinises whatever species fall underneath it. Similarly, this chapter throws quadrats over a few global hotspots using various case-studies in order to understand how nationalists have deployed animals. Lifting the quadrats, we look at practices of breeding, slaughtering and eating animals and find wild and domestic animals, the tamed and the untamed, including the kinds of animals with which we opened this chapter but many others too – rugby-playing gazelles, penguins, skuas, trout, rhinos, whales, beavers, polar bears, kangaroos, and even Nazi cows.

Herderian herds

Can animals be nationalists? The question is not as absurd as it might seem. From some evolutionary theorists has arisen the argument that national or ethnic attachment is a form of evolved altruism among group-living animals. Usually such large agglomerations occur among mammals 'in the form of herds . . . in which the average individual gains directly from joining the group. Rarely does membership in such a herd involve costs comparable to the self-sacrifice of those willing to die for their national pride'.[2] It has been argued, however, that if there is a biological basis for group strife it should be understood within the context of humanity's quest for identity. Nationalism exists as extensions of the normal human (or animal?) desire to protect the group – the strong 'affective need to delimit a social cosmos of conspecifics with whom he can share interpretations of his socially constructed world'.[3] Nationalism and its hypertrophies (like xenophobia or racism) thus seems (to many theorists, such as Perry Anderson) a very human construct – but this position has been attacked by controversial populists such as Robert Ardrey and more serious researchers, such as Konrad Lorenz and Lionel Tiger; Ardrey and others were essentially using 'animal nationalism' to argue that humans were hardwired to seek territorial control.[4]

In navigating this debate one remembers uneasily the warring chimpanzee tribes described by pioneering primatologist Jane Goodall. She witnessed a four-year civil war for territory involving kidnapping, rape, and murder.[5] The 'Gombe Chimpanzee War' that Goodall described raged from 1974 to 1978, a violent conflict between two groups in Tanzania's Gombe Stream National Park. The Kasakela (in the north) and the Kahama (in the south) had previously been a single, unified community, but the chimps dispersed into northern and southern factions. Hostilities erupted in January 1974, when a raiding sortie of six adult Kasakela males killed a young Kahama male. By 1976, the war had gained full-throttled momentum with groups of Kasakela unleashing almost daily cross-border incursions into Kahama territory. Over the next four years, all of the Kahama adult males were killed by the Kasakela males. Of the Kahama females: one was killed outright, two went missing mysteriously, and three were kidnapped, beaten and raped by the Kasakela males. The Kasakela then took over the Kahama's erstwhile territory. Alas, the war (like many human wars) was for nothing. With the Kahama gone, the Kasakela's range now bordered the more populous and powerful Kalande, who quickly forced the Kasakela to relinquish their newly conquered territory. Scientists and the public were initially astonished by Goodall's fieldnotes – as chimpanzees had been seen as inherently gentle creatures. But similar outbreaks have been recorded over time and the broad consensus is now that chimpanzees (like humans) aggressively defend territories against outside groups and struggle for dominance over neighbouring groups,[6] basing their decisions to attack strangers on strategic assessments of the strength of their largely male coalitions.[7] In fact, the uneasy feeling about parallels between the two species grows because of the familiarity of chimpanzee warfare: we recognise their silent patrols and tactical attempts to isolate and undermine their enemies – because they parallel our own. There were the usual casualties of war and war crimes: adults and babies were cannibalised during and after mêlées. Killing thus emerges for them – as it does for us – as a consequence of having 'turf', living in separate groups, and the vicissitudes of volatile power relations. It is questionable whether this can be defined as nationalism – although a lively literature has arisen defending the animal roots of human nationalism – this naturalisation of nationalism serves to legitimise in many quarters the aggressive defence of national borders. Nevertheless, whether or not they can be nationalist (in even a crude sense) themselves, this chapter will show that animals play a very lively role in a nation's foundation and edifice, both materially and, particularly, symbolically.

'Nationalism is a dangerous animal'[8]

The very first human to use the word 'nationalism' was Johann Gottfried von Herder (1744–1803), who understood it as a vigorous attachment to one's own nation, based on (at least etymologically) a birth group or a blood-related group, which could (he lamented) also turn into chauvinism against other nations.[9] Most subsequent philosophers have embraced the cosmopolitan narrative of a shared history and identity. Perhaps only Herder has offered the most enduring philosophical intervention in the other direction, as he conceptualised the nation as a major unit of social analysis or, indeed, as the basic 'unit' of humanity.[10] Isaiah Berlin later interpreted this as purely cultural nationalism, but there are elements of political nationalism useful in our analysis.[11] Herder associated nations with particular terrains, marked by climate and topography – national landscapes.[12] Even when people were dispersed or migrated, he still thought them linked to their original homeland, which imprinted onto their sensibilities as children, permeated their thought and language and thus got passed down 'from generation to generation' even if people left that landscape by emigrating.

Despite Herderian notions of enduring generational transfer, nation-states are an historically relatively recent phenomenon: they are not eternal, despite their claims to the contrary. Ernest Gellner argued that, although nationalists pretend that nations were always there, 'in the very nature of things [as it were, in Herderian terms], only waiting to be "awakened" ... from their regrettable slumber, by the nationalist "awakener".'[13] As Ernest Renan reminds one: 'Nations are not something eternal. They have begun, they will end'.[14] He could have added: not anytime soon, though. Nationalism is not a spent force: as Serbia/Bosnia, the newly liberated republics of the Soviet Union, South Sudan, Scotland, Brexit and innumerable other examples demonstrate. While globalisation and multi-culturalism are powerful forces, nothing suggests that nationalism will be displaced or overcome in the near future.

Neither can one make an argument for increasing global orderliness: nationalism is a rough beast. Nations and territories do not neatly correspond: people spill over borders, loyalties stretch across boundaries or proliferate within them – all in complex ways. The simple territorially and homogenous nation-state is largely a myth and the existence of national minorities is almost inescapable. Even Herder conceded the 'imperfect alignment of state and nation', given the messy realities of the real world it is a multi-nation state that seeks to set up structures of self-government for different national groups, to respond to 'heterogeneities in national belonging'.[15] Herder sternly disapproved of the 'wild mixing of various races and nationalities under one sceptre', while strongly approving of cultural diversity in separate spheres, and cultural determinism.[16] It is a starting point to understand – given the modern global order – both the unavoidability of national identity and its undeniable power, both covert and manifest. Nationalism spills over theoretical borders too. Of course, there is no direct cut-off point between patriotism–nationalism–jingoism–xenophobia; they exist on a continuum.[17] Nationalism (on this shifting spectrum) is a resurgent force, despite Trotsky's wishful thinking in consigning it to the 'ash heap of history'. Politicians, as inveterate scavengers – together with raccoons, foxes and bears – have long overturned and rooted through the dustbins of history.

Another point to ponder is that nationalism only works on the presumption that humans alone are individuals and agentive – both ideas have been challenged from an animal studies perspective that reminds one that species are constructed categories. Species spill over bio-borders too. Donna Haraway has, for example, noted that we need to think about 'terrain politics', which recognises that bodies are composed of different species at different levels – apparently autonomous bodies are really overlapping ecosystems of parasites, pathogens and microscopic biota.[18] Humans are walking multi-species compilations – internally cosmopolitan despite our narrow definition of self. This certainly extends Herder's argument that humans are the only cosmopolitan species, whereas other species are specific, linked irrevocably to their own environments. He declared: 'Human beings should live everywhere on earth, while every animal species merely has its land and its narrower sphere'.[19] But animals ignore Herder's localism all the time, as this chapter will explore when discussing exotic or alien species. As noted earlier in this chapter, most philosophers have embraced the cosmopolitan narrative of a shared global human history and identity, but it is challenging to push the idea of eco-cosmopolitanism as a counterweight to 'animal' nationalism. While it is a relatively new concept that still needs theorisation, eco-cosmopolitanism pushes one to think past narrow nationalism, to challenge 'nationalist political conflicts over environment and take account of the planetary ecological systems that must be assessed by any cultural production attempting to introduce an environmental ethic'.[20] From this perspective, Ahuja looked at animals who defy all borders and travel vast distances: the cetaceans. He analysed the 2009 Oscar-winning documentary *The Cove*, which looks at dolphin-hunting practices in Japan, to offer a critique of nationalism's legitimation of violence towards (some) animals. Ahuja argues that cetaceans, who travel vast oceanic distances around the planet, are somehow not part of the imaginings that form the foundation of nations.[21]

Yet, actually, cetaceans are very much bound up in constructing countries.[22] Whales are sites and symbols for the 'material exercise of national sovereignty', including the 'sovereign right' to 'noncriminally put to death', in Derrida's term, meaning to engage in state-sanctioned violence.[23] For example in Japan, although few still desire to eat whale flesh, whaling is about far more than merely meat. After World War II, when a defeated Japan needed protein, the American occupying authorities advised that whale meat should become a staple in school lunches. Whale meat then became for the first time widespread nationally as a part of the Japanese diet. A generation later, under a 1986 ban on commercial whaling by the International Whaling Commission, Japan was still permitted to engage in ostensible 'scientific whaling' and to sell the meat afterwards. The country's whale consumption crested in 1962 at 226,000 tons, then dropped to a mere 15,000 tons in 1985, the year *before* the ban. Some argue that the Japanese stopped consuming whale meat as the country recovered from the war and turned to more popular meat sources, such as beef. Nowadays, Japan remains pro-whaling because it

> evokes a sense of nationalism. Japan does not want to stop whaling simply because it is told to do so by Western countries, including those that encouraged Japanese to eat whale meat after the war, when other food sources were scarce.[24]

As Ayako Okubo, from the Ocean Policy Research Foundation, observed: 'It's not because Japanese want to eat whale meat. It's because they don't like being told not to eat it by foreigners'.[25]

Cock and bull stories: gender, class and nationalism

Foreigners telling people what to do about animals has a long history. Janet Davis has shown how the American colonial authorities often used animals as a proxy form of government and to legitimise colonial rule as benign stewardship.[26] From the end of the nineteenth century, the American Society for the Protection of Animals, established in 1866, spread its dominion to Cuba, Puerto Rico, the Philippines – the new dominions of the United States. Its views on anti-cruelty worked in tandem with new colonial laws designed to refashion the freshly acquired territories, to 'promote a better state of things wherever the authority of the Nation is established'.[27] Animal advocacy had a long relationship with power, especially the power inherent to scripting the nation.[28] Of course, the historical spread of humanitarianism transnationally also played an important role – with anti-slavery and then animal welfare.[29] The new American authorities banned cockfighting, with heavy fines of $500 and jail time of up to six months. Cockfighting, as Clifford Geertz showed 40 years ago, had long been fundamental to the story that some nations – such as the Balinese – told themselves about how their society was structured, helping shape their national self-identity.[30] Similarly, cockfighting was integral to the gendered and classed self-understanding of participants in the new American colonies. The men involved projected much of their own masculinised identity onto the fighting roosters. The main fight could be between two parties or multiple entrants, but in each fight, two cocks (armed with natural spurs or metal razor spurs) were matched by weight and presented by handlers, allowed to give each other a few pecks and then released to fight until the conclusion: running away, refusal to fight, defeat or death. Davis has shown how this worked as a kind of 'animal nationalism' with supporters, opponents and participants projecting gendered and classed 'ideologies of nation' onto the roosters. The fights were more than avian-advanced avarice or ambition or aggression – at stake were also political claims about 'citizenship' and 'national belonging'.[31] Defenders of the pursuit were cockfight nationalists intent on defending the sport as a legitimate struggle for sovereignty and simultaneously resisting their 'othering' by the state. On the opposite side, agents of the state created a pecking order of 'animal kindness', buttressing their claims of 'benevolent stewardship' over the other nations. Interestingly, local men did not object to the banning of bullfighting under the same suite of laws, as it had long been seen as the hated symbol of their previous oppressors, the Spanish. Bullfighting was seen as the realm of the hated nobility and Roman Catholic Church, whereas roosters were cheap to own – they were fecund and tough, which is why the irascible birds were able to follow commerce and conquest globally after originating in South East Asia.[32] Thus colonial authorities wielded overt power over 'animal welfare' in order to refashion their subjects 'Good people'. But what about inventing 'Good animals'?

The good animals?

One of the critical building blocks of nationalism is a state-sponsored and media-propagated celebration of a defined territory. Often this is described as territorial possession over a 'natural' environment, which is rhetorically described as having shaped the 'national character'. Such natural symbolism is vital in inventing and then curating a shared national identity. As a key theorist of nationalism, Anthony Smith argues that, together, these symbols 'constitute an important force for social solidarity, transformation, and renewal . . . necessary for the establishment of social cohesion, the legitimisation of institutions and of political authority, and the inculcation of beliefs and conventions of behaviour'.[33] National symbols are not only displayed in the most palpable ways: armies marching or in jingoistic displays of national flag-waving but also, in Billig's terms, the most banal and quotidian circumstances and ubiquitous but unremarked-upon icons – such as the 'national animals' incorporated into the Coat of Arms.[34] In Canada there has been recent controversy over the national symbol chosen in 1975 – the beaver – on the grounds that it resembles, as a conservative senator put it in 2011, a 'dentally defective rat' who simply vandalises the environment.[35] The senator proposed the polar bear, 'with its strength, courage, . . . and dignity', which critics warned would be an unfortunate symbol if they followed trends predicted by ecologists and became extinct. There were several dissenters: a member of Parliament maintained that dislodging the beaver would ignore the animal's impact on Canada's history, as it was 'the relentless pursuit of beaver that opened the great Northwest' (early colonists moved into the country's extremities to trap beavers for their pelts). A local natural history professor at Carleton University countered that the national emblem was not just a question of history. Instead he found the beaver ontologically apposite for the national *Geist*: 'They are like Canadians. Their demeanour is very pleasant', before adding, 'Polar bears inspire fear'.[36] Most national leaders like their national animals to be terrifying. Iconic beasts are frequently not indigenous, but are usually predators. Many European countries, for example, are represented by a lion or an eagle – they appear in at least 39 of the world's national symbols.

An oddly non-threatening national animal for a redoubtable state was South Africa's springbok (Afrikaans: *spring* meaning leap; *bok* meaning antelope), a graceful gazelle that became a symbol of (white) South Africa in the early twentieth century, appearing on the coat of arms and a number of South African sports teams, most prominently the national rugby team (a sport central to the identity of white, male South Africans). In fact, the springbok has been the emblem of the South African National Rugby team since it was introduced in 1906. After apartheid's demise, the new African National Congress government declared that teams were to be known as the Proteas, an indigenous flower. At the last moment, then-president Nelson Mandela allowed the rugby team to stay the 'Springboks', as a gesture of goodwill to the mainly white (and largely Afrikaner) rugby supporters, stating 'there is a real possibility that if we accept the Springbok we will unite our country as never before'. On the day of the final, President Mandela famously strode out onto the field wearing a Springbok jersey and cap to hand over the trophy to the victorious (white Afrikaans) Springbok captain. Under the spirit of a rainbow nation, the 'Boks' became reimagined as the

Africanised version of 'springboks' – the '*Amabokoboko*'.[37] Twenty years later, with the rainbow faded to a grey economic outlook and amid protests at the slow pace of transformation in rugby (as a proxy for the slow pace of transformation in broader society) the Protea replaced the Springbok as the national emblem. The Springbok did not go extinct: its home range moved from its traditional place on the left breast of the jersey, to the right breast (alongside the Protea) for international matches. The emblem issue occasionally resurfaces as a proxy for debates over nation-building.

Sometimes the 'Good Animals' are not emblematic but rather, real creatures, actively introduced to colonise a new space.[38] For example, in Australia – just as in other colonial spaces – the settlers sought to make themselves feel *at* home, by making it *like* home.[39] Whereas at first a certain pragmatism pervaded, with native animals such as the kangaroo at least providing a source of food before sufficient livestock could be imported, as the colony became more established there was an increasing desire to import Britain into the new landscape by importing British wildlife: among many others, songbirds, rabbits, foxes, brown trout and rainbow trout.[40] By the 1860s, acclimatisation societies institutionalised the importation of British beasts, but also, interestingly, exotica from other colonies, including springbok from South Africa.[41] But, while such aliens were nurtured, natives were ruthlessly suppressed in the 'fauna wars'; wombats and bilbies were killed for their digging, grazing marsupials for their conflict with sheep, and various carnivores for stock depredation.[42] However, by the early twentieth century there was political opposition to native animal slaughter and increasing accord on the need for native animal protection. By the mid-twentieth century, 'World War II reinforced Australian nationalism, and the post-war collapse of the British Empire forced Australians to reconstruct their national identity'.[43] Nationalism was one of the drivers behind redefining ecological policy and protection of native animals, re-categorising them as worthy of protection. Thus, because of shifts within nationalism, native animals could shape-shift between 'Bad' and 'Good' animals.

The bad animals – the Herd Reich?

The Good animals of one state may become the reviled Bad animals of the next regime. This is illustrated by the story of a restoration project that had much in common with nationalist Herderian quests for origin and authenticity.[44] As noted, Herder developed the idea of organic nationalism, in which the state partly derives its legitimacy from historic cultural and hereditary groups. It has been argued that Nazi ideas of a Germanic identity drew on Herder's romantic quest for the eternal *geist*. One such project was run by the brothers Lutz and Heinz Heck, of the Berlin and Munich zoos. Both were well connected to the Nationalist Socialist elite and, in line with the Nazi ecomythography, they celebrated autochthonous animals. For the 1936 Olympics in Berlin, Lutz Heck fashioned a Teutonic zoo, with 'Wolf Rock' at its hub, surrounded by what they considered quintessentially 'German' animals such as bears and lynxes. But the Heck brothers also sought to resurrect the long-dead and half-mythic beasts found in the nineteenth century romantic opera of Richard Wagner, who came to be idolised by the Nazi party. Both Nietzsche and Wagner espoused an ancient reverence for the animal spirit. Wagner's operatic heroes and villains battled each other in a darkly preternatural world, which prized fantasy over banal reality by reviving and, indeed, re-creating traditional Norse and Teutonic mythology.

Lutz Heck simply adapted a traditional method of selective breeding animals to accentuate certain traits: 'What my brother and I now had to do was to unite in a single breeding stock all those characteristics of the wild animal which are now found only separately in individual animals'.[45] Even an apparently vanished animal's genes might be found in the gene pool of closely related kin or direct descendants, so if he focused on slowly 'breeding back' animals most similar to their extinct forebears, over time he would re-establish their pure ancestral being.[46] The Heck brothers tried to revive the aurochs (the wild ancestor of domestic cattle), the wisent (a forest dwelling bison) and the tarpan (an ancient horse breed) by ostensibly breeding back to primordial purity, to purge the degeneration inherent in domestication. These beasts were intended to re-wild the forests of the Third Reich as living totems to its power. The Hecks worked under the patronage of Hermann Göring, who also revived for himself a title itself extinct for two centuries: '*Reichsjägermeister*' ('The Reich's Master of the Hunt'). Together they tried to repopulate the *urwald* forest landscape with animals from the romantic Wagnerian imagination.[47] Some of his back-bred animals were released into the newly conquered Białowieża forest in Poland. Heck recalled:

> In my youth my imagination was caught by the famous description in [Wagner's] Nibelungenlied of Siegfried's hunt in the forest ... I was interested above all in the two huge wild oxen, which ... are regarded as the most powerful representatives of primeval German game – the European bison and the aurochs.[48]

The ethologist Konrad Lorenz argued in a key article, illustrated with photographs from Lutz Heck's zoo, that 'civilized' animals and humans were analogous.[49] He maintained that the domesticated beast and the urbanised human both suffered the retention of immature features into adulthood, degeneration of the muscles and morals, and a marked increase in libido. He saw domestication as a degenerative disintegration; the Hecks were confronting this disintegration by breeding 'national' animals back towards the 'original'. Yet the Hecks bred an irony. In attempting to revive the pure and primitive aurochs, they actually created a hybrid mongrel of modern breeds. Some labelled the project a ruse that created new breeds as mere facsimiles of extinct ones. Most of the ancient creatures were only briefly brought back. The aurochs released into the captured Polish forest were shot by hungry soldiers for food. When the Allies bombed Berlin in January 1944, the zoo animals burned and bled to death in their cages. Some escaped, briefly, and scattered. Lutz Heck's son had to shoot the stampeding aurochs.

The Heck brothers' vision was essentially of nationalist expansion through animals, territorially and temporally, across the borders into Poland's Białowieża forest and back in time to revive extinct beasts. In a sense it was a bloody remaking of history, landscape and body echoing the Nazi project itself. Indeed, some Polish green groups, for example, still actively resist the backbred beings as foreign forgeries.[50] Some zoologists certainly prefer to speak of 'near-tarpans' or 'neo-aurochsen'. But despite the ideological baggage, four decades after the war, Heck cattle started spreading out across Europe in a range of restorative projects. Current nomenclature no longer differentiates the aurochs as a species separate from domestic cattle. The '*Bos primigenius*' lost its vaunted exclusive scientific status. Significantly, in an act that shows how animals can transcend their ideological heritage, in the *Oostvaardersplassen* in the Netherlands they were introduced as eco-proxies, useful substitutes for the Ice Age mega-fauna that once nibbled down the meadow grasses.[51] However, nationalism prevailed; when a conservationist brought a few over to his farm in Devon in 2009, the British press (from the *Daily Mail* to the *Guardian*) reported on this bovine invasion of 'Nazi cows' with a mixture of knee-jerk nationalism and satire: 'Giant Nazi cows on the loose in Britain', 'Nazi "Super Cows" Shipped to Devon Farm', 'Farmer brings "Nazi" cows back to Britain after 2,000 years'; the *Daily Mail's* contribution, 'In an English field, the cattle created by Hitler', was accompanied by a picture of the Heck cattle captioned with the British tabloid's traditional pun, 'We were only following udders'.[52]

From rebirth to death?

A significant facet in understanding nationalism's relationship with animals is looking at how animals are not only bred, but how they die. Staying with Germany for this example; in 1995, a federal German court banned Muslims from *schächten* – slaughtering animals without prior stunning, ruling that the practice was not a religious necessity and therefore unprotected by freedom of religious expression in the constitution.[53] This was overturned seven years later, in 2002, as halal slaughter without stunning the beast was seen as integral to freedom of religion. David Smith traces the practice back a generation to the 1980s and shows that objections sometimes had xenophobic or racist rhetoric.[54] In fact, religious slaughter had been allowed in the Weimar Republic, and one of the Nazis' first changes to the law (targeted, of course, at Jews) in 1933 was a directive specifying compulsory stunning of all slaughter animals. There followed a raft of animal protectionist laws by the Nazis, which were overturned by the Allies in 1946. The Federal Court of Justice (*Bundesgegerichtshof*) confirmed that the Nazis' law had been an instrument of intra-national nationalism, a violent measure aimed at Jews, and confirmed toleration of *schächten*. But, as the Muslim population increased in West Germany from 6,500 (in 1961) to 1.8 million (in 1989), the biggest welfare group, the German Animal Protection Association, turned its attention to this section of the population. West Germany's nationality laws were based not on birth/residency but on 'blood', so resident Muslims could not access citizens' public services or vote. The growing population and rising unemployment became linked in many people's minds and triggered a national debate in the 1980s on what it meant to be 'German'. Discussion centred on the unGermanness of the 'barbaric' practice of inflicting unneeded pain and fear upon the beast. This was mobilised as a trope of distinction between German and non-German. Adherents of animal-protectionism, Smith notes, supported an ideology of cultural homogeneity. Essentially – in their minds – foreigners could only become nationalised if they repudiated their ideas about animals and embraced German values of compassionate citizenry (in a parallel to the cockfighting laws discussed earlier).

For almost two decades, state authorities refused to issue permits for halal slaughter. Then in 2002, a Muslim butcher raised the issue to the level of a constitutional complaint. The court ruled that religious freedom of expression necessitated allowing halal slaughter and acknowledged that there was not yet scientific consensus over whether stunning spares animals' pain. As Smith argues, this decision 'finally slaughtered the animal protectionists' holy cow of western, "humane" and "conventional" slaughter with stunning'.[55] But then the court revealed its own political nationalist interest in the matter, concluding that the right of Muslims to practise halal slaughter aided their assimilation into German society.

Joeys and jingos: the national stomach and the politics of food

Just as Smith had examined slaughtering animals, Charlotte Craw went one step further and reflected on the nationalist politics of *eating* them.[56] Craw has explored the alignment of nationalist narratives and recipes using 'indigenous animals'; using kangaroo meat qualifies a dish as 'Australian' and somehow environmentally sound. She notes that the native, the natural and the nation have become intertwined. Animals framed as 'natural' and very 'other' to the human realm of politics, were actually deployed in questions of settler belonging. Craw uses a popular recipe book, 'the bible of contemporary Australian home cooking', to understand how consuming kangaroo meat became a soothing solution to an uncomfortable disquiet over national identity.[57] Such nostalgic deployment of kangaroo meat legitimised a particular conception of nationalised identity for (white) Australians anxious over their 'place' in the country.

This 'food nationalism' can also affect animals. In 2014, for example, the inmates of Russia's Moscow Zoo, one of Europe's oldest, were caught up in a quasi-Cold War fracas. The Kremlin announced a curb on Western imports, which suddenly made zoo fodder 'forbidden fruit', after an embargo on food imports from the United States, the European Union and other Western countries intended to be political retaliation towards nations critical of Russia's reaction to Ukraine's insurgency.[58] But the diplomatic blow also hit furry stomachs at the zoo. The animals were used to cosmopolitan dining: 'The sea lions crack open Norwegian shellfish. The cranes peck at Latvian herring. The orangutans snack on Dutch bell peppers. Now the venerable Moscow Zoo needs to find politically acceptable substitutes to satisfy finicky animal palates . . . '.[59] The animals 'don't like Russian food,' a zoo spokesperson admitted. The Russian Bear, symbolising Russian 'virility and independence' was, ironically, one of the animals worst affected.[60]

What is especially important for dissecting animals as categories here (quite literally – in the case of the kangaroo-meat recipes) is that, as discussed earlier in the chapter, 'exotic' and 'native' are historically loaded terms – they carry a heavy history. This burden of the past carries into the present, particularly in battles over national identity. As Marcus Hall observed about projecting human political anxieties onto animals: 'Natives and exotics are us . . . '.[61] Kenneth Olwig has also demonstrated that discourses over the dangers and perils of alien species bleed into (sometimes quite literally) violent rhetoric over native-alien discourse.[62] Olwig notes that the scientists who fret about the penetration by invasive exotica are often blithely unaware of overlaps with national chauvinists. But nationalists have certainly drawn on the work of scientists on ecological imperialism and the supposed threat of foreign races to the native populations.[63] In similar vein, Duncan Brown has asked 'Are Trout South African?' He uses this as a lens into exploring the politics of acclimatising trout, a 'non-native' species, just as in the earlier Australian example, which has operated as a metaphor for understanding a search for identity within a white settler society. Naturalists and settler ideologues both preferred to see 'nature' as an 'empty space' for better 'breeds' – be they fish or human. Brown argues further that the history of trout in South Africa can also be understood as that of a 'rainbow of hope' rising above narrow-minded claims of national identity and 'belonging'. These are incredibly important questions to ask about nationhood, given South Africa's ugly exhibitions of extreme xenophobia – from violent attacks on African 'foreigners' in 2008 and 2015, in particular, to more stealthy refusals to employ them in key sectors, seeing them as threats to national security.

Animal whites?

Staying with South Africa, historical anthropologists Jean and John Comaroff have focused on newspaper coverage of South African ecological 'news', and explored public panics over the threat of alien species to native ecosystems.[64] They have theorised the 'ecology of nationhood' to explain a 'new post-racist form of racism' in which anxieties of belonging are projected onto nature itself, to ostensibly de-politicise a highly charged racial issue. Certainly, there is an element of claims of autochthony through a 'benevolent stewardship' like the kind described earlier in the chapter of the US officials over their cruel cockfighting colonies; white citizens often claim 'belonging' through protecting and policing 'nature'. A variation of this kind of moral panic is the threat of the alien (human) to the Good Animal-citizens.[65] This is entangled in the politics of human belonging too. For example, in South Africa at the moment there is a political and highly racialised debate being waged in the press with conservation discourses over, ironically, 'black' and 'white' rhinos (*Diceros bicornis* and *Ceratotherium simum*, respectively). One politician, Gayton McKenzie (of the newly minted Patriotic Alliance) is on record as declaring that he feels he must 'actually pray every night for a white rhino to die' . . .

> [b]ecause when the last white rhino is dead, maybe people will start caring about the coloured[66] man in this country . . . . Between April 2014 and April 2015, there are six coloured guys that die every day due to gang violence. Half a rhino died per week during that year. But everywhere, you hear save the rhino'.[67]

(In fact, the white rhino is the least endangered, at 20,000 plus, but 'white rhino' makes for better newspaper fodder and social media copy than 'black rhino', which is critically endangered at about 5,000).[68] Recently, the rhino-poaching crisis has been caught up in intra-national debates. Historically, South Africa has used military force rather than diplomacy with neighbouring states and, similarly, antipoaching has been enforced harshly. Contemporary antipoaching overlaps with political unease over

Figure 2.1 Bumper sticker, Kimberley, South Africa, January 2014.
Photo by author.

border safety, and this has precipitated the 'rhinofication' of South African security. Humphreys and Smith argue that militarised efforts to protect rhino confront the reality of a large and largely African class, which (for several generations) has been barred from wildlife management by white regimes.[69] Tellingly, the head of the Kruger National Park's antipoaching activities is a retired apartheid general, whose rhetoric suggests he is approaching antipoaching as a new Border War: ' . . . South Africa, a sovereign country, is under attack from armed foreign nationals. This should be seen as a declaration of war against South Africa by armed foreign criminals'.[70] Of course, this is not to suggest that rhino poaching is an invented crisis. The numbers killed are staggering; in 2014 alone, 1,215 rhinos were killed in South Africa. The number of carcasses of poached rhinos in Kruger Park (a game reserve that is itself a borderland with Mozambique) rose from ten in 2007 to 827 in 2014.[71] But equally staggering are the human casualties: as many as 500 poachers have been killed since 2010 in the Kruger alone. Bluen has argued that the 'rhino war' contains elements of a white 'xenophobia', particularly because most of the poachers are black men from Mozambique.[72] The poachers are certainly 'othered', there is even talk of 'exterminating' them – they can be 'noncriminally put to death' in the eyes of many (mainly white) South Africans.[73] In claiming stewardship, in a form of intra-national nationalism, white South Africans are also insisting on their right to 'belong' (as in Figure 2.1 above). Further, the (largely) white public concern shared through, for example, dressing their vehicles as rhinos[74], putting a symbolic red plastic rhino horn on the front of their cars, thereby almost therianthropically 'becoming' rhinos or at least inhabiting them.

Native species? Race, settlers and species[75]

In the above example, 'bad non-citizens' have been killed – rhetorically and literally – to protect the rhino as a quintessentially 'good' citizen-animal. But sometimes, in protecting the nation's fantasies about itself, the animals have to be killed too. In a case-study of the Prince Edward Islands of sub-Antarctica under South African rule, Van der Watt and Swart have shown how animals can be stunt-doubles in a time-honoured mythic melodrama nations need to perform in inventing themselves. Nationalism is not only a 'dangerous animal', it is dangerous to animals, as shown below.[76]

South Africa took possession of the islands in the 1940s and almost at once references were made to the 'newest citizens of South Africa'. Pictures were taken of naval officers literally shaking hands with (flabbergasted but unresisting) penguins. This was, however, the very problem with these new colonial subjects: they were too submissive. They exhibited 'Island tameness'– the propensity of isolated populations of animals to lose their suspicion of potential predators, including humans. They were thus almost too perfect as colonial subjects – incapable of any resistance. But this did not fit the nationalist narrative, which was predicated on the notion of frontier conquest and romantic Herderian nationalism.[77] The nation needed an enemy.[78] Luckily, one presented itself in the form of the brown skua, a kleptoparasitic bird, known to savage penguin chicks. These insurgent skuas made possible a re-enactment of the conventional conquest narrative. By shooting them in vast numbers, the colonisers were able to repel and then repress these rebels. 'The 'good' animal-citizens (the penguins) and the 'bad' animal-citizens (the skuas) both facilitated a

> psychosocial process of colonisation, enabling the men stationed on the island to act out a comforting and legitimising narrative of conquest. So entrenched was the frontier myth that it was a story the settlers needed to tell on a sub-Antarctic island, with one key difference: without human characters, the local fauna had to play the key roles of subject, in order to allow settler agency and the fiction of colonial victory.[79]

The anthropomorphism was necessary to invent new subject-citizens to 'people' the islands, to then govern and control.

As illustrated above, anthropomorphism is useful, but, as indicated below, theriomorphism is vital. In the Antarctic avian example, it was a nationalist narrative that forced animals to play the role of people, but the reverse has happened; people have been compelled to become animals. Of course, in the example of rhinos, some sectors *chose* to become animals, but only high-prestige 'Good Animals'. Sometimes, however, humans have been re-categorised (against their will) along with the Bad Animals, as a threat to the nation. Integral to the process of inventing a nation is categorising and then vilifying its so-called enemies. Sometimes this dehumanisation is waged against external enemies, as in 'trophy photographs' of American military torturing Iraqi prisoners in Abu Ghraib prison, of a naked Iraqi man forced to crawl on the floor on all fours, with a dog-leash around his neck, as part of animalising 'the other', here as a tamed pet. Sometimes the dehumanisation is against internal enemies as a form of intra-national nationalism (as in reinventing Jews as *Untermenschen*, as vermin and as Lorenz's degenerate domestic animals, as discussed earlier in the chapter). Dehumanisation is useful; it overcomes the normal human revulsion against murder, it facilitates 'noncriminally putting to death'. In April 1994, when South Africa was celebrating the end of apartheid with the election of Nelson Mandela, Rwanda, a central African state, saw the genocide of an ethnic minority, the Tutsis. In 100 days, from April to July 1994, the country's Hutu paramilitary, *Interahamwe* ('We who strike together'), butchered about 800,000 Tutsis (and Hutus). At the time, the genocide was presented as the consequence of ancient 'ethnic' or even 'tribal' animosity, between Tutsi and Hutu locked together in the same nation-state. However, evidence from the UN Tribunal established that this was false. In reality, the genocide was methodically enforced by a group of disaffected military officers. At least in part they were able to persuade Hutu to kill Tutsi friends, family and strangers, through the rhetoric of 'othering'.[80] To make the genocide thinkable, differential forms of national citizenship were imagined and propagated, with Tutsis re-categorised as animals, becoming a means of legitimising the slaughter. Tutsis were at first referred to as evil people but this soon escalated to 'cockroaches'.[81] The instigators depicted them as vermin that must be exterminated for the sake of saving humans or, even, humanity. This permitted and, indeed, necessitated 'noncriminally putting them to death'.

Conclusion – beastly nationalism?

Animals do not respect national borders, as the examples of the insouciantly roving Ustin and Kuzya illustrate, but borders respect animals. In fact, animals help police, celebrate and move them, literally and figuratively. As discussed, a key and critical facet of the nation is its possession and patrolling of a specific geographic territory. The discourse of nationalism then insists on a defined 'natural territory', in part, at least, to discuss just how unnatural and even accidental the nature of its borders are. As Lord Salisbury sardonically observed in 1890:

> We have been engaged in drawing lines upon maps where no white man's feet have ever trod; we have been giving away mountains and rivers and lakes to each other, only hindered by the small impediment that we never knew exactly where the mountains and rivers and lakes were.[82]

In the mountains and rivers and lakes were finned, furred and feathered future 'citizens' of these arbitrarily defined states. The natural part was (and is) not only used as a sleight of hand or alibi for camouflaging the arbitrary delineations, but also to actively promote citizenship. In other words, animals can be mobilised in the state-sponsored construction of the identity of belonging and, as the flipside of the coin, the identity of difference. An important argument, significant for animal-sensitive historians, is that a species is not so much simply an ecological fact, but also a political decision.[83] Their identity is at least as historical as it is biological. Species are imagined just as nations are. But to say something is 'imagined' is not to say it is not powerful, nor real to those who believe. Nostalgia helps reify the imagined identity, it papers over cracks of actual heterogeneity, in a nation-state or in a herd of animals. In essence, 'animals and their bodies appear to be one site of struggle over the protection of national identity and the production of cultural difference'.[84] These animal-citizens – the Good and the Bad, the real and the invented, the alien and the native – play a part in the buttressing of the nation's story it tells about itself. To end where we began, we return to the animal as proxy for the nation-state. To turn back to the sports pages from this week, one reads of yet another rugby victory: 'Lions make nation proud'.

And, of course, in their way, they have.

Notes

1 M. Billig, *Banal Nationalism*, London: Sage, 1995.
2 M.A. Warnecke, R.D. Masters, and G. Kempter, 'The roots of nationalism: nonverbal behavior and xenophobia', *Ethology and Sociobiology* 13, 4 (1992): 267–282.
3 V. Reynolds, V. Falger, and I. Vine (eds.), *The Sociobiology of Ethnocentrism: Evolutionary Dimensions of Xenophobia, Discrimination, Racism and Nationalism*, London: Croom Helm, 1987, 93.
4 R. Ardrey, *The Territorial Imperative: A Personal Inquiry into the Animal Origins of Property and Nations*, London: Collins, 1967; K. Lorenz, *On Aggression*, New York: Bantam, 1967; D. Morris, *The Naked Ape*, New York: Dell, 1969; L. Tiger, *Men in Groups*, New York: Random House, 1970.
5 J. Goodall, *The Chimpanzees of Gombe: Patterns of Behavior*. Cambridge MA: Harvard University Press, 1986; J. Goodall, *Through a Window: My Thirty Years with the Chimpanzees of Gombe*, New York: Houghton Mifflin Harcourt, 2010.
6 M. Wilson *et al.* 'Lethal aggression in Pan is better explained by adaptive strategies than human impacts', *Nature* 513, 7518 (2014): 414–417, 513.
7 M.L. Wilson and R.W. Wrangham, 'Intergroup relations in chimpanzees', *Annual Review of Anthropology* 32, 1 (2003): 363–392.
8 As Bob Geldof noted, in a sweary appeal to Scotland to not vote for independence from the United Kingdom.
9 J.G. Herder, *Outline of a Philosophy of the History of Man*, trans. T. Churchill, London: Joseph Johnson, 1800; first published 1784–1791; A. Patten, '"The most natural state": Herder and nationalism', *History of Political Thought* 31, 4 (2010): 657–689, 657.
10 Patten, '"The most natural state"', 657; R. White, 'Herder: On the Ethics of Nationalism', *Humanitas* 18, 1 (2005): 166–181.
11 I. Berlin, *Vico and Herder: Two Studies in the History of Ideas*, London: Hogarth Press, 1976.
12 Patten, '"The most natural state"', 667.
13 E. Gellner, *Nations and Nationalism*, Oxford: Oxford University Press, 1983, 48.
14 In H.K. Bhabha (ed.), *Nation and Narration*, New York: Routledge, 1990, 20.
15 Patten, '"The most natural state"', 688, 689.
16 F.M. Barnard (ed.), *Herder's Social and Political Thought*, Oxford: Oxford University Press, 1965, 324
17 G. Orwell, 'Notes on nationalism', in *Such, Such Were the Joys*, New York: Harcourt, Brace and Co., 1953, 96.
18 Cited in M. Grebowicz and H. Merrick, *Beyond the Cyborg: Adventures with Donna Haraway*, New York: Columbia University Press, 2013.
19 Quoted in N. Ahuja, 'Species in a planetary frame: eco-cosmopolitanism, nationalism, and "The Cove"', *Tamkang Review* 42, 2 (2012): 13–32, 15.
20 Ahuja, 'Species in a planetary frame', 26–27.
21 For the imagining of nations see the classic, B. Anderson, *Imagined Communities: Reflections on the Origin and Spread of Nationalism*, New York: Verso, 1991.
22 A. Brydon, 'Icelandic nationalism and the whaling issue', *North Atlantic Studies*, 2, 1–2 (1990): 185–191.

23 U. Heise, *Sense of Place and Sense of Planet: The Environmental Imagination of the Global*, New York: Oxford University Press, 2008.
24 K. Takahara, 'Whaling—for nationalism or science?', *The Japan Times*, 25 December 2007.
25 N. Onishi, 'For Japan, defense of whaling scratches a nationalist itch', *The New York Times*, 13 March 2007.
26 J. Davis, 'Cockfight nationalism: blood sport and the moral politics of American Empire and nation building', *American Quarterly* 65, 3 (2013): 549–574.
27 Davis, 'Cockfight nationalism', 549.
28 S. Swart, '"It is as bad to be a black man's animal as it is to be a black man": the politics of species in Sol Plaatje's *Native Life in South Africa*', *Journal of Southern African Studies* 40, 4 (2014): 689–705.
29 I. Tyrrell, *Reforming the World: The Creation of America's Moral Empire*, Princeton NJ: Princeton University Press, 2010.
30 C. Geertz, 'Deep play: notes on the Balinese cockfight', *Daedalus* 101, 1 (1972): 1–37.
31 Davis, 'Cockfight nationalism'.
32 Davis, 'Cockfight nationalism'.
33 A. Smith, *Nationalism: Theory, Ideology, History*, Cambridge: Polity Press, 2001, 521.
34 Billig, *Banal Nationalism*.
35 *Canadian Press*, 27 October 2011.
36 *BBC News*, 29 October 2011.
37 D. Booth, 'Mandela and Amabokoboko: nationalising South Africa', *Indicator* 13, 2 (1996): 19–22. Ironically, Springbok are one of the few antelope species experiencing a demographic boom.
38 T. Dunlap, 'Australian nature, European culture: Anglo settlers in Australia', *Environmental History Review* 17, 1 (1993): 25–48; S. White, 'British colonialism, Australian nationalism and the law: hierarchies of wild animal protection', *Monash University Law Review* 39 (2013): 452–472.
39 S. Swart, *Riding High: Horses, Humans and History in South Africa*, Johannesburg: Witwatersrand University Press, 2010, 20.
40 T. Flannery, *The Future Eaters: An Ecological History of the Australasian Lands and People*, Chatswood NSW: Reed New Holland, 1994, 355.
41 Sometimes they also promoted indigenous plants such as the wattle – so they were not always about suppressing native flora and fauna. See L. Robin, 'Nationalising nature: wattle days in Australia', *Journal of Australian Studies* 26, 73 (2002): 13–26.
42 P. Olsen, *Upside Down World: Early European Impressions of Australia's Curious Animals*, Canberra ACT: National Library of Australia, 2010, 10–11.
43 Dunlap, cited in White, 'British colonialism', 471.
44 This section is drawn directly from S. Swart, 'Frankenzebra: Dangerous knowledge and the narrative construction of monsters', *Journal of Literary Studies*, 30, 4, 2015 and S. Swart, 'Zombie Zoology: the Quagga and the history of reanimating animals', in S. Nance (ed.), *The Historical Animal*, Syracuse, NY: Syracuse University Press, 2015.
45 L. Heck, *Animals: My Adventure*, trans. E.W. Dickes, London: Methuen, 1954, 143.
46 Heinz crossed Highland, Hungarian and Corsican cattle, while Lutz mated Spanish and French cattle.
47 For a pioneering study see P. Viereck, *Metapolitics: The Roots of the Nazi Mind*, New York: Capricorn Books, 1941, revised version, 1965. For a recent analysis see M. Wang, 'Heavy breeding: the heck "Aurochs" and the quest for biological unity', *Cabinet*, 45 (2012).
48 Quoted in Wang, 'Heavy breeding'.
49 K. Lorenz, 'Durch domestikation verursachte störungen arteigenen verhaltens', *Zeitschrift fur Angewandte Psychologie und Charakterjunde* 59 (1940): 2–81.

50 Some criticism has been simply of the methodology (rather than the politics) of the Heck programmes as early as the 1950s. See T. van Vuure, 'History, morphology and ecology of the aurochs (*Bos primigenius*)', available at http://members.chello.nl/~t.vanvuure/oeros/uk/lutra.pdf. Recently, mitochondrial DNA analysis has shown a possible Near Eastern Neolithic origin for domestic cattle with possibly no clear demonstration of domestication of European aurochs – which would have destroyed the Heck Project ontologically.

51 S. Zimov, 'Pleistocene park: return of the mammoth's ecosystem', *Science* 308, 5723 (2005): 796–798

52 *Metro*, 21 April 2009; *Constantine Report*, 22 April 2009; *The Telegraph*, 21 April 2009; *Daily Mail*, 21 April 2009.

53 D. Smith, '"Cruelty of the worst kind": religious slaughter, xenophobia, and the German Greens', *Central European History* 40, 1 (2007): 89–115. For a longer term, historical perspective on *schächten*, see D. Brantz, 'Stunning bodies: animal slaughter, Judaism, and the meaning of humanity in Imperial Germany', *Central European History* 35, 2 (2002): 167–194.

54 This section derives from Smith, '"Cruelty of the worst kind"'.

55 Smith, '"Cruelty of the worst kind"', 113.

56 C. Craw, 'The ecology of emblem eating: environmentalism, nationalism and the framing of kangaroo consumption', *Media International Australia* 127, 1 (2008): 82–95.

57 Craw, 'Ecology of emblem eating', 82.

58 *The Telegraph*, 8 August 2014.

59 M. Birnbaum, 'After Russia bans Western food, Moscow Zoo animals need a new diet', *The Washington Post*, 8 August 2014.

60 *The Telegraph*, 8 August 2014.

61 M. Hall, 'The native, naturalized and exotic – plants and animals in human history', *Landscape Research* 28, 1 (2003): 5–9, 9.

62 K. Olwig, 'Natives and aliens in the national landscape', *Landscape Research* 28, 1 (2003): 61–74.

63 G. Groening and J. Wolschke-Bulmahn, 'Some notes on the mania for native plants in Germany', *Landscape Journal* 11, 2 (1992): 116–126.

64 J. Comaroff and J. Comaroff, 'Naturing the nation: aliens, apocalypse and the postcolonial state', *Journal of Southern African Studies* 27, 3 (2001): 233–265.

65 B. Büscher, '"Rhino poaching is out of control!" Violence, race and the politics of hysteria in online conservation', *Environment and Planning A* 48, 5 (2016): 979–998.

66 The term 'coloured' refers to mixed race South Africans rather than blacks, as in some other global contexts. Terms such as 'non-white', 'non-European', 'Bantu', and 'coloured' are products of South Africa's highly racialised history with the authoritarian classification of people along racial lines (giving priority to whites). See M. Adhikari, *Not White Enough, Not Black Enough: Racial Identity in the South African Coloured Community*, Athens, OH: Ohio University Press, 2005.

67 R. Poplak, 'Trainspotter: fringe festival – how Gayton McKenzie spells the onset of the coalition era', *Daily Maverick,* 27 July 2016.

68 In fact, the term 'white' is believed to derive from the Dutch/Afrikaans wijd/*wyd* or wide, referring to their wide upper lips, as opposed to the pointed mouths of the black rhino.

69 E. Lunstrum, 'Conservation meets militarisation in Kruger National Park: historical encounters and complex legacies', *Conservation & Society* 13, 4 (2015): 356–369.

70 The South African Border War, 1966 to 1989, in South West Africa and Angola— a conflict between South Africa and local independence movements were opposing illegal South African control over them, after the United Nations withdrew legal sanction for South Africa's grip on South West Africa (now Namibia).

71 B. Büscher and M. Ramutsindela, 'Why southern Africa's peace parks are sliding into war parks', *Sunday Times*, 17 February 2016; B. Büscher and M. Ramutsindela, 'Green violence: rhino poaching and the war to save Southern Africa's peace parks,' *African Affairs* 115, 458 (2016): 1–22.

72 K.-J. Bluen, '"Rhino wars": a manifestation of white supremacy and xenophobia', *Daily Maverick*, 28 July 2016.

73 Bluen, '"Rhino wars"'; J. Humphreys and M.L.R. Smith, 'The "rhinofication" of South African security', *International Affairs* 90, 4 (2014): 795–818; B. Büscher and M. Ramutsindela, 'Green violence'.

74 The manufacturers note: 'Whether you drive a macho 4x4 or a slick sedan, these plastic Rhinoses will mark you as a friend of the rhino. Made from recycled and recyclable polypropylene, the Rhinose has four attachment points enabling it to be securely fixed to your vehicle's grille with cable ties'. See www.rhinorage.org/Media-office-article.aspx?id=26, last accessed 7 March 2016.

75 This section is drawn directly from L. Van der Watt and S. Swart, 'The South African Prince Edward Islands and the making of sub-Antarctic environments, 1947–1995' (draft).

76 Van der Watt and Swart, 'South African Prince Edward Islands'.

77 M. Legassick, 'The frontier tradition in South African historiography', in S. Marks and A. Atmore (eds.), *Economy and Society in Pre-Industrial South Africa*, London: Longman, 1980: 44–79.

78 D. Day, *Conquest: How Societies Overwhelm Others*, Oxford: Oxford University Press, 2008, 23.

79 Van der Watt and Swart, 'South African Prince Edward Islands'.

80 H. Hintjens, 'When identity becomes a knife: reflecting on the genocide in Rwanda', *Ethnicities* 1, 1 (2001): 25–55.

81 A. De Swaan, 'Widening circles of disidentification: on the psycho- and sociogenesis of the hatred of distant strangers –reflections on Rwanda', *Theory, Culture & Society* 14, 2 (1997): 105–122.

82 Quoted in R. McCorquodale and R. Pangalangan, 'Pushing back the limitations of territorial boundaries', *European Journal of International Law* 12, 5 (2001): 867–888, 867.

83 Swart, *Riding High*, Chapter Seven.

84 G. Elder, J. Wolch, and J. Emel, 'Race, place, and the bounds of humanity', *Society & Animals* 6, 2 (1998): 183–202, 184.

References

Adhikari, M. *Not White Enough, Not Black Enough: Racial Identity in the South African Coloured Community*, Athens: Ohio University Press, 2005.

Ahuja, N. 'Species in a planetary frame: eco-cosmopolitanism, nationalism, and "The Cove"', *Tamkang Review* 42, 2 (2012): 13–32.

Anderson, B. *Imagined Communities: Reflections on the Origin and Spread of Nationalism*, New York: Verso, 1991.

Ardrey, R. *The Territorial Imperative: A Personal Inquiry into the Animal Origins of Property and Nations*, London: Collins, 1967.

Barnard, F.M. (ed.) *Herder's Social and Political Thought*, Oxford: Oxford University Press, 1965.

BBC News. 'Canadian senator wants polar bear as new emblem', *BBC News*, 29 October 2011, available at www.bbc.co.uk/news/world-us-canada-15503106, last accessed 6 March 2017.

Berlin, I. *Vico and Herder: Two Studies in the History of Ideas*, London: Hogarth Press, 1976.

Bhabha, H.K. (ed.) *Nation and Narration*, New York: Routledge, 1990.

Billig, M. *Banal Nationalism*, London: Sage, 1995.

Birnbaum, M. 'After Russia bans Western food, Moscow Zoo animals need a new diet', *The Washington Post*, 8 August 2014.

Bluen, K.-J. '"Rhino wars": a manifestation of white supremacy and xenophobia', *Daily Maverick*, 28 July 2016.

Booth, D. 'Mandela and Amabokoboko: nationalising South Africa', *Indicator* 13, 2 (1996): 19–22.

Brantz, D. 'Stunning bodies: animal slaughter, Judaism, and the meaning of humanity in Imperial Germany', *Central European History* 35, 2 (2002): 167–193.

Brydon, A. 'Icelandic nationalism and the whaling issue', *North Atlantic Studies*, 2, 1–2 (1990): 185–191.

Büscher, B. '"Rhino poaching is out of control!" Violence, race and the politics of hysteria in online conservation', *Environment and Planning A* 48, 5 (2016): 979–998.

Büscher, B. and Ramutsindela, M. 'Green violence: rhino poaching and the war to save Southern Africa's peace parks,' *African Affairs* 115, 458 (2016): 1–22.

Büscher, B. and Ramutsindela, M. 'Why southern Africa's peace parks are sliding into war parks', *Sunday Times*, 17 February 2016.

Canadian Press. 'Nicole Eaton, Canadian Senator, new national symbol should be a polar bear', *The Canadian Press*, 27 October 2011.

Comaroff, J. and Comaroff, J. 'Naturing the nation: aliens, apocalypse and the postcolonial state', *Journal of Southern African Studies* 27, 3 (2001): 233–265.

Craw, C. 'The ecology of emblem eating: environmentalism, nationalism and the framing of kangaroo consumption', *Media International Australia* 127, 1 (2008): 82–95.

Davis, J. 'Cockfight nationalism: blood sport and the moral politics of American Empire and nation building', *American Quarterly* 65, 3 (2013): 549–574.

Day, D. *Conquest: How Societies Overwhelm Others*, Oxford: Oxford University Press, 2008.

De Swaan, A. 'Widening circles of disidentification: on the psycho- and sociogenesis of the hatred of distant strangers – reflections on Rwanda', *Theory, Culture & Society* 14, 2 (1997): 105–122.

Dunlap, T. 'Australian nature, European culture: Anglo settlers in Australia', *Environmental History Review* 17, 1 (1993): 25–48.

Elder, G., Wolch, J., and Emel, J. 'Race, place, and the bounds of humanity', *Society & Animals* 6, 2 (1998): 183–202.

Flannery, T. *The Future Eaters: An Ecological History of the Australasian Lands and People*, Chatswood NSW: Reed New Holland, 1994.

Geertz, C. 'Deep play: notes on the Balinese cockfight', *Daedalus* 101, 1 (1972): 1–37.

Gellner, E. *Nations and Nationalism*, Oxford: Oxford University Press, 1983.

Goodall, J. *The Chimpanzees of Gombe: Patterns of Behavior*. Cambridge MA: Harvard University Press, 1986.

Goodall, J. *Through a Window: My Thirty Years with the Chimpanzees of Gombe*, New York: Houghton Mifflin Harcourt, 2010.

Grebowicz, M. and Merrick, H. *Beyond the Cyborg: Adventures with Donna Haraway*, New York: Columbia University Press, 2013.

Groening, G. and Wolschke-Bulmahn, J. 'Some notes on the mania for native plants in Germany', *Landscape Journal* 11, 2 (1992): 116–126.

Hall, M. 'The native, naturalized and exotic – plants and animals in human history', *Landscape Research* 28, 1 (2003): 5–9.

Heck, L. *Animals: My Adventure*, trans. E.W. Dickes, London: Methuen, 1954.

Heise, U. *Sense of Place and Sense of Planet: The Environmental Imagination of the Global*, New York: Oxford University Press, 2008.

Herder, J.G. *Outline of a Philosophy of the History of Man*, trans. T. Churchill, London: Joseph Johnson, 1800; first published 1784–91.

Hintjens, H. 'When identity becomes a knife: reflecting on the genocide in Rwanda', *Ethnicities* 1, 1 (2001): 25–55.

Humphreys, J. and Smith, M.L.R. 'The "rhinofication" of South African security', *International Affairs* 90, 4 (2014): 795–818.

Legassick, M. 'The frontier tradition in South African historiography', in S. Marks and A. Atmore (eds.), *Economy and Society in Pre-Industrial South Africa*, London: Longman, 1980, 44–79.

Lorenz, K. 'Durch domestikation verursachte störungen arteigenen verhaltens', *Zeitschrift fur Angewandte Psychologie und Charakterjunde* 59 (1940): 2–81.

Lorenz, K. *On Aggression*, New York: Bantam, 1967.

Lunstrum, E. 'Conservation meets militarisation in Kruger National Park: historical encounters and complex legacies', *Conservation & Society* 13, 4 (2015): 356–369.

Marks, S. and Atmore, A. (eds.) *Economy and Society in Pre-Industrial South Africa*, London: Longman, 1980.

McCorquodale, R. and Pangalangan, R. 'Pushing back the limitations of territorial boundaries', *European Journal of International Law* 12, 5 (2001): 867–888.

Morris, D. *The Naked Ape*, New York: Dell, 1969.

Olsen, P. *Upside Down World: Early European Impressions of Australia's Curious Animals*, Canberra ACT: National Library of Australia, 2010.

Olwig, K. 'Natives and aliens in the national landscape', *Landscape Research* 28, 1 (2003): 61–74.

Onishi, N. 'For Japan, defense of whaling scratches a nationalist itch', *The New York Times*, 13 March 2007.

Orwell, G. 'Notes on nationalism', in *Such, Such Were the Joys*, New York: Harcourt, Brace and Co., 1953.

Patten, A. '"The most natural state": Herder and nationalism', *History of Political Thought* 31, 4 (2010): 657–689.

Poplak, R. 'Trainspotter: fringe festival – how Gayton McKenzie spells the onset of the coalition era', *Daily Maverick*, 27 July 2016.

Reynolds, V., Falger, V., and Vine, I. (eds.) *The Sociobiology of Ethnocentrism: Evolutionary Dimensions of Xenophobia, Discrimination, Racism and Nationalism*, London: Croom Helm, 1987.

Robin, L. 'Nationalising nature: wattle days in Australia', *Journal of Australian Studies* 26, 73 (2002): 13–26.

Smith, A. *Nationalism: Theory, Ideology, History*, Cambridge: Polity Press, 2001.

Smith, D. '"Cruelty of the worst kind": religious slaughter, xenophobia, and the German Greens', *Central European History* 40, 1 (2007): 89–115.

Swart, S. *Riding High: Horses, Humans and History in South Africa*, Johannesburg: Witwatersrand University Press, 2010.

Swart, S. '"It is as bad to be a black man's animal as it is to be a black man": the politics of species in Sol Plaatje's *Native Life in South Africa*', *Journal of Southern African Studies* 40, 4 (2014): 689–705.

Swart, S. 'Frankenzebra: dangerous knowledge and the narrative construction of monsters', *Journal of Literary Studies* 30, 4 (2015): 45–70.

Swart, S. 'Zombie zoology: the Quagga and the history of reanimating animals', in S. Nance (ed.), *The Historical Animal*, Syracuse, NY: Syracuse University Press, 2015, 54–71.

Takahara, K. 'Whaling—for nationalism or science?', *The Japan Times*, 25 December 2007.

Telegraph. 'Russian bear grumbles as food sanctions hit Moscow zoo', *The Telegraph*, 8 August 2014.

Tiger, L. *Men in Groups*, New York: Random House, 1970.

Tyrrell, I. *Reforming the World: The Creation of America's Moral Empire*, Princeton: Princeton University Press, 2010.

Van der Watt, L. and Swart, S. 'The South African Prince Edward Islands and the making of sub-Antarctic environments, 1947–1995' (draft).

van Vuure, T. 'History, morphology and ecology of the aurochs (*Bos primigenius*)', available at http://members.chello.nl/~t.vanvuure/oeros/uk/lutra.pdf, last accessed 7 March 2017.

Viereck, P. *Metapolitics: The Roots of the Nazi Mind*, New York: Capricorn Books, 1941; revised version, 1965.

Wang, M. 'Heavy breeding: the heck "Aurochs" and the quest for biological unity', *Cabinet* 45, (2012).

Warnecke, M.A., Masters, R.D., and Kempter, G. 'The roots of nationalism: nonverbal behavior and xenophobia', *Ethology and Sociobiology* 13, 4 (1992): 267–282.

White, R. 'Herder: on the ethics of nationalism', *Humanitas* 18, 1 (2005): 166–181.

White, S. 'British colonialism, Australian nationalism and the law: hierarchies of wild animal protection', *Monash University Law Review* 39 (2013): 452–472.

Wilson, M.L. and Wrangham, R.W. 'Intergroup relations in chimpanzees', *Annual Review of Anthropology* 32, 1 (2003): 363–392.

Wilson, M.L., Boesch, C., Fruth, B., Furuichi, T., Gilby, I.C., Hashimoto, C., Hobaiter, C.L. et al. 'Lethal aggression in Pan is better explained by adaptive strategies than human impacts', *Nature* 513, 7518 (2014): 414–417.

Zimov, S. 'Pleistocene park: return of the mammoth's ecosystem', *Science* 308, 5723 (2005): 796–798.

3
NEW POLITICAL HISTORY AND THE WRITING OF ANIMAL LIVES

Mieke Roscher

Introduction

There has been a heated debate among animal historians around the topic of the 'real' versus the symbolic animal, with some historians arguing that a history of animals can be nothing more than a representational recount of animal lives, the historian's role being that of a chronicler as well as interpreter.[1] This seems highly problematic both with regard to the responsibility of historians and to the objects of such conceptualisations (whether animal or other). More generally, what can be termed 'the representation debate' reveals difficulties central to the understanding of writing history. Historical approaches that claim to rely solely on the representational consideration of animals and that really record only human attitudes to animals might therefore be in need of an elaboration. Indeed, what is required is a fusion of historiographical approaches that take representation seriously, but which go further by also including the material life of the animal, namely the life of specific animals in historical contexts.

Practising history with regard to making visible the past lives of animals can draw on a number of concepts well established within the historical discipline. It can also profit from more recent historiographical debates which have been developed in view of changing societal conditions, activating concepts made available by the new political history and the cultural history of politics respectively, including other than human actors by expanding the focus on 'materiality' and the 'body'.[2] The animal, or so it may be suggested, meets the criteria of those possible beneficiaries of such new approaches in political history. Drawing on a set of concepts in a revised cultural political history, specifically the construction of reality through communicative and bodily processes on the one hand and the differentiation between political framings and 'politics as practice' on the other, a productive agenda for writing the lives of animals and of practising animal history is conceivable.

What is required in order to get to the core of animal history is thus a twofold approach that combines the *material* interaction between humans and animals (and the impact of these interactions on animal lives and bodies) with their discursively charged *representations*, or, to speak in terms of political history, the juxtaposition of symbolic action and social action. Through this lens a distinct *production* of animals (both materially and discursively) can be identified.[3] This production is manifested historically and thus needs careful examination, particularly with regard to the role of the animal in these meaning-making processes. Underlying this argument is the assumption that this production relies on a constant exchange with the animal. This exchange or co-production can further be regarded as a process of political negotiation via or with the animal.[4] Both of these processes are naturally bound to have very different consequences for the animals' lives and are in need of scrupulous historical disentanglement.

Relying on input from new political history as well as from material culture approaches, the history of the body and performativity studies, the substantive aim of this paper is to illustrate how the political meaning of animals is produced in this way, through practices of humans *and* other animals. This production of meaning has an explicit and versatile political agenda by which animals are directly affected and which animals also *effect*. This applies to normative measures as part of political decision-making processes such as animal welfare laws as well as philosophical and ethical conceptions about the role of the animal within the larger societal framework. Within this theoretical and historiographical scheme, the possibilities of conceptualising animals as political actors who help determine the political dimension of human–animal relationships come to light. To explicate this theoretical discussion I will rely on examples and sources from my own work on animals, more precisely on dogs and horses in the Third Reich. Through these examples, I want to demonstrate what needs to be considered empirically as well as methodologically when writing a political history of animals.

Political history and animals

Political history has dominated historiography from its inception in the Rankean tradition right from the start.[5] Seen as the recounting of diplomatic history, the history of political systems as well as of the history of political ideologies, this approach, although based primarily on empiricist ideas, clearly ignored animals. It also failed to take notice of workers, women and colonised people as actors of history. Although animals were frequent in political symbolism from antiquity onwards and appear as such in iconographic source material accordingly, serving as a medium of communication and perception, of structure and order and of interpreting the world, political history has tended to neglect them. This must appear strange in view of the fact that animals have also functioned as ubiquitous others, material evidence to justify and to explain all sorts of, predominantly political, ostracisms, demarcations and exclusion processes.[6] Here, animals functioned as surrogates, their bodies subject to the exercise of political control. Political power structures were clearly introduced or reinforced by way of controlling animals. Historically, this becomes apparent with the high profile of animal spectacles in Roman political life or the medieval animal trials.[7] Neither animals themselves nor their classification were subject only to an abstract symbolism. On the contrary, power was manifested through their physical subjugation, the interaction with the real, bodily animal. This remained valid for modern times. Throughout the eighteenth and nineteenth century, for instance, animals were widely used as a tool to demonstrate political order. The reorganisation of a society now expressed by new economic structures and newly formed (political) classes was a case in point.[8] It was first and foremost the working classes who were shunned for their perceived animality.[9] This was also bitter reality for colonised peoples in the age of imperialism.[10] Animalisation was the dominant trope in political as well as social exclusion. The same was true for exclusion based on racist belief systems. Furthermore, control over animals more often than not functioned as an extension of the policy-making process. Research has shown for example how colonial safaris within the British Empire, especially the hunting of big cats, was a political means for controlling colonial subjects, replacing native or princely hunting traditions, such as those exercised by the former Mughal rulers, with what was perceived as European and civilised forms of hunting.[11] A political history of the modern age, Kathleen Kete surmises, would just not be possible without paying attention to these animal-related encounters.[12] This is certainly the case for a political history of the Third Reich, where animal-related tropes dominated political discourses.[13] Some animals, such as certain dog breeds, were Germanised so as to become part of Hitler's plan for a thousand-year empire. But here again it was animals' material bodies that served to make these discourses a living reality.

New political history: what's in a name?

To follow Ranke's dictum, telling 'history how it actually happened, showing what really was', has played into the hands of those writing the history of 'great men' and 'events', but it has seen itself challenged by various moves within historiography, starting with the Annales school, but followed by the rise of new historicism and the development of social history more generally. The established strand of political history was thereby marked as outdated, precisely because it failed to recognise the communicative spaces and practices shaping political action.[14] But here again, animals remained outside the scope of historical considerations. Moreover, what has been labelled the 'new' political history did not have the lived relations of humans and animals in mind when insisting that practices of everyday life be included in the understanding of political communication. On the contrary, letting all too many actors into the frame of (cultural) history has been guarded against, for fear of 'cultural relativism'.[15] If everything has a history, the argument went, what is the point of writing it? If everything is political, what is non-political?[16] Focusing on animals as historical actors has thus become the subject of a wider historiographical debate around who to include and on what perspective to take in 'political' history. Still, it is worth turning, for the practice of writing animal lives, to the communicative spaces, the performances and the symbolism and semantics that the new political or cultural history of politics promised, beyond the more narrow definition of political theory, even if one must be aware of a potential watering down of the 'political'.[17] The existing structures of political power must always be carefully looked at. Saying that, we need clarification about what is meant by new political history before entering into a debate over how it can be made fruitful for writing animal history.

Firstly, it needs to be asserted that the terminology of political history was and still is strongly dependent on certain specific national traditions within the field of history, as well as on different political traditions as such. So whereas from the 1970s onwards there appeared to be a consensus that the *established* political history of the Rankean tradition had failed to incorporate socio-political structures, mentalities as well as cultural symbolism available to historical agents, there was much less agreement on which theoretical and methodological direction to take.[18] Where the French Annales School in its search for 'total history' wanted to do away with political history as such, the 'new political history' of the American tradition focused on more quantitatively orientated projects as well as on the 'infrapolitics' of the oppressed. In Britain, for a further contrast, political history was undermined by cultural history precisely because the construction of the political self and political space came to the forefront of the historian's interests.[19] This 'cultural history of politics' was influenced particularly by subaltern studies.[20] The constitution of identities and meanings also came into the focus of British historians.[21] The German historical profession and their insistence on the *Sonderweg* (literally: 'special path') took yet another tack, following both the history of everyday life and historical anthropology and turning political history into what has been termed 'the cultural history of the political,' in which the symbolic constitution of politics as well as the 'material organisation of political communication' was considered.[22]

Admittedly, these differences appear insignificant in comparison with the 'old' political history, but they are, at least in principle, willing to include 'agents of an entirely different kind' than human actors in their historiographical framework.[23] Furthermore, all include or tolerate a focus on communicative spaces, which may well include non-verbal communication and the space of social interaction.[24] Moreover, even with their diverse access to their fields of enquiry all approaches of a new political history find a common ground in their daring to go beyond pure culturalism inherent in many studies within a history aware of the cultural turn.[25]

Unfortunately, this still seems to remain 'theoretical', as more often than not historians following the new political history approach cling to the analysis of stately institutions, or, as Steinmetz and Haupt put it: 'governments, monarchs, parties, or parliaments (. . .) still get the bulk of attention in many new political histories'.[26] Nevertheless, the potential that the new political history offers in terms of opening up communicative spaces and scope of action beyond the institutionalised political process, especially for everyday practices, should be of interest as a heuristic tool for animal historians. Firstly, and rather traditionally, it offers the chance to look at how animals figured as subjects of political legislation, but secondly it can look at how animals figured in political semantics, and thirdly, much more in tune with an animal perspective, it can look at the bodily presences in everyday encounters that are the essence of the political.

These lines of argument can be illustrated for the attempts to write about animals in the Third Reich. Looking at domesticated animals who were said to be the beneficiaries of the Nazi animal welfare project, the myriad layers of politics resulting in their status are obviously open to analysis. Dogs and horses figured especially prominently in the political and propagandistic repertoire deployed by the Nazis. The *Reichstierschutzgesetz* (animal welfare law) of 1933 referenced the ideology of National Socialism more generally but also the alleged 'racial predisposition of the Germanic people to animal welfare' specifically, was mainly directed at their well-being.[27] The legislation listed many prohibitions against the use of animals and was allegedly passed to protect animals for their own sake.[28] In this context, a new political history approach seems to be valuable both for an understanding of a history of everyday life of the Third Reich as well as a history of animals. This further prompts the question of how animals' lives were constituted in the face of a totalitarian system which posed as the animals' friend: what can be said about their everyday experiences? Did these ideologically charged presumptions affect the animals' living conditions and, if so, in what way? The safeguarding and procreation of animals was declared one of the most important policies to be pursued as a matter of national defence.[29] But how was this reflected in their bodily experiences? And, of course, how can we get an animal dimension into these heavily politicised arguments?

This appears to be quite a task, considering that political theory has regarded the animal not as a participant in interactions defined as political, but rather and exclusively as an object of political decision making.[30] This is not surprising given that in an Aristotelian reading the *zoon politikon*, the political animal, is only ever of human form, whereas the animal is without a voice (*zoon alogon*) and therefore not part of political processes as such.[31] Mainstream political theory does not regard animals – neither entire species nor individual animals – as capable of being political. The Merriam-Webster dictionary gives among other entries the following definition for politics: 'the total complex of relations between people living in society'.[32] This society is thus understood as solely made up of humans. This is in line of what has been critiqued as an exclusionary zoopolitics, namely a Derridean analysis of the place of politics as the proper arena of the human. The dualistic framework of humanity and animality is therefore constitutive for humans to think of themselves as political and rational animals, in opposition to the animal that must be neither political nor rational.[33] Social theory has lately begun to include other entities, however, among them non-human animals, as basic bearers of agency. These theories have also left their mark on the new and cultural history, especially discourses of entanglements and performances. Seeing the political discourse as a social practice, that is, as essentially meaning the negotiation between the self and the other surely brings the animal onto the table of a new approach to political history.[34] This is where we might return to new political history defined as 'sociocultural history with the political brought in again'.[35] The entanglement of symbolic and physical acts, the performativity of ideology and subversion as well as the material side of politics, thus serves to characterise a historical programme well worth the attention of animal–human historians. In order to do this we must try to do away with a 'people-centred view that all but obscured the political work done by things, technologies and practices'.[36] With reference to this 'political work' it must be stated that by including the animals into a history of everyday life, one is not at all being 'counter-political', as some historians of the political claim the 'everyday' to be.[37] On the contrary, looking at microhistorical levels allows us to see how the political power structures have sieved through to the individual entities, the individual life, the ordinary. Looking at how politics mould specific entities at specific times is valid if we want to understand the reciprocity of social transformations. This is of course where animal historians and animal studies scholars generally have turned to actor-network-theory, and Bruno Latour specifically, to bring the animal as non-human-actor or agent into the frame.[38] However, we must not be tempted to take Latour as the only valuable authority in considering how material living beings influence other material living beings. There are a variety of historical-minded approaches that help to balance the important influence of the material. As Frank Trentmann writes: 'For historians, the question is less about *whether* than *how* we can bring matter back into a mind-centred study of politics, and what we might add.'[39] The same is relevant for animal histories and some of the suggestions proposed by Trentmann become valid here also. Firstly, he proposes the biography of things as a fruitful way to elaborate on objects as 'containers of association and values that carried with them potential repertoires of political action'.[40] The steps taken by animal biographers follow a similar direction yet also try to hint at the individuality of animal–human encounters. The alternative proposes to look at 'governmentality' in the material manifestation of power-relations found in the shaping of places, buildings and so on. The vibrant field of zoo history already shows how such a political order is exercised through the presence, ordering and classification of animals.[41] Challenges of course remain in determining exactly how power structures differ, for example in transnational perspectives. The zoo as a European phenomenon of the nineteenth century, exhibiting both the imperial as well as the bourgeois world in miniature form, has long ago been adapted and culturally transformed in order to be applicable to other cultures and other political systems. The value of a new political history approach infused with cultural history is that it is able to show how, for example, change in political systems trickles down to its single elements by highlighting how political symbols, rituals and practices become obsolete in view of new ones or remain stable even if the historical or cultural conditions change.[42] As an example, consider the establishment of a 'German Zoo' within the Berlin zoological garden in 1937, showcasing only Germanic animals, or Germanised animals such as wolves, bears and eagles: this is a phenomenon that distinctively followed the making of other political landscapes and hierarchical orders.[43]

Between the symbolic and the 'real' animal

As outlined above, new political history looks at semantics as well as material realities. This is where it seems most helpful for animal historians. When writing a history of animals, numerous writers seem to have been struck by the dilemma that they only appear to have access to human representations of an animal, rather than the animals themselves.[44] This in turn has led to frequent debates on the sources that animal historians use and the equally obvious problem that these sources are predominantly human-made and thus partial in an anthropocentric way.[45] However, what is assumed here rather high-handedly by critics of animal history is that a representation of an animal is not a real animal, but merely a symbolic construction. It is surely a legitimate historiographic response not to follow the path of the purely constructivist view and instead look for the real animal as a political actor within history. It is a challenge worth taking and one which I would argue is feasible, if only by pointing out in what instances and under which historical conditions animals in historical narratives merely figure as representations of human imagination. Analysing how animals served to convey metaphorical and visual meaning at particular points in time, within particular, diverse contexts is but one aspect in need of consideration when examining the political animal from an historian's perspective. Having said that, it is still important to illuminate what specific symbolic representations of the political were conveyed via the animal. This is why we should not do away with representationalism but *include* its insights in the overall analysis.[46] I want to stress that a new political history of animals is interested in getting to the core of animals symbolically and narratively, to uncover how animals function as regulators in the context of political and social knowledge and to categorise them according to their status as objects of cultural semantics. This has always to be considered, however, together with the need to bring together material traces and discursive iconographies. For animal history this means going beyond demarcating the 'animal' as the generic 'other'. The ultimate aim is to consider the material interactions through which the symbolic functional role of animals is manifested.

To return to the project of writing a political history of animals in the Third Reich, one would need to disentangle the distinctive discursive lines of animals and animality that fitted the nomenclature of National Socialism. So one of the most persuasive discourses apostrophised animals as part of the '*Volksgemeinschaft*' (folk community), something that raised their status above those humans declared subhuman. Notwithstanding this status, however, when the material animal was needed as a resource, this place in the folk community was routinely undermined. This happened for example in 1934 when an antivivisection clause passed as a propagandistic tool by the then still existing Prussian state, was secretly abolished in order to make way for the animal testing needed for war preparations.[47] Changing the law did not here change the semantic use of the animals, and their representation. Discourse and material realities could thus differ significantly, and it is the job of the animal historian following the lines of a new political history to uncover these discrepancies.

The practice/performative turn in animal history

Taking actor-network theory into account, animal studies scholars have routinely pointed to the potential of animals as agents in the process of generating knowledge. This should be expanded to the potential of animals to figure as agents in political processes as well. As Donna Haraway suggests, the interactive process of material-semiotic actors is to be understood and to be recognised as the 'apparatus of bodily production'.[48] Thereby, one is able to shed a light on the relational existences of humans and animals, their collective relationship.[49] While agreeing with Haraway that animals also shape and create their worlds socially, this interactive process between animal and human can be made subject to exploring the possibilities of exercising political influence without remaining stuck in subject-object dualisms.[50] The move from language to performance is thus to be seen in accordance with the shift from the representational to the material animal. As Karen Barad points out with respect to science studies, 'the move towards performative alternatives to representationalism shifts the focus from questions of correspondence between descriptions and reality (that is, do they mirror nature or culture?) to matters of practices/doings/actions'.[51]

A central vantage point of animal historiography highlights the diverse power structures underlying the human–animal relations that implicitly – because they are not controlled by the animals themselves – impress on political action.[52] In this sense, what is being proposed is in tune with approaches taken by the new political history in the course of which symbolic practices, semantics and rituals are analysed with a view of their inherent power relations and transformations, clearly operating outside of an understanding of politics solely based on political institutions.[53] This approach also agrees with wider shifts within the cultural historical profession, which turned from 'culture as discourse to culture as practice and performance'.[54] This is to some extent also true for political history. The single-minded focus on 'events' has been done away with in favour of a programme taking into account whole chains of events, processes and decisions, something that was accomplished by British and American historians long before it came to be accepted in German political historiography.[55] What seems to be important here is that by looking at *practices*, we do not turn a blind eye to human practices in favour of animal practices, but recognise instead, as Frank Trentmann stipulates with regard to the interaction of things and humans, that 'much everyday life involves routines that have a history and dynamic of their own and are often shared'.[56] By concentrating on shared experiences, the potential of focusing on practices involving animals becomes clear. Not only were these practices as part of everyday life far more subtly political than say the mass demonstrations and mass events carefully choreographed by the Nazi leadership, they also help to paint a much more vivid picture of what it meant to be human or animal at a particular point in time.

So the terminology of politics that is taken into account here explicitly targets encounters of conflict and negotiation processes, the articulation of interests, but also the pushing of boundaries. A new political history influenced by cultural studies approaches of accepting new and divergent actors in turn allows for a shift in perspectives by including the political animal and a political historiography of animals respectively. By that I mean that political order is constructed through symbolic action and performances. These actions are repeatedly exercised on animal bodies. However, they are also shared performatively by the animals themselves, in their role as 'meaning-making figures'.[57] They thereby function as a 'potential repertoire of political action'.[58] The ritualised petting of animals for example, which Adolf Hitler routinely practised with his dog, is, as Adorno and Horkheimer have so famously pointed out, a performance of political power: 'The idle stroking of children's hair and animal pelts signifies: this hand can destroy'.[59]

Performance as relational agency

Performativity relies on bodily interaction, it relies on some sort of relation, be it intentional or accidental. In this process the face-to-face interaction unfolds into what I would term relational agency. This relational agency exists between all beings or species, but in particular between concrete specimens of species, between a distinct animal and a distinct human. By way of taking into account the relations that surface between animals and humans, one is also able to show in which manner animals in diverse constellations of relationships have impressed on human subjects. A history of such relations would therefore do away with subject-object attributions and accept animals as active partners in this conjunction. Haraway therefore regards relationships as 'the smallest possible unit of analysis'.[60] David Gary Shaw also talks of '*unities* – in which especially close, disciplined actors are produced', and Steinbrecher of 'interaction fabrics' between animal and human, enmeshed in non-verbal communication which could be accounted for by historical analysis.[61] Every relationship, including that of animals and humans, Steinbrecher claims, should be contemplated as interactive and reciprocal.[62] This aspect is underlined by Emma Power in her interpretation of the domestication process. Domestication, she argues, is not a process by human actors forced onto animals, but, on the contrary, a dynamic practice which relied on the exchange between the species: 'Domestication is not a finished or stable relation, but must be continuously negotiated and held in place'.[63] Co-evolution, to take up another term made prominent by animal historians in recent years, is therefore not to be seen as purely biological but as a cultural process as well. The network of relations must therefore be viewed both with regard to the individual as well as to society. As Edward Russell states: 'Historians would have nothing to study without coevolution, because human beings probably would not exist'.[64] By this, animals are elevated to 'intimate partners' in the historical development of the human species, as active contributors within the 'co-constitutive relationship'.[65] In this sense, agency is always to be characterised as essentially relational: 'There is no agency that is not interagency', as Vinciane Despret reminds us.[66] Within animal historiography this relational approach sits well with the methodology taken by social as well as political historians, in which the microhistorical focus on social action is always aligned to the macro level of social and political institutions. This also holds true for a particular approach to the study of practices, or *praxiography*. 'Praxiography might provide new ways of opening up historical power relations by looking at the relationship between practices of knowledge production and the representation of the body that is produced', argues Pascal Eitler.[67] For the exercise of animal history, this means to take seriously the shifts that occur between the semantic typifications and the material realities that accompany certain practices. This praxiography without a doubt subscribes to the recognition of inscribed power relations in practices and to the political aspect of the relations shaping those practices. These practices change over time and thus not only allow for a study of different relationships between humans and specific animals but also considers the implications for specific animals or animal species. It is the effects of such practices on the production of animal bodies, that this approach is interested in.[68] Praxiography also clarifies the fact that writing the history of animals implies typically narrowing down the scope of writing to the history of those animals with whom humans live in close contact and with whom they build relationships. It asks also for a 'small-scale history' which takes the 'micro-processes of everyday life' seriously.[69]

Concentrating on practices instead of actors, as Pascal Eitler suggests, makes this clear precisely because it helps historians to ascribe the production of subjectivity to acts exercised by actors.[70] The same has been said about privileging practices before structures: 'practice emerges here as the space in which a meaningful intersection between discursive constitution and individual initiative occurs'.[71] Focusing on the situated spaces, the encounter, the practice rather than on proving an actors intentionality has led to whole sets of studies promoting the 'doings' of the participants and entities respectively: doing gender, doing culture and doing politics are just a few of these approaches.[72]

Applying the material culture approach: bringing Haraway into history

The practice turn has recently also been made fruitful with regard to taking a new look at material interactions in the shape of both material culture studies and what has been termed new materialism. The latter can be defined using the words of Clever and Ruberg:

> Instead of assuming (hierarchical) differences between entities beforehand, new materialists study the performance of differences in these ever-changing, shifting realities. This directs the focus to encounters, practices, and moments where matter and culture are *acting* together, producing meaning or a reality in that moment.[73]

In this reading, new materialism widens the scope of activities and practices to be considered without however rendering the differences meaningless (and thus ignoring power structures). In short, it 'pays attention to matter, movement, and difference'.[74] Whereas material networks history relies on the concept of the 'co-construction' of networks, which can be historically analysed, Haraway uses the concept of co-constitutive relationships to explain the shared history of humans and animals.[75] As these relations rely on both material (bodily) as well as social (and therefore both cultural and political) interactions, Haraway speaks of 'naturalcultural contact zones' that constitute the loci of historical interplay between the species, or between specific members of specific species in temporal-spatial specific contexts to be more precise.[76] She also famously claims that the 'material-semiotic nodes or knots' require consideration when aiming at the full meaning of animals and this may also be applied to the historical study of animals.[77] However, when practising such a history we are still in need of sources that illustrate the symbolisms as well as the material functions of animals. This is why the material has once more been at the centre of animal historians' attention.[78]

Furthermore, the specific localities assume a whole new relevance when looking at animal history. It is no wonder then that some of the most exciting new works in historical animal studies are composed by animal geographers.[79] Haraway sees these places, however, just as a gateway to the 'mortal world-making entanglements' she is really interested in.[80] These entanglements, she claims, influence all beings regardless of their status as objects or subjects. And this is why she speaks of a co-history of humans and (some) animals.[81] This resonates with the central themes of Actor-Network-Theory (ANT), but seems more applicable since it refers to the corporality of the entities, which in turn are defined and produced by multiple material practices. Nicki Charles and Bob Carter have recently also propagated a reading of agency as inherently entangled, in which collectives and face-to-face relations appear 'historically contingent and variable'.[82] As James Epstein adds: 'The politics of meaning and the meaning of politics are intertwined'.[83] The meaning of animals, their symbolism, is therefore also bound up with their place both in political rhetoric and practice. Furthermore, politics have a 'material essence' both with regard to action as well as reaction.[84] As Trentmann makes clear: 'The material is recognised as a conduit of political processes that helps shape (and not just reflect) political identities, concerns, and fields of action'.[85] Melanie Rock and Gwendolyn Blue have also argued for an extension of the political publics to include animals because of their inherent materiality and of the space they occupy in these multi-species political discourses, an 'assemblage of bodies, practices and technologies that are brought together by a particular issue'.[86] This is of course again in tune with Latour who wants to introduce to the political arena all those non-human things that people are attached to.[87]

Animal history as body history

One aspect of the material that can be made fruitful for animal–human historians is the turn to the body. Historical approaches touching on the body have been made prominent time and again since the late 1990s to the point where Roy Porter called it 'the historiographical dish of the day'.[88] Aligned with a re-application of Foucauldian programmes of biopolitics, which is as a disciplinary force in contrast to zoopolitics directed at both animals and humans, the body is seen as shaped and governed by discursive strategies resulting in practices which can readily be regarded as political.[89] Here again, however, a reading influenced by a cultural history approach of the body as essentially constructed led to a debate on the solely representational character of the body as source and a call of historians to consider the corporeality of the human body with real experiences which needed consideration. This also holds true, of course, for animal histories, albeit the fact that body history curiously concentrated until recently solely on the human body. Stressing the corporality of animal bodies with real experiences is an important step for a validity of material encounters without however falling back to biological essentialisms which enforces the status of animals as the ultimate, naturalised other. Sensing the danger of such essentialism, Pascal Eitler calls instead for seeing 'bodies as a kind of surface in its ongoing materialization and not as a kind of container in its seemingly ahistorical stability'.[90] This is where approaches of a new political history come in, where the negotiation processes that precede these 'ongoing materializations' are analysed. Thereby, 'an understanding of the body that is neither static nor coherent' can be accomplished.[91] As Etienne Benson points out, it is also possible to filter out the solidity and corporality of the animal in written sources without returning to representationalism and thereby to a semantic field fully occupied by human exceptionalism.[92] A new political history of animals would then, just as body history, not be confined to collecting empirical data in the archives, nor to 'decoding "representations"'. It would 'make sense of the interplay between the two'.[93] It is after all the living interdependency between the animal and the human that affects human life profoundly. These interdependencies and effects are not to be reduced to the social, however, but need to be expanded to the realm of the political, as they are both the result of conflictual relations and normative regulations. Animals in these interdependencies should not be reduced to mere 'presentationalisms' void of agency or, indeed, political meaning.[94] This is because not only the social but also the political is constantly influenced by our bodily interaction with animals.[95] Having said this, it can be regarded as one of the most convincing arguments for including animals in the register of political history that they figure so prominently in rituals, meticulously structured and choreographed evidences of power, in which they have been given a distinct role and denied agency or where their agency was forcefully infringed upon as part of the political semiotic system. The politics of controlling the body, 'the power realities produced by the exercise of the state's authority over the bodies of its subjects', for example, a field of enquiry that was opened up by historians of the body, is thus also accessible to animal history.[96] This is especially relevant with regard to the history of the breeding of animals, a topic most relevant when writing a political history of animals in the Third Reich. From as early as 1937 breeders were asked to specifically create horses that would conform to the demands of both military and economy and to eradicate any deficiencies still to be observed especially in draught horses.[97] Those 'deficiencies' ranged from height, ossifications and spavin to 'wrong' temperament.[98] What was asked for instead was, aside from the right build, a pliable, modest character and an undemanding nature. The body was thus a battlefield for the economic and political agendas of the Third Reich: and this was particularly true for animals.

Conclusion: applying the new political history approach

Practising animal history through including the concepts of political history means accepting the animal as a subject of political interaction. It comes, however, with a distinctly challenging programme for the historian as it combines discursive and empiricist approaches. These approaches are in turn influenced by what has been called new political history or the cultural history of the political. Methodologically, this approach tries to bridge the gap between the course followed mainly by literary scholars and historians of ideas on the one hand, which foreground only the representational character of animals, and an actor-focused research promoted by social historians on the other. It is vital to incorporate what one could term the discursive middle, in which the conditions and practices that *produce* the semantic field in the first place are closely scrutinised. This is why a threefold approach is proposed here. Firstly, historians need to critically recount the spatial and physical presence of animals and their actions, all of which can be found in the diverse sources available to animal historians. Secondly, the specific production of animals – both physically through breeding and selection as well as symbolically by the ascribing of properties and characteristics – as a result of human–animal relations needs to be considered. Thirdly, the endowing of animals with a discursive *charge* should be reflected upon. To be able to get to the impact and impressions of the 'real' animals, it is necessary to consider their entangled meanings at specific times. Naturally enough, we need to consider how the discursive shifts in turn impact on the material object. A political history of animals would therefore turn to the power-relations inherent in specific animal–human constellations. It would look at the (social) practices solidifying or questioning the production of power relations and thereby at the production of specific animals at specific times. Thus it would ask for the communicative spaces semantically underlining or undermining these practices.

Reflecting on the writing of a new political history of animals in the Third Reich we can see how this would mean looking at how the changing power relations from one regime to another carried implications for various human–animal relations, enabling and requiring a comparative approach. For example, the *Gleichschaltung* (the political streamlining of political institutions and societies) heavily affected the agrarian, veterinarian and animal welfare institutions but it also influenced the life of animals politically and physically. The changing breeding laws, the privileging of certain breeds and certain species for that matter, changed the life of those animals.

The symbolism communicated via animals again played heavily on the semantics of Nazi politics. Dogs and horses were routinely declared as comrades in the fight, especially on the front lines, and attributed with 'Germanic' qualities. These politics were ritually enforced, for instance, by 'paying tribute' to war horses or publicising letters of Wehrmacht soldiers praising horses' courage, loyalty and honour. The political language defining animals focused on their role in society, even if it was merely symbolical. The shift from being comrades to being a member firstly of the *Volksgemeinschaft* (folk community) and secondly of the 'community of fate' had drastic effects on animals' treatment.[99] Some animals were included in the mythology of the *Volksgemeinschaft*. Besides dogs and horses other working animals such as oxen and cows were seen as doing their bit to further the nationalist ideology by working for the German cause.[100] Discursively inserting some animals into this community was part of Nazi propaganda. This is not a particular feature of the Third Reich, of course, but national socialist propaganda made special use of animals, incorporating them into the 'speech acts' that have long been the field of investigation by political historians. Their impacts on the lives of animals (or even on that of humans) is still a field in need of further investigation and one to which animal historians could contribute significantly. The semantics of 'vermin' for example were triggered not only by the discourses on hygiene that characterised the end of the nineteenth century and which surely encouraged the debates on racial hygiene in the Third Reich, but also impacted on the life of animals declared to be vermin.[101] It is of some importance in this context that the German term for breed is the same as that of 'race', as the Nazis transferred many of their ideas on racial politics from the animal kingdom. Classifications and forms of social order were thus intrinsically intertwined.

Moreover, in 1942 when food became scarce, a discussion arose which generally questioned the keeping of pets. Hitler intervened personally in fear of the emotional consequences for the German people. Instead, a law was passed in May of 1942, banning Jews from keeping pets, be they dogs, cats or birds. As Maren Möhring concludes, these animals taken from the Jewish population were seen as contaminated, as surplus mouths to feed and thus could not count on being included in the realm of animals declared worthy of protection under animal welfare legislation.[102] There were two sides to this coin, however. When in February of 1940 a mass mustering with over 5,000 dogs took place, the '*Hundewelt*' claimed that all 'bastard dogs' or mongrels were to be refused enlistment and also that it would not be worth feeding them.[103] It was only the pure-bred dogs who could hope to die a hero's death at the front. The same was true for horses, of which only the 'pure race' was valued. Breeders were called upon not to trait on bloodlines causing the 'production' of inferior animals, a practice which would counter the political cause of National Socialism.[104] The ubiquitous political semantics of racialised inclusion and exclusion found in such source material strongly hint at the importance of animals for the wider rhetoric of the Third Reich. The very accessibility of animal bodies made them test subjects for practical eugenics.

These semantics were also enforced by the bodily performances of the animals, which in turn were used to claim the willingness of animals to contribute to the Nazi project. Bodies in action again helped to underline metaphorics. Long after the Third Reich had fallen, the German shepherd dog has remained the symbol of Nazi brutality and of the fatal allegiance of Germans to the regime.[105] The visual aspects of this semantic field thereby open up a whole genre of sources for the historian to use. Pictures of prized breeding animals, military honours or mobilisation and conscription of dogs and horses were frequently to be found not only in animal welfare magazines, but also in the publications of the agrarian institutions. Moreover, the political and societal institutions helping to frame these semantics are a starting point for analysis. In claiming, for example, that the love of animals was inherently German, both the animal welfare as well as the veterinarian lobby supported the regime in their projects of exclusion and inclusion.[106] Political institutions influenced animal lives and were concurrently influenced by their symbolic values and presences.

Lastly, the material consequences resulting from political decision-making processes and political acts of speech might differ from the intentions of the laws passed or the normative settings and the propaganda that followed from intentionally covering up the material realities. Declaring horses and dogs comrades, for example, hid the fact that thousands of horses died in the first days of the war alone. As early as 1939, horse breeder associations were alarmed about the waste of animal life, more often than not caused by overworking.[107] Moreover, the *Reichstierschutzgesetz* did not prevent animal experiments. On the contrary, animals were routinely used for experimentation justified by the war efforts. Furthermore, not all dogs were lucky enough to be included in the mythology of camaraderie. The slaughtering of dogs for food was still a common practice especially in rural regions. Veterinarians were thus frequently called for the inspection of dog meat to state whether or not it was fit for human consumption. Even if the total numbers of dogs slaughtered (2,328 in 1935) seems small it still contradicted propagandistic efforts to raise the status of the dog as a part of the *Volksgemeinschaft*.[108]

All in all, what has been argued for in this chapter is that by turning to the political, using approaches offered by the new political history that consider semiotics, symbolism and representation but also corporal interactions and practices and the 'real' animal, a 'co-history' of species can be presented, one that does not ignore the living experiences of relationships. To exemplify my arguments I have made use of sources from the Third Reich and thus positioned my line of thought in the context of high politics of a totalitarian regime. There is, of course, room for looking at other political animals at other times and in other, less extreme, regimes. Philip Howell has, for example, placed his history of dogwalking the Victorian city into the political framework of liberalism and thereby the 'creation of the responsible subjects'.[109] Through the practice of walking dogs certain liberal freedoms were performatively evoked. Muzzling of dogs on the other hand was at the same time seen as infringement by the authorities or as a sign of a well-disciplined, civilised people. The debate over muzzling, as Howell suggests, can therefore be read with regard to the 'governmentality' of the liberal city'.[110] A new political history of animals understood as a cultural history of the political such as presented in both examples would look therefore at all aspects of the political and it does so from multiple perspectives. Not only does it focus on the framework, but also the processes and institutions involved, considering structures as well as agents. In doing so, it agrees with new materialist approaches while moving from representationalism to performativity.[111]

Notes

1 Arguing for the representational character of animal history are, most prominently, E. Fudge, 'A left-handed blow: writing the history of animals', in N. Rothfels (ed.), *Representing Animals*, Bloomington IN: Indiana University Press, 2002, 3–18, and D. Brantz, 'Introduction' in D. Brantz (ed.), *Beastly Natures: Animals, Humans, and the Study of History*, Charlottesville VA: University of Virginia Press, 2010, 1–13. A strong case for abandoning the representational perspective is P. Eitler, 'In tierischer Gesellschaft. Ein Literaturbericht zum Mensch-Tier-Verhältnis im 19. und 20. Jahrhundert', *Neue Politische Literatur* 54, 1 (2009): 207–224. An argument for bringing both perspectives together is H. Kean, 'The moment of Greyfriars Bobby: the changing cultural position of animals, 1800–1920', in K. Kete (ed.), *A Cultural History of Animals in the Age of Empire*, Oxford: Berg, 2007, 25–46.

2 P. Eitler, 'Animal history as body history: four suggestions from a genealogical perspective', *Body Politics* 2, 4 (2014): 259–274. Focusing on materiality and the body has been at the centre of a number of recent studies including: J.B. Landes, P.Y. Lee, and P. Youngquist (eds.), *Gorgeous Beasts: Animal Bodies in Historical Perspective*, University Park PA: Pennsylvania State University Press, 2012; L. Cox, 'Finding animals in history: veterinary artefacts and the use of material history', in S. Nance (ed.), *The Historical Animal*, Syracuse NY: Syracuse University Press, 2015, 99–117.

3 Eitler, 'Animal history as body history'.

4 K. Hobson, 'Political animals? On animals as subjects in an enlarged political geography', *Political Geography* 26, 3 (2007): 250–267.

5 G.G. Iggers and J.M. Powell, *Leopold von Ranke and the Shaping of the Historical Discipline*, Syracuse NY: Syracuse University Press, 1990; F. Gilbert, *History: Politics or Culture? Reflections on Ranke and Burckhardt*, Princeton NJ: Princeton University Press, 2014; K. Passmore, 'History and historiography since 1945', in R.E. Backhouse and P. Fontaine (eds.), *A Historiography of the Modern Social Sciences*, Cambridge: Cambridge University Press, 2014, 29–61.

6 K. Peggs, *Animals and Sociology*, Basingstoke: Palgrave Macmillan, 2012. For an historical case study see M. Fissell, 'Imagining vermin in early modern England', *History Workshop Journal* 47, 1999, 1–29.

7 For the arena: D.G. Kyle, 'Animal spectacles in ancient Rome: meat and meaning', in T.F. Scanlon (ed.), *Sport in the Greek and Roman Worlds: Greek Athletic Identities and Roman Sports and Spectacle, Volume 2*, Oxford: Oxford University Press, 2014, 269; A. Futrell, *Blood in the Arena: The Spectacle of Roman Power*, Austin TX: University of Texas Press, 2000. On animal trials: P. Dinzelbacher, 'Animal trials: a multidisciplinary approach', *Journal of Interdisciplinary History* 32, 3 (2002): 405–442; P. Beirnes, 'The law is an ass: Reading E.P. Evans' *The Medieval Prosecution and Capital Punishment of Animals*', *Society & Animals* 2, 1 (1994): 27–46.

8 B.N. Fielder, 'Animal humanism: race, species, and affective kinship in nineteenth-century abolitionism', *American Quarterly* 65, 3 (2013): 487–514; E.U. Da Cal, 'The influence of animal breeding on political racism', *History of European Ideas* 15, 4–6 (1992): 717–725; K. Coulter, 'Herds and hierarchies: class, nature, and the social construction of horses in equestrian culture', *Society & Animals* 22, 2 (2014): 135–152; P. Howell, 'The dog fancy

at war: breeds, breeding, and Britishness, 1914–1918', *Society & Animals* 21, 6 (2013): 546–567; A. Skabelund, 'Breeding racism: the imperial battlefields of the "German" shepherd dog', *Society & Animals* 16, 4 (2008): 354–371; D. Brantz, 'Stunning bodies: animal slaughter, Judaism, and the meaning of humanity in imperial Germany', *Central European History* 35, 2 (2002): 167–193.

9 D. Herzog, *Poisoning the Minds of the Lower Orders*, Princeton NJ: Princeton University Press, 1998.

10 K. Kete, 'Animals and human empire', in K. Kete (ed.), *A Cultural History of Animals in the Age of Empire*, Oxford: Berg, 2007, 1–23; S. Sivasundaram, 'Imperial transgressions: the animal and human in the idea of race', *Comparative Studies of South Asia, Africa and the Middle East* 35, 1 (2015): 156–172; J. Saha, 'Among the beasts of Burma: animals and the politics of colonial sensibilities, c. 1840–1940', *Journal of Social History* 48, 4 (2015): 910–932.

11 J. Sramek, '"Face him like a Briton!": Tiger hunting, imperialism, and British masculinity in colonial India, 1800–1875', *Victorian Studies* 48, 4 (2006): 659–680; C. McKenzie, 'The British big-game hunting tradition: masculinity and fraternalism with particular reference to the Shikar Club', *The Sports Historian* 20, 1 (2000): 70–96.

12 K. Kete, 'Animals and ideology: the politics of animal protection in Europe', in Rothfels, *Representing Animals*, 19–34.

13 B. Sax, *Animals in the Third Reich*, London: Continuum, 2000; M. Roscher, 'Das nationalsozialistische tier: Projektionen von Rasse und Reinheit im Dritten Reich', *TIERethik* 13, 2 (2016): 30–48.

14 W. Steinmetz and H.-G. Haupt, 'The political as communicative space in history: the Bielefeld approach', in W. Steinmetz, I. Gilcher-Holtey, and H-G. Haupt (eds.), *Writing Political History Today*, Frankfurt: Campus Verlag, 2013, 11–36.

15 P. Burke, 'Overture: the new history, its past and its future', in P. Burke (ed.), *New Perspectives on Historical Writing*, Cambridge: Polity, 1992, 1–24, 3.

16 T. Mergel, 'Überlegungen zu einer Kulturgeschichte der Politik', *Geschichte und Gesellschaft* 28, 4 (2002): 574–606, 586.

17 U. Frevert, 'Neue Politikgeschichte: Konzepte und Herausforderungen', in U. Frevert and H.-G. Haupt (eds.), *Neue Politikgeschichte. Perspektiven einer Historischen Politikforschung*, Frankfurt: Campus Verlag, 2005, 7–26, 23; see also Burke, 'Overture', 2.

18 Steinmetz and Haupt, 'The political as communicative space', 11.

19 Steinmetz and Haupt, 'The political as communicative space', 13–15; see also D. Wahrman, 'The new political history: a review essay', *Social History* 21, 3 (1996): 343–354.

20 Burke, 'Overture', 103.

21 S. Fielding, 'Looking for the "New Political History"', *Journal of Contemporary History* 42, 3 (2007): 515–524, 516.

22 Steinmetz and Haupt, 'The political as communicative space', 18.

23 Steinmetz and Haupt, 'The political as communicative space', 20.

24 L. Schorn-Schütte, 'Historical political research', in Steinmetz, *Writing Political History Today*, 369–382, 374. B. Stollberg-Rilinger, 'Was heißt Kulturgeschichte des Politischen?' in B. Stollberg-Rilinger (ed.), *Was heißt Kulturgeschichte des Politischen?* Berlin: Duncker & Humblot, 2005, 9–27, 14.

25 See L. Hunt and V.E. Bonnell (eds.), *Beyond the Cultural Turn: New Directions in the Study of History and Culture*, Berkeley CA: University of California Press, 1999. Also: G.M. Spiegel (ed.) *Practicing History: New Directions in Historical Writing after the Linguistic Turn*, New York: Routledge, 2005.

26 Steinmetz and Haupt, 'The political as communicative space', 20.

27 Senatspräsident F. Grau, 'Die rassische Bedingtheit des deutschen Menschen zum Tierschutz', *Reichstierschutzblatt* 1, (1939): 2.

28 For a discussion see Sax, *Animals in the Third Reich*; F. Uekötter, *The Green and the Brown: A History of Conservation in Nazi Germany*, Cambridge: Cambridge University Press, 2006.
29 P. Eipper, *Das Haustierbuch,* Berlin: Deutscher Verlag, 1943, 15.
30 A. Cochrane, *An Introduction to Animals and Political Theory*, London: Palgrave Macmillan, 2010.
31 See S.R. Clark, *The Political Animal: Biology, Ethics and Politics*, London: Routledge, 2002.
32 'Politics', available at www.merriam-webster.com/dictionary/politics, last accessed 16 March 2016.
33 P. Llored, M. Chrulew, and B. Buchanan, 'Zoopolitics', *SubStance* 43, 2 (2014): 115–123.
34 D. Haraway, *Primate Visions: Gender, Race, and Nature in the World of Modern Science*, New York: Routledge, 1989.
35 H.T. Velde, 'The opening up of political history', in Steinmetz et al., *Writing Political History Today*, 383–395, 393.
36 F. Trentmann, 'Political history matters: everyday life, things, and practices', in Steinmetz et al., *Writing Political History Today*, 397–408, 397.
37 Trentmann, 'Political history matters, 399.
38 See specifically B. Latour, *Reassembling the Social: An Introduction to Actor-Network-Theory*, Oxford: Oxford University Press, 2005.
39 Trentmann, 'Political history matters', 402.
40 Trentmann, 'Political history matters', 403.
41 M. Roscher, 'Curating the body politic: the spatiality of the zoo and the symbolic construction of German nationhood (Berlin 1933–1961)', in J. Bull, T. Holmberg, and C. Åsberg (eds.), *Animals and Place: Lively Cartographies of Human-Animal Relations*, London: Ashgate, 2017: 115–136.
42 Stollberg-Rilinger, 'Kulturgeschichte des Politischen', 21.
43 Roscher, 'Curating the body politic'.
44 See most prominently Fudge, 'Left-handed blow'. See also Brantz, 'Introduction', 10.
45 On the debate on sources, see H. Kean, 'Challenges for historians writing animal–human history: what is really enough?', *Anthrozoös* 25, Sup.1 (2012): 57–72.
46 For this approach see Kean, 'Greyfriars Bobby'; also see D. Donald, *Picturing Animals in Britain, 1750–1850*, New Haven CT: Yale University Press, 2007.
47 Uekötter, *The Green and the Brown*.
48 Haraway, *Primate Visions*, 310.
49 P. Eitler and M. Möhring, 'Eine Tiergeschichte der Moderne: theoretische Perspektiven', *Traverse* 15, 3 (2008): 91–105, 97.
50 Eitler and Möhring, 'Eine Tiergeschichte', 98.
51 K. Barad, 'Posthumanist performativity: toward an understanding of how matter comes to matter', *Signs* 28, 3 (2003): 801–831.
52 Hobson, 'Political animals', 251.
53 Frevert, 'Neue Politikgeschichte', 23.
54 G.M. Spiegel, 'Introduction', in Spiegel, *Practicing History*, 1–31, 3.
55 Mergel, 'Kulturgeschichte der Politik', 574.
56 Trentmann, 'Political history matters', 407.
57 Haraway, *Primate Visions*, 5.
58 Trentmann, 'Political history matters', 408.
59 T.W. Adorno and M. Horkheimer, *Dialectic of Enlightenment*, Palo Alto CA: Stanford University Press, 2002, 210.
60 Haraway, *Primate Visions*, 20.
61 D.G. Shaw, 'The torturer's horse: agency and animals in history', *History and Theory* 52, 4 (2013): 146–167, 163; A. Steinbrecher, '"They do something": ein praxeologischer

Blick auf Hunde in der Vormoderne', in F. Elias *et al.* (eds.), *Praxeologie: Beiträge zur interdisziplinären Reichweite praxistheoretischer Ansätze in den Geistes- und Sozialwissenschaften*, Berlin: De Gruyter, 2014, 29–51, 29.
62 '"They do something"', 51.
63 E. Power, 'Domestication and the dog: embodying home', *Area* 44, 3 (2012): 371–378, 371.
64 E. Russell, 'Coevolutionary history', *American Journal of History* 119, 5 (2014): 1514–1528.
65 B. Walker, 'Animals and the intimacy of history', *History and Theory* 52, 4 (2013): 45–67, 67; Haraway, *Primate Visions*, 208.
66 V. Despret, 'From secret agents to interagency', *History and Theory* 52, 4 (2013): 29–44, 44.
67 I. Clever and W. Ruberg, 'Beyond cultural history? The material turn, praxiography, and body history', *Humanities* 3, 4 (2014): 546–566, 562.
68 See most prominently Eitler, 'Animal history as body history'.
69 J. Brewer, 'Microhistory and the histories of everyday life', *Cultural and Social History* 7, 1 (2014): 87–109.
70 Eitler, 'Animal history as body history', 263.
71 Spiegel, 'Introduction', 20.
72 S. Hirschauer, 'Praktiken und ihre Körper: über materielle Partizipanden des Tuns', in K.H. Hörning and J. Reuter (eds.), *Doing Culture: Neue Positionen zum Verhältnis von Kultur und Sozialer Praxis*, Bielefeld: transcript, 2004, 73–91, 73.
73 Clever and Ruberg, 'Beyond cultural history', 551; see also T. Bennett and P. Joyce, 'Material powers: introduction', in T. Bennett and P. Joyce (eds.), *Material Powers: Cultural Studies, History and the Material Turn*, London: Routledge, 2010, 1–23.
74 Clever and Ruberg, 'Beyond cultural history', 552.
75 J. Murdoch, 'Ecologising sociology: actor-network theory, co-construction and the problem of human exceptionalism', *Sociology* 35, 1 (2001): 111–133.
76 Haraway, *Primate Visions*, 7.
77 D. Haraway, *When Species Meet*, Minneapolis MN: University of Minnesota Press, 2008, 4.
78 Landes, Lee and Youngquist, *Gorgeous Beasts*.
79 Most prominently C. Philo and C. Wilbert (eds.), *Animal Spaces, Beastly Places: New Geographies of Human-Animal Relations*, London: Routledge, 2000; J. Wolch and J. Emel (eds.), *Animal Geographies: Place, Politics, and Identity in the Nature-Culture Borderlands*, London: Verso, 1998. For more recent examples see P. Atkins (ed.), *Animal Cities: Beastly Urban Histories*, Farnham: Ashgate, 2012; H. Buller, 'Animal geographies I', *Progress in Human Geography* 38, 2 (2013): 308–318; P. Howell, *At Home and Astray: The Domestic Dog in Victorian Britain*, Charlottesville VA: University of Virginia Press, 2015; J. Lorimer and C. Driessen, 'From "Nazi Cows" to cosmopolitan "ecological engineers": specifying rewilding through a history of heck cattle', *Annals of the American Association of Geographers* 106, 3 (2016): 631–652.
80 Haraway, *When Species Meet*, 4.
81 Haraway, *When Species Meet*, 12.
82 B. Carter and N. Charles, 'Animals, agency and resistance', *Journal for the Theory of Social Behaviour* 43, 3 (2013): 322–340.
83 J. Epstein, 'Introduction: new directions in political history', *Journal of British Studies* 41, 3 (2002): 255–258.
84 Trentmann, 'Political history matters', 300.
85 Trentmann, 'Political history matters', 307.
86 G. Blue and M. Rock, 'Animal publics: accounting for heterogeneity in political life', *Society & Animals* 22, 5 (2014): 503–519.

87 B. Latour, 'From realpolitik to dingpolitik', in B. Latour and P. Weibel (eds.), *Making Things Public: Atmospheres of Democracy*, Cambridge, MA: MIT Press, 2004, 14–41.
88 R. Porter, 'History of the body reconsidered', in P. Burke (ed.), *New Perspectives on Historical Writing*, Cambridge: Polity Press, 2001, 232–260, 236.
89 R. Cooter, 'The turn of the body: history and the politics of the corporal', *ARBOR Ciencia: Pensiamiento y Cultura* 186, 743 (2010), 393–405; Clever and Ruberg, 'Beyond cultural history'. For a general discussion of the term in the context of animal rights discourse see D. Wadiwel, 'Three fragments from a biopolitical history of animals: questions of body, soul, and the body politic in Homer, Plato, and Aristotle', *Journal for Critical Animal Studies* 6, 1 (2008): 17–39.
90 Eitler, 'Animal history as body history', 268.
91 I. Clever, *Practice Matter(s), Exploring Practice Theories of the Body for Body History*, unpublished MA Thesis, Faculty of Humanities, University of Utrecht, 2013, 24.
92 E. Benson, 'Historiography, disciplinarity, and the animal trace', in L. Kalof and G.M. Montgomery (eds.), *Making Animal Meaning*, East Lansing MI: Michigan State University Press, 2011, 3–16, 4.
93 Porter, 'History of the body reconsidered', 211.
94 Cooter, 'The turn of the body', 400.
95 D. Haraway, *The Companion Species Manifesto: Dogs, People and Significant Otherness*, Chicago IL: Prickly Paradigm Press, 2003.
96 Porter, 'History of the body reconsidered', 225.
97 'Niederschrift über die Besprechung, betreffend Versorgung des Heeres mit Kaltblutpferden am Sonnabend, den 19. Juni 1937' [Meetings on the contribution of heavy horses to the army, 19 June 1937], German National Archives (henceforth BArch) R 68 I/118.
98 BArch R 68 I/118. Spavin is a disease of the hock joint of horses in which enlargement occurs.
99 The term 'community of fate' replaced the 'folk community' concept in the last months of the war but was equally vague and nebulous in its meaning: see M. Steber and B. Gotto, *Visions of Community in Nazi Germany: Social Engineering and Private Lives*, Oxford: Oxford University Press, 2014, 40.
100 *Reichstierschutzblatt* 4, 1940.
101 Mergel, 'Kulturgeschichte der Politik', 599. Sax, *Animals in the Third Reich*; M. Urban, *Von Ratten, Schmeißfliegen und Heuschrecken. Judenfeindliche Tiersymbolisierungen und die postfaschistischen Grenzen des Sagbaren*, Konstanz/München: UVK Verlagsgesellschaft, 2014.
102 M. Möhring, '"Herrentiere" und "Untermenschen": zu den Transformationen des Mensch-Tier-Verhältnisses im nationalsozialistischen Deutschland', *Historische Anthropologie* 19, 2 (2011): 240–241.
103 '5,000 Berliner Hunde werden gemustert' (5,000 dogs are being mustered)', *Die Hundewelt (The Dog World)* 16, 4 (1940): 41.
104 Eipper, *Das Haustierbuch*, 113.
105 Skabelund, 'Breeding racism', 358.
106 Roscher, 'Curating the Body Politic'.
107 'Feldpostbrief Nr. 15818 an Herrn Major Buhle (Field post letter from Major Buhle)', 17 November 1939, BArch R 68 I/105.
108 *Berliner Tierärztliche Wochenschrift* 51, 1935, 835.
109 Howell, *At Home and Astray*, 151.
110 Howell, *At Home and Astray*, 170.
111 Barad, 'Posthumanist performativity', 803.

References

Adorno, T.W. and Horkheimer, M. *Dialectic of Enlightenment*, Palo Alto CA: Stanford University Press, 2002.

Atkins, P. (ed.), *Animal Cities: Beastly Urban Histories*, Farnham: Ashgate, 2012.

Barad, K. 'Posthumanist performativity: toward an understanding of how matter comes to matter', *Signs* 28, 3 (2003): 801–831.

Beirnes, P. 'The law is an ass: Reading E.P. Evans' the medieval prosecution and capital punishment of animals', *Society & Animals* 2, 1 (1994): 27–46.

Bennett, B. and Joyce, P. 'Material powers: introduction', in T. Bennett and P. Joyce (eds.), *Material Powers: Cultural Studies, History and the Material Turn*, London: Routledge, 2010, 1–23.

Benson, E. 'Historiography, disciplinarity, and the animal trace', in L. Kalof and G.M. Montgomery (eds.), *Making Animal Meaning*, East Lansing MI: Michigan State University Press, 2011, 3–16.

Blue, G. and Rock, M. 'Animal publics: accounting for heterogeneity in political life', *Society & Animals* 22, 5 (2014): 503–519.

Brantz, D. 'Stunning bodies: animal slaughter, Judaism, and the meaning of humanity in imperial Germany', *Central European History* 35, 2 (2002): 167–193.

Brantz, D. 'Introduction' in D. Brantz (ed.), *Beastly Natures: Animals, Humans, and the Study of History*, Charlottesville VA: University of Virginia Press, 2010, 1–13.

Brewer, J. 'Microhistory and the histories of everyday life', *Cultural and Social History* 7, 1 (2014): 87–109.

Buller, H. 'Animal geographies I', *Progress in Human Geography* 38, 2 (2013): 308–318.

Burke, P. 'Overture: the new history, its past and its future', in P. Burke (ed.), *New Perspectives on Historical Writing*, Cambridge: Polity, 1992, 1–24.

Carter, B. and Charles, N. 'Animals, agency and resistance', *Journal for the Theory of Social Behaviour* 43, 3 (2013): 322–340.

Clark, S.R. *The Political Animal: Biology, Ethics and Politics*, London: Routledge, 2002.

Clever, I. *Practice Matter(s), Exploring Practice Theories of the Body for Body History*, unpublished MA Thesis, Faculty of Humanities, University of Utrecht, 2013.

Clever, I. and Ruberg, W. 'Beyond cultural history? The material turn, praxiography, and body history', *Humanities* 3, 4 (2014): 546–566.

Cochrane, A. *An Introduction to Animals and Political Theory*, London: Palgrave Macmillan, 2010.

Cooter, R. 'The turn of the body: history and the politics of the corporal', *ARBOR Ciencia: Pensiamiento y Cultura* 186, 743 (2010), 393–405.

Coulter, K. 'Herds and hierarchies: class, nature, and the social construction of horses in equestrian culture', *Society & Animals* 22, 2 (2014): 135–152.

Cox, L. 'Finding animals in history: veterinary artefacts and the use of material history', in S. Nance (ed.), *The Historical Animal*, Syracuse NY: Syracuse University Press, 2015, 99–117.

Da Cal, E.U. 'The influence of animal breeding on political racism', *History of European Ideas* 15, 4–6 (1992): 717–725.

Despret, V. 'From secret agents to interagency', *History and Theory* 52, 4 (2013): 29–44.

Dinzelbacher, P. 'Animal trials: a multidisciplinary approach', *Journal of Interdisciplinary History* 32, 3 (2002): 405–442.

Donald, D. *Picturing Animals in Britain, 1750–1850*, New Haven CT: Yale University Press, 2007.

Eipper, P. *Das Haustierbuch*, Berlin: Deutscher Verlag, 1943.

Eitler, P. 'In tierischer Gesellschaft. Ein Literaturbericht zum Mensch-Tier-Verhältnis im 19. und 20. Jahrhundert', *Neue Politische Literatur* 54, 1 (2009): 207–224.

Eitler, P. 'Animal history as body history: four suggestions from a genealogical perspective', *Body Politics* 2, 4 (2014): 259–274.
Eitler, P. and Möhring, M. 'Eine Tiergeschichte der Moderne: theoretische Perspektiven', *Traverse* 15, 3 (2008): 91–105.
Epstein, J. 'Introduction: new directions in political history', *Journal of British Studies* 41, 3 (2002): 255–258.
Fielder, B.N. 'Animal humanism: race, species, and affective kinship in nineteenth-century abolitionism', *American Quarterly* 65, 3 (2013): 487–514.
Fielding, S. 'Looking for the "New Political History"', *Journal of Contemporary History* 42, 3 (2007): 515–524.
Fissell, M. 'Imagining vermin in early modern England', *History Workshop Journal* 47, (1999): 1–29.
Frevert, U. 'Neue Politikgeschichte: Konzepte und Herausforderungen', in U. Frevert and H.-G. Haupt (eds.), *Neue Politikgeschichte. Perspektiven einer Historischen Politikforschung*, Frankfurt: Campus Verlag, 2005, 7–26.
Fudge, E. 'A left-handed blow: writing the history of animals', in N. Rothfels (ed.), *Representing Animals*, Bloomington IN: Indiana University Press, 2002, 3–18.
Futrell, A. *Blood in the Arena: The Spectacle of Roman Power*, Austin TX: University of Texas Press, 2000.
Gilbert, F. *History: Politics or Culture? Reflections on Ranke and Burckhardt*, Princeton NJ: Princeton University Press, 2014.
Grau, F. 'Die rassische Bedingtheit des deutschen Menschen zum Tierschutz', *Reichstierschutzblatt* 1, (1939): 2.
Haraway, D. *Primate Visions: Gender, Race, and Nature in the World of Modern Science*, New York: Routledge, 1989.
Haraway, D. *The Companion Species Manifesto: Dogs, People and Significant Otherness*, Chicago IL: Prickly Paradigm Press, 2003.
Haraway, D. *When Species Meet*, Minneapolis MN: University of Minnesota Press, 2008.
Herzog, D. *Poisoning the Minds of the Lower Orders*, Princeton NJ: Princeton University Press, 1998.
Hirschauer, S. 'Praktiken und ihre Körper: über materielle Partizipanden des Tuns', in K.H. Hörning and J. Reuter (eds.), *Doing Culture: Neue Positionen zum Verhältnis von Kultur und Sozialer Praxis*, Bielefeld: transcript, 2004, 73–91.
Hobson, K. 'Political animals? On animals as subjects in an enlarged political geography', *Political Geography* 26, 3 (2007): 250–267.
Howell, P. 'The dog fancy at war: breeds, breeding, and Britishness, 1914–1918', *Society & Animals* 21, 6 (2013): 546–567.
Howell, P. *At Home and Astray: The Domestic Dog in Victorian Britain*, Charlottesville VA: University of Virginia Press, 2015.
Hunt, L. and Bonnell, V.E. (eds.), *Beyond the Cultural Turn: New Directions in the Study of History and Culture*, Berkeley CA: University of California Press, 1999.
Iggers, G.G. and Powell, J.M. *Leopold von Ranke and the Shaping of the Historical Discipline*, Syracuse NY: Syracuse University Press, 1990.
Kean, H. 'The moment of Greyfriars Bobby: the changing cultural position of animals 1800–1920', in K. Kete (ed.), *A Cultural History of Animals in the Age of Empire*, Oxford: Berg, 2007, 25–46.
Kean, H. 'Challenges for historians writing animal—human history: what is really enough?', *Anthrozoös* 25, Sup.1 (2012): 57–72.
Kete, K. 'Animals and ideology: the politics of animal protection in Europe', in N. Rothfels (ed.), *Representing Animals*, Bloomington IN: Indiana University Press, 2002, 19–34.

Kete, K. 'Animals and human empire', in K. Kete (ed.), *A Cultural History of Animals in the Age of Empire*, Oxford: Berg, 2007, 1–23.

Kyle, D.G. 'Animal spectacles in ancient Rome: meat and meaning', in T.F. Scanlon (ed.), *Sport in the Greek and Roman Worlds: Greek Athletic Identities and Roman Sports and Spectacle*, Volume 2, Oxford: Oxford University Press, 2014, 269–295.

Landes, J.B., Lee, P.Y., and Youngquist, P. (eds.), *Gorgeous Beasts: Animal Bodies in Historical Perspective*, University Park PA: Pennsylvania State University Press, 2012.

Latour, B. 'From realpolitik to dingpolitik', in B. Latour and P. Weibel (eds.), *Making Things Public: Atmospheres of Democracy*, Cambridge, MA: MIT Press, 2004, 14–41.

Latour, B. *Reassembling the Social: An Introduction to Actor-Network-Theory*, Oxford: Oxford University Press, 2005.

Llored, P., Chrulew, M., and Buchanan, B. 'Zoopolitics', *SubStance* 43, 2 (2014): 115–123.

Lorimer, J. and Driessen, C. 'From "Nazi Cows" to cosmopolitan "ecological engineers": specifying rewilding through a history of heck cattle', *Annals of the American Association of Geographers* 106, 3 (2016): 631–652.

McKenzie, C. 'The British big-game hunting tradition: masculinity and fraternalism with particular reference to the Shikar Club', *The Sports Historian* 20, 1 (2000): 70–96.

Mergel, T. 'Überlegungen zu einer Kulturgeschichte der Politik', *Geschichte und Gesellschaft* 28, 4 (2002): 574–606.

Möhring, M. '"Herrentiere" und "Untermenschen": zu den Transformationen des Mensch-Tier-Verhältnisses im nationalsozialistischen Deutschland', *Historische Anthropologie* 19, 2 (2011): 240–241.

Murdoch, J. 'Ecologising sociology: actor-network theory, co-construction and the problem of human exceptionalism', *Sociology* 35, 1 (2001): 111–133.

Passmore, K. 'History and historiography since 1945', in R.E. Backhouse and P. Fontaine (eds.), *A Historiography of the Modern Social Sciences*, Cambridge: Cambridge University Press, 2014, 29–61.

Peggs, K. *Animals and Sociology*, Basingstoke: Palgrave Macmillan, 2012.

Philo, C. and Wilbert, C. (eds.), *Animal Spaces, Beastly Places: New Geographies of Human-Animal Relations*, London: Routledge, 2000.

Porter, R. 'History of the body reconsidered', in P. Burke (ed.), *New Perspectives on Historical Writing*, Cambridge: Polity Press, 2001, 232–260.

Power, E. 'Domestication and the dog: embodying home', *Area* 44, 3 (2012): 371–378.

Roscher, M. 'Curating the body politic: the spatiality of the zoo and the symbolic construction of German nationhood (Berlin 1933–1961)', in J. Bull, T. Holmberg, and C. Åsberg (eds.), *Animals and Place: Lively Cartographies of Human-Animal Relations*, London: Ashgate, 2017, 115–136.

Roscher, M. 'Das nationalsozialistische Tier: Projektionen von Rasse und Reinheit im Dritten Reich', *TIERethik* 13, 2 (2016): 30–48.

Russell, E. 'Coevolutionary history', *American Journal of History* 119, 5 (2014): 1514–1528.

Saha, J. 'Among the beasts of Burma: animals and the politics of colonial sensibilities, c. 1840–1940', *Journal of Social History* 48, 4 (2015): 910–932.

Sax, B. *Animals in the Third Reich*, London: Continuum, 2000.

Schorn-Schütte, L. 'Historical political research', in W. Steinmetz, I. Gilcher-Holtey, and H-G. Haupt (eds.), *Writing Political History Today*, Frankfurt: Campus Verlag, 2013, 369–382.

Shaw, D.G. 'The torturer's horse: agency and animals in history', *History and Theory* 52, 4 (2013): 146–167.

Sivasundaram, S. 'Imperial transgressions: the animal and human in the idea of race', *Comparative Studies of South Asia, Africa and the Middle East* 35, 1 (2015): 156–172.

Skabelund, A. 'Breeding racism: the imperial battlefields of the "German" shepherd dog', *Society & Animals* 16, 4 (2008): 354–371.

Spiegel, G.M. 'Introduction', in G.M. Spiegel (ed.), *Practicing History: New Directions in Historical Writing after the Linguistic Turn*, New York: Routledge, 1–31.

Spiegel, G.M. (ed.) *Practicing History: New Directions in Historical Writing after the Linguistic Turn*, New York: Routledge, 2005.

Sramek, J. '"Face him like a Briton!": Tiger hunting, imperialism, and British masculinity in colonial India, 1800–1875', *Victorian Studies* 48, 4 (2006): 659–680.

Steber, M. and Gotto, B. *Visions of Community in Nazi Germany: Social Engineering and Private Lives*, Oxford: Oxford University Press, 2014.

Steinbrecher, A. '"They do something": ein praxeologischer Blick auf Hunde in der Vormoderne', in F. Elias, A. Franz, H. Murmann, and U.W. Weiser (eds.), *Praxeologie: Beiträge zur interdisziplinären Reichweite praxistheoretischer Ansätze in den Geistes- und Sozialwissenschaften*, Berlin: De Gruyter, 2014, 29–51.

Steinmetz, W. and Haupt, H.-G. 'The political as communicative space in history: the Bielefeld approach', in W. Steinmetz, I. Gilcher-Holtey, and H-G. Haupt (eds.), *Writing Political History Today*, Frankfurt: Campus Verlag, 2013, 11–36.

Stollberg-Rilinger, B. 'Was heißt Kulturgeschichte des Politischen?', in B. Stollberg-Rilinger (ed.), *Was heißt Kulturgeschichte des Politischen?* Berlin: Duncker & Humblot, 2005, 9–27.

Trentmann, F. 'Political history matters: everyday life, things, and practices', in W. Steinmetz, I. Gilcher-Holtey, and H-G. Haupt (eds.), *Writing Political History Today*, Frankfurt: Campus Verlag, 2013, 397–408.

Uekötter, F. *The Green and the Brown: A History of Conservation in Nazi Germany*, Cambridge: Cambridge University Press, 2006.

Urban, M. *Von Ratten, Schmeißfliegen und Heuschrecken. Judenfeindliche Tiersymbolisierungen und die postfaschistischen Grenzen des Sagbaren*, Konstanz/München: UVK Verlagsgesellschaft, 2014.

Velde, H.T. 'The opening up of political history', in W. Steinmetz, I. Gilcher-Holtey, and H-G. Haupt (eds.), *Writing Political History Today*, Frankfurt: Campus Verlag, 2013, 383–395.

Wadiwel, D. 'Three fragments from a biopolitical history of animals: questions of body, soul, and the body politic in Homer, Plato, and Aristotle', *Journal for Critical Animal Studies* 6, 1 (2008): 17–39.

Wahrman, D. 'The new political history: a review essay', *Social History* 21, 3 (1996): 343–354.

Walker, B. 'Animals and the intimacy of history', *History and Theory* 52, 4 (2013): 45–67.

Wolch, J. and Emel, J. (eds.), *Animal Geographies: Place, Politics, and Identity in the Nature-Culture Borderlands*, London: Verso, 1998.

4
PUBLIC HISTORY AND HERITAGE
A fruitful approach for privileging animals?

Hilda Kean

Introduction

I start this chapter with some non-human animal protagonists and some definitions. For the former we have a small terrier dog who grieved over the corpse of his human companion; a donkey who alongside a human medical orderly helped rescue wounded soldiers at Gallipoli; various Norwegian brown rats, not of the fancy variety but the type who cause terror amongst many humans; and last but not least some long dead, and now taxidermied, polar bears. I will discuss these beings later in this chapter but have deliberately placed them here to indicate both their importance in this piece of writing and also as an indication of the focus I have chosen to adopt as a historian who seeks, at the bare minimum, to privilege the role of animals in the creation of histories. As I have discussed elsewhere, while debates around the nature of the materials used in the creation of histories involving animals are important – materials always are, whatever sort of history is being created – what is probably more important is the stance of the historian, her aims and objectives, the decisions she takes in developing particular arguments and employing specific materials and the way such work is presented and to whom.[1]

Like many with an academic background who choose to work within the broad framework of animal studies I also work within other 'disciplinary' areas or 'sub-fields' of history, particularly those of 'public history' and heritage, not least because of the scarcity of employment at present for those simply working in the field of historical animal studies. Thus routinely I am faced with apparently contradictory and conflicting ways of approaching subject matter. This is a problem experienced by many working in the fields of 'history' within both the Humanities and Social Studies areas. Here, however, I am routinely faced with apparently contradictory and conflicting ways of approaching the subject matter of 'history'. It is nevertheless felt particularly acutely within pubic history, since it is by definition 'inclusive' and 'democratised', but its 'public' is typically ill-defined, and it is notoriously capable of being co-opted by authority, in the form of 'heritage' and narratives of national identity. All the same, perhaps the challenge of 'public history' can be preserved or reclaimed – and the attempt to include *other* animals in these 'public histories' might be one particularly instructive way to do so.

The term public history confusingly, but perhaps not surprisingly, has different emphases in different cultural contexts. While Britain routinely produces heritage workers, museum curators, local historians and community practitioners who create history and put it to work in the world, in north America and Australasia there are often professional historians who define themselves in this way and are employed as such by local and national government institutions and businesses. The north American National Council on Public History (NCPH) established in 1980 to bring together a range of United States agencies and stake holders offers one description of the field, namely that 'All share an interest and commitment to making history relevant and useful in the public sphere' and that 'public history describes the many and diverse ways that history is put to work in the world'.[2] In this context the 'world' is taken to mean sites outside the academic lecture room and 'put to work' suggests that the practice has some sense of function or meaning beyond an intrinsic search for knowledge. Tactfully the Australian leading public historian Paul Ashton defines public history as an 'elastic nuanced and contentious term' that can be 'broadly defined as an array of practices that communicate and engage with historical meanings in the public sphere'. But, as he also acknowledges, it is 'the practice of historical work in a wide range of forums and sites which involves the negotiation and different understandings about the nature of the past and its meaning and uses in the present'.[3] Although some have emphasised the employment status of the historian, particularly stressing the work of those employed outside academia, for example in museums or archives,[4] given the fluidity of employment and funding regimes, more recently the focus has been on the places in which historical meaning is created or, more conservatively, the audiences for such knowledge. At its narrowest a definition of public history embraces the presentation of aspects of the past to a wide audience outside the confines of a seminar room.[5] At its most dynamic it involves individuals, groups and communities in the construction of their own histories.[6] This latter approach has been famously promoted by Ronald Grele as a participatory historical culture.[7] What such apparently different approaches have in common, however, is an implicit understanding that the way in which knowledge is created is key – process rather than research per se is central to a public history discourse. Often cited here is the work of the late British historian Raphael Samuel who emphasised the possibilities of history made by people (and not 'professional historians' alone) explaining that the creation of history by a 'thousand different hands' resulted in a *social* form of knowledge.[8] By opening up the categorisation of those making history – 'the who' – epistemology – 'the what' – is also changed. Running alongside this line of argument is an awareness of the way in which the past is contested: different meanings and strong feelings that can make history making unstable (and even career breaking).[9] In a new collection on public history, the author, aiming to demonstrate that historians should participate in a public understanding of the past, argues, 'Historians should accept that they do not work for the sake of history only, to advance historical research but for and with others'.[10]

As will be evident from the brief summary above, public historians approach their work not around particular subject matter per se but from a perspective of the process of creating meaning or disseminating ideas with a particular emphasis on accessibility. However, despite what might be viewed as a broadly progressive sense of epistemology, analysis of the role of non-human animals has yet to be a routine analytic feature of key journals such as *The Public Historian* where animals are noticeable by their distinct absence.[11] Non-human animals seem then to mark the limits of the ambition of inclusiveness, let alone that of participation in public history.

Those working within a broad framework of animal studies also, of course, have different emphases but many would acknowledge that animals as some sort of subject *matter* – rather than *process* as such – is key. Nevertheless, there are some complementarities. There are those who, like many public historians, see a role for themselves within a social and political context outside academic study per se. Jonathan Balcombe has explained this as an approach that seeks to 'parlay existing theory into action, and to do our bit to change the tide for animals'.[12] This trajectory has been emphasised in a recent book by Nik Taylor, where she has expressed her 'unease with the majority of animal studies scholarship that remains divorced from the reality of animal lives' and warns against scholarship 'falling into the trap of contemplation without action'.[13] Contemplation and introspection are certainly present within the field of animal studies, sometimes to the extent of work being esoteric and divorced from any engagement with living animals. Too often an emphasis on theoretical precision and the need to repeat in almost mantra-like fashion the work of mainly continental European philosophers – without applying this to the lived experience past or present of non-human animals – can create a context far removed from putting such meaning, to again quote the NCPH, 'to work in the world'.[14] For example, a framework very different from that of 'the world' was envisaged in the introduction to a recent animal–human history collection *The Historical Animal* that, having drawn analogies with feminist and environmental history, concluded with the phrase ' . . . for any group to achieve their justice – whatever their particular "justice" may be – they must have their history written and accepted *within the academy*' (my emphasis).[15] The author here is certainly not ignoring animals but still privileges academic boundaries as a framework for situating 'justice' rather than engagement with 'the world'. Creating a *real* impact outside academia (rather than just ticking a box for UK universities' funding requirements) might mean not just looking at the dissemination of 'boundaried' knowledge but instead an engagement with those outside the seminar walls with those who have different contributions to make to historical meaning – and understanding of the lives of non-human animals and their treatment.

Animals in the creation of national histories

In *practice* there is far more blurring between the processed-based approach of public historians and the sometimes more esoteric world of animal studies than I might have suggested above, but rather than seeking to juxtapose abstract definitions I intend instead to focus on different animals who, in their own way, have played significant roles in the past, and to consider how their lives and narratives might be approached from different perspectives. Certainly, if we think of public history as demonstrating the importance of the past in different national public contexts there is a plethora of examples of *practice* to animals to choose from. Many nations have consciously chosen to incorporate individual animals, especially those possessing names, into their commemorative cultures and histories. Consider the 'first dogs' of the first families, the fascination with the past animals, usually dogs, who have lived with American Presidents. Notwithstanding the bizarre Christmas videos of George W. Bush and his dogs Miss Beazley and Barney around the Christmas tree,[16] we can agree with Helena Pycior that, 'each first dog had a history, a personality, a disposition suitable to the bustle of the White House . . . and a role in the history of the United States . . . '[17] Equally acknowledged in North American popular memory are Stubby the guard dog who saved lives on the battlefields of the First World War by his vigilance, or Balto, the Alaskan malamute, who with other dogs and human mushers saved the isolated town of Nome by bringing the diphtheria vaccine across an arduous journey in the 1920s.[18] Both of these dogs, in their own ways, continue to be popular today either in taxidermied form in the Smithsonian or in a bronze sculptural depiction of Balto in New York's Central Park.[19] In such examples we may be looking at nothing but representations but, as Diana Donald has convincingly argued, we need to

> take representations of animals as what they purport to be, and analyse them for what they truly contain: evidence of human convictions and emotions about other species. Fragmented, obscure, deeply conflicting as this evidence may be, it offers the only possibility of recovering a key aspect of history which has, as yet, hardly begun to be understood.[20]

And in the case of stuffed animals like Balto, Rachel Poliquin has argued that for all that 'taxidermied animals have been transfigured by the fervour of human longing' these animals are 'never just cultural objects but are rather provocative animal-things imbued with both the longing to capture animal life immortally and the longing to see the living animal again'.[21]

So animals do participate, if unwillingly, in one form of public history. Given the relatively recent origins of the state of Australia and particularly its intention to create a separate identity from Britain in the aftermath of the First World War, Australia is arguably the best example of the ways that animals have been consciously used to create national histories separate from British traditions.[22] Certainly animals have played important roles in the nation-forming fiction of Banjo Patterson and Henry Lawson. Lawson's memorial by George Lambert in Sydney's Domain with a proud dog certainly reflects his stories of the outback that featured animals in key narratives. This is an appropriate location for a memorial to this resolutely urban author who created an idealised past for the new colony while rarely straying from his Sydney home.[23]

Consider too the effects of the journalist, Charles Bean, who can reasonably be defined as a public historian, who did so much to create and document the ANZAC spirit as an identity separate from Britain especially employing the Australian and New Zealand military experience in the battles at Gallipoli during the 1914–18 war. He was largely responsible for both the establishment of the Australian War Memorial in Canberra that functions both as a major museum and one of the most popular in Australia and also the national archives for war records that is frequently used by a range of history practitioners.[24] The emphasis here was upon re-creating a wartime experience by collecting 'everything connected with the War' with the intention that in the future soldiers would visit with their friends and children 'and there revive the past'.[25] Significantly, animals who had played a wartime role were also requisitioned for the museum: much discussion took place on how to 'preserve indefinitely' a messenger dog, carrier pigeon and the head of Sandy,[26] who was a bay gelding horse born in 1908 and was some 15.2 hands tall,[27] serving in Egypt with Major General Sir William Throsby Bridges and had then travelled to Britain. The horse of the commander of the Australian first division at Gallipoli was the only one of some 170,000 horses to return to Australia after the war.[28] Extensive quarantine and complicated logistical procedures enabled the horse to return – together with Private Jordan 'who understands the animal well' – to Australia.[29] By 1922 the now elderly horse was killed 'for humane reasons' and the new Australian War Memorial determined to acquire part of his body, as this 'would make an interesting exhibit'.[30] Such dead animal heroes were seen as helping to build a distinctive Australian identity particularly amongst young people. In addition to these animal 'exhibits' there were intricate diorama displays of particular battles including models of soldiers and animals. What is striking here is not the development of a museum per se but a recognition that ordinary soldiers' *own* memorabilia (such as cones from the 'Lone Pine Ridge') would form an integral part of the collections. Such items could be duplicates since they carried with them different stories from the soldiers who had collected them.[31] Animals serving alongside the military were to be an integral part of this project from the outset. Thus in the same way that the warfare of the 1914-18 war was conducted in 'more than human public spaces' so too was this most prestigious new museum explicitly incorporating animals into the state's official past. This participatory and open approach was a very different stance to that of the British state over the same war.[32] Within this 'open' approach to history-making, non-human animals were embraced. They became not mere accessories but active participants in the creation of national histories.

The donkey I referred to at the start of this chapter was equally an important figure in the creation of such new nation formation. This particular donkey working alongside a medical orderly, Jack Simpson Fitzpatrick (commonly known as Simpson), rescuing the wounded under heavy bombardment in so-called Shrapnel Gully in the battlefields of Gallipoli has become an integral – and enduring – part of the nation's past. Simpson and his donkey were first recognised in the public commemorative landscape of the 1930s with a small memorial outside the Melbourne War Memorial.[33] This partnership of man and animal – neither would have existed without the other – has been replicated in their representation: they are always presented together (and have been re-created in different sites).[34]

From the 1980s there has been a revival of interest in ANZAC day despite – or perhaps because of – the deaths of the last human veterans. This has suggested 'in part an emotional need for structure and tradition'.[35] The 1988 ceremonies witnessed an unveiling of a larger version of the iconic original memorial of Simpson and the donkey alongside the Australian War Museum, appealing particularly to children. The sculptor, Peter Corlett, commented that he envisaged the statue as 'not unlike the image of Christ entering Jerusalem'. The donkey was to be 'small yet sturdy and reliable, with a look of reluctant co-operation about him'. The re-worked memorial has proved to be popular. Children treated the representation of the donkey affectionately, stroking his nose so extensively that it has been worn smooth. The animal was key to the form of the artwork while the overall intention of the artist was to produce a work celebrating 'a personal compassion of common *humanity*'.[36] Simpson is unlikely to have been incorporated in the way he has within the national sense of the past *without* his donkey; yet, according to the artist's words, if not in the minds of the numerous children who enjoy the sculpture, the 'animal' plays a secondary role to the idea of 'humanity'. The trope of animals working alongside humans in war does suggest an agency of sorts, albeit one not independent of humans.[37] This has been demonstrated in subsequent Australian war commemorations, not least the 'Animals in War' memorial by Steven Mark Holland unveiled in the same site in 2009 (Figure 4.1). Here the accompanying plaque refers to animals who 'served alongside Australians' and 'performed many essential duties' including those who 'lived with the Australians as mascots or companions'.[38] Interestingly here the 'emotional work' of animals as well as the more utilitarian role of, say, mine detection is acknowledged.

Figure 4.1 Steven Mark Holland, *Memorial to Animals in War*, Sculpture Garden, Australian War Memorial, Canberra, Australia, unveiled 2009.

Author's photograph.

The initial statue in Melbourne had been created at the impetus of Philadelphia Robertson, secretary general of the Australian Red Cross 'to lead our thoughts into the quiet ways of compassion and kindness'.[39] Museum practitioners and politicians initiated the 1988 version at the Australian War Memorial in Canberra.[40] There have also been, for example, recent campaigns by the descendants of those who had served in the Australian Light Horse in the First World War to erect an appropriate monument to Sandy – the horse whose head was acquired by the Australian War Memorial – at the spot where his body was buried at Maribyrnong, in Victoria, where there was a Remount Depot paddock. As a local resident argued, campaigners wanted to stop the site from becoming 'just another piece of housing estate'.[41] Here a dead horse, representing the ANZAC moment of nation formation, was appropriated to create a community identity that also appealed to national sentiments. While the campaigners were not directly successful, the VicUrban, the state government developer, agreed to recognise the horse by naming a road on the estate in his memory.[42]

I am not arguing that there is a more benign approach towards animals exhibited nor in such memorials that Australian animal welfare or animal rights legislation is leading the world. But rather that an acknowledgment of the presence of animals in heritage works designed to create national identity – and to create an 'entry point' to important features of historical national memory, particularly for children and those unused to visiting museums – should be recognised and analysed by those working as animal–human historians.[43] I note too that such creations of public sentiment towards a lowly donkey in the nation's past do not necessarily relate to positive sentiments towards the treatment of donkeys in Australia in the present. Indeed Australian-based Jill Bough has argued that the majority of the population has little knowledge of, or interest in, the shooting from helicopters of hundreds of thousands of wild donkeys, especially in Western Australia and the Northern Territory.[44] I am suggesting that those interested in animal studies and particularly animal–human history should view such commemorative developments as a positive starting point in the public domain for exploring the meaning of the animal–human relationship across time. We might also observe that these sentiments were developed outside, to quote Raphael Samuel, 'the conventions and the coldness of the seminar room'.[45] While there are various caveats around the particular concept of animal agency being promoted in such representations – for example the continuing privileging of the human position within such an animal–human relationship. This should not detract from the fact that modern audiences *are* given information about the past that includes animals as active participants in the creation of the nation's past. We might then go further than acknowledging only a public display of an animal–human bond to a deeper analysis of the nature of the relationship, questioning the human position and drawing attention to the negative – as well as the positive – role of representation in masking, in this example, exploitation. In this way, at least some of the aims of public history might be endorsed.

Ignoring the archive: the dog at the Eureka Stockade

I now want to take further the exploration of how awareness of the historical role of animals – and perhaps their representation – is often absent from the work of social historians even when contemporary materials provide such 'evidence'. As I argued at the start of this chapter, the stance of the historian is critical. Thus an a priori awareness of the role of animals in creating societies, such as that contained in the perspective of many within the animal studies field, might be valuable in challenging accepted approaches.

I thus turn to a particular example of a dog, a recently restored statue and a different national history – also in Australia. In summary, the Eureka Stockade was erected in 1854 on the goldfields of Ballarat some 115 kilometres northwest of Melbourne in Victoria. Prospectors – or 'diggers', the word that became incorporated into Australian English as a badge of national male identity – were obliged to pay taxes in order to dig (rather than to pay taxes on what was actually obtained from the land). The workers saw this as unjust since one could be obliged to pay even if nothing was mined. Moreover although they were obliged to pay taxes they had no political representation.[46] Breaking point was reached in early December 1854 and it was resolved to resist physically oppressive state forces. A barricade (or stockade) was erected around the workers' camp and was defended by diggers against attacks by the military. As a result many diggers were either killed outright or later died of their wounds. Although some of the leaders were brought to court for treason there was found to be no case to answer and all were acquitted. This is the briefest summary of the events at Ballarat, which have become 'a key event in the development of Australian democracy and Australian identity'.[47] These dramatic events have been contested by historians and had various interpretations, as public history often bears witness.[48] Speaking from a conservative position, Spate argued that the incident 'hardly bears the weight sometimes placed upon it'; 'It was dramatic in a country whose history lacks spectacular event of this sort, but hardly a turning-point in Australian history'.[49] Leading Australian historian, Stuart Macintyre, has by contrast declared the Eureka Stockade to be a 'formative event in the national mythology' noting that:

> Radical nationalists celebrated it as a democratic uprising against imperial authority and the first great event in the emergence of the labour movement. The Communist Party's Eureka Youth League invoked this legacy … so did the right-wing National Front, while revisionist historians have argued that the rebellion should be seen as a tax revolt by small businesses.[50]

For some, the Eureka events have been interpreted as an Australian version of British Chartism[51] while feminists have recently sought to acknowledge the role of women in the rebellion and thus incorporate them within a historically radical past.[52] Significantly the events of December 1854 have been acknowledged to be part of a broader cultural heritage that exists – and is certainly known about – inside and *outside* academic circles.

Still, despite the plethora of *academic* articles re-interpreting this event for the present there has, to date, been scant acknowledgment or analysis by such experts of the presence of a small terrier dog at the stockade. Such a dog did exist and was fulsomely acknowledged at the time. Only a few days after the event the local newspaper the *Geelong Advertiser and Intelligencer* published a letter giving an eye-witness account of the aftermath of the military attack:

> Poor women crying for absent husbands, and children frightened into quietness.
> I, sir, write disinterestedly, and I hope my feelings arose from a true principle;

but when I looked at that scene, my soul revolted at such means being so cruelly used by a government to sustain the law. A little terrier sat on the breast of the man I spoke of, and kept up a continuous howl: it was removed, but always returned to the same spot; and when his master's body was huddled, with the other corpses, into the cart, the little dog jumped in after him, and lying again on his dead master's breast, began howling again.

'The master' – not personally known to the letter writer – was described as

a stout-chested fine fellow, apparently about forty years old, [who] lay with a pike beside him: he had contusions in the head, three strokes across the brow, a bayonet wound in the throat under the ear, and other wounds in the body – I counted fifteen wounds in that single carcase.

Neither dog – nor man – were named. It was, however, the dog's physical position and behaviour that caused him to be noticed. Raffaello Carboni, a man who identified himself as both a digger and an anarchist reproduced this account some weeks later in a contemporary pamphlet. His lengthy description includes amongst other things the names of the dead diggers and their nationalities.[53] It is seen as a sufficiently reputable 'source' for it still to be quoted in twenty-first century analyses and used as evidence for a range of interpretations.[54] There is no reason therefore to doubt his account of the stockade's dog.

A similar account was published on the fiftieth anniversary in the *Geelong Advertiser* of 6 December 1904. Here one correspondent recorded his memory of the event 50 years before:

I saw a little terrier whining piteously beside his dead master. While viewing this solemn scene a dray arrived in which was placed the body of the man who in life was the owner of the dog. When the little terrier saw his master removed his grief knew no bounds. Those interested tried to drive him away: they could not beat him back. He got into the dray and sat upon his master's breast, revealing in most unmistakable language that this master was taken away from him. No human being could have lamented more at the loss of their dearest relative or friend than that affectionate and faithful dog bewailed the loss of his master.[55]

Clearly those who witnessed and then recorded their observations were sympathetic to the diggers' cause rather than the authorities'. The language of grief, exemplified here by howling, wailing, whining, is a cross-species emotion. In this instance the vocal dog seemed to express publicly the more silent emotion of the human eyewitnesses.[56] These are not the accounts of 'detached' historians.[57] The recent publication of the Eureka Stockade Memorial Trust has tried to explain the impact of the memory of the dog, noting, 'Unlike others of the dead making their final journey, at least this particular digger had a mourner whose grief made a lasting impression on all who witnessed it'.[58] Moreover, given that many of the wounded men were not given medical treatment but summarily dispatched, Paul Williams suggests that 'If the dog had been human he would have almost certainly been killed'.[59] That is, the dog is simultaneously an empathetic part of the scene but detached from the slaughter by virtue of not being human.

The broad description of the dog in 1904 is the same as that recorded contemporaneously but, importantly, does not use identical language which suggests that the dog had not simply passed into folklore but had been actually seen and remembered by another observer.[60] The presence of a small terrier dog grieving over the dead body of his human companion was thus acknowledged in the public domain as an aspect of the stockade worth recording at the contemporary moment – and some 50 years later. This lasting animal presence is not some post-humanist reappraisal: even for conventional historians who tend to privilege 'primary sources' above all else, there is evidence from the local press, invariably used on such occasions, that the dog existed and was deemed to perform an historic role in the overall events. In the twenty-first century *academic* accounts the dog is noticeable by his absence. In stark contrast those working in the broad sphere of public history have positively acknowledged the dog's presence albeit not exploring trans-species emotion in any depth.

This is obvious from the revamped memorial, at the new Museum of Australian Democracy at Eureka (MADE) located on the site of the stockade, and unveiled in December 2014, which features two aspects – the memorial of the dog and the 22 pikes (Figure 4.2). (The latter represented 22 people as supposedly 15 different nationalities of the dead.)[61] Importantly the dog has not been reduced to merely some sort of symbol of canine loyalty or grief. Indeed the public acknowledgment and memorialisation of the dog led to a posthumous award of a Purple Cross awarded to the 'real' dog by the Australian RSPCA in 1997. (This highest Australian honour for a non-human animal has also been previously posthumously awarded to Simpson's donkey, the hero of Gallipoli, as discussed above.)[62] So the representation has had the effect here of leading to awareness of the presence and agency of a specific 'real' animal. The plaque unveiled with the memorial initially in 1999 reads, 'It honours a loyal and faithful animal, and commemorates the sacrifice of those pikemen who heroically defended the Eureka stockade on Sunday 3 December 1854'.[63]

That the dog's documented, 'historical' presence has been brought into the present and given a privileged role has little to do with cultural or labour historians or animal studies scholars. Rather it has come about through those working in the role of public historians creating a new museum at the supposed site and commissioning an art work. The focus of the museum itself had been controversial as Anne Beggs Sunter has thoroughly analysed. As she notes, there were 'differences in the objective of funding bodies, management, professional curators, citizens, tourists and descendants of those who fought at Eureka'.[64] In discussing the composition of the committee to oversee the project, Beggs Sunter notes that there was no academic historian – nor a representative 'from the Left side of politics'.[65] At the original unveiling in 1999 were present the Irish ambassador and the Premier of Victoria with blessings given by local bishops and a rabbi.[66] To some extent the inclusion of a representation of a non-human animal, a dog, was less controversial (and no doubt cheaper to reproduce) than one or more three-dimensional human figures. In such a contested narrative who would be represented? Which narrative would they embody? – questions that Gervase Phillips discusses in this volume.[67] What is missing here is a perspective drawn from animal studies although what we are presented with is surely a version of

Figure 4.2 Pikeman's Dog Memorial, created by Charles Smith and Joan Walsh-Smith, located on the site of the Museum of Australian Democracy at Eureka in Ballarat, December 2014.

Author's photograph.

what Urbanik and Morgan call human-spatial-dog-politics.[68] It is not simply that the dog is incorporated into commemorative space but that the space itself becomes cross-species.

The example of the Eureka dog also shows that it is not simply historians who create history. Indeed many would agree with Jeremy Black that they rarely do so.[69] The pikeman's dog is now part of modern Australia's commemorative history and landscape, both – I emphasise – by his own actions, his agency – but also because contemporary writers noted his actions and, in turn, those interested in the importance of the wider event recognised his role in the narrative. The broad configuration of public history might help us explore such approaches to animal–human history more effectively than social or cultural history alone. Still it is also an area that would benefit from an animal studies perspective including, perhaps, an explicit *challenge* to existing frameworks for the creation of popular narratives rather than a simple incorporation into existing tropes.[70]

The rats in Sydney's Hyde Park Barracks: making animals an integral part of museum historiography

I now turn to a very different example drawn from Australian public history practice, namely the rats in the Hyde Park Barracks. I do this not because I have any particular allegiance pertinently towards museum practice in Australia but because this is one of the most innovative public history approaches towards animals in museums and heritage buildings that I have witnessed to date. It draws upon concepts of material culture, art and animal agency and the explicit notion that historical meaning is constructed. Whilst non-human animals, or parts of them, have long been part of the public exhibitionary complex, this is a highly distinctive approach. Here the practice of generations of rats is highlighted. The rats who accumulated and kept traces of material under the floorboards are prominently acknowledged in practice and displays at the museum. The Hyde Park Barracks is a building that fulfilled various state functions since its role as the first convict barracks in the colony in 1819. It was later used to house mainly Irish female immigrants and destitute and aged women and orphans. From the late nineteenth century to the 1970s it was used as legal offices and courtrooms.[71] Its latest reincarnation as a museum had a fortuitous 'moment', in the rise of artworks that have increasingly played with the relationship between the ordinary and process, thus creating different perceptions of time and the past.[72] The imaginative approach was directed by Peter Emmett who conceived of the Barracks as a theatre set, believing, in Kate Gregory's words that entering the Barracks 'should be a three dimensional sensory, spatial and corporeal experience of the past'.[73] As display boards explain, the theoretical approach of the museum is based on 'Each mark, relic or word gives us hints about past lives and experiences. We invite you to join the historical process of piecing together the present traces of the past'.[74] Thus an active role is envisaged for the human visitor. As one writer has analysed, visitors 'find themselves in the midst of an archaeological dig'.[75] The rats were occupants of the building alongside humans and their role in exposing layers of meaning as quasi-public historians *themselves* is key to the museum's presentations. The rats are acknowledged as having played an active part in the creation of meaning in the place. In their movement through the building and their engagement with humans they accumulated scraps of clothing, food and bedding to make nests. Many everyday items were discovered under the floorboards – bonnets, aprons, shirts, shoes, stockings – not least because of the rats' activity.[76] It was the animal process of accumulation and collecting and then a human recognition of its historical value that allowed the archaeological service to document ordinary everyday lives at the Barracks in the past.[77] Moreover, for some years live rats – sadly not the 'authentic' Norwegian brown rats but the 'friendlier' domestic agouti rats – were kept in a displayed burrow/play area in a glass case in the ticket office. All visitors were obliged to acknowledge the animals' presence as they gathered to buy tickets for the museum.[78] Despite the various articles that criticise the general conceptual outlook of Emmett at Hyde Park Barracks (and later the Museum of Sydney) there has apparently yet to be any scholarly analysis or even mention of the role of the rats in this overall framework, which is to say public historians working *analytically* (as opposed to being museum curators etc.) have failed to engage with the underlying processes of historical meaning created in the museum – despite its explicit declaration.[79]

Here an understanding of the behaviour of rats – their agency if you will – and their practice of creating nests from a range of available material – and also their 'ancestral' occupation of the built environment – led to an imaginative construction of the past lived experience of the building. Yet, frustratingly in this instance, analysis of practice has not led to an awareness of the role of the rats despite the 'evidence' presented in the galleries. Despite documentation of the role of their ancestors in the creation of the past, in the present the rats are written out of scholarly analysis of the creation of the process of meaning at the Barracks, albeit being promoted by those public historians and archaeologists developing the site itself. Animal studies scholars who grapple with the role of animals in the archive might well add an understanding of the too easily overlooked role of rats.[80]

Individualising the generic: animal studies and polar bears

My final detailed example refers to mainstream practice in museums and the way in which this has been subverted – though again not by professional historians, but by artists. No one who has lived in Britain in the last few decades should be the least surprised about the power of the artistic imagination upon the public consciousness and public funding particularly through the Heritage Lottery Fund. Public museums and art galleries were created at a time of nation formation, particularly in Europe during the late eighteenth and early nineteenth century. Institutions such as the British Museum or National Gallery were features that ensured that the visitor engaged with (and was educated by) civilising aspects away from the quotidian.[81] People, it has been argued, come to know the meaning of a nation (or locality) 'partly through the objects and artefacts which have been made to stand for and symbolize its essential values'.[82] Animals formed an integral part of such collections, as we have seen in the Australian context, but also in specific national natural history museums and in local museums. Recently there have been some attempts to use the enduring popularity of taxidermied animals that formed a key part of such collections in new ways. The collection of the natural history museum in Kassel in Germany, for example, displays regional natural history from the Paleozoic period to the present with taxidermied animals placed in authentic locations and times of the year as a way of re-contextualising them for a more environmentally conscious present. More imaginatively, in a recent special exhibition in this museum on sex and evolution, animals of various species were displayed in various acts of copulation, which, if nothing else, captured popular attention.[83] Another example of re-using museums' collections of taxidermied animals has been found in the work of Bryndis Snaebjornsdottir and Mark Wilson,[84] 'Nanoq: flat out and bluesome'. Described by historical geographer David Matless as a 'document . . . which offers an exemplary case of the arts of collection, documentation and design',[85] one of the main aims of the work was to reveal the way in which the bodies of polar bears had become tangible and uncomfortable documents of a difficult past history.[86] Although this work has usually been discussed as a work of art,[87] it nevertheless was also an exploration of the sites in which stuffed polar bears are kept and seen by the public in museums and historic houses. As Hansen has put it:

> In their 'original' display cases, each individual stuffed bear symbolizes 'bear-ness', with this 'bear-ness' residing close to the skin. While serialization suggests that one bear, one specimen, remains interchangeable by standing in for an entire group, it is, ironically, by showing several specimens together that *nanoq* makes this serialization break down as one starts to notice the animals' individual features.[88]

That is, the conventional 'animal material' of nineteenth-century western natural history museums has been re-appropriated to present animals not as generic specimens but as former living beings with individual traits.[89] Snaebjornsdottir/ Wilson's work consisted of 34 individual taxidermied polar bears – collected from museum displays, storage rooms, workshops undergoing restoration, or private houses – together with their individual histories. In the process of this, different readings and contextualisation were given to the animals. By tracing the history of 'a cultural afterlife' the animals became transformed from an anonymous 'specimen' to some form of individual being.[90] Thus the museum proved to be both a site of animal material but also of the creation of new meaning drawn from such material. The *public* space for such work defied any particular academic boundaries both in its subject matter and approach – and location of display.[91]

This is a very different approach to the more conventional one argued by Swinney: that the celebrity of an individual animal in a museum menagerie exists because of their status prior to death – and transitions into an object of display.[92] Amongst other things, the work of Snaebjornsdottir/Wilson explores the very concept of being an animal in a museum. In their imaginative use of almost anonymised 'specimens', that was the norm of nineteenth-century natural history collections they have both challenged the way such polar bears were looked at and, importantly, have suggested new ways of thinking with existing taxidermied animals in museums. That is, they have provided concepts that public historians can appropriate using 'stock' that already exists but with different analytical approaches.[93]

There have been several other examples of creative work privileging animals in public museums. Thus from 2011 to 2013 the National Army Museum in London used the popularity of the play and then film of 'War Horse' to mount an exhibition entitled, 'War horse: fact or fiction?' There were displays that focussed on individual horses, rather than, say, the generic role of cavalry horses including: Napoleon's mount Marengo whose skeleton was displayed in London in 1832, Jimson the mule who served with the Middlesex Regiment in India and the South African Wars and who received medals for his work and Sefton of the Household Cavalry injured by an IRA bomb in London in 1982. The focus on the individual and not merely the group also helped create a sense of empathy and identification missing from conventional military history. The majority of the material was, inevitably, drawn from human constructed sources, such as paintings, but an artwork by Laura Antebi of a large horse made of wire stumbling upon barbed wire evoked far more than the textual explanation of the suffering caused to horses through such entrapment. The National Army museum exhibition attempted throughout to privilege horses rather than to

Figure 4.3 Harrie Fasher, *Silent Conversation*, 2014, from *Spirited: Australia's Horse Story*, National Museum Australia, Canberra, exhibition 11 September 2014 to 9 March 2015. Author's photograph. Courtesy of National Museum Australia.

speak of the work of soldiers with them. Near the end of the exhibition was a large horizontal display cabinet consisting of rows of small white outline horses inviting visitors to remember the role of horses in war.[94] Significantly individuals, including specific non-human animals, were privileged. Artwork designed to evoke an empathetic response challenged the visitor to look at warfare generally and the First World War in particular in different ways to the norm.

More recently the exhibition 'Spirited: Australia's Horse Story' at the National Museum of Australia in 2014–15 has tackled the difficult task of trying to show the role of horses as active protagonists in the development of the nation – with a focus upon horses rather than people's perception of them per se (Figure 4.3).[95] Artworks played around with different ideas of power, for example, an outline metallic human figure being forced to be the focus of a larger metallic horse's gaze or huge moving images of wild horses unrestrained by humans. In this spirit carriages were not seen as vehicles with absent 'operators' but models of horses were included to demonstrate the effect of the weight upon their bodies. Thus, the public historians working in these locations that draw on artistic representations to create new ways of thinking historically about animals.

Some concluding thoughts

If we return to the initial ideas in this chapter of both putting history to work in the world and of creating scholarship exploring the reality of animal lives, we might now conclude that there is more potential in a relationship between the approaches of animal studies researchers and public historian practitioners. The process basis of public history can indeed provide scope for the development of histories exploring animal–human relationships and the material on which this is founded. To date this is an undeveloped area but one in which those with an interest in debates within animal studies – agency, representation, the materials for privileging animals – might play a useful role. Some small developments indicate tentative ways forward. The National Museum of Animals and Society, which has previously existed only online, is now physically based in Los Angeles and is primarily devoted to campaigning for the rights of actually existing animals. The museum has seen the importance of recording and disseminating the long history of campaigns for animals: 'We exist to preserve, interpret and share our inspiring legacy of animal protection, to nurture current and future generations' overall awareness about animals in society and to empower change'.[96] Thus, as Keri Cronin notes in her chapter in this volume, the museum has organised online exhibitions including those on the Band of Mercy and campaigns aimed at children to establish the long traditions of such work. Online, or digital, history as demonstrated here might be a valuable way of collecting and collating and sharing material and ideas internationally. Certainly the plethora of blogs and initiatives from animal enthusiasts such as the online Ernest Bell, the Henry Salt library archive and the Humanitarian League indicates the breadth of interest in the role of the past in the present.[97] Those drawn to a site primarily for information around vegetable-based food can also read about past campaigns (and recipes!)[98] In such practical ways history is not seen as discrete from present activity but rather a foundation for it.

Notes

1 H. Kean, 'Challenges for historians writing animal–human history: what is really enough?', *Anthrozoos* 25, S1 (2012): s57–s72.
2 National Council on Public History, n.d. 'What is public history', available at http://ncph.org/what-is-public-history/about-the-field/, last accessed 19 August 2017.
3 P. Ashton, 'Public history' in A. Clark and P. Ashton (eds.), *Australian History Now*, Sydney: New South Publishing, 2013, 167–180, 169, 179.
4 For discussion of these definitions see H. Kean and P. Martin (eds.), *The Public History Reader*, Abingdon: Routledge, 2013, xvi–xviii.
5 See for example J. Tosh, *Why History Matters*, Basingstoke: Palgrave Macmillan, 2008, 119.
6 Ludmilla Jordanova has suggested that public history can be a tool of political establishments as well as radical history movements. She argues that a focus on the way the past can be 'open-ended' and 'public property' should mean that historians see their activities in a wider perspective and raise questions about the practice of history. L. Jordanova, *History in Practice*, London: Arnold Publishers, 2000, 141–143.
7 R.J. Grele, 'Clio on the road to Damascus: a national survey of history as activity and experience', *The Public Historian* 72, 1 (2000): 31–34. See also M. Frisch, *A Shared Authority: Essays on the Craft and Meaning of Oral and Public History,* Buffalo NY: State University of New York Press, 1990.
8 R. Samuel, *Theatres of Memory: Past and Present in Contemporary Culture*, London: Verso, 1994, 8.
9 One of the best publicised cases is of the presentation of the Enola Gay at the Smithsonian Institute and the ensuing ructions. See amongst others, Jordanova, *History in Practice*,

156–159; M. Wallace, *Mickey Mouse History and Other Essays on American Memory*, Philadelphia PA: Temple University Press, 1996, 269–318. This including the sacking of the director of the National Museum of Australia and a state inquiry into the portrayal of Australia's past at the museum. In Australia acrimonious debates about the contested nature of modern Australia's origins – and its relationship with indigenous peoples – as portrayed, inter alia, at the National Museum of Australia led to a state inquiry into the portrayal of Australia's past at the museum and the sacking of the director. Such controversies were called the 'History Wars' and this was not necessarily just hyperbole. See G. Hansen, 'White hot history: the review of the National Museum of Australia', *Public History Review* 11, (2003): 39–50; D. Casey, 'Culture wars: museums, politics and controversy', *New Museum Developments and the Culture Wars*, special issue of *Open Museum Journal* 6, (2003): 8–10; S. Macintyre and A. Clark, *The History Wars*, Melbourne: Melbourne University Press, 2003.

10 T. Cauvin, 'Introduction' in T. Cauvin (ed.), *Public History: A Textbook of Practice*, Abingdon: Routledge, 2016, 1–25, 2.

11 *The International Journal of Heritage Studies* has, however, made a tentative foray into this area with a series of articles, including those on zoo heritage and commemorative animal statues.

12 J. Balcombe, 'Concluding remarks: from theory to action: an ethologist's perspective', in N. Taylor and T. Signal (eds.), *Theorizing Animals: Re-thinking Humanimal Relations*, Leiden: Brill, 2011, 281–289, 288.

13 N. Taylor, *Humans, Animals, and Society: An Introduction to Human–Animal Studies*, Brooklyn NY: Lantern Books, 2013, 168–169.

14 ncph.org/what-is-public-history/about-the-field/.

15 S. Nance, 'Introduction', in S. Nance (ed.), *The Historical Animal*, Syracuse NY: Syracuse University Press, 2015, 1–16, 16.

16 Original official white house video from 2009 archived and represented at www.youtube.com/watch?v=7vaFAy6eIU8 site, last accessed 20 June 2016.

17 H. Pycior, 'The public and private lives of "Private Dogs"', in D. Brantz (ed.), *Beastly Natures: Animals, Humans, and the Study of History*, Charlottesville VA: University of Vi.inia Press, 2010, 176–203, 199; See also H. Pycior, 'The making of the "First Dog": President Warren G. Harding and Laddie Boy', *Society and Animals* 13, 2 (2005): 109–138.

18 M. Lemish, *War Dogs: Canines in Combat*, Washington DC: Brassey's, 1996, 25–27; H. Kean, 'Balto, the Alaskan dog and his statue in New York's Central Park: animal representation and national heritage', *International Journal of Heritage Studies* 15, 5 (2009): 413–430. See also an analysis of Hatchiko in mid-twentieth-century Japan in A. Skabelund, *Empire of Dogs: Canines, Japan, and the Making of the Modern Imperial World*, New York: Cornell University Press, 2011, 145ff.

19 For an image of Stubby, see http://amhistory.si.edu/militaryhistory/collection/object.asp?ID=15 site, last accessed 18 August 2017.

20 D. Donald, *Picturing Animals in Britain, 1750–1850*, New Haven CT: Yale University Press, 2007, vi.

21 R. Poliquin, *The Breathless Zoo: Taxidermy and the Cultures of Longing*, University Park PA: Pennsylvania University Press, 2012, 223.

22 See here A. Franklin, *Animal Nation: The True Story of Animals and Australia*, Sydney: University of New South Wales Press, 2006. On memorials, see R. Searby, 'Red dog, horses and Bogong moths: the memorialisation of animals in Australia', *Public History Review* 15, (2008): 117–134.

23 H. Kean, 'Public history and two Australian dogs: Islay and the dog on the tucker box', *ACH: The Journal of the History of Culture in Australia* 24–25, (2006): 135–162, 142.

24 H. Kean and P. Ashton, 'Introduction: people and their pasts and public history today', in H. Kean and P. Ashton (eds.), *Public History and Heritage Today: People and their Pasts*, Basingstoke: Palgrave Macmillan, 2012, 1–20, 11.
25 Minutes of the Australian War Memorial Committee 26 June 1018, Australian War Memorial, 170 1/1.
26 Director to curator in Sydney 23 October 1925, Australian War Memorial 315, 328 002 001 01.
27 Certificate A.P.04 B.E.F 17/1/1918 in Australian War Memorial 13 7026/2/31.
28 C. Coulthard-Clark, 'One came home,' *Wartime* 19, (2002): 37–39. During the 1920s and 30s Dorothy Brooke located many overworked former cavalry horses in Egypt and founded the Old War Horse Memorial Hospital in Cairo: see H. Kean, *Animal Rights: Social and Political Change in Britain since 1800*, London: Reaktion Books, 1998, 179.
29 H. Kendall (?) to HQ AIF, Australian Corps Memorandum, 28 February 1917, Australian War Memorial 13 7026/2/31.
30 Apparently the now elderly horse's condition and the cost of paying a taxidermist to mount the whole body led just to the head being mounted, at a cost of £75. (Minutes of Finance sub-committee of Australian War Museum, 12 September 1922, and 19 March 1923, Australian War Memorial 170 2/1.)
31 General correspondence file of Bean, Australian War Memorial 93 4/6/1. For a modern analysis of the role of objects in generating memory in museums see G. Kavanagh, *Dream Spaces: Memory and the Museum*, London: Bloomsbury, 2000.
32 By way of contrast see the letter of 1923 from Arthur Leetham, Royal United Service Institute, Whitehall to the director of the museum, regarding the war museum in Crystal Palace then in the process of moving: 'The British public have not taken to that museum at all. I think the real truth is that they want to forget about the war instead of being reminded of it. History only repeats itself. It was not until 50 years after the Napoleonic Wars that any interest was exhibited in such relics, and I am of the opinion that it will be another 50 years before this nation will really be interested in the museum of the great war'. See Australian War Memorial 93, 7/1/243.
33 The original, unveiled in 1936, was aimed at women with its focus on nursing rather than a combat soldier: see B. Scates, *A Place to Remember: A History of the Shrine of Remembrance*, Melbourne: Cambridge University Press, 2009, 158–159. The secretary-general of the Australian Red Cross, Philadelphia Robertson, wrote that 'A memory to Simpson, the donkey man ... will provide the human touch ... The patient donkey with the Red Cross brassard beneath his long ears, adds an inimitable touch to the whole picture. Children seeing the Shrine will be awed into reverence by its greatness. Simpson, with his donkey and its pathetic burden will appeal to the child's natural love of animals and sympathy with all suffering. To all of us, amid the stress and turmoil of everyday life, the memorial with its gentle story, should lead our thoughts into the quiet ways of compassion and kindness': Philadelphia Robertson to E. Preston Wells, 7 March 1935, Simpson Collection: *Argus*, 28 October 1933 as quoted in Scates, *A Place to Remember*, 159.
34 See, for instance, the recreation from trees at Lakes Entrance, Victoria.
35 P. Ashton and P. Hamilton, *History at the Crossroads: Australians and the Past*, Ultimo, New South Wales: Halstead Press, 2010, 49.
36 Peter Corlett, 'Simpson and his donkey: a proposal', November 1986, Commission File 89/1234 Australian War Memorial. See H. Kean, 'Animals and war memorials: different approaches to commemorating the human-animal relationship', in R. Hediger (ed.), *Animals and War: Studies of Europe and North America*, Boston MA: Brill, 2012, 237–260.
37 The 'A is for Animals travelling exhibition of 2009' and the accompanying catalogue of the Australian War Memorial analyses the way 'Animals have worked alongside

Australians in war for over one hundred years'. *A is for Animals. An A to Z of Animals in War*, Canberra: Australian War Memorial, 2009, 2.

38 See Kean, 'Animals and war memorials'.
39 Philadelphia Robertson to E. Preston Wells, 7 March 1935, Simpson Collection: *Argus*, 28 October 1933 as quoted in Scates, *A Place to Remember*, 159.
40 See P. Cochrane, *Simpson and the Donkey: The Making of a Legend*, Melbourne: Melbourne University Press, 1992.
41 *The Age*, 23 October 2005; 'Diggers push to honour Gallipoli horse Sandy in new suburb', *Sydney Herald* 24 April 2009, available at www.awm.gov.au/articles/encyclopedia/horses/sandy, last accessed 25 August 2017. Thanks to Rose Searby for drawing my attention to this.
42 K. Lahey, 'Old warhorse to leave his mark on new suburb', *The Age,* 7 May 2009, available at www.theage.com.au/national/old-warhorse-to-leave-his-mark-on-new-suburb-20090506-avcm.html, last accessed 25 August 2017.
43 See for example the popularity of stories by Henry Lawson and Banjo Patterson in which animals feature prominently. For a discussion of the iconic role of The Dog on the Tucker Box, a fictional dog featuring in many Australian pioneer myths, see Kean, 'Public history and two Australian dogs'. Also see in this volume Liv Emma Thorsen on Barry and his role in Swiss culture.
44 J. Bough, *Donkey*, London: Reaktion Books, 2011, 96–99.
45 R. Samuel (ed.), *History Workshop: A Collectanea 1967–1991*, Oxford: History Workshop, 1991, 11.
46 This had been a key radical cause highlighted, for example by John Hampden in the English Civil War with the epithet 'No taxation without representation' and was frequently appropriated for different causes including the campaign in Britain for women's suffrage in the early twentieth century. As most of the diggers were immigrants from the British Empire this political aim would have been well known amongst them.
47 Australian Government, 'Eureka Stockade': www.australia.gov.au/about-australia/australian-story/eureka-stockade, last accessed 25 March 2017.
48 Particularly useful are A. Beggs-Sunter, 'Contested memories of Eureka: museum interpretations of the Eureka Stockade', *Labour History* 85, (2003): 29–46; A. Beggs-Sunter, 'Eureka: gathering the "oppressed of all nations"', *Journal of Australian Colonial History* 10, 1 (2008): 15–34.
49 O.H.K. Spate, *Australia*, London: Ernest Benn, 1968, 44; see also the view of conservative historian H.G. Turner that this was 'our own little rebellion', H.G. Turner, *Our Own Little Rebellion: The Story of the Eureka Stockade*, Melbourne: Whitcomb and Tombs, 1913, as quoted in P.A. Pickering, 'Ripe for a republic': British radical responses to the Eureka Stockade', *Australian Historical Studies*, 34, 121 (2003): 69–90.
50 S. Macintyre, *A Concise History of Australia*, Cambridge: Cambridge University Press, 2016, 90.
51 Thus Jupp has characterised the background of Ballarat miners seeing them as one third English (although also noting Irish and Chinese backgrounds) stating that 'They brought with them radical and Chartist traditions which were to upset the oligarchic political system and establish one of the first democracies in the world based on manhood suffrage and the secret ballot', J. Jupp, *The English in Australia*, Cambridge: Cambridge University Press, 2004, 73. See also Pickering 'Ripe for a republic'.
52 C. Wright, '"New brooms they say sweep clean": women's political activism on the Ballarat Goldfields, 1854', *Australian Historical Studies* 39, 3 (2008): 305–321.
53 Carboni used the report of the political leader Peter Lalor, declaring that of the 22 dead, 10 were from the island of Ireland, 1 from England, 1 Scotland, 1 Prussia, 1 Wurtemberg, 2 Canada, and several unknown places. R. Carboni, *The Eureka Stockade*, Melbourne, 1855, 98–99. According to Pickering, citing the Victorian Royal Commission, some 50%

who had taken the oath under the flag of the Southern Cross to rebel were Irish. Pickering, 'Ripe for a republic,' 78.

54 Thus Wright, 'New brooms', 312, uses Carboni's account (p.44) to argue that, 'Some women wanted to be paid-up members of the Ballarat Reform League, a privilege that they were denied'.

55 As quoted in K. Prato, *The Pikeman's Dog: A Poem*, unnumbered page one Ballarat: self-published, n.d. (A local history of 1887 also mentions the dog: W.B. Withers, *History of Ballarat*, Ballarat: Niven and Co, 1887, 120, as quoted in P. Williams, *The True Story of the Pikeman's Dog*, Ballarat: Eureka Stockade Memorial Trust, 1999, 10.

56 See, for example, M.C. Nussbaum, *Upheavals of Thought*, Cambridge: Cambridge University Press, 2001, 90–92; W.M. Reddy, *The Navigation of Feeling: A Framework for the History of Emotions*, Cambridge: Cambridge University Press, 2001, xi.

57 I am not suggesting that historians should be 'detached' but rather that this is the default (and often unthought out) position of mainstream historians. By way of contrast public historians and heritage historians are more likely to look empathetically at emotional responses. See Kavanagh, *Dream Spaces* or the monumental work of Laurajane Smith on people's responses to museums, arguing that that visitors' engagement is not necessarily about learning as such but is an emotional experience: L. Smith, 'Emotion, affect and registers of engagement at heritage sites', unpublished paper, University College London, Archaeology Department public lecture, 21 May 2013.

58 Williams, *True Story*, 12.

59 Williams, *True Story*, 17.

60 For discussion of individual and transmitted stories see, for example, the work of A. Portelli, *The Death of Luigi Trastulli and Other Stories: Form and Meaning in Oral History*, New York: SUNY Press, 1991.

61 According to the sculptors of the memorial, Joan Walsh Smith and Charles Smith, 15 nationalities took part in the rebellion of 1854, available at http://monumentaustralia.org.au/themes/culture/animals/display/30234-the-pikeman%60s-dog 2010, last accessed 20 August 2017. Pickering, 'Ripe for a Republic,' by way of contrast, emphasises the 'Britishness' of the occasion.

62 Williams, *True Story*, 18.

63 http://monumentaustralia.org.au/themes/culture/animals/display/30234-the-pikeman%60s-dog, last accessed 29 September 2016.

64 Beggs-Sunter, 'Contested memories', 31.

65 At the time the state government was run by the Liberals. (In an Australian context this is the name of the mainstream right-wing party – equivalent to British Conservatives.) See Beggs-Sunter, 'Contested Memories', 34. However, the Eureka Stockade Memorial Trust numbered the distinguished historian Professor John Molony amongst its ranks. As an interview with him shows he acknowledges the presence of the dog in his forthright analysis of the Eureka Stockade. www.youtube.com/watch?v=LUGr8wDv_2c, last accessed 22 June 2016.

66 Williams, *True Story*, 19,

67 See H. Kean, 'The dog and cat massacre of September 1939 and the People's War', *European Review of History: Revue Européenne d'Histoire*, 22, 5 (2015): 741–756.

68 J. Urbanik and M. Morgan, 'A tale of tails: the place of dog parks in the urban imaginary', *Geoforum* 44, (2013): 292–302, 301.

69 J. Black, *Using History*, London: Hodder Arnold, 2005, 2.

70 See H. Kean, *The Great Cat and Dog Massacre*, Chicago IL: University of Chicago Press, 2018, for an attempt to challenge notions of the Second World War on the Home Front as a 'good war' through the inclusion of domestic animals within the narrative.

71 K. Gregory, 'Art and artifice: Peter Emmett's curatorial practice in the Hyde Park Barracks and Museum of Sydney', *Fabrications* 16, 1 (2006): 1–22, 5.
72 See, for example, D. Dean and R. Williams, 'Critical cloth: to be continued . . . ' and 'The time I'm taking: sewing Proust', in Kean and Martin (eds.), *Public History Reader*, 224–232.
73 As quoted in Gregory, 'Art and artifice', 6.
74 Display board entitled 'Layers', viewed by author at the Barracks, December 2014.
75 M.K. Stenglin, 'Space odyssey: towards a social semiotic model of three-dimensional space', *Visual Communication* 8, 1 (2009): 35–64.
76 Sadly this process of collection and accumulation is not even mentioned in P. Davies, 'Clothing and textiles at the Hyde Park Barracks Destitute Asylum, Sydney, Australia', *Post-Medieval Archaeology* 47, 1 (2013): 1–16.
77 Kean and Martin, *Public History Reader*, xiv–xvi.
78 Sadly the rats' case was removed a couple of years ago. They were left to die out and were not replaced. From conversations with staff in December 2014 it seems that the member of staff most fond of the animals had left and no one was keen to take over their role.
79 I have previously discussed the rats in my introduction to Kean and Martin, *The Public History Reader*.
80 See, for example, Z. Tortorici, 'Animal archive stories: species anxieties in the Mexican National Archives', in Nance (ed.), *Historical Animal*, 75–98.
81 Perhaps the key work on this theme is C. Duncan, *Civilizing Rituals: Inside Public Art Museums*, London: Routledge, 1995.
82 S. Hall, 'Whose heritage? Un-settling 'the heritage', re-imagining the post nation', in J. Littler and R. Naidoo (eds.), *The Politics of Heritage: The Legacies of Race,* Abingdon: Routledge, 2005, 23–35, 25.
83 www.naturkundemuseum-kassel.de/museum/sonderausstellung/ausstellungen/SexEvolution.php, last accessed 6 July 2016.
84 http://snaebjornsdottirwilson.com/, last accessed 25 August 2017.
85 D. Matless, 'Book review: *Nanoq: Flat Out and Bluesome: A Cultural Life of Polar Bears*, by Bryndís Snæbjörnsdóttir and Mark Wilson', *Cultural Geographies* 16, 4 (2009): 538–539.
86 G. Aloi, *Art and Animals*, London: I.B. Tauris, 2011, 39.
87 S. Baker, *Artist/ Animal*, Minneapolis MN: University of Minnesota Press, 2013, 217–9; G. Aloi, 'Deconstructing the animal in search of the real', *Anthrozoös* 25, S1 (2012): s73–s90, s74–s76; R. Hansen, 'Animal skins in contemporary art', *Journal of Visual Art Practice* 9, 1 (2010): 9–16.
88 Hansen, 'Animal skins in Contemporary Art', 14.
89 S.T. Asma, *Stuffed Animals and Pickled Heads*, Oxford: Oxford University Press, 2001, 3–46.
90 Aloi, 'Deconstructing the animal', s75.
91 Snaebjornsdottir/Wilson's ongoing interest in taxidermy is also reflected in the artists' film *Between you and me*. Here a seal is taxidermied over a three-hour period in which, they suggested, the seal became 'part of its own creation' and the creation of space to think through and this challenged the idea of the animal and the human 'with which we populate our intellect and our experience'. See Baker, *Artist /Animal*, 217.
92 G.N. Swinney, 'An afterword on afterlife', in S.J.M.M. Alberti (ed.), *The Afterlives of Animals*, Charlottesville VA: University of Virginia Press, 2011, 219–223, 222–223.
93 The possibility of animal biography was the focus of *Animal Biographies: Recovering Animal Selfhood through Interdisciplinary Narration?,* a conference organised by the Human–Animal Studies Centre at the University of Kassel in March 2016.

94 For a fuller account, see Kean, 'Challenges for historians', s66–s67. See also D. Pakeman, 'Fact and fiction: reinterpreting animals in a national museum', *Society and Animals* 21, 6 (2013): 591–593.
95 www.nma.gov.au/exhibitions/spirited, last accessed 10 September 2015.
96 www.museumofanimals.org/, last accessed 10 July 2016.
97 John Edmundson regularly posts extracts from collected archival material, particularly aimed at an activist readership who visit the vegan website Happy Cow: www.happycow.net/reviews/the-humanitarian-league-kowloon-39395, last accessed 10 July 2016.
98 www.happycow.net/blog/ernest-bell/.

Bibliography

Aloi, G. *Art and Animals*, London: I.B. Tauris, 2011.
Aloi, G. 'Deconstructing the animal in search of the real', *Anthrozoös* 25, S1 (2012): s73–s90.
Asma, S.T. *Stuffed Animals and Pickled Heads*, Oxford: Oxford University Press, 2001.
Ashton, P. 'Public history', in A. Clark and P. Ashton (eds.), *Australian History Now*, Sydney: New South Publishing, 2013, 167–180.
Ashton, P. and Hamilton, P. *History at the Crossroads: Australians and the Past*. Sydney: Halstead Press, 2010.
Baker, S. *Artist/ Animal*, Minneapolis MN: University of Minnesota Press, 2013.
Balcombe, J. 'Concluding remarks: from theory to action: an ethologist's perspective', in N. Taylor and T. Signal (eds.), *Theorizing Animals: Re-thinking Humanimal Relations*, Leiden: Brill, 2011, 281–289.
Beggs-Sunter, A. 'Contested memories of Eureka: museum interpretations of the Eureka Stockade', *Labour History* 85, (2003): 29–46.
Beggs-Sunter, A. 'Eureka: gathering "the Oppressed of All Nations"', *Journal of Australian Colonial History* 10, 1 (2008): 15–34.
Black, J. *Using History*, London: Hodder Arnold, 2005.
Bough, J. *Donkey*, London: Reaktion, 2011.
Carboni, R. *The Eureka Stockade*, Melbourne, 1885.
Casey, D. 'Culture wars: museums, politics and controversy', *New Museum Developments and the Culture Wars*, special issue of *Open Museum Journal* 6, (2003): 8–10.
Cauvin, T. 'Introduction', in T. Cauvin (ed.), *Public History: A Textbook of Practice*, Abingdon: Routledge, 2016, 1–25.
Cochrane, P. *Simpson and the Donkey: The Making of a Legend*, Melbourne: Melbourne University Press, 1992.
Coulthard-Clark, C. 'One came home,' *Wartime* 19, (2002): 37–39.
Davies, P. 'Clothing and textiles at the Hyde Park Barracks Destitute Asylum, Sydney, Australia', *Post-Medieval Archaeology* 47, 1 (2013): 1–16.
Dean, D. and Williams, R. 'Critical cloth: to be continued . . . ' and 'The time I'm taking: sewing Proust', in H. Kean and P. Martin, *Public History Reader*, Abingdon: Routledge, 2013, 224–232.
Donald, D. *Picturing Animals in Britain, 1750–1850*, New Haven CT: Yale University Press, 2007.
Duncan, C. *Civilizing Rituals: Inside Public Art Museums*, London: Routledge, 1995.
Franklin, A. *Animal Nation: The True Story of Animals and Australia*, Sydney: University of New South Wales Press, 2006.
Frisch, M. *A Shared Authority: Essays on the Craft and Meaning of Oral and Public History*, Buffalo NY: State University of New York Press, 1990.
Gregory, K. 'Art and artifice: Peter Emmett's curatorial practice at the Hyde Park Barracks and Museum of Sydney', *Fabrications* 16, 1 (2006): 1–22.

Grele, R.J. 'Clio on the road to Damascus: a national survey of history as activity and experience', *The Public Historian* 72, 1 (2000): 31–34.

Hall, S. 'Whose heritage? Un-settling 'the heritage', re-imagining the post nation', in J. Littler and R. Naidoo (eds.), *The Politics of Heritage: The Legacies of Race*, Abingdon: Routledge, 2005, 23–35.

Hansen, G. 'White hot history: the review of the National Museum of Australia', *Public History Review* 11, (2003): 39–50.

Hansen, R. 'Animal skins in contemporary art', *Journal of Visual Art Practice* 9, 1 (2010): 9–16.

Jordanova, L. *History in Practice*, London: Arnold Publishers, 2000.

Jupp, J. *The English in Australia*, Cambridge: Cambridge University Press, 2004.

Kavanagh, G. *Dream Spaces: Memory and the Museum*, London: Bloomsbury, 2000.

Kean, H. *Animal Rights: Social and Political Change in Britain since 1800*, London: Reaktion Books, 2000.

Kean, H. 'Public history and two Australian dogs: Islay and the dog on the tucker box', *ACH: The Journal of the History of Culture in Australia* 24–25, (2006): 135–162.

Kean, H. 'Balto, the Alaskan dog and his statue in New York's Central Park: animal representation and national heritage', *International Journal of Heritage Studies* 15, 5 (2009): 413–430.

Kean, H. 'Challenges for historians writing animal–human history: what is really enough?', *Anthrozoös* 25, S1 (2012): s57–s72.

Kean, H. 'Animals and war memorials: different approaches to commemorating the human-animal relationship', in R. Hediger (ed.), *Animals and War*, Boston MA: Brill, 2012, 237–260.

Kean, H. 'The dog and cat massacre of September 1939 and the People's War', *European Review of History: Revue Européenne d'Histoire* 22, 5 (2015): 741–756.

Kean, H. *The Great Cat and Dog Massacre*, Chicago IL: University of Chicago Press, 2018.

Kean, H. and Ashton, P. 'Introduction: people and their pasts and public history today', in H. Kean and P. Ashton (eds.), *Public History and Heritage Today: People and their Pasts*, Basingstoke: Palgrave Macmillan, 2012, 1–20.

Kean, H. and Martin, P. (eds.), *The Public History Reader*, Abingdon: Routledge, 2013.

Lemish, M. *War Dogs: Canines in Combat*, Washington DC: Brassey's, 1996.

Macintyre, S. *A Concise History of Australia*, fourth edition, Cambridge: Cambridge University Press, 2016.

Macintyre, S. and Clark, A. *The History Wars*, Melbourne: Melbourne University Press, 2003.

Matless, D. 'Book review: *Nanoq: Flat Out and Bluesome: A Cultural Life of Polar Bears*, by Bryndís Snæbjörnsdóttir and Mark Wilson', *Cultural Geographies* 16, 4 (2009): 538–539.

Nance, S. 'Introduction', in S. Nance (ed.), *The Historical Animal*, Syracuse NY: Syracuse University Press, 2015, 1–16.

Nussbaum, M.C. *Upheavals of Thought*, Cambridge: Cambridge University Press, 2001.

Pakeman, D. 'Fact and fiction: reinterpreting animals in a national museum', *Society and Animals* 21, 6 (2013): 591–593.

Pickering, P.A. '"Ripe for a republic": British radical responses to the eureka stockade', *Australian Historical Studies* 34, 121 (2003): 69–90.

Poliquin, R. *The Breathless Zoo: Taxidermy and the Cultures of Longing*, University Park PA: Pennsylvania University Press, 2012.

Portelli, A. *The Death of Luigi Trastulli and Other Stories: Form and Meaning in Oral History*, New York: SUNY Press, 1991.

Prato, K. *The Pikeman's Dog: A Poem*, Ballarat: self-published, n.d.

Pycior, H. 'The making of the "First Dog": President Warren G. Harding and Laddie Boy', *Society & Animals* 13, 2 (2005): 109–138.

Pycior, 'The public and private lives of "Private Dogs"', in D. Brantz (ed.), *Beastly Natures: Animals, Humans, and the Study of History*, Charlottesville VA: University of Virginia Press, 2010, 176–203.

Reddy, W.M. *The Navigation of Feeling: A Framework for the History of Emotions*, Cambridge: Cambridge University Press, 2001.

Samuel, R. (ed.), *History Workshop: A Collectanea 1967–1991*, Oxford: History Workshop, 1991.

Samuel, R. *Theatres of Memory: Past and Present in Contemporary Culture*, London: Verso, 1994.

Scates, B. *A Place to Remember: A History of the Shrine of Remembrance*, Cambridge: Cambridge University Press, 2009.

Searby, R. 'Red dog, horses and Bogong moths: the memorialisation of animals in Australia', *Public History Review* 15, (2008): 117–134.

Skabelund, A. *Empire of Dogs: Canines, Japan, and the Making of the Modern Imperial World*, New York: Cornell University Press, 2011.

Spate, O.H.K. *Australia*, London: Ernest Benn, 1968.

Stenglin, M.K. 'Space odyssey: towards a social semiotic model of three-dimensional space', *Visual Communication* 8, 1 (2009): 35–64.

Swinney, G.N. 'An afterword on afterlife', in S.J.M.M. Alberti, The *Afterlives of Animals*, Charlottesville VA: University of Virginia Press, 2011, 219–233.

Taylor, N. *Humans, Animals, and Society: An Introduction to HumanAnimal Studies*, Brooklyn NY: Lantern Books, 2013.

Tortorici, Z. 'Animal archive stories : species anxieties in the Mexican National Archives', in S. Nance (ed.), *The Historical Animal*, Syracuse NY: Syracuse University Press, 2015, 75–98.

Tosh, J. *Why History Matters*, Basingstoke: Palgrave Macmillan, 2008.

Turner, H.G. *Our Own Little Rebellion: The Story of the Eureka Stockade*, Melbourne: Whitcomb and Tombs, 1913.

Urbanik, J. and Morgan, M. 'A tale of tails: the place of dog parks in the urban imaginary', *Geoforum* 44, (2013): 292–302.

Wallace, M. *Mickey Mouse History and Other Essays on American Memory*, Philadelphia PA: Temple University Press, 1996.

Williams, P. *The True Story of the Pikeman's Dog: The Rebels' Dog with the Royal Award*, Ballarat: Eureka Stockade Memorial Trust, 1999.

Withers, W.B. *History of Ballarat*, Ballarat: Niven and Co, 1887.

Wright, C. '"New brooms they say sweep clean": women's political activism on the Ballarat Goldfields, 1854', *Australian Historical Studies* 39, 3 (2008): 305–321.

5

WILDLIFE CONSERVATION AS CULTURAL MEMORY

Jan-Erik Steinkrüger

At the beginning of her introductory book on geographies of human–animal relations, *Placing Animals*, Julie Urbanik writes:

> Animals surround me right now as I write these words. Inside are three cats; sculptures of elephants, cats, water buffalo, frogs, birds, and an octopus; photos of cheetahs, elephants, seals, giraffes, and all sorts of birds; and a painting of coyotes.[1]

As I write these lines I recall her words and in a similar way I am surrounded by my two cats, I can hear a dog barking on the street, and can see the zebra mask my wife and I brought back from our last vacation. This is, however, just one sense of the animals surrounding me, since these are only the ones physically in the here and now, forgetting all the past animals I carry with me. So I remember our first dog, who used to pick me up at school when I was six or seven. I also think of the time my budgie was eaten by the neighbour's cat, the feathers still hanging out of her mouth when I got home. I think of the bunny my wife had as a child, although I never met it. I am not only surrounded by animals here and now, but also in memories, my own as well as in those stories told to me.

Just like my personal memory, our cultural memory teems with animal life. Animals are used as symbols on statues, monuments and paintings, representing the qualities associated with an animal species, or continents, countries, and cities, or just depicting a once-loved animal companion next to its human counterpart. Some nonhuman animals are commemorated in their own right: individuals like Hamish McHamish – a ginger cat who lived nomadically in the Scottish town of St. Andrews, visiting the houses and businesses on South Street – or Greyfriars Bobby in Edinburgh, who is depicted in a statue and immortalised in children's books.[2] Other animals are commemorated as collectives, for their services to humans, such as animals in war or at work, such as pit ponies, and some as reminders of the extinction of species.[3] The Mass Extinction Monitoring Observatory (MEMO), for instance, located on the Isle of Portland on England's south coast, shows carvings of all the plants and animals that have become extinct in modern times, and is probably the largest and most expensive project of this kind today.[4] A memorial that combines all of these perspectives on animals, however, is the *Halfautomatische Troostmachine* ('semiautomatic comforting machine') built on the site of a former zoo bear pit in Maastricht. Planned in 1997 and realised in 2001 by the artist Michel Huisman, it features a bear statue on a bench outside the pit depicting Jo, the last bear who lived in the pit and was moved to Utrecht in 1993. In the former compound, which was part of a small zoo, extinct animals are depicted in the moat surrounding the figures of a woman and a dead giraffe. Thus the *Halfautomatische Troostmachine* simultaneously commemorates the individual bear Jo, the former zoo of Maastricht, the treatment of animals in zoos, and the extinction of animal species.

Hilda Kean has examined in detail the depiction and commemoration of animals as sculptures, in memorials and other forms of memory-work, though mostly in an urban context.[5] What interests me in this chapter, however, is the extent to which not only statues, monuments and other memorials but also wildlife conservation programmes might be considered a form of cultural memory. Looking at a broad range of wildlife projects from national parks to the reintroduction of animal species, the conservation of animals shows an obvious similarity to archives in the attempt to preserve an inheritance for later generations. Besides these clear parallels between natural and cultural heritage, a commitment which is explicitly demonstrated in UNESCO's 1972 *Convention concerning the Protection of the World Cultural and Natural Heritage*, I would like to instance the many entanglements of wildlife conservation in forms of cultural memory.[6] Animals are involved not only in archives of genetic information, but also narratives of humans and human–animal relations. Before looking into the relevant historiography, and toponymy, landscapes, and the role of the animal as a mediator of cultural memory, I will briefly introduce the work of Jan and Aleida Assmann, who despite having never written on animals, have nevertheless introduced a broad conception of cultural memory that is fundamental to the following argument.

Cultural memory

It is due to the works of Jan and Aleida Assmann that research on memorialisation and commemoration has gained the importance and analytical depth it possesses in recent German cultural and historical studies.[7] Drawing on the sociologist Maurice Halbwachs' concept of 'collective memory' and the historian Aby Warburg's concept of 'social memory' (and thus arguing for the importance of collectives, in contrast to an individual's mental capacity), Assmann and Assmann coined the term 'cultural memory'.[8] 'Cultural memory' for them is also a reply or an alternative to Pierre Nora's famous *lieux de mémoire*, whose overemphasis on the role of national commemoration betrays the lack of a deeper theorisation of memory.[9] In their contribution, Assmann and Assmann distinguish three levels of memory associated with different times, identities, and forms of memory. Firstly, there is the level of *individual memory* as 'a matter of our neuro-mental system'.[10] It is one's own inner capacity to remember and, as Jan Assmann writes, the only form of memory recognised under the term until the 1920s. So my personal memories of my childhood dog would count as such, though I mostly remember the stories my mother and sister told of him, which could thus be considered *communicative memory*, the second of the Assmanns' levels. This equates to Halbwachs' 'collective memory': here, memory is not merely an individual mental capacity but bound up with communication and socialisation – as my childhood stories suggest. It is what, dialectically, makes a social group as well as being necessarily made by a social group. Jan and Aleida Assmann particularly associate this process with the timespan of oral history, communicated in an intergenerational dialogue.[11] But Halbwachs differentiated his idea of 'collective memory' from traditions, which Jan and Aleida Assmann posit as a separate form of collective memory, placing *cultural memory* as a third, cultural or fully 'social' level. It is Warburg's concept of social memory that they credit for first identifying and interpreting the kind of cultural objectifications taking place at this level, as symbolic carriers of memory *through* multiple generations.[12] So whereas individual memory is embodied and collective or communicative memory is bound up with everyday interaction and communication, social or cultural memory tends to become disembodied and institutionalised:

> It is exteriorized, objectified, and stored away in symbolic forms that, unlike the sounds of words or the sight of gestures, are stable and situation-transcendent: they may be transferred from one situation to another and transmitted from one generation to another.[13]

There are several aspects of this argument worthy of elaboration. Firstly, Assmann and Assmann's concept of cultural memory is underpinned by a semiotic understanding of culture, in which social groups constantly refer to and define themselves through a shared set of codes materialised in texts, monuments, pictures or even landscapes. Cultural memory, therefore, 'exists in the forms of narratives, songs, dances, rituals, masks, and symbols; specialists such as narrators, bards, mask-carvers, and others are organized in guilds and have to undergo long periods of initiation, instruction, and examination'.[14] Aleida Assmann also goes on to emphasise the inability to remember everything: 'When thinking about memory, we must start with forgetting. [. . .] In order to remember some things, other things must be forgotten. Our memory is highly selective. Memory capacity is limited by neural and cultural constraints such as focus and bias'.[15] Like other scholars on social memory, she considers forgetting as normal and remembering as the exception. Just as an individual who may remember certain events, places, and so on, but cannot remember all the other events and places in his or her past, cultural memory runs through a selection process of what to remember and what to forget. Thirdly, Aleida Assmann usefully distinguishes between passive and active forms of remembering and forgetting. Whereas passive forgetting is a non-intentional act of falling out of sight by loss or misplacement, active forgetting is the intentional act of trashing and destroying:

> Acts of forgetting are a necessary and constructive part of internal social transformations; they are, however, violently destructive when directed at an alien culture or a persecuted minority. Censorship has been a forceful if not always successful instrument for destroying material and mental cultural products.[16]

In a similar vein the border between passive and active memory is the distinction of passive storage of the past as potential cultural memory – which she calls *archive* – and the active usage of the past as cultural memory – which she calls *canon*:

> The institutions of active memory preserve the *past as present* while the institutions of passive memory preserve the *past as past*. The tension between the pastness of the past and its presence is an important key to understanding the dynamics of cultural memory. These two modes of cultural memory may be illustrated by different rooms of the museum. The museum presents its prestigious objects to the viewers in representative shows which are arranged to catch attention and make a lasting impression. The same museum also houses storerooms stuffed with other paintings and objects in peripheral spaces such as cellars or attics which are not publicly presented.[17]

In summary, cultural memory for Jan and Aleida Assmann plays an important role in the working of the signifying system of a society or culture. In its different forms it produces and reaffirms the collective identity of a group by giving it its (official) history. Cultural memory, however, is a necessarily selective process of active and passive forgetting and remembering, which raises the question which past is actively remembered and which actively or passively forgotten and why. Although Assmann and Assmann mostly focus on human history these questions also apply to a more than human history. From the perspective of an animal–human historian we can, for instance, ask which animals – either collectively or individually – are actively remembered, and which are, actively or passively, forgotten.

Historiographies and historical narratives of wildlife conservation

In Jan and Aleida Assmann's understanding of cultural memory the line between history and memory ultimately dissolves: historiography as an active act of doing history and transferring the past into the present in a selective process serves as a key form of cultural memory. As Jan Assmann emphasises, however, not all history is memory, but only history in relation to the question of identity:

> Memory is [historical] knowledge with an identity-index, it is knowledge about oneself, that is, one's own diachronic identity, be it as an individual or as a member of a family, a generation, a community, a nation, or a cultural and religious tradition.[18]

History evolves to memory when it serves as the history of someone and becomes part of an identity discourse as in discourses of national identity: 'Nation-states produce narrative versions of their past which are taught, embraced, and referred to as their collective autobiography. National history is taught via history textbooks, which have been appropriately termed "weapons of mass instruction"'.[19] The official version of history is not only written and taught, but alternative versions of the past become overwritten and ignored.

Even wildlife protection may become part of a national narrative, as Julie M. Weiskopf shows with the example of postcolonial, national discourse in Tanzania during the 1960s. As a newly founded state with about 120 ethnic groups, the socialist government of Tanzania and its educational institutions focused on creating a unified national identity after colonialism and searched for embodiments of it by taking cultural components from across the country and making them properly 'Tanzanian'. As in other nation-building processes, officials identified regional customs such as dances to form a canon of Tanzanian traditions. In Tanzanian national discourse wildlife was appropriated in a similar manner. It was framed as a national heritage by taking 'a region-specific resource and reimagin[ing] it as the collective and shared property of every member of the nation'.[20] To do this the Swahili word *urithi*, which means 'heritage' as well as 'inheritance' was employed, referring to Tanzanian's wild animals. The protection of wild animals was made a legacy and an obligation from precolonial times: 'National *urithi* endowed Tanzanians with ties that reached across generations, as the country's current wildlife was the legacy of previous generations' good management. [. . .] Wildlife as national *urithi* thus gave the present generation shared ancestors'.[21] The protection of wildlife involved not only the natural but also the national, cultural heritage of Tanzania. It was not an end in itself, but was also a national duty. The narrative of wildlife protection as part of Tanzanian national identity not only reaffirmed the national identity, however, but legitimised Tanzania's efforts in wildlife conservation in its national parks and game reserves.

As the example of Tanzania shows, wildlife conservation may be entangled into the historiographies of nations, as part of their identity discourse. Wildlife conservation, however, is not only part of (other) histories, but has histories of its own. The conservation of wildlife, therefore, may not only be part of a national cultural memory, but the historiographies of wildlife conservation themselves can be considered a form of identity discourse. Almost all conservation projects from national parks to species reintroduction programmes present their history in brochures and on their webpages; many of them being written not by academic historians, but by those working in the field. For Lawrence Rakestraw, this is often in the projects' self-interest: 'Professional conservationists are historically minded, since resource management combines the past, present, and future in its planning and administration'.[22] To successfully manage even the most modest conservation project, one has to know the impact of previous events to plan for the future. The publication of the history, though, serves another purpose: conservation projects 'try to justify their own actions or those of their agencies'.[23] The intention of telling history is either to confirm the success of conservation or to underline the necessity for further support and continued funding. To do so, conservation is either placed in the narrative of successful, ongoing protection efforts, or, alternatively, it is set in contrast to a previous status.

The emphasis of tradition is what Jörn Rüsen considers a *traditional type* of historical narrative and historical consciousness:

> When historical consciousness furnishes us with traditions, it reminds us of origins and the repetition of obligations [. . .]. Traditional orientations present the temporal whole, which makes the past significant and relevant to present

actuality and its future extension as a continuity of obligatory cultural life patterns over time.[24]

Such is the case in the above example of Tanzania, where today's wildlife protection is narrated as an ancestry obligation from precolonial times. The second line of argument of demarcation is what Rüsen calls a *genetic narrative*. In these narratives it

> is change itself that gives history its meaning. […] The future surpasses, indeed "outbids", the past in its claims on the present – a present conceptualized as an intersection, an intensely temporalized mode, a dynamic transition. This is the quintessential form of a kind of modern historical thought shaped by the category of progress […].[25]

The most radical form of these traditional narratives of wildlife conservation is the myth of a premodern or precolonial time of a natural state in which human and nonhuman animals coexisted peacefully. Such a narrative is used in the example cited above of Tanzanian national discourse, when referring to a precolonial tradition and obligation of wildlife protection. The naïve hypothesis behind this depiction is that indigenous societies per se have or at least had a higher degree of ecological sustainability. This assumption, however, is questionable, as it is founded on idealised and romanticised ideas of indigenous societies, abstracting from their histories and inner differences.[26] For Catherine Nash the deconstruction of such simplified, traditional narratives is one of the central tasks for (critical) environmental histories:

> Environmental history can offer a powerful critique of modern capitalism and colonialism but also challenge the romanticisation of pre-modernity and pre-colonial societies and so counter the primitivising claims of some environmental philosophies. Like the postcolonial project of criticising the material and cultural oppression of colonialism without positing a model of a true and static pre-colonial culture that can be recovered, environmental history can critique modern environmental damage while challenging the notion of a pristine nature in harmony with pre-modern native people.[27]

In this myth of pristine harmony, nature and culture before the advent of modernity and colonialism are considered static and effectively timeless. In this traditional narrative of conservation there is thus no (noteworthy) ecological or environmental or indeed animal–human history before the era of modernity, and nothing therefore to commemorate. Nature and with it animals and their relation to humans become ahistorical.

Whereas traditional historical narratives underestimate or deny change – or argue for a return to a previous state – *genetic* historical narratives of conservation overestimate change by mistakenly equating it with progress. The teleological orientation here is evident. Today's efforts on behalf of wildlife protection and conservation, in such genetic narratives, are often seen as important milestones and precursors for positive future developments. Such is the case for example in Robert Brown's *Conservation Timeline*, which summarises the 'milestones' of conservation since the 1990s:

> Throughout the 1990s to the present, conservationists and national leaders worldwide have become increasingly aware of the mounting threats to wildlife and habitats, including human population growth, resource extraction, habitat fragmentation, climate change, and loss of biodiversity. Efforts to address these threats and live sustainably will continue for decades to come.[28]

Besides the teleological, thoroughly modernist undertone in the line of argument in Brown's and similar historiographies of wildlife conservation the emphasis on societies' attitudes and awareness towards the environment is striking. For Jeanne Kay both are basic and recurrent themes in conservation historiography, based on the assumption that attitude and awareness determine the use of and ultimate impact upon those environments. For her, this widespread assumption runs counter to empirical evidence and is simply based on wishful thinking: 'Scholars who are concerned conservationists may dislike the idea that the best one can hope for by way of sound planetary management is that it will follow resource deterioration, and even then, some cultures will fatalistically adjust to deteriorated resources'.[29]

As shown with Rüsen's differentiation of traditional and genetic historical narratives, historiographies of wildlife conservation typically use the past either as a positive role model or as a preliminary stage for today's and future conservation efforts to legitimise wildlife conservation. Both examples of historiographies described – Tanzanian national discourse on the one hand, and Brown's milestones on the other – mirror the presence in historical periods, especially in the colonial era, in which wildlife population declined due to overuse and mismanagement. It is only in the contrast to these negative historical predecessors – or a problematic interim period in Tanzanian national discourse – that the necessity of conservation becomes tangible. Only the positive and negative historical narratives together form an argument for conservation and build a canon of cultural memory of wildlife conservation. With the example of national parks in mind, Justin Reich shows, though, that it is sometimes rather the absence than the presence of the past that is associated with nature and wildlife conservation: '[T]he historiography of the national parks, while focusing on how parks *preserve* landscapes, continues to underemphasise how these places *create* new landscapes'.[30] The role humans played in the creation of 'wildlife' is neglected and with it the animal–human history becomes a non-history of a pristine nature.

Naming places of wildlife conservation

Historical narratives of places are often reflected in their toponomies. As Whelan argues, the names of places 'act as a spatialization of memory and power, making tangible specific narratives of nationhood and reducing otherwise fluid histories into sanitized, concretized myths that anchor the projection of national identity onto physical territory'.[31] Toponymy, the study of place names, has increasingly brought attention to the politics of place-naming practice in the last decades building on concepts from postcolonial and gender studies.[32] In focus are the 'nationalisation' of street names by erasing colonial street names, for example in Singapore, or the renaming of streets from East Berlin's communist past after the German reunion during the 1990s.[33] Whereas street names and even stadium names have been in focus, the names of animal conservation areas, and the usage of animal names has scarcely been noticed. Just like other place names, however, the names of national parks, nature reserves, and wildlife sanctuaries enact and evidence power relations.

Looking at the toponymy of wildlife conservation areas, many are named after their founders, sponsors, former landowners or chief of states. Such is the case for Kruger National Park, named after Paul Kruger (1825–1904), the president of the Transvaal Republic from 1883 to 1900, who proclaimed parts of today's national park a government wildlife park in 1898. Jane Carruthers has shown that despite the official narrative of Kruger as a nature enthusiast, he not only lagged behind public opinion on wildlife conservation, but had to be forced into the establishment of the refuge. In her interpretation, this was part of an Afrikaner Nationalist political strategy for an increase in international acceptance of the apartheid regime to name the park after Kruger and make him the key actor in its founding history.[34] As shown by this example such toponyms not only commemorate certain individuals, but often reflect and reaffirm the power relations within colonial regimes or of a politically and financially dominant reigning class; in the case of Kruger National Park both at once.

From a postcolonial perspective even more interesting are conservation sites named after ethnic groups that formerly owned or occupied the territory before it was proclaimed a nature conservation area. In these cases, it is important to note by and after whom and in whose language a park was named, since often different ethnic groups might have been traversing the same territory beforehand and ethnical borders might have blurred between them. By highlighting one indigenous group, the presence of others is overwritten and neglected; crossings and overlaps between groups become ignored or sanitised. A most peculiar case is that of Yosemite National Park. The name was given to Yosemite Valley by L.H. Bunnell of the Mariposa Battalion in 1851 in honour of the tribes they were about to drive from the valley. 'Yohhe'meti', however, was not an autonym by a group themselves, but a xenonym for a multi-tribal group of renegades given to them by surrounding Mewok tribes and translating to 'those who kill' or 'grizzly bears', '[f]erocious translations for a tribe that most ethnographers describe as essentially peaceful – but a tribe that would, when confronted, fiercely defend its homeland' as Tracy Salcedo-Chourré writes.[35] By using xenonyms instead of autonyms it is not so much the indigenous group itself, but its perception by others which is remembered, again defined by the perpetrator not the perpetrated; it is the subaltern spoken of, not spoken with.

The naming of wildlife preservation areas just like other places becomes a theatre for the negotiation of difference and power relations. They commemorate the ruling and forget those expropriated, expelled or even killed in the process. Nonhuman animals, however, are scarcely mentioned in the names of these areas. Their histories have so far been also neglected, their pasts have been written out of such naming, a counter discourse still pending.

Conservation landscapes as cultural memory

Besides names of landscapes, the image of landscapes and the landscape itself serve as signifiers in a cultural system, as Denis Cosgrove and James S. Duncan have argued in several of their works.[36] Duncan writes for instance that 'The landscape [. . .] is one of the central elements in a cultural system, for as an ordered assemblage of objects, a text, it acts as a signifying system through which a social system is communicated, reproduced, experienced, and explored'.[37] Consequently, landscapes may also be anchors for memory.[38] As many studies have shown, our individual memory works spatially rather than temporally: 'We remember events and people by locating them in particular places, landscapes, and organizations of space rather than by reference to time or date'.[39] Similarly our cultural memory remembers spatially: the pictures of certain landscapes become inscribed into our cultural heritage. Especially our perception of nature is still formed by romanticism's ideas of the ideal natural landscape without humans (and thus without history). These also influence how we perceive and therefore realise nature conservation sites.

A prime example for the conjunctions of landscape and cultural memory in nature conservation is Serengeti National Park, which has been a UNESCO natural world heritage site since 1981. Roderick P. Neumann sees the establishment of Serengeti National Park as 'a process of nature production rather than nature preservation'.[40] To fulfil a European idea of African nature, the area which was to become Serengeti National Park had to be cleansed of the people who lived there and effectively sanitised; in sum, 'the idea of nature as a pristine, empty African wilderness was largely mythical and could only become a reality by relocating thousands of Africans whose agency had in fact shaped the landscape for millenia'.[41] It was not only the people, however, but also their history and their relationship to nonhuman animals which had to be neglected.

The myth of the Serengeti as untouched nature dates back to its first descriptions by Oscar Baumann (1864–1899), an Austrian traveller and one of the first Europeans to set foot in the region, in the 1870s. In it he describes the landscape as vast wilderness, 'unaware that the orchard-like appearance of the open savanna was a remnant of [. . .] traditional burns of the grasslands'.[42] In contrast to his description and common belief even today the open savanna was never just a natural landscape, but a cultural landscape, 'no less a product of human agency than the Rhine Valley, the Bavarian Alps, or any other iconic region revered by German hikers and mountaineers'.[43] Ikoma, Ikizu and Nata, who had occupied the Western Serengeti's short-grass savanna for centuries until drought and disease as well as Maasai raids and Western colonisers had driven them off the land in the second half of the nineteenth century, attracted wildlife and controlled tsetse and ticks with these fires and shaped the landscape: 'This human ecology had linked hunter-gatherers, pastoralists, farmers and wildlife for millennia even though Europeans deemed it to be inefficient and wasteful. Indeed, humans and animals had coevolved on the Serengeti plains'.[44]

As Neumann highlights, early preservation ideas also subsumed the people as part of the primeval nature:

> Within an evolutionary view of culture (then widely accepted among educated Europeans) hunters and gatherers and pastoralists were considered to

be living more off the fruits of Nature than their own labour. People of these cultures, therefore, would not necessarily disrupt the landscape aesthetic.[45]

Ironically it was the evidence of their influence on the landscape, which led to their movement.

One of the most influential for the popularisation of the image of the Serengeti was Bernhard Grzimek (1909–1987), zoo director of the Frankfurt Zoo and most famous in Germany for his television programme *Ein Platz für Tiere* (*A Place for Animals*) which aired from 1956 to 1987. With his television shows and documentaries, Grzimek 'probably raised more money for conservation, educated more people about nature, and twisted more arms of more African bureaucrats than any man in history'.[46] It was his Academy Award winning documentary *Serengeti darf nicht sterben* (*Serengeti shall not die*) in 1959, which drew international attention to the Serengeti National Park. From 1957 to 1959 Grzimek and his son, Michael Grzimek (1934–1959), launched a series of surveys on animal migration patterns in the Serengeti National Park after the British colonial government had decided on a reduction of the park's size to make space for a permanent homeland for Maasai herders. The surveys resulted in a demarcation based on Grzimek's results.

> This process was documented in their book and Oscar-winning documentary film [...] which remained unfinished when Michael Grzimek died in a small plane crash in early January 1959, a tragedy that helped to draw even greater European sympathy for the animal protection cause.[47]

Serengeti Shall Not Die became one of the first documentary movies on the Serengeti and also one of the first movies explicitly promoting wildlife conservation. It set the tone for a whole genre:

> The narrative suggests that animals can be saved only by establishing parks, aided by the efforts of people like Grzimek, who perform difficult and selfless acts in harnessing science and technology for the task. [...] The image of the Serengeti landscape (and any African park) in these films is entirely wild and natural, without history or social context. They describe a landscape broken into ecological zones – plains, water holes, and hills – but devoid of names or information that would differentiate one place from another either in time or space. [...] These potently symbolic images of the Serengeti as one of the "last nooks of paradise", a wild Africa, existing in its pristine state since the dawn of time, proved influential in creating the global perception of the Serengeti landscape.[48]

In contrast to this globally influential narrative of an environment without history and without people, stand the collective memory of Ikoma, Nata, Ikizu, Ishenyi, and Ngoreme, who used to live in parts of today's park and still live at its western border. During her field work with a group of Ikoma, Shetler notes:

> In contrast to Grzimek's images, the elders see a differentiated social landscape that also includes wildlife. [...] Standing on the higher places, they looked

across the landscape and named the areas settled by different clans, often associated with hills. They uncovered the remains of rock walls that were once fortresses to protect the people from Maasai raids in the late nineteenth century.[49]

Humans in Grzimek's narrative of the Serengeti are only shown either as hunter-gatherer people endangered and part of the pristine nature like the animals or as outside threats to the animal population 'reinforcing the belief that African peoples had no place in a landscape designated by God to protect the animals'.[50] Cultural heritage is mentioned scarcely at all in his movies, barely noting German colonial history in the region and entirely lacking reference to its black African history.[51] Thomas Lekan concludes:

> Grzimek sought to break with colonialist exoticism and racism in his depictions of the African wilderness. However, his tendency to privilege the eternal cycles of 'nature' over the vagaries of human history reinscribed rather than confronted Germany's troublesome environmental legacy in East Africa, and this in turn aided the expulsion of the Maasai and others from the Serengeti and exacerbated the asymmetries of power and wealth created by the tourist economy in the region.[52]

In Grzimek's wildlife documentaries, as in many afterwards, temporality is reduced mostly to the annual cycle of the seasons and the never-ending cycle of death and renewal eliding 'the vagaries of linear, human time, particularly the colonialist violence and postwar struggles that had shaped this region before the Grzimeks' arrival'.[53] The Serengeti shown in Grzimek's movies has never become the way it is, but always was this way, in an Africa without history. It is a pristine nature, in which neither indigenous humans nor nonhuman animals had history before colonialism.

Grzimek, and the many wildlife documentaries following his example, shaped the common belief that 'what ought to be seen in Africa were animals, not people' and that this animal wildlife is timeless and ahistorical, only bound to the circle of life and the change of seasons.[54] During the 1960s *Serengeti Shall Not Die* not only led to an increase in safari tourism especially in Tanzania and the Ngorongoro region, but also in a renaissance of zoological gardens across Europe and the founding of so-called 'safari parks' – zoo-like enterprises, in which the visitors travel through the compounds with their own car.[55] His image of the Serengeti has become part of a shared cultural memory of the Serengeti – or even of African savannas in general – paradoxically by concealing the precolonial and colonial histories of it. At the same time, however, Bernhard Grzimek and the movie *Serengeti Shall Not Die* have become part of cultural memory themselves: both are inscribed into the history of German wildlife conservation sometimes considered an important pioneer for the German green movement:

> West Germans who grew up between the 1950s and 1980s remember Grzimek fondly as the avuncular 'animal whisperer' whose extemporaneous, professorial style and passion for animal protection helped to transform

many straight-laced boys and girls of the Adenauer era into the firebrand ecological activists of the Brandt years.[56]

At the same time the documentary and its director are inscribed into the Serengeti National Park itself as one can read on the park's official webpage:

> Dr. Grzimek had more effect on wildlife conservation in Africa, and especially in Tanzania and the Serengeti, than any other individual. Today his legacy races across those endless plains and roars at the African moon. Everyone who stands in awe at the unfolding spectacle of the Serengeti owes a debt of gratitude for the life and work of Bernhard Grzimek.[57]

Animals as cultural memory

As the example of Serengeti National Park shows, not only the historiographies and names of conservation projects, but even the landscape of a conservational area, its image and lastly our (tourist) gaze at it can be considered a form of cultural memory.[58] In this last section, however, I will argue that even the animal itself has cultural memory inscribed into it. Not only the *Convention concerning the Protection of the World Cultural and Natural Heritage* already mentioned at the beginning of the chapter, but also the shared terminology of conservation and preservation, handle wildlife as if they were archive records or museum exhibits, either presented as part of an exhibition or stored in an archive – as 'genetic heritage', say – for later generations to rediscover.[59] The animal individuals presented to the audience in a national park or other wildlife conservation project – whether they are exhibited on a guided tour, presented in brochures, or on webpages – are, just like zoo animals, supposed to *stand for* their animal species in its entirety. As Stephen H. Spotte has argued for zoos, however, the relation between an animal individual as a signifier for a species and the species as a whole is questionable.[60] At the same time the animal individual not only represents its species, but the success in the species' conservation and the people involved in it.

Such is the case in the reintroduction of the Przewalski's horse. For zoologists, it is considered a prime example of a rescue which would not have been possible without the existence of zoological gardens.[61] Brent Huffman writes: '[S]everal ungulates owe their continued existence to captive breeding, including the Przewalski's horses [. . .]. These species were once extinct in the wild, but zoos have preserved them all and reintroduced them to their native ranges'.[62] Today the Przewalski's horse (*equus ferus przewalskii* Poliakov, also *equus ferus hagenbecki* Matschie) is considered to be the only extant wild horse.[63] Its specific importance for biologists lies in the species' ancestry to the domestic horse as Klaus-Dieter Budras *et al.* emphasise: 'It can be regarded as a representative of a group of related species, which were once widely distributed over Europe and Asia and from which the domestic horse derived'.[64] Przewalski's horses, whether held in zoological gardens, in semi-reserves or reserves, are therefore not only considered representatives of their own species, but of wild horses in general. As a 'pre-domestic' horse they additionally become 'a window into a lost past' or even 'pristine nature' before domestication. Przewalski's horses are therefore not only a genetic storehouse, but as a 'living fossil' represent an evolutionary heritage and at the same time a memory of the act of domestication. Paradoxically, this 'wild' ancestor of the domestic horse only survived through captive breeding and in part through crossbreeding with domestic horses. In an aporia, Przewalski's horses are thus ancestor and descendant, wild and domestic, past and future.

There had been no sightings of the Przewalski's horse outside of human custody since the late 1960s, so that it became categorised as 'extinct in the wild' by the IUCN.[65] With the founding of a semi-reserve in the Netherlands, reintroductory efforts began in the 1980s leading to the first releases into the wild in Hustain Nuruu Park in Mongolia during the early 1990s. Today the status of the Przewalski's horses is changed to 'endangered'. The lineage of all of the Przewalski's horses living today (around 2,000) can be traced back to thirteen individual animals. All of these animals 'responsible' for the species' survival were held in zoological gardens:

> Of the 53 animals recorded in the studbook as having been brought into zoological collections in the west, only 12 contribute any genes to the current living population. Of these, 11 were brought into captivity in 1899–1902 and the last of them died in 1939. The one wild horse that has been bred into the population since then is the mare 231 Orlitza III, captured as a foal in 1947. A thirteenth founder is stallion 56 Halle I, born in 1906 in Halle (Germany) to a wild caught stallion and a domestic Mongolian mare, which was one of the foster mothers used to nurse the Przewalski's foals during their journey to European collectors.[66]

The commemoration of these thirteen 'forefathers' also commemorates the role zoological gardens played in the reintroduction. The success of the Przewalski's horse breeding programme becomes a key argument in the legitimisation of zoological gardens' role as a 'Noah's Ark' in 'undoing the past for a better future'.[67] As Cornelius Holtorf argues, though, the role of zoological gardens is rather ambivalent:

> Zoos today are proud to make a contribution (however small) to the conservation of endangered species or species already extinct in the wild. This concerns the continuity of gene pools that have emerged over long evolutionary periods of time but, in the end, have not survived in the wild, often because of human intervention. The course of history is reversed, as it were, by reintroduction of species into their habitats where they had become extinct [...]. A second chance is not given to animal individuals but to the species and, thus, to evolution as a whole.[68]

Not only is the individual Przewalski's horse held in a zoo reintroduced into the wild, but it is supposed to represent the species as well as its reintroduction as well as the role the zoos played in it. Lastly it also represents the humans involved in the process. At the turn of the twentieth century, the animal trader and later zoo founder Carl Hagenbeck (1844–1913) was the chief importer for Mongolian wild horses.[69] Most of the Przewalski's horses caught in the wild and brought to European and American collectors and zoos were traded by him; many dying during the transport.[70]

The eleven Przewalski's horses, however, who were the basis of the breeding programme, also stem from Hagenbeck. For this 'contribution' to the conservation the *Verband der Zoologischen Gärten e.V.*, the German union of zoological gardens, write on their webpage on Przewalski's horses: 'Dem Przewalskipferd wäre es nicht anders ergangen, hätten sich nicht Baron Falz-Fein und Carl Hagenbeck darum bemüht, Wildpferde aus der Mongolei zu erhalten' (The Przewalski's horse would not have been any better off, if Baron Falz-Fein and Carl Hagenbeck had not strived to get wild horses from Mongolia).[71] The history in this and similar descriptions of Hagenbeck's influence on Przewalski's horse population justifies the hunt, trade and collection retrospectively: 'Though today we disapprove of these practices, they were after all for the better good'.

Conclusion

The *Halfautomatische Troostmachine*, discussed at the start of this chapter, commemorates the individual bear Jo and the appalling conditions in which he lived, the equally terrible treatment of animals in zoos (especially at the beginning of the twentieth century), and the extinction of animal species through humans. The individual Przewalski's horse, on the other hand, is used as a representation of the achievements in the conservation of an extinct animal species which is supposedly only possible through zoological gardens and their acquisitions at the beginning of the twentieth century. Whereas the first narrative critically unfolds a past, which would be otherwise forgotten, the second narrative has to conceal the role humanity played in the Przewalski's horse's extinction in the first place to highlight the human achievement. The role of the nonhuman animal in this history is reduced to the genealogical tree of the Przewalski's horses' breeding book.

With this chapter I aimed to present an overview of the many entanglements of wildlife conservation and cultural memory. As the examples of Kruger, Grzimek and Hagenbeck show, human individuals and their biographies are inscribed into conservation projects, in the projects' names, into our understanding of a 'wild' landscape, or even into the animal itself. At the same time, we can differentiate between a memory of conservation and a memory through conservation. The narrative of a tradition as well as the narrative of change in wildlife conservation used or abused history to justify conservation efforts. Indifference to this conservation was also used as part of a search for an identity in Tanzania or to give purpose to zoological gardens. Wildlife conservation, however, is not only bound to memory, but to forgetting too. To become a wildlife conservation area, the human imprint typically becomes neglected or alternatively sanitised following the seductive but erroneous notion that 'wilderness has no history'.

The aim of future research in animal–human histories could be to emphasise the role individual animals held in wildlife conservation projects and to show the shared histories of humans and nonhuman animals before and during wildlife protection. A future emancipatory political project would be to not only make accessible indigenous human histories but also nonhuman animal histories, by naming projects after individual animals and rejecting the representation of 'natural' landscapes. After all wilderness has histories, nonhuman as well an animal–human histories.

Notes

1 J. Urbanik, *Placing Animals: An Introduction to the Geography of Human–Animal Relations*, Lanham MD: Rowman & Littlefield, 2012, xi.
2 H. Kean, 'The moment of Greyfriars Bobby: the changing cultural position of animals, 1800–1920', in K. Kete (ed.), *A Cultural History of Animals in the Age of Empire*, Oxford: Bloomsbury, 2007, 31–33. H. Kean, 'An exploration of the sculptures of Greyfriars Bobby, Edinburgh, Scotland, and the Brown Dog, Battersea, South London, England', *Society & Animals* 11, 4 (2002): 353–373.
3 For the 'Animals in War' memorial in London see: H. Kean, 'Traces and representations: animal pasts in London's present', *London Journal* 36, 1 (2001): 65–68. A rather new example of a memorial for pit ponies is the *The Pit Pony Experience* unveiled in November 2015 in Collinsville, Australia. It commemorates the last working pit ponies in Australia, Wharrier and Mr. Ed, who retired in 1990: see http://pitponyexperience.com.au/, last accessed 27 September 2016. On the history of pit ponies see C. Thompson, *Harnessed: Colliery Horses in Wales*, Cardiff: National Museum of Wales, 2008.
4 A.C. Willox, 'Climate change as the work of mourning', *Ethics & the Environment* 17, 2 (2012): 137–164, 152; K.H. Redford, K. Aune, and G. Plumb, 'Hope is a bison', *Conservation Biology* 30, 4 (2016): 689–691, 689.
5 H. Kean, 'Traces and representations: animal pasts in London's present', *London Journal* 36, 1 (2011): 54–71; H. Kean, 'Balto, the Alaskan dog and his statue in New York's Central Park: animal representation and national heritage', *International Journal of Heritage Studies* 15, 5 (2009): 413–430; H. Kean, 'Commemorating animals: glorifying humans? Remembering and forgetting animals in war memorials', in M. Andrews, C. Bogati Jewitt, and N. Hunt (eds.), *Lest We Forget: Remembrance and Commemoration*, Stroud: History Press, 2011, 60–70; H. Kean, 'Animals and war memorials: different approaches to commemorating the human–animal relationship', in R. Hediger (ed.), *Animals and War*, Boston: Brill, 2012, 237–260.
6 For a similar comparison of zoos and heritage see: T. Axelsson and S. May, 'Constructed landscapes in zoos and heritage', *International Journal of Heritage Studies* 14, 1 (2008): 43–59, C. Holtorf and O. Ortman, 'Endangerment and conservation ethos in natural and cultural heritage: the case of zoos and archaeological sites', *International Journal of Heritage Studies* 14, 1 (2008): 74–90.
7 J. Assmann, *Das Kulturelle Gedächtnis: Schrift, Erinnerung und Politische Identität in Frühen Hochkulturen*, München: Beck, 1992; A. Assmann, *Erinnerungsräume: Formen und Wandlungen des Kulturellen Gedächtnisses*, München: Beck, 1999; A. Assmann, *Cultural Memory and Western Civilization: Functions, Media, Archives*, Cambridge: Cambridge University Press, 2011.
8 M. Halbwachs, *Das Gedächtnis und Seine Sozialen Bedingungen*, trans L. Geldsetzer, Frankfurt am Main: Suhrkamp, 1985; in English, M. Halbwachs, *On Collective Memory*, trans L.A. Coser, Chicago IL: University of Chicago Press, 1992. Translated from: M. Halbwachs, *Les Cadres Sociaux de la Mémoire*, Paris: Presses Universitaires de France, 1952. E.H. Gombrich, *Aby Warburg: An Intellectual Biography*, London: Warburg Institute, 1970, 323ff.
9 P. Nora (ed.), *Les Lieux de Mémoire I: La République*, Paris: Gallimard, 1984; P. Nora (ed.), *Les Lieux de Mémoire II: La Nation*, Paris: Gallimard, 1986; P. Nora (ed.), *Les Lieux de Mémoire III: Les Frances*, Paris: Gallimard, 1992.
10 J. Assmann, 'Communicative and cultural memory', in A. Erll and A. Nünning (eds.), *Cultural Memory Studies: An International and Interdisciplinary Handbook*, Berlin: De Gruyter, 2008, 109–118, 109.
11 Assmann, 'Communicative and cultural memory', 113.
12 Assmann, 'Communicative and cultural memory', 110.

13 Assmann, 'Communicative and cultural memory', 111.
14 Assmann, 'Communicative and cultural memory', 112.
15 Assmann, 'Canon and archive', in Erll and Nünning (eds.), *Cultural Memory Studies*, 97–107, 97.
16 Assmann, 'Canon and archive' 98.
17 Assmann, 'Canon and archive'.
18 Assmann, 'Communicative and cultural memory', 114.
19 Assmann, 'Canon and archive', 101.
20 J.M. Weiskopf, 'Socialism on safari: wildlife and nation-building in postcolonial Tanzania, 1961–77', *Journal of African History* 56, 3 (2015): 429–447, 438.
21 Weiskopf, 'Socialism on safari', 438.
22 L. Rakestraw, 'Conservation historiography: an assessment', *Pacific Historical Review* 41, 3 (1972): 271–288, 273.
23 Rakestraw, 'Conservation historiography'.
24 J. Rüsen, 'Historical consciousness: narrative structure, moral function, and ontogenetic development', in P. Seixas (ed.), *Theorizing Historical Consciousness*, Toronto: University of Toronto Press, 2004, 63–85, 71. See also J. Rüsen, *Zeit und Sinn: Strategien historischen Denkens*, Frankfurt am Main: Fischer Taschenbuch Verlag, 1990.
25 J. Rüsen, 'Historical consciousness', 76–77.
26 B. Maragia, 'The indigenous sustainability paradox and the quest for sustainability in post-colonial societies: is indigenous knowledge all that is needed?', *Georgetown International Environmental Law Review* 18, 2 (2006): 197–248, 221–225; R.E. Johannes, 'Introduction', in R.E. Johannes (ed.), *Traditional Ecological Knowledge: A Collection of Essays*, Gland: IUCN, 1989, 7.
27 C. Nash, 'Environmental history, philosophy and difference', *Journal of Historical Geography* 26, 1 (2000): 23–27, 25. Also see M. Leach and C. Green, *Gender and Environmental History: Moving beyond the Narratives of the Past in Contemporary Women–Environment Policy Debates*, London: IDS Publications, 1995.
28 R. Brown, 'A conservation timeline: milestones of the model's evolution', *The Wildlife Professional* 4, 3 (2010): 28–31, 31.
29 J. Kay, 'Preconditions of natural resource conservation', *Agricultural History* 59, 2 (1985): 124–135, 135.
30 J. Reich, 'Re-creating the wilderness: shaping narratives and landscapes in Shenandoah National Park', *Environmental History* 6, 1 (2001): 95–117, 96.
31 Y. Whelan, 'Mapping meanings in the cultural landscape', in G. Ashworth and B. Graham (eds.), *Senses of Place: Senses of Time*, Aldershot: Ashgate, 2005, 61–71, 62.
32 For an overview of critical place-name studies see: R. Rose-Redwood, D. Alderman, and M. Azaryahu, 'Geographies of toponymic inscription: new directions in critical place-name studies', *Progress in Human Geography* 34, 4 (2010): 453–470.
33 B. Yeoh, 'Street-naming and nation-building: toponymic inscriptions of nationhood in Singapore', *Area* 28, 3 (1996): 298–307; M. Azaryahu, 'German reunification and the politics of street names: the case of East Berlin', *Political Geography* 16, 6 (1997): 479–493.
34 J. Carruthers, 'Dissecting the myth: Paul Kruger and the Kruger National Park', *Journal of Southern African Studies* 20, 2 (1994): 263–283; J. Carruthers, *The Kruger National Park: A Social and Political History*, Pietermaritzburg: University of Natal Press, 1995.
35 T. Salcedo-Chourré, *Historic Yosemite National Park: The Stories Behind One of America's Great Treasures*, Guilford CT: Rowman & Littlefield, 2016, 2.
36 On landscape semiotics see: D.E. Cosgrove, 'The myth and the stones of Venice: an historical geography of a symbolic landscape', *Journal of Historical Geography* 8, 2 (1982): 145–169; D.E. Cosgrove, *Social Formation and Symbolic Landscape*, Madison WI: University

of Wisconsin Press, 1984; D.E. Cosgrove, 'Prospect, perspective and the evolution of the landscape idea', *Transactions of the Institute of British Geographers* 10, 1 (1985): 45–62; D.E. Cosgrove, 'Landscape studies in geography and cognate fields of the humanities and social sciences', *Landscape Research* 15, 3 (1990): 1–6; J.S. Duncan, *The City as Text: The Politics of Landscape Interpretation in the Kandyan Kingdom*, Cambridge: Cambridge University Press, 1990.
37 Duncan, *The City as Text*, 17.
38 J. Assmann, 'Communicative and cultural memory', 111; on the linkage of landscape and memory see C. Holtorf and H. Williams, 'Landscapes and memories', in D. Hicks and M. Beaudray (eds.), *Cambridge Companion to Historical Archaeology*, Cambridge: Cambridge University Press, 2006, 235–253.
39 G. Bachelard, *The Poetics of Space*, trans. M. Jolas, New York: Orion Press, 1964; F.S. Yates, *The Art of Memory*, Chicago IL: University of Chicago Press, 1966; G. Johnson, *In the Place of Memory: How We Build the World Inside Our Heads*, New York: Knopf, 1991; J.B. Shetler, *Imagining Serengeti: A History of Landscape Memory in Tanzania from Earliest Time to the Present*, Athens OH: Ohio University Press, 2007, 20.
40 R.P. Neumann, 'Ways of seeing Africa: colonial recasting of African society and landscape in Serengeti National Park', *Ecumene* 2, 2 (1995): 149–169, 150.
41 Neumann, 'Ways of seeing Africa', 150.
42 T. Lekan, '*Serengeti Shall Not Die*: Bernhard Grzimek, wildlife film, and the making of a tourist landscape in East Africa', *German History* 29, 2 (2011): 224–364, 243.
43 Lekan, '*Serengeti Shall Not Die*', 244.
44 Lekan, '*Serengeti Shall Not Die*', 243.
45 Neumann, 'Ways of seeing Africa', 163.
46 J.S. Adams and T.O. McShane, *The Myth of Wild Africa: Conservation Without Illusion*, Berkeley CA: University of California Press, 1992, 50.
47 Lekan, '*Serengeti Shall Not Die*', 225.
48 Shetler, *Imagining Serengeti*, 2.
49 Shetler, *Imagining Serengeti*, 4.
50 Lekan, '*Serengeti Shall Not Die*', 239.
51 Lekan, '*Serengeti Shall Not Die*', 241–243.
52 Lekan, '*Serengeti Shall Not Die*', 230.
53 Lekan, '*Serengeti Shall Not Die*', 232.
54 Lekan, '*Serengeti Shall Not Die*', 260; also see R. Koshar, '"What ought to be seen": tourists' guidebooks and national identities in modern Germany and Europe', *Journal of Contemporary History* 33, 3 (1998): 323–340.
55 The safari park in Hodenhagen, Germany founded in 1974 is even explicitly called Serengeti Park. J-E. Steinkrüger, *Thematisierte Welten: Über Darstellungspraxen Zoologischer Gärten und Vergnügungsparks*, Bielefeld: transcript, 2013, 267–268.
56 Lekan, '*Serengeti Shall Not Die*', 225. Also: J.I. Engels, 'Von der sorge um tiere zur sorge um die umwelt: tiersendungen als umweltpolitik in Westdeutschland zwischen 1950 und 1980', *Archiv für Sozialgeschichte* 43 (2003): 297–323.
57 A. Root, 'Professor Dr. Dr. Bernhard Grzimek', www.serengeti.org/p_grzimek.html, last accessed 9 June 2016.
58 J. Urry, 'The tourist gaze and the "environment"', *Theory, Culture & Society* 9, 3 (1992): 1–26; and J. Urry and J. Larsen, *The Tourist Gaze 3.0*, London: SAGE, 2011.
59 C. Holtorf, 'The zoo as a realm of memory', *Anthropological Journal of European Cultures* 22, 1 (2013): 89–114, 106.
60 S.H. Spotte, *Zoos in Postmodernism: Signs and Simulation*, Madison NJ: Fairleigh Dickinson University Press, 2006.

61 See for example W. Zimmermann, 'Przewalskipferde auf dem weg zur wiedereinbürgerung – verschiedene projekte im vergleich', *Zeitschrift des Kölner Zoo* 48, 5 (2005): 183–209, 183.
62 B.A. Huffman, 'Husbandry and care of hoofstock', in M.D. Irwin, J.B. Stoner and A.M. Cobaugh (eds.), *Zookeeping: An Introduction to the Science and Technology*, Chicago IL: University of Chicago Press, 2013, 266–277, 276.
63 O.A. Ryder, 'Przewalski's horse: prospects for reintroduction into the wild', *Conservation Biology* 7, 1 (1993): 13–15, 13.
64 K.-D. Budras, K. Scheibe, B. Patan, W.J. Streich, and K. Kim, 'Laminitis in Przewalski horses kept in a semireserve', *Journal of Veterinary Science* 2, 1 (2001): 1–7, 1.
65 I. Bouman and J. Bouman, 'The history of Przewalski's horse', in L. Boyd and K. Houpt (eds.), *Przewalski's Horse: The History and Biology of an Endangered Species*, Albany NY: SUNY Press, 1994, 5–38; S.R.B. King, 'Extinct in the wild to endangered: the history of Przewalski's Horse (*equus ferus przewalskii*) and its future conservation', *Mongolian Journal of Biological Sciences* 3, 2 (2005): 37–41; Ryder, 'Przewalski's Horse'.
66 S. Wakefield, J. Knowles, W. Zimmermann, and M. van Dierendonck, 'Status and action plan for the Przewalski's horse (equus ferus przewalskii)', in P.D. Moehlman (ed.), *Equids: Zebras, Asses and Horses: Status Survey and Conservation Action Plan*, Cambridge: IUCN, 2002, 82–92, 85.
67 Holtorf and Williams, 'Landscapes and memories', 252.
68 Holtorf, 'The zoo as a realm of memory', 106–107.
69 On Carl Hagenbeck see: E. Ames, *Carl Hagenbeck's Empire of Entertainments*, Seattle WA: University of Washington Press, 2008; N. Rothfels, *Savages and Beasts: The Birth of the Modern Zoo*, Baltimore MD: Johns Hopkins University Press, 2002; L. Dittrich and A. Rieke-Müller, *Carl Hagenbeck (1844–1913): Tierhandel und Schaustellungen im Deutschen Kaiserreich*, Frankfurt am Main: Lang, 1998; H. Thode-Arora, *Für Fünfzig Pfennig um die Welt: Die Hagenbeckschen Völkerschauen*, Frankfurt am Main: Campus-Verlag, 1989. See also J. Kolbas, 'The Mongolian wild horse', *Focus on Geography* 47, 1 (2002): 26–29, 27.
70 Bouman and Bouman, 'The history of Przewalski's horse'.
71 Verband der Zoologischen Gärten, 'Urwildpferd, przewalskipferd, takhi', available at www.zoodirektoren.de/index.php?option=com_k2&view=item&id=185:przewalskipferd, last accessed 9 June 2016.

Bibliography

Adams, J.S. and McShane, T.O. *The Myth of Wild Africa: Conservation Without Illusion*, Berkeley CA: University of California Press, 1992.

Ames, E. *Carl Hagenbeck's Empire of Entertainments*, Seattle WA: University of Washington Press, 2008.

Assmann, A. *Erinnerungsräume: Formen und Wandlungen des Kulturellen Gedächtnisses*, München: Beck, 1999.

Assmann, A. 'Canon and archive', in A. Erll and A. Nünning (eds.), *Cultural Memory Studies: An International and Interdisciplinary Handbook*, Berlin: De Gruyter, 2008, 97–107.

Assmann, A. *Cultural Memory and Western Civilization: Functions, Media, Archives*, Cambridge: Cambridge University Press, 2011.

Assmann, J. *Das Kulturelle Gedächtnis: Schrift, Erinnerung und Politische Identität in Frühen Hochkulturen*, München: Beck, 1992.

Assmann, J. 'Communicative and cultural memory', in A. Erll and A. Nünning (eds.), *Cultural Memory Studies: An International and Interdisciplinary Handbook*, Berlin: De Gruyter, 2008, 109–118.

Axelsson, T. and May, S. 'Constructed landscapes in zoos and heritage', *International Journal of Heritage Studies* 14, 1 (2008): 43–59.

Azaryahu, M. 'German reunification and the politics of street names: the case of East Berlin', *Political Geography* 16, 6 (1997): 479–493.

Bachelard, G. *The Poetics of Space*, trans. M. Jolas, New York: Orion Press, 1964.

Bouman, I. and Bouman, J. 'The history of Przewalski's horse', in L. Boyd and K. Houpt (eds.), *Przewalski's Horse: The History and Biology of an Endangered Species*, Albany NY: SUNY Press, 1994, 5–38.

Brown, R. 'A conservation timeline: milestones of the model's evolution', *The Wildlife Professional* 4, 3 (2010): 28–31.

Budras, K-D., Scheibe, K., Patan, B., Streich, W.J., and Kim, K. 'Laminitis in Przewalski horses kept in a semireserve', *Journal of Veterinary Science* 2, 1 (2001): 1–7.

Carruthers, J. 'Dissecting the myth: Paul Kruger and the Kruger National Park', *Journal of Southern African Studies* 20, 2 (1994): 263–283.

Carruthers, J. *The Kruger National Park: A Social and Political History*, Pietermaritzburg: University of Natal Press, 1995.

Cosgrove, D.E. 'The myth and the stones of Venice: an historical geography of a symbolic landscape', *Journal of Historical Geography* 8, 2 (1982): 145–169.

Cosgrove, D.E. *Social Formation and Symbolic Landscape*, Madison WI: University of Wisconsin Press, 1984.

Cosgrove, D.E. 'Prospect, perspective and the evolution of the landscape idea', *Transactions of the Institute of British Geographers* 10, 1 (1985): 45–62.

Cosgrove, D.E. 'Landscape studies in geography and cognate fields of the humanities and social sciences', *Landscape Research* 15, 3 (1990): 1–6.

Dittrich, L. and Rieke-Müller, A. *Carl Hagenbeck (1844–1913): Tierhandel und Schaustellungen im Deutschen Kaiserreich*, Frankfurt am Main: Lang, 1998.

Duncan, J.S. *The City as Text: The Politics of Landscape Interpretation in the Kandyan Kingdom*, Cambridge: Cambridge University Press, 1990.

Engels, J.J. 'Von der sorge um tiere zur sorge um die umwelt: tiersendungen als umweltpolitik in Westdeutschland zwischen 1950 und 1980', *Archiv für Sozialgeschichte* 43 (2003): 297–323.

Gombrich, E.H. *Aby Warburg: An Intellectual Biography*, London: Warburg Institute, 1970.

Halbwachs, M. *Das Gedächtnis und Seine Sozialen Bedingungen*, trans L. Geldsetzer, Frankfurt am Main: Suhrkamp, 1985.

Halbwachs, M. *On Collective Memory*, trans L.A. Coser, Chicago IL: University of Chicago Press, 1992.

Halbwachs, M. *Les Cadres Sociaux de la Mémoire*, Paris: Presses Universitaires de France, 1952.

Holtorf, C. 'The zoo as a realm of memory', *Anthropological Journal of European Cultures* 22, 1 (2013): 89–114.

Holtorf, C. and Ortman, O. 'Endangerment and conservation ethos in natural and cultural heritage: the case of zoos and archaeological sites', *International Journal of Heritage Studies* 14, 1 (2008): 74–90.

Holtorf, C. and Williams, H. 'Landscapes and memories', in D. Hicks and M. Beaudray (eds.), *Cambridge Companion to Historical Archaeology*, Cambridge: Cambridge University Press, 2006, 235–253.

Huffman, B.A. 'Husbandry and care of hoofstock', in M.D. Irwin, J.B. Stoner, and A.M. Cobaugh (eds.), *Zookeeping: An Introduction to the Science and Technology*, Chicago IL: University of Chicago Press, 2013, 266–277.

Johannes, R.E. 'Introduction', in R.E. Johannes (ed.), *Traditional Ecological Knowledge: A Collection of Essays*, Gland: IUCN, 1989.

Johnson, G. *In the Place of Memory: How We Build the World Inside Our Heads*, New York: Knopf, 1991.

Kay, J. 'Preconditions of natural resource conservation', *Agricultural History* 59, 2 (1985): 124–135.

Kean, H. 'Traces and representations: animal pasts in London's present', *London Journal* 36, 1 (2001): 65–68.

Kean, H. 'An exploration of the sculptures of Greyfriars Bobby, Edinburgh, Scotland, and the Brown Dog, Battersea, South London, England', *Society & Animals* 11, 4 (2002): 353–373.

Kean, H. 'The moment of Greyfriars Bobby: the changing cultural position of animals, 1800–1920', in K. Kete (ed.), *A Cultural History of Animals in the Age of Empire*, Oxford: Bloomsbury, 2007, 31–33.

Kean, H, 'Balto, the Alaskan dog and his statue in New York's Central Park: animal representation and national heritage', *International Journal of Heritage Studies* 15, 5 (2009): 413–430.

Kean, H. 'Commemorating animals: glorifying humans? Remembering and forgetting animals in war memorials', in M. Andrews, C. Bogati Jewitt, and N. Hunt (eds.), *Lest We Forget: Remembrance and Commemoration*, Stroud: History Press, 2011, 60–70.

Kean, H, 'Traces and representations: animal pasts in London's present', *London Journal* 36, 1 (2011): 54–71.

Kean, H. 'Animals and war memorials: different approaches to commemorating the human-animal relationship', in R. Hediger (ed.), *Animals and War*, Boston: Brill, 2012, 237–260.

King, S.R.B. 'Extinct in the wild to endangered: the history of Przewalski's Horse (*equus ferus przewalskii*) and its future conservation', *Mongolian Journal of Biological Sciences* 3, 2 (2005): 37–41.

Kolbas, J. 'The Mongolian wild horse', *Focus on Geography* 47, 1 (2002): 26–29.

Koshar, R. '"What ought to be seen": tourists' guidebooks and national identities in modern Germany and Europe', *Journal of Contemporary History* 33, 3 (1998): 323–340.

Leach, M. and Green, C. *Gender and Environmental History: Moving beyond the Narratives of the Past in Contemporary Women–Environment Policy Debates*, London: IDS Publications, 1995.

Lekan, T. '*Serengeti Shall Not Die:* Bernhard Grzimek, wildlife film, and the Making of a Tourist Landscape in East Africa', *German History* 29, 2 (2011): 224–364.

Maragia, B. 'The indigenous sustainability paradox and the quest for sustainability in postcolonial societies: is indigenous knowledge all that is needed?', *Georgetown International Environmental Law Review* 18, 2 (2006): 197–248.

Nash, C. 'Environmental history, philosophy and difference', *Journal of Historical Geography* 26, 1 (2000): 23–27.

Neumann, R.P. 'Ways of seeing Africa: colonial recasting of African society and landscape in Serengeti National Park', *Ecumene* 2, 2 (1995): 149–169, 150.

Nora, P. (ed.), *Les Lieux de Mémoire I: La République*, Paris: Gallimard, 1984.

Nora, P. (ed.), *Les Lieux de Mémoire II: La Nation*, Paris: Gallimard, 1986.

Nora, P. (ed.), *Les Lieux de Mémoire III: Les Frances*, Paris: Gallimard, 1992.

Rakestraw, L. 'Conservation historiography: an assessment', *Pacific Historical Review* 41, 3 (1972): 271–288.

Redford, K.H., Aune, K., and Plumb, G. 'Hope is a bison', *Conservation Biology* 30, 4 (2016): 689–691.

Reich, J. 'Re-creating the wilderness: shaping narratives and landscapes in Shenandoah National Park', *Environmental History* 6, 1 (2001): 95–117.

Rose-Redwood, R., Alderman, D., and Azaryahu, M. 'Geographies of toponymic inscription: new directions in critical place-name studies', *Progress in Human Geography* 34, 4 (2010): 453–470.

Rothfels, N. *Savages and Beasts: The Birth of the Modern Zoo*, Baltimore MD: Johns Hopkins University Press, 2002.

Rüsen, J. *Zeit und Sinn: Strategien historischen Denkens*, Frankfurt am Main: Fischer Taschenbuch Verlag, 1990.

Rüsen, J. 'Historical consciousness: narrative structure, moral function, and ontogenetic development', in P. Seixas (ed.), *Theorizing Historical Consciousness*, Toronto: University of Toronto Press, 2004, 63–85.

Ryder, O.A. 'Przewalski's horse: prospects for reintroduction into the wild', *Conservation Biology* 7, 1 (1993): 13–15.

Salcedo-Chourré, T. *Historic Yosemite National Park: The Stories Behind One of America's Great Treasures*, Guilford CT: Rowman & Littlefield, 2016.

Shetler, J.B. *Imagining Serengeti: A History of Landscape Memory in Tanzania from Earliest Time to the Present*, Athens OH: Ohio University Press, 2007.

Spotte, S.H. *Zoos in Postmodernism: Signs and Simulation*, Madison NJ: Fairleigh Dickinson University Press, 2006.

Steinkrüger, J-E. *Thematisierte Welten: Über Darstellungspraxen Zoologischer Gärten und Vergnügungsparks*, Bielefeld: transcript, 2013.

Thode-Arora, H. *Für Fünfzig Pfennig um die Welt: Die Hagenbeckschen Völkerschauen*, Frankfurt am Main: Campus-Verlag, 1989.

Thompson, C. *Harnessed: Colliery Horses in Wales*, Cardiff: National Museum of Wales, 2008.

Urbanik, J. *Placing Animals: An Introduction to the Geography of Human-Animal Relations*, Lanham MD: Rowman & Littlefield, 2012.

Urry, J. 'The tourist gaze and the "environment"', *Theory, Culture & Society* 9, 3 (1992): 1–26.

Urry, J. and Larsen, J. *The Tourist Gaze 3.0*, London: SAGE, 2011.

Wakefield, S., Knowles, J., Zimmermann, W., and van Dierendonck, M. 'Status and action plan for the Przewalski's horse (equus ferus przewalskii)', in P.D. Moehlman (ed.), *Equids: Zebras, Asses and Horses: Status Survey and Conservation Action Plan*, Cambridge: IUCN, 2002, 82–92.

Weiskopf, J.M. 'Socialism on safari: wildlife and nation-building in postcolonial Tanzania, 1961–77', *Journal of African History* 56, 3 (2015): 429–447.

Whelan, Y. 'Mapping meanings in the cultural landscape', in G. Ashworth and B. Graham (eds.), *Senses of Place: Senses of Time*, Aldershot: Ashgate, 2005, 61–71.

Willox, A.C. 'Climate change as the work of mourning', *Ethics & the Environment* 17, 2 (2012): 137–164.

Yates, F.S. *The Art of Memory*, Chicago IL: University of Chicago Press, 1966.

Yeoh, B. 'Street-naming and nation-building: toponymic inscriptions of nationhood in Singapore', *Area* 28, 3 (1996): 298–307.

Zimmermann, W. 'Przewalskipferde auf dem weg zur wiedereinbürgerung – verschiedene projekte im vergleich', *Zeitschrift des Kölner Zoo* 48, 5 (2005): 183–209.

6
THE EXPERIMENTAL ANIMAL
In search of a moral ecology of science?

Robert G.W. Kirk

We cannot properly understand animal–human history in the modern period without addressing the scientific use of animals. Animal research has been a prominent object of concern, criticism and protest within the academy and society and as such it has played a formative role in the development of the field of 'animal' studies. Indeed, to understand *why* a volume such as this exists one would have to consider the history of societal responses to animal research. It is in the encounter between the experimental animal and the experimenter that the boundary between animal and human has been made and remade countless times over. Why do we experiment on animals? Because animals are physiologically like humans. Why do we experiment on animals? Because animals are ethically different to humans. Animal research concerns the ongoing negotiation of similitude and difference across human and animal, always tentative and always with societal and ethical consequence. More than any other site, it is the experimental encounter where we can see situated relational interdependencies across species being negotiated and transformed with full acknowledgement of their complexity and tentative nature. As Lynda Birke, Arnold Arluke and Mike Michael have argued, '[a]s the laboratory animal is made and unmade, so too is the identity of the lay public'.[1] It is for this reason animal research has been and remains one of the most misunderstood, contentious and polarising of animal–human relationships. Science, in sum, has been one of the most prominent catalysts and contexts for the problematisation of animal–human relationships; yet it has equally provided many of the tools and discourses of critique through fields such as ethology and animal welfare science. To understand animal–human history we would do well to start with the role of animals in science.

The experimental animal was a condition of possibility for many fields of science, not least 'scientific' medicine.[2] Animals were the object and means of study within natural history and anatomical observation, whilst the finches, pigeons and other species that provided Charles Darwin with inspiration and evidence for the theory of evolution by natural selection clearly played a fundamental role in shaping modernity.[3] Animals were fundamental to the development of the sciences of animal behaviour, ethology, primatology and related fields, all of which contribute to a fuller understanding of animal–human history broadly conceived.[4] The history of taxonomy, for instance, demonstrates not only the centrality of animals within nineteenth-century science but the extent to which science is enmeshed within wider societal and cultural trends.[5] Whilst all of these areas are integral to the history of science this chapter focuses on the use of animals within a cluster of sciences which we might, at the risk of slight ahistoricism, think of as the 'biomedical' sciences. There are a number of overlapping reasons for this focus. Without the experimental animal, it is hard to imagine how the biomedical sciences would have come into being.[6] Without the biomedical sciences, the modern world as we know it would not have come into being. And without the experimental use of animals within the biomedical sciences, debates about human–animal relations as well as the academic and political discourse of human–animal studies, would be very different indeed.

This chapter is structured around the conceit that social history and the history of science have approached animal research from distinct directions which, whilst productive and appropriate for their respective object of concern and audience, only provide partial accounts of the role of science as a driver of change within animal–human history. It proceeds in two substantive parts before concluding. The first part reviews how the experimental animal tends to be sublimated within social history as concern for the animal is read against wider societal themes such as class, gender, and race. In the second part, an overview of the historiography of science is presented to show how animals have been included within histories of the production of scientific knowledge in such a way that the wider societal themes fade out of analysis. Where broader social considerations are retained they rarely engage with how social values are enacted in the work of animal research. As such, both literatures address the history of animal research without necessarily bringing core moral and ethical questions to the fore of their analysis. In conclusion, it is suggested that synthesising the two by framing analysis around a 'moral ecology of science' would produce something greater than the sum of the parts of real value to understanding animal–human history more broadly. Moreover, such a move would align historical accounts of animals in science with the methodological, analytic and moral/ethical concerns that shape and drive scholarship from the social sciences and other fields within 'animal studies'.

Histories of the experimental animal *as concern for the social*

Human use of nonhuman animals to understand biological life generally and human life specifically has a long history.[7] This chapter focusses on the nineteenth and twentieth century, as animal bodies were established as a basic resource for experimental research in the then emergent life sciences during this 'modern' period. Broad changes in medical thinking and practice across the nineteenth century have been characterised as 'the disappearance of the sick man from medical cosmology' by the medical sociologist Nicholas Jewson and famously titled by Michel Foucault the 'birth of the clinic'.[8] These creative periodisations attempt to capture a tapestry of trends most prominent of which have been the decentring of patient experience in the diagnosis of illness and the shift toward understanding diseases as immanent entities in themselves locatable within the body.[9] Alongside the formation of new specialisms such as physiology and bacteriology, these trends worked to transform medicine from an art grounded in experience to a science based on experiment. Whereas the former relied on learning from lectures, texts and existing knowledge, the latter sought original knowledge through empirical observation and, crucially, experimentation. This move from valorising what *was* known to seeking what *was not* in medical thought and education formed a critical condition of possibility for the emergence of the 'experimental' animal.[10]

Early nineteenth-century post-revolutionary France, or more specifically Paris, took centre stage in the emergent new 'experimental' medicine.[11] Pioneers such Francois Magendie (1783–1855) and his successor Claude Bernard (1813–1878) established France at the forefront of the new science of physiology, as Louis Pasteur (1822–1985) and Emile Roux (1853–1933) did with bacteriology.[12] The authority of these new sciences rested in innovative medical research practices which, in turn, relied on nonhuman animals as resources and experimental tools. By mid-century, use of animals for experimentation, or 'vivisection' as it was then known, was established as a 'French' science.[13] Immediately, vivisection associated with a wave of radical societal transformations few of which went uncontested and none of which developed in isolation. Whilst historians of science and medicine have worked to locate 'French' medicine within the revolutionary politics of its time, seeking to show scientific and societal values to be deeply interwoven, it is social historians who have focussed on how moral values shaped societal responses to vivisection.[14] However, social history tends to read nineteenth-century opposition to animal research, or the 'antivivisection' movement, as indicative of, and to some extent driven by wider (which is to say human) societal concerns.

If France was the birthplace of vivisection then Britain would appear to be the origin of political and social objections to animal research (although this may be more an effect of historiography than an accurate account of the development of antivivisection). In the British context, opposition to vivisection emerged in Britain in relation to (and subsequently became entangled with) wider concerns about animal cruelty. In February 1825, for example, the Irish parliamentarian and campaigner against animal cruelty Richard Martin (1754–1834) concluded his introduction of a bill to abolish bear-baiting to the House of Commons with reference to Magendie who he labelled a 'disgrace to society' for performing 'experiments so atrocious as almost to shock belief'.[15] Magendie had visited London the previous year to demonstrate his scientific work. At the time, public demonstrations of new scientific knowledge were common, serving to enhance personal standing and the authority of science more generally across society. Crowds who attended these events were drawn by a complex mixture of the desire to learn but also be entertained. This allowed reformers like Martin, who were committed to alleviating cruelty to animals, to equate vivisection with 'cruel' sporting practices like animal-baiting; both appeared to be exercises in animal cruelty for human pleasure. Yet, for social history, this antivivisectionist sentiment was not merely about animal cruelty. At a time when anti-French sentiment remained a powerful force in English culture, one can read Magendie and vivisection not just as symbols of brutality and perversion but as specifically a French form of post-revolutionary brutality suggestive of the generalised perversion of French culture.

By the mid to late nineteenth-century, as English protest against vivisection developed a distinctive identity within the broader animal cruelty reform movement, anti-French sentiment had become a powerful rhetorical frame for antivivisectionist discourse. The presentation of 'vivisection' as particular to French physiological science shaped early British antivivisectionist discourse in such a way that the wider political movement can and has been read as a predominantly anti-French crusade.[16] Frances Power Cobbe (1822–1904), perhaps the most prominent antivivisectionist, is illustrative. Cobbe frequently characterised vivisection as a French corruption of science arguing 'as a rule that the most cultivated are the most merciful' yet in 'France, alas! It is men of science – men belonging to the learned professions – who disembowel living horses and open the brains of dogs'.[17] The English medical profession was equally quick to appropriate societal aversions toward animal cruelty together with anti-French sentiment when the status of English scientific medicine was at stake. The French origins of vivisection were a much-used rhetorical resource in the long-running squabble between the English physiologist Sir Charles Bell and Magendie which was at its height between 1822 and 1842.[18] This dispute revolved about who first identified and separated motor and sensory nerve roots, which was the basis for what is now recognised as the 'Bell-Magendie Law'.[19] Where Magendie's claim rested on vivisection, Bell in contrast had worked with dead or at worst insensible animals. Bell presented his refusal to work with living animals as fundamental not only to his moral position as a scientist but the rigour of the scientific work itself:

> After refraining long, on account of the unpleasant nature of the operation, I at last opened the spinal canal of the rabbit ... the creature still crawled ... I was deterred from repeating the experiment by the protracted cruelty of the dissection. I reflected that an experiment would be satisfactory if done on an animal recently knocked down and insensible; that whilst I experimented on a living animal, there might be a trembling or action excited in the muscles by touching a sensitive nerve, which motion it would be difficult to distinguish from that produced more immediately through the influence of the motor nerves.[20]

As the dispute with Magendie developed, Bell increasingly presented himself as adhering to a deductive anatomical approach as opposed to vivisection, eventually becoming quite opposed to the notion he was an 'experimentalist' at all.[21] Bell cultivated the notion that abhorrence toward vivisection was an English virtue which guaranteed rather than hindered the quality of the nation's science.[22] Rhetorically, this allowed supporters of Bell to mobilise anti-French and antivivisectionist sentiments to belittle Magendie's claim to scientific priority.[23] Accordingly, historians have argued that anti-French sentiment was a powerful factor in shaping the development and reception of early antivivisectionism in Britain. Whilst such analysis has clear literary and cultural importance, its effect is to obscure both concern for the animal and the animal itself in favour of far more human concerns of national identity, social standing and cultural politics.

In a comparable move, social history has also shown how antivivisectionist discourse embodied wider political concerns regarding the place of women in nineteenth-century society. In a sensitive analysis connecting Victorian (and later Edwardian) innovations in gynaecological medical practices to tropes within pornography and wider literature, Lansbury has argued that for English middle-class women 'to protest against vivisection was to challenge a world of male sexual authority and obscenity which they sensed unconsciously, even if they had no direct experience of it'.[24] In this way women and animals were increasingly aligned through the identification of the oppression of women in society with the vivisected animal in science. The entanglement of early antivivisectionist and feminist politics was not specific to England. Antivivisectionist protest in late-nineteenth America has similarly been characterised by social historians as a 'particularly female concern, pitting women against the exclusively male medical research establishment'.[25] In *fin de siècle* France, too, existing historiography would suggest that it 'was not lost on feminists that the powerlessness and suffering inflicted on animals by the experimental vivisectionist had a parallel in the way females were treated by hysteria doctors'.[26] Indeed, this association was so pronounced that across national contexts proponents of vivisection responded to their critics by characterising antivivisection as an irrational sentimentality common in women but unbecoming in men. Some went further still, asserting that the excessive love of animals intrinsic to antivivisection was a mental pathology. The French psychologist Pierre Janet thought antivivisectionism to be a specific form of feminine hysteria which he named 'la zoophilie' whilst the American neurologist Charles Loomis Dana claimed the same of 'zoo-phil-psychosis'.[27] Again, these nuanced studies make important contributions to social historical understanding of gender and feminist politics. Yet, whilst it is not their intent, the consequence of bringing gender to the analytic fore is to shift attention away from the animal, which is reduced to a cypher for the expression of concerns over the gendered human. Finn's study of antivivisection and feminism in *fin de siècle* France is representative, concluding that '[i]n ridiculing the vanity of vivisectionist doctors in print, in interrupting their experiments, batting them with umbrellas and trashing their labs, French feminists were in fact striking a blow for their own gender'.[28]

In sum, social and literary historical accounts of antivivisection tend to construe opposition to animal research as symbolic of wider, human, societal concerns such as those of nation and gender. In addition to nation and gender, the early history of animal research has been read against the values of race and changing understanding of the nature of civilisation, all ordered hierarchically within Victorian culture through the assumption that the capacity to experience pain was felt most keenly by the most evolved (and thus most 'civilised') forms of life.[29] Class, too, has been mobilised to explain and understand how nineteenth-century objections to animal research became entangled with movements to alleviate cruelty to animals. As Harriet Ritvo has *persuasively* argued, for Victorian culture '[c]ruelty to animals was supposed to characterise the most dangerous members of society, not those on whose responsible shoulders the social structure rested'.[30] In the minds of middle-class Victorians animal cruelty represented the threat of social disorder emanating from the lower classes.[31] At a time when science was gaining ever greater social status, scientists having the prestige and social leadership associated with the clergy and clerisy, to suggest that science involved the everyday practice of animal cruelty was to reveal a threat to society itself. Accordingly, the historian Richard D. French concluded that '[a]ntivivisectionists foresaw the cold, barren, alienation of a future dominated by the imperatives of technique and expertise. It was not experiments on animals they were protesting, it was the shape of the century to come'.[32]

It is unclear to what extent social history intends to make a hard assentation that human concerns for human values lie at the heart of opposition to animal research. Hilda Kean, for instance, in her analysis of the relationship of socialist and feminist politics to that of animal advocacy in the Edwardian period, argues that political association with human concerns does not imply a diminishment of a concern for the animal in the thought and actions of the historical actors under study.[33] Others are not so clear: perhaps because the archive is silent when asked such evaluative questions. Nevertheless, the consequence of foregrounding human cultural concerns for *historiography* is to diminish the explanatory capacity of social history to seriously interrogate how, why, and to what consequence human concern for nonhuman animals may serve as a primary motivating force of historical change. Inevitably, any discursive reduction of the animal, making it serve as a cypher for human political and societal concerns, produces what Erica Fudge has labelled histories of animals which are actually 'histories of human attitudes toward animals'.[34] The question as to what extent the animal has disappeared from historiography as a result of the narrative framing of social history or because animals were never really present in the historical processes being examined all too often is left unclear. At best, we might conclude that the place of the animal within social history is sublimated toward all too human concerns (not least those of class, race and gender). As such, the narrative framing of social history renders the historical actor incapable of embodying or expressing an authentic concern for the nonhuman animal in itself. Feminist middle-class Victorian women may well have been 'striking a blow for their gender'. Antivivisectionists of all sexes and social backgrounds may well have been 'protesting . . . the shape of the century to come'. But such explanations say little as to how these and other historical actors related to and understood animals *as animals* and perhaps as constituent parts of 'society'. The history of animal experimentation, as presented by social history, has struggled to engage meaningfully with the extent to which the animal may have been more than a symbol for human values and concerns. To address such a question would require the animal to be placed at the centre of the historical narrative. Moreover, it would be to make animals the analytic focus of new investigations of the social and society. Investigations orientated toward understanding how nonhuman animals have shaped human history beyond their ready representation of human concerns. Such an endeavour would imply radically rethinking the humanistic limit of our historical imagination to move toward the writing of 'more than human histories'.[35] Here, approaches from the history of science may have something to offer.

Histories of the experimental animals *as concern for science*

The history of science presupposes that 'science' is no different from any other human activity; science forms part of human culture. As such, 'science' can and should be studied historically. Just as one need not be an economist to study economic history or have served in the military to understand military history one need not be a scientist to investigate the history of science. The same methodologies and analytic approaches can be applied to the history of science as one would apply to any other field of history. Nevertheless, many historians continue to set the history of 'science' apart from History proper; they do so for many reasons, but two reasons in particular are of interest. First, the history of science has, historically, been more open than other historical fields to finding common cause with diverse theorists across the philosophy and sociology of science. Second, and interrelatedly, to render science open to historical study is to trouble a fundamental division of academic labour where ontology is assumed to be the province of the sciences whereas the humanities confine their interest to the vagaries of culture. Both of these characteristics are shared by – and have in many ways been inspirational to – scholars across the eclectic field of human–animal, more-than-human, and multispecies studies. Once it is recognised, as Jamie Lorimer concisely expresses the notion, that the 'world is hybrid – neither social nor natural', then the inclusion of animals in our historical narratives becomes not just possible but a necessity.[36]

The historical study of science must, through its very *raison d'être*, radically depart from an understanding of science on its own terms. To recognise the historicity of scientific knowledge is to reject the claim that science as a body of knowledge has access to the uncontaminated 'truth' about what nature really is through virtue of a set of practices and stances situated outside of human culture.[37] For this reason, the history of science presupposes that scientific knowledge is embedded within and inevitably contaminated by the social and cultural contexts of its production. To claim that 'science is social relations', as one influential early radical science movement pioneer memorably proclaimed, or to say scientific knowledge is in some way a 'social construction', is far from uncontentious, as it directly challenges the authority of scientific knowledge.[38] This in essence was the argument at the heart of the 'science wars' which played out across the 1980s and 1990s.[39] Whilst historians of science were much less active combatants than anthropologists, sociologists and others who self-identified with the social studies of science cause, as a field its claim to historical credibility was nevertheless at stake. More pertinent to present purposes, this was the context in which a series of innovative ways of approaching and understanding science were forged, which have proved subsequently to be intellectual catalysts for scholars interested in the 'animal question'.

One such work is Donna Haraway's *Primate Visions*, which mobilised the history of science to intervene in and contribute to the formation of feminist science studies. *Primate Visions* presents a highly contentious but equally influential approach to understanding science encapsulated by questions such as '[w]hat may count as nature for late industrial people . . . For whom and at what cost . . . In what specific places, out of which intellectual histories, and with what tools is nature constructed?'[40] For Haraway, science is storytelling – a statement which contrary to how it is often understood in no way intends to demean the importance or authority of scientific knowledge. To say science is storytelling is merely to recognise that science, like all human activities, is an outcome of human creativity and thus embedded in human values and culture. Haraway meticulously reconstructs how primatology was forged in gendered, colonial, and racial contexts, all collectively shaping and driving changing understandings of 'nature'. Each account of nature produced gave form to a specific way of doing primatology, serving certain interests and ends over others. In Haraway's hands the history of science became a tool for political intervention, and in subsequent years her work has been recognised and deployed as such within the now burgeoning field of animal studies. Arguably, *Primate Visions* remains the most commanding exemplar of what the history of science can contribute to animal studies as an academic and political programme.[41] Haraway's work remains distinctive in her elegant weaving of material and semiotic analysis to produce historically sensitive accounts of 'technoscience'.[42]

Arguably, neither historians of science nor emergent historians of animals have fully embraced the potential of Haraway's trajectory or fully reckoned with its challenges. If we are to accept the historicity of science and the hybridity of nature and culture then it becomes impossible (or at least disingenuous) to make any unreflective or uncritical resort to 'science' as a means to ground animal advocacy politics or chart new more-than-human futures. More problematic for the historian is that to do so is to knowingly embrace ahistorical explanatory frameworks. Accordingly, historical writing should be cautious in its embracement of contemporary scientific knowledge. In their desire to find the otherwise absent animal in the archive some historians have drawn on the contemporary knowledge of animal ethology, behaviour and welfare.[43] To extrapolate and apply scientific knowledge in this way implies such knowledge to be a universal truth transcendent of history. As historians, however, we know better. This raises an open question as to the limits and limitations of historical practice.

A second way of thinking about and working on science which emerged from the 1980s and 1990s is the work of Bruno Latour and his followers which continues to be referred to colloquially as Actor-Network Theory (ANT).[44] Like Haraway, Latour presents a material-semiotic method which challenges simple dichotomies of human–animal, nature–culture. However, whereas Haraway retains a political and thus radical element to her work, ANT all too often falls flat in its tendency toward apolitical descriptive narrative. Within ANT all 'actors' within a 'network' are described in the same terms; thus all actors whether human or nonhuman can possess 'agency'. This suggests ANT has value for animal studies, which it does. However, ANT is severely limited in what it can do, and has been much misunderstood. One problem is derived from the name; ANT is a methodology, not a theory. As such it is incapable of explanation and so any potential for political or ethical intervention is curtailed. ANT produces description. Within ANT, for example, 'agency' has a specific meaning stripped of conscious intent. An 'actor' is merely an object that modifies another object. From the perspective of ANT everything is a potential 'actor'. The value of this approach is that it facilitated a material turn within the history of science. Yet it did so at the cost of erasing meaning and thus politics in favour of pragmatic description. Consequently, whilst ANT has encouraged historiography to include the animal within accounts of the history of science, it simultaneously, in strong contrast to Haraway, depoliticised such scholarship – rendering mute its potential to take moral, ethical or political standpoints.

One can see this effect in Robert Kohler's account of the early to mid-twentieth-century development of drosophila genetics.[45] In an attempt to distinguish his approach from predecessors both in the older 'history of ideas' tradition and comparatively more recent 'social constructivist' approach, Kohler establishes that he has no interest in 'knowledge production'.[46] Kohler framed his account as an 'empirical' study of 'experimental practice' focussed on 'the material culture, social conventions and moral ordering of experimental production'.[47] Accordingly, he brings the animal to the fore as a means to explore the material culture of science in a direct retort to radical social constructivists (which in itself shows that the inclusion of nonhuman animals is not in itself a radical intervention). *Lords of the Fly* examines the role of the fly in shaping the scientific work of T.H. Morgan, the social organisation of his laboratory, and the moral rules governing the drosophila community. By transposing E.P. Thompson's concept of the 'moral economy' to scientific practice, Kohler argues that a specific set of practices and expectations characterises the social relations of the drosophila community.[48] Moreover, he carefully shows how the biological nature of drosophila gave shape to the 'moral economy' of drosophila research. It was, for instance, the biological fecundity of the fly that produced a moral order characterised by a collaborative ethos, reciprocity, the free exchange of fly stocks and disclosure of experimental plans and findings. Flies reproduced at such a rate that more mutants were identified than could ever be successfully investigated by a single research group. With more work than human workers there was no impediment to sharing the tools of the trade. Research questions were owned by specific research communities, but the flies became communal property. Kohler reconstructs how these moral 'codes' of research conduct contributed to the drosophilists forming a distinctive communal identity. As such, the social practices of drosophila researchers owed their origin to the distinctiveness of the drosophila fly. Kohler equally demonstrates how the fly 'impelled Morgan to abandon experimental evolution for the neo-Mendelian variety of experimental heredity'.[49] In this way drosophila 'took over' Morgan's laboratory, contributing to a research trajectory within which the fly would flourish and in doing so significantly shape the development of genetic science (and by extension our understanding of the 'human').

In seeking to turn back the historiographic tide of sociological reductionism Kohler brought drosophila to the fore, but he framed the fly as a scientific tool which operated as something akin to a social technology. Rather than valorising the 'agency' of the fly (a term that Kohler actually avoids) it is the biological and material properties of drosophila which are shown to be determining factors of both scientific production and the social relations of science. In this way, Kohler is less interested in developing an ANT-like approach than he is in promoting a turn to the material culture of science which subtly reasserts the naturalistic narrative. Kohler's message is that nature, in the form of the fly, determines knowledge production as well as the social (or 'moral') economy of science. In a sense, the fly was no more than a marker for a 'nature' which determined scientific knowledge whilst contributing to the constitution of human social and moral values, but in doing so remained outside of the same. Tellingly, Kohler shows no concern for the fly. The question as to what extent moral, social and cultural values might become embedded in the nonhuman material culture of experimental science, whether this be fly or other material tools and technologies, is left unanswered.[50] Here we can see that the history of science provides fertile ground for empirically exploring human–animal relations and is custodian of a number of approaches for capturing and reading the 'agency' (or contributions) of animals to human culture. Yet, the *raison d'être* of the history of science all too often prevents such studies from exploring how moral values and ethical concerns might operate within scientific epistemology, practice and knowledge production. But this is just a fly, one might think. We ask too much. What scope is there for *including* concern for the fly within the moral economy rather than framing the fly merely as an external factor in the shaping of the moral economy of science? Perhaps more than one might think.

If one includes animal care practices within the history of scientific knowledge production (which I would argue certainly should be the case) then a different set of questions emerge which collectively present an alternative way of scientifically relating to flies. How does one accommodate, breed, feed, protect and promote the welfare of experimental animals? These and related questions were increasingly asked by scientists in the opening decades of the twentieth century, eventually catalysing the formation of a sub-field named 'laboratory animal science' tasked with finding "scientific" approaches to the health, management, care and latterly welfare of experimental animals.[51] The formation of 'laboratory animal science' in the 1940s and 50s was not only a response and outcome of animal research but a conscious attempt to make a 'science' of animal care. As such, it is one of the first coherent and systematic expressions of what today we would call 'animal welfare science'. In the earliest discourse of laboratory animal science drosophila appear alongside other minor and major species of experimental animal. For instance, drosophila appear in *The UFAW Handbook on the Care and Management of Laboratory Animals* (1957) alongside guinea-pigs, mice (of various varieties), rats, voles, foxes, ferrets, minks, sheep, pigs, goats, horses, fowl, pigeons, canaries, reptiles, amphibia, cats, dogs, monkeys and primates and others, each recognised to have specific husbandry, management and care needs.[52] The Universities Federation for Animal Welfare (UFAW) is a self-styled 'scientific' animal welfare organisation, which played an important role in developing a 'science' of animal welfare in the mid twentieth century. The *UFAW Handbook* was one of the first general textbooks addressing the practical care of laboratory animals. At the same time, it applied and promoted UFAW's distinctive view of experimental epistemology which assumed that a moral concern for the animal operated as a guarantor of the quality and reliability of scientific knowledge.[53] In sum, a history of the material culture of animal research could (and arguably should) include consideration of changing practices of care; from basic husbandry to the promotion of animal health and 'welfare'. Doing so would expand Kohler's use of 'moral economy' so as to include animals. Moreover, it would expand the reach of the concept in such a way that it would usefully approximate Lorraine Daston's otherwise quite distinct sense of the moral economy of science as 'a web of affect-saturated values'.[54]

Kohler was far from alone amongst historians of science in bringing the experimental animal to the fore only to neglect the role of affect, care and moral values in the epistemological and material work of scientific knowledge production. A 1993 collection of themed papers, appearing in the *Journal of the History of Biology*, collectively explored the question of 'the right organism for the job' investigating to what extent an experimental system ('job') was defined and remade by the experimental organism ('tool') and vice versa. Each emphasised the human labour involved in constructing an experimental system and experimental organism which together produced reliable, reproducible scientific knowledge.[55] A similar approach characterised *The Right Tool for the Job: At Work in Twentieth-Century Life Sciences*, within which a range of contributors sought to explore the material culture of scientific production. This volume probed the factors that made the 'right tool' for an experimental 'job' to demonstrate the situated complexity of 'rightness'. Each contribution captured the multiple practical, material, economic and social factors of 'the conditions of production' which serve as the respective conditions of possibility for situated scientific knowledge. The aim was to show how practical experimental work was 'co-constructed' with scientific theory within what the editors described as:

> an ecology of knowledge ... including an ecology of the contents of scientific knowledge, but also an ecology of the *conditions of its production* – an ecology of scientific activity/practice/work.[56]

On the wave of a historiographic turn to the material culture of science which swept into the history of the life sciences in the 1990s, a number of authors brought the animal to the fore, developing and adapting methodological and analytic approaches which include the role of animals in historical accounts of scientific knowledge production. Excluded, however unconsciously, from this 'ecology' of scientific knowledge production was any productive engagement with the role of affective or moral values broad enough to include the nonhuman animal. Why? One compelling explanation emerges from the agenda behind this work. As Paolo Palladino noted at the time

> problems of sociological reductionism will not be resolved by simply shifting the focus of work in the history of science away from ideas and institutions onto such organisms or any other crucial tools of scientific practice ... to acknowledge the autonomy of technologies of production, and yet withhold critical analysis of the social relationships embedded in these technologies, amounts to an equally reductionist technological determinism.[57]

The historiographic turn to material culture had, in its retort radical social construction, turned too far in favour of approaching science on its own terms. And as Daston acknowledges

> [w]e are heirs to a tradition that ... opposes facts to values ... [e]motions may fuel scientific work by supplying motivation, values may infiltrate scientific products as ideology or sustain them as institutionalized norms, but neither emotions nor values intrude upon the core of science.[58]

Accordingly, affective concern or moral values cannot be admitted a role in the ecology of scientific knowledge if one approaches science on its own terms of representation.

Historians of science attentive to the animal have, however, included other societal values within their work thereby evading (to differing extents) Palladino's critique that a technological determinism was replacing a sociological determinist explanatory framework within studies of the material culture of science. Bonnie Tocher Clause, for instance, examined how wider social and economic trends, such as scientific management philosophy and the economics of mass-production, influenced the development of the 'Wistar Rat' (one of the first widely used 'standard' research animals).[59] Standardisation, a major theme within the history of science, is critical for the reliability of scientific knowledge as standards allow accurate communication and transmission of knowledge.[60] Standardisation of measurement, techniques and standard tools enables situated scientific work conducted in different times and places to become stabilised to such a point that agreement about experimental outcomes can occur. As such, for animals to serve as reliable 'tools' within scientific research, they too had to be standardised.[61] Natural inherent variation within any population of animals for this reason posed a particular problem for the use of experimental animals. Regardless of species, from drosophila through to higher mammals, all individuals from a given population were expected to respond to the same event in the same way. Otherwise it would be equivalent to every laboratory having their own system of measurement: communication and verification of experimental results would become extremely challenging. One approach to 'standardising' experimental animals was to create populations with the same genotype. One of the earliest 'standardised' animals of this type was the 'Wistar Rat': inbred over multiple generations so as to produce genetic homogeneity. In reconstructing the history of the Wistar Rat, Clause draws affinities between science and wider social trends such as industrial production. Clause shows how the primary characteristics of the Wistar Rat, 'uniformity of product, standards of quality, and efficiency of production', were adapted from management literature inspired by Frederick W. Taylor's philosophy of 'scientific' management and applied to great effect to the production of scientific knowledge.[62] As a result, a population of rats was fundamentally changed to become a new form of life, neither entirely natural nor a product purely of human design, appropriate to and identified by their place in scientific research.

A similar argument informs Karen Rader's account of Clarence Cook Little and the Jackson Laboratory – one of the earliest and foremost commercial producers of experimental mice. Rader elegantly examines the transformation of common mice into highly standardised experimental tools, attentive to the development of techniques of intensive inbreeding supported by industrial production and commercialisation. Rader carefully narrates historical change against the context of disciplinary formation (genetic and cancer research), transformations in the institutional and infrastructural organisation of science and its funding, as well as wider economic and social change within the USA.[63] Whilst Rader writes firmly within the framing of an 'ecology of knowledge', acknowledging that the 'inbred laboratory mouse began as medical and remains primarily so', she extends her reach to tentatively engage with social history and consider their 'cultural legacy'.[64] Rader, for example, explores how the case for federal support of the Jackson Laboratory was made on the grounds that mice had little societal value. Consequently, as a research tool, mice evaded antivivisectionist criticism that tended to appeal to public sentiment through a focus on 'pet' animals such as the dog. Rader charts how the ways in which society values (or fails to value) a species impacts upon what can and cannot be done to that species.[65] By revealing how the societal niche occupied by mice was transformed into political capital and used rhetorically to gain economic support and promote scientific endeavour, Rader provides tantalising glimpses at how scientific identity may have been shaped by societal values and perceived moral consequences of animal research.[66] Nevertheless, we learn little about how such values operated on the micro level; how moral values and ethical concerns may have shaped the material culture of scientific production in everyday practice. The intrusion of wider social themes shifts the narrative focus away from the micro studies of the material culture of science. As such, the question of how affective relationships and the lived experience of working with and caring for experimental mice may have shaped the 'ecology of scientific knowledge' is left unexplored.

A slightly different though not unrelated approach to animals within the history of science explored investigates their increasing use as 'models' across the twentieth century. One motivation of such work is to realign the material production of scientific knowledge with the history of changing scientific epistemology and theories (the 'intellectual' components of science that social constructivist and material culture approaches sought to move beyond). Rachel A. Ankeny and Sabina Leonelli have argued that 'model organisms' are a distinctive category of experimental animal characterised by their explicit role to facilitate comparative modes of research. Model organisms model specific objects; serving as an epistemological and ontological bridge between research tool and object of research, animal and human. Model organisms, Ankeny and Leonelli argue, are identified through reference to their 'representational scope' (how far results from a model can be generalised) and 'representational target' (the object to be understood through use of the model).[67] When applied historically this approach interrogates the material culture of scientific production by probing the conditions of validity for a given model. Working at the intersection of the history and philosophy of science, Ankeny and Leonelli are interested in the epistemic commitments which accompany the use of model organisms; their aim is to understand the epistemological rules which govern the validity of animal research. Here, historical approaches allow Ankeny and Leonelli to demonstrate how societal structures, relations and values become entangled within the epistemological work of animal research. They show, for instance, how the construction of models for complex behavioural conditions such as alcoholism place emphasis on the situatedness of the animal, resulting in the experimental environment as much as the animal itself being standardised.[68] In a superlative series of articles exploring the work of John B. Calhoun and the pathological consequence of crowding, Edmundo Ramsden, sometime collaborator with Ankeny and Leonelli, has revealed how the epistemological demands of behavioural research necessarily expanded the vision of researchers so as include the environment as a means to control and standardise the animal body.[69] Whilst Ramsden stops short of considering the moral or ethical consequences of the wider impact of the experimental environment upon the animal, this question has increasingly been taken up by social scientists and is deserving of rigorous historical attention (a theme of my own work).[70]

Why, we might ask, are sociologists of science beginning to probe the role of affect, emotion and welfare concerns within the epistemology and material practice of animal research whereas the history of science has been slow to engage with such questions? One possibility is that historians of science all too often continue to work with a vision of science which is too close to that of science's own terms; as Daston reminds us, 'we are heirs to a tradition where facts are opposed to values' and so 'neither emotions nor values intrude upon the core of science'.[71] Commonly, emotion is considered a challenge to the production of scientific knowledge as it concerns subjective states, introduced through practices and an accompanying language which places 'truth' in the eye of the individual beholder as opposed to 'objective' verifiable evidence. Historians of science tend to mirror their scientific actors predominantly because their evidence is often a representation of the ideal as opposed to a record of the actual. Sociological, anthropological and ethnographic studies of animal research have the advantage of observing science as it happens for what it is; whereas historians are confined to studying scattered remnants of representations of what science was meant to be. Where emotion appears in existing historiography on animal research it tends to be framed in such a way as to conform closely to the sciences' own terms; emotions are problematic and they are recognised only insofar as they have to be controlled and removed from the experimental encounter. The behavioural sciences, for instance, emphasise the role of the environment in shaping behaviour; thus Ramsden, in studying behavioural scientists such as Calhoun, argues that controlling the environment is important to the material production of scientific 'objectivity' (which it was). Similarly, Otniel Dror found that early twentieth-century physiologists acknowledged the emotional experience of research animals and used it as a conceptual, rhetorical, political, and practical tool in their work. Emotion, up to and including suffering, was prominent within physiological discourses because researchers recognised affective states impacted on their object of study; as Dror shows, '[p]hysiological knowledge demanded pain-free animals'.[72] For physiologists, acknowledging and controlling animal emotion brought additional political advantages in serving as a counter to antivivisection critique. Safeguarding experimental animals by minimising exposure to suffering was not just a moral good but a scientific necessity.[73] In a systematic and nuanced study of the physiologist I.P. Pavlov, Daniel Todes goes further, to show how animal emotion has played a productive role in the ecology of scientific knowledge. Contrary to the strict opposition of values to facts, Todes reveals how informal acknowledgment of animal emotion provided scope for flexibility in interpreting the results of animal-based research. Within Pavlov's laboratory, animals who appeared 'happy' were considered healthy and thus 'normal', providing reliable data. However, where animals displayed unexpected results these could be discounted if their appearance was judged emotionally aberrant.[74] In this way, animal emotion played an important and productive epistemological role within the 'everyday' practice of Pavlov's science (albeit in ways that were unacknowledged in published works).[75]

The history of science has developed a number of methodological and analytic approaches which include the animal within the historiography of science. However, this has been achieved without making the animal of the human–animal relationship the *object* of investigation. Historians of science remain focussed on the production of scientific knowledge; the animal enters their vision only to the extent it plays a role in the 'ecology of scientific knowledge'. Animals only *matter* in these accounts to the extent that they shape or are shaped by science. Social and culturally orientated historians of science have been more attentive to broader political, societal, economic and cultural themes that shape the broader landscape of animal research. Susan Lederer, for example, has shown how scientific publication practices have been shaped by the culture of antivivisection as journal editors responded to public criticism of animal research by instituting policies which diminished the visibility of animals' representation in scientific papers; for instance photos were discouraged 'when the condition of the animal is unsightly'.[76] Such studies, however, in moving to the macro scale of social relations, tend to engage with cultural representations and appropriation of animals. As a result, experimental animals are displaced within these historical narratives in much the same way as they have been within social history. Ultimately, for much of the historiography of science, science remains an all-too-human activity.

Conclusion: And say the laboratory animal responded? A path to the moral ecology of science

Theoretical approaches developed within animal studies and related fields suggest the animal is worthy of study in itself; this is a political as much as an intellectual standpoint. The history of science has been slow to respond to this challenge but there is no reason why the historical study of science should be an exception. On the contrary, the work of Donna Haraway is testament to the capacity of the history of science to be political. More than a testament, in asking '[w]hen we have never been human, what is to be done?' Haraway invites the history of science to take a stance.[77] What would the history of science look like if we were to take seriously an approach which framed the 'ecology of scientific knowledge' as a genuinely relational and situated process through which the human and animal were made and remade over time? There is evidence to suggest that affective, moral and ethical values shape the choice of species scientists choose to work with and in so doing change the way scientists understand their own identity as well as how society values the species under study. None other than Claude Bernard, successor to Magendie and the villain of many nineteenth-century antivivisectionist narratives, refused to work with monkeys on the apparent grounds that the species too closely resembled humanity.[78] What does this mean for how Bernard understand both humanity and the 'nonhuman' primate? We might ask the same of Bell: what was it about his encounter with experimental animals which led him to respond as he did? If the material culture of experimental practice (or 'moral economy of science') is as critical as historians of science have claimed in shaping the 'ecology of scientific knowledge', then the question of how affective, moral, and ethical values have been enacted within, and thus transformed by, animal research, becomes an urgent area of historical inquiry. This would productively align the macro-concerns of social historians with the micro-concerns of historians of science to reveal how the values of science and those of society co-develop over time; shaping and being shaped by animal research. What we begin to see here is neither a moral economy of science nor an ecology of scientific knowledge. Rather, it is the potential to develop a 'moral ecology of science'.

A moral ecology of science would be sensitive to the 'moral economy' in the sense of Kohler and that of Daston. It would include the embodied experience of affect and emotion as well as the moral, cultural and other subjective values as situated positive components of the ecology of scientific production. Within the frame of a moral ecology of science, historical analysis would be extended to encompass questions of how the embodied emotion alongside affective, moral and other values shape and are shaped by human–animal experimental encounter which in turn drives scientific activity and knowledge production.[79] Such an approach would not only catalyse new historical questions but could serve to align approaches and concerns of the history of science with those of social history to produce more than the sum of their parts. To sketch an example, social historians have explained why dogs, cats and equines possessed privileged ethical status in late nineteenth-century discourses and regulations around animal research – because of the status these species held within everyday society.[80] We might, then, ask why, in the closing decades of the twentieth century, nonhuman primates had become the species of most concern within the discourses opposing animal research? Unlike nineteenth-century dogs, cats and equines, late twentieth-century nonhuman primates were not active visible components of everyday life in 'modern' urban society. So where might we find an answer? Arguably, heightened societal concerns for nonhuman primates as a species of privileged ethical value historically emerged through their use as experimental animals. It was the knowledge thereby gained of their cognitive, behavioural and social complexity which served as the conditions of possibility for social movements such as the Great Ape Project.[81]

From this perspective, the *raison d'être* of the use of animals within scientific research contains its own negation; species are used because of their proximity to the human. The more that proximity is experienced and understood the more difficult it becomes to sustain ethical arguments for their continued use. Evidence can be found in the 1979 report of a UK governmental inquiry into the LD50 test – a procedure which at the time had faced strong criticism from the reinvigorated animal advocacy movement. The scientific use of nonhuman-primates was not in any way related to the LD50 test and formed no part of the inquiry. Nevertheless, quite outside its remit, and responding to the testimony of scientists and technicians who worked with nonhuman primates, the report highlighted that:

> primates are in terms of evolution closer to man than cats or dogs and so possibly more likely to experience pain and apprehension to the same extent as a human being. Those who have worked with them, we are told, often feel a particular affinity with and sympathy for them which they do not feel for other species.[82]

As a result, nonhuman primates were included with the small group of highly protected species within the then regulatory framework for animal research in the UK, in essence gaining a privileged ethical position which dogs, cats, asses and mules had enjoyed since 1876. Nonhuman primates gained this status not through the imposition of social values external to science but rather through recognition of emergent relational and situated values shared by science and society.

What scientists, animal technicians and care staff had articulated in 1979 of their own accord was then a concern for the nonhuman primate. Moreover, what they reported was a recognition of the capacity of nonhuman primates to respond as opposed to merely react to an experimental encounter. In conclusion, I would argue that one approach to the historical study of a 'moral ecology of science' would be to borrow and repurpose the Derridean question: and say the animal responded?[83] Within the history of science, how have the responses of experimental animals been productively recognised; not to close them down but to productively open them up as drivers of historical change? And to what effect? In what ways have scientists, technicians and related researchers recognised the responses of experimental animals and thereby learned to better relate responsibly toward those animals? Taking up such questions would bring the history of science into dialogue with broader work across the humanities and social sciences which seeks to understand animals generally and animal research specifically, not least the influential work of Vinciane Despret, who mobilises the history of science to make a plea to resist the removal of passion from knowledge production:

> to 'de-passion' knowledge does not give us a more objective world, it just gives us a world 'without us'; and therefore, without 'them' – lines are traced so fast. And as long as this world appears as a world 'we don't care for', it also becomes an impoverished world, a world of minds without bodies, of bodies without minds, bodies without hearts, expectations, interests, a world of enthusiastic automata observing strange and mute creatures; in other words, a poorly articulated (and poorly articulating) world.[84]

If further impetus was desired for understanding the history of animal research through a moral ecology of science, attentive to the productive role of affect, emotion, moral and other subjective values, then this would be it.

Notes

1 L. Birke, A. Arluke, and M. Michael, *The Sacrifice: How Scientific Experiments Transform Animals and People*, West Lafayette IN: Purdue University Press, 2007, 187.
2 A. Cunningham (ed.), *The Laboratory Revolution in Medicine*, Cambridge: Cambridge University Press, 1998.
3 F.J. Sulloway, 'Darwin and his finches: the evolution of a legend', *Journal of the History of Biology* 15, 1 (1982): 1–53; J.A. Secord, 'Nature's fancy: Charles Darwin and the breeding of pigeons', *Isis* 72, 2 (1981): 162–186 (but see B. Theunissen, 'Darwin and his pigeons: the analogy between artificial and natural selection revisited', *Journal of the History of Biology* 45, 2 (2012): 179–212). For the role of dogs in Darwin's thought see P. Howell, *At Home and Astray: The Domestic Dog in Victorian Britain*, Charlottesville VA: University of Virginia Press, 2015, 102–124.
4 A classic overview of the history of behavioural science is R. Boakes, *From Darwin to Behaviourism*, Cambridge: Cambridge University Press, 2008. For ethology see R.W. Burkhardt, *Patterns of Behavior: Konrad Loren, Niko Tinbergen and the Founding of Ethology*, Chicago IL: University of Chicago Press, 2005. For an insightful history of changing relations of the epistemologies of field and laboratory see R.E. Kohler, *Landscapes and Labscapes: Exploring the Lab-field Border in Biology*, Chicago IL: University of Chicago Press, 2002.

5 An excellent example is J.F.M. Clark, *Bugs and the Victorians*, New Haven CT: Yale University Press, 2003.
6 W.F. Bynum, '"C'est un malade": animal models and concepts of human diseases', *Journal of the History of Medicine and Allied Sciences* 45, 3 (1990): 397–413.
7 See A.H. Maehle and U. Trohler, 'Animal experimentation from antiquity to the end of the eighteenth century', in N.A. Rupke (ed.), *Vivisection in Historical Perspective,* London: Routledge, 1987, 14–47; A. Guerrini, *Experimenting with Humans and Animals: From Galen to Animal Rights*, Baltimore MD: Johns Hopkins University Press, 2003.
8 N.D Jewson, 'The disappearance of the sick-man from medical cosmology, 1770–1870', *Sociology* 10, 2 (1976): 225–244; M. Foucault, *The Birth of the Clinic*, London: Routledge, 1997 [originally published 1973].
9 Jewson and Foucault remain powerful frames for medical history in spite of their respective claims resting more on conceptual elegance than empirical evidence: see M.E. Fissell, 'The disappearance of the patient's narrative and the invention of hospital medicine', in R. French and A. Wear (eds.), *British Medicine in an Age of Reform*, London: Routledge, 1991, 91–109.
10 For an overview of medical history see W.F. Bynum *et al.*, *The Western Medical Tradition: 1800 to 2000*, Cambridge: Cambridge University Press, 2006.
11 D.B. Weiner and M.J. Sauter, 'The city of Paris and the rise of clinical medicine', *Osiris* 18, (2003): 23–42.
12 J.E. Lesch, *Science and Medicine in France: The Emergence of Experimental Physiology, 1790–1855*, Cambridge MA: Harvard University Press, 1984; W.F. Bynum, *Science and the Practice of Medicine in the Nineteenth Century*, Cambridge: Cambridge University Press, 1994.
13 Vivisection, from the Latin *v vus* (living) and *sectio* (cutting), referred literally to the cutting of living bodies. Over time, the necessity of surgery decreased dramatically across the varied scientific uses of animals. Consequently, 'vivisection' became a less useful description of scientific practice. Nevertheless, vivisection continued to be used by those opposed to animal research long after scientific discourse abandoned the term.
14 In an otherwise fascinating account of the way French medicine shaped and was shaped by the turbulent politics of early nineteenth-century France, Jacyna describes how a contemporary commentator acknowledged Magendie's many contributions to physiological knowledge, before noting that few liked 'this pitiless assassin of poor dogs, the only true friends we have in this world' but without examining what this might mean. See L.S. Jacyna, 'Medical science and moral science: the cultural relations of physiology in Restoration France', *History of Science* 25, 2 (1987): 111–146, 137.
15 Quoted in Guerrini, *Experimenting*, 70.
16 C.A. Recarte, 'Anti-French discourse in the nineteenth-century British antivivisection movement', *Atlantis* 36, 1 (2014): 31–49.
17 F.P. Cobbe, 'The rights of man and the claims of brutes', *Fraser's Magazine* 68, (1863): 586–602, reprinted in S. Hamilton (ed.), *Animal Welfare and Antivivisection 1870–1910: Nineteenth-Century Women's Mission, Volume 1: Frances Power Cobbe*, London: Routledge 2004, 1–49.
18 C. Berkowitz, *Charles Bell and the Anatomy of Reform*, Chicago IL: University of Chicago Press, 2015.
19 C. Berkowitz, 'Disputed discovery: vivisection and experiment in the 19th century', *Endeavour* 30, 3 (2006): 98–102.
20 C. Bell, *The Nervous System of the Human Body*, London: Henry Renshaw, 1844, 25.
21 G. Rice, 'The Bell-Magendie-Walker controversy', *Medical History* 31, 2 (1987): 190–200, 198, n. 32.

22 Subsequent British vivisectionists in contrast made a virtue of the humanitarian goals of animal research; see for instance R. Boddice, 'Vivisecting Major: a Victorian gentleman scientist defends animal experimentation, 1876–1885', *Isis* 102, 2 (2011): 215–237.
23 See for example 'On experiments on living animals', *London Medical Gazette* 20 (1937): 804–808; P.F. Cranefield, *The Way In and the Way Out: Francois Magendie, Charles Bell and the Roots of the Spinal Nerves*, New York: Futura, 1974.
24 C. Lansbury, 'Gynaecology, pornography, and the antivivisection movement', *Victorian Studies* 28, 3 (1985): 413–437, 422. See also C. Lansbury, *The Old Brown Dog: Women, Workers, and Vivisection in Edwardian England*, Madison WI: University of Wisconsin Press, 1985.
25 C. Buettinger, 'Women and antivivisection in late nineteenth-century America', *Journal of Social History* 30, 4 (1997): 857–872.
26 M.R. Finn, 'Dogs and females: vivisection, feminists and the novelist Rachilde', *French Cultural Studies* 23, 3 (2012): 190–201, 197.
27 C. Buettinger, 'Antivivisection and the charge of zoophil-psychosis in the early twentieth century', *The Historian* 55, 2 (1993): 277–288.
28 Finn 'Dogs and females', 198.
29 See L. Bending, *The Representation of Bodily Pain in Late Nineteenth-Century English Culture*, Oxford: Oxford University Press, 2000.
30 H. Ritvo, *The Animal Estate: The English and Other Creatures in the Victorian Age*, London: Penguin, 1990, 156; H. Ritvo, *Noble Cows and Hybrid Zebras: Essays on Animals and History*, Charlottesville VA: University of Virginia Press, 2010, esp. chapter 5, 73–90.
31 J. Turner, *Reckoning with the Beast: Animals, Pain and Humanity in the Victorian Mind*, Baltimore MD: Johns Hopkins University Press, 1980.
32 R. D. French, *Antivivisection and Medical Science in Victorian Society*, Princeton NJ: Princeton University Press, 1975, 412. This remains the definitive historical study of antivivisection in the late nineteenth century.
33 H. Kean, 'The "smooth cool men of science": the feminist and socialist response to vivisection', *History Workshop Journal* 40 (1995): 16–38.
34 E. Fudge, 'A left-handed blow: writing the history of animals', in N. Rothfels (ed.), *Representing Animals*, Indianapolis IN: Indiana University Press, 2002, 3–18, 6–7.
35 Which is to say histories not of animals per se, not of animals in place of humans, but rather histories that recognise that the human is materially and symbolically created and sustained through its relationships with other than human historical actors.
36 J. Lorimer, *Wildlife in the Anthropocene: Conservation After Nature*, Minneapolis MN: University of Minnesota Press, 2015, in addition to being an excellent argument for rethinking the ontological status of 'wildlife' equally provides a lucid overview of how different and often challenging literatures can be brought together around shared themes of hybridity.
37 For instance, Donna Haraway characterised narratives which separate the knowing subject from the object known so as to produce 'objective' science as performing an 'illusion' akin to the 'god trick'. On this reading objectivity is rendered immanent, situated in particular practices, places and times. See D. Haraway, 'Situated knowledges: the science question in feminism and the privilege of partial perspective', *Feminist Studies* 14, 3 (1988): 575–599, 582.
38 R.M. Young, 'Science is social relations', *Radical Science Journal* 5, (1977): 65–129.
39 For a lucid overview of the core issues within this historiographic trend, together with analysis of the subsequent 'science wars' of the 1990s, see I. Hacking, *The Social Construction of What?* Cambridge MA: Harvard University Press, 1999.

40 D. Haraway, *Primate Visions: Gender, Race, and Nature in the World of Modern Science*, London: Routledge, 1989, 1.
41 In challenging simple dualisms such as nature-culture, human-animal, sex-gender, Haraway opens fertile ground for rethinking human relations to animals and remaking the world we share whilst simultaneously undermining any uncritical resort to 'science'. Some primatologists, however, reacted unfavourably to what they saw as an attack on the scientific credibility of their work, see for instance M. Cartmill, 'Review: Primate Visions: Gender, Race, and Nature in the World of Modern Science', *International Journal of Primatology* 12, 1 (1991): 67–75. Others were more favourable, see in particular S.C. Strum and L.M. Fedigan (eds.), *Primate Encounters: Models of Science, Gender and Society*, Chicago IL: University of Chicago Press, 2000.
42 Characteristic of Haraway's writing, 'technoscience', alongside terms such as 'naturecultures', challenges the way language reifies dichotomy. For an introduction to her thought, see D. Haraway, *The Haraway Reader*, London: Routledge, 2003.
43 For example E. Fudge, 'Milking other men's beasts', *History and Theory* 52, 4 (2013): 13–38; S. Nance, *Entertaining Elephants: Animal Agency and the Business of the American Circus*, Baltimore MD: Johns Hopkins University Press, 2013.
44 Latour has continuously fought and lost a battle to extract himself from the work which made his name, as one writing that 'there are four things that do not work with actor-network theory; the word actor, the word network, the word theory and the hyphen' (see 'On recalling ANT', *Sociological Review* 47, S1 (1999): 15–25). For a lengthy and lucid critique and re-presentation of his earlier work see B. Latour, *Reassembling the Social: An Introduction to Actor-Network-Theory*, Oxford: Oxford University Press, 2007.
45 R. Kohler, *Lords of the Fly: Drosophila Genetics and the Experimental Life*, Chicago IL: University of Chicago Press, 1994.
46 J. Harwood, *Styles of Scientific Thought: The German Genetics Community, 1900–1933*, Chicago IL: University of Chicago Press, 1993.
47 Kohler, *Lords of the Fly*, 3.
48 E.P. Thomson used 'moral economy' to capture the normative social values which governed a local economy most famously in his example of eighteenth-century food riots. See E.P. Thompson, 'The moral economy of the English crowd in the eighteenth century', *Past and Present* 50 (1971): 76–136.
49 Kohler, *Lords of the Fly*, 50.
50 A pertinent and interesting element of Latour's thought is his challenge to the assumption that technologies belong in the realm of means whereas questions of moral value apply to ends. Thus technologies can embody moral values. See for instance B. Latour, 'Morality and technology: the end of the means', *Theory, Culture and Society* 19, 5–6 (2002): 247–260. In my own work I extend this argument to show how technologies such as the laboratory animal cage 'materialise' societal and moral values. The same could be said of the various technologies that facilitate companion animal relations (e.g. dog leads). See for example R.G.W. Kirk, 'Care in the cage: materializing moral economies of animal care in the biomedical sciences, c.1945', in K. Bjørkdahl and T. Druglitrø (eds.), *Animal Housing and Human–Animal Relations: Politics, Practices and Infrastructures*, London: Routledge, 2016, 167–184, 167–168.
51 R.G.W. Kirk, 'A brave new animal for a brave new world: the British Laboratory Animals Bureau and the constitution of international standards of laboratory animal production and use, circa 1947–1968', *Isis* 101, 1 (2010): 62–94.
52 A.N. Worden and W. Lane-Petter, *The UFAW Handbook on the Care and Management of Laboratory Animals*, London: UFAW, 1957, 859–867.

53 R.G.W. Kirk, 'The invention of the 'stressed animal' and the development of a science of animal welfare, 1947–86', in D. Cantor and E. Ramsden (eds.), *Stress, Shock, and Adaptation in the Twentieth Century*, Rochester NY: University of Rochester Press, 2014, 241–263.
54 Whereas Kohler consciously adapts his understanding of 'moral economy' from the work of E.P. Thompson, Daston, in contrast, appears to have coined the term independently – only latterly realising that her appeal 'to "economies" of affects and values has little to do with Thompson's accounts of corn markets and the tradition of "setting the price" by persuasion or riot, although it does appeal to a broader sense of "legitimizing notion"': see L. Daston, 'The moral economy of science', *Osiris* 10 (1995): 2–24.
55 M. Lederman and R.M. Burian, 'The right organism for the job', *Journal of the History of Biology* 26 (1993): 235–367.
56 A.E. Clarke and J. Fujimura (eds.), *The Right Tool for the Job: At Work in Twentieth-Century Life Sciences*, Princeton NJ: Princeton University Press, 1992, 4–5.
57 P. Palladino, 'Review: bringing the world into the laboratory, or the (ir)resistible rise of Drosophila-melanogaste', *British Journal for the History of Science* 29, 2 (1996): 217–221, 221.
58 Daston, 'Moral economy', 3.
59 B.T. Clause, 'The Wistar rat as a right choice: establishing mammalian standards and the ideal of a standardized mammal', *Journal of the History of Biology* 26, 2 (1993): 329–349.
60 See S.L. Star and M. Lampland (eds.), *Standards and Their Stories: How Quantifying, Classifying, and Formalizing Practices Shape Everyday Life*, Ithaca NY: Cornell University Press, 2008.
61 C.A. Logan, 'Before there were standards: the role of test animals in the production of empirical generality in physiology', *Journal of the History of Biology* 35, 2 (2002): 329–363.
62 Clause, 'The Wistar rat', 348–349.
63 K. Rader, *Making Mice: Standardizing Animals for American Biomedical Research, 1900–1955*, Princeton NJ: Princeton University Press, 2004.
64 Rader, *Making Mice*, 251.
65 In contrast to Britain, during the period of Rader's study American animal research was loosely and diversely governed by state laws but no federal law existed to govern tensions between scientific and societal values until 1966. As enacted, the Animal Welfare Act (1966) established minimum 'standards' of care and management for animals but defined the term animal in such a way as to exclude a number of commonly used experimental animal species including mice.
66 Rader, *Making Mice*, 152–153.
67 R.A. Ankeny and S. Leonelli, 'What's so special about model organisms?' *Studies in History and Philosophy of Science Part A* 42, 2 (2011): 313–323.
68 S. Leonelli, R.A. Ankeny, N.C. Nelson, and E. Ramsden, 'Making organisms model human behavior: situated models in North-American alcohol research, 1950-onwards', *Science in Context* 27, 3 (2014): 485–509.
69 See for instance E. Ramsden, 'From rodent utopia to urban hell: population, pathology, and the crowded rats of NIMH', *Isis* 102, 4 (2011): 659–688.
70 See C. Friese, 'Realizing potential in translational medicine: the uncanny emergence of care as science', *Current Anthropology* 54, S7 (2013): S129–S138; N. Nelson, 'Model homes for model organisms: intersections of animal welfare and behavioral neuroscience around the environment of the laboratory mouse', *BioSocieties* 11, 1 (2016): 46–66. See R.G.W. Kirk, 'Between the clinic and the laboratory: ethology and pharmacology in the work of Michael Robin Alexander Chance, c.1946–1964', *Medical History* 53, 4 (2009): 513–536.
71 Daston, 'Moral economy of science', 2.
72 O.E. Dror, 'The affect of experiment: the turn to emotions in Anglo-American physiology, 1900–1940', *Isis* 90, 2 (1999): 205–237, 210.

73 Dror, 'The affect of experiment', 233–236.
74 D.P. Todes, *Pavlov's Physiology Factory: Experiment, Interpretation, Laboratory Enterprise*, Baltimore MD: Johns Hopkins University Press, 2002.
75 I have observed similar uses of anthropomorphic language and recognition of animal emotion; see for example R.G.W. Kirk, 'In dogs we trust? Intersubjectivity, response-able relations, and the making of mine detector dogs', Journal of the History of the Behavioral Sciences 50, 1 (2013): 1–36.
76 S.E. Lederer, 'Political animals: the shaping of biomedical research literature in twentieth-century America', *Isis* 83, 1 (1992): 61–79, 71.
77 N. Gane, 'When we have never been human, what is to be done? Interview with Donna Haraway', *Theory, Culture & Society* 23, 7–8 (2006): 135–158.
78 J. Schiller, 'Claude Bernard and vivisection', *Journal of the History of Medicine and Allied Sciences* 22, 3 (1967): 246–260, 255, n. 88. Bernard's view is distinctive in that the monkey was not a species that arrowed particular concern within the antivivisectionist movement; the latter privileged dogs, horses and equines and cats as deserving of particular moral concern.
79 My own work has tentatively developed in this direction; for example Kirk, 'In dogs we trust?'.
80 See French, *Antivivisection*, esp. 394–395. Species also shaped the practice of Victorian animal research: see R. Boddice, 'Species of compassion: aesthetics, anaesthetics, and pain in the physiological laboratory', *19: Interdisciplinary Studies in the Long Nineteenth Century*, 15 (2012).
81 P. Singer and P. Cavalieri (eds.), *The Great Ape Project: Equality Beyond Humanity*, London: Fourth Estate, 1993.
82 *Report on the LD50 Test Presented to the Secretary of State by the Advisory Committee on the Administration of the Cruelty to Animals Act 1876*, London: HMSO, 1979, 17–18.
83 J. Derrida, *The Animal That Therefore I Am*, New York: Fordham University Press, 2008, 119–140. But see Haraway's important corrective in D. Haraway, *When Species Meet*, Minneapolis MN: University of Minnesota Press, 2008, 19–20.
84 V. Despret, 'The body we care for: figures of anthro-zoo-genesis', *Body & Society* 10, 2 (2004): 111–134, 131.

Bibliography

Ankeny, R.A. and Leonelli, S. 'What's so special about model organisms?' *Studies in History and Philosophy of Science Part A* 42, 2 (2011): 313–323.

Bending, L. *The Representation of Bodily Pain in Late Nineteenth-Century English Culture*, Oxford: Oxford University Press, 2000.

Bell, C. *The Nervous System of the Human Body*, London: Henry Renshaw, 1844.

Berkowitz, C. 'Disputed discovery: vivisection and experiment in the 19th century', *Endeavour* 30, 3 (2006): 98–102.

Berkowitz, C. *Charles Bell and the Anatomy of Reform*, Chicago IL: University of Chicago Press, 2015.

Birke, L., Arluke, A., and Michael, M. *The Sacrifice: How Scientific Experiments Transform Animals and People*, West Lafayette IN: Purdue University Press, 2007.

Boakes, R. *From Darwin to Behaviourism*, Cambridge: Cambridge University Press, 2008.

Boddice, R. 'Vivisecting Major: a Victorian gentleman scientist defends animal experimentation, 1876–1885', *Isis* 102, 2 (2011): 215–237.

Boddice, R. 'Species of compassion: aesthetics, anaesthetics, and pain in the physiological laboratory', *19: Interdisciplinary Studies in the Long Nineteenth Century*, 15 (2012).

Buettinger, C. 'Antivivisection and the charge of zoophil-psychosis in the early twentieth century', *The Historian* 55, 2 (1993): 277–288.

Buettinger, C. 'Women and antivivisection in late nineteenth-century America', *Journal of Social History* 30, 4 (1997): 857–872.

Burkhardt, R.W. *Patterns of Behavior: Konrad Lorenz, Niko Tinbergen and the Founding of Ethology*, Chicago IL: University of Chicago Press, 2005.

Bynum, W.F. '"C'est un malade": animal models and concepts of human diseases', *Journal of the History of Medicine and Allied Sciences* 45, 3 (1990): 397–413.

Bynum, W.F. *Science and the Practice of Medicine in the Nineteenth Century*, Cambridge: Cambridge University Press, 1994.

Bynum, W.F., Hardy, A., Jacyna, S., Lawrence, C., and Tansey, E.M. *The Western Medical Tradition: 1800 to 2000*, Cambridge: Cambridge University Press, 2006.

Cartmill, M. 'Review: Primate visions: gender, race, and nature in the world of modern science', *International Journal of Primatology* 12, 1 (1991): 67–75.

Clark, J.F.M. *Bugs and the Victorians*, New Haven CT: Yale University Press, 2003.

Clarke, A.E. and Fujimura J. (eds.), *The Right Tool for the Job: At Work in Twentieth-Century Life Sciences*, Princeton NJ: Princeton University Press, 1992.

Clause, B.T. 'The Wistar rat as a right choice: establishing mammalian standards and the ideal of a standardized mammal', *Journal of the History of Biology* 26, 2 (1993): 329–349.

Cobbe, F.P. 'The rights of man and the claims of brutes', in S. Hamilton (ed.), *Animal Welfare and Antivivisection 1870–1910: Nineteenth-Century Women's Mission, Volume 1: Frances Power Cobbe*, London: Routledge, 2004, 1–49.

Cranefield, P.F. *The Way In and the Way Out: Francois Magendie, Charles Bell and the Roots of the Spinal Nerves*, New York: Futura, 1974.

Cunningham, A. (ed.), *The Laboratory Revolution in Medicine*, Cambridge: Cambridge University Press, 1998.

Daston, L. 'The moral economy of science', *Osiris* 10 (1995): 2–24.

Derrida, J. *The Animal That Therefore I Am*. New York: Fordham University Press, 2008.

Despret, V. 'The body we care for: figures of anthro-zoo-genesis', *Body & Society* 10, 2–3 (2004): 111–134.

Dror, O.E. 'The affect of experiment: the turn to emotions in Anglo-American physiology, 1900–1940', *Isis* 90, 2 (1999): 205–237.

Finn, M.R. 'Dogs and females: vivisection, feminists and the novelist Rachilde', *French Cultural Studies* 23, 3 (2012): 190–201.

Fissell, M.E. 'The disappearance of the patient's narrative and the invention of hospital medicine', in R. French and A. Wear (eds.), *British Medicine in an Age of Reform*, London: Routledge, 1991, 91–109.

Foucault, M. *The Birth of the Clinic*, London: Routledge, 1997.

French, R.D. *Antivivisection and Medical Science in Victorian Society*, Princeton NJ: Princeton University Press, 1975.

Friese, C. 'Realizing potential in translational medicine: the uncanny emergence of care as science', *Current Anthropology* 54, S7 (2013): S129–S138.

Fudge, E. 'A left-handed blow: writing the history of animals', in N. Rothfels (ed.), *Representing Animals*, Indianapolis IN: Indiana University Press, 2002, 3–18.

Fudge, E. 'Milking other men's beasts', *History and Theory* 52, 4 (2013): 13–38.

Gane, N. 'When we have never been human, what is to be done? Interview with Donna Haraway', *Theory, Culture & Society* 23, 7–8 (2006): 135–158.

Guerrini, A. *Experimenting with Humans and Animals: From Galen to Animal Rights*, Baltimore MD: Johns Hopkins University Press, 2003.

Hacking, I. *The Social Construction of What?* Cambridge MA: Harvard University Press, 1999.

Haraway, D. 'Situated knowledges: the science question in feminism and the privilege of partial perspective', *Feminist Studies* 14, 3 (1988): 575–599.
Haraway, D. *Primate Visions: Gender, Race, and Nature in the World of Modern Science*, London: Routledge, 1989.
Haraway, D. *The Haraway Reader*, London: Routledge, 2003.
Haraway, D. *When Species Meet*, Minneapolis MN: University of Minnesota Press, 2008.
Harwood, J. *Styles of Scientific Thought: The German Genetics Community, 1900–1933*, Chicago IL: University of Chicago Press, 1993.
Howell, P. *At Home and Astray: The Domestic Dog in Victorian Britain*, Charlottesville VA: University of Virginia Press, 2015.
Jacyna, L.S. 'Medical science and moral science: the cultural relations of physiology in Restoration France', *History of Science* 25, 2 (1987): 111–146.
Jewson, N.D. 'The disappearance of the sick-man from medical cosmology, 1770–1870', *Sociology* 10, 2 (1976): 225–244.
Kean, H. 'The "smooth cool men of science": the feminist and socialist response to vivisection', *History Workshop Journal* 40 (1995): 16–38.
Kirk, R.G.W. 'Between the clinic and the laboratory: ethology and pharmacology in the work of Michael Robin Alexander Chance, c.1946–1964', *Medical History* 53, 4 (2009): 513–536.
Kirk, R.G.W. 'A brave new animal for a brave new world: the British Laboratory Animals Bureau and the constitution of international standards of laboratory animal production and use, circa 1947–1968', *Isis* 101, 1 (2010): 62–94.
Kirk, R.G.W. 'In dogs we trust? Intersubjectivity, response-able relations, and the making of mine detector dogs', *Journal of the History of the Behavioral Sciences* 50, 1 (2013): 1–36.
Kirk, R.G.W. 'The Invention of the 'stressed animal' and the development of a science of animal welfare, 1947–86', in D. Cantor and E. Ramsden (eds.), *Stress, Shock, and Adaptation in the Twentieth Century*, Rochester NY: University of Rochester Press, 2014, 241–263.
Kirk, R.G.W. 'Care in the cage: materializing moral economies of animal care in the biomedical sciences, c.1945', in K. Bjørkdahl and T. Druglitrø (eds.), *Animal Housing and Human– Animal Relations: Politics, Practices and Infrastructures*, London: Routledge, 2016, 167–184.
Kohler, R. *Lords of the Fly: Drosophila Genetics and the Experimental Life*, Chicago IL: University of Chicago Press, 1994.
Kohler, R.E. *Landscapes and Labscapes: Exploring the Lab-Field Border in Biology*, Chicago IL: University of Chicago Press, 2002.
Lansbury, C. 'Gynaecology, pornography, and the antivivisection movement', *Victorian Studies* 28, 3 (1985): 413–437.
Lansbury, C. *The Old Brown Dog: Women, Workers, and Vivisection in Edwardian England*, Madison WI: University of Wisconsin Press, 1985.
Latour, B. 'On recalling ANT', *Sociological Review* 47, 1 (1999): 15–25.
Latour, B. 'Morality and technology: the end of the means', *Theory, Culture and Society* 18, 5/6 (2002): 247–260.
Latour, B. *Reassembling the Social: An Introduction to Actor-Network-Theory*, Oxford: Oxford University Press, 2007.
Lederer, S.E. 'Political animals: the shaping of biomedical research literature in twentieth-century America', *Isis* 83, 1 (1992): 61–79.
Lederman, M. and Burian, R.M. 'The right organism for the job', *Journal of the History of Biology* 26, (1993): 235–367.
Leonelli, S., Ankeny, R.A., Nelson, N.C., and Ramsden, E., 'Making organisms model human behavior: situated models in North-American alcohol research, 1950-onwards', *Science in Context* 27, 3 (2014): 485–509.

Lesch, J.E. *Science and Medicine in France: The Emergence of Experimental Physiology, 1790–1855*, Cambridge MA: Harvard University Press, 1984.

Logan, C.A. 'Before there were standards: the role of test animals in the production of empirical generality in physiology', *Journal of the History of Biology* 35, 2 (2002): 329–363.

Lorimer, J. *Wildlife in the Anthropocene: Conservation After Nature*, Minneapolis MN: University of Minnesota Press, 2015.

Maehle, A.H. and Trohler, U. 'Animal experimentation from antiquity to the end of the Eighteenth Century', in N.A. Rupke (ed.), *Vivisection in Historical Perspective*, London: Routledge, 1987, 14–47.

Nance, S. *Entertaining Elephants: Animal Agency and the Business of the American Circus*, Baltimore MD: Johns Hopkins University Press, 2013.

Nelson, N. 'Model homes for model organisms: intersections of animal welfare and behavioral neuroscience around the environment of the laboratory mouse', *BioSocieties* 11, 1 (2016): 46–66.

Palladino, P. 'Review: bringing the world into the laboratory, or the (ir)resistible rise of drosophila-melanogaste' *British Journal for the History of Science* 29, 2 (1996): 217–221.

Rader, K. *Making Mice: Standardizing Animals for American Biomedical Research, 1900–1955*, Princeton NJ: Princeton University Press, 2004.

Ramsden, E. 'From rodent utopia to urban hell: population, pathology, and the crowded rats of NIMH', *Isis* 102, 4 (2011): 659–688.

Recarte, C.A. 'Anti-French discourse in the nineteenth-century British Antivivisection movement', *Atlantis* 36, 1 (2014): 31–49.

Rice, G. 'The Bell-Magendie-Walker controversy', *Medical History* 31, 2 (1987): 190–200, 198, n. 32.

Ritvo, H. *The Animal Estate: the English and Other Creatures in the Victorian Age*, London: Penguin, 1990.

Ritvo, H. *Noble Cows and Hybrid Zebras: Essays on Animals and History*, Charlottesville VA: University of Virginia Press, 2010.

Rupke, N.A. (ed.), *Vivisection in Historical Perspective*, London: Routledge, 1987.

Schiller, J. 'Claude Bernard and vivisection', *Journal of the History of Medicine and Allied Sciences* 22, 3 (1967): 246–260.

Secord, J.A. 'Nature's fancy: Charles Darwin and the breeding of pigeons', *Isis* 72, 2 (1981): 162–186.

Singer, P. and Cavalieri, P. (eds.), *The Great Ape Project: Equality Beyond Humanity*, London: Fourth Estate, 1993.

Star, S.L. and Lampland, M. (eds.), *Standards and Their Stories: How Quantifying, Classifying, and Formalizing Practices Shape Everyday Life*, Ithaca NY: Cornell University Press, 2000.

Strum, S.C. and Fedigan, L.M. (eds.), *Primate Encounters, Models of Science, Gender and Society*, Chicago IL: University of Chicago Press.

Sulloway, F.J. 'Darwin and his finches: the evolution of a legend', *Journal of the History of Biology* 15, 1 (1982): 1–53.

Theunissen, B. 'Darwin and his pigeons: the analogy between artificial and natural selection revisited', *Journal of the History of Biology* 45, 2 (2012): 179–212.

Thompson, E.P. 'The moral economy of the English crowd in the eighteenth century', *Past and Present* 50 (1971): 76–136.

Todes, D.P. *Pavlov's Physiology Factory: Experiment, Interpretation, Laboratory Enterprise*, Baltimore MD: Johns Hopkins University Press, 2002.

Turner, J. *Reckoning with the Beast: Animals, Pain and Humanity in the Victorian Mind*, Baltimore MD: Johns Hopkins University Press, 1980.

Weiner, D.B. and Saunter, M.J. 'The city of Paris and the rise of clinical medicine', *Osiris* 18 (2003): 23–42.
Worden, A.N. and Lane-Petter, W. *The UFAW Handbook on the Care and Management of Laboratory Animals*, London: UFAW, 1957.
Young, R.M. 'Science *is* social relations', *Radical Science Journal* 5 (1977): 65–129.

7
ANIMALS IN THE HISTORY OF HUMAN AND VETERINARY MEDICINE

Abigail Woods

Introduction

Medicine is, by definition, a human-led endeavour. While animals have always suffered from disease, they only became participants in human and veterinary medicine when humans began to pay attention to their health and attempt to learn about and intervene in it. Historical analysis shows that this occurred particularly when human interests were threatened by the state of animal health, and when humans perceived benefits to arise from understanding and manipulating it. As objects of medicine, animals were refashioned into tools and targets of disease investigation, regulation and management. Their bodies, minds and lived experiences were profoundly affected by these transformations. However, animals were not only shaped by human/veterinary medicine, they also shaped it. Through their selection and use as raw material for experiments, they moulded the development of medical science. As a result of the investigations performed upon them, and in their ability to spread diseases to humans, they altered the state of human health, while as victims of disease they influenced animal health practices, policies and the people concerned with them.

The histories of animals and human/veterinary medicine are therefore deeply intertwined. The purpose of this chapter is to review what is known about their shared histories, to reflect on authors' approaches to the subject, and to identify some promising lines of recent and future enquiry. Focusing particularly on nineteenth and twentieth-century Western Europe and North America, it proceeds by discussing three animal roles that feature repeatedly in histories of human and veterinary medicine: as experimental material, transmitters of disease to humans, and victims of disease. The first role was co-constitutive with human medicine, the third with veterinary medicine, and the second straddled their boundaries. Each will be explored in turn. Taking up Hilda Kean's argument that while animals shape history, their contributions are only revealed by the humans that generate narratives about them, this account also identifies the contemporary agendas that inspired and shaped historians' narratives.[1]

Although historically, animals and medicine were intimately linked, the same cannot be said for the scholarly fields devoted to their investigation. In fact there is a striking disconnect between medical history and human–animal history. Each has its own journals, societies, methods, intellectual priorities, traditions and historiographies, which delineate authors' interests in, and approaches to, animals in medicine. To date, animals in medicine have attracted far more attention from medical than human–animal historians, which is surprising when one considers the extent to which animals shaped and were shaped by medicine.[2] Their neglect within human–animal history cannot be attributed to a lack of resources, because as subjects of newspaper reporting, government statistics, policy documents, veterinary case books, scientific journal articles, medical textbooks, and museum display, animals left rich traces on the medical historical record.[3] Rather, it may reflect human–animal historians' preferences for studying wild and pet animals rather than the rodents, horses and farmed livestock that were important to medicine, and for focusing on the symbolic aspects of animals rather than the material properties on which medicine depended.[4]

In comparison, medical historians have placed a greater emphasis on the materiality of animals and devoted considerable attention to horses, livestock and rodents. Whereas scholars in human–animal studies agonise long and hard about whether animals, as products of nature, can exert agency over human culture, medical historians see no contradiction in regarding them as 'biotechnologies' positioned between nature and culture.[5] As early converts to Latour's Actor-Network Theory, they readily acknowledge that animals – along with other material objects – possess agency, but unlike human–animal historians, they have not debated the nature of that agency, and remain largely untouched by the latter's efforts to bring animals from the margins to the centre of historical analysis.[6] Nor have animals benefitted from democratising tendencies within medical history, which have inspired the foregrounding of experiences of other marginalised groups such as working-class women, ethnic minorities and colonised peoples.[7] Consequently, while medical historians recognise the importance of animals, they usually treat them not as subjects with their own histories but as passive participants in human histories. The conclusion identifies some recent exceptions to this medical historical approach, and offers suggestions for how to build upon them in order to develop a richer, more wide-ranging account of animals within the history of human/veterinary medicine.

Experimental material

The most widely recognised role that animals performed within medical history was that of experimental material. Historians have written extensively about how scientists manipulated animals within their laboratories in order to illuminate the structure and function of healthy bodies, the nature and causes of disease, and how to prevent and manage it both medically and surgically.[8] They generally assume that the goal of such experiments was to advance human health, and that the status of the animal subject was that of human proxy or 'model'. They also identify many criticisms that resulted from using animals for experimental purposes, and efforts to control or minimise that use.[9]

Present-day agendas are partly responsible for the attention devoted to this subject. Recurrent debates about the validity of animal experiments have inspired interest in previous controversies, while the significance of animal experiments to medical science today has encouraged historians to investigate how this situation arose. Investigations have been aided by the rich resources generated by past debates and scientific enquiries. In the majority of historical writings, animals feature as shadowy, passive canvases on which medical scientists built knowledge, disciplines and reputations. Their 'disappearance' reflects how scientists de-constituted their bodies into anatomical components and physiological forces.[10] However, some authors award them greater prominence by analysing how scientists and anti-vivisectionists felt about animals, how scientists sourced, maintained, fashioned and manipulated them; and how animals influenced scientific objectives, methods and results.[11]

The use of animals for experimental purposes dates back to Greek times, but only became a mainstream feature of medical science during the nineteenth and twentieth centuries, particularly in Western Europe and North America. One key historical development was the emergence of experimental physiology as a field of scientific enquiry.[12] Typically, its scientists sought to determine how bodies worked by manipulating or disrupting particular functions and observing the results in experimental animals.[13] This was a distinctively different approach to the 'hospital medicine' favoured by clinicians, who sought to learn about disease by observing patients in life and dissecting their bodies after death. Experimental physiology therefore effected the 'disappearance' of patients as well as the dismembering of animal bodies.[14]

Experimental physiology emerged first in France at the turn of the nineteenth century, both within veterinary schools – which had facilities for experimenting on horses – and in the Paris School of Medicine, which offered training in surgical skills that some doctors subsequently applied to experimental animals.[15] It then spread to Germany, where experiments were characterised by the diversity of the species employed.[16] For Claude Bernard (1813–78), the leading French advocate of experimental physiology, animal experiments were entirely justified because human experiments were unethical, and the mere observation of human bodies could not reveal their functions.[17] He claimed that 'to learn how man and animals live, we cannot avoid seeing great numbers of them die'.[18] The experiences of experimental animals themselves were unimportant, for the scientist 'no longer hears the cry of animals, he no longer sees the blood that flows, he sees only his idea and perceives only organisms concealing problems which he intends to solve'.[19] Somewhat different opinions were voiced in Britain during the 1820s following a visit by Bernard's teacher, François Magendie (1783–1855), who performed experimental demonstrations on dogs. Spokespeople for the incipient movement for the protection of animals from cruelty criticised the suffering he inflicted, while the Scottish anatomist, Charles Bell – who claimed priority over Magendie in discovering the function of the spinal nerve roots – asserted that bodily function could be worked out equally well through the dissection of dead animals.[20]

These sentiments were one reason why experimental physiology was slow to take off in Britain compared with France and Germany. However, by the 1870s it had won several influential exponents, notably Michael Foster, who established a research school at Cambridge University, and John Burdon Sanderson, the first Professor-Superintendent of the Brown Institute of Comparative Pathology in London, and from 1874, Professor of Physiology at University College London. To train beginners in the skills required for animal experiment they and their physiologist colleagues published in 1873 a *Handbook for the Physiological Laboratory*. Its descriptions were graphic (for example in outlining physiological changes witnessed during animal asphyxiation), and it made few references to anaesthesia.[21]

The *Handbook* inspired the emergence of anti-vivisectionist organisations which incorporated men and women of diverse political views who claimed to speak for animals and actively opposed experiments upon them. They directed their efforts primarily at dogs: the experimental frog had few defenders.[22] They questioned the necessity for experiment, its morality and scientific utility. Imagining their pet dogs, and – in the case of women – themselves as patients undergoing similar treatment at the hands of male doctors, they condemned the scientists responsible, and voiced fears that they would extend their experimental activities to vulnerable humans, notably women and working-class men. The controversy culminated in legal restrictions to the performance of animal experiments in Britain under the 1876 Cruelty to Animals Act.[23] Similar protests emerged a little later in the USA, and caused editors of scientific journals to take preventive action. Through amending the content of articles received for publication they sought to disguise the details of experiments performed upon animals in order to defuse anti-vivisectionist critique.[24]

The emergence of bacteriology under Louis Pasteur (1822–95), Robert Koch (1843–1910) and others, was another key context in which animals were transformed into medical experimental material.[25] Inspired by the notion that infectious diseases were caused by germs, medical scientists used a range of animal species to culture, isolate and identify them, and to develop, test and standardise protective vaccines and sera. Experiments usually proceeded by injecting or inoculating animals and then killing them and subjecting their bodily tissues and fluids to pathological and bacteriological analysis.[26] Bruno Latour conceptualises these developments in terms of the recruitment of non-human and human agents into networks, which Pasteur used to dominate nature within the laboratory and thereby generate a new role for bacteriology within society. As laboratory experimental material and farmyard recipients of anthrax vaccination, animals were crucial to this process and thereby bridged the realms of nature and culture.[27]

The use of experimental animals as sources of biological material for use in humans actually pre-dated bacteriology. Edward Jenner had shown in 1796 that humans inoculated with lymph taken from the pustules of cows suffering from cowpox were immune to smallpox infection. Although this method – the original 'vaccination' – won the support of government and the mainstream medical establishment, it also caused considerable alarm, which persisted throughout the century and fuelled opposition to compulsory smallpox vaccination. Critics highlighted its transgression of the human–animal boundary, and voiced fears about its brutalising effects and possible transmission of disease. From the 1880s, bacteriological methods were applied to the collection of cowpox lymph. Large numbers of calves were purchased and housed in experimental vaccination stations. Scientists made multiple wounds on their bellies, inoculated them with smallpox lymph, extracted fluid from the blisters that developed, and treated it with glycerine to kill extraneous bacteria.[28]

This development foreshadowed the production of serum from horse bodies, for the purpose of protecting human bodies against diphtheria, tetanus and other infectious diseases. At the turn of the twentieth century, serum production became an industrialised process in which horses were employed as 'manufacturing units' and had large quantities of blood extracted repeatedly from their bodies.[29] Smaller animals such as guinea pigs were used to ensure the safety and standardise the quality of sera, and subsequently other biological products such as hormones and insulin that were developed in the 1920s and 30s.[30] As their manufacture expanded, so, too, did demand for experimental animals. In early twentieth-century Britain, the usual supplies of rodents from fancy breeders were quickly exhausted and the quality of experimental results declined. Stray dogs could not be used, as the 1906 Dogs Act (which was passed partly due to fears that lost pets might be used for experiments) prevented the police from handing them over to scientists. This situation spurred scientists to develop and co-ordinate more reliable supplies of higher quality animals, and on occasions to breed their own.[31] Trade in animals developed on a large scale from the 1950s and fuelled their use for screening and for clinical trials of drugs produced by the burgeoning pharmaceutical industry. Animals thereby supported and were increasingly consumed by 'big biomedical science'.[32]

Several authors have explored the social historical processes by which certain animals came to be regarded as the 'right tools for the job' of experimental research.[33] Initially, cost and ease of acquisition were important, as was the biology of the animal: did it permit experimenters who possessed certain skill-sets to investigate their chosen problems? Was its biology sufficiently close to that of humans to permit the extrapolation of findings across species, and was the animal physically and temperamentally suited to experimental use?[34] To enable extrapolation to humans, human diseases were induced artificially in animals. However, the biological resemblance of these animal 'models' to humans was often contested. While scientists' criticisms centred on the validity of particular models, anti-vivisectionists challenged the underpinning principle that animals could act as human proxies.[35] As experiments proceeded during the late nineteenth and early twentieth centuries, scientists gathered more data about the bodies and habits of their selected species, and learned how to manipulate them through inbreeding to better to suit their purposes.[36] This was a self-reinforcing process that 'locked in' scientists to using particular species for particular lines of scientific enquiry: xenopus toads to diagnose pregnancy, frogs to study muscular action, guinea pigs for scurvy, mice for cancer, and rats for behavioural psychology.[37] At the same time, the expansion and specialisation of biomedical science led scientists to seek out new medical and surgical 'jobs' to which animal 'tools' could be applied. Rats and mice were particularly versatile. Through inbreeding, strain selection, and latterly by genetic manipulations, they were further refashioned and standardised to better suit scientists' needs.[38]

Scientists' utilitarian attitudes to experimental animals did not necessarily exclude more affective relationships with them. In testifying before the Royal Commission that gave rise to the 1876 Cruelty to Animals Act, several British scientists expressed their personal fondness for dogs but were still prepared to experiment on them for the greater good. They saw no contradiction between loving their pet dogs and experimenting on other dogs: how they treated them revolved around the question of how dogs could best serve mankind.[39] Likewise, at the turn of the twentieth century, the Russian physiologist Ivan Pavlov surgically refashioned dogs into 'particular kinds of "machines" designed and produced in the laboratory to generate particular kinds of facts'.[40] However, his scientific assistants also named their dogs and recognised their distinctive personalities, which could influence physiological functioning and hence responses to experiments.[41]

In Britain and the USA during the late nineteenth and early twentieth centuries, physiologists began to invoke animal emotions as an explanation for experimental results and to adjust their experimental practices in efforts to accommodate and control them, for example by handling animals frequently to accustom them to humans.[42] British scientists also grew concerned with how the laboratory's physical and social environment might affect the experimental performance of animals. During the 1950s they articulated this concern using the prevailing language of stress, and used it as a basis for developing a new science of animal welfare, which sought more reliable scientific results through the redesign of laboratories and animal houses, and the professionalisation of their staff. In turning ethical concern for animals into a scientific necessity, animal welfare science refashioned scientists' relationships with experimental animals and the animals' lived experiences.[43]

However, the field was unable to dispel attacks by the later twentieth-century movements for animal liberation and animal rights, which opposed animal experimentation on principle.[44] Targets included the 1984 transplantation by Californian doctors of a baboon heart into a baby girl dying of heart failure. While researchers rejected the allegation that xenotransplantation was unacceptable, they decided that for ethical and other reasons, future organs should be sourced from pigs rather than primates.[45] This was not the first time that human–animal relationships had influenced the choice of experimental animal. In 1950s Switzerland, scientists investigating new forms of fracture repair initially performed clinical research on dogs. However, they soon turned to sheep, because, although biologically sheep had dissimilar metabolisms to dogs and were more difficult to fashion into experimental surgical material, scientists found it easier to maintain emotional distance from them.[46]

Disease transmitters

The histories of human and veterinary medicine come together in the exploration of a second important role played by animals: that of disease transmitter to humans. The diseases in question are known as 'zoonoses' on account of their ability to spread between humans and animal. Biologically, zoonoses have always existed. However, Western medical scientists and governments began to perceive them as particularly pressing problems during the later nineteenth century, when the new science of bacteriology identified their common microbial causes in humans and animals, and when the increasing movement of animals and their products by railways and steamships generated new opportunities for disease to spread.[47] They responded by incorporating zoonotic diseases within the new research and policy domains of 'comparative pathology,' and 'veterinary public health,' respectively.[48]

These domains generated rich documentary records that are readily accessible to historians. Inspired by the late twentieth-century resurgence of zoonotic disease, and the discoveries that HIV/AIDS evolved from a disease of non-human African primates, SARS from a disease of civets, and new variant CJD from 'mad cow disease' or BSE, scholars have used these resources to investigate antecedents to present-day concerns.[49] Their accounts usually focus on research and policy, and reduce animals to the bodily products that were implicated in the spread of disease to humans: meat, milk, wool, faeces and saliva. In revealing the types of zoonotic diseases that humans perceived as problems at particular points in time, these accounts cast valuable light on how animals influenced human health, and how humans lived with and depended on animals.

The most problematic zoonotic diseases of the late nineteenth century were anthrax, glanders, tuberculosis and rabies. In humans, anthrax presented as 'woolsorters disease' (a fatal pneumonia associated with the growing textile industry) and 'malignant pustule' (a skin disease). Its increasing incidence resulted from the growth of the global wool trade, which exposed Western wool workers to spores contained in the fleeces of Asian and South African sheep.[50] Glanders was a fatal respiratory disease spread by horses to humans who worked closely with them, such as grooms. It was particularly a problem in cities such as London, where stables were expanding in size and number to accommodate the increasing numbers of horses needed to serve growing human populations.[51]

Suspicions that tuberculosis could spread from cows to humans via meat pre-dated Robert Koch's 1882 claim that the same bacterium was responsible for disease in both species. Subsequently, milk was identified as a dangerous substance. In Britain, the consumption of both products was increasing due to growing affluence, the development of the railway milk trade, and the popularity of dairy farming, to which farmers turned in response to a collapse in arable prices. Another factor which contributed to the spread of tuberculosis between cows, and from cows to humans, was the tendency (especially in cities) to house dairy cows indoors within poorly ventilated sheds. Efforts to understand and control tuberculosis in cows featured rival claims to expertise over their diseased bodies. Veterinarians asserted their knowledge of tuberculosis in cows, while public health doctors professed a superior understanding of the risk of spread to humans. In their efforts to win government recognition and employment, all displayed greater concern about the threat that cows posed to public health than working-class consumers, for whom price and availability of meat trumped quality.[52]

Rabies is a rare example of a disease studied both by medical historians and human–animal historians.[53] Although it rarely killed humans, rabies aroused disproportionate fear and attention owing to the horrific manner of death and its potential conveyance by 'man's best friend'. Nineteenth-century rabies scares coincided with the evolution of pet-keeping and the pedigree dog fancy. By transforming dogs into bestial killers, the disease challenged human efforts to reshape and domesticate them. In blaming urban street dogs for rabies spread, commentators drew on wider fears of their human equivalents, the undisciplined, threatening lower and criminal classes. Efforts to control rabies through the enforced muzzling of dogs reveal marked contrasts in how public health doctors and dog owners perceived them. For the former, dogs were potential conduits of disease, therefore they and their owners had to be disciplined. For the latter, dogs were family members whose control by government amounted to unjustifiable state intervention in the private sphere.[54]

The significance of these zoonotic diseases waned during the early twentieth century owing to the success of policies applied to their control. Despite much controversy, the muzzling of dogs, along with leashing, licensing, and (from the 1930s) vaccination led to the decline of rabies.[55] Anthrax was managed through the disinfection of fleeces and livestock vaccination. Mallein and tuberculin were used to identify and remove horses and cows infected with glanders and tuberculosis respectively, while milk supplies were made safe through pasteurisation.[56] However, new zoonotic diseases then emerged in response to the changing ways in which humans farmed and slaughtered livestock.

Starting in the inter-war years, and accelerating after the Second World War, economic pressures and scientific and technical breakthroughs encouraged a trend towards larger farms in which animals were kept within more confined spaces. These conditions facilitated the spread of campylobacter and salmonella bacteria, which caused few symptoms in animals but potentially severe food poisoning in humans. Further spread occurred as a result of unhygienic animal carcass handling within increasingly industrialised slaughterhouses.[57] One response to this and to other problems of health and productivity within intensive farming systems was the liberal use of antibiotics, but from the 1960s this generated fears that bacterial resistance would develop and threaten human health.[58] Intensive farming was also blamed for the BSE epidemic that emerged in 1980s Britain. It transpired that in a cost-saving attempt to improve livestock productivity, ruminant tissues containing the BSE agent had been recycled into meat and bone meal and fed back to cows. Herbivores were thereby turned into carnivores, and the humans that consumed them exposed to the risk of new variant CJD.[59] While BSE has all but disappeared, the other diseases remain, and form a conduit for ongoing concerns about how animals are treated on farms.[60]

Disease victims

A third, much-studied role performed by animals within the history of human/veterinary medicine was that of disease victim. Like the other roles, it was created by humans. Animals became victims not because of their biological vulnerability to disease, but because humans noticed, cared, and were motivated to take action. The more highly they valued animals, and the greater the risk and impact of animal diseases, the more likely they were to intervene. They managed disease victims in two distinctive ways: through public policies that counteracted the spread of infectious diseases among animal populations, and through private interventions in the health of particular animals, flocks or herds. Historical analysis focuses largely on the former because, in contrast to the latter, public policies targeted high-profile diseases and inspired well-documented controversies. Historians have used these documents to illuminate wider developments in international trade, agriculture, colonialism, understandings of disease, the growth of government and its use of expertise. Unfortunately, in so doing, they rather overlook the effects of these policies and diseases on animals themselves.[61]

Policies for the control of contagious animal diseases emerged in the eighteenth century in response to the highly fatal, contagious cattle plague or rinderpest, which swept across Western Europe. They were extended in the later nineteenth century, when increased animal movements associated with colonial expansion, military campaigns, the development of railways and steamships, and the feeding of rapidly expanding urban populations, enabled this and other diseases to spread. Cattle plague invaded Asia, Europe and Africa, and there was a marked increase in the incidence of contagious bovine pleuro-pneumonia, foot and mouth disease, sheep scab, Texas Fever (in North America), and trypanosomiasis, horse sickness and East Coast Fever (in Southern Africa). Similar 'stamping out' principles were applied in all cases. Derived from efforts to counteract earlier epidemics of human bubonic plague, they focused on the bodies of animals that were vulnerable to – or capable of – transmitting infection. Horses and livestock were quarantined or slaughtered, and restrictions placed upon their movements on and off infected farms and in the surrounding area. Where parasites were implicated, animals were forcibly dipped in chemical solutions and limits placed on their use of grazing pastures.[62]

The alarm that these diseases inspired, and the many wide-ranging, costly efforts to control them indicate how heavily humans relied on healthy animals for food, draught power, military power, economic investment, income-generation and cultural capital. Ambitious veterinarians sought to capitalise on this reliance by lobbying for government employment in the making and implementation of animal health policy. However, diseased animal bodies frequently eluded their control. This was partly because owners and carers evaded government regulations, and also because disease manifested unexpectedly in animals. At the turn of the twentieth century, each additional disease that the British government elected to control brought new difficulties for vets as animals' variable symptoms, post-mortem appearances and unexpected vulnerabilities to infection undermined veterinary diagnoses and epidemiological predictions.[63] In certain countries, from the late nineteenth century, vaccines and sera were developed and adopted as substitutes, replacements or antecedents to the stamping-out policy. They were used particularly where diseases were prevalent, and where – as in colonial contexts – resistant publics and a lack of veterinary manpower prevented governments from exerting substantial control over animal bodies.[64]

In their efforts to manage contagious animal diseases, governments attached little significance to the health of individual animals, whose status mattered only insofar as it indicated the health of other animals. Policies aimed not to cure or protect individuals, but to contain and ideally eradicate infection from animal populations, regions and nations. To this end, individual animal bodies were manipulated, medicated or destroyed. While disease control policies were ostensibly fashioned in accordance with economic logic and the biological properties of disease, they actually reinforced existing hierarchies in the value placed upon animals (and their owners). Animals belonging to wealthy elites were protected at the expense of those owned by grass-roots and (in colonial contexts) indigenous producers. The inequalities inherent in these policies were recognised at the time, and led to frequent controversy and occasional rebellion.[65] While some historians have chosen to celebrate their eventual success, it is important to recollect the costs they inflicted on both animals and humans.[66]

These costs were demonstrated most forcefully by the 2001 UK epidemic of foot and mouth disease. This was a highly contagious and largely non-fatal condition that had entered the country only once in the previous 33 years. When deciding how to contain its rapid spread, the government rejected vaccination because under international trading rules, a lengthy trade ban would apply to those larger farmers who exported to FMD-free countries. Instead, it opted to 'stamp out' disease using compulsory slaughter on an unprecedented scale. The policy brought death to over 10 million sheep and cows and untold distress to their owners and carers. Government decision-making was supported by epidemiological models which reduced animals to mere abstractions. However the processes of slaughtering and disposal – which were depicted graphically in the local, national and international media – made their corporeal realities impossible to ignore. Human and material resources proved inadequate to the task, and the delays that set in enabled the further spread of disease. When the disease was finally stamped out, commentators highlighted the absence of animals: the silent farmyards and the empty fields.[67]

Animal victims of less dramatic diseases such as endemic respiratory and gastro-intestinal infections, mastitis, lameness and infertility, were generally ignored by the state. Both in the pre-modern and modern eras, decisions upon their management fell to owners and carers. These humans could choose to save money or prevent suffering by destroying sick animals; they could cut their losses by selling sick animals to unsuspecting buyers, or they could transform animals into patients by attempting their treatment. The treatments they applied are richly documented within Byzantine and Arabic manuscripts, popular almanacs and published manuals, farriers' and vets' case books, bills and veterinary practice records, and oral histories.[68] Prior to the twentieth century, medical interventions were frequent, varied and heroic. Animals were bled, dosed with medicine balls, drenches and drinks, given enemas, and rubbed with lotions, liniments and caustic substances that were intended to raise blisters on the skin. Their births were assisted, their wounds dressed and fractures set. To manage lameness, horses' hooves were reshod and their lower limbs subjected to surgical interventions that included the use of hot irons to cauterise tendons. To increase their productivity and manageability, horses and farmed livestock were routinely castrated. During the mid twentieth century, drugs prepared by pharmaceutical companies (most notably antibiotics) began to replace home-made and patent remedies.[69] In addition, developments in anaesthesia – which did not become a routine veterinary practice for decades after its 1840s discovery – enabled more extensive surgical interventions such as orthopaedic operations.[70]

Many of these interventions appear brutal in retrospect, and may have enhanced rather than diminished animal suffering. However, rather than attributing them to the ignorance and callousness of animal healers in an age less enlightened than our own, it is important to evaluate them according to the standards of the time. Animal healing often drew on the rationales and practices of human medicine. Interventions were supported by custom, experience and prevailing understandings of disease. While there were complaints about the ignorance and cruelty of animal healers, these should not be taken at face value because healers operated within a fiercely competitive 'veterinary marketplace' in which they sought to advance their own profiles by denigrating their rivals.[71] This was a common strategy among veterinary surgeons, who emerged as a new body of healers in the late eighteenth and early nineteenth century. Evidence suggests that in the nineteenth century their claims to superiority were overstated, and that there was considerable overlap between their practices and those of unqualified healers. Vets continued to face competition from 'castrators' and unqualified charity workers well into the twentieth century.[72]

In deciding whether to transform animal disease victims into patients, and how to manage their diseases, animal carers and health experts were influenced by the functions that animals performed for humans, and the social, economic and cultural value awarded to them.[73] Human dependence on horses for sport, transport and military strength meant that they formed the dominant species of animal patient until displaced by the internal combustion engine. Farmed livestock became particularly important during and after the Second World War, when food shortages and post-war reconstruction placed a premium upon their health. The individual attention they received diminished as farms grew larger, and health interventions were redirected towards the flock or herd. As suppliers of meat and milk, cows generally received more attention than pigs, sheep, and especially chickens. The treatment of these sick animals had utilitarian objectives. By contrast, the treatment of pets – which became particularly important patients during the later twentieth century – was guided by an affective 'economy of love' that reflected their movement into the home and status as family members.[74]

Reflection

As this chapter demonstrates, there is an extensive body of literature that addresses the history of animals in human and veterinary medicine. Written largely by medical historians, it is shaped by the quantity and accessibility of archival sources, the authors' disciplinary perspectives, and by contemporary problems in health and medicine that encouraged them to select certain topics and modes of enquiry. In focusing particularly on three key roles played by animals – as experimental material, transmitters of disease to humans, and victims of animal disease – this literature offers important insights into the history of human–animal relationships and the ways in which animals shaped and were shaped by human/veterinary medicine. The chapter will conclude by highlighting some of the problems with this approach, recent attempts to address them, and where the future of the field might lie.

It is, of course, impossible for historians to escape the influence of the present on the writing of the past. There are obvious reasons why historians investigate well-documented subjects, and it cannot be denied that historically animals did play important roles as experimental material, transmitters of disease to humans, and victims of animal disease. However, in deciding to focus their attention upon these roles, and in the manner in which they portray them, medical/veterinary historians display a human-centred perspective that runs counter to the agendas of much human–animal history.[75] When considering the transformation of animals into medical objects, such historians focus on the achievement of human ends: experimental animals were fashioned into 'laboratory models' of diseased humans in order to advance human health; animals that transmitted disease were targeted because of the risks they posed to human health; and animal disease victims attracted attention because they disrupted human utilitarian and affective relationships with them.

While this perspective reflects the views of many human historical actors, it tends to overlook the animals themselves, and what disease, its investigation and management meant for them. It neglects to consider contexts in which humans regarded animals not simply as passive objects of human intervention but as active medical subjects, and it oversimplifies what, at the time, was often a very complex set of health relationships between humans and non-human animals, that were not confined to the contexts of laboratory experiments, zoonotic disease control and the management of animal patients. Recent scholarship is just beginning to illustrate these claims. For example, several authors have shown that while dogs did indeed 'model' for humans in laboratory investigations into insulin treatment, orthopaedic surgery and transplant surgery, later in the twentieth century clinical trials and experiences in humans were used to inform the application of these measures within the expanding field of pet medicine. In these circumstances, human animals effectively acted as 'models' for dog diseases.[76] One animal species could also model for others, such as ferrets employed by British scientists in the 1920s for the testing of dog distemper vaccine. In the same context, dogs simultaneously performed roles as experimental material and patients.[77]

In the mid twentieth-century study of zoonotic malaria, scientists in the USA constructed humans and monkeys not as disease victims and transmitters, but as parasitic 'co-hosts' whose disease relationships they viewed as constitutive with their evolutionary relationships, each shedding light on the other.[78] Concurrently, in using birds to 'model' malaria in humans, other scientists pushed beyond a simple focus on disease transmission to explore the more complex relationships between parasites, hosts and their environments. Here, they made a virtue of the fact that their experimental models were not standardised but rather highly variable, like the humans they modelled.[79] Meanwhile, in the context of post-World War Two global health, animals with zoonotic diseases were subjected to health interventions not simply because of their ability to transmit diseases to humans, but because they themselves were sick, and therefore less capable of producing meat and milk for consumption by humans.[80]

Also, animal diseases did not have to be zoonotic for them to influence human health. During the 1880s, efforts to counteract rickets that developed spontaneously in lions and monkeys housed within the London Zoological Gardens shaped ideas about human rickets, while the effects of myxomatosis on rabbit populations in the 1950s led investigators to suggest how human evolution had been moulded by past encounters with disease.[81] Inferences could be drawn in the opposite direction. Charles Darwin used studies of asylum patients to interpret animal emotions, while British asylum doctor Walter Lauder Lindsay studied asylum patients to learn about animal behaviour, and animal behaviour to learn about asylum patients.[82] Such investigations both reflected and reconfigured perceived boundaries between human and non-human animals.

In addition, recent scholarship reveals how animals actively moulded their construction and management as patients. In the nineteenth-century London Zoological Gardens, elite medical men who attempted to use the stethoscope, apply anaesthesia and perform minor operations were impeded by their animal patients' propensities to struggle and bite.[83] Elsewhere, animals encouraged clinical interventions by exhibiting disease symptoms that attracted the attention of carers and veterinary surgeons. For example in the 1960s, the failure of American house cats to urinate in places designated by humans led their carers to present them at veterinary clinics. This forced vets who had previously taken little interest in cats to perform investigations that led to the identification of a 'Feline Urological Syndrome'.[84] Likewise, following the veterinary repair of their fractured limbs, pet dogs sometimes exhibited pain behaviours that, in causing their carers to seek veterinary aid, challenged veterinarians' faith in radiographic images as an 'objective' indicator of animal clinical status.[85] Interestingly, accounts of these developments have been written primarily by veterinarians-turned-historians, whose historical writing has perhaps been informed by their rich personal experiences of the agency that animals can exert within clinical encounters.

In transcending the dominant anthropocentric framework of medical history, these novel lines of enquiry reveal the variety of historically neglected roles that animals played within the history of human/veterinary medicine in addition to those of experimental material, disease transmitters and disease victims. In the few examples outlined above, animals featured as beneficiaries of therapies 'modelled' on humans, as shapers of human nutritional status and food production systems, as forgers of disease categories and health interventions, as sources of comparative and evolutionary thinking across species, and as shapers and products of their (diseased) environments. These findings suggest the need to move beyond the standard historical categories into which medical historians have placed animals, and to think more imaginatively about their contributions to human/veterinary medicine.

This need is reinforced by the present-day human health agenda known as 'One Health'. Since its emergence in the early twenty-first century, One Health has pursued an expansive vision of improving health and wellbeing through studying problems at the interface of humans, animals and their environments.[86] Advocates justify its integrated approach by reference to multiple present-day connections between human and animal health, ranging from the joint threats posed by climate change, food insecurity and emerging diseases, to the ways in which spontaneous instances of animal disease can elucidate analogous diseases in humans, and human surgical advances inform treatment of pets. In highlighting the richness of human–animal health connections, and the fact that many health problems do not privilege humans but are shared across species, this agenda throws into sharp relief the narrowness of historians' anthropocentric approaches to animals in human/veterinary medicine and the need for fresh thinking about them.

Adopting a more animal-centred approach would not only generate new historical perspectives on animals but also on medicine. In pushing scholars to move beyond the much-studied fields of experimental medicine and government policy to consider the more-than-human dimensions of pathology, epidemiology, parasitology, psychiatry and other areas of medicine, which were pursued not just in laboratories but also in fields, zoos, asylums and dairies, it promises to disrupt established ideas about what constituted human medicine and its relationships with veterinary medicine.[87] To develop this line of analysis it is important to bring human–animal history and medical history closer together. Medical historians' concern with the materiality of animal bodies and their skill in interpreting the traces that animals left on the medical historical record can complement and be complemented by human–animal historians' interest in animal agency, animal experiences and subjectivities. Although requiring both sets of scholars to move beyond the constraints of their disciplinary frameworks and to question their preconceptions about the nature of history, a combined approach to the subject promises more than the sum of its parts. Ranging widely across domesticated and wild animal species, it would enable the development of a rich medical history of animals and a truly animal history of medicine.

Notes

1 H. Kean, 'Challenges for historians writing animal–human history: what is really enough?', *Anthrozoös* 25, sup.1 (2012): 57–72. For a different perspective on this subject, see R.G.W. Kirk and M. Worboys, 'Medicine and species: one medicine, one history?', in M. Jackson (ed.), *The Oxford Handbook of the History of Medicine*, Oxford: Oxford University Press, 2011, 561–577.

2 For example, K. Rader, *Making Mice: Standardizing Animals for American Biomedical Research, 1900–55*, Princeton NJ: Princeton University Press, 2004; S. Jones, *Death in a Small Package: A Short History of Anthrax*, Baltimore MD: Johns Hopkins University Press, 2010; K. Brown and D. Gilfoyle (eds.), *Healing the Herds: Disease, Livestock Economies, and the Globalization of Veterinary Medicine*, Athens OH: Ohio University Press, 2010; A. Woods, M. Bresalier, A. Cassidy, and R. Mason Dentinger, *One Health and its Histories: Animals and the Shaping of Modern Medicine*, Basingstoke: Palgrave, 2017, 27–70.

3 E. Benson, 'Animal writes: historiography, disciplinarity, and the animal trace', in L. Kalof and G.M. Montgomery (eds.), *Making Animal Meaning*, East Lansing MI: Michigan State University Press, 2011, 3–16.

4 See the chapter by Mieke Roscher, 'New political history and the writing of animal lives' in this volume.

5 E. Russell, 'Introduction', in S. Schrepfer and P. Scranton (eds.), *Industrializing Organisms: Introducing Evolutionary History*, London: Routledge, 2003, 3–16.

6 B. Latour, *The Pasteurization of France*, trans. A. Sheridan and J. Law, London: Harvard University Press, 1988, was a particularly influential text within medical history. See also: Kean, 'Challenges for historians'; Benson, 'Animal writes'; D. Brantz, 'Introduction', in D. Brantz (ed.), *Beastly Natures. Animals, Humans, and the Study of History*, London: University of Virginia Press, 2010, 1–13; E. Fudge, 'A left-handed blow: writing the history of animals', in N. Rothfels (ed.), *Representing Animals*, Bloomington IN: Indiana University Press, 2003, 3–18. On agency see also Philip Howell, 'Animals, agency, and history' in this volume.

7 J.H. Warner, 'The uses of patient records by historians: patterns, possibilities and perplexities', *Health and History* 1, 2/3 (1999): 101–111; E. Hurren, '"Abnormalities and deformities": the dissection and interment of the insane poor, 1832–1929', *History of Psychiatry* 23, 1 (2012): 65–77.

8 For overviews of this topic and reviews of recent literature see: A. Guerrini, *Experimenting with Humans and Animals: From Galen to Animal Rights*, Baltimore MD: Johns Hopkins University Press, 2003; I. Löwy, 'The experimental body', in R. Cooter and J. Pickstone (eds.), *Companion Encyclopedia of Medicine in the Twentieth Century*, London: Routledge, 2003, 435–449; K. Rader, 'Scientific animals: The laboratory and its human-animal relations, from Dba to Dolly', in R. Malamud (ed.), *A Cultural History of Animals in the Modern Age*, London: Bloomsbury, 2007, 119–137; T. Schlich, E. Mykhalovskiy, and M. Rock, 'Animals in surgery – surgery in animals: nature and culture in animal–human

relations and modern surgery', *History and Philosophy of the Life Sciences* 31, 3/4 (2009): 321–354; N.H. Franco, 'Animal experiments in biomedical research: A historical perspective', *Animals* 3, 1 (2013): 238–273; A. Woods, 'Between human and veterinary medicine: the history of animals and surgery', in T. Schlich (ed.), *Palgrave Handbook of the History of Surgery*, London: Palgrave, 2017, 115–132.
9 See the chapter by Robert Kirk in this volume.
10 P. White, 'The experimental animal in Victorian Britain', in L. Daston and G. Mitman, *Thinking with Animals: New Perspectives on Anthropomorphism*, New York: Columbia University Press, 2005, 59–81.
11 For instance, see the chapters in N. Rupke (ed.), *Vivisection in Historical Perspective*, London: Routledge, 1990; D. Todes, 'Pavlov's physiology factory', *Isis* 88, 2 (1997): 205–246; Rader, *Making Mice*.
12 Guerrini, *Experimenting with Humans and Animals*.
13 W.F. Bynum, '"C'est une malade": animal models and concepts of human diseases', *Journal of the History of Medicine and Allied Sciences* 45, 3 (1990): 397–413.
14 N.D. Jewson, 'The disappearance of the sick-man from medical cosmology, 1770–1870', *Sociology* 10, 2 (1976): 225–244.
15 P. Elliot, 'Vivisection and the emergence of experimental physiology in nineteenth-century France', in N. Rupke (ed.), *Vivisection in Historical Perspective*, London: Routledge, 1990, 48–77. J. Lesch, *Science and Medicine in France: The Emergence of Experimental Physiology, 1790–1855*, London: Harvard University Press, 1984.
16 C. Logan, 'Before there were standards: the role of test animals in the production of empirical generality in physiology', *Journal of the History of Biology* 35, 2 (2002): 329–363.
17 Guerrini, *Experimenting with Humans and Animals*, 70–92.
18 Claude Bernard, *An Introduction to the Study of Experimental Medicine*, trans. H.C. Greene, New York: Dover, 1957, 99.
19 Bernard, *Introduction to the Study of Experimental Medicine*, 103.
20 A. Guerrini, 'Animal experiments and antivivisection debates in the 1820s', in C.K. King and J.R. Goodall, *Frankenstein's Science: Experimentation and Discovery in Romantic Culture, 1780–1830*, Aldershot: Ashgate, 2008, 71–85.
21 E.E. Klein, J. Burdon-Sanderson, M. Foster, and T.L. Brunton, *A Handbook for the Physiological Laboratory*, London: J. and A. Churchill, 1873.
22 White, 'Experimental animal', 59–81.
23 R. French, *Antivivisection and Medical Science in Victorian Society*. London: Princeton University Press, 1975, 112–158; C. Lansbury, *The Old Brown Dog: Women, Workers, and Vivisection in Edwardian England*, London: University of Wisconsin Press, 1985; Rupke (ed.), *Vivisection in Historical Perspective*; H. Kean, 'The "smooth cool men of science": the feminist and socialist response to vivisection', *History Workshop Journal* 40 (1995): 16–38; H. Kean, *Animal Rights: Political and Social Change in Britain since 1800*, London: Reaktion, 1998, 96–112.
24 S. Lederer, 'Political animals: The shaping of biomedical research literature in twentieth-century America', *Isis* 83, 1 (1992): 61–79.
25 Guerrini, *Experimenting with Humans and Animals*, 93–113; C. Gradmann, 'Experimental life and experimental disease: the role of animal experiments in Robert Koch's medical bacteriology', *BIF Futura* 18 (2003): 80–88.
26 Bynum, 'C'est une malade', 397–413.
27 Latour, *Pasteurization of France*.
28 N. Durbach, *Bodily Matters: The Anti-Vaccination Movement in England, 1853–1907*, Durham NC: Duke University Press, 2004, 124–126; S.L. Kotar and J.E. Gessler, *Smallpox: A History*, Jefferson NC: McFarland & Company, 2013, 284–287.

29 J. Simon, 'Monitoring the stable at the Pasteur Institute', *Science in Context* 21, 2 (2008): 181–200.
30 Löwy, 'The experimental body', 435–449.
31 E.M. Tansey, 'Protection against dog distemper and dogs protection bills: the Medical Research Council and anti-vivisectionist protest, 1911–33', *Medical History* 38, 1 (1994): 1–26; R.G.W. Kirk, '"Wanted – standard guinea pigs": standardization and the experimental animal market in Britain ca.1919–1947', *Studies in History and Philosophy of Science Part C* 39, 3 (2008): 280–291.
32 Löwy, 'The experimental body', 435–449.
33 A.E. Clarke and J.H. Fujimura (eds.), *The Right Tools for the Job: At Work in the Twentieth Century Life Sciences*, Princeton NJ: Princeton University Press, 1992; Rader, 'Scientific animals', 119–137.
34 F. Holmes, 'The old martyr of science: the frog in experimental physiology', *Journal of the History of Biology* 26, 2 (1993): 311–328.
35 Löwy, 'The experimental body', 435–449.
36 B. Clause, 'The Wistar Rat as a right choice: establishing mammalian standards and the ideal of a standardized mammal', *Journal of the History of Biology* 26, 2 (1993): 329–349.
37 R. Ankeny and S. Leonelli, 'What's so special about model organisms?', *Studies in History and Philosophy of Science Part A* 42, 2 (2011): 313–323.
38 Rader, *Making Mice*; I. Löwy and J-P. Gaudillière, 'Disciplining cancer: mice and the practice of genetic purity', in J-P. Gaudillière and I. Löwy (eds.), *The Invisible Industrialist: Manufactures and the Production of Scientific Knowledge*, Basingstoke: Macmillan, 1998, 209–249.
39 White, 'Experimental animal', 74; R. Boddice, 'Vivisecting major: a Victorian gentleman scientist defends animal experimentation, 1876–1885', *Isis* 102, 2 (2011): 215–237.
40 Todes, 'Pavlov's physiology factory', 221.
41 Todes, 'Pavlov's physiology factory', 205–246.
42 O.E. Dror, 'The affect of experiment: the turn to emotions in Anglo-American physiology, 1900–1940', *Isis* 90, 2 (1999): 205–237.
43 R.G.W. Kirk, 'The invention of the "stressed animal" and the development of a science of animal welfare, 1947–86', in D. Cantor and E. Ramsden (eds.), *Stress, Shock, and Adaptation in the Twentieth Century*, Rochester NY: University of Rochester Press, 2014, 241–263.
44 P. Singer, *Animal Liberation*, London: Cape, 1976; T. Regan, *The Case for Animal Rights*, Berkeley CA: University of California Press, 1983.
45 C. Remy, 'The animal issue in xenotransplantation: controversies in France and the United States', *History and Philosophy of the Life Sciences* 31, 3/4 (2009): 407–432.
46 M. Schlünder and T. Schlich, 'The emergence of "implant-pets" and "bone-sheep": animals as new biomedical objects in orthopedic surgery (1960s-2010)', *History and Philosophy of the Life Sciences* 31, 3/4 (2009): 433–466.
47 A. Hardy, 'Animals, disease and man: making connections', *Perspectives in Biology and Medicine* 46, 2 (2003): 200–215; M. Harrison, *Contagion: How Commerce has Spread Disease*, New Haven CT: Yale University Press, 211–246.
48 L. Wilkinson, *Animals and Disease: An Introduction to the History of Comparative Medicine*, Cambridge: Cambridge University Press, 1992; S. Jones, *Valuing Animals: Veterinarians and their Patients in Modern America*, Baltimore MD: Johns Hopkins University Press, 2003; D. Brantz, 'Animal bodies, human health, and the reform of slaughterhouses in nineteenth-century Berlin', *Food and History* 3, 2 (2005): 193–215.
49 H. Ritvo, 'Animal planet', *Environmental History* 9, 2 (2004): 204–220.
50 Jones, *Anthrax*.
51 Anon, *Animal Health: A Centenary, 1865–1965*, London: HMSO, 1965, 195–201.

52 K. Waddington, *The Bovine Scourge: Meat, Tuberculosis and Public Health, 1850–1914*, Woodbridge: Boydell Press, 2006; K. Waddington, 'The dangerous sausage: diet, meat and disease in Victorian and Edwardian Britain', *Cultural and Social History* 8, 1 (2011): 51–71.

53 D.J. Haraway, *The Companion Species Manifesto: Dogs, People, and Significant Otherness*, Chicago IL: Prickly Paradigm Press, 2003.

54 There is an extremely extensive literature on the history of rabies. Key works include: J. Walton, 'Mad dogs and Englishmen: the conflict over rabies in late Victorian England', *Journal of Social History* 13, 2 (1979): 219–239; K. Kete, 'La rage and the bourgeoisie', *Representations* 22 (1988): 89–107; H. Ritvo, *The Animal Estate: The English and Other Creatures in the Victorian Age*, Cambridge MA: Harvard University Press, 1987, 167–204; N. Pemberton and M. Worboys, *Mad Dogs and Englishmen: Rabies in Britain, 1830–2000*, Basingstoke: Palgrave Macmillan, 2007; P. Teigen, 'Legislating fear and the public health in Gilded Age Massachusetts', *Journal of the History of Medicine and Allied Sciences* 62, 2 (2007): 141–170; P. Howell, *At Home and Astray: The Domestic Dog in Victorian Britain*, Charlottesville VA: University of Virginia Press, 2015, 150–174.

55 M. Cassier, 'Producing, controlling and stabilizing Pasteur's anthrax vaccine: creating a new industry and a health market', *Science in Context* 21, 2 (2008): 253–278; Howell, *At Home and Astray*; Pemberton and Worboys, *Mad Dogs and Englishmen*.

56 Jones, *Anthrax*; K. Waddington, 'To stamp out "so terrible a malady": bovine tuberculosis and tuberculin testing in Britain, 1890–1939', *Medical History* 48, 1 (2004): 29–48; A. Olmstead and P. Rhodes, *Arresting Contagion: Science, Policy, and Conflicts over Animal Disease Control*, Cambridge MA: Harvard University Press, 2015.

57 A. Hardy, *Salmonella Infections, Networks of Knowledge, and Public Health in Britain, 1880–1975*, Oxford: Oxford University Press, 2014.

58 R. Bud, *Penicillin: Triumph and Tragedy*, Oxford: Oxford University Press, 2007.

59 P. Van Zwanenberg and E. Millstone. *BSE: Risk, Science and Governance*, Oxford: Oxford University Press, 2005.

60 For example see Felicity Lawrence, 'If consumers knew how farmed chickens were raised, they might never eat their meat again', *Guardian*, 24 April 2016, available at www.theguardian.com/environment/2016/apr/24/real-cost-of-roast-chicken-animal-welfare-farms, last accessed 11 August 2016.

61 For a discussion of the extensive literature on these diseases, see A. Woods, 'Animals and disease', in M. Jackson (ed.), *Routledge History of Disease*, Abingdon: Routledge, 2016, 147–164.

62 Woods, 'Animals and disease'.

63 A. Woods, 'From practical men to scientific experts: British veterinary surgeons and the development of government scientific expertise, c1878–1919', *History of Science* 51, 4 (2013): 457–480.

64 Woods, 'Animals and disease', 147–164.

65 C. Bundy, '"We don't want your rain, we won't dip": popular opposition, collaboration and social control in the anti-dipping movement, c1908–16', in W. Beinart and C. Bundy (eds.), *Hidden Struggles in Rural South Africa*, London: Currey, 1987, 191–221; P. Phoofolo, 'Epidemics and revolutions: the rinderpest epidemic in late nineteenth-century southern Africa', *Past and Present* 138 (1993): 112–143; A. Woods, *A Manufactured Plague: The History of Foot and Mouth Disease in Britain*, London: Earthscan, 2004.

66 Olmstead and Rhodes, *Arresting Contagion*, 278–301.

67 C. Chapman and J. Crowden, *Silence at Ramscliffe: Foot and Mouth in Devon*, Oxford: Bardwell Press, 2005; M. Doring and B. Nerlich (eds.), *The Social and Cultural Impact of Foot-and-Mouth Disease in the UK in 2001: Experiences and Analyses*, Manchester: Manchester University Press, 2009.

68 See, W. Beinart and K. Brown, *African Local Knowledge and Livestock Health*, Woodbridge: Boydell and Brewer, 2013; L.H. Curth, *The Care of Brute Beasts: A Social and Cultural Study of Veterinary Medicine in Early Modern England*, Leiden: Brill, 2010; L.H. Curth, *'A Plaine and Easie Waie to Remedie a Horse': Equine Medicine in Early Modern England*, Leiden: Brill, 2013; M. MacKay, 'The rise of a medical specialty: the medicalisation of elite equine care c.1680–c.1800', unpublished PhD thesis, University of York, 2009; A. McCabe, *A Byzantine Encyclopaedia of Horse Medicine: The Sources, Compilation, and Transmission of the Hippiatrica*, Oxford: Oxford University Press, 2007; H.A. Shehada, *Mamluks and Animals: Veterinary Medicine in Medieval Islam*, Leiden: Brill, 2013; A. Woods and S. Matthews, '"Little, if at all, removed from the illiterate farrier or cow-leech": the English veterinary surgeon, c.1860–85, and the campaign for veterinary reform', *Medical History* 54, 1 (2010): 29–54.

69 T. Corley and A. Godley, 'The veterinary medicine industry in Britain, 1900–2000', *Economic History Review* 64, 3 (2011): 832–854.

70 Woods, 'Between human and veterinary medicine'.

71 L.H. Curth, 'The care of the brute beast: animals in the seventeenth-century medical marketplace', *Social History of Medicine* 15, 3 (2002): 375–392; MacKay, 'Rise of a medical specialty'.

72 Woods and Matthews, "Little, if at all"; A. Gardiner, 'The "dangerous" women of animal welfare: how British veterinary medicine went to the dogs', *Social History of Medicine* 27, 3 (2014), 466–487.

73 Jones, *Valuing Animals*, 63–90.

74 C. Degeling, 'Negotiating value: comparing human and animal fracture care in industrial societies', *Science, Technology, & Human Values* 34, 1 (2009): 77–101; Jones, *Valuing Animals*; Schlünder and Schlich, "Implant-pets"; J. Swabe, *Animals, Disease and Human Society: Human–Animal Relations and the Rise of Veterinary Medicine*, London: Routledge, 2002.

75 Fudge, 'A left-handed blow'.

76 Schlich, Mykhalovsky and Rock, 'Animals in surgery'; Degeling, 'Negotiating value'; A. Gardiner, 'The animal as surgical patient: a historical perspective in the twentieth century', *History and Philosophy of the Life Sciences* 31, 3/4 (2009): 355–376.

77 M. Bresalier and M. Worboys, '"Saving the lives of our dogs": the development of canine distemper vaccine in interwar Britain', *British Journal for the History of Science* 47, 2 (2014): 305–334.

78 R. Mason Dentinger, 'Patterns of infection and patterns of evolution: how a malaria parasite brought "monkeys and man" closer together in the 1960s', *Journal of the History of Biology* 49, 2 (2016): 359–395.

79 L. Slater, 'Malarial birds: modeling infectious human disease in animals', *Bulletin of the History of Medicine* 79, 2 (2005): 261–294.

80 M. Bresalier, 'World hunger and the healthy animal: the multiple roles of livestock in post-war malnutrition', in A. Woods, M. Bresalier, A. Cassidy, and R. Mason Dentinger, *One Health and its Histories: Animals and the Shaping of Modern Medicine*, Basingstoke: Palgrave, 2017, 119–160.

81 P. Erikson and G. Mitman, 'When rabbits became human (and humans, rabbits): stability, order, and history in the study of populations', *Working Papers on The Nature of Evidence: How Well Do 'Facts' Travel*, London: London School of Economics, 2007; A. Woods, 'Doctors in the zoo: connecting human and animal health in British zoological gardens, c1828–1890', in A. Woods, M. Bresalier, A. Cassidy, and R. Mason Dentinger, *One Health and its Histories: Animals and the Shaping of Modern Medicine*, Basingstoke: Palgrave, 2017, 27–70.

82 A. Pearn, '"This excellent observer . . .": the correspondence between Charles Darwin and James Crichton Brown', *History of Psychiatry* 21, 2 (2010): 160–175; E. Gray, 'Animals and the asylum: a comparative approach to the science of the mind', unpublished paper presented to 'Science in the Asylum' Conference, Wakefield, 2012.
83 Woods, 'Doctors in the zoo'.
84 S. Jones, 'Framing animal disease: housecats with feline urological syndrome, their owners, and their doctors', *Journal of the History of Medicine and Allied Sciences* 52, 2 (1997): 202–235.
85 C. Degeling, 'Picturing the pain of animal others: rationalising form, function and suffering in veterinary orthopaedics', *History and Philosophy of the Life Sciences* 31, 3/4 (2009): 377–403.
86 J.E. Zinsstag, D. Waltner-Toews, and M. Tannera, 'From "One Medicine" to "One Health" and systemic approaches to health and wellbeing', *Preventive Veterinary Medicine* 101, 3 (2011): 148–156; E.P.J. Gibbs, 'The evolution of One Health: a decade of progress and challenges for the future', *Veterinary Record* 174, 4 (2014): 85–91; A. Cassidy, 'One Health? Building an interdisciplinary bandwagon at the interfaces of animal health, human health and the environment', in S. Frickel, M. Albert, and B. Prainsack (eds.), *Investigating Interdisciplinary Research: Theory and Practice across Disciplines*, New Brunswick NJ: New Jersey: Rutgers University Press, 2016, 213–236.
87 Woods, Bresalier, Cassidy and Mason Dentinger, *One Health*.

References

Ankeny, R. and Leonelli, S. 'What's so special about model organisms?', *Studies in History and Philosophy of Science Part A* 42, 2 (2011): 313–323.

Anon. *Animal Health: A Centenary, 1865–1965*, London: HMSO, 1965.

Beinart, W. and Brown, K. *African Local Knowledge and Livestock Health*, Woodbridge: Boydell and Brewer, 2013.

Benson, E. 'Animal writes: historiography, disciplinarity, and the animal trace', in L. Kalof and G.M. Montgomery (eds.), *Making Animal Meaning*, East Lansing MI: Michigan State University Press, 2011, 3–16.

Bernard, C. *An Introduction to the Study of Experimental Medicine*, trans. H.C. Greene, New York: Dover, 1957.

Boddice, R. 'Vivisecting major: a Victorian gentleman scientist defends animal experimentation, 1876–1885', *Isis* 102, 2 (2011): 215–237.

Brantz, D. 'Animal bodies, human health, and the reform of slaughterhouses in nineteenth-century Berlin', *Food and History* 3, 2 (2005): 193–215.

Brantz, D. 'Introduction', in D. Brantz (ed.), *Beastly Natures. Animals, Humans, and the Study of History*, London: University of Virginia Press, 2010, 1–13.

Bresalier, M. and Worboys, M. '"Saving the lives of our dogs": the development of canine distemper vaccine in interwar Britain', *British Journal for the History of Science* 47, 2 (2014): 305–334.

Bresalier, M. 'World hunger and the healthy animal: the multiple roles of livestock in post-war malnutrition', in A. Woods, M. Bresalier, A. Cassidy, and R. Mason Dentinger (eds.), *One Health and its Histories: Animals and the Shaping of Modern Medicine*, Basingstoke, Palgrave: Basingstoke, 2017, 119–160.

Brown, K. and Gilfoyle, D. (eds.), *Healing the Herds: Disease, Livestock Economies, and the Globalization of Veterinary Medicine*, Athens OH: Ohio University Press, 2010.

Bud, R. *Penicillin: Triumph and Tragedy*, Oxford: Oxford University Press, 2007.

Bundy, C. '"We don't want your rain, we won't dip": popular opposition, collaboration and social control in the anti-dipping movement, c1908–16', in W. Beinart and C. Bundy (eds.), *Hidden Struggles in Rural South Africa*, London: Currey, 1987, 191–221.

Bynum, W.F. '"*C'est une malade*": animal models and concepts of human diseases', *Journal of the History of Medicine and Allied Sciences* 45, 3 (1990): 397–413.

Cassidy, A. 'One Health? Building an interdisciplinary bandwagon at the interfaces of animal health, human health and the environment', in S. Frickel, M. Albert, and B. Prainsack (eds.), *Investigating Interdisciplinary Research: Theory and Practice across Disciplines*, New Brunswick NJ: Rutgers University Press, 2016, 213–236.

Cassier, M. 'Producing, controlling and stabilizing Pasteur's anthrax vaccine: creating a new industry and a health market', *Science in Context* 21, 2 (2008): 253–278.

Chapman, C. and Crowden, J. *Silence at Ramscliffe: Foot and Mouth in Devon*, Oxford: Bardwell Press, 2005.

Clarke, A.E. and Fujimura, J.H. (eds.), *The Right Tools for the Job: At Work in the Twentieth Century Life Sciences*, Princeton NJ: Princeton University Press, 1992.

Clause, B. 'The Wistar Rat as a right choice: establishing mammalian standards and the ideal of a standardized mammal', *Journal of the History of Biology*, 26, 2 (1993): 329–349.

Corley, T. and Godley, A. 'The veterinary medicine industry in Britain, 1900–2000', *Economic History Review* 64, 3 (2011): 832–854.

Curth, L.H. 'The care of the brute beast: animals in the seventeenth-century medical marketplace', *Social History of Medicine* 15, 3 (2002): 375–392.

Curth, L.H. *The Care of Brute Beasts: A Social and Cultural Study of Veterinary Medicine in Early Modern England*, Leiden: Brill, 2010.

Curth, L.H. *'A Plaine and Easie Waie to Remedie a Horse': Equine Medicine in Early Modern England*, Leiden: Brill, 2013.

Degeling, C. 'Negotiating value: comparing human and animal fracture care in industrial societies', *Science, Technology, & Human Values* 34, 1 (2009): 77–101.

Degeling, C. 'Picturing the pain of animal others: rationalising form, function and suffering in veterinary orthopaedics', *History and Philosophy of the Life Sciences* 31, 3/4 (2009): 377–403.

Doring, M. and Nerlich, B. (eds.), *The Social and Cultural Impact of Foot-and-Mouth Disease in the UK in 2001: Experiences and Analyses*, Manchester: Manchester University Press, 2009.

Dror, O.E. 'The affect of experiment: the turn to emotions in Anglo-American physiology, 1900–1940', *Isis* 90, 2 (1999): 205–237.

Durbach, N. *Bodily Matters: The Anti-Vaccination Movement in England, 1853–1907*, Durham NC: Duke University Press, 2004.

Elliot, P. 'Vivisection and the emergence of experimental physiology in nineteenth-century France', in N. Rupke (ed.), *Vivisection in Historical Perspective*, London: Routledge, 1990, 48–77.

Erikson, P. and Mitman, G. 'When rabbits became human (and humans, rabbits): stability, order, and history in the study of populations', *Working Papers on The Nature of Evidence: How Well Do 'Facts' Travel*, London: London School of Economics, 2007.

Franco, N.H. 'Animal experiments in biomedical research: a historical perspective', *Animals* 3, 1 (2013): 238–273.

French, R. *Antivivisection and Medical Science in Victorian Society*. London: Princeton University Press, 1975, 112–158.

Fudge, E. 'A left-handed blow: writing the history of animals', in N. Rothfels (ed.), *Representing Animals*, Bloomington IN: Indiana University Press, 2003, 3–18.

Gardiner, A. 'The animal as surgical patient: a historical perspective in the twentieth century', *History and Philosophy of the Life Sciences* 31, 3/4 (2009): 355–376.

Gardiner, A. 'The "dangerous" women of animal welfare: how British veterinary medicine went to the dogs', *Social History of Medicine* 27, 3 (2014), 466–487.

Gibbs, E.P.J. 'The evolution of One Health: a decade of progress and challenges for the future', *Veterinary Record* 174, 4 (2014): 85–91.

Gradmann, C. 'Experimental life and experimental disease: the role of animal experiments in Robert Koch's medical bacteriology', *BIF Futura* 18, (2003): 80–88.

Gray, E. 'Animals and the asylum: a comparative approach to the science of the mind', unpublished paper presented to 'Science in the Asylum' Conference, Wakefield, 2012.

Guerrini, A. *Experimenting with Humans and Animals: From Galen to Animal Rights*, Baltimore MD: Johns Hopkins University Press, 2003.

Guerrini, A. 'Animal experiments and antivivisection debates in the 1820s', in C.K. King and J.R. Goodall, *Frankenstein's Science: Experimentation and Discovery in Romantic Culture, 1780–1830*, Aldershot: Ashgate, 2008, 71–85.

Haraway, D.J. *The Companion Species Manifesto: Dogs, People, and Significant Otherness*, Chicago IL: Prickly Paradigm Press, 2003.

Hardy, A. 'Animals, disease and man: making connections', *Perspectives in Biology and Medicine* 46, 2 (2003): 200–215.

Hardy, A. *Salmonella Infections, Networks of Knowledge, and Public Health in Britain, 1880–1975*, Oxford: Oxford University Press, 2014.

Harrison, M. *Contagion: How Commerce has Spread Disease*, New Haven CT: Yale University Press, 211–246.

Holmes, F. 'The old martyr of science: the frog in experimental physiology', *Journal of the History of Biology*, 26, 2 (1993): 311–328.

Howell, P. *At Home and Astray: The Domestic Dog in Victorian Britain*, Charlottesville VA: University of Virginia Press, 2015.

Hurren, E. '"Abnormalities and deformities": the dissection and interment of the insane poor, 1832–1929', *History of Psychiatry* 23, 1 (2012): 65–77.

Jewson, N.D. 'The disappearance of the sick-man from medical cosmology, 1770–1870', *Sociology* 10, 2 (1976): 225–244.

Jones, S. 'Framing animal disease: housecats with feline urological syndrome, their owners, and their doctors', *Journal of the History of Medicine and Allied Sciences* 52, 2 (1997): 202–235.

Jones, S. *Valuing Animals: Veterinarians and their Patients in Modern America*, Baltimore MD: Johns Hopkins University Press, 2003.

Jones, S. *Death in a Small Package: A Short History of Anthrax*, Baltimore MD: Johns Hopkins University Press, 2010.

Kean, H. 'The "smooth cool men of science": the feminist and socialist response to vivisection', *History Workshop Journal* 40, (1995): 16–38.

Kean, H. *Animal Rights: Political and Social Change in Britain since 1800*, London: Reaktion, 1998, 96–112.

Kean, H. 'Challenges for historians writing animal–human history: what is really enough?', *Anthrozoös* 25, sup.1 (2012): 57–72.

Kete, K. 'La rage and the bourgeoisie', *Representations* 22 (1988): 89–107.

Kirk, R.G.W. '"Wanted – standard guinea pigs": standardization and the experimental animal market in Britain ca.1919–1947', *Studies in History and Philosophy of Science Part C* 39, 3 (2008): 280–291.

Kirk, R.G.W. 'The invention of the "stressed animal" and the development of a science of animal welfare, 1947–86', in D. Cantor and E. Ramsden (eds.), *Stress, Shock, and Adaptation in the Twentieth Century*, Rochester NY: University of Rochester Press, 2014, 241–263.

Kirk, R.G.W. and Worboys, M. 'Medicine and species: one medicine, one history?', in M. Jackson (ed.), *The Oxford Handbook of the History of Medicine*, Oxford: Oxford University Press, 2011, 561–577.

Klein, E.E., Burdon-Sanderson, J., Foster, M., and Brunton, T.L. *A Handbook for the Physiological Laboratory*, London: J. and A. Churchill, 1873.

Kotar, S.L. and Gessler, J.E. *Smallpox: A History*, Jefferson NC: McFarland & Company, 2013.
Lansbury, C. *The Old Brown Dog: Women, Workers, and Vivisection in Edwardian England*, London: University of Wisconsin Press, 1985.
Latour, B. *The Pasteurization of France*, trans. A. Sheridan and J. Law, London: Harvard University Press, 1988.
Lawrence, F. 'If consumers knew how farmed chickens were raised, they might never eat their meat again', *Guardian*, 24 April 2016, available at www.theguardian.com/environment/2016/apr/24/real-cost-of-roast-chicken-animal-welfare-farms, last accessed 11 August 2016.
Lederer, S. 'Political animals: the shaping of biomedical research literature in twentieth-century America', *Isis* 83, 1 (1992): 61–79.
Lesch, J. *Science and Medicine in France: The Emergence of Experimental Physiology, 1790–1855*, London: Harvard University Press, 1984.
Logan, C. 'Before there were standards: the role of test animals in the production of empirical generality in physiology', *Journal of the History of Biology* 35, 2 (2002): 329–363.
Löwy, I. 'The experimental body', in R. Cooter and J. Pickstone (eds.), *Companion Encyclopedia of Medicine in the Twentieth Century*, London: Routledge, 2003, 435–449.
Löwy, I. and Gaudillière, J-P. 'Disciplining cancer: mice and the practice of genetic purity', in J-P. Gaudillière and I. Löwy (eds.), *The Invisible Industrialist: Manufactures and the Production of Scientific Knowledge*, Basingstoke: Macmillan, 1998, 209–249.
MacKay, M. 'The rise of a medical specialty: the medicalisation of elite equine care c.1680–c.1800', unpublished PhD thesis, University of York, 2009.
Mason Dentinger, R. 'Patterns of infection and patterns of evolution: How a malaria parasite brought "monkeys and man" closer together in the 1960s', *Journal of the History of Biology* 49, 2 (2016): 359–395.
McCabe, A. *A Byzantine Encyclopaedia of Horse Medicine: The Sources, Compilation, and Transmission of the Hippiatrica*, Oxford: Oxford University Press, 2007.
Olmstead, A. and Rhodes, P. *Arresting Contagion: Science, Policy, and Conflicts over Animal Disease Control*, Cambridge MA: Harvard University Press, 2015.
Pearn, A. '"This excellent observer . . .": the correspondence between Charles Darwin and James Crichton Brown', *History of Psychiatry* 21, 2 (2010): 160–175.
Pemberton, N. and Worboys, M. *Mad Dogs and Englishmen: Rabies in Britain, 1830–2000*, Basingstoke: Palgrave Macmillan, 2007.
Phoofolo, P. 'Epidemics and revolutions: the rinderpest epidemic in late nineteenth-century southern Africa', *Past and Present* 138 (1993): 112–143.
Rader, K. *Making Mice: Standardizing Animals for American Biomedical Research, 1900–55*, Princeton NJ: Princeton University Press, 2004.
Rader, K. 'Scientific animals: the laboratory and its human–animal relations, from Dba to Dolly', in R. Malamud (ed.), *A Cultural History of Animals in the Modern Age*, London: Bloomsbury, 2007, 119–137.
Regan, T. *The Case for Animal Rights*. Berkeley CA: University of California Press, 1983.
Remy, C. 'The animal issue in xenotransplantation: controversies in France and the United States', *History and Philosophy of the Life Sciences* 31, 3/4 (2009): 407–432.
Ritvo, H. *The Animal Estate: The English and Other Creatures in the Victorian Age*, Cambridge MA: Harvard University Press, 1987.
Ritvo, H. 'Animal planet', *Environmental History* 9, 2 (2004): 204–220.
Rupke, N. (ed.), *Vivisection in Historical Perspective*, London: Routledge, 1990.
Russell, E. 'Introduction', in S. Schrepfer and P. Scranton (eds.), *Industrializing Organisms: Introducing Evolutionary History*, London: Routledge, 2003, 3–16.

Schlich, T., Mykhalovskiy, E., and Rock, M. 'Animals in surgery – surgery in animals: nature and culture in animal–human relations and modern surgery', *History and Philosophy of the Life Sciences* 31, 3/4 (2009): 321–354.

Schlünder, M. and Schlich, T. 'The emergence of "implant-pets" and "bone-sheep": animals as new biomedical objects in orthopedic surgery (1960s–2010)', *History and Philosophy of the Life Sciences* 31, 3/4 (2009): 433–466.

Shehada, H.A. *Mamluks and Animals: Veterinary Medicine in Medieval Islam*, Leiden: Brill, 2013.

Simon, J. 'Monitoring the stable at the Pasteur Institute', *Science in Context* 21, 2 (2008): 181–200.

Singer, P. *Animal Liberation*, London: Cape, 1976.

Slater, L. 'Malarial birds: modeling infectious human disease in animals', *Bulletin of the History of Medicine* 79, 2 (2005): 261–294.

Swabe, J. *Animals, Disease and Human Society: Human-Animal Relations and the Rise of Veterinary Medicine*, London: Routledge, 2002.

Tansey, E.M. 'Protection against dog distemper and dogs protection bills: the Medical Research Council and anti-vivisectionist protest, 1911–33', *Medical History* 38, 1 (1994): 1–26.

Teigen, P. 'Legislating fear and the public health in Gilded Age Massachusetts', *Journal of the History of Medicine and Allied Sciences* 62, 2 (2007): 141–170.

Todes, D. 'Pavlov's physiology factory', *Isis* 88, 2 (1997): 205–246.

Van Zwanenberg, P. and Millstone, E. *BSE: Risk, Science and Governance*, Oxford: Oxford University Press, 2005.

Waddington, K. 'To stamp out "so terrible a malady": bovine tuberculosis and tuberculin testing in Britain, 1890–1939', *Medical History* 48, 1 (2004): 29–48.

Waddington, K. *The Bovine Scourge: Meat, Tuberculosis and Public Health, 1850–1914*, Woodbridge: Boydell Press, 2006.

Waddington, K. 'The dangerous sausage: diet, meat and disease in Victorian and Edwardian Britain', *Cultural and Social History* 8, 1 (2011): 51–71.

Walton, J. 'Mad dogs and Englishmen: the conflict over rabies in late Victorian England', *Journal of Social History* 13, 2 (1979): 219–239.

Warner, J.H. 'The uses of patient records by historians: patterns, possibilities and perplexities', *Health and History* 1, 2/3 (1999): 101–111.

White, P. 'The experimental animal in Victorian Britain', in L. Daston and G. Mitman, *Thinking with Animals: New Perspectives on Anthropomorphism*, New York: Columbia University Press, 2005, 59–81.

Wilkinson, L. *Animals and Disease: An Introduction to the History of Comparative Medicine*, Cambridge: Cambridge University Press, 1992.

Woods, A. *A Manufactured Plague: The History of Foot and Mouth Disease in Britain*, London: Earthscan, 2004.

Woods, A. 'From practical men to scientific experts: British veterinary surgeons and the development of government scientific expertise, c1878–1919', *History of Science* 51, 4 (2013): 457–480.

Woods, A. 'Animals and disease', in M. Jackson (ed.), *Routledge History of Disease*, Abingdon: Routledge, 2016, 147–164.

Woods, A. 'Between human and veterinary medicine: the history of animals and surgery', in T. Schlich (ed.), *Palgrave Handbook of the History of Surgery*, London: Palgrave, 2017, 115–132.

Woods, A. 'Doctors in the zoo: connecting human and animal health in British zoological gardens, c1828–1890', in A. Woods, M. Bresalier, A. Cassidy, and R. Mason Dentinger, *One Health and its Histories: Animals and the Shaping of Modern Medicine*, Basingstoke: Palgrave, 2017, 27–70.

Woods, A. and Matthews, S. '"Little, if at all, removed from the illiterate farrier or cow-leech": the English veterinary surgeon, c.1860–85, and the campaign for veterinary reform', *Medical History* 54, 1 (2010): 29–54.

Woods, A., Bresalier, M., Cassidy, A., and Mason Dentinger, R. *One Health and its Histories: Animals and the Shaping of Modern Medicine*, Basingstoke: Palgrave, 2017.

Zinsstag, J.E., Waltner-Toews, D., and Tannera, M. 'From "One Medicine" to "One Health" and systemic approaches to health and wellbeing', *Preventive Veterinary Medicine* 101, 3 (2011): 148–156.

8
ANIMAL MATTER IN MUSEUMS
Exemplifying materiality[1]

Liv Emma Thorsen

Live and dead animals are with us and around us. Innocently and unconsciously, animals have left material sources such as horns, bones, hides, and shells. If animals themselves do not leave documents, the historian's most prominent sources, there are nevertheless several other ways to encounter their historical existence. The animals of past times subsist as natural matter, for instance, in old photographs, dusty registers, and fragile letters; remnants from encounters between humans and animals which can tell us something about animals' unnatural history, as historian Nigel Rothfels claims.[2] This chapter will give emphasis to the potential of museum objects as sources for an animal–human history, exploring objects in cultural history museums and natural history museums, institutions that store a variety of objects made of animal remains, ranging from stuffed animals to utility shafts of bone, from viscera in spirit to breeches of canine leather. The examples discussed in this chapter are things made of organic material derived from animals, either objects made to reshape the once-living animal, or objects composed exclusively or partly of animal matter. The question is what kind of knowledge may such objects provide, beyond their form, shape, materials, and technique.

The lives of wild as well as domestic animals, their corpses and their place in tradition, imagination and beliefs have been given a wide range of material expressions throughout history. However, the word 'animal' is not even indexed in the *Handbook of Material Culture*, first published in 2006.[3] In his introduction to the handbook, Christopher Tilley nevertheless challenges the opposition between things and persons by pointing to animals as a kind of border case, being neither one nor the other:

> The object and the objectivity of things supposedly stand opposed to the subject and the subjectivity of persons. From this perspective, persons are animated and alive, while the things, whatever they may be, are simply static and dead: kick a stone or a pot and you won't hurt or offend it. Yet even in simple and empirical terms, a host of borderline cases, such as animals or technological extensions of persons, challenge the opposition.[4]

Animals are here considered as something distinctively *in between*. Animals work undauntedly to maximize their well-being, for instance, something considered in the language of 'agency'. But if agency also may be assigned to *things*, following the lead of 'the material turn' in the humanities and social sciences, how might we characterise the agency of this genre of museum objects?

To ascribe agency to things means to contemplate their materiality, which is the central aim of this chapter. An understanding of material agency can hardly be separated from the difficult business of *matter*.[5] Materiality implies a relation between the material object and people, and establishes the material object in a historical, social and cultural context.[6] When studying material objects as materiality, the task is then to identify materials as significant and meaningful in these contexts: 'All materials have their properties which may be described but only some of these materials are significant to people'.[7] Following this injunction, the objects that are presented and exemplified in this chapter are carefully chosen because of the significance of their material properties. To allude to the material objects desired by collectors and destined for the early modern cabinets of curiosity, for instance, these material qualities were supposed to arouse wonder and invite attention, to provoke investigation and prompt reflection about the world.[8]

Studying material things as meaningful elements in a wider historical and cultural context furthermore implies a kind of vicarious agency – their provocation to interpretation *by* somebody, *for* some purpose. Writing and reflecting about the meaningfulness and materiality of museum objects contributes to keeping them visible and prevents them from falling into oblivion. As stated by the critic Miguel Tamen, interpretable objects attract 'friends'.[9] This making of friends by material things testifies to a society engaged in interpretation and in attributing a kind of intentionality to the objects they are in this way befriending.[10] The mission of such societies of friends is precisely to keep the objects 'alive'. Inspired by Tamen, science historian Lorraine Daston turns to the things themselves to scrutinise why certain objects attract friends, and she is arrested by their sheer *materiality*: 'The capacity to call such a society of friends into existence is as much a part of a thing's thingness, of its reverberations in the world, as its material properties like weight and chemical composition'.[11] Daston's personal selected things are the unique glass flowers at the Harvard Museum of Natural History in Cambridge, Massachusetts. In contrast to these famous glass flowers, the chosen objects that will be presented in this chapter are, except perhaps for the preserved dogs in the Natural History Museum at Tring, little known to the public, some of them being permanently exiled to a museum storeroom. However, even if they may look like humble things at first encounter they are nevertheless worthy of befriending, because, to paraphrase Daston, they are as I shall show 'irresistibly interpretable'.[12]

This chapter stresses animal matter and its repercussions on the scholar as a starting point for a discussion of materiality. First, the cultural history museum and the natural history museum will be presented as places that contain animal matter and treasuries for scholars engaged in the cultural histories of animals. Next, a biography of Bella, a stuffed dog in a museum storeroom, will serve as a primer to different perspectives on museum animals and materiality, leading to a discussion of taxidermy as both handicraft and a category of things still closely associated with animals and animality.

With the trajectory of Bella in mind I will then discuss how animal matter is embedded in culture and society, exemplified by evocative, talkative and 'knotted' animal things. Finally, the chapter touches on the ethical questions animal museum objects may provoke.

Animal matters in museums: across categories

With a wording taken from Chris Philo and Chris Wilbert, museums of cultural history and natural history may be described as 'beastly places'.[13] However, contrary to their idea of beastly places as territories in which animals can live according to their natural needs with a minimum of human interference, museums are places that demonstrate the numerous ways animals have been merged and incorporated in culture, and likewise, though less investigated, their importance and influence on society. In the museum the objects have been ordered, classified, defined and categorised. Museum objects are, however, also confined by their classificatory categories. Looking for the materiality of animal matters typically implies the crossing of these categories.

During the sixteenth and seventeenth centuries, collecting precious and rare objects was intrinsically connected with a princely way of living. To collect was, according to Paula Findlen, 'a precise mechanism to transform knowledge into power'.[14] In order to raise the visitor's curiosity, the favoured principle of exposing and exhibiting objects was 'the close juxtaposition of contrasting'.[15] At the end of the eighteenth century in Europe many princely collections were split up and systemised according to the Enlightenment visions of taxonomic order.[16] Things stemming from nature were increasingly separated from art objects. The historical and symbolic connections between object, collection and owner were thus ruptured when the objects were inserted in the new knowledge regimes. The *ippopotamo* in the *Museo Zoologica* 'La Specola' in Florence, one of the oldest European public natural history museums and today part of Universitá di Firenze, will serve as an example.

When Florence's new natural history museum opened its doors on 21 February 1775, with the impressive official name *L'Imperiale Regio Museo di Fisica e Storia Naturale*, the public was introduced to an institution that precisely realised the Age of Enlightenment's new museum ideal.[17] The museum was open to one and all, and its activities were organised according to new scientific principles. Commissioned by the Grand Duke of Tuscany, the medical doctor and natural scholar Giovanni Targioni Tozzetti put together a catalogue over a period of two years, from 1763 to 1764, of what he designated the 'natural products' in the princely collections. Most came from the now-extinct Medici family's cabinets of curiosity in the Uffizi galleries and the Palazzo Pitti.

In the preface to the catalogue, Tozzetti recommends that the general public should have access to these unique natural objects. Seven years later, the young Grand Duke Peter Leopold of Habsburg-Lorraine decided to put all the natural science objects in a separate museum. The construction of an astronomical observatory also brought astrology and meteorology into the museum's sphere of concern. Completed in 1789, the observatory gave the museum the popular name 'La Specola'. In the same year, the adjoining Giardino del Boboli was made into a botanical garden and associated with the institution. Thus the museum covered all the branches of natural history, while the Medicis' huge collections of art and precious items were put on display in the Uffizi and the Pitti Palace. To the visitor, however, the unique historical complexity of the Specola collections may confound the idea that 'nature' is presented here. For instance, decorated and engraved shells of *nautilus pompilius* and a valve of a freshwater bivalve with Buddha figures covered with mother-of-pearls are clearly artistically elaborated objects, but these were considered predominantly things of *nature* and directed to the collections in 'La Specola' accordingly.

The object that is probably most resistant to this categorisation, however, is La Specola's hippopotamus, approximately 300 years old, its venerable age revealed through the execution of its preservation, which further suggests that its executors had never seen the animal alive. The museum states that the origin and death of the hippo is unknown. What is known, however, is that the mount did belong to the Medici collections and it is easy to connect the pachyderm to the early baroque royal court culture of Cosimo III (1670–1723), and to the cultural history of exotic, wild animals in Europe.[18] Thus cages for wild animals were placed in the Giardino di Boboli for the enjoyment of the Florentine court. According to anecdote, the hippo belonged to this menagerie, and it is claimed to have lived in one of the garden fountains.[19] Not much else is known, however. The specimen proves that the hippo was not fully grown when it died, and it has a mark around its neck that has been interpreted as coming from some kind of harness, though this is now contested by the museum after a restoration of the hippo finished in 2012.

Little is known about the menagerie in the Boboli garden, but in a brief description from 1757 it is stated that the *serraglio* also contained a separate section with stuffed animals.[20] Cosimo III was a prince who spent time and money on collecting live animals – but also in presenting them after death for display, an act that shows how rare and expensive the noble collectors of this time considered these animals to be. Live hippopotamuses have been extremely rare in Europe, so exquisite that when a hippo calf arrived in London Zoo in 1850, it was claimed to be the first hippo seen in Europe after the age of the Romans. This makes the hippopotamus in La Specola an especially interesting and valuable object for both natural history *and* cultural history.[21]

Interestingly the recent restoration of the hippo has revealed that two styles of preparation are apparent in this specimen, from the seventeenth and eighteenth centuries respectively.[22] When the specimen was moved from the Grand Duke's collection to be exposed in the new natural history museum, the highly skilled craftsmen of the famous anatomical ceroplastics in La Specola remodelled the hippo's head using wax on a wooden frame. More importantly, this was part of a crucial change of focus. The specimen in La Specola was initially preserved in order to allow a precious individual animal to be admired in a princely cabinet even in its afterlife, but in the systematic exhibition it was reduced to acting as a representative of its species. All the same, after its restoration in 2012, the hippo was displayed together with an ornamental arrangement of hippopotamus teeth, an object stemming from the late nineteenth-century collection of the Duke of Turin's hunting trophies; so the museum has re-established a link between this impressive species and the princely tradition of self-presentation by means of dead animals.

Consider a second example, which in contrast to the mount of the rare and valuable hippo, is chosen from the multitude of vernacular things stored in cultural history museums, namely knives. Accession number NF 2007–0817AC (Norsk Folkemuseum) is an assemblage of twelve table knives, produced by Moss & Gambles, Sheffield, England, and by Henckels, Solingen, Germany around 1900.[23] The knives look pretty much alike, having a blade of steel (not stainless) with a rounded end and stamped with the manufacturer's trademark, and with handles made of bone. The Sheffield knives are a bit longer than the German ones, but both were common goods in Norway around 1900. They are still to be found in Norwegian kitchen drawers, and are frequently sold in antique shops and flea markets. Of particular interest when examining animals and materiality are these bone handles. What significance do these fragments of animal matter have for a discussion of the history of animals? As mass-produced things the knives are not especially interesting per se. If it is possible to maintain that this set of table knives reverberate in the world, to follow Daston, it is largely because the material of their handles connects them to the animal-industry by the turn of the twentieth century.

The crucial thing is what happens when we turn our attention from relation to substance, from seeing the knives only as imported common goods, to contemplating the material of the handles. This means using the knives as a *pars pro toto* – as a few of millions of ordinary table knives with handles of bone, most often either bone from horse or cow, a commonplace of what we can talk of as an animal-industrial economy. At the end of the nineteenth century the development of the great industrial cities in the US and Europe depended heavily, for instance, on horsepower, making bone from horse a cheap and easily available raw material.[24] In 1900, 130,000 horses worked in New York, 74,000 in Chicago, and in London 50,000 horses were used just for transporting people. Around 1900, the urban horse had been made a commodity – but not only as a living animal. Working horses lived short lives, partly because of hard work, but also because of the value of their carcasses:

> Rendering plants shaved the hair to be used for cushions. (...) Hair also became a stiffener for plaster and was made into blankets. Skinners cut the hide off, using the rump portion of the hide for highly valued cordovan leather. They boiled hooves to extract oil, especially for glue but also for gelatin. Renderers boiled the carcass in a pressure boiler to separate flesh from bones and carved the leg bones into knife handles and combs.[25]

Other products sourced from dead horses were bootblack, carbonate of ammonia, phosphorus for matches, pet food, soap, and candles.

Here are twelve different products extracted from the horse carcass, then. Some were perishable consumer goods, while others were used for the production of more durable objects such as the handles. The horse's materiality thus demonstrates how animal matter exists historically and continues today to be entangled in complex, extensive networks. But how far can horse matter such as, say, gelatine be followed?[26] What we can say is that from economies such as the food, pharmaceutical, cosmetic and weapon industries, to religious and ethical dietary restrictions, animal matter is everywhere.

Special things: the poet's dog Bella

Animal museum matter may be both naturalised and unique. Take a third example, the dog belonging to the Norwegian romantic poet Henrik Wergeland (1808–1845). On 6 July 1845, six days before his death, Wergeland (1808–1845) wrote his last letter.[27] The addressee was Halvor H. Rasch at the Zoological Collections of the Royal Frederick University in Christiania (today Oslo) and the topic was Wergeland's dog Bella. In the letter Bella was bequeathed to the collections. The dog, Wergeland explained, 'deserved a place in them as a skeleton and stuffed as type for the antique canine form on bas-reliefs'. And, he continued, 'If you want it, take it at once, because it disturbs me in my scant sleep'.[28] Whether the 9-year-old Bella was allowed to die a natural death or she was put down immediately after being given to the Zoological Collections is not known. But the remains were to be inserted in the collections after Bella's hide was stuffed. The fragile body still exists, not as a scientific specimen but as object 'NF 1902–0211', currently stored in a refrigerated room in the Norsk Folkemuseum in Oslo.[29] The skeleton has disappeared. The accession number informs us that Bella was transferred from the Zoological Collections to the Folkemuseum in 1902. The body, though bulky and badly mounted, has a clear resemblance to sighthounds, being a bit larger than a whippet. The skin is greyish brown and dappled. Her glass eyes are missing.

The museum storeroom is a terminal station for many objects but also a point of departure. An approach to opening up the categories in which museum things are inscribed is to follow the trajectories or biographies of the objects, if possible all the way from live animals to museum items.[30] As stated by the anthropologist Arjun Appadurai, the meaning of things is 'inscribed in their forms, their uses, their trajectories'.[31] In this regard, Bella has a double biography, one that highlights her existence as an individual, and one that emphasises her as a museum object. The transfer here of the stuffed dog from a museum of nature to one of culture is particularly significant, as it eroded its legitimacy as a specimen and destabilised its meaning. In the zoological collections the remnants of the pet dog Bella had been neutralised and naturalised, to make her represent a type of *Canis lupus familiaris*. In the Folkemuseum, however, the stuffed dog became an item on a par with the poet's other belongings preserved therein.

The stuffed Bella sheds light on her potential as a museum object. For many years the dog was displayed in Wergeland's arbour. The octagonal small, wooden hut had been moved to the Folk Museum in 1902, the same year as Bella was transported from the university in the centre of Oslo to the peninsula of Bygdøy. Inside the arbour the stuffed animal was displayed together with others of Wergeland's belongings; here the dog was reduced to a prop in a tableau performing the poet's summer study. Exposed to shifting temperatures through many years the body deteriorated badly and was finally stored properly in a cold storeroom.[32]

To Wergeland, Bella had meant different things. He was himself a collector of nature, alive and dead; to make his dog a scientific specimen was a logical consequence of his engagement in natural history. Bella's destiny may be interpreted as a rational and unsentimental way to handle the body of a dead animal. When the dog was alive, Wergeland had written the beautiful stanza 'I lower my sorrows in my dog's eye like into a deep well'.[33] However, his strong affinity to dogs and to animals and nature in general did not prevent him from considering his pet dog Bella an interesting contribution to a natural history collection: namely, to add to our knowledge of the hunting hounds of antiquity. We on the other hand are inclined to see the individual *Bella*, Henrik Wergeland's dog, a beloved pet known to us from his writings, and the act of objectifying and transforming her to a thing, either as specimen or property, contrasts strongly with how the great majority of Norwegians deposit their dead dogs today.[34] Judged by the way we handle the bodies of our dead pet dogs, the dog as a sentient being seems to be closer to a human than in Wergeland's times. Whether our feelings towards dogs are more sincere today than then, is, however, harder to tell.

Why and for what purpose is this miserable-looking, poorly upholstered body, close to 200 years old, of a dog called Bella, a thought-provoking thing? Bella's story is really about animal matter in transition in space and time. It exemplifies brilliantly the degree to which our understanding of a material object is deduced from where it is situated or located, in the case of Bella the natural history museum versus the folk museum. It is also, and maybe even more suggestively, a lesson about shifting emotions and the historicity in humans' feelings towards dogs. The biography of Bella, alive and dead, demonstrates the antagonistic ways humans have handled dogs and treated dogs, an animal that has been moved along an axis with instrumentality and sentimentality as its extremes.

Today no casual visitor can see the real object, but Bella is virtually present at Digitalt Museum, the electronic database of the Norwegian cultural history museums. The virtual appearance of Wergeland's dog reinforces her prospects of gaining new friends and maybe of telling new tales.

Transformations: upholstering and taxidermy

In one sense, stuffed animal bodies stand out as the ultimate objectification of animals where animal matter in museums is concerned. Whether we are reminded of life or rather death is, however, a moot point. The objectified animal may have been seen as 'the remnant of life'; to Victorians 'the taxidermy specimen realized the vitality within the remaining fur and feathers', historian Ann C. Colley claims.[35] Taking the opposing view, the art historian Rachel Poliquin stresses death as the foremost property of taxidermy: 'its realism is deadly'.[36] Whether a taxidermy animal suggests life or death is perhaps, however, a question about *quality*. 'Mounts are intended to be "resurrections", as close to life as possible,' science historian Samuel Alberti unequivocally states.[37] But the remains of Bella attract attention because she was a national skald's pet, and we contemplate her eeriness accordingly. The trouble with Bella is that her badly mounted skin, and the general decay of the object, make her a travesty of a dog and expose her definitive deadness. The illusion of life that pulls thousands of children to the stuffed animals in dioramas and glass cases in natural history museums around the world is particularly absent in this specimen. What remains is death.

The object Bella is, then, a piece of upholstery. Old animal mounts have lumpy and lifeless forms because the technique was simply to fill a hide, for instance with straw, which makes the body shrink, or with plaster, which makes the hide crack. Taxidermy at its best has been considered an art.[38] The core of taxidermy is to eradicate allusions to the death of the animal. The term itself comes from the Greek, being composed of 'taxis' which means movement, and 'derma' which means skin. The combination of the two means moving or manipulating the skin or the hide on a manikin in order to recreate the shape of the once-living animal.[39]

Biographies of zoological specimens may be described as '*material* knowledge in transit, bringing experiences of nature with them to different sites and audiences'.[40] This can be elaborated further, for biographies of zoological specimens are typically fragmented knowledge. What is seldom reflected on when contemplating exhibitions of animals in glass cases is that what we see are body *fragments*: a giraffe's hide, an eagle's skin. Natural history museums are filled with nature, and the problem is really how to move nature into the museum. To succeed in this endeavour, nature must be processed and transformed to manageable pieces that can function as scientific data. A great deal of work is invested to save fragments of the original animal, and the information they contain. Mammal and bird skins are stored flat in cabinets, bones put carefully in boxes and on shelves, soft tissue soaked in liquor, the temperature in the storerooms controlled. Each fragmented animal is being held together by means of registers, field notes, photographs, measurements, scientific articles and the like.

The arrangement of animal matter, not merely its preservation, is an essential lesson. To take an example: the Gothenburg Natural History Museum displays a splendid mounted bull elephant, shot in Angola on 4 December 1948 by museum taxidermist David Sjölander.[41] The animal was flayed, the hide treated with 4 kilograms of phenol and 100 kilograms of salt. After two weeks the skeleton had been thoroughly cleansed and the transportation back to Sweden could begin. Some of the bones were so huge that they had to be sawn. 'The elephant is a particularly popular dismembered animal', Kalof and Fitzgerald state in their analysis of hunting trophy photographs.[42] As taxidermy, however, the Gothenburg mounted elephant is made of fragments from *three* separate elephants: skin from the Angola bull, tusks from a second animal, and the characteristic hairs on the tail from a third. The complete skeleton with tusks is stored in the museum's Bone Cellar. Another example is the walrus, another taxidermy eye-catcher in the museum, shot on 9 January 1927 in the archipelago north of Gothenburg, the body transported to the museum the following day. The walrus's hide was mounted, the intestines soaked in liquor and the bones placed in the Bone Cellar.

As previously argued, materiality may be studied as a relation between matter or materials and people. The materiality of a taxidermy animal body in a natural history museum works within a triangle composed of the mounted specimen, the absent and idiosyncratic and once-alive animal, and the observer. The mounted animals crowding together in the glass cases are didactic objects made to represent their species. However, the very idea of a species is an abstraction, as Jeremy Mynott claims in his book *Birdscapes*:

> But what is that we are identifying or failing to identify, anyway? For most purposes we seem to be more interested in the bird as a representative of a

species rather than as an individual. That's what we name, count, admire, conserve or eat. (...) The idea of a species is after all an abstraction, (...), a convenient way of relating a lot of birds that share certain common properties.[43]

The essence of the process to convert an animal into one or several specimens is 'the very act of removal' according to Alberti.[44] Scars, bodily defects caused by bone fractures, bullet injuries, and holes in hides have carefully been patched up on the taxidermy body. Through the act of removal and preservation, the animal is thus cleansed of meanings that might connect the beast to society and culture, its history partly erased: 'For, if objects are to act as data, they need to be impartial – their constructedness needs to be hidden by those whose credibility depends upon them', claims Alberti.[45]

To 'naturalise' is another verb used for mounting animals, expressing the taxidermist's purpose: to achieve a result that presents the animal in a natural state. But to what degree does an individual animal function fully as a neutral illustration of the idealised species? High quality taxidermy makes the animal look alive again but the use of real skins presupposes death and undermines the neutrality of the object. But even a single flat skin in a museum series can be a carrier of information for 'telling complex histories of human–animal encounter, cohabitation, and estrangement', as Patchett, Foster and Lorimer demonstrate in their biography of a harrier skin.[46] Information about earlier life clings to the animal fragments in the natural history collections.

In contrast to scientific models made of wood, wax, ceramics or plaster, being simulacra or imitations of an original, stuffed animals have skin and fur that once belonged to a live animal, pretending to be the real thing. They possess an 'uncanny animal-thingness', to quote Rachel Poliquin: 'This uncanny animal-thingness has the power to provoke, to edify, and even to undermine the validity of its own existence'.[47] A stuffed animal is a crafted thing, yet one of its properties is its volatility. Taxidermy's purpose is to arrange skins, but a skin can be arranged several times. A mount can be dismantled. The skin is of value to the natural history museum, not the animal object per se except for specimens of extinct or famous animals. And even the skin of a historical specimen from a famous animal can be rearranged, like the rescue dog Barry in the Natural History Museum of Bern.[48]

Poliquin, moreover, expresses the uncertainty that sticks to the materiality and meaning of stuffed animals: 'Animal or object? Animal and object? This is the irresolvable tension that defines all taxidermy'.[49] This tension leads Poliquin into seven different interpretations of taxidermy, each coloured by what she calls 'a particular longing':[50]

> All taxidermy is a disorientating, unknowable thing. All taxidermy is driven to capture animal beauty. It is always a spectacle, whose meaning depends in part on the particularity of the animal being displayed. It is motivated by the desire to tell ourselves stories about who we are and about our journey within the larger social and natural world. It is driven by what lies beneath the animal form, by the metaphors and allegories we use to make our world

make sense. And finally, taxidermy is always a gesture of remembrance: the beast is no more.[51]

To understand the materiality of taxidermied animals one must then ask for the reason why the animal was preserved, and then ask what the object means today.[52] Poliquin's seven interpretive categories are wonder, beauty, spectacle, order, narrative, allegory and remembrance. If we return to the animal-thing Bella, she definitely arouses both wonder and remembrance by virtue of being the relics of Henrik Wergeland's last companion animal. The dog was preserved to represent a canine type of antiquity and to be displayed in a natural history museum, but ultimately did not fit into the scientific taxonomies. As an animal-thing she is a travesty of a dog and the reverse of beauty. Bringing these elements together makes a narrative comprising the dog and the poet, attitudes to animals in the past and the present, an experience of distance in time and mentality.

Evocative and talkative things: dogs at Tring

In the flow of scholarship that has followed in the wake of the material turn in humanities and social sciences, many accounts explore carefully picked objects, objects that are attributed the power to talk, to evoke and to bring to mind. According to psychologist Sherry Turkle evocative objects are things that unite emotion and intellect:

> We find it familiar to consider objects as useful or aesthetic, as necessities or vain indulgences. We are on less familiar ground when we consider objects as companions to our emotional lives or as provocations to thought. The notion of evocative objects brings together these two less familiar ideas, underscoring the inseparability of thought and feeling in our relationship to things. We think with the objects we love; we love the objects we think with.[53]

Evocative things are mnemonic. They assist our memories helping and provoking us to think and remember. A hearing-impaired man explained to a journalist what his personal belongings meant to him. He expressed the link between things, memory and thought that we learn from Turkle's text but in this case experienced as a repetitive everyday task:

> I love to collect things, you know because I can't hear I need a lot to look at. I observe things, touch things, sniff on things and communicate with them. There's not a thing here without a personal value. When I dust, old memories pop up and make me happy. I love to dust.[54]

His statement adds a new potential to dull dusting: to dust is to keep the connection between things and memory present and awake.

When considering the expressive potential in things, Turkle gives prominence to the psychological quality of an object. Lorraine Daston, on the other hand, emphasises its materiality. I will claim that the objectified Bella, given her status of pet, is an evocative object. But Bella is also one of the kind of things that talk, or rather make us talk about them, a *chimera*. The essence of the chimera is composition, Daston states:

> Things that talk are often chimeras, composites of different species. The difference in species must be stressed: the composites in question don't just weld together different elements of some kind (for example, the wood, nails, glue and paint stuck together to make a chair); they straddle boundaries between kinds. Art and nature, persons and things, objective and subjective are somehow brought together in these things, and the fusions result in considerable blurring of outlines.[55]

A chimera is a being composed of parts from different animals. Originally a Greek term, the chimera was a monstrous animal, half lion and half goat, with a serpent's tail. The key aspect about chimera-like things, in Daston's words, is that they 'straddle boundaries between kinds', *and* they straddle boundaries drawn between classes or species.[56] They thus transcend boundaries and connect commonly separated elements. Because chimerical objects challenge boundaries and categories, they attract attention. Daston maintains that chimerical objects bind materiality and meaning together.[57] She also claims that the speech of objects is derived from the particular characteristics of the objects, properties that fit with the cultural purposes they are part of and participate in, or participated in. Hence, we must know the changing contexts to make things speak.

Stuffed animals are material chimeras. As physical natural history objects they can be touched, moved, rebuilt and viewed, all according to the purpose. To the visitor they tell about fauna and also mobilise perceptions, narratives and emotions.[58] Stuffed animals resist standard classification according to the nature–culture dichotomy. They raise the question of what kind of artefact we are dealing with: are they cultural objects, natural objects or rather hybrids that interact between nature and non-nature, where non-nature points towards the social and cultural conditions of natural science, as well as toward art and notions about the relationship between people and animals?

Talkative things thus catch our attention because they connect nature and culture, blur boundaries and combine elements that often are separate. Bella as history and materiality pulls together nature and culture, pet and specimen, museum registers and poetry, upholstery and flesh and blood. Chimera alludes to composition and monster. In this discussion it should be observed that chimera also claims a signification that refers to imagination, creative thought and inventiveness. This establishes a connection between Turkle's notion of 'evocative things' and Daston's understanding of 'things that talk'. But sight precedes speech, especially in museum displays. Evocative and talkative things first speak to the eye: 'Speaking to the eye beyond speaking to the brain I would think would be of the very greatest benefit for my readers'. These were the words of Italian scientist and taxidermist Paolo Savi in his introductory chapter to *Ornithologia Toscana*.[59]

The stuffed dogs exhibited in the Natural History Museum's collection at Tring, in Hertfordshire, England, certainly speak to the eye. European museum collections – be they in natural history museums or cultural history museums – very seldom contain stuffed dogs or other domesticated animals, and it is even more rare to see them displayed. A famous exception, however, is the Dog Collection at Tring.[60] During the years 1900–1915, Richard Lydekker (1849–1915) of the Natural History Museum (part of the British Museum until 1963) was in charge of the Collection of Domesticated Animals.[61] The collection was planned with skins and skeletons 'to form a nucleus of a study series', added with a 'collection of photographs of modern breeds (. . .). When practicable, the various breeds should be represented with skins and skeletons of well-known animals – more especially prize-winners'.[62] Such a collection, he hoped, 'in the course of time will be of the highest value to the breeder, as well as to the student of variation'.[63] The dogs that today are shown at Tring were formerly part of an exhibition of domesticated animals displayed in the Central and North Halls of the Natural History Museum in London.[64] In the 1950s there was an ongoing discussion about the possibility of making Tring into a museum of domesticated animals. This failed: the exhibition was dismantled in 1959, only the dog collection transferred to its present home at Tring.[65]

Today the display of stuffed dogs at Tring most of all offers an instructive and unique demonstration of the exterior changes the exposed breeds have undergone during the last hundred years. The exhibition may be interpreted as an illustrative and thought-provoking installation of the aesthetic manipulation of the so-called purebred dog. Short snouts are getting shorter, curved legs more curved, small loins and hind limbs smaller, wide skulls wider, under-hung jaws even more under-hung, which has been the case of the English bulldog. As Lydekker ascertained in his description of the breed already in 1908: 'These features are exaggerated in the modern breed, which is useless for fighting'.[66]

The dogs were mounted by the famous taxidermy workshop Rowland Ward Ltd.[67] Ward provided stuffed specimens to The Natural History Museum in London and to natural history museums all over Europe. The second important client group was big game hunters. Similar to the preferred posture given to wild mammals, the dogs are mounted standing, and they don't carry any pointers to domestication and tameness such as a collar. Trophy taxidermy has also influenced the mounting of the dogs: a head of a King Charles Cavalier mounted on a wooden plaque opens the visitor's eyes wide.

When assembling the collection of domestic animals Lydekker aimed at prize-winning individuals. In fact a high number of the dogs displayed in the Tring museum had been exhibited successfully in dog shows in their lifetime. Several of them had been famous award-winning show and racing dogs, and several had been at their best when they died, very often due to canine distemper. In this period canine distemper became steadily more common in the British Isles, and a vaccine against the illness did not exist.

The most prominent of the exhibited dogs are: Mick the Miller, who in his lifetime was a shining star after the first greyhound racing stadium was opened in Manchester in 1926 (between the years 1928 and 1931 he won 46 out of 61 races), the greyhound Fullerton (1887–1899) who lost just two of his 33 races, and the English bulldog Nuthurst Doctor (1901–1909), 26 times a champion, a winner of 700 other prizes, and declared Best in Show at the Kennel Club's exhibition at the

Crystal Palace in 1907. Other dogs are distinguished because they were the first example of a breed presented in England, for example the Pekingese male Ah Cum, imported from China in 1896.[68] The Australian feral dingo and 'pariah' dogs from India and Turkey were included in the collection to emphasise the variation of the species and for a pointed contrast between the purebred and the mongrel.

Taxidermied wild animals generally fit well in natural history museums, being the places these objects are expected to occupy. Domestic animals have been less sought-after. One important reason for this is the great variety of breeds in a single species, another is that the breeds have been continuously altered by their domestication. The dog as a species is specifically problematic to stuff and put on display because of its cultural significance in Western countries. To the Victorians, '(a) home was the dog's proper place'.[69] Today the dog is frequently referred to as a member of the family. An animal that is so closely associated with the intimacy of home and family is not expected to be objectified. The taxidermied dogs in the natural history museum at Tring thus emphatically, with Daston's words, 'straddle boundaries between kinds'. The Tring dogs, preserved in the museum vitrine, address us simultaneously as specimens of breeds but also as individuals mentioned by name, each with a curriculum vitae that tells the dates of the dog's birth and death, data about their triumphs in the show ring or at the racing track plus the breeder's and the owner's names. The pedigree that placed the dog socially and culturally and made them 'pure' in contrast to the undocumented cur has followed the dead animal. The dogs' importance as cultural things is also accentuated by the fact that after the taxidermist had completed his work the preserved body was inspected by a dog show judge for quality.

In the museum the dogs have once more been put on display: they are still showpieces as they were in their lifetime. 'A preserved dog will always stand out as something different', Rachel Poliquin states in her discussion of the Tring dogs, hinting at the dog's importance as a pet and a friend:

> While the emotionality surrounding perpetual pets makes them particularly disturbing, even the dogs in The Dog Collection at Tring are disquieting. Dogs are our companion species, our ancient partners in work and life, and probably humans' first nonhuman friends. Perhaps the human–dog bond is too intimate for such post-mortem bodily invasion.[70]

To their owners the prize-winning dogs were, maybe pets, but surely tools for gaining social prestige and economic reward. For the majority of dog lovers who see the stuffed dogs today they are more likely to be considered 'matter out of place'.[71]

The dogs at Tring are evocative objects in flux between nature and culture. Championship was the standard for a good and correct animal. When Lydekker collected the dogs, prize-winning and purebred dogs were integrated in the upper classes' conspicuous consumption producing social status. Lydekker's intention was that the dog collection 'in the course of time' should function as a materialised guide for good breeding.[72] But time has taken the breeds on show at Tring far from the standards of a hundred years ago. The importance of the collection today is mainly to demonstrate human manipulation of canine matter by selective breeding, an instructive installation of what, according to Yi-Fu Tuan, may be labelled 'dominant affection' or 'affective dominance'.[73]

Knotted: dog fur

Humans, animals and objects are all 'products of their relating', and one type of relation is a knot.[74] 'The world is a knot in motion', Donna Haraway states in *The Companion Species Manifesto*.[75] This highly compressed formulation refers to two essential postulates in her text: first, beings do not exist alone and isolated but are entangled in other beings and objects by what Haraway calls prehensions or graspings. The second point is that neither live creatures nor dead objects have an isolated beginning or ending. As she declares: 'There are no pre-constituted subjects and objects, and no single sources, unitary actors, or final ends'.[76] In her book *Wild Animal Skins in Victorian Britain* Ann C. Coley demonstrates how big game hunters mapped their routes by marking the sites where the animals had been killed. Killing also comprised flaying and curing of the skins in camp: 'their course (was charted) through their encounters with wild skins'.[77] Such 'hunting maps' both materialise and visualize, by virtue of the object map, the interlocking of wild skins, colonialism and empire. Animal skins are highly movable and entangled objects. Here a Norwegian peasant's winter cap lined with dog fur and stored in the Trøndelag Folkemuseum, Norway, serves, like the stuffed hide of Bella, as a door opener to reach a better understanding of the contradictory attitudes to animals in the past, and especially to dogs.

The cap is made of red wool cloth lined with lamb fur, while the ear pads are lined with dog fur. The local term is 'hundskinnshuv', roughly translated as dog-skin cap. The cap is approximately 150 years old and was added to the collections in 1920. It was manufactured at a time when taking care of hides from dogs was as common as using skin and fur from other domestic animals.

Figuring in the General Register as number TF 810, the catalogue card contains interesting information about the use of dog fur among the peasants in the community of Røros before 1877. This was the year the community got a railway connection, and with the railway new commodities such as mass-produced clothes became available and consequently replaced the traditional clothing. Consulting the register we learn that a cap made of dog fur was part of the peasants' winter costume when driving to church and on festive occasions. Dog fur was, in other words, for high festivals and celebrations: it was exclusive.

The cap was worn together with an ankle-length overcoat made of dog fur. The hands were protected from the cold by mittens made of dog fur lined with lambskin, and on their feet they wore high boots trimmed with a brim of dog fur. Class also enters; only wealthy peasants could afford the dog fur costume. Those with less money had to content themselves with travelling furs of reindeer or sheep. This means that the skin of ruminants such as reindeer and sheep was of less value than that of the carnivore dog, not to mention travelling furs of wolf skin that were even more rare and expensive. A dog fur costume was a sign of social and economic power, a conspicuous indicator of class.[78]

By whom and where were dog furs made? The museum register gives the answer. The skins were from 'genuine sámi dogs' and the costumes were sold at the annual winter market in Røros. Here Norwegians and Swedes met, peasants as well as sámi people. The expression 'genuine sámi dogs' indicates that the costumes were sámi products, with fur from the small spitz dogs used by the sámi as herding dogs. Peasants in northern Sweden also raised dogs for their fur.[79] This was fur from larger dogs called 'grey-dogs'. Their grey coat was very similar to that of the 'grey legs', the feared wolf.[80] In 1876 the Swedish zoologist P.O. Olsson wrote that quite a lot of the population in Jämtland kept dogs '. . . mainly because their coat rends expensive and excellent fur'.[81] Greydogs were the ancestors of the Elk Hound, the most prominent of the five Norwegian national breeds.[82]

Unravelling object TF810 brings together people, animals and things that are related in human and beastly hierarchies and situated in time and place. The cap was part of an economic and rational culture in which animals primarily were of utility and the dog a domestic animal among other domestic animals. Skin, fur, wool and fat from dogs were all utilised.[83] While in a Norwegian valley peasants were still wearing dog-skin caps, dog owners from the upper and middle classes in other European countries had already started to 'domesticate animal death': to bury their pet dogs and raise tombstones on the graves.[84]

Animal matter: power and emotion

Dog-skin caps, taxidermied animals, cutlery, upholstered pets, fragments of exotic animals – all are glimpses of singular elements in a vast multitude of objects made from animal materials, most of them stored out of sight of the public. During recent years museums have worked to digitalise their collections to make them more accessible. On the other hand, objects are being taken out of displays because they are assumed to be offensive to visitors. 'The museum object is shaped by and shaping of visitors' attention. At the same time, these objects are animated by the museum, its practices and procedures, its classifications and its display techniques', Michelle Henning claims.[85] To display human matter is controversial today, and maybe it is only a question of time before taxidermied animals will be removed from the glass cabinets. As demonstrated previously, the objects selected have been labelled evocative, talkative, chimerical, knotted, and hybrid because their properties trigger emotions, tickle the curiosity, and invite conversations and discourse. Yet embedded in these examples of animal materiality are also questions that involve power and sentiment.

'Contact with power often ends in death. What once was alive becomes inanimate matter. Thus trees turn into table and chairs, animals into meat and leather', Yi-Fu Tuan states in his influential work *Dominance and Affection: The Making of Pets*.[86] Tuan's concern is to highlight how humans' affection and love for vulnerable creatures also contain elements of dominance and cruelty. In this way, animal matter in museums makes human power over animals visible, undeniable and ubiquitous.

Contrary to Tuan's dark vision of the totally controlled animal squeezed between love and dominance is the use of animals in sámi reindeer nomadic culture in Finnmark, Norway. Until the 1950s the reindeer was the principal element in a quotidian technology based on inter-relationship and inter-dependence between humans and animals.[87] From the reindeer the nomadic families received food and clothing. Everything digestible of the animal was utilised for food: the meat was salted, dried or smoked. The female reindeers were milked and with the fat milk they either made cheese or the milk was dried in reversed reindeer stomachs. The same with the blood, so the small working herding dogs would have blood in their daily diet the whole year through. Both summer and winter costumes were made of carefully chosen parts of the reindeer's coat. Babies and small children's clothes were made of skin from newborn reindeer calves, and winter shoes were made of skin from the reindeer's skull. A thick layer of reindeer skins covered the tent floor during the winter season. The reindeer has also been tamed to serve as a draught animal, the lasso was earlier made of sinews. Horn and bones have been used for making vernacular objects such as spoons, handles, and needle-cases. Animal matter holds together the reindeer nomadic family lives. In this perspective not only humans but also the humble animal things wield power.

Daniel Miller has claimed 'that the best way to understand, convey and appreciate our humanity is through attention to our fundamental materiality'.[88] Our relationship to material things has profound consequences for future life on earth, but before addressing materialism as a political issue, Miller calls for a consideration of 'the consequences of our materiality and of material culture for a more profound understanding of what we our selves are'.[89] In other words, to be a human is to live by and with what Miller calls 'stuff'.

Synonyms for 'stuff' are paraphernalia, junk, mess, gear, material, substance, matter, things, objects, articles, packages, bits and pieces. In the examples discussed in this chapter, stuff or whatever we choose to label the materiality we live with and in, animal and human are profoundly entangled. The logic of the museum is to detach things from their former relations in order to obtain ultimate storage suitable to the materials of the objects. To critically question the materiality of the objects means to restore their power as related matter. The Sheffield and Solingen knives are certainly pieces of commonplace paraphernalia, their handles are made from bones that once supported some beasts' warm and working bodies. This re-establishes a connection between the object and the once-animated animal and makes it ontologically stand out from objects made of stone, metal or plant material. When Miller asks us to consider 'the consequences of our materiality' we might feel that this is very close to the commonplace acknowledgment of humanity's dependence on animals. 'What we our selves are' cannot be imagined without including (other) animals. Animal matter, animal matters, are neither innocent nor neutral. This will become more evident and urgent as the history of animals is being written, step by step.

Notes

1 I wish to thank Kristin Asdal, Inger Johanne Lyngø and especially Karen Rader for constructive comments, and Philip Howell for making the text linguistically consistent.
2 N. Rothfels, *Savages and Beasts: The Birth of the Modern Zoo*, Baltimore MD: Johns Hopkins University Press, 2002, 6. Rothfels mentions environments such as museums, books, circuses and zoos as places where animals' unnatural history unfold.
3 C. Tilley, W. Keane, S. Küchler, M. Rowlands, and P. Spyer (eds.), *Handbook of Material Culture*, London: Sage, 2006.

4 Tilley *et al. Handbook of Material Culture*, 3.
5 Cultural historian B. Rogan says: 'It seems by the way to be clear that the concept (materiality) is used in different ways, both as a processual concept which aims to grasp the relation between things and persons, or the 'social life' of things related to the social life of humans, but also as a concept which says something about the physical substance of things'/'Det synes imidlertid klart at begrepet brukes på ulike måter, både som et prossesuelt begrep som prøver å fange opp relasjonen mellom ting og mennesker, eller tingenes 'sosiale liv' i relasjon til menneskers sosiale liv, men også som et begrep som sier noe om tingenes fysiske substans': B. Rogan, 'Et faghistorisk etterord om materiell kultur og kulturens materialitet', in S.-A. Naguib and B. Rogan (eds.), *Materiell Kultur & Kulturens Materialitet*, Oslo: Novus Forlag, 2011, 313–385. Dudley stresses the same duality when defining materiality: 'What, though, precisely is this "materiality"? In part at least it connotes the form and the materials of which an object consists, together with the techniques by which it may have been made or formed, any additions or presentational conventions (such as a frame) which may have been added to it, and all and any traces of the passage of time, and, especially, physical human interaction. Materiality implies, too, though, engagement – be it cognitive, emotional, or imaginative alone (. . .) or physically, bodily participative as well (. . .)': S.D. Dudley, *Museum Materialities: Objects, Engagements, Interpretations*, London: Routledge, 2010, 7. A strong argument for studying the properties of materials instead of materiality is given by T. Ingold, 'Materials against materiality', *Archaeological Dialogues*, 14, 1 (2007): 1–16.
6 C. Tilley, 'Materiality in materials', *Archeological Dialogues* 14, 1 (2007): 16–20.
7 Tilley, 'Materiality in materials', 17.
8 For the early modern collections in Italy, see P. Findlen, *Possessing Nature: Museums, Collecting, and Scientific Culture in Early Modern Italy*, Berkeley CA: University of California Press, 1996; S.M. Pearce, *Museums, Objects, and Collections: A Cultural Study*, Washington DC: Smithsonian Institution Press, 1992, 91–98.
9 M. Tamen, *Friends of Interpretable Objects*, Cambridge MA: Harvard University Press, 2001.
10 Tamen, *Friends of Interpretable Objects*, 4.
11 L. Daston (ed.), *Things that Talk. Object Lessons from Art and Science*, New York: Zone Books, 2004, 228.
12 Daston, *Things that Talk*, 229.
13 C. Philo and C. Wilbert (eds.), *Animal Spaces, Beastly Places: New Geographies of Human–Animal Relations*, London: Routledge, 2000.
14 Findlen, *Possessing Nature*, 23.
15 K. Whitaker, 'The culture of curiosity', in N. Jardine, J.A. Secord, and E.C. Spary (eds.), *Cultures of Natural History*, Cambridge: Cambridge University Press, 1996, 75–90.
16 A. MacGregor, *Curiosity and Enlightenment: Collectors and Collections from the Sixteenth to the Nineteenth Century*, New Haven CT: Yale University Press, 2007; Pearce, *Museums, Objects, and Collections*, 98–115.
17 S. Battaglini, G. Bianucci, M. Cerri, M. Dellacasa, A. Iacopini, C. Nocchi, P. Orlandi, E. Palagi, F. Strumia, and M. Zuffi, 'Il Museo di Storia Naturale e del Territorio', in P. Meletti (ed.), *Arte e Scienza nei Musei dell'Università di Pisa*, Pisa: Edizioni Plus, 2002, 97–140.
18 M.M. Simari, 'Serragli a Firenze al tempo dei Medici' in *Natura Viva in Casa Medici*, Firenze: Centro Di della Edifimi, 1985, 99, 23–31.
19 G. Batini, *Firenze Curiosa*, Firenze: Bonechi Editori, 1972, 25–30.
20 Batini, *Firenze Curiosa*.
21 For a more extensive presentation of the biography of the hippopotamus in 'La Specola' see L.E. Thorsen, 'The hippopotamus in the Florentine zoological museum "La Specola": a

discussion of stuffed animals as sources of cultural history', *Museologia Scientifica: Rivista dell'A.N.M.S.* 21, 2 (2006): 269–281.

22 'L'ippopotamo de "La Specola" torna in esposizione dopo mesi di assenza', 10 September 2012, available at www.nove.firenze.it/b212102051-l-ippopotamo-de-la-specola-torna-in-esposizione-dopo-mesi-di-assenza.htm, last accessed 17 March 2017.

23 See examples of common table knives produced in Sheffield and Solingen here: http://digitaltmuseum.no/011023244099?page=43&query=kniv&pos=1008, last accessed 17 March 2017.

24 The section about the commodifying of the urban horse draws on C. McShane and J.A. Tarr, *The Horse in the City: Living Machines in the Nineteenth Century*, Baltimore MD: Johns Hopkins University Press, 2007, 16, 18–36.

25 McShane and Tarr, *The Horse in the City*, 29

26 Gelatine or gelatin is made from the skin of horses, cattle and pigs.

27 For Wergeland, see http://global.britannica.com/biography/Henrik-Arnold-Wergeland, last accessed 17 March 2017.

28 '. . . fortjener Plads der som Skelett og udstoppet som Typus for den antikke hundeform på Basrelieferne': L. Amundsen and D.A. Seip (eds.), *Henrik Wergelands Skrifter*, Oslo: J.W. Cappelens forlag, 1962, Volume 8, 239.

29 Norsk Folkemuseum is Norway's largest open air and cultural history museum, founded in 1894.

30 S.J.M.M. Alberti (ed.), *The Afterlives of Animals*, Charlottesville VA: University of Virginia Press, 2011; L.E. Thorsen, *Elephants Are Not Picked From Trees: Animal Biographies in Gothenburg Natural History Museum*, Aarhus: Aarhus University Press, 2014.

31 A. Appadurai, *The Social Life of Things: Commodities in a Cultural Perspective*, Cambridge: Cambridge University Press, 1986, 5.

32 See pictures of Bella at the Norsk Folkesuseum here: http://digitaltmuseum.no/011023128033?name=%22hunder%22&pos=1, last accessed 17 March 2017.

33 'I min Hunds Øje sænker jeg mine Sorger som i en dyb Brønd'. From the poem 'Mig selv', 1841.

34 L.E. Thorsen, *Hund! Fornuft og Følelser*, Oslo: Pax Forlag, 2001, 247–273; L.E. Thorsen, 'Dead dogs: utility and emotions', *Ethnologia Scandinavica* 31 (2001): 109–117.

35 A.C. Colley, *Wild Animal Skins in Victorian Britain: Zoos, Collections, Portraits, Maps*, Burlington: Ashgate, 2014, 97.

36 R. Poliquin, *The Breathless Zoo: Taxidermy and the Cultures of Longing*, University Park PA: Pennsylvania University Press, 2012, 108.

37 S.J.M.M. Alberti, 'Constructing nature behind glass', *Museum and Society* 6, 2 (2008): 73–97, 81.

38 P.A. Morris, *A History of Taxidermy: Art, Science and Bad Taste*, Ascot: MPM Publishing, 2010.

39 Morris, *History of Taxidermy*, 8.

40 Alberti, *Afterlives of Animals*, 4.

41 This discussion of examples from the Gothenburg Natural History Museum is based on L.E. Thorsen, *Elephants Are Not Picked From Trees*.

42 Kalof and Fitzgerald classify trophy photograph motives according to three conventions: the newly killed animal prior to dismemberment; the killed animal and the white hunter, the latter sometimes posing on top of the fallen body with the cut-off tail in his hand, and the cutting up of the body with displays of tusk, head and feet; tail, tusks, head and feet members give an indication of size. See L. Kalof and A. Fitzgerald, 'Reading the trophy: exploring the display of dead animals in hunting magazines', *Visual Studies* 18, 2 (2003): 112–122.

43 J. Mynott, *Birdscapes: Birds in Our Imagination and Experience*, Princeton NJ: Princeton University Press, 2009, 58–59.
44 Alberti, 'Constructing nature behind glass', 82.
45 Alberti, 'Constructing nature behind glass', 81.
46 M. Patchett, K. Foster, and H. Lorimer, 'The biographies of a hollow-eyed Harrier', in Alberti, *Afterlives of Animals*, 110–134. The authors underline the importance of well-curated collections and easy access to data as premises for animal biography studies in natural history collections.
47 R. Poliquin, 'The matter and meaning of museum taxidermy', *Museum and Society* 6, 2 (2008): 123–134, 127.
48 The most famous Swiss rescue dog, named Barry, was born in 1800 and died in 1814, and his stuffed skin has been on display in the Natural History Museum of Bern since 1815. The skin has been rearranged twice, the last time in 1923 when the mount was done to make the dog look like the modern Saint Bernard breed. Barry became a legend in his lifetime, and has been kept alive in stories, poems, pictures, and, notably, through the museum's own memory work. The dog's bicentennial anniversary was celebrated by reconstructing the body once again, this time on paper. See M. Nussbaumer, *Barry vom Grossen St. Bernhard*, Bern: Naturhistorisches Museum der Burgergemeinde Bern, 2000; L.E. Thorsen, 'A dog of myth and matter: Barry the Saint Bernard in Bern', in LE. Thorsen, K. Rader, and A. Dodd (eds.) *Animals on Display: The Creaturely in Museums, Zoos, and Natural History*, University Park PA: Pennsylvania University Press, 2013, 128–153.
49 Poliquin, *Breathless Zoo*, 12.
50 Poliquin, *Breathless Zoo*, 6.
51 Poliquin, *Breathless Zoo*, 7.
52 Poliquin, *Breathless Zoo*, 7.
53 S. Turkle, *Evocative Objects: Things We Think With*, Cambridge MA: MIT Press, 2007, 8.
54 'Jeg elsker å samle på ting, jeg må ha masse å se på når jeg ikke hører, vet du. Jeg observerer ting, tar på ting, lukter på ting og kommuniserer med dem, det finnes ikke en eneste ting her som ikke har personlig verdi. Når jeg tørker støv, dukker gamle minner opp og gjør meg glad. Jeg elsker å tørke støv': N.-C. Ihlen-Hansen in 'Fransk Las Vegas på Vestli', *Aftenposten*, 3 October 2008, available at www.aftenposten.no/norge/Fransk-Las-Vegas-pa-Vestli-277206b.html, last accessed 17 March 2017.
55 Daston, *Things That Talk*, 21.
56 Daston, *Things that Talk*.
57 Daston, *Things that Talk*, 10.
58 S.T. Asma offers an adequate expression of the emotional sensation visitors may feel in the natural history museum: 'Most nature museums – and this goes back to the curiosity cabinets of the Renaissance and early Enlightenment – do not really titillate the appetites, as in the case of consumer manipulation. The feeling of wonder, or the sensation of the marvelous, *is* emotional and can intoxicate, but unlike the appetites, it has no obvious object or specifiable goal. (. . .) Enthusiasm (the word means "to be filled with the gods") is an emotion that museums often engender, and it suggests that one momentarily loses oneself to something bigger – in a word, transcendence': S.T. Asma, *Stuffed Animals and Pickled Heads: The Culture and Evolution of Natural History Museums*, Oxford: Oxford University Press, 2001, 34, emphasis in original.
59 'Il parlare all'occhio oltre il parlare alla mente, credei dovesse esser della più grande utilità per i mei lettori, (. . .)': P. Savi, *Ornitologia Toscana ossia Descrizione e storia degli uccelli che trovansi nella Toscana con l'aggiunta delle descrizione di tutti gli altri*, Pisa: Dalla Tipografia Nistri/Fratelli Nistri, 1827, XII.

60 The collections and the museum were established by Lionel Walter Rothschild, biographed in M. Rothschild, *Dear Lord Rothschild: Birds, Butterflies and History*, London: Hutchinson, 1983. He bequeathed the collection to the British Museum.
61 Lydekker worked for the Director and Keeper of Zoology, Ray Lankester. For domesticated animals in the British Natural History Museum see W.T. Stearn, *The Natural History Museum at South Kensington*, London: The Natural History Museum, 1981, 183–185; for the Dog Collection, see K. Dennis-Bryan and J. Clutton-Brock, *Dogs of the Last Hundred Years at the British Museum (Natural History)*, London: British Museum, 1988.
62 R. Lydekker in A.C.L.G. Günther, *The History of the Collections Contained in the Natural History Departments of the British Museum*, Volume II, London, 1906, 67.
63 R. Lydekker in Günther, *The History of the Collections*, 68.
64 Apart from dogs, breeds of cattle, sheep, goats, cats, ferrets, guinea pigs, rabbits, pigeons, poultry, ducks, geese and canaries were displayed. See R. Lydekker, *A Guide to Domesticated Animals (other than Horses)*, London: British Museum, 1908.
65 British Museum (Natural History) Archives, DF 1004/cp/721 Tring Museum of Domestic Animals 1950–1960; See Stearn, *Natural History Museum*, 185.
66 Lydekker, *Guide to Domesticated Animals*, 40.
67 P.A. Morris, *Rowland Ward: Taxidermist to the World*, Lavenham: Lavenham Press, 2003.
68 Dennis-Bryan and Clutton-Brock, *Dogs of the Last Hundred Years*, 98. For the Pekingese, see S. Cheang, 'Women, pets and imperialism: the British Pekingese dog and nostalgia for old China', *Journal of British Studies* 45, 2 (2006): 359–387.
69 H. Kean, *Animal Rights: Political and Social Change in Britain Since 1800*, London: Reaktion, 1998, 88. See also P. Howell, *At Home and Astray: the Domestic Dog in Victorian Britain*, Charlottesville VA: University of Virginia Press, 2015, 73–75.
70 Poliquin, *Breathless Zoo*, 215.
71 M. Douglas, *Purity and Danger*, London: Routledge, 1966.
72 R. Lydekker in Günther, *The History of the Collections*, 68.
73 Y.-F. Tuan, *Dominance and Affection: the Making of Pets*, New Haven CT: Yale University Press, 1984.
74 D. Haraway, *The Companion Species Manifesto: Dogs, People, and Significant Otherness*, Chicago IL: Prickly Paradigm Press, 2003, 7.
75 Haraway, *Companion Species Manifesto*.
76 Haraway, *Companion Species Manifesto*, 6.
77 Colley, *Wild Animal Skins*, 154.
78 In the Swedish novel *Ormens väg på Hälleberget (The Way of the Serpent)* (1984/1990) by Torgny Lindgren, the cruel and despotic merchant Karl Orsa always wears an overcoat of dog fur when he visits his poor tenants' hut, forcing the women to have sex with him to pay their debts. Dog furs are also mentioned and attributed to well-off people in other Nordic novels set in the nineteenth century. The connnection between power and lack of empathy symbolised in the dog fur overcoat is also demonstrated in Lindgren's autobiography *Minnen* (2010). Lindgren notes how his grandfather bought a litter of sámi dogs, and when they were grown up, they were slaughtered and their skins used to make an overcoat.
79 C.R. Sundström, *Handbok för Hundvänner*, Stockholm: Gernandts Boktryckeri–Aktiebolag, 1889, 124; E. Johansson, *Skogarnas fria Söner*, Nordiska Museets Handlingar, 118, Kristianstad: Nordiska Museet, 1994; I. Svanberg, *Hästslaktare och Korgmakare: Resursutnyttjande och Livsstil Bland Sockenlappar*, Umeå: Johan Nordlander-sällskapet, 1999.
80 It is probable that several overcoats in Norwegian museums catalogued as wolf fur are in fact made of dog fur.
81 Olsson, quoted in Svanberg, *Hästslaktare och Korgmakare*, 87.

82 The correct name of the Elk Hound should be Elk Dog.
83 Even as late as the 1950s, Norwegian farm dogs could be skinned and the skin used to sit on or as bedside rugs. For the use of dog fur in England see: Kean, *Animal* Rights, 73–74; K. Thomas, *Man and the Natural World: Changing Attitudes in England 1500–1800*, Oxford: Oxford University Press, Penguin, 1996, 340, n. 340.
84 Howell, *At Home and Astray*, 147.
85 M. Henning, *Museums, Media and Cultural Theory*, London: Open University Press, 2006, 11.
86 Tuan, *Dominance and Affection*, 12.
87 Ø. Vorren and E. Manker, *Samekulturen: En kulturhistorisk oversikt*, second edition, Tromsø, Bergen, and Oslo: Universitetsforlaget, 1976, 30–81.
88 D. Miller, *Stuff*, Cambridge: Polity Press, 2010, 4.
89 Miller, *Stuff*, 5.

Bibliography

Alberti, S J.M.M. 'Constructing nature behind glass', *Museum and Society* 6, 2 (2008): 73–97, 81.
Alberti, S.J.M.M. (ed.), *The Afterlives of Animals*, Charlottesville VA: University of Virginia Press, 2011.
Amundsen, L. and Seip, D.A. (eds.), *Henrik Wergelands Skrifter*, Volume 8, Oslo: J.W. Cappelens forlag, 1962.
Appadurai, A. *The Social Life of Things: Commodities in a Cultural Perspective*, Cambridge: Cambridge University Press, 1986.
Asma, S.T. *Stuffed Animals and Pickled Heads: The Culture and Evolution of Natural History Museums*, Oxford: Oxford University Press, 2001.
Batini, G. *Firenze Curiosa*, Firenze: Bonechi Editori, 1972, 25–30.
Battaglini, S., Bianucci, G., Cerri, M., Dellacasa, M., Iacopini, A., Nocchi, C., Orlandi, P., Palagi, E., Strumia, F., and Zuffi, M., 'Il Museo di Storia Naturale e dei Territorio', in P. Meletti (ed.), *Arte e Scienza nei Musei dell'Università di Pisa*, Pisa: Edizioni Plus, 2002, 97–140.
Cheang, S. 'Women, pets and imperialism: the British Pekingese dog and nostalgia for old China', *Journal of British Studies* 45, 2 (2006): 359–387.
Colley, A.C. *Wild Animal Skins in Victorian Britain: Zoos, Collections, Portraits, Maps*, Burlington: Ashgate, 2014.
Daston, L. (ed.), *Things that Talk. Object Lessons from Art and Science*, New York: Zone Books, 2004.
Dennis-Bryan, K. and Clutton-Brock, J. *Dogs of the Last Hundred Years at the British Museum (Natural History)*, London: British Museum, 1988.
Douglas, M. *Purity and Danger*, London: Routledge, 1966.
Dudley, S.D. *Museum Materialities: Objects, Engagements, Interpretations*, London: Routledge, 2010.
Findlen, P. *Possessing Nature: Museums, Collecting, and Scientific Culture in Early Modern Italy*, Berkeley CA: University of California Press, 1996.
Günther, A.C.L.G. *The History of the Collections Contained in the Natural History Departments of the British Museum*, Volume II, London, 1906.
Haraway, D. *The Companion Species Manifesto: Dogs, People, and Significant Otherness*, Chicago IL: Prickly Paradigm Press, 2003.
Henning, M. *Museums, Media and Cultural Theory*, London: Open University Press, 2006.
Howell, P. *At Home and Astray: the Domestic Dog in Victorian Britain*, Charlottesville VA: University of Virginia Press, 2015.
Ingold, T. 'Materials against materiality', *Archaeological Dialogues* 14, 1 (2007): 1–16.

Johansson, E. *Skogarnas fria Söner*, Nordiska Museets Handlingar, 118, Kristianstad: Nordiska Museet, 1994.

Kalof, L. and Fitzgerald, A. 'Reading the trophy: exploring the display of dead animals in hunting magazines', *Visual Studies* 18, 2 (2003): 112–122.

Kean, H. *Animal Rights: Political and Social Change in Britain Since 1800*, London: Reaktion, 1998, 88.

Lydekker, R. *A Guide to Domesticated Animals (other than Horses)*, London: British Museum, 1908.

MacGregor, A. *Curiosity and Enlightenment: Collectors and Collections from the Sixteenth to the Nineteenth Century*, New Haven CT: Yale University Press, 2007.

McShane, C. and Tarr, J.A. *The Horse in the City: Living Machines in the Nineteenth Century*, Baltimore MD: Johns Hopkins University Press, 2007.

Miller, D., *Stuff*, Cambridge: Polity Press, 2010.

Morris, P.A. *Rowland Ward: Taxidermist to the World*, Lavenham: Lavenham Press, 2003.

Morris, P.A. *A History of Taxidermy: Art, Science and Bad Taste*, Ascot: MPM Publishing, 2010.

Mynott, J. *Birdscapes: Birds in Our Imagination and Experience*, Princeton NJ: Princeton University Press, 2009.

Nussbaumer, M. *Barry vom Grossen St. Bernhard*, Bern: Naturhistorisches Museum der Burgergemeinde Bern, 2000.

Patchett, M., Foster, K., and Lorimer, H. 'The biographies of a hollow-eyed Harrier', in S.J.M.M. Alberti, (ed.), *The Afterlives of Animals*, Charlottesville VA: University of Virginia Press, 2011, 110–134.

Pearce, S.M. *Museums, Objects, and Collections: A Cultural Study*, Washington DC: Smithsonian Institution Press, 1992, 91–98.

Philo, C. and Wilbert, C. (eds.) *Animal Spaces, Beastly Places: New Geographies of Human-Animal Relations*. London: Routledge, 2000.

Poliquin, R. 'The matter and meaning of museum taxidermy', *Museum and Society* 6, 2 (2008): 123–134.

Poliquin, R., *The Breathless Zoo. Taxidermy and the Cultures of Longing*, University Park PA: Pennsylvania University Press, 2012.

Rogan, B., 'Et faghistorisk etterord om materiell kultur og kulturens materialitet', in S.-A. Naguib and B. Rogan (eds.), *Materiell Kultur & Kulturens Materialitet*, Oslo: Novus Forlag, 2011, 313–385.

Rothfels, N. *Savages and Beasts: The Birth of the Modern Zoo*, Baltimore MD: Johns Hopkins University Press, 2002.

Rothschild, M. *Dear Lord Rothschild: Birds, Butterflies and History*, London: Hutchinson, 1983.

Savi, P. *Ornitologia Toscana ossia Descrizione e storia degli uccelli che trovansi nella Toscana con l'aggiunta delle descrizione di tutti gli altri*, Pisa: Dalla Tipografia Nistri/Fratelli Nistri, 1827, XII.

Simari, M.M. 'Serragli a Firenze al tempo dei Medici', in *Natura Viva in Casa Medici*, Firenze: Centro Di della Edifimi, 1985, 99, 23–31.

Stearn, W.T. *The Natural History Museum at South Kensington*, London: The Natural History Museum, 1981.

Sundström, C.R. *Handbok för Hundvänner*, Stockholm: Gernandts Boktryckeri–Aktiebolag, 1889.

Svanberg, I. *Hästslaktare och Korgmakare: Resursutnyttjande och Livsstil Bland Sockenlappar*, Umeå: Johan Nordlander-sällskapet, 1999.

Tamen, M. *Friends of Interpretable Objects*, Cambridge MA: Harvard University Press, 2001.

Thomas, K., *Man and the Natural World: Changing Attitudes in England 1500–1800*, Oxford: Oxford University Press, Penguin, 1996.

Thorsen, L.E. 'Dead dogs: utility and emotions', *Ethnologia Scandinavica* 31 (2001): 109–117.
Thorsen, L.E. *Hund! Fornuft og Følelser*, Oslo: Pax Forlag, 2001.
Thorsen, L.E. 'The hippopotamus in the Florentine zoological museum "La Specola": a discussion of stuffed animals as sources of cultural history', *Museologia Scientifica: Rivista dell'A.N.M.S.* 21, 2 (2006): 269–281.
Thorsen, L.E. 'A dog of myth and matter: Barry the Saint Bernard in Bern', in L.E. Thorsen, K. Rader, and A. Dodd (eds.), *Animals on Display: The Creaturely in Museums, Zoos, and Natural History*, University Park PA: Pennsylvania University Press, 2013, 128–153.
Thorsen, L.E. *Elephants Are Not Picked from Trees: Animal Biographies in Gothenburg Natural History Museum*, Aarhus: Aarhus University Press, 2014.
Tilley, C. 'Materiality in materials', *Archeological Dialogues* 14, 1 (2007): 16–20.
Tilley, C., Keane, W., Küchler, S., Rowlands, M., and Spyer, P. (eds.), *Handbook of Material Culture*, London: Sage, 2006.
Tuan, Y-F. *Dominance and Affection: the Making of Pets*, New Haven CT: Yale University Press, 1984.
Turkle, S., *Evocative Objects: Things We Think With*, Cambridge MA: MIT Press, 2007.
Vorren, Ø. and Manker, E. *Samekulturen: En kulturhistorisk oversikt*, second edition, Tromsø, Bergen, and Oslo: Universitetsforlaget, 1976.
Whitaker, K. 'The culture of curiosity', in N. Jardine, J.A. Secord, and E.C. Spary (eds.), *Cultures of Natural History*, Cambridge: Cambridge University Press, 1996, 75–90.

PART II

Problems and paradigms

9
ANIMALS, AGENCY, AND HISTORY

Philip Howell

Introduction

Most of us who have written and taught animal–human history will have at one time or other encountered profound scepticism at the very idea that animals have agency, even before we come to whether such agency might be accessible to historians. These objections are usually conjoined. Thus the author of a 1974 spoof in the *Journal of Social History* asserted the 'full historical power' of the domestic animals he (she?) was purporting to consider.[1] This 'strangely prophetic' text now serves as an instructive prolegomenon to the subsequent development of animal–human history, to the extent that for many practitioners today the 'full historical power' – or the historical agency – of nonhuman animals is not in the least bit controversial.[2] Given the passage of time, it is as a result almost exponentially dispiriting to see the same gesture trotted out in the recent hoaxing of the German journal *Totalitarianism and Democracy*. In a 'Plea against Academic Conformism', 'Christiane Schulte' and her (his?) collaborators denounce what they see as the 'anti-humanism' inherent in 'Human–Animal Studies', singling out for opprobrium the 'thesis of animal "agency"'.[3] Each burlesque, for all their forty years' distance, attacks not merely the enterprise of animal studies, but the project of an animal–human *history*. They do this – from opposite ends of the political spectrum – by labelling the historical study of animal agency no more than a fad or a freak: condemning liberal-progressive pieties on the one hand, spurious radicalism on the other.

The question for today's historians is not, however, whether or not nonhuman animals have agency. The risk in any such catechism is of rehearsing and rehashing anthropocentric attitudes.[4] Attempting to 'recover' animals' historical agency would only be to reproduce the assumptions that 'made it possible to ask such a question in the first place' – so Walter Johnson remarked about chattel slaves in the United States; the real question is 'to ask what historians mean (and what they miss) when they talk about "agency"'.[5] That is, as Drew Swanson has recently written, 'animal agency is real, whether or not historians recognize and theorize it; the challenge is making this agency do historical work'.[6] In setting out to review this 'historical work', convinced that animals' agency is 'an empirical question rather than a philosophical or ontological presupposition' I lay out three distinct, if necessarily interrelated, approaches to the problem of researching and narrating animals' historical agency, highlighting examples and exemplars as I do so.[7] Nevertheless, since part of the problem has always been that widely divergent and incompatible conceptions of agency are involved, I have to begin by setting out as briefly and as straightforwardly as I can some of the most important genealogies of 'agency'.

Agency, anthropocentrism, and some alternatives

Firstly, talk of 'agency' inevitably calls to mind the thoroughly overdetermined notions of free will and moral responsibility, for all that these ideas raise more problems than answers when applied to animals and their histories.[8] In a recent discussion of contemporary racehorses as performers and protagonists, Shelly R. Scott asserts that 'with agency comes choice and responsibility because it is rooted in free will', but immediately signals our difficulties with a reference to her animal subjects, as animals, not being allowed 'free reign'.[9] A simple typo, for sure, but an instructive one, for it enacts the familiar contrast between the sovereign human subject ('reign') and the very constraints ('rein') that we associate with nonhumans.[10] If we take, say, Rousseau's definition of the 'freedom of will' as the freedom to disobey the law of nature – the possession of 'moral liberty' as opposed to 'natural liberty' – then such 'free will' by definition excludes nonhuman animals.[11] In ethical terms, no nonhuman animal can ever be more than a 'moral patient' (a thing or being towards which 'moral agents' have responsibilities).

If we prefer, we can substitute for 'free will' any one of the other 'occult' qualities that have been put forward as exclusively human possessions.[12] In the Cartesian tradition, it is the human capacity to *reason* that famously sets humans apart and alone. Descartes' views on animals are readily simplified, even traduced, but the standard interpretation of the Cartesian method has not been much more than modified.[13] Here, the Cartesian subject (autonomous, sovereign, individual) is made dependent upon an a priori separation from the Cartesian object (automata, determined, inferior) – among whose ranks we must of course number every single other animal.[14] We can nuance this basic argument by appealing to a spectrum or hierarchy of attributes, with nonhuman animals lacking what are usually referred to as the higher- or second-order attributes that define full personhood.[15] The question of 'agency' sometimes revolves around whether other animals can be said to exercise their actions in a mutual, meaning-full, world, one in which the mirrored agency of others is fully recognised – but the answer cometh that they cannot. In Heidegger's phenomenology, to take an idiosyncratic but iconic argument, the 'knowing agent' of the Cartesian tradition is replaced with the world-shaping 'engaged agent', but nonhuman animals are regarded as being so very 'poor in world' that to talk of their 'freedom' or 'agency' would be patently absurd.[16] In this zero-sum game our sovereign agency as human individuals seems to depend on (other) animals being relegated en masse to their own, distinctly inferior, 'kingdom'. Humans may be supposed to exercise sovereign agency over other animals precisely to demonstrate our capacity for 'self-rule', and to shore up the defences against a Hobbesian state of nature in which true freedom is impossible.[17] Human sovereignty arguably descends from the very possibility of a property right in animals, conferring as it does so an *historical* life that is denied to those constitutive others who possess only a brute, creaturely, existence.[18]

In social theory and social history, to take a different tack entirely, agency can be conceived of as the complement and correction to an overweening emphasis on the structuring power of 'society' or 'culture' (or, less often, 'nature'). In the 'structure-agency' debate, so-called, agency refers to the 'negative capacity' of individuals to empower themselves beyond the constraints of their social and institutional worlds, to 'co-constitute' rather than simply be determined by those 'social' structures. An influential emphasis has been on the role of the individual as an active social agent in promoting historical change, in negotiating the power of cultures, institutions, of society itself, and in resisting even the most oppressive and seemingly authoritarian regimes.[19] This is a more likely resource for animal–human historians than the abstractions of moral philosophy, not least because agency defined in this way became a master category of the New Social History, a movement to which the historical concern with animals is in some senses an extension.[20] The expansion of the category of personhood, and the focus on collective as well as individual agencies, especially that of the marginalised and the oppressed, the anonymous and brutalised masses, is promising – for just as we have been taught to understand that even the most downtrodden of peoples, the most swinish of multitudes, have not been utterly deprived of agency or power or historical significance, so have animal–human historians been at pains to argue that neither are nonhuman animals wholly subjugated.

Once again, however, the anthropocentric presumptions of our theories are disabling, as we might perhaps expect from a self-consciously 'social' theory and 'social' history. For Marx, for example, the human animal can develop into an historical individual only through the structures of human society, for even where animals live collectively they lack the productive labour that comes from conscious, collective human activity.[21] Marianne Elisabeth Lien has recently pointed out how this contrast between man and animal in Marx (even in the more nature-focussed, early Hegelian Marx) is enacted through the notion of agency, so that '"making history" through consciously working on his or her surroundings delineates Anthropos as an object of study'.[22] It is not really surprising that in the working out of the structure-agency debates animals have routinely been excluded. The political theorist Alex Callinicos all too grandly asserts, for instance, that 'the task of the historian is [to] uncover the eternal conflict between human agents and the objective conditions of their existence'.[23] As a noted practitioner, William Sewell's words might carry more authority with historians, but he too has proved unwilling to include nonhuman others, stating that 'a capacity for agency – for desiring, for forming intentions, and for acting creatively – is inherent in all humans. . . . a capacity for agency is as much a given for humans as the capacity for respiration'.[24] Such interventions exemplify the thwarted promise of both social theory and social history for any more-than-human history. The problem lies, as it does with metaphysical speculations, in the anthropocentric presuppositions written into the notion of agency from the start, which is to say: anthropocentrism in, anthropocentrism out. Here, 'agency' is so tightly defined that no nonhuman animal, nothing *but* a human being, could ever make history.

What if we turn, instead, to what has been called 'deep history'?[25] Attempts to avoid both the anthropocentric abstractions of moral philosophy and the etiolated conception of agency derived from classical social theory might be pursued by looking to work on agency and action in the behavioural and life sciences, and beyond (including those historical disciplines that have paid more than passing attention to the physical sciences, such as archaeology and anthropology).[26] We would still have a distinction between 'differentialists', who insist on nonhumans' lack of agency, and their 'assimilationist' critics, affirming a spectrum of capacities shared by all animals. So the distinctiveness of human beings in the development of the complex sociocognitive phenomenon referred to by Albert Bandura as 'self-agency' might be set against the recognition of a vast range of 'self-directed agents', of which humans are only the most sophisticated.[27] These discussions inevitably involve the modelling and specification of the precise level of self-awareness, self-reflexivity, and self-control required, and it may be asking too much of historians to be very familiar with these discussions.[28] But while we must be aware of the dangers of cherry-picking conclusions from the natural sciences and their allied disciplines and subdisciplines, we should at least be able to take stock of how humans' capacities have evolved alongside and in contradistinction to that of other animals.[29] As Steve Best puts it, the task would then be to interpret history

> not from an evolutionary position that reifies human agency as the autonomous actions of a Promethean species, but rather from a co-evolutionary perspective that sees nonhuman animals as inseparably embedded in human history and as dynamic agents in their own right.[30]

Doing 'deep history' is not simply adding the insights of 'natural' science to 'history' and the humanities, however – this would simply be to follow, rather listlessly, the *pas de deux* of 'nature' and 'culture'.[31] It is abundantly clear, if 'restoring to humans and non-humans a common fate' is our aim, that we have to rethink the nature–culture opposition, even if, especially if, 'human agency' is at stake.[32] The profound rethinking and redistribution of agency that comes from such an ambition is deeply disorientating to those who see any compromising of human privilege merely as a species of 'antihumanism'.[33] The sociologist Frank Furedi, for instance, laments what he supposes is the very 'annihilation of human agency' in any 'posthumanist' 'Big History':

> What is really at stake here is not the timescales being investigated by history, but the nature of historical imagination itself. The new historical outlooks seek to shift the focus of history away from any human-centred approach to the past, and towards the depiction of material and natural processes as the key influences on history. According to this viewpoint, anthropocentrist history, as the Big History people call it, is a conceit, since human beings have actually had very little to do with the really important events of the past 13 billion years. In effect, what used to be understood as history becomes a minor sub-branch of geology and biology. The emphasis on Big or Long or Deep history is underwritten by an (often unconscious) impulse to downgrade the humanist ideal of *people* making history.[34]

For Furedi, history by definition should have as its focus the 'story and development of humanity', seemingly to the exclusion of the history of everything else.[35] This is a quite impossible stance, however, and one that animal–human historians should summarily reject.[36] We simply cannot filter out a 'pure' human world from a world of animals and things:

> The world is filled not, in the first instance, with facts and observations, but with *agency*. The world, I want to say, is continually *doing things*, things that bear upon us not as observation statements upon disembodied intellects but as forces upon material beings ... Much of everyday life, I would say, has this character of coping with material agency, agency that comes at us from outside the human realm and that cannot be reduced to anything within that realm.[37]

Andrew Pickering's work in science studies (from which these words are taken) is a particularly useful reference point, but we should also mention the sociology of science associated with Bruno Latour and his colleagues (so-called 'Actor-Network Theory' or ANT), the 'vital materialism' of the philosopher Jane Bennett and others involved in the 'material turn', the various attempts to go beyond language to the embodiment of experience collected under the unsatisfactory rubric of 'non-representational theory', or – for the very enthusiastic – the virtually uncategorisable work of the philosophers Gilles Deleuze and Felix Guattari (whose discussion of 'becoming-animal' is particularly relevant).[38] It is impossible to sum up such diverse work here, not to mention their points of difference, save to say that agency is no longer considered as a property or possession of a few, but is rather inherent in the world and its myriad relationships – thus Pickering refers to 'dances of agency', Latour *et al.* to 'networks', and Deleuze and Guattari to 'assemblages'.[39] There are also important links to the theory of 'affordances', which refers to the opportunities offered by the environments from which no animal or organism can be separated: that is, it is the *relations* between organisms and their surroundings (objects, other organisms, opportunities), as they are sensed and perceived, that make action possible and thus make up what we call agency.[40] The central point, however, is that agency is better seen as the product of the *relations* between a whole series of agents in a dynamic system.[41] In the very plainest terms, agency is out there in the world rather than in us (and us alone) as human beings: as Jane Bennett reminds us, 'There was never a time when human agency was anything other than an interfolding network of humanity and nonhumanity'.[42]

Historicising animal agencies

A relational and situated definition of agency, one that happily extends past the borders of the human, and is installed in the world we all inhabit, is surely to be preferred to the anthropocentric alternatives we inherit from moral philosophy and social theory. Even if we accept these accounts, though, and they have become somewhat dulled by repetition, how can we incorporate their insights into our animal–human histories? Some have argued that we simply cannot. The historian Ingrid Tague, for instance, as a prologue to a fine study of pets in eighteenth-century Britain, states the problem with such clarity and conviction that it justifies lengthy quotation:

> This work both engages with and departs from much of the work in animal studies when it comes to the question of animal agency . . . Animals have had a significant impact on human history, . . . Nevertheless, we cannot write a history of animals in the same way that it is possible to write human history. We do not have access to animal experiences even to the extent that we have access to the experiences of the poor and illiterate, who also left no written records. We can only explain animal behavior with reference to our own, human thoughts and feelings . . . As a historian, then, I focus unapologetically on humans. I am interested in animals primarily because of their impact on human life, rather than the other way around – not because I think animals are unimportant, but because ultimately the study of history must be a study of humans.[43]

This is a stance that parallels, in part, the position taken by Erica Fudge in her landmark essay 'A left-handed blow': that the history of animals is strictly speaking 'impossible', given our dependence as historians on textual sources and conventions.[44] We will see shortly that this does not in fact mean that historians cannot speak of animal agency, as Tague supposes, but it is worth stressing at this point that even Fudge's measured reservations about the history of animals are not beyond challenge. Other historians have pointed out that archives both familiar and unfamiliar provide palpable and prolific traces of animals' agency.[45] We are enjoined, moreover, to read our sources in different ways, not merely carefully brushing history 'against the grain' but also, rather more energetically, rowing 'against the current'.[46] It has been persuasively argued that animal–human historians should make more use of oral history, ethnography, and literary sources, of material culture and its 'vibrant matter', as well as cultivating new ways of looking and new ways of writing, particularly about the sensory impact of animals.[47] All are very effective strategies to combat the anthropocentrism of conventional history, and to enlarge our accounts of animals' agency.

Ascribed animal agencies

If we move to the specific ways in which animal agency may be narrated by historians, however, we should start with what I would call *ascribed agencies* (the plural is of course a gesture towards the problems in essentialising 'agency'). For even if we admit Tague's reservations, and the arguments for the centrality of representation, histories of how animal agency has been understood are plainly possible. Indeed, the conditions under which nonhuman animal agency has historically been recognised and authorised must be one of the principal subjects for any animal–human history worth the name. This is how Susan Pearson and Mary Weismantel put it: 'Instead of understanding agency as a transcendent feature of being – one we can see anywhere if only we look hard enough – we would do better to ask how agency has been defined historically, and how agentive powers have been constructed and distributed through social formations'.[48] This formulation does not have to mean the discursive and social construction of animal agency alone, but it is clear that historians can contribute and have contributed to such accounts.[49] Peter Dinzelbacher's discussion of the famous trials of animals in the European Middle Ages, for instance, is advertised as a contribution not to the history of animals per se but rather to the history of *mentalities*.[50] Even if we do not accept at face value the notion that priests, lawmakers and laypeople endowed pigs, dogs, horses, oxen, cats, fish, even swarms of insects, with moral agency and responsibility, the historical fact that culpability for crimes and sins could in some circumstances be extended to nonhumans is striking, and deserves our attention as historians of attitudes if not necessarily of the animals themselves.[51]

A particularly important example of this *ascription* of animals' agency is the individuation of animals, their endowment with character and personality. A certain individuality and quasi-personhood has long been conferred on breed animals, animals in warfare, and many others, with companion animals, zoo animals, and performing animals perhaps the very best exemplars. Animal performers and celebrities are specially blessed, or cursed, with such accoutrements of agency: and many have left accounts of themselves, via human amanuenses, in the form of animal biographies and 'autobiographies'.[52] The most well known is Jumbo, the Barnum circus elephant and first international animal superstar, who was biographed shortly after his tragic death in 1885.[53] Narratives written by humans about named animals, even from the animal's perspective, do not attest to animal agency in themselves, of course: we are always conscious that humans are speaking for these animals. When Jumbo's keeper Matthew Scott writes that 'If poor, dear old Jumbo could but speak he would join in what I say', even the most naïve reader might be expected to demur.[54] The fact that many such animal biographies are part of a genre of 'it-narratives' (or 'novels of circulation', in which nonhuman animals take their place alongside other objects passed around as property from one owner to another) suggests that animals are reduced to the status of things as much as they are raised to that of persons.[55] Focussing on the learned pigs, horses, dogs, and even geese that were a passing fad on the eighteenth-century British stage, Monica Mattfield reflects that real animal agency is not espoused but effaced.[56] The most violent erasure of the animal occurs when such names as 'Jumbo' – or we can think of 'Shamu' the orca in our own day – function as trademarks or brands.[57] Here the property of a name becomes only another detachable thing to be commodified and circulated, principally for human purposes and profit.

All the same, we have to be careful that we do not, as historians, reproduce this effacing of animal agency even as we recognise the power of representation. Speaking *for* animals does not have to reduce animals to mere objects, 'active phantoms' at best.[58] Sympathy or sentiment may constitute a distinctive counter-tradition, one that at its most progressive is able to 'cut across even the bounds of species to establish a shared first-person form of life'.[59] As Keri Cronin points out, the representation of speaking animals 'allowed readers and activists to recognize animal agency, but also existed as a site in which to imagine further articulation of nonhuman agency and voice'.[60] Writing about animals' agency might well function as the subversive exploration of the speculative space of human and animal nature, taking in 'the dissonant, the unconventional, the aberrant, and the unbounded'.[61] Indeed, we do not have to choose between the history of the representation of animal agency and the history of that agency itself, for they are always inseparable. Nonhuman animals are not merely passive objects of knowledge, lay or scientific, but have actively contributed, through their actions, physical traits, and their nonhuman charisma to the stories told about them, including their *histories*.[62] In Erica Fudge's words, 'the production of meaning and order is the work of many, and not always human, agents'.[63] It is vital for the historian to accept that animals have the power to enter the space of human consciousness, 'to pry apart forms of agency and the human subject', rather than their animality merely being colonised and constructed and coded by cultural forms.[64] Or, as Laura Brown pleasingly puts it, 'imaginary animal-kind has both created complex human society and also given animals themselves a role in human history – the potential to affect and alter human culture'.[65]

If I can single out just one text as exemplary of this focus on ascribed agencies in animal–human history, it would be Fudge's work on the discourse of reason in early modern England, and her 2006 book *Brutal Reasoning* in particular.[66] Fudge examines a very familiar theme, the role of reason in making out distinctions between humans and animals, and its role in silencing and erasing animals from history.[67] But she approaches this task by exploring the range of ways in which early modern people (laypeople as well as 'experts') raised the capacity of nonhuman animals to reason, and the possibility of human beings not having, losing, or taking leave of their rationality. Fudge sets out then precisely to challenge the effacement of the animal from history, the positioning of historiography itself as a Cartesian discourse, by allowing this thoroughly ambiguous history of perceptions of animality and humanity to raise questions about 'agency' itself:

> A broader notion of agency might allow us a way of rethinking not only how we conceptualize the arrangements of culture and the structures of thought that organize humans' perception of animals and of themselves in the past – it might also allow us to rethink how it is that we understand the history of being human, and from that gain a better understanding of what it means to be a human now.[68]

Agonistic animal agencies

This important qualification of the degree of anthropocentrism involved in representations of animal agency takes us closer to what we can think of as the direct, proactive historical agency of nonhuman animals – though I prefer to speak here of *agonistic animal agencies* (again preferring the ambiguous and indeterminate plural). Here, the emphasis is less on the ascription of agency by human beings (however collaborative) as on the actions of nonhuman animals themselves – particularly insofar as these actions push back against the pressures and presumptions of the human-dominated world. The historian Dorothee Brantz notes that one of the problems we face is that historians such as William Sewell have not granted animals the ability to transform human structures, taking us explicitly back to the terms of the structure-agency debate.[69] Susan Nance takes a similar tack in drawing a distinction between 'agency' and 'power', insofar as animals' agency is restricted when compared to humans' physical and imaginative organisation of the world and its inhabitants.[70] These arguments and distinctions are hardly unimpeachable, but their intent is clear enough: animal–human historians should seek to demonstrate the role of animals not only in but also *against* a human-dominated world.

The most obvious example in the historiography is the theme of *resistance*. We might recall that the pseudonymous 'Charles Phineas' mocked the very notion, speaking of animals' 'constant but concealed rebellion', but a number of academics and activists have fleshed out this theme entirely sincerely and seriously, passionately and politically.[71] For some, this claim revolves around the disruptive existence of animals who simply refuse to cooperate with the projects and plans of human beings – not just the 'wild' animals formally placed outside the lines of civilisation (and who 'fought back . . . with fang and claw' to avoid becoming captives and commodities), nor their 'liminal' cousins who live in human spaces without being under human control, but also those 'domesticated' and most obviously dominated nonhumans.[72] Thus, in a discussion of attempts to extend control and civility over early nineteenth-century New York City's swinish multitudes, Catherine McNeur can assert that it was not only hog owners who opposed the moral and sanitary plans of the respectable: the pigs themselves 'stubbornly grunted in resistance'.[73] This is an appealing image, but it is not merely a rhetorical flourish – animal–human historians have been quick to argue that animals actively resisted their subordination. David Gary Shaw's formulation of animals as history's 'secret agents' makes this point memorably and subtly: for him, and others, nonhuman animals *became* historical subjects *through* resistance, however cryptically.[74]

Such resistance may be thought of as predominantly subversive, a weapon of the brutalised and the weak, expressed in footdragging (hoofdragging?) rather than in open revolt. It is clear though that for others a more collective and conscious resistance is envisaged. In the introduction to his book *Fear of an Animal Planet*, for instance, Jason Hribal is introduced, rather jarringly, as the Michelet of the animal rebels whom he portrays as self-consciously and purposefully 'making their own history'.[75] Hribal could hardly be more unequivocal: 'They have a conception of freedom and a desire for it. They have agency'.[76] This refrain becomes positively anthemic in the hands of Matthew Candelaria, who writes of 'vermin' (in the terms of human disdain) exhibiting 'an agency that is above and beyond that of other animals . . . potent symbols of the animal subject: free of human bondage, masters of their world and ours'.[77] There is a tendency in such hyperbole to up the historical ante, to see 'resistance' as a kind of animal freedom-fighting, and animal–human history as a chronicle of animal mutinies and *émeutes*. Indeed, the slogan (borrowed from Emma Lazarus) of contemporary critical animal studies – 'none are free until all are free' – suggests this characteristic elision of agency with 'freedom'. The problem, as Walter Johnson argued with regard to slave revolts, is 'the absence of a detailed consideration of politics in any notion of "agency" which conflates activity with "resistance"'.[78] There is an inevitable tendency to portray lack of overt resistance as acceptance of the conditions of existence, of cooperation or even collaboration: as Vinciane Despret has noted, 'When animals do what they know is expected of them, everything begins to look like a machine that is functioning, and their obedience looks "mechanical", a word that conveys its meaning very well'.[79] In short, the uncritical adoption of 'resistance', wearing its ethical and normative judgements on its sleeve, runs the risk of reducing the actions of animals to '(resistant) features of the system that enslaved them'.[80] We might reasonably question not just the possibility but the politics of adopting the 'animal standpoint' in this fashion.[81]

A discussion of animals' agency as historical actors surely does not have to be narrated in precisely the same terms as human riots, revolts, and revolutions for it to be worthy of recording. There has been for instance a productive turn in animal–human history to understanding the *specificity* of animals' existence, attempting to consider their species-life rather than their collectively subjugated status. This necessitates placing some of our attention and effort as historians into understanding the *nature* of these animals. Kelly Enright is right to insist on the need for animal–human historians to understand animals as animals, to evaluate their actions in their irreducible specificity, for 'understanding animal behavior is integral to understanding what people saw and what they did not see when looking at animals'.[82] Perhaps the main avenue here has been through a turn to animal welfare science (AWS), and the signal example of this approach is Susan Nance's recent monograph on the agency of elephants in the golden age of the American travelling circus.[83] On the one hand, Nance provides us with a detailed exploration of how animal individuality and agency functioned within the generic conventions, audience expectations, and corporate needs of the circus in its heyday, and she persuasively portrays the performances of elephant 'characters' as trapped within these conventions as much as they were by the bars of their cages. Thus the elephant functioned, Nance argues, in one of two roles: either as the genial or jovial elephant presented to the public as part of the business of the circus as usual, or alternately as the 'rogue' or 'mad' elephant who ran amok when things went wrong. What Nance does, without implying that social and cultural constructions are everything, is to show that the elephant's individual agency was principally *perceived* by circus audiences and readers through these discursive lenses, with the results both reinforcing and qualifying human power and privilege: the conjoining of elephant and human agency as a 'battle of wills' acknowledges animals' agency as much as it affirms human mastery – for there would be no spectacle at all without the threat and the thrill of the animal turning on his or her 'master'.[84]

Nance is at pains to insist on the reality of animals' lives, actions, and experiences, however, and to show that this elephant agency can be reconstructed, with care. She does this by turning to the insights of contemporary ethology and animal welfare, confident in the belief that no evolutionary change can be rapid enough to invalidate this understanding of elephant behaviour. By doing so Nance can speak about elephants rejecting their routines and their trainers' demands: 'elephants periodically altered or rejected movements that were uncomfortable, tiring, seemingly pointless, or otherwise undesirable in some way we cannot know'.[85] In her most explicit formulation, Nance suggests that these circus elephants were engaged in 'rejecting the conditions of their experience'.[86] Nance does not buy into all the connotations and pitfalls of 'resistance', but she can stress, bolstered with ethological authority, that captive elephants exercised an agency that was a central part of the history of the travelling circus:

> Elephants owned by these companies did not collectively and consciously resist circus management as a group of humans might, by sabotaging key equipment, engaging in slowdowns or strikes, or simply quitting. Yet the

routines of their captivity caused elephants to behave in species-typical ways that often produced the same effects.[87]

Assembled agencies

Nance's approach, persuasive as it is, is not the only way of writing of animals' agency in history, however. For a start, her account focusses on animals 'exotic' to the shores on which they ended up, their 'otherness' firmly part of their entertainment appeal, and their 'training' a brutal affair of ropes, pulleys and hooks. As a history of animal–human interaction, we are never allowed to forget that this is indeed a 'battle of wills' between an animal that ought to be in the wild and its masters. Accordingly, this narrative of agency feels at times too close to that described by the liberal political philosophers Sue Donaldson and Will Kymlicka as characteristic of traditional animal rights theory (ART), where there is a strict divide between animals that should be 'allowed' to live 'independently', and those that we illegitimately domesticate and dominate.[88] Donaldson and Kymlicka prefer to put the focus on the very different obligations we have to other animals depending on the specific relations and interactions we have with them, with all the consequences this has for how we understand animal agency:

> The capacity for agency seems to vary widely amongst animals. An adaptive and social animal like a dog, rat, or crow is capable of great behavioural flexibility, of choosing between options depending on context and needs. Other animals are more tightly 'scripted'; they are 'niche specialists' who cannot readily adapt to changes in their environment, either because their needs are inflexible, or because they lack the cognitive flexibility to explore alternatives. But any plausible theory of animal rights must be attentive to the potential for animal-initiated forms of interaction, and for animal agency in response to human-initiated interaction.[89]

What other histories of animal agencies might be told, bearing in mind these strictures on the variety and complexity of our relationships with other animals? The final thematic that I want to put forward here, and in some ways I think it is the most useful and nuanced, focusses on the ways in which animals' agency should not be thought of in agonistic terms, set apart from the complex mesh of relationships between people and other animals. Consonant with what has been argued above, perhaps the most important responsibility on the historian is to consider instead the 'embedding' or 'distribution' of agency within heterogeneous assemblages of people, nonhuman animals, and environments: this is the focus on what I would like to call here *assembled agencies* in animal–human history.

Let us take 'domesticated' and 'liminal' animals in turn, as illustrations of these histories and geographies of assembled animal–human agency. One obvious example is the agency involved in the relationship between human beings and domestic animals. We might think in one register of animal agencies utilised in the service of humans – consider the histories of war or police dogs, for example – but should these examples be considered still too subordinate, too instrumentalised, consider the training of animals as assistants or companions.⁹⁰ The emphasis on companionship is something that many historians have explored in some depth, myself included.⁹¹ I have discussed for instance the ways in which the simple business of taking the dog for a walk became, in the crises represented by the rabies panics in late nineteenth-century Britain, politically or 'biopolitically' problematic.⁹² With Michel Foucault's theorisation of 'governmentality' in mind (that is, the ways in which governments enter into calculated apportionments of responsibility to their subjects), I extend his focus on the 'conduct of conduct' to the animals at the other end of the leash: their *conduct* (their actions, comportment, appearance – their agency, if you will) is inseparable from that of their human companions, who need to demonstrate to the representatives of the state and to their fellow citizens that they are, complementarily, 'responsible owners'. The agency of the dog – his or her ability to enjoy the open air and to escape the confines of the house – is both compromised by fears about vicious and rabid animals in the public streets and enabled by the actions of their human companions. In this 'assemblage' of agencies the 'conduct of conduct of conduct' (here I have pointedly risked the *reductio ad absurdum*) links the state, the human being, and the nonhuman animal.⁹³

For the uncommitted, the case of guide dogs may be rather simpler, for it is particularly obvious that the human being has to be trained alongside her or his animal assistant, and therefore that agency can in no wise be equated with autonomy – here the agency of the (disabled) human is dependent in large part upon the agency of the animal. As the relational theories of agency described above suggest, *dependency* and *agency* are not exclusive. Sue Donaldson and Will Kymlicka borrow the concept of 'dependent agency' from disability studies, arguing that the political agency of nonhuman animals might be nurtured in the same way that some humans may trust in our assistance and love, in eliciting or interpreting their interests, preferences, and goals.⁹⁴ We can readily see, as historians, how the agency of animals and humans has been assembled in these ways, even to the extent that animal and human exhibit a kind of hybrid agency. The modern guide dog movement, for example, began in 1929 with the work of the dog breeder and philanthropist Dorothy Harrison Eustis at the first *Seeing Eye* schools in Nashville and New Jersey.⁹⁵ Mrs Eustis's initial inspiration will serve to illustrate, even to the most confirmed anthropocentrist, the usefulness of the concept of 'dependent agency':

> It was as though a complete transformation had taken place before my eyes. One moment it was an uncertain blind man, tapping with a cane, the next it was an assured person, with his dog firmly in hand and his head up, who walked toward us quickly and firmly, giving his orders in a low confident voice. That one quick glimpse of the crying need for guidance and companionship in the lonely, all-enveloping darkness stood out clearly before my swimming eyes. To think that one small dog could stand for so much in the life of a human being, not only in his usual role of companion but as his eyes, sword, and shield and buckler!⁹⁶

Instead of considering animals' agency in these situations as no more significant than that of a cane or a stick, we should recognise a reciprocal training in acts of communication, even the creation of 'moral beings capable of being endowed with certain rights and duties'.[97]

What, finally, of 'liminal' (or 'commensal') animals – those who exist alongside us but not in any straightforward sense *with* us?[98] These are often animals that we write off as 'pests' or 'vermin', animals who cannot easily be individualised, let alone loved, species that we are tempted to think of as little above automata. But these are also animals whose agency is assembled with ours. One final exemplar is Dawn Day Biehler's *Pests in the City*: a history of flies, bedbugs, roaches and rats in late nineteenth- and twentieth-century America.[99] These animals choose to inhabit what we like to think of as 'our' spaces, but without choosing to engage with human beings much beyond the opportunities that we offer. They are dependent on us nevertheless, and on the jerry-built landscapes we have constructed – for by accident human beings have created a host of spaces, microgeographies, 'affordances', for these animals to inhabit, survive, propagate, and flourish. Flies, for Biehler, are iconic 'agents of interconnection', but all her 'pests' are 'entangled' with urban history, even as these animals showed scant respect for its anthropocentric narration, as they 'scurried, hitchhiked, scuttled, and buzzed across the borders of public and private space'.[100] Flies and bedbugs, rats and roaches are not, to return to Matthew Candelaria's paean to non-human animal agency, 'free of human bondage'.[101] What the historian has to do instead is recognise, with Biehler, how their agential histories are bound up with, 'assembled' with, that of the city, and with the fate of the (typically racialised) urban poor, with the state, and indeed with our historically evolving *knowledge* of animal nature. Indeed, what makes Biehler's account so peculiarly instructive is that she brings together the stresses on ascribed and agonistic agencies described above, showing for instance how our human knowledge of these animals and their agency is central to this history – without taking this as an ethological truth about their nature, nor discounting the active agency of these animals themselves.[102] Thus Biehler runs the agency of flies – to take her first 'pest' – against the developing understanding, in entomology, pest control, and sanitary reform, of the 'agency of flies' (and she makes a point of noting that this was a phrase used by turn-of-the-century American social investigators and urban health officers). In so doing Biehler reconstructs the historical ascription of flies' agency while at the same drawing on the benefits of entomological understanding of the nature of flies. In other words – in contrast I think to Nance, who separates ethology from history – Biehler integrates our knowledge of animal agency with the historical significance of that agency. She shows how that knowledge about flies and their agency was operationalised, in order to police people as much as pests, and to extend the purview of the state. What we have, ultimately, is a dynamic history of the agency of flies and other 'pests', as we understand such agency now, and as people in the past understood it.

Conclusions

There is signal worth in ending with the agency of flies – because of their seeming historical insignificance, their resistance to the kind of ascriptions of agency with which I began this chapter. These sovereign and imperial genealogies of agency would seem at first sight to offer little or nothing for animal–human history, reminding us only of that 'immensely powerful alliance of intellectual forces' that has 'conspired against the view that animals could truly be agents'.[103] Many of the arguments that have traditionally clothed human beings with 'agency' now look, however, at best well-worn and at worst distinctly shoddy. The life sciences, the development of 'deep history', work in science studies and beyond – point to a *relational* conception of agency that is far more inclusive, and at the same time, far more demanding of us as historians. The three pathways that I have separated out here depend in part on precisely where we align ourselves with regard to the more or less anthropocentric accounts and definitions of 'agency', and though I have forwarded *assembled agencies* as a way to the most critical and effective histories, this is not to discount the productive possibilities for animal–human histories of the other options. I know also that in drawing such clear distinctions I risk simplification, for these approaches are often interrelated. Still, it is essential for the historian to be as clear as possible about the presuppositions of his or her research, about what is ultimately being claimed in the name of agency, not least because it is all too easy for both supporters and antagonists of animal–human history to select definitions to suit their different interests. The issue remains what we take such 'agency' to mean, how the agency of nonhuman animals can and should be related to the agency possessed and practised by human beings – and, most importantly for us, how we might, as historians, study and narrate this agency or agencies. The responsibilities of the historian are obvious, for 'historians working with the idea of agency across species must still tell stories'.[104] My colleague Hilda Kean is surely right to put the stress on 'the choices, agency if you will, of those seeking to transform such actions into history'.[105] One last instance of 'dependent agency', and not the least important, is the reliance of nonhuman animals on responsible and informed historians for narrating their contribution to history.

Notes

1 C. Phineas, 'Household pets and urban alienation', *Journal of Social History* 7, 3 (1974): 334–343, 343.
2 E. Fudge, 'A left-handed blow: writing the history of animals', in N. Rothfels (ed.) *Representing Animals*, Bloomington, IN: Indiana University Press, 2002, 3–18, 5.
3 C. Schulte, 'Der deutsch-deutsche Schäferhund –Ein Beitrag zur Gewaltgeschichte des Jahrhunderts der Extreme', *Totalitarismus und Demokratie* 2 (2015): 319–334. The article is not accessible online but can be found here: www.enricoheitzer.de/2016/02/18/sch%C3%A4ferhund-gate/, last accessed 11 July 2016. 'Schulte and friends' have explained and justified their hoax in the articles 'Commissar Rex an der Mauer erschossen' and 'Holen wir uns die Agency zurück' available at www.heise.de/tp/artikel/47/47395/1.html and www.heise.de/tp/artikel/47/47395/2.html, last accessed 11 July 2016.
4 Z. Tortorici and M. Few, 'Writing animal histories', in M. Few and Z. Tortorici (eds.), *Centering Animals in Latin American History*, Durham NC: Duke University Press, 2013, 1–28, 14.
5 W. Johnson, 'On agency', *Journal of Social History* 37, 1 (2003): 113–124, 114.
6 D.A. Swanson, 'Mountain meeting ground: history at an intersection of species', in S. Nance (ed.), *The Historical Animal*, Syracuse NY: Syracuse University Press, 2015, 240–257, 214.
7 E. Benson, 'Animal writes: historiography, disciplinarity, and the animal trace', in L. Kalof and G.M. Montgomery (eds.), *Making Animal Meaning*, East Lansing MI: Michigan State University Press, 2011, 3–16, 7.

8 For 'free will', see R. Kane (ed.), *The Oxford Handbook of Free Will*, second edition, Oxford: Oxford University Press, 2011. The 'moral agency' of nonhuman animals is attracting increasingly substantial discussion: see M. Bekoff and J. Pierce, *Wild Justice: The Moral Lives of Animals*, Chicago IL: University of Chicago Press, 2009; G. Clement, 'Animals and moral agency: the recent debate and its implications', *Journal of Animal Ethics* 3, 1 (2013): 1–14; P. Shapiro, 'Moral agency in other animals', *Theoretical Medicine and Bioethics* 27, 4 (2006): 257–273.
9 S.R. Scott, 'The racehorse as protagonist: agency, independence, and improvisation', in S.E. McFarland and R. Hediger (eds.), *Animals and Agency: An Interdisciplinary Exploration*, Leiden: Brill, 2009, 45–65, 47.
10 Even of course if the claim to sovereign absolutism is evidently delusory: think of Shakespeare's un-kinged Richard II, brought to the level or lower of his roan Barbary: 'I was not made a horse,/And yet I bear a burthen like an ass' (*Richard II* V. v. 92–93).
11 R. Wokler, 'Rousseau's two concepts of liberty' in G. Feaver and F. Rosen (eds.), *Lives, Liberties and the Public Good: New Essays in Political Theory for Maurice Cranston*, London: Palgrave Macmillan, 1987, 61–100.
12 For 'occult qualities', see J. Rodman, 'The liberation of nature?' *Inquiry* 20, 1–4 (1977): 83–131, 91.
13 For a recent reaffirmation, see M.R. Miller, 'Descartes on animals revisited', *Journal of Philosophical Research* 38 (2013): 89–114.
14 K. Oliver, *Animal Lessons: How They Teach Us to be Human*, New York: Columbia University Press, 2009, 26.
15 We can cite the cognitive capacity for self-interpretation, the 'beliefs' necessary even to have 'desires', the fundamental preconditions for the ownership of experience, for 'self-ownership', and so on. See as an example the positions taken by the philosopher Donald Davidson and his recent interrogator Helen Steward on 'propositional attitudes': D. Davidson, 'Rational animals', *Dialectica* 36, 4 (1982): 317–327; H. Steward, 'Animal agency', *Inquiry* 52, 3 (2009): 217–231.
16 See C. Taylor, 'Engaged agency and background in Heidegger', in C. Guignon (ed.), *The Cambridge Companion to Heidegger*, second edition, Cambridge: Cambridge University Press, 2006, 202–221.
17 S. Donaldson and W. Kymlicka, 'Unruly beasts: animal citizens and the threat of tyranny', *Canadian Journal of Political Science* 47, 1 (2014): 23–45, 28.
18 D.J. Wadiwel, 'The war against animals: domination, law and sovereignty', *Griffith Law Review* 18, 2: (2009): 283–297, 158. See also D.J. Wadiwel, 'The will for self-preservation: Locke and Derrida on dominion, property and animals', *SubStance* 43, 2 (2014): 147–161.
19 Johnson, 'On agency', 189. See P. Burke, *History and Social Theory*, Cambridge: Polity, 2005, 136, on the 'return of the actor'.
20 See H. Ritvo, 'History and animal studies', *Society and Animals* 10, 4 (2002): 403–406; S. Swart, '"But where's the bloody horse?": textuality and corporeality in the "animal turn"', *Journal of Literary Studies* 23, 3 (2007): 271–292.
21 'The animal is immediately one with its life-activity. It does not distinguish itself from it. It is *its life-activity*. Man makes his life-activity the object of his will and consciousness' (Marx, *Economic and Philosophic Manuscripts* (1844), quoted in A. Callinicos, *Making History: Agency, Structure, and Change in Social Theory*, second edition, Leiden: Brill, 2004, 23.
22 M.E. Lien, *Becoming Salmon: Aquaculture and the Domestication of a Fish*, Berkeley CA: University of California Press, 2015.
23 Callinicos, *Making History*, 2.

24 W.H. Sewell, 'A theory of structure: duality, agency, and transformation', *American Journal of Sociology* 98, 1 (1992): 1–29. Sewell doubles up on his anthropocentrism by insisting that only human beings could count as the collective agents necessary for historical action: 'Agency entails an ability to coordinate one's actions with others and against others, to form collective projects, to persuade, to coerce, and to monitor the simultaneous effects of one's own and others' activities' (21).

25 See D.L. Smail, *On Deep History and the Brain*, Berkeley CA: University of California Press, 2008; D.L. Smail, 'Neuroscience and the dialectics of history', *Análise Social* 47, 4 (2012): 894–909. For a contrast, and how not to do 'deep history', see D. Laibman, *Deep History: A Study in Social Evolution and Human Potential*, Albany NY: SUNY Press, 2007. Laibman's rational choice model of human evolution is clear from the very outset that 'Humans . . . have the capacity (and necessity) for *agency* in a way that other animal species do not' (9).

26 'Hominins have always been constituted by the agency of persons and things. Our history is a material history, not just a succession of thoughts or speech acts. If deep time is to figure in our histories, then we need narratives that can triangulate between agents and materials': A. Shryock, T.R. Trautmann, and C. Gamble, 'Imagining the human in deep time', in A. Shryock and D.L. Smail (eds.), *Deep History: The Architecture of Past and Present*, Berkeley CA: University of California Press, 2011, 21–54, 30. See also M.H. Johnson, 'Conceptions of agency in archaeological explanation', *Journal of Anthropological Archaeology* 8, 2 (1989): 189–211.

27 I give these two references simply as contrasting examples of such work on agency: A. Bandura, 'Toward a psychology of human agency', *Perspectives on Psychological Science*, 1, 2 (2006): 164–180; W.D. Christensen and C.A. Hooker, 'Self-directed agents', *Canadian Journal of Philosophy* 31, Sup. 1 (2001): 18–52.

28 See P. Haggard and B. Eitam, *The Sense of Agency*, Oxford: Oxford University Press, 2015.

29 T. Newton, 'The turn to biology', *The Sociological Review Monographs* 64 (2016): 117–133.

30 S. Best, 'The rise of critical animal studies: putting theory into action and animal liberation into higher education', *Journal of Critical Animal Studies* 7, 1 (2009): 9–52, 17. Relevant work in the life sciences and beyond takes in neuroscience, cognitive science, psychology, cybernetics, phenomenological biology, ecological psychology, ethology, animal welfare science.

31 *Pas de deux* is borrowed from P. Descola, *The Ecology of Others*, Chicago IL: Prickly Paradigm Press, 2013, 85.

32 Descola, *Ecology of Others*, 63. D. Brantz, 'Introduction', in D. Brantz (ed.), *Beastly Natures: Animals, Humans, and the Study of History*, Charlottesville VA: University of Virginia Press, 2010, 1–13, 4.

33 For 'posthumanism' critique of humanistic visions of subjectivity coincident with conscious agency and dominion over the natural world, see R. Braidotti, *The Posthuman*, Cambridge: Polity, 2013, 101, and N.K. Hayles, *How We Became Posthuman: Virtual Bodies in Cybernetics, Literature, and Informatics*, Chicago IL: University of Chicago Press, 1999, 288.

34 F. Furedi, '"Big History": the annihilation of human agency', 24 July 2013, available at www.spiked-online.com/newsite/article/frank_furedi_on_history/13844#.VzCVVRUrL_8, last accessed 11 July 2016.

35 Furedi, 'Big History'.

36 As Susan Nance puts it, 'there has never been any purely human space in world history. We must account for nonhumans as living beings – not merely representations – in order to find the fullest possible explanation of history and to avoid simply engaging in self-flattery

or self-deception': S. Nance, *Entertaining Elephants: Animal Agency and the Business of the American Circus*, Baltimore MD: Johns Hopkins University Press, 2013, 7.
37 A. Pickering, *The Mangle of Practice: Time, Agency, and Science*, Chicago IL: University of Chicago Press, 1995, 6, emphasis in original.
38 Excellent introductions are afforded by B. Latour, *Reassembling the Social: An Introduction to Actor-Network Theory*, Oxford: Oxford University Press, 2005; J. Bennett, *Vibrant Matter: A Political Ecology of Things*, Durham NC: Duke University Press, 2010; N. Thrift, *Non-Representational Theory: Space, Politics, Affect*, second edition, London: Routledge, 2007, but there is no real alternative to diving straight in to G. Deleuze and F. Guattari, *A Thousand Plateau: Capitalism and Schizophrenia*, Minneapolis MN: University of Minnesota Press, 1987.
39 Thus Marianne Elisabeth Lien, considering the farming of salmon, sees the agency of fish as 'a distributed property of the entire salmon assemblage' (Lien, *Becoming Salmon*, 168).
40 For James Gibson's theory of affordances, first published in 1979, see J.J. Gibson, *The Ecological Approach to Visual Perception*, classic edition, New York: Psychology Press, 2015; see also A. Chemero, 'An outline of a theory of affordances', *Ecological Psychology* 15, 2 (2003): 181–195. Such ideas are influenced by earlier work by Jacob von Uexkül, and the Husserlian concept of *Umwelt*.
41 Other ways of expressing this 'relational agency' are these terms, among others: 'embedded agency'; 'extended agency'; 'distributed agency'; 'dependent agency'; 'lateral agency'.
42 Bennett, *Vibrant Matter*, 21.
43 I.H. Tague, *Animal Companions: Pets and Social Change in Eighteenth-Century Britain*, University Park PA: Penn State University Press, 2015, 9. Tague accepts of course that her eighteenth-century animal companions were 'living, breathing beings that had a direct impact on the lives of the humans with whom they interacted' (8), but she insists that we cannot speak of their historical agency.
44 Fudge, 'A left-handed blow'.
45 Benson, 'Animal writes'. See also Z. Tortorici, 'Animal archive stories: species anxieties in the Mexican national archives', in S. Nance (ed.), *The Historical Animal*, Syracuse NY: Syracuse University Press, 75–98, 95, on the 'reverberations of individual connections with images of animals, textual representations of animals, and animals living in the past'.
46 Fudge, 'A left-handed blow', 14; J. Soluri, 'On edge: fur seals and hunters along the Patagonian littoral, 1860–1930', in M. Few and Z. Tortorici (eds.), *Centering Animals in Latin American History*, Durham NC: Duke University Press, 2013, 243–369, 263.
47 Benson, 'Animal writes'; S.J. Pearson and M. Weismantel, 'Does "the animal" exist? Toward a theory of social life with animals', in D. Brantz (ed.), *Beastly Natures: Animals, Humans, and the Study of History*, Charlottesville VA: University of Virginia Press, 2010, 17–37; Bennett, *Vibrant Matter*. See also N. Rothfels, 'Touching animals: the search for a deeper understanding of animals', in Brantz (ed.), *Beastly Natures*, 38–58, and S. Swart, 'Zombie zoology: history and reanimating extinct animals', in S. Nance (ed.), *The Historical Animal*, Syracuse NY: Syracuse University Press, 2015, 54–71, 70.
48 Pearson and Weismantel, 'Does "the animal" exist?' 27.
49 For social or 'cultural construction' of agency, see J.W. Meyer and R.L. Jepperson, 'The "actors" of modern society: the cultural construction of social agency', *Sociological Theory* 18, 1 (2000): 100–120.
50 P. Dinzelbacher, 'Animal trials: a multidisciplinary approach', *Journal of Interdisciplinary History* 32, 3 (2002): 405–421. On animal trials, see the classic works by E.P. Evans, *The Criminal Prosecution and Capital Punishment of Animals: The Lost History of Europe's Animal Trials*, London: Faber and Faber, 1987, and W.W. Hyde, 'Prosecution and punishment of

animals and lifeless things in the Middle Ages and modern times,' *University of Pennsylvania Law Review* 64, 7 (1916): 696–730, together with more recent reflections: P.S. Berman, 'Rats, pigs, and statues on trial: the creation of cultural narratives in the prosecution of animals and inanimate objects', *New York University Law Review* 69 (1994): 288–326; G. Teubner, 'Rights of non-humans: electronic agents and animals as new actors in politics and law', *Journal of Law and Society* 33, 4 (2006): 497–521.

51 A contemporary comparison is the jarring use of the word 'murder' by the film director Werner Herzog, referring to the bear that killed the animal activist Timothy Treadwell. See also D. Lulka, 'Consuming Timothy Treadwell: redefining human agency in light of Herzog's *Grizzly Man*', in S.E. McFarland and R. Hediger (eds.), *Animals and Agency: An Interdisciplinary Exploration*, Leiden: Brill, 2009, 67–88.

52 On 'animal celebrities', see D.C. Giles, 'Animal celebrities', *Celebrity Studies* 4, 2 (2013): 115–128; L. Brown, *Homeless Dogs and Melancholy Apes: Humans and Other Animals in the Modern Literary Imagination*, Ithaca NY: Cornell University Press, 2010, 113–143; H. Keenleyside, 'The first-person form of life: Locke, Sterne, and the autobiographical animal', *Critical Inquiry* 39, 1 (2012): 116–141. For an example of the 'animal apparatus' of Hollywood 'stardom', see C.E. White, 'Tony the wonder horse: a star study', in S. Nance (ed.), *The Historical Animal*, Syracuse NY: Syracuse University Press, 2015, 289–306. Some performing animals might be considered as doubly endowed with agency – as animals who were attractions in their own right, and as animal actors represented in their biographies as reflecting on their career on the boards: see M. Dobson, 'A dog at all things: the transformation of the onstage canine, 1550–1850', *Performance Research* 5, 2 (2000): 116–124.

53 For recent biographical and quasi-biographical attention see P. Chambers, *Jumbo: This Being the True Story of the Greatest Elephant in the World*, London: Andre Deutsch, 2007; S. Nance, *Animal Modernity: Jumbo the Elephant and the Human Dilemma*, Houndmills: Palgrave Macmillan, 2015; J. Sutherland, *Jumbo: The Unauthorised Biography of a Victorian Sensation*, London: Aurum Press, 2013.

54 M. Scott, *Autobiography of Matthew Scott, Jumbo's Keeper*, Bridgeport CT: Trow's Printing Company, 1885, 96.

55 An introduction to 'it-narratives': M. Blackwell (ed.), *The Secret Life of Things: Animals and Objects in Eighteenth-Century Fictions of Circulation*, Lewisburg PA: Bucknell University Press, 2007.

56 M. Mattfield, '"Genus porcus sophisticus": the learned pig and the theatrics of national identity in late eighteenth-century London', in L. Orozco and J. Parker-Starbuck (eds.), *Performing Animality: Animals in Performance Practices*, Houndmills: Palgrave Macmillan, 2015, 57–76, 66.

57 On the representation and effacement of animals see: S. Baker, *The Postmodern Animal*, London: Reaktion, 2000; J. Berger, *Why Look at Animals?* London: Penguin, 2009; A.M. Lippit, *Electric Animal: Toward a Rhetoric of Wildlife*, Minneapolis MN: University of Minnesota Press, 2000; N. Rothfels (ed.), *Representing Animals*, Bloomington IN: Indiana University Press, 2002.

58 Lippit, *Electric Animal*, 54. An example: Rebecca Onion persuasively argues that the agency of sled dogs is central to the stories that were told about Alaska, about the frozen North, about American whiteness and masculinity, but she goes on to aver that 'in these stories, the actions of the dogs are useful more for human thought than for the animals themselves, leaving their actual agency up to question': R. Onion, 'Sled dogs of the American North: on masculinity, whiteness, and human freedom', in S.E. McFarland and R. Hediger (eds.), *Animals and Agency: An Interdisciplinary Exploration*, Leiden: Brill, 2009, 129–155, 154.

59 Keenleyside, 'The first-person form of life', 140.
60 J.K. Cronin '"Can't you talk?" Voice and visual culture in early animal welfare campaigns', *Early Popular Visual Culture* 9, 3 (2011): 203–223, cited in H. Kean, 'Challenges for historians writing animal–human history: what is really enough?' *Anthrozoös* 25, Sup 1 (2012): s57–s72, s59.
61 Brown, *Homeless Dogs*, 2; see also V. Richter, *Literature After Darwin: Human Beasts in Western Fiction, 1859–1939*, Houndmills: Palgrave, 2011.
62 For 'nonhuman charisma', see J. Lorimer, *Wildlife in the Anthropocene: Conservation after Nature*, Minneapolis MN: Minnesota University Press, 2015. For science, Donna Haraway has argued that great apes were not passive agents of knowledge, and contributed 'authorship' to scientific narratives: D. Haraway, *Primate Visions: Gender, Race, and Nature in the World of Modern Science*, New York: Routledge, 1989.
63 E. Fudge, *Brutal Reasoning: Animals, Rationality, and Humanity in Early Modern England*, Ithaca NY: Cornell University Press, 2006, 191–192.
64 S. McHugh, 'Literary animal agents', *PMLA* 124, 2 (2009): 487–495.
65 Brown, *Homeless Dogs*, 18.
66 Fudge, *Brutal Reasoning*.
67 In such a forbiddingly presumptive discourse, reason is turned into 'an inherent possession of the individual, rather than the product of actions or of a network that relies on and includes animals': Fudge, *Brutal Reasoning*, 191.
68 Fudge, *Brutal Reasoning*, 188.
69 Brantz, 'Introduction', 3.
70 S. Nance, 'Introduction', in S. Nance (ed.), *The Historical Animal*, Syracuse NY: Syracuse University Press, 2015, 1–16, 3; Nance, *Entertaining Elephants*, 97.
71 Phineas, 'Household pets', 343.
72 The quotation is from D.E. Bender, *The Animal Game: Searching for Wildness at the American Zoo*, Cambridge MA: Harvard University Press, 2016, 52.
73 C. McNeur, *Taming Manhattan: Environmental Battles in the Antebellum City*, Cambridge MA: Harvard University Press, 2014, 27, 39.
74 D.G. Shaw, 'The torturer's horse: agency and animals in history', *History and Theory* 52, 4 (2013): 146–167; V. Despret, 'From secret agents to interagency', *History and Theory* 52, 4 (2013): 29–44.
75 J. St. Clair, in J. Hribal (ed.), *Fear of the Animal Planet: The Hidden History of Animal Resistance*, Petrolia CA: Counterpunch, 2010, 16.
76 Hribal, *Fear of the Animal Planet*, 26.
77 M. Candelaria, 'The microgeography of infestation in relationship spaces', in S.E. McFarland and R. Hediger (eds.), *Animals and Agency: An Interdisciplinary Exploration*, Leiden: Brill, 2009, 301–320, 302.
78 Johnson, 'On agency', 115.
79 Despret, 'From secret agents to interagency', 43.
80 Johnson, 'On agency', 116.
81 For the 'animal standpoint', see the passionate advocacy of Best, 'The rise of critical animal studies', 17: 'Whereas nearly all histories, even so-called 'radical' narratives, have been written from the human standpoint, a growing number of theorists have broken free of the speciesist straightjacket to examine history and society from the standpoint of (nonhuman) animals. This approach, as I define it, considers the interaction between human and nonhuman animals – past, present, and future – and the need for profound changes in the way humans define themselves and relate to other sentient species and to the natural world as a whole'. Critical reflections on perspectivity and agency can be accessed in Despret, 'From secret agents to interagency'.

82 K. Enright, 'Why the rhinoceros doesn't talk: the cultural life of a wild animal in America', in Brantz (ed.), *Beastly Natures*, 108–126. Helen Cowie rightly reminds us (with zoo and menagerie captives in mind) that 'As real living beasts . . . exotic animals also exerted some agency over their interactions with the public, connecting with spectators on a more visceral level as huge, ferocious, noisy or hungry beings who could be fed, ridden or touched': H. Cowie, *Exhibiting Animals in Nineteenth-Century Britain: Empathy, Education, Entertainment*, Houndmills: Palgrave Macmillan, 2014, 5–6.

83 Nance, *Entertaining Elephants*. For an introduction to AWS see M.S. Dawkins, 'A user's guide to animal welfare science', *Trends in Ecology & Evolution* 21, 2 (2006): 77–82.

84 Nance, *Entertaining Elephants*, 127.

85 Nance, *Entertaining Elephants*, 154.

86 Nance, *Entertaining Elephants*, 10.

87 Nance, *Entertaining Elephants*, 174.

88 S. Donaldson and W. Kymlicka, *Zoopolis: A Political Theory of Animal Rights*, Oxford: Oxford University Press, 2011.

89 Donaldson and Kymlicka, *Zoopolis*, 66.

90 C. Pearson, 'Dogs, history, and agency', *History and Theory* 52, 4 (2013): 128–145; N. Pemberton, 'Hounding Holmes: Arthur Conan Doyle, bloodhounds and sleuthing in the late-Victorian imagination', *Journal of Victorian Culture* 17, 4 (2012): 454–467, N. Pemberton, 'Bloodhounds as detectives' dogs, slum stench and late-Victorian murder investigation', *Cultural and Social History* 10, 1 (2012): 69–91.

91 P. Howell, *At Home and Astray: The Domestic Dog in Victorian Britain*, Charlottesville VA: University of Virginia Press, 2015; K. Kete, *The Beast in the Boudoir: Petkeeping in Nineteenth-Century Paris*, Berkeley CA: University of California Press, 1994; Tague, *Animal Companions*.

92 P. Howell, *At Home and Astray*, 150–173.

93 Howell, *At Home and Astray*, 151–152.

94 For 'dependent agency' see Donaldson and Kymlicka, *Zoopolis*, 104–108.

95 See M. Ascarelli, *Dorothy Harrison Eustis and the Story of the Seeing Eye*, West Lafayette IN: Purdue University Press, 2010.

96 Ascarelli, *Dorothy Harrison Eustis*, 35.

97 See Haraway, *When Species Meet*; C. Wolfe, *Zoontologies: The Question of the Animal*, Minneapolis MN: Minnesota University Press, 2003, 95.

98 A.H. Gibson, 'Beasts of burden: feral burros and the American West', in S. Nance (ed.), *The Historical Animal*, Syracuse NY: Syracuse University Press, 2015, 38–53, 40. See also K. Nagy and P.D. Johnson, *Trash Animals: How We Live with Nature's Filthy, Feral, Invasive, and Unwanted Species*, Minneapolis MN: University of Minnesota Press, 2013.

99 D.D. Biehler, *Pests in the City: Flies, Bedbugs, Cockroaches, and Rats*, Seattle WA: University of Washington Press, 2013.

100 Biehler, *Pests in the City*, 4.

101 Candelaria, 'The microgeography of infestation', 302. But see also 305: 'the vermin demonstrate their agency and actively participate with humans in the habiting of space'.

102 Biehler also draws on what we know of flies to relate urban history from their point of view, choosing to use 'who' and 'he' and 'she' instead of 'which' and 'that' and 'it', even in the case of maggots emerging from wet sludge: Biehler, *Pests in the City*, 33.

103 Steward, 'Animal agency', 228.

104 Swanson, 'Mountain meeting ground', 256.

105 Kean, 'Challenges for historians', s60.

References

Ascarelli, M. *Dorothy Harrison Eustis and the Story of the Seeing Eye*, West Lafayette IN: Purdue University Press, 2010.

Baker, S. *The Postmodern Animal*, London: Reaktion, 2000.

Bandura, A. 'Toward a psychology of human agency', *Perspectives on Psychological Science* 1, 2 (2006): 164–180.

Bekoff, M. and Pierce, J. *Wild Justice: The Moral Lives of Animals*, Chicago IL: University of Chicago Press, 2009.

Bender, D.E. *The Animal Game: Searching for Wildness at the American Zoo*, Cambridge MA: Harvard University Press, 2016, 52.

Bennett, J. *Vibrant Matter: A Political Ecology of Things*, Durham NC: Duke University Press, 2010.

Benson, E. 'Animal writes: historiography, disciplinarity, and the animal trace', in L. Kalof and G. M. Montgomery (eds.), *Making Animal Meaning*, East Lansing MI: Michigan State University Press, 2011, 3–16.

Berger, J. *Why Look at Animals?* London: Penguin, 2009.

Berman, P.S. 'Rats, pigs, and statues on trial: the creation of cultural narratives in the prosecution of animals and inanimate objects', *New York University Law Review* 69 (1994): 288–326.

Best, S. 'The rise of critical animal studies: putting theory into action and animal liberation into higher education', *Journal of Critical Animal Studies* 7, 1 (2009): 9–52.

Biehler, D.D. *Pests in the City: Flies, Bedbugs, Cockroaches, and Rats*, Seattle WA: University of Washington Press, 2013.

Blackwell, M. (ed.), *The Secret Life of Things: Animals and Objects in Eighteenth-Century Fictions of Circulation*, Lewisburg PA: Bucknell University Press, 2007.

Braidotti, R. *The Posthuman*, Cambridge: Polity, 2013.

Brantz, D. 'Introduction', in D. Brantz (ed.), *Beastly Natures: Animals, Humans, and the Study of History*. Charlottesville VA: University of Virginia Press, 2010, 1–13.

Brown, L. *Homeless Dogs and Melancholy Apes: Humans and Other Animals in the Modern Literary Imagination*, Ithaca NY: Cornell University Press, 2010.

Burke, P. *History and Social Theory*, Cambridge: Polity, 2005.

Callinicos, A. *Making History: Agency, Structure, and Change in Social Theory*, second edition, Leiden: Brill, 2004.

Candelaria, M. 'The microgeography of infestation in relationship spaces', in S.E. McFarland and R. Hediger (eds.), *Animals and Agency: An Interdisciplinary Exploration*, Leiden: Brill, 2009, 301–320.

Chambers, P. *Jumbo: This Being the True Story of the Greatest Elephant in the World*, London: Andre Deutsch, 2007.

Chemero, A. 'An outline of a theory of affordances', *Ecological Psychology* 15, 2 (2003): 181–195.

Christensen, W.D. and Hooker, C.A. 'Self-directed agents', *Canadian Journal of Philosophy* 31, Sup. 1 (2001): 18–52.

Clement, G. 'Animals and moral agency: the recent debate and its implications', *Journal of Animal Ethics* 3, 1 (2013): 1–14.

Cowie, H. *Exhibiting Animals in Nineteenth-Century Britain: Empathy, Education, Entertainment*, Houndmills: Palgrave Macmillan, 2014.

Cronin, J.K. '"Can't you talk?" Voice and visual culture in early animal welfare campaigns', *Early Popular Visual Culture* 9, 3 (2011): 203–223.

Davidson, D. (1982) 'Rational animals', *Dialectica* 36, 4 (1982): 317–327.

Dawkins, M.S. 'A user's guide to animal welfare science', *Trends in Ecology & Evolution* 21, 2 (2006): 77–82.

Deleuze, G. and Guattari, F. *A Thousand Plateau: Capitalism and Schizophrenia*, Minneapolis MN: University of Minnesota Press, 1987.

Descola, P. *The Ecology of Others*, Chicago IL: Prickly Paradigm Press, 2013.

Despret, V. 'From secret agents to interagency', *History and Theory* 52, 4 (2013): 29–44.

Dinzelbacher, P. 'Animal trials: a multidisciplinary approach', *Journal of Interdisciplinary History* 32, 3 (2002): 405–421.

Dobson, M. 'A dog at all things: the transformation of the onstage canine, 1550–1850', *Performance Research* 5, 2 (2000): 116–124.

Donaldson, S. and Kymlicka, W. *Zoopolis: A Political Theory of Animal Rights*, Oxford: Oxford University Press, 2011.

Donaldson, S. and Kymlicka, W. 'Unruly beasts: animal citizens and the threat of tyranny', *Canadian Journal of Political Science* 47, 1 (2014): 23–45.

Enright, K. 'Why the rhinoceros doesn't talk: the cultural life of a wild animal in America', in D. Brantz (ed.), *Beastly Natures: Animals, Humans, and the Study of History*, Charlottesville VA: University of Virginia Press, 2010, 108–126.

Evans, E.P. *The Criminal Prosecution and Capital Punishment of Animals: The Lost History of Europe's Animal Trials*, London: Faber and Faber, 1987.

Fudge, E. 'A left-handed blow: writing the history of animals', in N. Rothfels (ed.), *Representing Animals*, Bloomington IN: Indiana University Press, 2002.

Fudge, E. *Brutal Reasoning: Animals, Rationality, and Humanity in Early Modern England*, Ithaca NY: Cornell University Press, 2006.

Furedi, F. '"Big History": the annihilation of human agency', 24 July 2013, available at www.spiked-online.com/newsite/article/frank_furedi_on_history/13844#.VzCVVRUrL_8, last accessed 11 July 2016.

Gibson, A.H. 'Beasts of burden: feral burros and the American West', in S. Nance (ed.), *The Historical Animal*, Syracuse NY: Syracuse University Press, 2015, 38–53.

Gibson, J.J. *The Ecological Approach to Visual Perception*, classic edition, New York: Psychology Press, 2015.

Giles, D.C. 'Animal celebrities', *Celebrity Studies* 4, 2 (2013): 115–128.

Haggard, P. and Eitam, B. *The Sense of Agency*, Oxford: Oxford University Press, 2015.

Haraway, D. *Primate Visions: Gender, Race, and Nature in the World of Modern Science*, New York: Routledge, 1989.

Hayles, N.K. *How We Became Posthuman: Virtual Bodies in Cybernetics, Literature, and Informatics*, Chicago IL: University of Chicago Press, 1999.

Howell, P. *At Home and Astray: The Domestic Dog in Victorian Britain*, Charlottesville VA: University of Virginia Press, 2015.

Hribal, J. *Fear of the Animal Planet: The Hidden History of Animal Resistance*, Petrolia CA: Counterpunch, 2016.

Hyde, W.W. 'Prosecution and punishment of animals and lifeless things in the middle ages and modern times,' *University of Pennsylvania Law Review* 64, 7 (1916): 696–730.

Johnson, M.H. 'Conceptions of agency in archaeological explanation', *Journal of Anthropological Archaeology* 8, 2 (1989): 189–211.

Johnson, W. 'On agency', *Journal of Social History* 37 (2003): 113–124.

Kane, R. (ed.), *The Oxford Handbook of Free Will*, second edition, Oxford: Oxford University Press, 2011.

Kean, H. 'Challenges for historians writing animal-human history: what is really enough?' *Anthrozoös* 25, Sup 1 (2012): s57–s72.

Keenleyside, H. 'The first-person form of life: Locke, Sterne, and the autobiographical animal', *Critical Inquiry* 39, 1 (2012): 116–141.
Kete, K. *The Beast in the Boudoir: Petkeeping in Nineteenth-Century Paris*, Berkeley CA: University of California Press, 1994.
Laibman, D. *Deep History: A Study in Social Evolution and Human Potential*, Albany NY: SUNY Press, 2007.
Latour, B. *Reassembling the Social: An Introduction to Actor-Network Theory*, Oxford: Oxford University Press, 2005.
Lien, M.E. *Becoming Salmon: Aquaculture and the Domestication of a Fish*, Berkeley CA: University of California Press, 2015.
Lippit, A.M. *Electric Animal: Toward a Rhetoric of Wildlife*, Minneapolis MN: University of Minnesota Press, 2000.
Lorimer, J. *Wildlife in the Anthropocene: Conservation after Nature*, Minneapolis MN: Minnesota University Press, 2015.
Lulka, D. 'Consuming Timothy Treadwell: redefining human agency in light of Herzog's *Grizzly Man*', in S.E. McFarland and R. Hediger (eds.), *Animals and Agency: An Interdisciplinary Exploration*, Leiden: Brill, 2009, 67–88.
Mattfield, M. '"Genus porcus sophisticus": the learned pig and the theatrics of national identity in late eighteenth-century London', in L. Orozco and J. Parker-Starbuck (eds.), *Performing Animality: Animals in Performance Practices*, Houndmills: Palgrave Macmillan, 2015, 57–76.
McHugh, S. 'Literary animal agents', *PMLA* 124, 2 (2009): 487–495.
McNeur, C. *Taming Manhattan: Environmental Battles in the Antebellum City*, Cambridge MA: Harvard University Press, 2014.
Meyer, J.W. and Jepperson, R.L. 'The "actors" of modern society: the cultural construction of social agency', *Sociological Theory* 18, 1 (2000): 100–120.
Miller, M.R. 'Descartes on animals revisited', *Journal of Philosophical Research* 38 (2013): 89–114.
Nagy, K. and Johnson, P.D. *Trash Animals: How We Live with Nature's Filthy, Feral, Invasive, and Unwanted Species*, Minneapolis MN: University of Minnesota Press, 2013.
Nance, S. *Entertaining Elephants: Animal Agency and the Business of the American Circus*, Baltimore MD: Johns Hopkins University Press, 2013.
Nance, S. *Animal Modernity: Jumbo the Elephant and the Human Dilemma*, Houndmills: Palgrave Macmillan, 2015.
Nance, S. 'Introduction', in S. Nance (ed.), *The Historical Animal*, Syracuse NY: Syracuse University Press, 2015, 1–16.
Newton, T. 'The turn to biology', *The Sociological Review Monographs* 64 (2016): 117–133.
Oliver, K. *Animal Lessons: How They Teach Us to be Human*, New York: Columbia University Press, 2009.
Onion, R. 'Sled dogs of the American North: on masculinity, whiteness, and human freedom', in S.E. McFarland and R. Hediger (eds.), *Animals and Agency: An Interdisciplinary Exploration*, Leiden: Brill, 2009, 129–155.
Pearson, C. 'Dogs, history, and agency', *History and Theory* 52, 4 (2013): 128–145.
Pearson, S.J. and Weismantel, M. 'Does "the animal" exist? Toward a theory of social life with animals', in D. Brantz (ed.), *Beastly Natures: Animals, Humans, and the Study of History*, Charlottesville VA: University of Virginia Press, 2010, 17–37.
Pemberton, N. 'Bloodhounds as detectives' dogs, slum stench and late-Victorian murder investigation', *Cultural and Social History* 10, 1 (2012): 69–91.
Pemberton, N. 'Hounding Holmes: Arthur Conan Doyle, bloodhounds and sleuthing in the late-Victorian imagination', *Journal of Victorian Culture* 17, 4 (2012): 454–467.

Phineas, C. 'Household pets and urban alienation', *Journal of Social History* 7, 3 (1974): 334–343.

Pickering, A. *The Mangle of Practice: Time, Agency, and Science*, Chicago IL: University of Chicago Press, 1995.

Richter, V. *Literature after Darwin: Human Beasts in Western Fiction, 1859–1939*, Houndmills: Palgrave, 2011.

Ritvo, H. 'History and animal studies', *Society and Animals* 10, 4 (2002): 403–406.

Rodman, J. 'The liberation of nature?' *Inquiry* 20, 1–4 (1977): 83–131.

Rothfels, N. (ed.), *Representing Animals*, Bloomington IN: Indiana University Press, 2002.

Rothfels, N. 'Touching animals: the search for a deeper understanding of animals', in D. Brantz (ed.), *Beastly Natures: Animals, Humans, and the Study of History*, Charlottesville VA: University of Virginia Press, 2010, 38–58.

Schulte, C. 'Der deutsch-deutsche Schäferhund—Ein Beitrag zur Gewaltgeschichte des Jahrhunderts der Extreme', *Totalitarismus und Demokratie* 2 (2015): 319–334, available at www.enricoheitzer.de/2016/02/18/sch%C3%A4ferhund-gate/, last accessed 11 July 2016.

Scott, M. *Autobiography of Matthew Scott, Jumbo's Keeper*, Bridgeport CT: Trow's Printing Company, 1885.

Scott, S.R. 'The racehorse as protagonist: agency, independence, and improvisation', in S.E. McFarland and R. Hediger (eds.), *Animals and Agency: An Interdisciplinary Exploration*, Leiden: Brill, 2009, 45–65.

Sewell, W.H. 'A theory of structure: duality, agency, and transformation', *American Journal of Sociology* 98, 1 (1992): 1–29.

Shapiro, P. 'Moral agency in other animals', *Theoretical Medicine and Bioethics* 27, 4 (2006): 257–273.

Shaw, D.G. 'The torturer's horse: agency and animals in history', *History and Theory* 52, 4 (2013): 146–167.

Shryock, A., Trautmann, T.R., and Gamble, C. 'Imagining the human in deep time', in A. Shryock and D.L. Smail (eds.), *Deep History: The Architecture of Past and Present*, Berkeley CA: University of California Press, 2011, 21–54.

Smail, D.L. *On Deep History and the Brain*, Berkeley CA: University of California Press, 2008.

Smail, D.L. 'Neuroscience and the dialectics of history', *Análise Social* 47, 4 (2012): 894–909.

Soluri, J. 'On edge: fur seals and hunters along the Patagonian littoral, 1860–1930', in M. Few and Z. Tortorici (eds.), *Centering Animals in Latin American History*, Durham NC: Duke University Press, 2013, 243–369.

Sutherland, J. *Jumbo: The Unauthorised Biography of a Victorian Sensation*, London: Aurum Press, 2013.

Swanson, D.A. 'Mountain meeting ground: history at an intersection of species', in S. Nance (ed.), *The Historical Animal*, Syracuse NY: Syracuse University Press, 2015, 240–257.

Steward, H. 'Animal agency', *Inquiry* 52, 3 (2009): 217–231.

Swart, S. '"But where's the bloody horse?": textuality and corporeality in the "animal turn"', *Journal of Literary Studies* 23, 3 (2007): 271–292.

Swart, S. 'Zombie zoology: history and reanimating extinct animals', in S. Nance (ed.), *The Historical Animal*, Syracuse NY: Syracuse University Press, 2015, 54–71.

Tague, I.H. *Animal Companions: Pets and Social Change in Eighteenth-Century Britain*, University Park PA: Penn State University Press, 2015.

Taylor, C. 'Engaged agency and background in Heidegger', in C. Guignon (ed.), *The Cambridge Companion to Heidegger*, second edition, Cambridge: Cambridge University Press, 2006, 202–221.

Teubner, G. 'Rights of non-humans: electronic agents and animals as new actors in politics and law', *Journal of Law and Society* 33, 4 (2006): 497–521.

Thrift, N. *Non-Representational Theory: Space, Politics, Affect*, second edition, London: Routledge, 2007.

Tortorici, Z. 'Animal archive stories: species anxieties in the Mexican national archives', in S. Nance (ed.), *The Historical Animal*, Syracuse NY: Syracuse University Press, 2015, 75–98.

Tortorici, Z. and Few, M. 'Writing animal histories', in M. Few and Z. Tortorici (eds.), *Centering Animals in Latin American History*, Durham NC: Duke University Press, 2013, 1–28.

Wadiwel, D.J. 'The war against animals: domination, law and sovereignty', *Griffith Law Review* 18, 2 (2009): 283–297.

Wadiwel, D.J. 'The will for self-preservation: Locke and Derrida on dominion, property and animals', *SubStance* 43, 2 (2014): 147–161.

White, C.E. 'Tony the wonder horse: a star study', in S. Nance (ed.), *The Historical Animal*, Syracuse NY: Syracuse University Press, 2015, 289–306.

Wokler, R. 'Rousseau's two concepts of liberty' in G. Feaver and F. Rosen (eds.), *Lives, Liberties and the Public Good: New Essays in Political Theory for Maurice Cranston*, London: Palgrave Macmillan, 1987, 61–100.

Wolfe, C. *Zoontologies: The Question of the Animal*, Minneapolis MN: Minnesota University Press, 2003.

10
REPRESENTING ANIMALS IN THE LITERATURE OF VICTORIAN BRITAIN

Jennifer McDonell

I begin with two iconic images of the Victorian era (Figure 10.1, Figure 10.2). The first is a photograph of Queen Victoria with one of her favourite border collies, Sharp (1866–79), who is seated on a gothic chair resembling a throne and leaning into his dour mistress's breast. The second is of the celebrity elephant Jumbo, who tragically died after being hit by a freight locomotive, a death that is all too neatly emblematic of nineteenth-century industrialisation. As they merge into each other, Sharp and his mistress embody Victorian domesticity in all its glaring contradictions, with Sharp standing in as a confidante and honorary royal and as a model of the obedient and loyal subject, an emblem of how good breeding anchors the bourgeois home.[1] Born around 1861 in what is now Eritrea, Jumbo was violently separated from his mother by hunters and sent to the Jardin des Plantes in Paris before being relocated to the London Zoo, where he was tortured by night for seventeen years to make him docile by day. When Jumbo became violent in middle age, he was bought by P.T. Barnum and emerged as one of the most lucrative circus acts of Barnum's 'Greatest Show on Earth', that is, until 1885 when he wandered onto a railway track in Ontario, Canada. Jumbo's body was subsequently dissected, with its parts attaining historical and cultural afterlife as museum specimens and taxidermied exhibits.[2] The real animals in these images represent extremes of sentiment and violence, the homely and the exotic, sympathetic interdependence with, and instrumental use of animals by humans that was in many ways characteristic of Victorian Britain.

The burgeoning field of Animal Studies (alternatively Human Animal Studies) is a vibrant, varied domain of methodological convergences and divergences, united by a shared concern with studying the species interdependence of human and animal lives. This chapter will attempt to provide an overview of significant developments and preoccupations in Animal Studies in so far as these have influenced research in Victorian literature, while also suggesting some possible future directions the field may take. Animal Studies scholarship in recent decades has rightly attempted to challenge long-unquestioned habits of constructing the 'human' in opposition to the homogenous category of 'the Animal'. The philosopher Jacques Derrida designates that category with a capital 'A' in the general singular, enclosed

Figure 10.1 Queen Victoria and Sharp, Balmoral Castle, 1866.
Courtesy W. and D. Downey / Stringer / Getty Images.

by the definite article to foreground the abstracted nature of a concept that allows humans to characterise members of particular nonhuman species as biological and transcultural constants.[3] In light of this long-standing dichotomy, one of the ongoing challenges for Animal Studies and literary analysis is how to think about animals *as animals* rather than simply as symbols or metaphors to explain primarily human concerns.

A remarkable menagerie of creatures can be found across all Victorian literary genres, a ubiquity that is in part traceable to the visibility of a wide range of animal species – especially domestic animals – in the everyday lives of the Victorians as raw material, labour, transport, food, clothing, entertainment, companionship, and scientific knowledge produced through animal observation and experimentation. The cities, towns and villages in which Victorian writers were born and bred were as much spaces occupied by animals as by people in a way that is alien to much contemporary experience. London and other major British cities were in every sense anthrozootic cities: urban environments defined by the interaction and interdependency of humans

Figure 10.2 Jumbo and his keeper Matthew Scott. Barnum poster, c. 1882.

Courtesy of the John and Mable Ringling Museum of Art.

and other animals.[4] Yet as George Levine observes of Victorian literature 'one looks hard to find encounters with animals that register the integrity of the animal itself'.[5] This is related to a broader problem which Levine and others have identified: the difficulty of representing nonhuman animals in human language, shaped by human intentions and attitudes. In this sense, what commentators have identified as 'the animal turn' in recent humanities and social sciences scholarship evinces how 'non human animals have become a limit case for theories of difference, otherness, and power'.[6]

Within contemporary theory, new materialists and animal theorists share, to use Rosi Braidotti's term, a 'post-anthropocentric' approach to matter and life.[7] For instance, in their introduction to *The Multispecies Salon*, Eben Kirksey, Craig Schuetze, and Stefan Helmreich question Bruno Latour's proposal to bring nonhumans into the democratic political process by assigning human 'spokespeople' to represent them. Citing historian Timothy Mitchell's playful reformulation of Gayatri Spivak's famous question 'Can the subaltern speak?' as 'Can the mosquito speak?', they compare the difficulties of speaking for and with other species to those we face when representing other people and cultures.[8] In view of these problems of representation, Kirksey and Helmreich suggest that researchers in the field attend less to trying to speak for nonhumans, and more to examining what it means for humans to live with them.[9] Taking inspiration from cultural critic Donna Haraway's theorisations of living with nonhumans in *The Companion Species Manifesto* and *When Species Meet*, the emerging discourse of multispecies ethnography has proposed not simply a recognition of nonhuman agents still on the margins of discourses of animality – whether plants, microorganisms, or reviled and loathed species – but also an understanding of the intricate, continually fluctuating relationships and interdependencies of humans and nonhumans across multiple species, usually in highly variable cultures and ecosystems.[10]

Accordingly, one of the most persistently used rhetorical figures in Animal Studies scholarship is 'entanglement'. The term is usually used to convey the idea that all species are unavoidably connected and interdependent with many others.[11] The value of the term lies in its emphasis on non-essentialist, non-anthropocentric relationality. In Anna Tsing's oft-quoted words, '*Human nature is an interspecies relationship*'.[12] Entanglement also contains within its range of meanings the idea of ensnarement or confusion, and can conceivably be extended to include the condition of captivation and captivity experienced by so many creatures represented in nineteenth-century literary texts. We are yet to see what insights a more robust dialogue between the nineteenth-century literary field and the ethnographic field might produce. Once we are done deconstructing the human–animal distinction and deploying new rhetorical figures to describe complex interconnectedness, it is often difficult to determine how exactly to proceed to a literary criticism that 'begins with relationships rather than with an essence of the actors'.[13]

The literature of Victorian Britain is vast, and this chapter is not intended to be a comprehensive overview of animals in the writing of the period. Rather, I will focus on three key problems that have preoccupied literary Animal Studies scholarship over the past three decades: representation, in particular the relationship between anthropomorphism and anthropocentrism; the role of animals as historical agents – as active, significant, and sometimes purposeful creatures worthy of sustained analytical attention; and the place of emotion and feeling in literary analysis, particularly in relation to sentimentality, an affective structure that is almost axiomatically Victorian and that is commonly associated with human–pet relationships. I will take my examples primarily from the popular Victorian genre of animal autobiography, Lewis Carroll's *Alice* books, and from the writing of Charles Dickens, whose name is almost synonymous with Victorian London.[14] An assumption that underpins this chapter is that understanding Victorian perceptions of animals is inseparable from understanding human self-conception in the same period, and that the impact of animals on Victorian Britain's imagination and artistic practices has significant implications for an understanding of its social and cultural life, and vice versa.

Thinking seriously about human–animal relations in Victorian writing also raises questions about interdisciplinarity. Current animal-focused research in Victorian literary studies has drawn on sources not only from such cognate disciplines as history, philosophy, or feminism but also from scientific disciplines including biology, zoology, primatology, ethology, ecology, and comparative psychology. The interdisciplinarity that has long been associated with Victorian literature – especially in its evolution as 'Victorian studies' and 'Victorian literature and culture' – derives from the sense of the uncontainability of the history of ideas and social and cultural life within the constraints of analytic singularity. This interdisciplinarity also finds a precedent in the Victorian period: George Henry Lewes, John Ruskin, John Stuart Mill, and Leslie Stephen, among others, wrote as authoritatively and prolifically about literature and art as of science and politics, while periodicals such as the *Cornhill*, the *Fortnightly*, the *Strand* and more short-lived journals, such as Dickens' *Household Words* and *All the Year Round*, in many ways anticipate the multidisciplinary research environment in which we now find ourselves. If the work of literary criticism consists in making visible what was previously invisible, audible what was inaudible, perceptible what was imperceptible, then the animals who are everywhere present in Victorian writing, but largely occluded in the history of literary criticism, have a claim to be taken seriously as literary subjects and as agents in historical processes.[15]

In this sense there is a close connection between noticing what is chronically overlooked and pursuing social justice, which in turn has implications for the way we as Victorianists pursue research and the kind of sources we consider relevant. For instance, the deployment of animal metaphor and symbol can lead us back to human concerns or, alternatively, to consider the materiality of animals in relation to situated knowledges and practices (in place, time, and social relations) that otherwise may remain invisible. In Dickens' *Bleak House*, for instance, the bird-like Miss Flite, former ward of the state, keeps symbolic caged birds with names including 'Hope', 'Youth', 'Waste', 'Cunning', 'Sheepskin', 'Wigs' and 'Jargon', who are liberated only a few lines after the judgement in *Jarndyce vs Jarndyce* is announced.[16] Among the man-made objects and abstract nouns which lend their names to Miss Flite's birds are a number of animal materials: 'Sheepskin', as the narrator often reminds us, is the material upon which legal documents are written, while 'Wigs' were often made of horsehair. The circulation of things deriving from animal bodies in Victorian fiction, including decorative and consumer goods, suggests intersections between Animal Studies and 'thing theory' or 'object-oriented inquiry', which might be explored in future research.[17] Models may be found in Katherine Grier's work on nineteenth-century American pet-keeping and Kathleen Kete's on pet-keeping in nineteenth-century Paris, which identify a wide range of potentially relevant sources, from newspaper reports and pet-keeping guidebooks to postcards and taxidermy, as well as pet accessories.[18]

A consideration of Dickens' extensive exploitation of the structural and behavioural characteristics of barnacles in *Little Dorrit* (1857) to satirise – through the Barnacle family and the figure of the Circumlocution Office – governmental nepotism and mismanagement might lead us to Darwin's *Monograph* (1851–54) on living barnacles (*Cirripedia*). The *Little Dorrit* narrator explains that having mastered the bureaucratic art of How Not To Do It, all the Barnacle family needed do was: '[s]tick on to the national ship as long as they could' and ensure that the Barnacle sinecure multiplies across the globe. *Little Dorrit* and Darwin's *Monograph* were both published in the 1850s at a time when market demand for popular books on seaside natural history had increased, largely because railroad development in the preceding decades put seaside visits within the reach of many Britons.[19]

Literal and figurative representations of animals in literary texts, however, are not easily disentangled. Dickens' satire of scientific education in *Hard Times* (1854) adopts a combative stance in relation to scientific nomenclature, and in doing so highlights the inherently unstable relationship between 'real' animals and their significations, the literal and the figurative, the connotative and denotative. In the opening chapter, the schoolmaster Thomas Gradgrind asks Sissy Jupe, who has grown up with horses in Sleary's circus, to define a horse. When she cannot, Gradgrind addresses the question to his more fact-minded student, Bitzer, who readily produces a lifeless definition:

> 'Quadruped. Graminivorous. Forty teeth, namely twenty-four grinders, four eye-teeth, and twelve incisive. Sheds coat in the spring; in marshy countries, sheds hoofs, too. Hoofs hard, but requiring to be shod with iron. Age known by marks in mouth.' Thus (and much more) Bitzer.
>
> 'Now girl number twenty,' said Mr Gradgrind. 'You know what a horse is.'[20]

Later in the novel, however, Bitzer proves no match for a real live dog and dancing horse, exposing the arrogance of Gradgrind's approving remark that Bitzer 'know[s] what a horse is'.[21] The real horses and dogs in Sleary's circus, with whom Sissy and others have emotionally and professionally meaningful affective relationships, are of course, figurative. The reader is meant to understand, however, that the scientific definition produced by Bitzer is a linguistic construct and the circus animals denote the 'real', the connotative value of a sign being context-dependent.

Dichotomies of reason and feeling, fact and fancy were commonplace in Victorian literature and print culture. The slipperiness of language evident in such dichotomies extends to the conventional, culturally entrenched opposition of 'human' and 'animal'. During the visit of the Ghost of Christmas Present in Dickens' *A Christmas Carol* (1843), Scrooge observes his nephew, Fred, entertain his sister and friends with a series of parlour games. They include a pared-down version of the guessing game Twenty Questions, in which it is elicited from Fred that he is 'thinking of an animal', which is:

> ... rather a disagreeable animal, a savage animal, an animal that growled and grunted sometimes, and talked sometimes, and lived in London, and walked about the streets, and wasn't made a show of, and wasn't led by anybody, and didn't live in a menagerie, and was never killed in a market, and was not a horse, or an ass, or a cow, or a bull, or a tiger, or a dog, or a pig, or a cat, or a bear.[22]

At last Fred's sister guesses that the 'animal' in question is none other than Fred's uncle Scrooge. The Victorian enthusiasm for such games as Twenty Questions and its variant, Animal, Vegetable or Mineral which assumed straightforward divisions between the animal, vegetable or mineral kingdoms, suggests a confidence in such eighteenth-century taxonomies of the natural world as Linnaeus's *Systema Naturae* of 1735 that insisted on distinct differences of kind between the human and nonhuman animals. The Twenty Questions sequence in *A Christmas Carol*, however, reminds readers that even in so seemingly hallowed a domesticated space as the Victorian middle-class home, and on such a quintessentially Dickensian occasion as Christmas, the boundaries separating humans, animals, and things are porous and unstable.

While nineteenth-century naturalists, comparative anatomists, and zoologists differed on various aspects of zoological classification and hierarchisation, humankind occupied an uncontested position at the apex of the animal kingdom. In this respect, nineteenth-century zoology – including works as different in intent and publication date as Thomas Bewick's *General History of Quadrupeds* (1790), Charles Darwin's *On the Origin of Species* (1859) or Arabella B. Buckley's popular zoological work for children, *The Winners in Life's Race, or The Great Backboned Family* (1883) – confirmed the unstated assumptions underpinning eighteenth-century systems of classification. These, as Harriet Ritvo points out, ranked animals not according to size, use, geography, or arbitrary factors such as alphabetical order but according to taxonomical hierarchies which confirmed 'the hegemonic relation of people to the rest of animate nature' as well as 'the relations between human groups'. The same system, which placed humankind at the apex of the animal kingdom, was used to construct and naturalise hierarchical social distinctions, including divisions between men and women and those between races.[23]

The Rambles of a Rat (1857) by Charlotte Maria Tucker (who wrote under the pseudonym A.L.O.E. ['A Lady of England']), explicitly aims to dispel prejudices against a largely unloved species, and remain true to the animal's habitat-influenced behaviour and species-specific disposition. However, under pressure of the author's evangelical beliefs, this popular story both reinforces and challenges dominant or 'hegemonic' middle-class values and prevailing social hierarchies in which rats remain 'the lowest forms of creation'.[24] An example of the popular genre of fictionalised animal autobiography, discussed further on, the story is narrated in the first person by Ratto, one of seven black rats born in a shed on the Thames, which he shares with a group of brown Norwegian rats and two abject, orphaned human children, one of whom is lame. As the author states in the 'Preface': 'I have indeed made rats talk, feel, and reflect, as those little creatures certainly never did; but the courage, presence of mind, fidelity, and kindness which I have attributed to my heroes, have been shown by real rats'.[25] The claim to facticity – the representation of 'real' rats and their mentalisms and emotional dispositions – is underpinned by the story's avowed dependence on a natural history bibliographic essay entitled 'Rats', which appeared in the *Quarterly Review* the same year *Rambles* was published. This aspiration to objectivity is undercut, however, by the author's admission that the most sensational passages of her declared source had to be omitted, a decision that suggests the difficulty of incorporating a loathed, feared and boundary-breaking species such as *rattus*, fully into human societies, both from a material and a conceptual point of view.

Tucker's polemical novel, in its blend of story and biological fact, illustrates the two-way cultural traffic that Gillian Beer has influentially argued was characteristic of Victorian science and literature: 'metaphors, myths and narrative patterns could move rapidly and freely to and fro between scientists and non-scientists'.[26] This observation requires some qualification. 'Amateur' natural history was perceived to be closer to literature in its reliance on affect and anecdote than it was to its more powerful rival, the rising field of biological sciences whose authority, it was hoped, would be grounded in the apparatus of rational and institutional knowledge.[27] Cannon Schmitt's discussion of the Victorian fascination with beetles provides one example of the shift from the study of nature being 'an amateur pursuit driven by affective attachments to being part of the apparatus of rational and institutional knowledge production'.[28] Furthermore, while the sciences and the humanities may have been on better speaking terms than they are today, recent scholarship has suggested that they were not only porous to each other's influence but were simultaneously defining their boundaries.[29]

The impact of evolution, especially Charles Darwin's theory of natural selection, on the literature and culture of Britain in the nineteenth century has been almost exhaustively examined.[30] Darwin's anti-teleological insights about evolution, common descent, and natural selection challenged powerful religious and secular dismissals of humans' organic relationship with animals and assumptions underpinning inherited mythologies, discourses, and narrative orders. *On the Origin of Species* and *The Descent of Man* presented a new balance between likeness and variability in natural history. While Darwin proposed that the human mind had evolved from animal forbears, he nonetheless asserted an 'immense' divergence in intellectual power between humans and other animals. Darwin's account itself evolved in relation to the work of other naturalists who recognised similarities between human and nonhuman animals, including Erasmus Darwin, Alfred Russell Wallace, 'the sponge philosopher' Robert Grant, and Robert Chambers, whose bestseller on transmutationism, *Vestiges of the Natural History of Creation* (1844), provoked fierce partisan debate at the time of its publication.[31] While some writers, such as John Ruskin, objected to the 'filthy heraldries which record the relation of humanity to the ascidian and the crocodile' the scientific fascination with human similarities to, and differences from, animals influenced many others.[32] That influence bred literary human–animal hybrids that trouble biological and social taxonomies: Robert Browning's man–beast Caliban, Rudyard Kipling's feral child Mowgli, H.G. Wells' 'Beast People' and Robert Louis Stevenson's simianised Mr Hyde. No other Victorian writer took this post-Lyellian, post-Darwinian understanding of the fragility of the categories 'human' and 'self' under the pressure of scientific knowledge and nomenclature more to the heart of his fictional universe than Lewis Carroll. Conceived in the 1860s, in the wake of *On the Origin of Species*, Alice finds herself in *Wonderland*, not in the benignly designed universe of natural theology but in a struggle for survival in which her body transforms in response to environmental stimuli. Confused by her morphological changes, she is unable to distinguish herself from other little girls nor as discrete from other animals. While she does not permanently change from child to beast, like Tom in Charles Kingsley's *Water Babies*, Alice in her meetings with Pigeon, the Caterpillar, white rabbit, Bill the lizard, the Cheshire cat and the enormous puppy who 'might be hungry', comes to understand herself as a clever animal in relation to other species, against whom she must defend herself, even aggressively if necessary.[33]

The ethical and moral dimensions of human–animal relations were also being examined in new ways in the late eighteenth and nineteenth centuries. Jeremy Bentham famously raised the ethical duty of humans to animals as early as 1780: 'the question is not, Can they *reason*? nor, Can they *talk*? but, Can they *suffer*?'[34] In the Utilitarian tradition Henry Sidgwick included animals in his ethics, concluding that it was 'arbitrary and unreasonable' to exclude from the ends of happiness 'the pleasure of any sentient being'.[35] In the mid-nineteenth century when animal slaughter was being brought under principles of instrumental rationality and bureaucratic control, Bentham's calculation of social goods and his social evils model proposed that, if all pain is an evil, then the pain and suffering caused to an animal by a human must also be an evil, regardless of the animal's capacity for reason. Reformers such as Richard Martin and William Wilberforce, leaders of the abolitionist movement, had begun to address animal abuse and neglect, leading to the passage of legislation such as Martin's Act (1822) to 'prevent the cruel and improper treatment of cattle' – the world's first animal welfare legislation – and the founding of protection societies such as the Society for the Prevention of Cruelty to Animals (SPCA, later the RSPCA) in 1824.[36] Utilitarianism was part of a transformation in general attitudes towards animals in the nineteenth century that saw increasing legislative control over the treatment of animals, and by the mid-nineteenth century the expression of violence towards animals was more regulated than ever before: laws forbade century-old sports such as bear-baiting, cockfighting, and dog-fighting. These developments did not, however, lead to the alleviation of suffering for the majority of animal species. Rather, the ruthless exploitation of animals in industry and transport, and the mass carnage of big game hunting and the increasing use of domestic animals, particularly dogs, in scientific experimentation, actually increased throughout the Victorian period. Meanwhile, the growth of empire and of commerce in such luxury trades as the import of ornamental feathers had a huge influence on animal destruction, as Robin Doughty and Nicholas Daly have shown.[37] There was also a rapid rise in unregulated pet-keeping and breeding of animals for show, the emergence of the first zoos and 'acclimatisation' programmes, and the development of the natural history museum using taxidermied specimens to offer crowd-pleasing dioramas (re)producing particular versions of the relationship between culture and nature.

Beginning in the 1870s, animal experimentation came to be more widely practised in British physiological laboratories, bringing into conflict scientific and humanitarian interests in the animal, as anti-vivisectionists and advocates of animal research debated their right to speak for the nonhuman animal. The practice of vivisection assumed a likeness between human and animal bodies while differentiating humans and animals based on ideas of soul or mind. Responses as diverse as Ouida's (pseudonym of Louise de la Ramé) anti-vivisection polemic *The New Priesthood: A Protest Against Vivisection* (1897) and H.G. Wells' *The Island of Dr Moreau* (1896), about a mad vivisectionist who works to surgically transform animals into humans, suggest the extent to which scientific discourse as it affected the welfare of animals was subjected to aesthetic and ethical scrutiny. Of interest to scholars in a variety of fields have been the vivisection debates of the later nineteenth century, with a strand of scholarship focusing on the 'Brown Dog Riots' of 1907 (about the treatment of a brown dog in a medical laboratory).[38]

Attitudes towards the killing of animals shifted in the Victorian period not only as a result of ethical concern for animal suffering but also because animal cruelty was believed to dehumanise humans.[39] The desire to prevent the sight of cruelty to animals motivated the ban on dog carts, the removal of slaughterhouses from public view, the 1857 bill that prevented children under 14 from witnessing slaughterhouse activities, the 1835 Act that made malicious and wanton cruelty to animals illegal, and the 1867 ban on public demonstrations of vivisection. Even such rescue projects as the Home for Lost and Starving Dogs – initiated in 1860 and established in Battersea in 1871 – represented an uneasy reconciliation between the humanitarianism that the Victorians were thought to have virtually invented with an instrumentalist ethos of how to deal with large numbers of unwanted animals on the streets.[40] The concern that witnessing animal cruelty would brutalise humans is evident not only in Dickens' representations of Smithfield market in *Oliver Twist* (1838), *Bleak House* (1853), *Great Expectations* (1861) and other novels, but also in his non-fiction writings about animal slaughter, such as the ironically titled, 'A monument of French folly' (1851), in which Dickens documents his inspection of Parisian abattoirs and praises their humane and efficient operations, but laments such cruel practices as the binding of calves' legs, which he attributes to peasant superstition.[41] In the co-written or 'composite' article (as Dickens called such collaborations), 'The heart of mid-London' (1851), cruelty towards animals is identified as a propensity of the lower classes. Dickens and Wills' spokesperson, the aptly named Mr Bovington, reports that drovers engage in such cruelties as dropping burning pitch on the backs of frantic livestock, and implies that their behaviour is akin to that of natives from the 'darkest' parts of the expanding British empire: they 'raved, shouted, screamed, swore, whooped, whistled, danced like savages'.[42] In 'A monument of French folly' Dickens notes that cruelty to animals has a negative effect on the formation of character: 'Hard by Snow Hill and Warwick Lane, you shall see the little children, inured to sights of brutality from their birth, trotting along alleys, mingled with troops of horribly busy pigs, up to their ankles in blood'.[43] Dickens' various representations of Smithfield, taken together, imply that what was at stake in the 'abomination of Smithfield' was the notion of civilisation itself. What appears to have most disturbed Dickens and many of his progressive contemporaries about drovers and urban butchers, is not the sacrifice of an animal for human consumption as such, but that human and beast appeared to have swapped roles: animal abusers and those who deal in nefarious trades associated with the slaughter of animals take on bestial, brutish characteristics attributed to animals such as bloodthirsty violence and uncontrollable instincts.

The *Smithfield Removal Act* predated by sixteen years the *Capital Punishment Amendment Act* 1868 which put an end to public executions in the United Kingdom. An idea of progressive 'civilisation' figured prominently in the reform arguments against public execution of humans and of animals, and was an important element in the interpretation of these changes. The Act, however, did not so much work to transform or eliminate practices of animal slaughter as to sequester them from view. Moreover, those who performed this work were often stigmatised as less than human, and were subjected to what Foucault identified as 'continuous and permanent systems of surveillance'.[44] Central to this process is the 'politics of sight', the term Timothy Pachirat uses to describe the dynamics by which two seemingly contradictory characteristics of the relationship between sight and power relate in practice. Drawing on the ideas of Norbert Elias, Pachirat argues that power operates through the creation of distance and concealment, and that our ideas of progress and civilisation are inseparable from, and perhaps even synonymous with, the concealment of what is rendered physically and morally repugnant.[45] For example, what once occurred in the open – sexual acts, spitting, defecating, killing animals, displaying animal parts such as whole animal heads at table – without provoking reactions of moral or physical disgust, has been increasing segregated, confined, and hidden from sight. Using Western etiquette manuals, among other evidence, Elias adduces manners surrounding the eating of meat as particular historical evidence: table portions as well as utensils have grown smaller and methods of preparation and carving have changed to ensure that 'while eating, one is scarcely reminded of its origin'.[46]

Elias's and Pachirat's observations are evidenced not only in the removal from sight of large-scale animal slaughter in mid-Victorian London, but also at the dinner table, as Dickens demonstrates in one of the most sinister Christmas dinners in Victorian fiction. In one of two dramatic sequences which turn on the consumption of pork in *Great Expectations*, the distance conventionally maintained between the meat on the table and its origins is erased. Wopsle and Pumblechook set Pip an exercise in counterfactual thinking, asking him to imagine what his life would be like as a 'four-footed Squeaker', with Pumblechook vividly evoking how 'the butcher would have come up to you as you lay in your straw . . . and he would have shed your blood and had your life'.[47] Pip, the human pig who ought to be grateful for Christmas dinner, is conflated with the animal pig who *is* Christmas dinner. This metaphorical transformation resonates with a later scene in which the bills clerk, Wemmick, serves up sausages made from a pig Pip has met on his hobby farm, impressing upon Pip that the meat he had eaten was 'a little bit of *him*. That sausage you toasted was his . . . Do try him if it is only for old acquaintance sake'.[48] The insertion of the personal pronouns 'him' and 'his' (emphasised by Dickens' italicisation) erases the distinctions that conventionally separate the domesticated animal as an individual 'acquaintance' from the animal as foodstuff destined for human consumption. In so doing, it further confuses the domestic sentiment associated with private space and the instrumental reason associated with public space, a division already allegorised in the sharp contrast between the character traits and values John Wemmick displays at home and in the professional world. The conflation of 'pig as pet or personage' with 'pig as pork' exposes public and private as inseparable, as interconnecting zones of circulation. It is as if an aspect of Smithfield market in the centre of London, which Pip encounters on his arrival in the city, has penetrated the domestic idyll of the 'castle'. In *The Sexual Politics of Meat*, Carol J. Adams explains that

> Behind every meal of meat is an absence: the death of the animal whose place the meat takes . . . . The function of the absent referent is to keep our "meat" separated from any idea that she or he was once an animal . . . to keep *something* from being seen as having been someone.[49]

While Dickens, in *Great Expectations*, is hardly recommending feminist vegetarianism of the kind Adams advocates, these passages not only underline the violence committed against the food animal in turning her or him into meat, but also draw attention to the unsettling idea that the consumption of a piece of sausage is the consumption of a being, and the consumption of the meaning of that being's death, thus altering the referent point of the meat.

As these examples suggest, the 'discourse of animality' was often used in Victorian writing as efficient shorthand for othering individuals and peoples – the poor, women, non-white or non-British subjects – and therefore authorising the oppression of humans by other humans. It is not surprising then that critics and theorists working in feminist, postcolonial, indigenous, queer, and critical race studies have concentrated on the use of zoological language to bestialise individuals and particular groups of people. As already pointed out, Victorian zoology and natural history operated to construct and naturalise racial, gender and class distinctions, and animals frequently served as figures of racial difference, social marginality, loss of identity and exploitation of women. Recent work in Victorian studies that brings renewed attention to intersections between race, species, and empire includes John Miller's *Empire and the Animal Body: Violence, Identity and Ecology in Victorian Adventure Fiction* (2012) and Shefali Rajamannar's *Reading the Animal in the Literature of the British Raj* (2012).[50] Miller focuses on ideologies of empire, hunting, and environmental destruction in the period 1860–1910 with an emphasis on exotic animals and imperial conquest in West Africa in the adventure fiction of R.M. Ballantyne, G.A. Henty, G.M. Fenn, Paul du Chaillu, H. Rider Haggard, and (beyond the Victorian period) John Buchan. Rajamannar's examination of animal narratives in the literature of the Raj covers a longer historical sweep and includes Kipling's *Jungle Book* and lesser known hunting narratives. Both Miller and Rajamannar highlight the interrelationship between biological and social categories: because the human/animal binary is unstable, textual representation can reinforce or undermine the ideological structures of imperial rule. These approaches continue the postcolonial dismantling of empire's logic of domination, while Miller's work also develops the recentring of the nonhuman in environmentally focused postcolonial criticism.

To counter essentialising views of cultures, we might consider that species difference is always in the process of being made, and that this process is not haphazard but is produced as an effect of power relationships. The dualisms that form such forceful undercurrents in Western culture – master and slave, male and female, white and non-white, reason and feeling, culture and nature, civilisation and savagery, subject and object, and human and animal – form an 'interlocking structure'.[51] The animal, therefore, is constituted not only through the human/animal dualism but by other pairs as well, including those relating to gender norms.[52] Drawing upon Animal Studies and queer theory, Monica Flegel, in *Pets and Domesticity in Victorian Literature and Culture: Animality, Queer Relations, and the Victorian Family* (2015), stresses the importance of the domestic pet in elucidating normative sexuality and (re)productivity within the familial home, and reveals how the family pet operates as a means of identifying aberrant, failed, or perverse familial and gender performances.[53] Flegel draws on texts by both canonical and non-canonical writers such as Clara Balfour, Juliana Horatia Ewing, E. Burrows, Bessie Rayner Parkes, Anne Brontë, George Eliot,

Frederick Marryat, and Charles Dickens, who speak to the centrality of the domestic pet to negotiations of gender, power, and sexuality within the home that both reify and challenge the imaginary structure known as the natural family in the Victorian period. Also focused on intersections of gender and animals, Josephine Donovan and other proponents of the feminist care tradition of animal ethics (among them Carol J. Adams, Marti Kheel and Val Plumwood) have resiled from the enlightenment tradition of seeking universal principles through abstract reasoning in favour of a contextual ethics, allowing for a narrative understanding of the particulars of a situation or a question. These approaches resist the 'logic of domination' that operates to reinforce sexism, racism, and speciesism alike, and have emphasised attention, compassion, and emotion in their analyses.[54] In this vein, Donovan's 'aesthetics of care' – based on the tradition of 'care ethics' in feminist theory – has produced sustained engagement with literary concepts such as *mimesis* and *katharis,* as well as readings of animals in nineteenth-century literary texts such as Tolstoy's *Anna Karenina* (1877). Donovan reads Tolstoy's famous essay 'What is Art?' as invoking 'vegetarian discourse', endorsing an 'ethics of care', and in his fiction, an empathetic and sensitive engagement with animals that challenges speciesist ideologies that view animals as merely objects for human use.[55]

To return to questions of agency raised in this chapter's opening, Dickens' engagement with Smithfield and with the killing and consumption of animals foregrounds instabilities inherent in the way the law of culture hierarchically arranges its species significations and values. As the only major Victorian author to represent human and animal relations at Smithfield market, his fiction and journalism on this subject reminds us that live animals, animal matter (or things), and human animals are co-constituted and function as a rapport of interconnecting forces, whether through cooperation or resistance; and that the 'humane' ideology espoused by Dickens and other reformers not only indexes generalised fears about degeneration and international competition but also, paradoxically, highlights the important role played by animal agents in human history. While there is not the space here to rehearse, in full, the range of positions on nonhuman agency, the argument that animals are agents is becoming ever more commonplace and forms part of a wider post-anthropocentric intellectual project that reconsiders the power and role of nonhuman forces in both the past and the present.[56] Mobilising a concept of animal agency in literary interpretation need not require that an animal consciously wills any specific change in the narrative. Indeed, the conventional understanding of agency as a capacity to effect change, which combines rational thought with conscious intention itself derives from an anthropocentric paradigm of enlightenment humanism.[57] As such, agency is a conception that is deeply embedded in humanist and Christian conceptions of human exceptionalism.

In resisting the classic understanding of agency as rational, intentional, and premeditated, Vinciane Despret explicates the concepts of interagency and *agencement*, the latter naming the rapport of forces that produces agency.[58] As well as considering Darwin's account of the reciprocity between orchids and their animal pollinators, Despret uses the example of animal resistance to illustrate

> ... that an animal resisting indeed appears as the very subject of the action, but it is not the same process as the one by which he/she becomes an agent.

"Agenting" (as well as "acting") is a relational verb that connects and articulates narratives (and needs "articulations"), beings of different species, things and contexts. There is no agency that is not interagency. There is no agency without *agencement,* a rapport of forces.[59]

Philip Armstrong has argued that Samuel Butler's insistence on the presence of 'mind' throughout the organic world in his utopian novels set in New Zealand – *Erewhon* (1872) and the revised and extended edition of *Erewhon* (1901) – which included two additional chapters that specifically focus on the question of whether the lives of animals have meaning or value beyond their use by human culture and agriculture – can be seen as an attempt to formulate a theory of networked agency *avant la lettre*.[60] Butler's unstable satiric structure disrupts accepted distinctions between conscious and unconscious behaviour, and proposes 'anthropomorphic accounts of various kinds of "mind" (consciousness, knowledge, desire, volition, choice, memory) and activity (poisoning, trapping, manufacturing, deceiving, hiding, showing off) at work amongst animals and plants'.[61] The same applies to the actions of many human characters in Victorian fiction – no more consistently than the animals do they exhibit rational agency in the classical sense. Dickens' London with its bad weather, crowding, noise, dirt, and danger, no less than the Brontës' fictionalised West Riding of Yorkshire, Thomas Hardy's Dorset, or Butler's New Zealand can be understood as interdependent networks of objects, animals, and humans responding to the exigencies of environment and the pressures of conflicting agencies. Butler's experience as a pastoralist in New Zealand, Armstrong writes,

> ... taught him that the relationship between humans and non-human nature is a field of possibilities in which agency emerges from interactions amongst a network of actors and events: the mindful decision-making of a single sheep; the co-operative social will of the flock; the barking of dogs; human behaviour that includes barking like dogs; the current of the river; the topography and vegetation of the riverbanks; and the delivery by the wind of attractive or aversive smells and sounds to the sheep.[62]

While not all Victorian literary texts offer relational and situated accounts of animal agency, many display a self-reflexivity about the pitfalls and potential of anthropomorphism, about the way in which common zoological metaphors appropriate animals as ciphers and alibis for human concerns. Lewis Carroll achieves this through nonsense and parody when, for example, Alice down the rabbit hole, attempts to recite a familiar poem, Isaac Watt's moral homily, 'Against Idleness and Mischief' (1715), which begins 'How doth the little busy bee'. Instead she recites a parody which retains some of Watt's original wording but omits the two stanzas about the application to human affairs of the bee's busy industry: 'How doth the little crocodile ... How cheerfully he seems to grin/How neatly he spreads his claws,/And welcomes little fishes in,/With gently smiling jaws'.[63] As one of many parodies of Victorian pedagogy (here recitation) and evolution in the Alice books, the noble insect is transformed into reptilian predation in a palimpsest that ironically draws attention to related but non-identical forms in a way that resembles evolution.[64]

When Boffin in Dickens' *Our Mutual Friend*, a work influenced by Darwinian naturalism, recommends bees as models of industry to the congenitally idle Eugene Wrayburn, he protests:

> I object on principle, as a two-footed creature, to being constantly referred to insects and four-footed creatures. I object to being required to model my proceedings according to the proceedings of the bee, or the dog, or the spider, or the camel.[65]

Instead of automatically dismissing anthropocentrism as a form of anthropomorphism, we might consider the potential for anthropomorphism to challenge the rigid distinctions we make between animal and human life.[66] In philosophy, for example, Jane Bennett uses biocentric anthropomorphism to discuss the materiality of nonhuman experience while Tess Cosslett in literary studies demonstrates how anthropomorphism in late eighteenth- and early nineteenth-century children's writing effectively created a sympathetic equivalence between human and animal suffering.[67] Among the most popular narrative forms in the nineteenth century were novels and fictional autobiographies with animal narrators – some, like Tucker's *The Rambles of a Rat*, aimed at children – a genre that focuses the question of anthropomorphism in an historically distinctive form. While many cultures have long-standing traditions of animals speaking and writing, in light of the Animal Studies project what, we may well ask, are the implications of human–animal ventriloquism for animals. Do nineteenth-century animal narrators reflect human consciousness, particularly that of marginal, disadvantaged human persons – women, children, servants, slaves, the elderly – or animal consciousness? Looking at a broad historical span of animal autobiography that goes back to earlier texts, Margo DeMello suggests that the genre demonstrates 'a new awareness of animal subjectivity, and a desire on the part of many animal lovers to give that subjectivity a voice'.[68] Taking a similar view, Marion Copeland maintains that animal autobiographies of horses dating back to *Black Beauty: The Autobiography of a Horse* (1877) 'make a claim not only for the sentience of the other-than-human animal but for its self-awareness, intelligence, grasp of past and future, as well as present, and understanding of the worlds, cultural and biological, in which it lives'.[69] There is no consensus on this point. Dog autobiographies such as Caroline Elizabeth Grey's *The Autobiography of Frank; the Happiest Dog that Ever Lived* (1861), Frances Power Cobbe's *Confessions of a Lost Dog* (1867), and Mrs E. Burrows' *Neptune, or the Autobiography of a New Foundland Dog* (1869) are ideologically contradictory tales that elicit sympathy for suffering individual canines and contribute to the humane movement while at the same time affirming the necessity of human power. Monica Flegel argues that while 'animal autobiographies can allow for a sympathetic imagining of victimization', these texts 'revel in the pleasure that can be produced by exerting control over the animal', thus allowing their female authors to align themselves with both the subjection of the animal and the power of the mistress-master.[70]

No less than *The Rambles of a Rat* or the dog autobiographies of Grey, Power Cobbe or Burrows, Anna Sewell's equine-centric blockbuster, *Black Beauty*, possibly the most famous animal narrative of the Victorian era, upholds 'systemic inequalities, be these speciesism, racism, classism, or sexism'.[71] This story of an ageing horse recalling his cruel past draws on the protest genre of the slave narrative to critique violence against animals and evoke sympathy for the suffering of horses exploited in urban employments such as drawing cabs and carts, and also the use of such devices as the curb bit and bearing rein (two popular harnessing devices which held the horse's head tightly erect, causing much pain to the animal) as a fashion accoutrement. Gina Dorré has discussed horse bodies as sites for the negotiation of hegemonic ideologies of class and gender, including the way both equine and female bodies are constrained by prevailing discourses of beauty in *Black Beauty*.[72] In contrast, Teresa Mangum points out how Sewell situates her speaking horses in the temporalities of the bildungsroman so that the animal is not absorbed into the human.[73] To read dog or horse autobiographies for how both animal and human lives are shaped through relations with animals is to subtly shift interpretation onto relationality rather than solely human concerns and preoccupations. If we resist the temptations of metonymy, and read an animal, such as Beauty as exceeding analogical reading, we open ourselves to modes of connection that acknowledge our shared bodily and temporal vulnerability or creatureliness.[74]

Vulnerability and risk are themes as central to queer, feminist, and disability studies as to Animal Studies. In *Precarious Life: The Powers of Mourning and Violence* and *Frames of War: When is Life Grievable?*, Judith Butler argues that mourning is a way of making connections, of establishing kinship, and of recognising the vulnerability and finitude of others.[75] These works insist that questions about who is entitled to mourn, and who is mournable, are at the heart of social intelligibility. As James Stanescu argues, disavowing mourning disavows the life of the other and cedes the one you care for as well as part of yourself into social unintelligibility.[76] Addressing in these works such human actions as war and racial profiling Butler has had little to say on the question of the animal. Nonetheless, her Levinasian-inspired ethics of interdependence, embodiment, vulnerability, and mourning provides a compelling incentive for thinking about the lives not only of humans, but also of animals.[77] Mourning the lives of animals can be a political act that produces communities of feeling, or we can forbid mourning and justify inflicting violence on vulnerable beings who cannot speak for themselves (at least in human language). The life of a beloved pet, a subject deemed to lead a trivial life, is definitionally considered less mournable than the life of a human animal. In this sense, I would argue that one of the most powerful forms of cultural disavowal for bereaved pet owners in the nineteenth century was the gendered construction of sentimentality.

Elegies, sonnets, short stories, and eulogies lamenting the death of pets proliferated throughout the nineteenth century, with even so unlikely a candidate as Matthew Arnold writing elegies on the deaths of his dachshunds, Geist and Kaiser, and a canary, Matthias ('Geist's Grave' [1881], 'Poor Matthias' [1882], and 'Kaiser Dead' [1887]). The writings of Jane Carlyle, Elizabeth Barrett Browning, Ouida and Michael Field, among others, provide situated accounts in which the expression of intense feelings, such as love or bereavement for a particular pet, is shadowed by a fear of being thought sentimental.[78] As a 'structure of feeling', sentimentality from the early nineteenth century onwards, as the voluminous literature on the topic shows, has been associated with the least authoritative expressions of cultural life: femininity, simple-mindedness, childishness, 'fancy', and idealism.[79] As Nicola Bown states, '[S]entimentality is excessive feeling evoked by unworthy objects; it is falsely idealising; it simplifies and sanitises; it is vulgar; it leads to cynicism; it is feeling on the cheap; it's predictable; it's meretricious.' Bown borrows these terms used in the denunciation of sentimentality from a range of literary critics including I.A. Richards, F.R. Leavis, Mary Midgley, Michael Tanner, and Aldous Huxley, making it difficult not to conclude that the word sentimentality has lost its historical validity and hence its analytic value.[80]

In light of common literary understandings of sentimentality, the idea that mourning for an animal is inherently sentimental in a pejorative sense rests on the speciesist assumption that passionate, individualised feeling towards nonhuman animals involves inappropriate or excessive feeling bestowed upon unworthy objects. This insight can be brought to bear on the way in which the discourse of sentimentality has functioned to disavow mourning for animal lives. As a term of approbation, sentimentality was not confined to companionate human and pet relationships. In nineteenth-century England the relationship that was established between women and irrational sentiment towards animals emerged at a time when the independent women's movement had managed to gain ground and women became increasingly active in the spheres of both animal advocacy and suffrage. Periodicals that covered the vivisection debate suggested, for example, that female opposition to animal experimentation was motivated by emotion, hysteria, sentimentalism or ignorance, all of which were opposed to rational science.[81] The resurgence of interest in the history of the emotions, including the place of sentiment and sentimentality in Victorian literature and culture, has begun to produce more historically nuanced critiques of the traditional scholarly tendency to conflate such categories as 'emotion', and 'sentimentality' and such actions as crying and tearfulness. Furthermore, in recent decades literary historians have argued that sentimental texts are atypically self-conscious about their ambition to 'radically reconceive civil relationships and collective obligations by disclosing the voices and interests of marginalised social subjects'.[82] These reconsiderations have not generally included animals, even though 'the engulfment of pets in the elaborate rituals and commodities unique to nineteenth-century mourning together signal a profound shift in human–animal relations during the nineteenth century'.[83]

Elizabeth Barrett Browning's correspondence on the subject of her dog Flush, Jane Carlyle's on the death of her Maltese half-cross Nero, Ouida's children's novel *A Dog of Flanders* (1872), and Michael Field's sonnet sequence on the death of the beloved pet Chow in the thirty poems of *Whym Chow: Flame of Love* (1914; written in 1906) can be cited as examples of texts that both reinforce and disrupt the cultural work attributed to sentimentality. Strong feelings of love and grief for their animal companions tip over into defiance of authority – of patriarchal norms, and into the adoption of unorthodox religious beliefs or the rejection of them altogether. John Ruskin had written to Katharine Bradley (or Michael Field) in December 1877 about her inordinate affection for a pet dog and her corresponding disaffection with Victorian religion: 'I don't care how much pain you are in – but that you should be such a fool as coolly to write to me that you had ceased to believe in God – and had found some comfort in a dog – <u>this</u> is <u>deadly</u>' (emphasis in the original).[84] Following upon the death of Nero, in 1860, Jane Welsh Carlyle speculates about his immortality and is grateful to her aunt, Grace Welsh, who 'gave me a reference to certain verses in Romans which seemed to warrant my belief in the immortality of animal life as well as human'.[85] Carlyle may have been clutching at straws in seeking Christian affirmation of species equality in the afterlife, but as numerous epitaphs in the Hyde Park Pet Cemetery show, she was not alone among bereaved Victorian pet owners, for whom the old question of the immortality of animal souls is sustained by a raft of unorthodox theological and spiritual speculation.[86]

Attention to such literary–historical case studies of human–animal relations discloses a nuanced vocabulary of feeling as a resource for an ethos of care towards animals: devotion, love, compassion, gratitude, melancholy, anxiety, grief, fear, guilt, desolation, shame, joy, and delight. In this respect the contemporary reassessment of the place of feeling and sentiment by philosophers and literary critics has an important application for the study of human–animal relations, and may serve as a corrective to the tendency to regard affects such as pity, sympathy, fondness, adoration, and compassion for animals not as mere 'inclinations' and sentiments but as an essential part of the substance of ethics itself.[87] There can, however, be no unproblematic ethics of care between humans and domestic dogs, and this tension can be traced in the Carlyle, Barrett Browning, and Field canine histories. The contradictions inherent in Elizabeth Barrett Browning's attitudes to pet-keeping, are evidenced in her sympathy for Flush's 'unnatural' situation as a sporting breed dog confined to an invalid's sick room as opposed to her representation of him as a refined, aristocratic fur baby who has repudiated the carnivorous virility of other animals, including her brother's Cuban bloodhound and Mastiff, and dogs of his own breed.[88] Memorialisation of the kind found in *Whym Chow: Flame of Love*, and in the Barrett Browning correspondence, involves idealising and isolating the beloved pet as a being apart from the animal world of stray dogs, hunted animals, work animals, and food animals.

Keith Thomas concludes his influential study of animals and society in England to 1800 by noting that the conflict between 'new sensibilities' towards the natural world, including animals, and the material realities of society with its growing cities and growing population, was not resolved: 'A mixture of compromise and concealment has so far prevented this conflict from having to be fully resolved. But the issue cannot be completely evaded and it can be relied upon to recur. It is one of the contradictions upon which modern civilization may be said to rest. About its ultimate consequences we can only speculate'.[89] Thomas might have made the same observation about England in 1837, the year Victoria ascended the throne, or 1901, the year of her death, although the forms that those compromises and concealments took are historically specific. Hazarding a generalisation, we might conclude that Victorian writing reveals the paradoxical mix of care, sentiment, indifference, and violence that might be said to typify relationships between humans and animals in a society profoundly uneasy about the distinct nature of humanity. The Victorians were what we have become: the compromises and concealments that characterised their often-contradictory attitudes towards animals are an important aspect of their legacy to globalising modernity.

Notes

1 See Adrienne Munich's analysis of domesticity and Queen Victoria's dogs in *Queen Victoria's Secrets*, New York: Columbia University Press, 1996, 127–155.
2 See P. Chambers, *Jumbo: the Greatest Elephant in the World*, London: André Deutsche, 2007 and J. Sutherland, *Jumbo: the Unauthorised Biography of a Victorian Sensation*, London: Aurum Press, 2014.
3 See J. Derrida, *The Animal That Therefore I Am*, ed. M.-L. Mallett, trans. D. Wills, New York: Fordham University Press, 2008, 34. For simplicity's sake, I will use 'animal' to mean 'nonhuman animal'. Animal Studies is used in its broadest, contemporary sense, to designate the multidisciplinary field known as Human–Animal Studies (HAS) – sometimes called anthrozoology – which is not to be confused with the scientific usage which refers to laboratory studies involving animals. Sometimes the related term, Critical Animal Studies, is used in Animal Studies scholarship, although CAS distinguishes itself from much mainstream human–animal studies by virtue of its commitment to an advocacy agenda. For a fuller discussion of the relationship between critical animal studies and human–animal studies see N. Taylor, *Humans, Animals and Society: An Introduction to Human–Animal Studies*, New York: Lantern Books, 2013, 155–169.
4 For an explanation of the 'anthrozootic city' see S.A. Miltenberger, 'Viewing the anthrozootic city: humans, domesticated animals, and the making of early nineteenth-century New York', in S. Nance (ed.), *The Historical Animal*, Syracuse NY: Syracuse University Press, 2015, 261–271, 262–263. The population of London doubled from 1800 to 1850, and the urban middle classes were exposed increasingly to the real and perceived dirt and disease associated with large numbers of animals confined in overcrowded spaces. As Ritvo states, the number of urban horses in Britain increased from about 350,000 in the 1830s to 1,200,000 at the beginning of the twentieth century, most of whom were used to haul omnibuses and other heavy vehicles in the growing towns: H. Ritvo, *The Animal Estate: The English and Other Creatures*, Cambridge MA: Harvard University Press, 1987, 311 n.1. On the numbers of horses see *Parliamentary Papers* 1873 (325) xiv, 3, 34. Railways temporarily increased the demand for horse transport; see H.J. Dyos and D.H. Aldcroft, *British Transport: An Economic History from the Seventeenth to the Twentieth Century*, Leicester: Leicester University Press, 1969, 213. In 1870 England, Wales, and Scotland contained 1,064,621 licensed dogs, with the number of unlicensed dogs being inestimably large (*Parliamentary Papers* 1877 (163) xlix, I). See also B. Harrison, 'Animals and the state in nineteenth-century England', in *Peaceable Kingdom: Stability and Change in Modern Britain*, Oxford: Clarendon Press, 1982, 83. In 1850 there were around 13,000 cows in London; and in 1841 some 2,764 'milk-sellers and cow keepers'. Enormous numbers of wild birds were snared and sold in the streets as pets – linnets, finches, larks (which were eaten), jackdaws, nightingales, sparrows, and starlings – some of which were subjected to cruel practices such as blinding and tongue splitting (N. Daly, *The Demographic Imagination and the Nineteenth-Century City: Paris, London, New York*, Cambridge: Cambridge University Press, 2015, 151, 156).
5 G. Levine, *Realism, Ethics and Secularism: Essays on Victorian Literature and Science*, Cambridge: Cambridge University Press, 2008, 251.
6 K. Weil, *Thinking Animals: Why Animal Studies Now?* New York: Columbia University Press, 2012, 5.
7 See R. Braidotti, *The Posthuman*, Cambridge: Polity Press, 2013, esp. 57–104.
8 E. Kirksey (ed.), 'Introduction', *The Multispecies Salon*, Durham NC: Duke University Press, 2014, 3–5.
9 E. Kirksey and S. Helmreich, 'The emergence of multispecies ethnography', *Cultural Anthropology* 25, 4 (2010): 545–576.

10 D.J. Haraway, *The Companion Species Manifesto: Dogs, People and Significant Otherness*, Chicago IL: Prickly Paradigm Press, 2003, and *When Species Meet*, Minneapolis MN: University of Minnesota Press, 2008.
11 For example, Karen Barad's concept of 'agential realism' introduces the idea of 'intra-action', as distinct from interaction, to express an already entangled state of agency: '"intra-action" *signifies the mutual constitution of entangled agencies*': K. Barad, *Meeting the Universe Halfway: Quantum Physics and the Entanglement of Matter and Meaning*, Durham NC: Duke University Press, 2007, 33, emphasis in original.
12 A. Tsing, 'Unruly edges: mushrooms as companion species', *Environmental Humanities* 1, 1 (2012): 141–154, 144, emphasis in original. See also D.J. Haraway, *When Species Meet*, Minneapolis MN: University of Minnesota Press, 2008, 19.
13 D. Lestel, 'Like the fingers of the hand: thinking the human in the texture of animality', in L. Mackenzie and S. Posthumus (eds.), *French Thinking about Animals*, trans. M. Chrulew and J. Bussolini, East Lansing MI: Michigan State University Press, 2015, 61–73, 64. French philosopher Dominique Lestel's work on ethology is productive to read together with multispecies ethnography, partly because of the emphasis both place on personhood as 'a relational narrative process' in which multispecies interactions are fundamentally constitutive (Lestel, 'Fingers of the Hand', 64). An important figure in what Brett Buchanan, Jeffrey Bussolini, and Matthew Chrulew have called an 'ethological revolution', along with Vinciane Despret, Isabelle Stengers, and Roberto Marchesini, Lestel's revisionist writing on animality and multispecies relationality is beginning to reach Anglophone readers. See B. Buchanan, J. Bussolini, and M. Chrulew, 'General introduction: philosophical ethology', *Philosophical Ethology I: Dominique Lestel*, special issue of *Angelaki: Journal of the Theoretical Humanities*, 19, 3 (2014): 1–3.
14 For a detailed discussion of dogs in Dickens' fiction and journalism see B. Gray, *The Dog in the Dickensian Imagination*, Aldershot: Ashgate, 2014, and P. Howell, 'Dogs in Dickensland: at home and astray with the Landseer of fiction' in *At Home and Astray: The Domestic Dog in Victorian Britain*, Charlottesville VA: University of Virginia Press, 2015, 25–49.
15 Jacques Rancière diagnoses the distribution of the perceptible as a political process in 'The Politics of Literature', in *The Politics of Literature*, trans. J. Rose, Cambridge: Polity Press, 2011, 4. For further discussion of this point in relation to literature see M. Ortiz-Robles, *Literature and Animal Studies*, London, Routledge, 2016, 144–145.
16 C. Dickens, *Bleak House*, ed. G. Ford and S. Monod, Norton critical edition, New York: W.W. Norton, 1977, 235.
17 See E. Freedgood, *The Ideas in Things: Fugitive Meaning in the Victorian Novel*, Chicago IL: Chicago University Press, 2009, and S. Amato, *Beastly Possessions: Animals in Victorian Consumer Culture*, Toronto: Toronto University Press, 2015.
18 See K.C. Grier, *Pets in America: A History*, Chapel Hill NC: University of North Carolina Press, 2005, and K. Kete, *The Beast in the Boudoir: Petkeeping in Nineteenth-Century Paris*, Berkeley CA: University of California Press, 1994.
19 See Jonathan Smith's discussion of these contexts in *Charles Darwin and Victorian Visual Culture*, Cambridge: Cambridge University Press, 2006, 64–68.
20 C. Dickens, *Hard Times*, Norton critical edition, third edition, eds. F. Kaplan and S. Monod, New York: Norton, 2001, ch. 2, 7–8.
21 Dickens, *Hard Times*, 8.
22 C. Dickens, *A Christmas Carol*, in *A Christmas Carol and Other Christmas Stories*, Oxford World Classics, ed. R. Douglas-Fairhurst, Oxford: Oxford University Press, 2008, 60.
23 Ritvo, *Animal Estate*, 15.
24 'Preface' to C. Tucker, *The Rambles of a Rat,* London: T. Nelson, 1857, v.

25 'Preface' to Tucker, *The Rambles of a Rat*, v.
26 G. Beer, *Darwin's Plots: Evolutionary Narrative in Darwin, George Eliot and Nineteenth-Century Fiction*, third edition, Cambridge: Cambridge University Press, 2009, 5.
27 For a discussion of Tucker's use of anecdote see J.A. Smith, 'Representing animal minds in early animal autobiography: Charlotte Tucker's *The Rambles of a Rat* and nineteenth-century natural history', *Victorian Literature and Culture* 43, 4 (2015): 725–744, 737–741. The popularity of natural history among the middle classes in the first half of the nineteenth century and its increasing decline in the face of the ascendance of professional biology has been documented by several historians of science. See Smith, 'Representing animal minds', 737–739; L.L. Merrill, *The Romance of Victorian Natural History*, New York: Oxford University Press, 1989; D.E. Allen, *The Naturalist in Britain: A Social History*, second edition, Princeton NJ: Princeton University Press, 1994; L. Barber, *The Heyday of Natural History, 1820–1870*, Garden City NY: Doubleday, 1980; J. Camerini, 'Remains of the day: early Victorians in the field', in B. Lightman (ed.), *Victorian Science in Context*, Chicago IL: University of Chicago Press, 1997, 354–377.
28 C. Schmitt, 'Victorian beetlemania', in D.D. Morse and M.A. Danahay (eds.), *Victorian Animal Dreams: Representations of Animals in Victorian Literature and Culture*, Aldershot: Ashgate, 2007, 35–51, 36.
29 Jessica Straley, for example, has discussed the children's literature of Margaret Gatty, Charles Kingsley, Lewis Carroll, Kipling, and Frances Hodgson Burnett in the contexts of the animal child recapitulating the course of human evolution and Victorian pedagogy. 'Victorian children's texts', Straley states, 'made literary experience the pivotal mechanism of human evolution, capable of teaching the child how to retract his bestial "tail" and how to enter instead into a higher, distinctly human world of extraordinary, edifying, and imaginative "tales"': see J. Straley, *Evolution and Imagination in Victorian Children's Literature*, Cambridge: Cambridge University Press, 2016, 25–26. For challenges to the 'one culture' model of Beer and Levine see G. Dawson, *Darwin, Literature and Victorian Respectability*, Cambridge: Cambridge University Press, 2007, and A. deWitt, *Moral Authority, Men of Science, and the Victorian Novel*, Cambridge: Cambridge University Press, 2013. The 'one culture' model is discussed in G. Levine (ed.), *One Culture: Essays in Science and Literature*, Madison WI: University of Wisconsin Press, 1987.
30 The scholarship on Darwin, evolution and Victorian literature is too extensive to list here. Some works I have in mind include C. Kenyon-Jones, 'Evolutionary animals: science and imagination between the Darwins' in *Kindred Brutes: Animals in Romantic-Period Writing*, Aldershot: Ashgate Press, 2001, 165–201; W. Abberley, *English Fiction and the Evolution of Language 1850–1914*, Cambridge: Cambridge University Press, 2015; S.G. Alter, *Darwinism and the Linguistic Image: Language, Race and Natural Theology in the Nineteenth Century*, Baltimore MD: Johns Hopkins University Press, 1999; D. Ospovat, *The Development of Darwin's Theory: Natural History, Natural Theology, and Natural Selection, 1838–1859*, Cambridge: Cambridge University Press, 1981, and J. Carroll, *Literary Darwinism: Evolution, Human Nature, and Literature*, London: Routledge, 2004.
31 See J.A. Secord, *Victorian Sensation: The Extraordinary Publication, Reception, and Secret Authorship of Vestiges of the Natural History of Creation*, Chicago IL: University of Chicago Press, 2001. On Darwin's precursors, see R. Stott, *Darwin's Ghosts: In Search of the First Evolutionists*, London: Bloomsbury, 2012.
32 J. Ruskin, *Love's Meinie*, Keston: Kent, 1873, 59.
33 For an overview of the literature on *Alice's Adventures in Wonderland* (1865) and *Through the Looking Glass, and What Alice Found There* (1872) and evolutionary theory see Straley, *Evolution and Imagination in Victorian Children's Literature*, 86–89. For extensive analysis of how Lewis Carroll's Alice books engage with the ideas of Charles Darwin and Thomas

Henry Huxley, among other thinkers, see G. Beer, *Alice in Space: The Sideways Victorian World of Lewis Carroll*, Chicago IL: Chicago University Press, 2016.

34 See J. Bentham, An *Introduction to the Principles of Morals and Legislation*, Oxford: Clarendon Press, 1823 [first printed 1780, first published 1780], reprint 1907, ch. 17, n. 122.

35 H. Sidgwick, *The Methods of Ethics*, seventh edition, London: Macmillan, 1907, 414.

36 The history of animal protection and its literature in the nineteenth century has been told by a number of scholars: see for example, H. Kean, *Animal Rights: Political and Social Change in Britain Since 1800*, London: Reaktion, 1998; J. Turner, *Reckoning with the Beast: Animals, Pain and Humanity in the Victorian Mind*, Baltimore MD: Johns Hopkins University Press, 1980; and K. Kete, 'Introduction: animals and human empire' in K. Kete (ed.), *A Cultural History of Animals in the Age of Empire*, Oxford: Berg, 2007, 1–24.

37 See R. Doughty, *Feather Fashions and Bird Preservation: A Study in Nature Protection*, Berkeley CA: University of California Press, 1975; and N. Daly, 'Fur and feathers: animals and the city in the anthropocene era' in Daly, *Demographic Imagination*, 148–188.

38 See C. Lansbury, *The Old Brown Dog: Women, Workers, and Vivisection in Edwardian England*, Madison WI: University of Wisconsin Press, 1985; and P. Mason, *The Brown Dog Affair*, London: Two Sevens Publishing, 1997.

39 See Ritvo, *Animal Estate*, 135.

40 Philip Howell has analysed the way in which the domestic image of Battersea Dogs' Home 'helped paper over its normal functions of policing, incarceration, and execution'. He also demonstrates how 'the discursive tropes regarding the *human* vagrant' were mapped onto street dogs at an 'important juncture for Victorian social policy'. See P. Howell, *At Home and Astray: The Domestic Dog in Victorian Britain*, Charlottesville VA: University of Virginia Press, 2015, 100, 83.

41 C. Dickens, 'A monument of French folly', *Household Words* 2, 50 (8 March 1851): 553–558, 555. For a more detailed discussion of Dickens' representation of Smithfield markets in his fiction see J. McDonell, 'Dickens and animal studies', in J. Jordan, R. Patten, and C. Waters (eds.), *Oxford Handbook to Charles Dickens*, Oxford: Oxford University Press, forthcoming 2018. For a discussion of how Dickens and other *Household Words* contributors writing on the subject of Smithfield 'both utilize and challenge standard humane rhetoric of the day' see R.D. Morrison, '*Household Words* and the Smithfield controversy at the time of the Great Exhibition', in L.W. Mazzeno and R.D. Morrison (eds.), *Animals in Victorian Literature and Culture: Contexts for Criticism*, London: Palgrave Macmillan, 2017, 41–63, 59.

42 C. Dickens and W.H. Wills, 'The heart of mid-London', *Household Words* 1, 6 (4 May 1850): 121–125, 122.

43 Dickens, 'Monument of French folly', 554.

44 M. Foucault, 'Two lectures', in C. Gordon (ed.), *Power/Knowledge: Selected Interviews and Other Writings 1972–77*, New York: Pantheon, 1980, 78–108, 105. See also M. Foucault, *Discipline and Punish: The Birth of the Prison*, trans. A. Sheridan, New York: Vintage, 1977.

45 T. Pachirat, *Every Twelve Seconds: Industrialized Slaughter and the Politics of Sight*, Haven CT: Yale University Press, 2011, 9–19.

46 See N. Elias, *The Civilizing Process*, Oxford: Blackwell, 2000, first published 1939, 102.

47 C. Dickens, *Great Expectations*, ed. M. Cardwell, Oxford: Clarendon Press, 1993, 27–28.

48 Dickens, *Great Expectations*, 371.

49 See C.J. Adams, *The Sexual Politics of Meat: A Feminist-Vegetarian Critical Theory*, 25th Anniversary Edition, London: Bloomsbury, 2015, xxiv.

50 J. Miller, *Empire and the Animal Body: Violence, Identity and Ecology in Victorian Adventure Fiction*, London: Anthem Press, 2012, and S. Rajamannar, *Reading the Animal in the Literature of the British Raj*, London: Palgrave Macmillan, 2012.

51 V. Plumwood, *Feminism and the Mastery of Nature*, London: Routledge, 1993, 43.

52 See, for example, C.J. Adams, *Neither Man nor Beast: Feminism and the Defense of Animals*, New York: Continuum, 1994; S. Kappeler, 'Speciesism, racism, nationalism ... or the power of scientific subjectivity', in C.J. Adams and J. Donovan (eds.), *Animals and Women: Feminist Theoretical Explorations*, Durham NC: Duke University Press, 1995, 320–352; and D.J. Haraway, *Primate Visions: Gender, Race, and Nature in the World of Modern Science*, New York: Routledge, 1989.

53 See M. Flegel, *Pets and Domesticity in Victorian Literature and Culture: Animality, Queer Relations, and the Victorian Family*, London: Routledge, 2015.

54 For further analysis of this position see Adams and Donovan, *Animals and Women*.

55 See J. Donovan, *The Aesthetics of Care: On the Literary Treatment of Animals*, London: Bloomsbury, 2016, 128.

56 See S.E. McFarland and R. Hediger (eds.), *Animals and Agency: An Interdisciplinary Exploration*, Leiden and Boston: Brill, 2009; and P. Howell, 'Animals, agency, and history' in this volume.

57 See P. Armstrong, *What Animals Mean in the Fictions of Modernity*, London: Routledge, 2008, 3. For a discussion of nonhuman agency in relation to place and space, see C. Philo and C. Wilbert, 'Animal spaces, beastly spaces: an introduction', in C. Philo and C. Wilbert (eds.), *Animal Spaces, Beastly Spaces: New Geographies of Human–Animal Relations*, London: Routledge, 2000, 1–34, 5.

58 V. Despret, 'From secret agents to interagency', *History and Theory*, 52, 4 (2013): 29–44. Despret is drawing on Deleuze, who had developed von Uexküll's notion of *umwelt*, which allows for the animal 'point of view', how an animal perceives according to what has meaning in its own world. See G. Deleuze and F. Guattari, *A Thousand Plateaus: Capitalism and Schizophrenia*, trans. B. Massumi, Minneapolis MN: Minnesota University Press, 1987, 260, 321, and von Uexküll, 1934, cited in Despret, 'From secret agents to interagency', 31, 37.

59 Despret, 'From secret agents to interagency', 44.

60 P. Armstrong, 'Samuel Butler's sheep', *Journal of Victorian Culture* 17, 4 (2012): 442–453, 452.

61 Armstrong, 'Samuel Butler's sheep', 451.

62 Armstrong, 'Samuel Butler's sheep', 453.

63 L. Carroll, *Alice's Adventures in Wonderland*, ed. P. Hunt, Oxford: Oxford University Press, 2009, 19.

64 Straley, *Evolution and Imagination in Victorian Children's Literature*, 101.

65 C. Dickens, *Our Mutual Friend*, ed. M. Cotsell, Oxford World's Classics edition, Oxford: Oxford University Press, 1989, 93.

66 On the relationship between anthropocentrism and anthropomorphism see L. Daston, 'Intelligences: angelic, animal, human', in L. Daston and G. Mitman (eds.), *Thinking with Animals: New Perspectives on Anthropomorphism*, New York: Columbia University Press, 2005, 37–58, 53; D. Ryan, *Animal Theory: An Introduction*, Edinburgh: Edinburgh University Press, 2015, 36–49.

67 J. Bennett, *Vibrant Matter: A Political Ecology of Things*, Durham NC: Duke University Press, 2010, 99. See T. Cosslett, *Talking Animals in British Children's Fiction, 1786–1814*, Farnham: Ashgate, 2006.

68 M. DeMello, 'Introduction', in M. DeMello (ed.), *Speaking for Animals: Animal Autobiographical Writing*, London: Routledge, 2013, 1–14, 4.

69 M. Copeland, '"Straight from the horse's mouth": equine memoirs and autobiographies', in DeMello (ed.), *Speaking for Animals*, 179–191, 180.

70 See M. Flegel, 'Mistresses as masters: voicing female power through the subject animal in two nineteenth-century animal autobiographies', in DeMello (ed.), *Speaking for Animals*, 89–101, 89–90.

71 N.C. Hansen, 'Horse talk: horses and human(e) discourses', in DeMello (ed.), *Speaking for Animals*, 207–229, 223.
72 G. Dorré, *Victorian Fiction and the Cult of the Horse*, Aldershot: Ashgate, 2006.
73 T. Mangum, 'Narrative dominion or the animals write back? Animal genres in literature and the arts', in K. Kete (ed.), *A Cultural History of Animals in the Age of Empire*, Oxford: Berg, 2007, 153–173, 161.
74 Anat Pick uses the term 'creaturely' to name practices and poetics that are attentive to 'the material, temporal, and vulnerable', and the embodied: see A. Pick, *Creaturely Poetics: Animality and Vulnerability in Literature and Film*, New York: Columbia University Press, 2011, 5.
75 See J. Butler, *Frames of War: When is Life Grievable?*, London: Verso, 2009, and *Precarious Life: The Powers of Mourning and Violence*, London: Verso, 2004.
76 See J. Stanescu, 'Species trouble: Judith Butler, mourning, and the precarious lives of animals', *Hypatia* 27, 3 (2012): 569–582, 567.
77 See C. Taylor, 'The precarious lives of animals: Butler, Coetzee, and animal ethics', *Philosophy Today* 52, 1 (2008): 60–72, and Stanescu, 'Species trouble'.
78 Michael Field was the pseudonym of Katharine Harris Bradley (1846–1914) and Edith Emma Cooper (1862–1913), celebrity authors and celebrity dog owners who, as poets, playwrights and diarists, lived and wrote together during the final decades of the nineteenth century up to World War I.
79 For Raymond Williams, literature provides 'often the only fully available articulation . . . of structures of feeling which as living processes are much more widely experienced': *Marxism and Literature*, Oxford: Oxford University Press, 1977, 133). Philip Armstrong has used Williams' concept of 'structures of feeling', referring to 'lived' or 'practical consciousness' prior to its ideological codification, to clarify how intimately the emergence of dispositions such as sympathy, sentimentalism, and nostalgia for nature have been tied up with human–animal relations in specific historical contexts and mediated through texts: see Armstrong, *What Animals Mean in the Fictions of Modernity*, 4. For a discussion of Philip Fisher's understanding of sentimentality as 'a politically radical technique' see Armstrong, *What Animals Mean in the Fictions of Modernity*, 165–167. See also F. Kaplan, *Sacred Tears: Sentimentality in Victorian Literature*, Princeton NJ: Princeton University Press, 1987; G. Stedman, *Stemming the Torrent: Expression and Control in Victorian Discourses on Emotion 1830–1872*, Aldershot: Ashgate, 2002; N. Bown (ed.), 'Rethinking Victorian sentimentality,' in *19: Interdisciplinary Studies in the Long Nineteenth Century* 4 (2007); C. Burdett, 'New agenda: sentimentalities: introduction', *Journal of Victorian Culture* 16, 2 (2011): 187–194; and B. Carney and C. Waters (eds.), 'Introduction: "Mr Popular Sentiment": Dickens and feeling', *19: Interdisciplinary Studies in the Long Nineteenth Century*, 14 (2012).
80 N. Bown, 'Introduction: crying over Little Nell', *19: Interdisciplinary Studies in the Long Nineteenth Century*, 4 (2007).
81 Claire Molloy has argued this case by demonstrating the way in which the vivisection debate was constructed in the media in England and the US from the mid-nineteenth century as a gendered issue whereby emotion and sentiment were configured in opposition to science and reason (*Popular Media and Animals*, London: Palgrave Macmillan, 2011, 27–28).
82 T. Menely, 'Zoöphilpsychosis: why animals are what's wrong with sentimentality', *Symploke* 15, 1–2 (2007): 244–267, 246. Also see J. Mason, *Civilized Creatures: Urban Animals, Sentimental Culture and American Literature 1850–1900*, Baltimore MD: Johns Hopkins University Press, 2005.
83 See T. Mangum, 'Animal angst: Victorians memorialise their pets', in D.D. Morse and M.A. Danahay (eds.), *Victorian Animal Dreams: Representations of Animals in Victorian Literature and Culture*, Aldershot: Ashgate, 2007, 15–34, 17.

84 John Ruskin to Katharine Bradley, 30 December 1877, cited in K. Bradley and E. Cooper, *Michael Field, the Poet: Published and Manuscript Materials*, edited by M. Thain and A.P. Parejo Vadillo, Peterborough ON: Broadview Press, 2009, 27, 308.
85 T. Holme, *The Carlyles at Home*, Oxford: Oxford University Press, 1965, 139.
86 See P. Howell, 'A place for the animal dead: pets, pet cemeteries and animal ethics in late Victorian Britain', *Ethics, Place and Environment*, 5, 1 (2002): 5–22.
87 Robert C. Solomon has made a case for regarding 'sentimental' emotions, both in response to literature and art, and in life more generally, as 'the precondition for ethical engagement': R.C. Solomon, *In Defense of Sentimentality*, New York: Oxford University Press, 2004, 4.
88 See J. McDonell, '"Ladies' pets" and the politics of affect: Elizabeth Barrett Browning and Jane Welsh Carlyle', *Australian Literary Studies* 25, 2 (2010): 17–34.
89 K. Thomas, *Man and the Natural World*, Harmondsworth: Penguin, 1983, 303.

References

Abberley, W. *English Fiction and the Evolution of Language 1850–1914*, Cambridge: Cambridge University Press, 2015.
Adams, C.J. *Neither Man nor Beast: Feminism and the Defense of Animals*, New York: Continuum, 1994.
Adams, C.J. *The Sexual Politics of Meat: A Feminist-Vegetarian Critical Theory*, 25th anniversary edition, London: Bloomsbury, 2015.
Adams, C.J. and Donovan, J. *Animals and Women: Feminist Theoretical Explorations*, Durham NC: Duke University Press, 1995.
Allen, D.E. *The Naturalist in Britain: A Social History*, second edition, Princeton NJ: Princeton University Press, 1994.
Alter, S.G. *Darwinism and the Linguistic Image: Language, Race and Natural Theology in the Nineteenth Century*, Baltimore MD: Johns Hopkins University Press, 1999.
Amato, S. *Beastly Possessions: Animals in Victorian Consumer Culture*, Toronto: Toronto University Press, 2015.
Armstrong, P. *What Animals Mean in the Fictions of Modernity*, London: Routledge, 2008.
Armstrong, P. 'Samuel Butler's sheep', *Journal of Victorian Culture* 17, 4 (2012): 442–453.
Barad, K. *Meeting the Universe Halfway: Quantum Physics and the Entanglement of Matter and Meaning*, Durham NC: Duke University Press, 2007.
Barber, L. *The Heyday of Natural History, 1820–1870*, Garden City NY: Doubleday, 1980.
Beer, G. *Darwin's Plots: Evolutionary Narrative in Darwin, George Eliot and Nineteenth-Century Fiction*, third edition, Cambridge: Cambridge University Press, 2009.
Beer, G. *Alice in Space: The Sideways Victorian World of Lewis Carroll*, Chicago IL: Chicago University Press, 2016.
Bennett, J. *Vibrant Matter: A Political Ecology of Things*, Durham NC: Duke University Press, 2010.
Bentham, J. *An Introduction to the Principles of Morals and Legislation*, Oxford: Clarendon Press, 1823 [first printed 1780, first published 1789], reprint 1907.
Bown, N. 'Introduction: crying over Little Nell', *19: Interdisciplinary Studies in the Long Nineteenth Century* 4 (2007).
Bown, N. (ed.) 'Rethinking Victorian sentimentality', *19: Interdisciplinary Studies in the Long Nineteenth Century* 4 (2007).
Bradley, K. and Cooper, E. *Michael Field, the Poet: Published and Manuscript Materials*, edited by M. Thain and A.P. Parejo Vadillo, Peterborough ON: Broadview Press, 2009.
Braidotti, R. *The Posthuman*, Cambridge: Polity Press, 2013.

British Parliamentary Papers 1873 (325).
British Parliamentary Papers 1877 (163).
Buchanan, B., Bussolini, J., and Chrulew, M. 'General introduction: philosophical ethology', *Philosophical Ethology I: Dominique Lestel*, Special issue of *Angelaki: Journal of the Theoretical Humanities* 19, 3 (2014): 1–3.
Burdett, C. 'New agenda sentimentalities: introduction', *Journal of Victorian Culture* 16, 2 (2011): 187–194.
Butler, J. *Precarious Life: The Powers of Mourning and Violence*, London: Verso, 2004.
Butler, J. *Frames of War: When is Life Grievable?*, London: Verso, 2009.
Camerini, J. 'Remains of the day: early Victorians in the field', in B. Lightman (ed.), *Victorian Science in Context*, Chicago IL: University of Chicago Press, 1997, 354–377.
Carney, B. and Waters, C. 'Introduction: "Mr Popular Sentiment": Dickens and feeling', *19: Interdisciplinary Studies in the Long Nineteenth Century* 14 (2012).
Carroll, J. *Literary Darwinism: Evolution, Human Nature, and Literature*, London: Routledge, 2004.
Carroll, L. *Alice's Adventures in Wonderland*, ed. P. Hunt, Oxford: Oxford University Press, 2009.
Chambers, P. *Jumbo: the Greatest Elephant in the World*, London: André Deutsch, 2007.
Copeland, M. '"Straight from the horse's mouth": equine memoirs and autobiographies', in M. DeMello (ed.), *Speaking for Animals: Animal Autobiographical Writing*, London: Routledge, 2013, 179–191.
Cosslett, T. *Talking Animals in British Children's Fiction, 1786–1814*, Aldershot: Ashgate, 2006.
Daly, N. *The Demographic Imagination and the Nineteenth-Century City: Paris, London, New York*, Cambridge: Cambridge University Press, 2015.
Daston, L. 'Intelligences: angelic, animal, human', in L. Daston and G. Mitman (eds.), *Thinking with Animals: New Perspectives on Anthropomorphism*, New York: Columbia University Press, 2005, 37–58.
Dawson, G. *Darwin, Literature and Victorian Respectability*, Cambridge: Cambridge University Press, 2007.
Deleuze, G. and Guattari, F. *A Thousand Plateaus: Capitalism and Schizophrenia*, trans. B. Massumi, Minneapolis MN: Minnesota University Press, 1987.
DeMello, M. (ed.) *Speaking for Animals: Animal Autobiographical Writing*, London: Routledge, 2013.
Derrida, J. *The Animal That Therefore I Am*, trans. D. Wills, New York: Fordham University Press, 2008.
Despret, V. 'From secret agents to interagency', *History and Theory* 52, 4 (2013): 29–44.
deWitt, A. *Moral Authority, Men of Science, and the Victorian Novel*, Cambridge: Cambridge University Press, 2013.
Dickens, C. and Wills, W.H. 'The heart of mid-London', *Household Words* 1, 6 (4 May 1850): 121–125.
Dickens, C. 'A monument of French folly', *Household Words* 2, 50 (8 March 1851): 553–558.
Dickens, C. *Bleak House*, ed. G. Ford and S. Monod, Norton critical edition, New York: W.W. Norton, 1977.
Dickens, C. *Our Mutual Friend*, ed. M. Cotsell, Oxford World's Classics Edition, Oxford: Oxford University Press, 1989.
Dickens, C. *Great Expectations*, ed. M. Cardwell, Oxford: Clarendon Press, 1993.
Dickens, C. *Hard Times*, Norton critical edition, third edition, eds. F. Kaplan and S. Monod, New York: W.W. Norton, 2001.
Dickens, C. *A Christmas Carol and Other Christmas Stories*, ed. R. Douglas-Fairhurst, Oxford: Oxford University Press, 2008.

Donovan, J. *The Aesthetics of Care: On the Literary Treatment of Animals*, London: Bloomsbury, 2016.

Dorré, G. *Victorian Fiction and the Cult of the Horse*, London: Routledge, 2006.

Doughty, R. *Feather Fashions and Bird Preservation: A Study in Nature Protection*, Berkeley CA: University of California Press, 1975.

Dyos, H.J. and Aldcroft, D.H. *British Transport: An Economic History from the Seventeenth to the Twentieth Century*, Leicester: Leicester University Press, 1969.

Elias, N. *The Civilizing Process*, Oxford: Blackwell, 2000, first published 1939.

Flegel, M. 'Mistresses as masters: voicing female power through the subject animal in two nineteenth-century animal autobiographies', in M. DeMello (ed.), *Speaking for Animals: Animal Autobiographical Writing*, London: Routledge, 2013, 89–101.

Flegel, M. *Pets and Domesticity in Victorian Literature and Culture: Animality, Queer Relations, and the Victorian Family*, London: Routledge, 2015.

Foucault, M. *Discipline and Punish: The Birth of the Prison*, trans. A. Sheridan, New York: Vintage, 1977.

Foucault, M. 'Two lectures', in C. Gordon (ed.), *Power/Knowledge: Selected Interviews and Other Writings 1972–77*, New York: Pantheon, 1980, 78–108.

Freedgood, E. *The Ideas in Things: Fugitive Meaning in the Victorian Novel*, Chicago IL: Chicago University Press, 2009.

Gray, B. *The Dog in the Dickensian Imagination*. Aldershot: Ashgate, 2014.

Grier, K.C. *Pets in America: A History*, Chapel Hill NC: University of North Carolina Press, 2005.

Hansen, N.C. 'Horse talk: horses and human(e) discourses', in M. DeMello (ed.), *Speaking for Animals: Animal Autobiographical Writing*, London: Routledge, 2013, 207–229.

Haraway, D.J. *Primate Visions: Gender, Race, and Nature in the World of Modern Science*, New York: Routledge, 1989.

Haraway, D.J. *When Species Meet*, Minneapolis MN: University of Minnesota Press, 2008.

Haraway, D.J. *The Companion Species Manifesto: Dogs, People and Significant Otherness*, Chicago IL: Prickly Paradigm Press, 2003.

Harrison, B. *Peaceable Kingdom: Stability and Change in Modern Britain*, Oxford: Clarendon Press, 1982.

Holme, T. *The Carlyles at Home*, Oxford: Oxford University Press, 1965.

Howell, P. 'A place for the animal dead: pets, pet cemeteries and animal ethics in late Victorian Britain', *Ethics, Place and Environment* 5, 1 (2002): 5–22.

Howell, P. *At Home and Astray: The Domestic Dog in Victorian Britain*, Charlottesville VA: University of Virginia Press, 2015.

Kaplan, F. *Sacred Tears: Sentimentality in Victorian Literature*, Princeton NJ: Princeton University Press, 1987.

Kappeler, S. 'Speciesism, racism, nationalism . . . or the power of scientific subjectivity', in C.J. Adams and J. Donovan (eds.), *Animals and Women: Feminist Theoretical Explorations*, Durham NC: Duke University Press, 1995, 320–352.

Kean, H. *Animal Rights: Political and Social Change in Britain Since 1800*, London: Reaktion, 1998.

Kenyon-Jones, C. *Kindred Brutes: Animals in Romantic-Period Writing*, Aldershot: Ashgate, 2001.

Kete, K. *The Beast in the Boudoir: Petkeeping in Nineteenth-Century Paris*, Berkeley CA: University of California Press, 1994.

Kete, K. 'Introduction: Animals and Human Empire', in K. Kete (ed.) *A Cultural History of Animals in the Age of Empire*, Oxford: Berg, 2007, 1–24.

Kirksey, E. (ed.) *The Multispecies Salon*, Durham NC: Duke University Press, 2014.

Kirksey, E. and Helmreich, S. 'The emergence of multispecies ethnography', *Cultural Anthropology* 25, 4 (2010): 545–576.

Lansbury, C. *The Old Brown Dog: Women, Workers, and Vivisection in Edwardian England*, Madison WI: University of Wisconsin Press, 1985.

Lestel, D. 'Like the fingers of the hand: thinking the human in the texture of animality', in L. Mackenzie and S. Posthumus (eds.), *French Thinking about Animals*, trans. M. Chrulew and J. Bussolini, East Lansing MI: Michigan State University Press, 2015, 61–73.

Levine, G. (ed.) *One Culture: Essays in Science and Literature*, Madison WI: University of Wisconsin Press, 1987.

Levine, G. *Realism, Ethics and Secularism: Essays on Victorian Literature and Science*, Cambridge: Cambridge University Press, 2008.

McDonell, J. '"Ladies' pets" and the politics of affect: Elizabeth Barrett Browning and Jane Welsh Carlyle', *Australian Literary Studies* 25, 2 (2010): 17–34.

McDonell, J. 'Dickens and animal studies', in J. Jordan, R. Patten, and C. Waters (eds.), *Oxford Handbook to Charles Dickens*, Oxford: Oxford University Press, (forthcoming 2018).

McFarland, S.E. and Hediger, R. (eds.) *Animals and Agency: An Interdisciplinary Exploration*, Leiden: Brill, 2009.

Mangum, T. 'Animal angst: Victorians memorialise their pets', in D.D. Morse and M.A. Danahay (eds.), *Victorian Animal Dreams: Representations of Animals in Victorian Literature and Culture*, Aldershot: Ashgate, 2007, 15–34.

Mangum, T. 'Narrative dominion or the animals write back? Animal genres in literature and the arts', in K. Kete (ed.), *A Cultural History of Animals in the Age of Empire*, Oxford: Berg, 2007, 153–173.

Mason, J. *Civilized Creatures: Urban Animals, Sentimental Culture and American Literature 1850–1900*, Baltimore MD: Johns Hopkins University Press, 2005.

Mason, P. *The Brown Dog Affair*, London: Two Sevens Publishing, 1997.

Menely, T. 'Zoöphilpsychosis: why animals are what's wrong with sentimentality', *Symploke* 15, 1–2 (2007): 244–267.

Merrill, L.L. *The Romance of Victorian Natural History*, New York: Oxford University Press, 1989.

Miller, J. *Empire and the Animal Body: Violence, Identity and Ecology in Victorian Adventure Fiction*, London: Anthem Press, 2012.

Miltenberger, S.A. 'Viewing the anthrozootic city: humans, domesticated animals, and the making of early nineteenth-century New York', in S. Nance (ed.), *The Historical Animal*, Syracuse NY: Syracuse University Press, 2015, 261–271.

Molloy, C. *Popular Media and Animals*, London: Palgrave Macmillan, 2011.

Morrison, R.D. '*Household Words* and the Smithfield controversy at the time of the great exhibition', in L.W. Mazzeno and R.D. Morrison (eds.) *Animals in Victorian Literature and Culture: Contexts for Criticism*, London: Palgrave Macmillan, 2017, 41–65.

Munich, A. *Queen Victoria's Secrets*, New York: Columbia University Press, 1996.

Ortiz-Robles, M. *Literature and Animal Studies*, London: Routledge, 2016.

Ospovat, D. *The Development of Darwin's Theory: Natural History, Natural Theology, and Natural Selection, 1838–1859*, Cambridge: Cambridge University Press, 1981.

Pachirat, T. *Every Twelve Seconds: Industrialized Slaughter and the Politics of Sight*, New Haven CT: Yale University Press, 2011.

Philo, C. and Wilbert, C. 'Animal spaces, beastly spaces: an introduction', in C. Philo and C. Wilbert (eds.), *Animal Spaces, Beastly Spaces: New Geographies of Human-Animal Relations*, London: Routledge, 2000, 1–34.

Pick, A. *Creaturely Poetics: Animality and Vulnerability in Literature and Film*, New York: Columbia University Press, 2011.

Plumwood, V. *Feminism and the Mastery of Nature*, London: Routledge, 1993.
Rajamannar, S. *Reading the Animal in the Literature of the British Raj*, London: Palgrave Macmillan, 2012.
Rancière, J. *The Politics of Literature*, trans. J. Rose, Cambridge: Polity Press, 2011.
Ritvo, H. *The Animal Estate: The English and Other Creatures in the Victorian Age*, Cambridge MA: Harvard University Press, 1987.
Ruskin, J. *Love's Meinie*, Keston: Kent, 1873.
Ryan, D. *Animal Theory: An Introduction*, Edinburgh: Edinburgh University Press, 2015.
Schmitt, C. 'Victorian beetlemania' in D.D. Morse and M.A. Danahay (eds.), *Victorian Animal Dreams: Representations of Animals in Victorian Literature and Culture*, Aldershot: Ashgate, 2007, 35–51.
Secord, J.A. *Victorian Sensation: The Extraordinary Publication, Reception, and Secret Authorship of Vestiges of the Natural History of Creation*, Chicago IL: University of Chicago Press, 2001.
Sidgwick, H. *The Methods of Ethics*, seventh edition, London: Macmillan, 1907.
Smith, J. *Charles Darwin and Victorian Visual Culture*, Cambridge: Cambridge University Press, 2006.
Smith, J.A. 'Representing animal minds in early animal autobiography: Charlotte Tucker's *The Rambles of a Rat* and nineteenth-century natural history', *Victorian Literature and Culture* 43, 4 (2015): 725–744.
Solomon, R.C. *In Defense of Sentimentality*, New York: Oxford University Press, 2004.
Stanescu, J. 'Species trouble: Judith Butler, mourning, and the precarious lives of animals', *Hypatia* 27, 3 (2012): 567–582.
Stedman, G. *Stemming the Torrent: Expression and Control in Victorian Discourses on Emotion 1830–1872*, Aldershot: Ashgate, 2002.
Stott, R. *Darwin's Ghosts: In Search of the First Evolutionists*, London: Bloomsbury, 2012.
Straley, J. *Evolution and Imagination in Victorian Children's Literature*, Cambridge: Cambridge University Press, 2016.
Sutherland, J. *Jumbo: The Unauthorized Biography of a Victorian Sensation*, London: Aurum Press, 2014.
Taylor, C. 'The precarious lives of animals: Butler, Coetzee, and animal ethics', *Philosophy Today* 52, 1 (2008): 60–72.
Taylor, N. *Humans, Animals and Society: An Introduction to Human–Animal Studies*, New York: Lantern Books, 2013.
Thomas, K. *Man and the Natural World*, Harmondsworth: Penguin, 1983.
Tsing, A. 'Unruly edges: mushrooms as companion species', *Environmental Humanities* 1, 1 (2012): 141–154.
Tucker, C. *The Rambles of a Rat*, London: T. Nelson, 1857.
Turner, J. *Reckoning with the Beast: Animals, Pain and Humanity in the Victorian Mind*, Baltimore MD: Johns Hopkins University Press, 1980.
Weil, K. *Thinking Animals: Why Animal Studies Now?*, New York: Columbia University Press, 2012.
Williams, R. *Marxism and Literature*, Oxford: Oxford University Press, 1977.

11

'AND HAS NOT ART PROMOTED OUR WORK ALSO?'

Visual culture in animal–human history

J. Keri Cronin

In October 1887 the editors of *The Animal World,* the official publication of Britain's Royal Society for the Prevention of Cruelty to Animals (RSPCA), published a lengthy article reviewing and reflecting upon many of the artworks exhibited at the annual Royal Academy exhibition at Burlington House in London.[1] While twenty-first century readers may find it somewhat strange that an animal advocacy publication would dedicate so much space to reviewing art, this was in fact not that unusual for nineteenth-century audiences. There are many important links between art and animal advocacy during this era, as those involved with organised animal advocacy saw tremendous potential for art to foster a sense of kindness and compassion in viewers and to challenge the status quo when it came to cruel treatment of animals. 'Noble men who devote themselves to the high calling of art', the writer for *The Animal World* opined, 'are teachers and prophets, whose influence is not less than that of philosophers, statesmen, and divines'.[2] Specific to the context of animal advocacy, the reviewer asked, 'and has not art promoted our work also?':

> The pencils of old masters, and those of a hundred modern animal painters, among whom Landseer will ever be prominent, have taught us to love animals, and when we cannot love, to be in sympathy with them as fellow creatures. The walls of the Academy year after year keep up this theme, and delineate particularly man's companionship with animals.[3]

As one might expect, the RSPCA's review of the Royal Academy exhibition specifically focused on the pictures of animals included in this show. Pictures such as Leonard Nightingale's *Welcome Morsels,* John Everett Millais's *The Nest,* Sidney Cooper's *Old Smithfield Market,* and Edmund Caldwell's *For the Safety of the Public* are among the paintings singled out by this review.

The following discussion uses this 1887 Royal Academy exhibition as a starting point for thinking through some of the ways in which art and visual culture can assist those of us who are interested in expanding animal–human history. What would art history look like if the 'question of the animal' were taken seriously? What would the writing of history look like if images were given the same level of consideration as other texts and archival material? What, if anything, can pictures of animals tell us about the histories and lived realities of animal–human relationships in previous eras? Paintings, drawings, prints, photographs, sculptures, and film clips are material objects that are always already a mediated way of accessing the information about the lives of those they represent. They are frames for seeing the world that are necessarily shaped by and inextricably linked to things such as politics, cultures, economics, and technologies – frames, in other words, that are driven by *human* concerns. Of course nonhuman animals figure largely in our politics, cultures, economics, and technologies, but these frames were developed by humans to make sense of *human* interactions, activities, and interests. How, then, can we turn to art and visual culture made in the past and ask those images to tell us something of the lives of animals from previous historical eras?

In the following discussion, I propose that visual culture is an important but often overlooked resource in the writing of human–animal histories. In many cases, as Steve Baker notes, our 'understanding of animals is shaped by representations rather than by direct experience of them'.[4] Further, as historian Samantha Cutrara has argued, imagery can be an important tool because pictures can create the potential for 'visualizing different pasts'.[5] What she means by this is that we need to be open to looking at images – really looking at them and not just repeating what we have been told about them – and thinking deeply and critically about what it is we are seeing, about what is represented in the frame but also about absences or gaps. What choices has the artist made and why? What can these choices tell us about dominant ideas regarding animal–human relationships during the time period in which the image was made? Cutrara also reinforces the notion that visual culture can be a platform for 'imagining different futures' which is a poignant reminder for those interested in animal–human history – our work has significant ramifications for the living, breathing animals that we currently share the planet with. Visual representations of animals are, therefore, an important consideration in animal–human history. Imagery can provide new ways of thinking about how humans and animals interacted in other time periods and can be a site from which different ways of imagining relationships with animals can be fostered.

What do we mean by the term 'visual culture'?

In much the same way that taking animals seriously has opened up new possibilities for doing animal–human history, in recent decades an expanded framework for the study and critical analysis of images has emerged across a number of academic disciplines. At the most basic level, when we talk about 'visual culture' we are typically talking about a broad range of images and image types. In the past, academic disciplines such as art history tended to limit the subject of analysis to images that fit into categories recognised as 'Art' – paintings, drawings, sculpture, etc. When one studies visual culture these kinds of images are still important, but now things such as advertisements, internet memes, protest images, film, fashion, graffiti, and scientific diagrams (to name but a few categories!) are also given serious scholarly consideration. Within this framework there is a recognition that images do not exist in a vacuum, and that different kinds of cultural representations influence and inform one another.

Foundational texts such as Gillian Rose's *Visual Methodologies* offer an important introduction to the use of images in the social sciences while, at the same time, scholars such as Nicholas Mirzoeff, Marita Sturken, and Lisa Cartwright have expanded ways of thinking about images in the humanities beyond what has traditionally been offered by the discipline of art history. There are, therefore, a wide range of ways in which scholars are thinking critically about and with images in the twenty-first century, but one of the defining features of visual culture is an emphasis on the ways in which the meanings of images shape and are shaped by 'the shared practices of a group, community, or society'.[6] Within this framework, historical, contextual, and visual analysis come together to emphasise different ways in which images can create and challenge dominant ideas. Further, there is increased recognition that the meaning of an image is not static and that the same meaning (or set of meanings) is not understood by all viewers. As Gillian Rose has argued, there are a range of different sites that need to be considered when thinking about the meaning of an image: 'the site(s) of the production of an image, the site of the image itself, and the site(s) where it is seen by various audiences'.[7] Further, Rose stresses the need to consider a range of 'modalities' that exist at each of these sites: technological, compositional, and social.[8] When we turn to visual culture as a way to think about human–animal history, then, these are some of the issues we need to keep in mind.

Animals, advocacy, and visual culture

There is, of course, a long history of nonhuman animals being represented in art and visual culture produced, collected, and curated by humans. Much of this work was created with little consideration of the impact it may have had on the living, breathing animals who existed outside of the picture frame. In recent years critics such as Randy Malamud have argued that this history of representation has obscured our understanding of animals both on an individual and on a species level. 'It is difficult for people to see animals,' Malamund posits, and one of the reasons he gives for this is the abundance of 'dense cultural constructions we impose on them'.[9] For Malamud this is more than an aesthetic issue. Rather, he argues that 'animals in visual culture thus suffer as a consequence of our habits of visualizing and acculturating them'.[10] There are, in other words, deep and profound ethical and ecological issues related to the ways in which humans have visually represented nonhuman animals.

Other scholars have taken a different approach and have argued that the history of art has been an important vantage point from which to trace the development of animal rights and animal liberation. Stephen Eisenman's *The Cry of Nature: Art and the Making of Animal Rights*, for example, makes the case that 'artists brought substantially different insights . . . to the definition and role of the animal – understandings based upon the unique, perceptual character of visual art'.[11] These insights, in turn, created a situation where new ways of thinking about 'the nature of animal psychology and physiology' began to be articulated in visual form.[12] Further, Eisenman argues that within this dynamic, animals were active participants and 'demanded their emancipation'.[13] Across Europe and North America in the nineteenth and early twentieth centuries, new ways of visually engaging with animals were being enacted – as the sites of raising, killing, and consuming animal bodies became transformed through the intertwined logics of modernism and capitalism, so too did the ways in which people visually encountered animals. As Eisenman writes,

> Animals themselves gathered in vast numbers and cacophonous in their outcries, were the avant-garde of the movement. By virtue of their species-natures, of course, they could not directly enter in to the political arena, but they attracted many articulate followers and supporters.[14]

In other words, the ways in which people visually engaged with animals gave rise to important milestones in the history of animal advocacy.

Visual culture, therefore, is a complex and often contested site from which to think about animal–human history. Images do not offer unmediated windows onto the past – we must always think critically about images we encounter in our research. What is certain, however, is that visual representations of animals always have 'real world' implications. As Jonathan Burt points out, 'animal imagery does not merely reflect human–animal relations and the position of animals in human culture, but is also used to change them'.[15]

Challenges and questions

Materials included in art gallery, museum, and archival collections tend to have a very anthropocentric focus, and traditional collecting and cataloguing practices can present distinct challenges for researchers seeking to access information about the lives (and deaths) of animals from previous historical periods as there inevitably are gaps in the records. The challenges of writing historical accounts that take animals seriously have been outlined by a number of scholars in recent years.[16] 'Animals do not leave documents', Erica Fudge reminds us, 'the only documents available to the historian in any field are documents written, or spoken, by humans'.[17] She also points out, however, the ways in which the histories of human and nonhuman animals are so intertwined that perhaps it is more accurate to refer to human culture as 'so-called human culture', something that is important to remember when we are doing animal–human history.[18] This observation underscores a primary objective for those of us trying to take animal histories seriously – we are like detectives opening up a 'cold case', and re-analysing the existing evidence from a different perspective. Traces of what we seek are there, but we need to reframe our investigations and we need to ask new questions.

So, what kinds of questions do we need to ask of visual images in order to arrive at what Fudge refers to as an 'interspecies competence', or 'a new way of thinking about and living with animals'?[19] To begin, we need to think critically about how any given representation might be related to the lived experiences of both those who have viewed it as well as the lived experiences of those who are included or implicated in the processes of representation happening within the image. On the most basic level, this means being aware of and attuned to the fact that throughout much of history the very materiality of art and image-making was (and still is) dependent upon the bodies of animals. Paintbrushes made with animal hair, pigments made from the crushed bodies of insects, paints that use egg as a binder, and gelatin-based film are examples of the kinds of materials and tools that artists have historically used. Art history, in other words, is a form of animal history. But this is not typically how it is taught. Rather, if animals are discussed at all in undergraduate art history classes or in textbooks focusing on canonical works of art, they are mentioned as important symbols for human ideas and narratives. As Diana Donald has pointed out, 'seldom has the representation of animals *per se* been thought worthy, or likely, to constitute the artist's principal intention; much less to be a proper object of consideration for the scholarly critic'.[20]

In the textbook I use in my nineteenth-century art history class, for example, the work of the celebrated British animal painter Edwin Landseer is briefly discussed – in a discussion of some of his best-known paintings, the author talks about the ways in which 'dogs personify humans', and that the 'instincts that Landseer's animals act on are ones that humans relate to'.[21] While these points offer one way of reading Landseer's work (the dominant one taken up by most art historians), they are not the only way to think about these pictures. As I have argued elsewhere, in the late nineteenth and early twentieth centuries many working in animal advocacy reproduced Landseer's paintings in their campaigns.[22] Simply put, this would not have happened if the only way to understand these pictures was as a comment on human culture and society. The reformers who so eagerly took up Landseer's work clearly saw other meanings in these images – they used these pictures to ask people to think about the dogs represented in them *as dogs*. In order to do animal–human history we likewise need to shift our framework and also take images of animals as a starting point to think about animals *as animals*. This includes not only thinking critically about what is (or is not) represented in the frame of the image but also about the materials used in the production of art and visual culture.

Second, we need to ask questions that can lead to detailed contextual and visual analysis of pictures. What do we see when we look at an image? How might someone occupying a different subject position see this image? What choices has the artist or image-maker made? Why were those choices made? How do the techniques and technologies used shape the way an image looks and, in turn, the way that the meaning of any given picture is negotiated by those who view it? What has been excluded from the frame? What are we not able to see, and why has the image-maker made those choices? How does the context in which an image is viewed shape the way that it is interpreted?

To answer these questions we need to first of all recognise that, like all texts, images are cultural objects and, as such, do not have inherent, concrete sets of meanings that accompany them. Images are not, and can never be, objective windows onto the past. Just as we know to analyse textual documents with a critical lens, so too must we become astute at visual and contextual analysis if we want images to assist us in continuing to piece together histories of human–animal relationships. While this may seem obvious when we are talking about paintings or sculptures – forms of visual culture, in other words, that are clearly the product of an artist's hand and imagination – we must also keep this in mind when we are considering camera-generated images. There is a tendency to assume that photographs and film are somehow *more true* than other forms of visual culture because of the mechanical nature of the camera and the indexical nature of the technologies of photography and cinema. However, as Allan Sekula points out in his classic essay 'On the invention of photographic meaning', 'the meaning of a photograph, like that of any other entity, is inevitably subject to cultural definition'.[23] Just like other forms of visual culture, photographs and film are shaped by many external factors such as advances or limitations in technology, as well as social, cultural, economic, and political frameworks. Further, as Jonathan Burt has argued, in many instances, the development of visual technology is, itself, dependent upon the bodies of animals.[24] In addition, the seemingly simple decisions a photographer makes about what she will or will not take a picture of and how she composes the shot are all important considerations to keep in mind as well. This is not to say that visual culture is 'fake', 'false', or unreliable. It can be as useful to historians as any other kind of text. While some visual examples may be more fabricated or manipulated than others, visual representations of animals can always be traced back to larger cultural conversations about animal–human relationships that are, themselves, subject to social, cultural, economic, and political frameworks.

When using visual culture to do animal–human history, we must be prepared to interrogate images, to think critically about them, and to ask deep questions about their creation, circulation, and consumption. We must also be prepared to recognise that a single image generates multiple and, at times, competing, sets of meanings. As W.J.T. Mitchell notes, pictures are 'complex individuals occupying multiple subject positions and identities'.[25] A critical analysis of images not only considers which reading(s) of any given picture is the most dominant and why, but also considers the inevitable additional meanings that accompanied (and continue to accompany) it. This is significant for any historical inquiry that is seeking a departure from the dominant historical narrative, as images can both reinforce and challenge the status quo. As Mitchell argues, 'images introduce new forms of value into the world, contesting our criteria, forcing us to change our minds . . . '[26] When it comes to animal–human history, imagery can be a site from which to not only reflect on the multiplicity of interwoven experiences that humans and animals have had in the past but also to imagine alternative ways of engaging with animals.

A Distinguished Member of the Humane Society

Images of animals can be recontextualised to reflect current and contemporary debates about how animals should be treated. Edwin Landseer's well-known painting, *A Distinguished Member of the Humane Society* (1831; Figure 11.1) serves as a good example here. There are a few different stories that exist which attempt to explain how it is that Landseer came to paint this picture. The most widely circulated of those stories tells of an encounter between the artist and a Newfoundland dog named Paul Pry.[27] The dog, we are told, was carrying a basket of flowers in his mouth and walking next to his human companion, Mrs Newman Smith.[28] There was, in other words, a real life, flesh-and-blood dog who inspired the painting of this picture. As Diana Donald has so eloquently described, part of the reason that so many people found this picture so appealing was the 'pure dogginess of its lovingly depicted

Figure 11.1 Edwin Landseer, *A Distinguished Member of the Humane Society*, exhibited at the Royal Academy Exhibition of 1838.

Courtesy Tate Gallery, London.

bloodshot eyes, pink protruded tongue, loose jowl and shaggy coat'.[29] But even though this picture evoked familiar characteristics of what viewers might think of when they thought of their canine companions – the 'pure dogginess' that Donald writes about – was this a true-to-life picture of Paul Pry? On the contrary, instead of faithfully painting his encounter with a specific dog, Landseer has instead represented this animal on the water's edge and presents to the viewer an image that is intended to speak of the heroic and legendary life-saving abilities of Newfoundland dogs in a more general sense – there is not a basket of flowers nor a human companion to be found in this scene! As Donald notes, it is 'this breed's famous life-saving feats in the water' that becomes the focus of this picture.[30]

Many who saw Landseer's painting when it was exhibited at the Royal Academy exhibition of 1838 would have known that the 'humane society' referred to in the title of the painting was the Royal Humane Society of Britain, an organisation formed in 1774 and originally called the Society for the Recovery of Persons Apparently Drowned. This information coupled with the fact that the particular breed of dog represented in this painting is a Newfoundland dog – a breed that has a reputation for marine rescue skills – may have shaped the dominant reading of this picture at the Royal Academy exhibition. In other words, those who saw this painting in that context would likely reflect on the ways in which dogs have been known to help humans in things such as marine rescue. However, we cannot be certain that all viewers would read the same picture in the same way. Perhaps some viewers were simply reminded of the fact that dogs tend to be good swimmers. Some might have been reminded of beloved childhood pets, and still others may have appreciated this picture strictly because of the artist's reputation and skill. In an article for the *Magazine of Art*, for example, Marion Harry Spielmann describes this picture as a 'masterpiece' because it is 'finely conceived and brilliantly executed'.[31] This multiplicity of potential meanings can be frustrating for historians who want to arrive at a singular, set meaning of an image. However, visual culture resists this kind of simplistic interpretation and, therefore, it is important for historians to sharpen their skills in visual and critical analysis so that they may begin to untangle the myriad ways in which any given image functions and creates meaning in each specific situation.

In the late nineteenth and early twentieth centuries many animal advocacy groups adopted *A Distinguished Member of the Humane Society* for campaign and educational purposes. Organisations such as The Victoria Street Society for the Protection of Animals from Vivisection used this image to make public pleas for compassion towards animals, in particular to ask those reading campaign leaflets to stop and recognise that animals used in vivisection were sentient beings and that scientific and medical experiments conducted on them were cruel and inhumane. When Landseer's image was reproduced in these contexts, new meanings were necessarily generated. The fact that this was a well-known picture certainly made it appealing to those who chose to reproduce it as part of animal advocacy campaigns, but we also have to remember that not all who saw this image in this context would have arrived at the intended meaning. When this picture was reduced in size and reproduced in black and white on the pages of an animal advocacy leaflet in the late nineteenth century, the conversations about it would have been very different from those that took place in front of the full-colour, oil-on-canvas painted version on display at the 1838 Royal Academy exhibition. This may seem like an obvious point, but the context of viewing and its subsequent role in the creation of meaning is frequently overlooked by those using images as historical documents. While some of the viewers who saw this image in a Victoria Street Society publication may have been prompted to think about the ways in which dogs help humans, their childhood pets, or the skill of the artist, the context in which the image was viewed – in this case, on the pages of an antivivisection leaflet – would also invite viewers to reflect on the ways in which dogs (and other animals) were treated in the vivisector's laboratory. While some might have come to the conclusion that it was perfectly fine for dogs to be experimented on, the advocates working under the banner of the Victoria Street Society, of course, hoped that images like this would garner more support for their anti-vivisection efforts.[32]

A Distinguished Member of the Humane Society does not depict laboratory scenes or gruesome images of graphic cruelty to animals.[33] Instead, those who chose to use this image for anti-vivisection advocacy purposes were hoping that viewers would reflect on how dogs could be selfless, loyal, brave, and heroic, and how they have frequently helped humans. 'How', the inclusion of this picture in this context seems to ask, 'can humans, in turn, be so cruel to dogs?' The use of Landseer by animal advocacy groups in the late nineteenth and early twentieth centuries worked particularly well because this was already a beloved and well-known image that had been reproduced through engravings and etchings throughout the nineteenth century.[34] The appropriation and repurposing of the image by groups such as the Victoria Street

Society added additional meanings to this familiar picture. Further, in the case of the original Landseer painting, the real-world referent was the dog Paul Pry. When the finished painting was first exhibited, however, this shifted to the dogs who work alongside humans in the context of marine rescue and was intended as a celebration of the heroism and bravery of these canine rescuers in a more general sense. When this picture was taken up later in the century in the context of animal advocacy, however, layers of meanings were added. This did not necessarily erase the previous interpretations and understandings of this picture – indeed, it would seem that it was so popular with those working in animal advocacy precisely because of Landseer's intended meaning. The idea that an animal who could be so loyal and brave could also be the victim of vivisection was what made these campaigns work.

Working with images

Erica Fudge has argued that we need to 'place ourselves next to the animals' when doing historical work.[35] Images can be important tools for doing this because pictures of animals have the ability to draw the viewer into the narrative being depicted. There is an important opportunity for an empathic connection between the viewer and the animal represented in the image. We are invited to pause and reflect on his or her situation and, quite often, this draws upon our previous knowledge of animals. A picture of a dog, in other words, may evoke memories of dogs we have encountered in our own lives – we may see Landseer's image and think about the brave and loyal dogs who worked alongside the Royal Humane Society of Britain, but we may also remember how the dog we had as a child loved to accompany us on trips to the beach and this could, in turn, lead to other memories and thoughts about dogs we have known and our relationships with them.

A viewer, in other words, has many different avenues through which to insert herself and her thoughts, knowledge, values, and memories into a picture and it is through these avenues that she can start to imagine new ways of engaging with both history and nonhuman animals. What constitutes 'kind', 'cruel', or 'inhumane' treatment of an animal is not a given and it varies depending upon historical, geographic, and cultural contexts. It also, in large part, depends on the species of animal under consideration. It is, therefore, these encounters between a viewer and an image that can expand our understanding of animal–human history.

So, how do we do this? What are the practical first steps a historian interested in animal–human history can take? This kind of work is not without its challenges. As mentioned above, archives, art galleries, and museums tend to have collections that centre on human narratives and achievements – even if records or traces of nonhuman animals are present they are likely organised and catalogued in such a way that makes doing animal–human history rather convoluted. For instance, the metadata or finding aids for a particular image or collection might not even mention animals, but this gap in the record-keeping does not mean they are actually absent. I recently encountered an archival photograph of a man posing with a horse-drawn sleigh in front of a building of historical significance to the local community in which the archive was situated. Both the building and the man were mentioned in the accompanying documents and metadata, but it was as if the horse was invisible.

He was not acknowledged even though he played a central role in the scene that was represented in the image – without a horse to pull the sleigh, the man would not have arrived at the building of interest! I would not have found this image by searching in the finding aids or catalogues – I found it simply by flipping through a file of material on an unrelated topic. I mention this anecdote to highlight that those interested in doing animal–human history need to be persistent and vigilant as they work through historical material. Representations of animals are abundant in most archives, but they often fall through the cracks of official organisational systems. Therefore, we need to think creatively about where we might encounter representations of animals in the existing historical records. As Susan Nance has noted, 'because we tend to mentally edit animals out as inconsequential, that evidence of animal life is often hidden in plain view in sources we do know'.[36]

There are many challenges faced by those trying to piece together animal–human history. Institutions that foreground animal–human history – institutions such as the American *National Museum of Animals & Society* – do exist, but they are few and far between.[37] Further, the archives of organisations focused on relationships between animals and humans (for example, animal advocacy organisations) are often understaffed or inaccessible to researchers. Smaller organisations from previous eras have sometimes closed and gone out of business, and finding traces of their work and advocacy/educational material can be hit-or-miss. At times, descriptions of images exist but there seems to be no physical trace of the original pictures these descriptions refer to. It is also important to be aware that collecting practices shape what was preserved. For example, in the case of animal advocacy, much of the material produced is ephemeral (pamphlets on cheap paper, for example), and, as such, these items have not always been collected, preserved, or valued in the same way as other forms of visual culture have been. And, finally, we need to look beyond the most famous or celebrated pictures that have been deemed worthy of study by art historical discourses. As the Landseer example above demonstrates, well-known and celebrated pictures can certainly provide a useful avenue for exploring animal–human histories, but, in many cases, pictures that were much discussed and widely circulated in previous eras are all but neglected in twenty-first century writings about images.

We need to cast a wide net if we are genuinely interested in thinking about animal–human histories through visual culture. As the example of the 1887 Royal Academy exhibition I began this chapter with demonstrates, exhibition reviews can be a useful tool for getting a sense of how specific images were exhibited and discussed in previous eras. In the case of animal-themed imagery, we need to be prepared to look beyond the expected sources of periodicals focused on art and culture. As we have seen, organisations such as the RSPCA also routinely wrote about pictures in previous eras. These alternative sources can provide different narratives about the pictures on display and these different kinds of conversations can open up new ways of thinking about old pictures.

Welcome Morsels

For the remainder of this essay I want to focus on two specific examples of artworks that were singled out in the RSPCA's review of the 1887 Royal Academy exhibition: Nightingale's *Welcome Morsels* (c.1887) and Caldwell's *For the Safety of the Public* (c.1887). These examples were two among many that were discussed in the review in *The Animal World*. My intention here is not to give a comprehensive synopsis of either the exhibition or the RSPCA's take on it. Rather, I have singled out a couple of pictures that, in the context of this chapter, can illustrate how we might start to think about art and visual culture as tools for framing animal–human histories.

Leonard Nightingale's *Welcome Morsels* (Figure 11.2) is a tender painting of a young girl offering food to two white goats.[38] Of this picture, the RSPCA reviewer expressed interest in obtaining copyright clearance to reproduce the painting in the *Band of Mercy*, a sister publication aimed at teaching children to be kind to animals.[39]

Figure 11.2 Leonard Nightingale, *Welcome Morsels*, exhibited at the Royal Academy Exhibition of 1887.

Collection: Christchurch Art Gallery Te Puna O Waiwhetu, Christchurch, New Zealand, reproduced with permission.

This kind of humane education was an important part of nineteenth-century animal advocacy, and often drew upon pictures to convey lessons of kindness and compassion to young people.

The relationship between humans and animals is the focus of Nightingale's picture. The girl stands with her back against a brick building, tentatively holding out some leafy green treats while the two goats – one smaller than the other, quite likely a mother and her kid – look at the girl and the food she is offering with great interest. Their heads are cocked and their ears are alert as they consider the offer. The two goats stand very close to one another, indicating a strong familial bond. There is, however, a safe distance between the girl and the goats – they have not yet decided whether or not to accept the treats. The goats, in other words, are shown as having agency, they are active participants in this exchange and are deciding how close they want to get to the girl. The title – *Welcome Morsels* – suggests that the goats are happy to be given food, but their body language indicates a bit of timidity as they assess the situation.

In the moment that Nightingale depicts, the relationship between the beings in this picture is still one that is characterised by a sense of uncertainty. The goats and the girl are tentatively checking one another out, assessing the situation, but there is no indication of a close relationship between the three pictured in this image. We might safely assume, in other words, that these goats are not this girl's pets, as the familiar tenderness that often accompanies pictures of children and their pets is absent in this image. What, then, is the relationship depicted here? A likely explanation given the history of nineteenth-century British agriculture is that these goats are being kept for either milk or meat, or both.[40]

Nightingale's *Welcome Morsels* was purchased immediately after the 1887 Royal Academy exhibition by Frederick Leighton, who was then the President of the Royal Academy. Leighton purchased the picture on behalf of the Canterbury Art Society and arranged for it to be shipped to New Zealand along with four other pictures from the same exhibition.[41] This painting was given to the Robert M'Dougall Art Gallery (now the Christchurch Art Gallery) in 1932 and it remains in this collection to the present day.[42] This painting, then, has been in New Zealand for most of its history. How does this context shape the way that this image has been read?

Goats are not native to New Zealand, and historical records point to this animal being introduced to the area by Captain James Cook in the eighteenth century.[43] Goats have been called 'the most destructive introduced herbivore', and there are now a large number of feral goats in New Zealand, many of whom are believed to be descendants from the original animals Cook brought with him.[44] The New Zealand Department of Conservation classifies these feral goats as 'pests' and is actively working to manage these populations as they are deemed a threat to native species.[45] The contrast between this ecological reality and the description of this image as being 'a small painting of quaint appeal' is significant.[46] Undoubtedly, at least some of those who viewed this painting in its New Zealand home would have had prior knowledge of the region's feral goat problem. As Kim Todd articulated in *Tinkering With Eden*, the relationships that exist between 'introduced' and 'native' species are always complex and often have colonial undertones. As Todd convincingly argues, the introduction of species to an area says a lot about how humans 'imagine their relationship with other species'.⁴⁷ But we also need to think about the agency and lived realities of the individuals at the heart of these tensions, both human and animal. What was the experience of those first goats introduced to New Zealand? Had they ever been on a boat before? Were they terrified? How well did they adapt to life in this unfamiliar landscape? What was life like for their descendants, the goats who were living in New Zealand in the nineteenth century when this picture arrived in that country? We may never be able to definitively answer these questions, but we can draw upon both existing historical records (documents related to Cook's voyage, for example) as well as research from the fields of biology and cognitive ethology to make some educated guesses about what these experiences might have been like for the goats of New Zealand. Since we are interested in animal–human history, we might also ask what life was like for the individual human citizens of New Zealand who shared their homeland with goats? At which points did the two species overlap and interact? How can Nightingale's painting help frame nineteenth-century discourses on introduced species and agricultural practices in New Zealand? How, in turn, can nineteenth-century agricultural and natural history writings from New Zealand help make sense of this picture?

Even though *Welcome Morsels* was painted in Britain and brought to New Zealand, many of those who viewed Nightingale's painting in its new home would undoubtedly have had their readings of this picture shaped by their individual and localised knowledge of goats in the New Zealand landscape. Some might have been from farming families, and the scene of a young girl attempting to foster a relationship with two goats might have made them smile wistfully. Others may have been government employees working actively to 'manage' feral goat populations in New Zealand, and Nightingale's picture may have conjured up more negative responses. Today many viewers undoubtedly look upon this picture as an example of sentimental Victorian art. For historians working on animal–human history, consideration of these different kinds of encounters are of prime importance.

For the Safety of the Public

Edmund Caldwell's picture entitled *For the Safety of the Public* (Figure 11.3) was also mentioned in the RSPCA review of the annual Royal Academy exhibition. Caldwell's painting is of a small fox terrier puppy wearing a muzzle so large that it stands in marked contrast to the diminutive size of his body. This picture was painted in direct response to a flashpoint incident in the history of human–animal relationships in England, and it is thematically related to debates about muzzling dogs to prevent the spread of rabies and hydrophobia in the second half of the nineteenth century.⁴⁸ Caldwell's painting focuses on a topic that was extremely contentious at the time, the mandatory muzzling of dogs in London due to fear of rabies and hydrophobia. In the summer of 1886 things reached a fevered pitch on this front due to the so-called 'mad-dog of Baker Street' incident.

The dog at the centre of this sad tale was a spaniel named Dash, the beloved companion of a woman who lived in the neighbourhood most famous for its association with Sir Arthur Conan Doyle's famous fictional detective, Sherlock Holmes. On the morning in question – 14 June 1886 – Dash was served his breakfast and then released

Figure 11.3 E. Gilbert Hester after Edmund Caldwell, print of *For the Safety of the Public* (original painting exhibited at the Royal Academy Exhibition of 1887). Collection of the author.

outside to get some exercise and fresh air as was his customary daily habit. When Dash set out that morning he was wearing the requisite muzzle, but at some point the muzzle became askew. Some reports say that this was because a group of local children were teasing him, others indicate it was because the muzzle was irritating him and he was rubbing it on the ground and the bushes in an attempt to get it off. Either way, the end result was that poor Dash was mistaken for a 'mad dog', and it didn't take long for the fear and panic to spread. Policemen were called to the scene, and, in their wisdom, decided to beat poor Dash to death with their truncheons. Dash's cries were, by all accounts, heartbreaking, and one can imagine how scared and confused he must have been. This was his neighbourhood and he went for a daily stroll around it. He had no reason to be afraid on his home turf. This horrific incident so upset a woman named Fannie Revell, upon whose doorstep this was taking place, that she ended up dumping a bucket of water on one of the officers in a futile attempt to stop the fatal beating.[49]

While Caldwell's picture did not depict the 'mad-dog of Baker Street' incident per se, it was thematically related to this episode. The title of the picture – *For the Safety of the Public* – was taken directly from the 'Muzzling Order' enacted by the Metropolitan Police, and the RSPCA reported that this picture was dedicated to police commissioner Sir Charles Warren who was the Chief Commissioner of Police in London at the time.[50] Many animal welfare groups active in London at this time were opposed to the muzzling order, often resorting to visual spectacle to make their point.[51] Caldwell's picture would have been part of this larger discourse and there would have been little doubt about the intended meaning of this picture in the minds of those who saw it at the Royal Academy exhibition of 1887.

As was the case with Landseer's *A Distinguished Member of the Humane Society*, there are many layers to this image. The original real-world referent for this picture was not Dash, but, rather, a puppy who belonged to a friend of the artist, a 'charming fox terrier'.[52] Caldwell had made 'several studies' of his friend's dog and these pictures combined with the 'anti-muzzling agitation of 1886' led to the creation of this piece.[53] When Caldwell showed this painting to his friend he would have, undoubtedly, recognised the direct link to his own puppy. He may also have thought of Dash, but this would be an additional layer of meaning. While this painting is of a fox terrier and Dash was a spaniel, there is no doubt that many who saw this picture in 1887 would have understood the connection the artist was making between the two animals. My point here, is that it becomes difficult to untangle and separate out the histories of Caldwell's friend's puppy and Dash and the many other dogs living in London at this time. A picture of an individual animal can tell us something about the individual, but it also becomes part of a larger discourse about the species that animal belongs to and how that type of animal is treated in a given geographical and historical context.

This painting generated considerable commentary, was voted 'best animal picture' in the 1887 Royal Academy exhibition by readers of the *Pall Mall Gazette*, and was described as an example of 'comic excellence'.[54] A columnist in the *Western Times* noted that all who saw this picture burst into 'fits of laughter', because it was 'so funny to see a tiny fox terrier behind a huge muzzle'.[55] But it wasn't all a laughing matter, and the *Western Times* writer concluded by linking Caldwell's picture back to the struggles dogs and their human companions had in London under the muzzling legislation at this time – 'It certainly counts *one* for the little dogs who have much to complain of under recent police regulations'.[56] Likewise, a reviewer in the *Morning Post* noted that Caldwell's picture provided a

> satirical allusion to the salutary police-regulations to which dogs were very properly subjected some time ago. In the ludicrous disproportion between the small, solitary puppy and the million-headed public, whose common enemy he is declared to be, dwells the fun of the picture.[57]

In other words, in the minds of many viewers and reviewers Caldwell's picture had important real-world connections to ongoing issues facing dogs and their human companions in late nineteenth-century London. These sorts of discussions of this picture provide further context for the history of the muzzling debate in London.

As one nineteenth-century art critic noted, *For the Safety of the Public* 'gained immense popularity' and the resulting etching of it 'commands a large sale'.[58] The original painting was purchased by the Baroness Burdett-Coutts, a wealthy woman who was involved in a number of philanthropic and charitable efforts, including animal advocacy.[59] Caldwell's picture was, therefore, viewed in many different contexts and, in each case, the viewer would bring his or her own ideas, thoughts, preconceived notions, memories, and experiences to the reading of this picture.

A few years later, in 1889, the contentious issue of muzzling dogs was raised in another image, this time one that appeared as a satirical image in *Moonshine* (Figure 11.4). Here the artist J.A. Shepherd plays upon Landseer's famous painting, *A Distinguished Member of the Humane Society*. As discussed above, by this time, Landseer's picture was well-known in Britain. Here Shepherd satirically refers to the muzzle as something that was 'presented by a grateful nation as a reward for his many acts of heroism'.[60] This image draws upon the sense of familiarity that nineteenth-century viewers would have with both the contentious issue of muzzling dogs and Landseer's *oeuvre* and, once again, this picture can serve as a launching point for consideration of the lived realities of dogs in the capital at this time.

While there are some thematic similarities between these three pictures by Landseer, Caldwell, and Shepherd, there is one primary difference that is of importance to this current discussion – Edwin Landseer is a well-known and celebrated figure in art

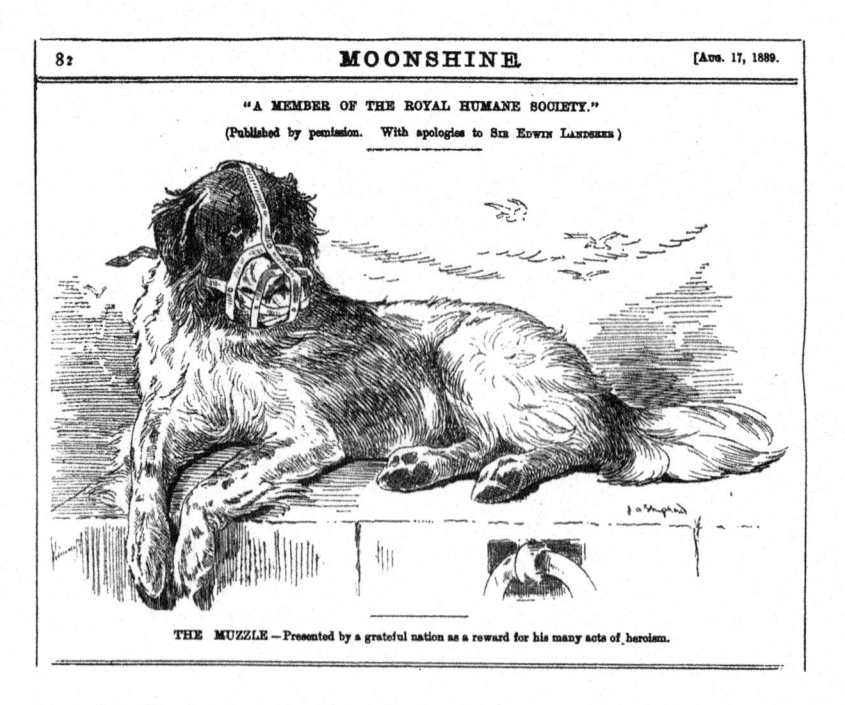

Figure 11.4 J.A. Shepherd, *A Member of the Royal Humane Society*, published in *Moonshine*, 17 August 1889.

historical discourses while the other two artists are not. *For the Safety of the Public* is an image that is barely acknowledged in the history of art. Caldwell's picture was very popular in its day – in large part owing to the centrality of the muzzling debates in London during the late nineteenth century – but the issue and this picture have faded from the minds of most people today. This example serves as an important reminder that if we are to use images to explore animal–human history we need to be willing to look beyond the art historical canon that has been passed down to twenty-first century readers. Instead, we need to take a look at primary sources and newspaper articles to help us discover a visual history that exists outside of the art history textbooks.

Conclusion

In their introduction to a special issue of *Visual Studies* in 2003, John Grady and Jay Mechling argue that in order to achieve a 'more complete and well-rounded understanding of animal human relations' we need 'scholarship that firmly puts animals in the picture, in the places they actually occupy in our lives and activities'.[61] It also means putting them in our histories, but, as discussed above, there are some distinct challenges to doing this. Scholars such as Susan Nance and Erica Fudge have noted that the repositories, documents, and material artefacts that collectively give testament to our histories are created, catalogued, valued, and maintained along distinctly human lines.[62] If, in other words, animals do not collect and curate historical and archival material, how are we ever to know about their history? And yet, as Nance and Fudge have also argued, there are creative and important ways in which we can go back to these already assembled collections with fresh eyes and approaches to look for traces of animal histories.

Likewise, in this chapter I have argued that images can offer alternatives to official anthropocentric histories. When we interrogate pictures with a focus on animal–human history we open up the possibility of thinking about interspecies relationships in new ways. Pictures can give us a glimpse into specific human–animal relationships, but they can also challenge what we think we know about a given story, and they can also foster imaginative ways of reconceptualising our relationships with nonhuman species.

In order to work with pictures in this way, we need to be open to thinking deeply and critically about visual culture and how meaning is made through imagery. This is not a simple or straightforward process and, as the examples above demonstrate, there are many different layers of meaning that need to be considered and negotiated. We need to ask ourselves what we see in the image and how what we see might either challenge or support assumptions and ideas we have about animals. We need to ask about the choices the image-maker made, and we need to recognise that what is excluded from an image is often as important as what is included. We need to consider the context of viewing and how the location and time frame in which one encounters the image can shape the reading of it. We need to be prepared to look between the lines and in the cracks, and to recognise that archives and repositories for images tend to be set up to tell human stories, but that doesn't mean they don't also offer useful insights for rethinking *animal* history if we know where and how to look.

And, finally, we need to be prepared to think about the animals whose lives are intertwined with these images. As Stephen Eisenman has noted, 'the image of animals, as well as their actual sight, sound and smell, has always been instrumental in their treatment by humans'.[63] In many cases images of animals do hold iconographic or symbolic meanings relating to human ideas, narratives, and interests, but we must not forget that they are still representations of animals and, as such, are part of a larger cultural framework that dictates how certain species are treated and valued. These representations, in other words, have real-life consequences for living, breathing, flesh-and-blood animals and, as such, we have an obligation to take them seriously.

Notes

1 This was the 119th annual exhibition of the Royal Academy, and it ran from May to August in 1887.
2 'A day at the Royal Academy', *Animal World* 18, 217 (1887): 147–149, 147.
3 'A day at the Royal Academy', 147.
4 S. Baker, 'Animals, representation, and reality', *Society & Animals* 9, 3 (2001): 189–201.
5 S. Cutrara, 'Using primary sources as a form of social justice: the role of archives, museums, and community collections in visualizing different pasts and imagining different futures', *Canada's History*, 31 March 2016, webinar, available at www.canadashistory.ca/Explore/Webinars/Using-primary-sources-as-a-form-of-social-justice, last accessed 24 April 2017.
6 M. Sturken and L. Cartwright, *Practices of Looking: An Introduction to Visual Culture*, second edition, New York: Oxford University Press, 2009, 3.
7 G. Rose, *Visual Methodologies: An Introduction to the Interpretation of Visual Materials*, second edition, London: Sage, 2007, 13.
8 Rose, *Visual Methodologies*, 13.
9 R. Malamud, *An Introduction to Animals and Visual Culture*, Basingstoke: Palgrave Macmillan, 2012, 19.
10 Malamud, *Introduction to Animals and Visual Culture*, 13.
11 S.F. Eisenman, *The Cry of Nature: Art and the Making of Animal Rights*, London: Reaktion, 2013, 18.
12 Eisenman, *Cry of Nature*, 197.
13 Eisenman, *Cry of Nature*, 11.
14 Eisenman, *Cry of Nature*, 197.
15 J. Burt, *Animals in Film*, London: Reaktion, 2002, 15.
16 See, for example F.L. Brown, *The City is More Than Human: An Animal History of Seattle*, Seattle WA: University of Washington Press, 2016; J. Dean, D. Ingram, and C. Sethna (eds.), *Animal Metropolis: Histories of Human–Animal Relations in Urban Canada*, Calgary: University of Calgary Press, 2017; E. Fudge, 'The history of animals', Ruminations H-Animal Network, 25 May 2006, available at https://networks.h-net.org/node/16560/pages/32226/history-animals-erica-fudge, last accessed 24 April 2017; E. Fudge, 'What was it like to be a cow? History and animal studies', in L. Kalof (ed.), *The Oxford Handbook of Animal Studies*, Oxford: Oxford University Press, 2017, 258–278; L. Kalof, *Looking at Animals in Human History*, London: Reaktion, 2007; H. Kean, 'Challenges for historians writing human–animal history: what is really enough?', *Anthrozoös* 25, S1 (2012): 57–72; S. Nance (ed.), *The Historical Animal*, Syracuse NY: Syracuse University Press, 2015; I.H. Tague, *Animal Companions: Pets and Social Change in Eighteenth-Century Britain*, University Park PA: Penn State University Press, 2015; H. Velten, *Beastly London: A History of Animals in the City*, London: Reaktion, 2013.

17 E. Fudge, 'A left-handed blow: writing the history of animals', in N. Rothfels (ed.), *Representing Animals*, Bloomington IN: Indiana University Press, 2002, 3–18, 5.
18 E. Fudge, 'Foreword', in M. Few and Z. Tortorici (eds.), *Centering Animals in Latin American History*, Durham NC: Duke University Press, 2013: ix–xi, ix. In recent years there has been a rise in the phenomenon of animals as artists. This is a somewhat controversial topic and one that is beyond the scope of this chapter. For more on this see J.K. Cronin, 'Animal artists: enrichment or exploitation', *Our Hen House*, 25 November 2013, available at www.ourhenhouse.org/2013/11/animal-artists-enrichment-or-exploitation/, last accessed 24 April 2017; A.B. Kaufman and J.C. Kaufman (eds.) *Animal Creativity and Innovation*, London: Academic Press, 2015.
19 Fudge, 'A left-handed blow', 11.
20 D. Donald, *Picturing Animals in Britain, 1750–1850*, New Haven CT: Yale University Press, 2007, vi.
21 P. Chu, *Nineteenth-Century European Art*, second edition, Upper Saddle River NJ: Pearson/Prentice Hall, 2006, 333.
22 J.K. Cronin, '"Popular affection": Edwin Landseer and nineteenth-century animal advocacy campaigns', in J. Castricano and L. Corman (eds.), *Animal Subjects 2.0*, Waterloo ON: Wilfrid Laurier University Press, 2016, 81–108.
23 A. Sekula, 'On the invention of photographic meaning', in V. Burgin (ed.), *Thinking Photography*, London: Palgrave, 1982, 84–109, 84.
24 J. Burt, 'The illumination of the animal kingdom: the role of light and electricity in animal representation', *Society & Animals* 9, 3 (2001), 203–228, 210. Burt argues that the work of people like Eadward Muybridge and Jules-Etienne Marey helped develop both photography of motion as well as motion pictures. The projects that Muybridge and Marey worked on often involved focusing the camera lens on the bodies of animals in motion and, as such, 'animals were an important motive force in driving the new technology' (210).
25 W.J.T. Mitchell, *What Do Pictures Want? The Lives and Loves of Images*, Chicago IL: University of Chicago Press, 2005, 47.
26 Mitchell, *What Do Pictures Want?*, 92.
27 Donald, *Picturing Animals in Britain*, 133.
28 M.H. Spielmann, '"A Distinguished Member of the Humane Society"', *Magazine of Art* (1891): 12–14, 12.
29 Donald, *Picturing Animals in Britain*, 133.
30 Donald, *Picturing Animals in Britain*, 133.
31 Spielmann, 'A Distinguished Member of the Humane Society', 12.
32 The position of the dog in the realm of (anti)vivisection discourses at this time was complex. On the one hand, dogs were frequently beloved pets and, as such, were symbolic not only of domesticity but also of the ways in which humans and animals could form deep emotional bonds with one another. See P. Howell, *At Home and Astray: The Domestic Dog in Victorian Britain*, Charlottesville VA: University of Virginia Press, 2015, 102–124, for vivisection as a 'distinctive threat to the Victorian home' (116). As such, this made representations of domestic dogs particularly useful in anti-vivisection literature. On the other hand, the long history of human–dog relationships 'meant physical and geographical as well as intellectual closeness' (Howell, *At Home and Astray*, 120) that led many vivisectors to turn to dogs as subjects in their experiments.
33 On graphic images in animal advocacy campaigns, see E. Aaltola, 'Animal suffering: representations and the act of looking'. *Anthrozoös* 27, 1 (2014), 19–31.
34 Spielmann, 'A Distinguished Member of the Humane Society', 12.
35 Fudge, 'A left-handed blow', 15.

36 S. Nance, 'Introduction', in S. Nance (ed.), *The Historical Animal*, Syracuse NY: Syracuse University Press, 2015, 1–16, 10.
37 For more on this LA-based museum, see www.museumofanimals.org/, last accessed 24 April 2017.
38 Nightingale was Principal of the Clapham School of Art in the late nineteenth and early twentieth centuries; see C. Holme (ed.) *Arts & Crafts: A Review of the Work Executed by Students in the Leading Art Schools of Great Britain and Ireland*, London: The Studio Ltd, 1916.
39 'A day at the Royal Academy', 147.
40 For more on the intertwined history of humans and goats, see J. Hinson, *Goat*, London: Reaktion, 2015.
41 'Art society', *The Press* [Canterbury, New Zealand] XLIV, 6820, 3 August 1887, 2.
42 For Leonard Charles Nightingale, 'Welcome Morsels', see http://christchurchartgallery.org.nz/collection/69-569, last accessed 24 April 2017.
43 G.M. Thomson, *The Naturalisation of Animals and Plants in New Zealand*, Cambridge: Cambridge University Press, 1922, 15.
44 D.R. Towns, D. Simberloff, and I.A.E. Atkinson, 'Restoration of New Zealand islands: redressing the effects of introduced species', *Pacific Conservation Biology* 3, 2 (1997): 99–124, 99.
45 New Zealand government, Department of Conservation, 'Animal pests A-Z', available at www.doc.govt.nz/nature/pests-and-threats/animal-pests/animal-pests-a-z/feral-goats/, last accessed 24 April 2017.
46 'M'Dougall Art Gallery', *The Press* [Canterbury, New Zealand] LXVII, 20577, 20 June 1932, 8.
47 K. Todd, *Tinkering With Eden: A Natural History of Exotics in America*, New York: W.W. Norton, 2001, 6.
48 See Howell, *At Home and Astray*, 150–173; N. Pemberton and M. Worboys, *Rabies in Britain: Dogs, Disease and Culture, 1830–2000*, Basingstoke: Palgrave Macmillan, 2013, 133.
49 G. Stock, E.E. Footner, F. Revell, C.A. Dawson, and A. Kingsford, 'The Baker Street "mad-dog" case', *The Spectator*, 24 July 1886: 989–990. The Victoria Street Society for the Protection of Animals from Vivisection published a leaflet outlining this case and distributed it free of charge: see 'Notes and Notices', *The Zoophilist* 6 (1886): 86.
50 F. Dolman, 'Humour at the Royal Academy', *Strand Magazine* 23 (1902): 603–610, 610; 'A day at the Royal Academy', 149.
51 H. Kean, *Animal Rights: Political and Social Change in Britain Since 1800*, London: Reaktion, 1998, 94, 147.
52 Dolman, 'Humour at the Royal Academy', 610.
53 Dolman, 'Humour at the Royal Academy', 610.
54 'Our academy competition', *Pall Mall Gazette* XLVI (1887): 1–2; Dolman, 'Humour at the Royal Academy', 610.
55 'Our ladies' column', *Western Times* (1887), 3.
56 'Our ladies' column', 3.
57 'St. James's Gallery', *Morning Post*, 2 July 1887, 3.
58 M. Spencer-Warren, 'The Baroness Burdett-Coutts', *Strand Magazine* 7 (1894): 348–360, 350.
59 Dolman, 'Humour at the Royal Academy', 610.
60 'A member of the Royal Humane Society', *Moonshine*, 17 August 1889, 82.
61 J. Grady and J. Mechling, 'Editors' introduction: putting animals in the picture', *Visual Studies* 18, 2 (2003): 92–95, 93.
62 Fudge, 'A left-handed blow'; Nance (ed.) *The Historical Animal*.
63 Eisenman, *Cry of Nature*, 15.

Bibliography

Aaltola, E. 'Animal suffering: representations and the act of looking'. *Anthrozoös* 27, 1 (2014), 19–31.
'A day at the Royal Academy', *Animal World* 18, 217 (1887): 147–149.
'A member of the Royal Humane Society', *Moonshine*, 17 August 1889, 82.
'Art society', *The Press* [Canterbury, New Zealand] XLIV, 6820, 3 August 1887, 2.
Baker, S. 'Animals, representation, and reality', *Society & Animals* 9, 3 (2001): 189–201.
Brown, F.L. *The City is More Than Human: An Animal History of Seattle*, Seattle WA: University of Washington Press, 2016.
Burt, J. 'The illumination of the animal kingdom: the role of light and electricity in animal representation', *Society & Animals* 9, 3 (2001): 203–228.
Burt, J. *Animals in Film*, London: Reaktion, 2002.
Chu, P. *Nineteenth-Century European Art*, second edition, Upper Saddle River NJ: Pearson-Prentice Hall, 2006.
Cronin, J.K. '"Popular affection": Edwin Landseer and nineteenth-century animal advocacy campaigns', in J. Castricano and L. Corman (eds.), *Animal Subjects 2.0*, Waterloo ON: Wilfrid Laurier University Press, 2016, 81–108.
Cronin, J.K. 'Animal artists: enrichment or exploitation', *Our Hen House*, 25 November 2013, available at www.ourhenhouse.org/2013/11/animal-artists-enrichment-or-exploitation/, last accessed 24 April 2017.
Cutrara, S. 'Using primary sources as a form of social justice: the role of archives, museums, and community collections in visualizing different pasts and imagining different futures', *Canada's History*, 31 March 2016, webinar, available at www.canadashistory.ca/Explore/Webinars/Using-primary-sources-as-a-form-of-social-justice, last accessed 24 April 2017.
Dean, J., Ingram, D., and Sethna, C. (eds.) *Animal Metropolis: Histories of Human-Animal Relations in Urban Canada*, Calgary: University of Calgary Press, Calgary, 2017.
Dolman, F. 'Humour at the Royal Academy', *Strand Magazine* 23 (1902): 603–610.
Donald, D. *Picturing Animals in Britain, 1750–1850*. New Haven CT: Yale University Press, 2007.
Eisenman, S.F. *The Cry of Nature: Art and the Making of Animal Rights*, London: Reaktion, 2013.
Fudge, E. 'Foreword', in M. Few and Z. Tortorici (eds.), *Centering Animals in Latin American History*, Durham NC: Duke University Press, 2013, ix–xi.
Fudge, E. 'A left-handed blow: writing the history of animals', in N. Rothfels (ed.), *Representing Animals*, Bloomington IN: Indiana University Press, 2002, 3–18.
Fudge, E., 'The history of animals', Ruminations H-Animal Network, 25 May 2006, available at https://networks.h-net.org/node/16560/pages/32226/history-animals-erica-fudge, last accessed 24 April 2017.
Fudge, E. 'What was it like to be a cow? History and animal studies', in L. Kalof (ed.), *The Oxford Handbook of Animal Studies*, Oxford: Oxford University Press, 2017, 258–278.
Grady, J. and Mechling, J. "Editors' introduction: putting animals in the picture', *Visual Studies* 18, 2 (2003): 92–95.
Hinson, J. *Goat*, London: Reaktion, 2015.
Holme, C. (ed.) *Arts & Crafts: A Review of the Work Executed by Students in the Leading Art Schools of Great Britain and Ireland*, London: The Studio Ltd, 1916.
Howell, P. *At Home and Astray: The Domestic Dog in Victorian Britain*, Charlottesville VA: University of Virginia Press, 2015.
Kalof, L. *Looking at Animals in Human History*, London: Reaktion, 2007.
Kaufman, A.B. and Kaufman, J.C. (eds.) *Animal Creativity and Innovation*, London: Academic Press, 2015.

Kean, H. 'Challenges for historians writing human-animal history: what is really enough?' *Anthrozoös* 25, S1 (2012): 57–72.

Kean, H. *Animal Rights: Political and Social Change in Britain Since 1800*, London: Reaktion, 1998.

'M'Dougall Art Gallery', *The Press* [Canterbury, New Zealand] LXVIII, 20577, 20 June 1932, 8.

Malamud, R. *An Introduction to Animals and Visual Culture*, Basingstoke: Palgrave Macmillan, 2012.

Mirzoeff, N. *The Visual Culture Reader*, third edition, London: Routledge, 2013.

Mitchell, W.J.T. *What Do Pictures Want? The Lives and Loves of Images*, Chicago IL: University of Chicago Press, 2005.

Nance, S. (ed.) *The Historical Animal*, Syracuse NY: Syracuse University Press, 2015.

Nance, S. 'Introduction', in S. Nance (ed.), *The Historical Animal*, Syracuse NY: Syracuse University Press, 2015, 1–16.

'Notes and Notices', *The Zoophilist* 6 (1886): 85–88.

'Our Academy competition', *Pall Mall Gazette* XLVI (1887): 1–2.

'Our ladies' column', *Western Times* (1887), 3.

Pemberton, N. and Worboys, M. *Rabies in Britain: Dogs, Disease and Culture, 1830–2000*, Basingstoke: Palgrave MacMillan, 2013.

Rose, G. *Visual Methodologies: An Introduction to the Interpretation of Visual Materials*, second edition, London: Sage, 2007.

Sekula, A. 'On the invention of photographic meaning', in V. Burgin (ed.), *Thinking Photography*, London: Palgrave, 1982, 84–109.

Spencer-Warren, M. 'The Baroness Burdett-Coutts', *Strand Magazine* 7 (1894): 348–360.

Spielmann, M.H. 'A Distinguished Member of the Humane Society', *Magazine of Art* (1891): 12–14.

'St. James's Gallery', *Morning Post*, 2 July 1887, 3.

Stock, G., Footner, E.E., Revell, F., Dawson, C.A., and Kingsford, A. 'The Baker Street "mad-dog" case', *The Spectator*, 24 July 1886: 989–990.

Sturken, M. and Cartwright, L. *Practices of Looking: An Introduction to Visual Culture*, second edition, New York: Oxford University Press, 2009.

Tague, I.H. *Animal Companions: Pets and Social Change in Eighteenth-Century Britain*, University Park PA: Penn State University Press, 2015.

Thomson, G.M. *The Naturalisation of Animals and Plants in New Zealand*, Cambridge: Cambridge University Press, 1922.

Todd, K. *Tinkering With Eden: A Natural History of Exotics in America*, New York: W.W. Norton, 2001.

Towns, D.R., Simberloff, D., and Atkinson, I.A.E., 'Restoration of New Zealand islands: redressing the effects of introduced species', *Pacific Conservation Biology* 3, 2 (1997): 99–124.

Velten, H. *Beastly London: A History of Animals in the City*, London: Reaktion, 2013.

12

WHEN ADAM AND EVE WERE MONKEYS

Anthropomorphism, zoomorphism, and other ways of looking at animals[1]

Boria Sax

Introduction

In September 1906, a pygmy named Ota Benga (Figure 12.1) was exhibited in the monkey house by the New York Zoological Park. Bones scattered around his enclosure, in the context of common racist stereotypes, suggested savagery and perhaps even cannibalism. His teeth had been filed to points, so they looked a bit like the fangs of a crocodile. An orangutan was placed in the cage, ostensibly to keep him company. Benga brought in huge crowds, but the exhibit immediately provoked protests, especially from the African-American community. After a while, Benga, who had up till then shown a pleasant disposition, became uncooperative and almost violent, so he was allowed to move freely on the grounds, but thousands of raucous tourists followed him about. After only three weeks, the zoo ceased to display Benga.[2]

It was not unusual for indigenous people such as the Inuit or Saami to be exhibited alongside beasts in the latter nineteenth and early twentieth centuries, although placing a human being in the monkey house had been unprecedented. The permeable boundary between human beings and animals was a constant source of uneasy, boisterous humour. It was not always easy to tell whether people were laughing at the animals, at themselves, or at society. It was not always easy to separate showmanship from science or entertainment from education. Perhaps the public enjoyed the presentation of Benga as a sort of proverbial 'wild man', including the titillating suggestion of cannibalism, while knowing full well that it was just a show.

When Benga departed from New York, the gap he left was filled within a few months by a popular chimpanzee named Baldy (Figure 12.2), who was constantly mentioned in the newspapers, and, though he did not cause much controversy, may well have been as big an attraction as the pygmy who preceded him. Like Benga, Baldy was originally from the Congo.

Figure 12.1 Ota Benga at the Bronx Zoo, 1906.
Courtesy Wikipedia.

Upon arriving at the Bronx Zoo in January 1907 at approximately the age of 4, he quickly acquired a reputation for unusual intelligence, and may have been accorded a status a bit above that of other animals. According to an article in a Jeffersonville, Indiana newspaper, Baldy was allowed to move freely throughout the monkey house when no visitors were present. One day he found a keeper's set of keys on a table, went to the keeper's room, tried a few keys in the lock until he found the one that fitted, opened the door and walked in. When he found the keeper washing his face with soap and then drying himself with a towel, Baldy immediately went to the sink and did the same.[3] He was becoming 'human'. Many such anecdotes were told of Baldy, who was studied by primatologists, fraternised with by zookeepers, and adored by the public. But several points in the news story strain credulity. Did the zoo really allow a chimpanzee that much freedom? Were those accomplishments real? In parts of the account at least, the journalist was probably conflating Baldy and Benga.

Figure 12.2 Postcard showing two pictures of Baldy in his zookeeper uniform, sold by the New York Zoological Park.

Courtesy Wildlife Conservation Society Archives.

Indigenous people on public display had been, at the time, shown in settings that emphasised their reputedly 'primitive' character. The apes, by contrast, were presented in ways that made them appear as 'civilised' as possible. In both instances, stereotypic images were used to construct a sort of 'missing link' between life in the wild and in modern society.[4] At many zoos around the turn of the century, apes were taught to smoke pipes or cigars, guzzle alcoholic drinks from bottles, type, play musical instruments, roller skate, and ride in carts drawn by dogs. At the New York Zoological Park, they would, among other acts, be displayed sitting at a table and drinking tea from fine china.[5] A newspaper article reported how Baldy was the first ape to learn to eat with a knife and fork. He was then assigned to teach this skill to the orangutans, who sat with him in chairs around a table. Soon, a quarrel broke out over food, and Baldy hit one of the orangs with a chair.[6]

At times Benga had been characterised by the zoo administration and the press as a 'zookeeper'. When criticised for racism, a menagerie official once explained, 'If Benga is in a cage, he is only there to look after the animals'.[7] The zoo later decided that Baldy would also be promoted to the rank of keeper, and he was given a custom-made uniform including shoes to wear on the job. Then it was time to show him about the entire zoo. Everything went well, and a crowd of over a thousand visitors soon gathered to watch, until Baldy entered the reptile house and was spooked by the anaconda. He tore off his shoes, ran off, and started climbing around the grounds, tearing his uniform to shreds, until the keepers finally managed to lead him back to the monkey house. Needless to say, the crowd loved the spectacle.[8]

Baldy continued to represent the zoo, often dressed in human clothes, and greeted visiting dignitaries including President Taft by shaking hands with them.[9]

After his release, Benga learned considerable English, moved to Virginia, took a job, and became accepted by the local community around Lynchburg, but committed suicide in 1916.[10] Baldy also became depressed, which might have been due to psychological trauma or, more likely, physical illness. A report in the *New York Zoological Society Bulletin* stated that he had become '. . . so savage at times that it is difficult to enter his cage'.[11] He died a week or two afterwards in January 1914, probably from simian tuberculosis.[12]

The zoo in the early twentieth century was, in many ways, unlike the sanitised institution that we know today. People would often put on formal attire to visit, but, otherwise, it was a pretty rowdy place, and there was a good deal of interaction between animals and human beings.[13] Despite the claim of being educational, the zoos were often not very different from the side shows, 'freak shows' if you will, in the circus. The zoo made little or no pretence of placing the animals in a natural environment. There was, from our contemporary point of view, amazingly little care taken for safety of either the animals or the people. One brilliant but eccentric herpetologist, Grace Wylie, at Chicago's Brookfield Zoo allowed poisonous snakes to move freely about her office and possibly beyond, convinced that they had been tamed.[14] The feeding of live rodents to anacondas and other snakes was at times a popular, though controversial, event, which brought gasps of horror and fascination.[15]

The traditional zoo is a very anthropocentric institution, since it assumes a sharp divide between the animals, who were there to be looked at, and human beings, who do the looking. The concept of 'anthropocentrism' can often seem very abstract and elusive, but, as I wish to show in this essay, its manifestations can be very tangible. These include perceived zoomorphic hybrids, such as Ota Benga, and anthropomorphic hybrids, such as Baldy. In the first instance, traits associated with animals are projected onto human beings. In the latter instance, human traits are attributed to animals. The way Baldy could immediately fill the role of Benga illustrates how zoomorphism and anthropomorphism address much the same need. Neither of these would be possible without the ontological division between the two realms of human beings, or 'civilisation', and animals, or 'nature'.[16]

What is anthropocentrism?

It is easy to use events of the past to foster a feeling of superiority, but much harder to apportion responsibility for them, and hardest of all to draw useful lessons. Many newspaper articles from the beginnings of the sojourns at the New York Zoological Park speak of both Benga and Baldy with affection, yet the treatment was of Benga was, in retrospect, very exploitative. Baldy was never, so far as we know, treated abusively, though perhaps the uncertain status between ape and human being was stressful for him as well. Should we blame the zoo authorities? The public? The spirit of the times? It could even be that Benga, despite his traumatised condition, knowingly acted out the role of a wild man, becoming a party to his own exploitation. It may also be that Baldy thought of himself as 'human' and behaved accordingly or at least enjoyed being the centre of attention. Spectators may have mistaken fear for excess energy or anxiety for merriment. At any rate, the anthropomorphic and zoomorphic displays addressed psychological needs that were ultimately a product of anthropocentrism. The ontological divide between the human and natural realms creates a need for mediators, which must be alienated from both domains.

The term 'anthropocentrism' literally means 'centred around human beings', and was initially a theological concept. It referred to the Jewish, Islamic, and Christian practice of attributing qualities borrowed from human society such as 'just' or 'righteous' to a transcendent God. The question addressed by philosophers such as Maimonides and Aquinas was whether this implicitly accorded an exaggerated importance to humanity, thus undermining our humility before the Deity.[17] The concept sank into obscurity during the Renaissance, as humankind, at least in the West, gained in collective self-confidence. It was revived in the early twentieth century, but it was used mostly to designate an exaggerated sense of human significance in relation to the natural world. Ecological thinkers such as Aldo Leopold and John Muir argued that all forms of life had value independent of their relationship to human beings, a position that came to be known as 'biocentrism'.[18] In the latter twentieth century, the concept of 'anthropocentrism' was also taken up by the animal rights movement, as a means to criticise a humanism that ignores or slights the interests of animals.[19]

In this chapter, I will use the term 'anthropocentrism' as it is understood by anthropologist Philippe Descola. This is one of a handful of ontologies with which cultures endeavour to make sense of the world. Others are animism, totemism, and analogism. All of these may be found to some degree in many, possibly all, human cultures, but one or another may predominate in certain times and places. Animism prevails in most of Africa and in most indigenous cultures of the Americas, while totemism does in the aboriginal culture of Australia; analogism is the norm in East Asia.

Only in the modern West is anthropocentrism the primary means of organising experience. It involves a sharp division of the world into the realms of humanity (i.e., 'civilisation') and nature.[20] Bruno Latour has written at length of how anthropocentrism, understood in this way, entails the endless task of trying to purify both the human and natural realms, yet constantly produces hybrids, since the division is highly artificial. The two domains are in perpetual contact in a virtually endless number of ways, so there are constant occasions for blending and merging. The methods of natural science, for example, are applied to society, thus undermining the idea of human autonomy. The methods of the humanities are then applied to science, which is pronounced 'socially constructed'.[21] Trying to keep the two realms pure is a bit like trying to keep sand from falling into the ocean or waves from breaking onto the land.

Understood in the broadest way, 'hybrids' would include sociobiology and deconstruction. In this chapter, however, I will use the word 'hybrid' in a less inclusive way than Latour, to refer to what I believe is a special instance of this blending. I have in mind figures that combine not only the domains but also the physical and social characteristics of both animals and human beings. One identity must be primary, whether it is as an animal, in the case of Baldy, or as a human, in the case of Benga. There is usually friction between the two identities as animal and human, which can result in laughter, pathos, aggression, or terror. Since both zoomorphism and anthropomorphism are based on an assumption of radical human distinctiveness, they are often, as examples in this chapter will demonstrate, found together. In many cases, one may even be substituted for the other, much as Baldy was used as the replacement for Benga.

The development of anthropocentrism

In the inner caverns of the cave paintings from Paleolithic Europe, there are relatively few hybrids of animals and human beings, but one is the famous 'sorcerer' at Trois Freres in France, which shows a man bearing the horns of a stag.[22] Early towns and cities, especially when surrounded by walls, mark off a human realm, distinct from the natural world that surrounds it. Composite figures of animals and people become more common in Neolithic times, and they then proliferate dramatically in the depictions of Egyptian deities, which frequently combine human bodies with animal heads. Thoth, the god of wisdom, often had the head of an ibis, and Anubis, god of the dead, had that of a jackal. But, while these figures blend the physical features of animals and people, it is very questionable whether the mixing extended to fundamental ontologies. The general absence of humour, revulsion, or fear suggests a lack of tension between their human and bestial identities.

In moderate instances, it can be very hard to distinguish anthropomorphism from empathy for animals or even distributed consciousness. There are legitimate debates about this today in the field of psychology, but when animals are depicted speaking human languages, wearing human clothes, or participating in parliamentary debates, the anthropomorphism is unmistakable. Both the Mesopotamians and Egyptians did, however, occasionally produce clearly anthropomorphic figures, cartoonish images of animals standing on two legs and acting 'human'. The best known example is the Sumerian Harp of Ur, now in the University of Pennsylvania Museum of Archeology, dated from around 2800 BCE. At the top is the golden head of a bull with a beard of lapis lazuli. Inlaid figures along the side depict as a lion, a bull, a deer, a scorpion, and a fox playing musical instruments, drinking from vessels, and conversing like people.[23]

Anthropocentrism intensifies in Greece, where the deities are consistently given human form. The Greek idealisation of the human figure seems intended in part to distinguish people sharply from simians and other animals by emphasising such features as high foreheads, ease of balance on two feet, and a relative lack of body hair. A very anthropomorphic portrayal of animals is found in the fables traditionally attributed to the half-legendary Aesop, a slave on the Isle of Samos in the seventh century, who was allegedly given his freedom and made advisor to the king for his skill in telling stories. These tales developed from the tradition of Sumero-Akkadian animal proverbs, but the degree to which Aesop's lions, donkeys, and foxes speak and interact like men and women had few if any recorded precedents.[24]

Zoomorphism, the sister quality to anthropomorphism, is a bit less dramatic in Greek culture, though it may be seen in many Greek myths of transformations. The sorceress Circe changed men into pigs and other animals. Zeus, who usually had a human form, changed himself into a swan to seduce the maiden Leda. His wife, Hera, changed Io, one of Zeus's mortal mistresses, into a heifer, and then sent a fly to drive her through the world. Zoomorphism is even raised to the level of philosophy when

Aristotle writes in *Politics* that non-Greeks, since they do not take part in political life, are essentially animals.[25]

Greco-Roman culture may border on being anthropocentric, but there is less ambiguity about Western culture in the modern period. When artists and writers of the Renaissance revived the Greek tradition of idealising the human form, it was an attempt to purify the human essence of bestial contamination. The same period brought the depiction of countless fantastical hybrids, figures that blended features of animals and human beings. These monsters appear in the margins of illuminated manuscripts and later in the work of artists such as Hieronymus Bosch, Martin Schongauer, and Pieter Bruegel the Elder.[26]

Many people read Descartes' *Discourse on Method* (first published 1637) as the manifesto of anthropocentrism, since he makes a very abrupt distinction between human beings, which have a soul, and all other creatures, which lack one. Although Descartes never denied that animals have emotions, he believed they were without reason or language and, therefore, completely lacking in autonomy, while people alone had free will.[27] Nevertheless, Descartes is often given too much credit or blame for ushering in the modern era. His readers were confined to the intellectual elite and, even there, most of his ideas were never very widely accepted.[28] But, although there have always been many countervailing tendencies, the abrupt distinction between civilisation and nature has gradually come to pervade Western intellectual life.

It is particularly difficult to lay aside anthropocentrism, since this is not only implicit in the way we answer ethical questions, it is even more central to the questions themselves. Suppose, for example, we ask whether it is ethical to hunt. Well, for whom? Nobody is likely to question the morality of a chameleon hunting flies or an American robin hunting worms. A few farmers might consider it wrong for wolves to hunt sheep, but most people would accept that as natural. Clearly, we mean the question to apply only to human beings, who live by a unique code. Should we decide that hunting is not ethical but make an exception for, say, American Indians, on the basis of their culture and history, we would at least partially dehumanise them. Anthropocentrism is inherent in the very idea of rights, which implicitly divides creatures into those that have them and those that do not, and that boundary itself is not affected at all by shifting certain animals such as apes and dogs from one side to the other.

Drolleries

The West has held what may well be a uniquely negative view of apes and monkeys at least since the Greco-Roman civilisation. Up through the Renaissance, scholars often quoted the dictum Cicero has attributed to Ennius in *De natura deorum*: *simia quam similis turpissima bestia nobis* ('The ape, vilest of beasts, so much resembles us').[29] The West has no simian culture heroes similar to Hanuman, who fights alongside Krishna in India or Old Monkey, who becomes a Buddha in China. It is a paradox that the evolutionary kinship of man and ape in evolution should have been discovered in precisely that part of the world where one might have expected it to encounter most resistance. Nowhere outside of Western culture has evolution been perceived as especially humbling to humankind.

For much of the Middle Ages, apes and monkeys in Western art were generally devils. These were, however, only vaguely simian figures which owed virtually nothing to observation and were based mostly on Greco-Roman mythological creatures such as satyrs or on Egyptian deities such as Thoth.[30] Tompkins observes that 'their dark, spidery bodies bristling with a vaguely sexualized menace ... seem to compress within itself everything in the natural world that was frightening or troubling to the Christian mind'.[31]

This changes around 1200, as macaques, imported and displayed to the public by travelling menageries, grow increasingly familiar.[32] Monkeys, since they were expensive and difficult to maintain, became a status symbol in the homes of aristocrats and some clergy, though other clergy railed against them as an indulgence.[33] In the drolleries, whimsical fantasies in the margins of illuminated manuscripts of the Middle Ages, monkeys were the animals depicted most frequently. They would be shown doing just about everything that people did, such as fighting with swords, jousting, dancing, playing bagpipes, or minding human babies, in a way that set a clear precedent for the anthropomorphised apes such as Baldy in zoos of the late nineteenth and early twentieth centuries.[34] Some of these pictures probably show acts by trained monkeys, which were taught to perform tricks such as somersaults and services such as collecting and eating lice.[35]

There is obviously a good deal of irony the illustrations, yet, as with apes like Baldy, it is not always clear at whom it is directed. Are the monkeys in illuminated manuscripts mocking human pretensions? Or is it the simians that are being mocked? In societies where weapons such as swords, activities such as hunting deer, and even the wearing of certain colours was prohibited to the peasantry, allowing monkeys to indulge in such acts freely could also have been a way of taunting the lower social orders. Perhaps, sometimes at least, the aristocrats were claiming a sort of solidarity with the natural world in their domination of the peasantry. Above all, however, the simians represent a primeval innocence, unimpeded by the bonds of law and social convention, like that of Adam before the Fall.

The monkeys of Eden

By the early modern period, the boundary between human beings and animals becomes a subject of contention, and zoomorphism becomes far more pronounced. Simians no longer represent demons but sinners.[36] Since, however, Christians related to God primarily as sinners, this made apes and monkeys into quintessential human beings. With sin came the possibility of redemption through repentance. Depictions of monkeys begin to take on complex, allegorical meanings, which are not easy to interpret, in the Renaissance and early modern periods. One example is a page from 'La Bible en Françoys', published by Verard Antoine in Paris around 1500 (Figure 12.3), which shows a scene of the Garden of Eden in a sphere that is emerging out of the root of a tree. Depicted in the centre of the sphere is the Tree of Knowledge, around which the serpent – which bears the torso and face of a woman – is coiled. On the left side of the tree is Adam and on the right is Eve, each of whom is holding an apple. A monkey eating an apple sits on the far right. Adam's gaze points to Eve, but both she and the serpent are looking over at the monkey. Eve is about to follow the example of the simian, after which Adam will copy her.

Figure 12.3 From the Bible initially published by Antoine Verard, 1510 edition. Courtesy Cambridge University Library.

The monkey is the major centre of attention here, not the first couple or the snake. The animal seems to bear much responsibility for the fall of humankind, yet there is nothing the least bit diabolical about it. On the contrary, the simian is portrayed with a good deal of affection. Its diminutive size suggests a child, and it could perhaps represent the future, the (somewhat degenerated) progeny of the first man and woman. The monkey, in other words, is all of us. The Fall is portrayed essentially as a natural event, without anguish or moralising. In the foreground in front of the tree is a panther, a traditional symbol of Christ, looking at Adam.[37]

This essential symbolism is made even more complex in an illustration to the Matthew Bible, first printed in 1537, by Erhard Altdorfer (Figure 12.4). Adam and Eve are sitting beneath an apple tree. Above them are two monkeys cavorting in the

Figure 12.4 Erhard Aldorfer, illustration showing Adam and Eve, from the Matthew Bible, first published in 1537.

Courtesy Cambridge University Library.

Figure 12.5 Jan Brueghel the Younger, 'Terrestrial Paradise', c.1620.

Courtesy Gemäldegalerie, Staatliche Museen zu Berlin, Preußischer Kulturbesitz, photographer Jörg P. Anders.

branches. The smaller monkey is giving an apple to the larger one, a very clear anticipation of original sin. God is looking down at the face of Adam, whose gaze is fixed on Eve. The first woman looks upward and points at a third monkey, smaller than the other two, which is hanging upside down from a branch.[38] That monkey seems to be an offspring of the simian couple, so perhaps Eve is asking Adam for a child. The way she is looking upwards suggests religious devotion, and, though the idea may at first seem blasphemous, it is not too far-fetched to see a symbolic relation between the baby monkey and Christ. It was, at any rate, entirely usual to view imagery of the natural world as a sort of book in which one might read religious parables.

Altdorfer may be the first landscape painter in Western art, and he was certainly among the first to consider the natural world an entirely worthy artistic subject. In his historical, religious, and mythological paintings, the trees and lakes in the background very often overshadow the human beings.[39] Like Eve in the woodcut, his attention very often turned away from people to the natural world. Perhaps he understood the biblical story of Eden as an allegory with significance that went beyond humankind to encompass animals and vegetation.

The depiction of simians by Jan Brueghel the Younger, unlike those of Verard and Altdorfer, is anthropomorphic, since it projects a human story onto a group of animals. A simian Adam and Eve possibly first appear in painting about 1620 in his 'Terrestrial Paradise' (Figure 12.5). It shows verdant forest in which the animals from lions to deer are living together peacefully in mated pairs. No human beings are present, but, in a high tree, one monkey is holding out an apple to her mate, as a red parrot, one of very few solitary animals in the picture, looks on.[40] All three animals are perched on a horizontal branch, and between the two monkeys rises a large twig, which resembles traditional depictions of the Tree of Knowledge. The two monkeys correspond to the first humans in the story of Eden, and they establish an iconographic pattern that will be repeated in many natural history books through at least the nineteenth century.

Man, ape, or satyr?

Throughout recorded history the status of human beings in relation to animals has been a point of ambiguity, and our own era is, in this respect, less different from previous ones than many people think.[41] Widely disseminated tales of talking animals and shape-changers in all eras have made human beings and animals appear to interact on an everyday basis. At the same time, there have been legal, religious, and traditional practices that differentiated radically between the human and animal realms. As long as the social order seemed relatively stable, and people believed it was ordained by God, questions of nomenclature were no more than intellectual exercises. But, as that order was increasingly questioned, these definitions increased in importance.

Before the work of Linnaeus in the early eighteenth century, there had been very little aspiration to a modern sort of scientific precision in the classification of animals and, for that matter, human beings. Designations were taken eclectically from old mythologies, biblical lore, traveller's tales, and observation. Labels such as 'human', 'wild man', 'ape', 'satyr', 'siren', and 'sphinx' were used fairly loosely, and they were not necessarily mutually exclusive. For many purposes, this informal system functioned pretty well, until explorers and traders created confusion by bringing back ever more accounts of exotic animals and people to Europe. Early modern culture faced a crisis of language that was, in many ways, similar to what we are experiencing today, as we struggle to make sense of a world in which robots are taking over many traditional roles of human beings. The old vocabularies were inadequate to integrate the new information. Reports constantly confused indigenous people, apes, and legendary creatures.

Early modern descriptions of apes reflect this consternation. The scientific study of simians dates from 1641, when the body of an ape was dissected by the Dutch anatomist Nicolaas Tulp. It may have been a chimpanzee, since he states that it came from Angola, but the picture that accompanied his description looks far more like an orangutan. He found that the anatomy of the creature was, in most respects, nearly identical to that of human beings, but concluded that it was the satyr of Greek mythology, because such creatures in Borneo reportedly captured and ravished women.[42]

The binomial classification of Linnaeus, in which all living things were included in a single system of hierarchic classification, was intended to banish such confusion by placing creatures in an unambiguous order, which would show the wisdom of God. Apes and human beings, however, did not seem to fit easily into his system of classification. Linnaeus troubled many of his contemporaries simply by including humankind in his taxonomy at all, thereby acknowledging that people are animals, but his love of order took precedence over his belief in human exceptionalism. Leaving men and women out would have made it impossible to address questions of human identity.

In the tenth edition of his *Systema Natura* (1758), which laid the foundation for modern taxonomy, Linnaeus classified human beings as primates, together with apes, monkeys, and bats. He further divided people into *Homo sapiens*, or people with knowledge, and *Homo troglodytes*, or cave dwellers. *Homo sapiens* was further divided into five subspecies. In addition to the Asian, European, American, and African varieties, there was an additional category called *Homo sapiens monstrosus*, which could accommodate any anthropoid figures that did not fit neatly into the other classes, such as Patagonian giants, people with birth defects, and, quite possibly, some apes.[43] *Systema Natura* may have changed the terms of the debates, yet it did nothing to alleviate the confusion.

Zoomorphic humans

At least until the early modern period, simians are conspicuously absent from most paintings of scenes such as Noah's Ark or the Garden of Eden, in which artists tried to show an inventory of the animal kingdom.[44] The reason for this absence is probably that artists felt they were already implicit in the human figures, in Noah, Adam, and Eve. While the relationship may not have been formally codified as a point of taxonomy, people intuitively felt that simians were not entirely distinct from men and women.

The idea of kinship between human beings and apes goes back to very early times, and observation of simians formed the basis of legends of giants, wild men, and other folkloric figures. Mythological figures such as satyrs, cynocephali, and sphinxes that were basically human in form have often been considered apes. According to many legends, simians were human beings that had degenerated or been punished for bad behaviour. In one, they were people who built the Tower of Babel, and then ran into the forest as it collapsed. In another, Enos, Adam's grandson, was punished by God for idolatry by being given the features of an ape, which were then passed on to his descendants.[45] In many legends from Northern Europe, Adam originally had a tail. In a story from the Talmud, God simply removes Adam's tail to increase his majesty by setting him apart from the animals. In some legends, Eve is made from Adam's tail rather from his rib, an idea used to explain why women are supposedly more bestial than men.[46]

The early modern shoemaker and folk poet Hans Sachs wrote that the apes were the result of a failed attempt to imitate the miracles of Jesus, when a smith placed his mother-in-law in a furnace and then doused the flames with water, believing this would make her young again. Her screams terrified members of her family, who, together with the elderly woman, all turned into apes.[47] Such tales are zoomorphic in that they transfer the behaviour and appearance of animals, in this case apes, to certain human beings. They regard the boundary between human beings and animals as being easily permeable, and consider human status as something that can only be maintained through vigilance.

One early work which combines anthropomorphic representation of animals with zoomorphic depiction of human beings is *Gulliver's Travels* by Jonathan Swift, first published in 1726–35. One of his journeys takes the hero, Gulliver, to the island ruled by talking horses called 'Houyhnhnms', who are notable for their high level of civilisation and generosity. Living alongside them are savage humans known as 'Yahoos', who wallow in filth and constantly fight over stones. Gulliver is taken under the protection of a horse, which becomes his 'master', and then attends a meeting where Houyhnhnms, debate whether to exterminate the Yahoos. One of those in attendance alleges that 'the Yahoos were the most filthy, noisome, and deformed animal that nature ever produced'.[48] The Yahoos were inspired by reports of 'primitive' people in exotic lands, and Swift was saying, in effect, that the level of civilisation rather than species determined the worth of a creature, and an animal such as a domestic horse counted for more than a savage.

Westerners of pre-modern times generally viewed history as a gradual process of degeneration that would lead ultimately to an apocalypse. In the latter eighteenth and through to about the mid-twentieth century, this progression, for many people at least, was turned around, becoming the ideal of progress. All along, people generally assumed that apes were similar yet inferior to human beings. If the world was getting worse, humans were becoming apes; if it was improving, apes were becoming human. When the outcome appeared uncertain, you might find elements of both.

For artists such as Altdorfer, zoomorphic representation of apes had been a means to comment on the universal human condition. Over the next several centuries it increasingly became a way of denigrating people, especially those of certain races or ethnicities. Black Africans were especially often portrayed with simian features, and so, to an extent, were East Asians, Germans, Jews and many other groups of people.[49] But, according to Curtis, in England,

> By the 1860s no respectable reader of the comic weeklies ... could possibly mistake the sinuous nose, long upper lip, huge projecting mouth, and jutting jaws as well as the sloping forehead for any other category of undesirable or dangerous human being than that known as Irish.[50]

For the most part, the caricatures of 'Negroes' in the American South or of the Irish in the English press were not very different from the anthropomorphised monkeys and apes of the modern era (Figure 12.6). All of these were frequently portrayed dancing, playing musical instruments, idling about, getting drunk, and fighting. While there were clear differences in emphasis, both the simian parodies and the racial stereotypes appeared to go about normal human activities without the accompanying cares, and both were viewed with a blend of scorn and muted admiration. But this sort of patronisation could easily give way to hatred. During World War II the Nazis depicted the races they considered 'degenerate' with simian features, while Americans portrayed the Japanese as monkeys.[51]

Figure 12.6. 'The ballot box of the future', cartoon from *The Day's Doings*, a newspaper published in London and sold in the United States, 1870.

Author's collection.

Anthropomorphic apes

From a zoomorphic perspective, apes and monkeys would be degenerate human beings, but, from an anthropomorphic point of view, they would be either primitive ones or children. In the Modern Period, the representation of monkeys would grow increasingly anthropomorphic. Artists would give monkeys and apes ever more attributes of human beings, though in ways that always accentuated, and virtually never placed in question, the inferior status of those simians.

The tradition of extreme anthropomorphism in the depiction of simians, established in drolleries of the late Middle Ages, expanded to other forms. In the rococo style of the eighteenth century, centred at the French court, simians were viewed essentially as playful, mischievous children. Pet monkeys were often portrayed in gardens or even in homes, to suggest a charming, if ultimately futile, revolt against the more stifling norms of society.[52] Depictions of apes and monkeys wearing clothes and engaged in human activities remained common in a variety of genres such as murals and Dutch tiles. In the early eighteenth century, the Meissen porcelain works in Dresden established a fashion for miniature sculptures of monkeys in the wigs and elegant jackets of aristocrats, playing musical instruments and dancing.[53]

As people began to think of history in terms of progress rather than decline, they increasingly portrayed apes as striving toward the condition of humanity (Figure 12.7). Just as the fruit suggested degeneration, a walking stick, enabling a primate to stand upright, suggested an aspiration toward evolutionary 'improvement'. Many, perhaps most, apes in illustrations from books of natural history of the latter eighteenth through to the mid-nineteenth centuries maintain human posture with the assistance of a cane. Occasionally, an ape will have a staff in one hand and a fruit in the other, as though to acknowledge the possibilities of both progress and decadence.

The motif of a simian Adam and Eve would appear regularly in illustrations to popular books of natural history throughout the Victorian era (Figure 12.8). The couple might be chimpanzees, orangutans, tamarins, howler monkeys, or any other variety of primate.[54] The smaller primate would have a more cunning expression and be holding out an apple, at times even offering it to the larger one. As the controversy about evolution in the nineteenth century intensified, the idea of Adam and Eve as apes combined the biblical and evolutionary perspectives. According to Corbey, 'By the nineteenth century, apes had begun to take over Adam's ancestral role'.[55] As Haraway puts it, 'Implicitly and explicitly, the story of the Garden of Eden emerges in the sciences of monkeys and apes, along with versions of the origins of society, marriage, and language'.[56] It is hard to know to what extent the religious references were conscious, but they probably comforted people by placing the relatively innovative idea of evolution in a familiar context. In assuming Adam's position as the progenitor of humankind, apes and monkeys inevitably also took over symbolism, themes, and motifs from the biblical story of the first couple. Most especially, attention to primates focused on loss of primeval innocence and acquisition of knowledge.

An apex of anthropomorphism came, as we have seen, in the late nineteenth and early twentieth centuries, when zoos constantly displayed simians clothed and engaged in human activities. That tradition was revived briefly in the 1970s, when efforts to teach human language to apes produced a generation of simian celebrities similar to those in zoos around the start of the twentieth century. Perhaps the most popular of

Figure 12.7 Illustration to Captain Cook's *Voyages*, 1785.
Author's collection.

Figure 12.8 Howler monkeys in the role of Adam and Eve. Illustration to *Geographical Distribution of Animals* by Adam White, 1867.
Author's collection.

these was Nim Chimpsky, whose role as a mediator between the human and bestial worlds makes him especially reminiscent of Baldy. Nim was raised as a human being, fed human food, dressed in human clothes, and imperfectly toilet-trained, before Herbert S. Terrace at Columbia University attempted to teach him a variant of American Sign Language. When his trainers reported dramatic initial success, Nim became a media star, and was also drawn into a vortex of personal feuds and academic politics. Eventually, Terrace concluded that Nim was mechanically repeating signs without understanding, and withdrew his original claims.[57] As researchers scaled back their initial contentions about the linguistic ability of apes, public interest in them also faded.[58]

Evolution

In the latter nineteenth century, there was a relatively brief return to the early medieval practice of showing apes as demonic, in reaction against Darwin's theory of evolution. The gorilla, especially, was often shown as a vicious monster, capable of killing indiscriminately and even raping human women.[59] Apart from this, however, the immediate impact of evolutionary theory on the depiction of apes, monkeys, and human beings is not easily apparent.[60] Many had already, as we have seen, generally thought of the boundary between humans and animals as permeable. Several thinkers such as Aelian, Plutarch, and Montaigne had already questioned, or at least significantly qualified, the idea of human superiority long before Darwin, and the theory of evolution did not immediately lead to any dramatic increase in such scepticism.[61] If human beings were animals, they had to be superior animals, the most 'advanced' on the proverbial 'scale of evolution'.[62]

Any doubts about human superiority were initially overpowered by the excitement that people felt at dramatic changes. When Darwin published his *On the Origin of Species* in 1859, steam power was transforming daily life, railroads were starting to link major urban centres, European colonial empires were expanding, and confidence in human progress was near an apex in the West. It would not be until around the end of the twentieth century that, facing the prospect of ecological disaster, many people would begin to seriously question the idea of human superiority.

Darwin, for all his importance as a scientist, was in ways a fairly typical Victorian gentleman who took the 'civilising' mission of the British Empire for granted. In his book *The Descent of Man*, we find the combination of anthropomorphism and zoomorphism that runs through modern culture, as he repeatedly contrasts the moral and intellectual refinement of certain animals, especially dogs and monkeys, with the crudeness of indigenous peoples. The book concludes,

> For my part, I would as soon be descended from that heroic little monkey who braved his dreaded enemy in order to save the life of his keeper . . . as from a savage who delights in torture of his enemies . . . and is haunted by the grossest superstitions.[63]

Beyond anthropocentrism

The display of Benga had been, or at least was sometimes rationalised as, an attempt to show the kinship of man and ape in Darwin's theory of evolution, and that surely applies to Baldy as well.[64] The nervous titters and slapstick routines that accompanied both exhibitions suggest that the zoo authorities and the public may have felt greater anthropological anxiety than they were aware of. Both exhibitions, especially that of Baldy, came on the eve of World War I, which marked the start of a gradual but intense disillusion with the idea of human exceptionalism, though it would often resurface in both open and covert ways.[65]

Both Benga and Baldy had been, at least since they were taken to the zoo, profoundly alienated figures, cut off from their original environments yet unable to adapt to their new one. The contexts in which they were exhibited were designed not to alleviate that alienation but to dramatise it. Benga was deprived of his humanity, while Baldy was severed from his simian character. Both were called 'zookeepers', but if Benga had only worn a uniform while Baldy had done without one, the displays would not have been nearly so dramatic. Their popularity may owe much to the way in which visitors to the zoo saw their own alienation as human beings from nature mirrored in the solitary figures. Although this was certainly not a matter of conscious intent, the exhibits may echo a religious paradigm that had been passed on over millennia. Within the world of zoo animals, Benga and later Baldy represented the human race, assigned dominion over lesser creatures, a bit like the Biblical Adam.

In summary, both zoomorphism and anthropomorphism are ways in which, after dividing the cosmos into the human realm or 'civilisation', ruled by autonomous choices, and nature, ruled by instinct and necessity, we create hybrid identities. Zoomorphism absorbs animals, or 'animalistic' traits, into the human sphere; anthropomorphism projects human traits into the natural realm. There is nothing fundamentally wrong with either of these processes, particularly when indulged in moderation, but in practice they are usually predicated on absurdly simplified notions of both human beings and animals.

Traditions that go back at least to the eighteenth century maintained that 'man is the tool-using animal'.[66] Researchers then very belatedly, in the later twentieth century, discovered the use and even the creation of tools by many other creatures such as apes, crows, and octopuses. In consequence, we raised the status of those creatures and started to think of them as at least partially 'human'. But the definition of 'man' as a 'tool-using animal' was, from the beginning, preposterously simplistic. It might, had it been accurate, set us somewhat apart from other beings, but it could not possibly have done any justice to the intricate blend of qualities that really do make human beings special. When we then partially extend this stereotypical definition to other animals, we inevitably stereotype them as well.

We may also say, following the tradition of Descartes, that, man is the animal with language. That claim has never been very widely accepted, and has now, at least in its extreme forms, been refuted in so many ways that it seems redundant even to list them. We not only share language with animals from vervet monkeys to ravens but also with computers and strands of DNA. A scholar might consider the electric impulses released by many fish, the colour changes of many lizards, and the chemical signals of many plants to be language, in that they can disseminate information with considerable precision.

But let us suppose for a moment that the definition of 'man' as the only animal with language were accurate. It would still do no justice whatsoever to the richness and complexity of human identity. What makes us special is not language so much as the things that we say by means of it. Following Chomsky, one might modify the initial definition and say that the unique feature of human beings is our grammar.[67] If true, it does not have the cosmic significance that polemicists for or against Chomsky (though not Chomsky himself) at times ascribe to it. While a remarkable ability, the use of grammar conveys no more superiority than the strength and suppleness of a spider's thread. When we base claims of status on such narrow criteria, we trivialise our human identity. If we then extend those claims to other creatures such as apes, we belittle them as well.

Zoomorphic hybrids are based on similarly stereotypical understandings. Suppose, for example, somebody calls a group of people 'apes'. Theoretically, this could mean all sorts of things, and by no means all of them are insulting. It might simply mean that the people in question are good at climbing or very strong. In practice, however, the words are certain to be understood in a derogatory way. We would take them to mean the individuals are crude, foolish, and impulsive.

We now seem to be as incapable as ever of viewing apes and monkeys as anything but incomplete human beings. We make a great deal of fuss, for example, about their tool use, but, while more sophisticated than many researchers had once anticipated, this is still an area in which people vastly excel them. The amazing leaps of gibbons among branches in the forest canopy, which no human being in his right mind would even attempt, are at least as impressive as elementary use of tools, yet human beings give gibbons very little credit for them.

We might do more justice to both other species and our own by viewing human beings as an amalgamation of features that are complex, elusive, mysterious, and utterly unique, yet impossible to capture in a simple formula. Humanity, in this sense, is in perpetual flux, and neither good nor bad. We might regard other creatures from monkeys to octopuses and butterflies in a similar way, without trying to reduce their existence to any single quality. There is nothing wrong with taking a degree of collective pride in our linguistic ability as human beings. If we can only do it without triumphalism and/or orgies of guilt, identifying the unique qualities of our species may help us to find our place in the community of living things. We should not judge people according to their resemblance to animals, nor animals by their similarity to human beings.

This, in my opinion, was intended by Pico della Mirandola in his *Oration on the Dignity of Man* of 1486, the original manifesto of Humanism, when, citing a Chaldean proverb, he proclaimed, 'Man is a living creature of varied, multiform, and ever-changing nature'.[68] This is clearly a description, not a definition by exclusion. Would Pico have extended this to other creatures such as apes or octopuses? My impression is that he would, though, because of Pico's cryptic style, that is not entirely clear. At any rate, we certainly can, and that would make both us and other living things a lot more interesting.

Notes

1 This chapter incorporates material from my review essay entitled 'The cost of human exceptionalism (review of *Spectacle: The Astonishing Life of Ota Benga* by Pamela Newkirk)', published in *Humanimalia* 7, 1 (2015) and available online at www.goo.gl/aAWrqc, accessed 24 August 2015. I would like to thank my wife, Linda Sax, for her help in editing

this chapter and for useful suggestions. It was she who first noticed the religious symbolism in some of the pictures of apes that I had collected from books of natural history.
2 P. Newkirk, *Spectacle: The Astonishing Life of Ota Benga*, New York: HarperCollins, 2015, 3–78; P.V. Bradford and H. Blume, *Ota: The Pygmy in the Zoo*, New York: St. Martin's Press, 1992, 179–204.
3 'Baldy also a Missing Link', *The Daily Reflector*, 11 February 1910, 1.
4 Bradford and Blume, *Ota*, 183.
5 These examples of ways in which simians were displayed are all depicted on postcards printed by prominent zoos in the latter eighteenth and early nineteenth centuries, which are in my private collection. The last example given may have been copied by keepers from displays in Britain and Continental Europe, where such shows were called 'chimpanzee tea parties'. See D. Hancocks, 'Zoo animals as entertainment exhibitions', in R. Malamud (ed.), *A Cultural History of Animals in the Modern Age*, Oxford: Berg, 2011, 95–118, 102–106.
6 '"Baldy" hits "Babe" with chair; reduced to nurse, he repents', *Portsmouth Daily Times*, 10 October 1910, 3.
7 Newkirk, *Spectacle*, 47, 50, 209–210. There are confused and contradictory accounts as to whether or to what extent Benga was held captive. We have no photographs of the enclosure where he was on display, and the issue may never be clarified entirely. For a rebuttal of the claims that he was held prisoner, see: M.S. Gabriel, 'Ota Benga having a fine time', *New York Times*, 13 September 1906, 6.
8 'Ape dislikes garb: simian protests against wearing guard's uniform; simian "Baldy" begins to disrobe in tree as big crowd follows and cheers', *The Goshen Mid-Week News-Times*, 3 October 1911, 7.
9 'Taft mits monkey at Bronx Zoo: feeds elephants and sees Roosevelt rhinoceros', *The Boston Post*, 24 May 1911, 16.
10 Newkirk, *Spectacle*, 242–246.
11 'The anthropoids', *New York Zoological Society Bulletin* 43, 1 (1914): 1078.
12 'Baldy of Bronx Zoo dead', *New York Times*, 21 January 1914, 7.
13 H. Ritvo, *The Animal Estate: The English and Other Creatures in Victorian England*, Cambridge MA: Harvard University Press, 1989, 205–242.
14 B. Sax, *Imaginary Animals: The Monstrous, the Wondrous and the Human*, London: Reaktion Books, 2013, 27–28; K.A. Menninger, 'Totemic aspects of contemporary attitudes towards animals', in G.B. Wilbur and W. Munsterberger (eds.), *Psychoanalysis and Culture*, New York: International Universities Press, 1951, 42–74, 62–63.
15 W. Blunt, *The Ark in the Park: The Zoo in the Nineteenth Century*, London: Hamish Hamilton/Tyron Gallery, 1976, 226; D. Rybot, *It Began Before Noah*, London: Michael Joseph, 1972, 145–146.
16 E. Fudge, *Perceiving Animals: Humans and Beasts in Early Modern English Culture*, Chicago IL: University of Illinois Press, 2000, 4–8.
17 E.J. Silverman, 'Anthropocentrism and the medieval problem of religious language', in R. Boddice (ed.), *Anthropocentrism: Humans, Animals, Environments*, London: Berg, 2011, 117–138, 117–134.
18 E.D. Jonge, 'An alternative to anthropocentrism: deep ecology and the metaphysical turn', in Boddice, *Anthropocentrism*, 307–320, 307–311.
19 T. Milligan, 'Speciesism as a variety of anthropocentrism', in Boddice, *Anthropocentrism*, 223–243, 223–226.
20 P. Descola, *Beyond Nature and Culture*, Chicago IL: University of Chicago Press, 2013, 91–231.
21 B. Latour, *We Have Never Been Modern*, trans. C. Porter, Cambridge MA: Harvard University Press, 1993, 10–59.

22 B. Sax, *The Frog King: Occidental Fables, Fairy Tales, and Anecdotes of Animals*, New York: Pace University Press, 1990, 126.
23 L. Kalof, *Looking at Animals in Human History*, London: Reaktion, 2007, 14–15.
24 B. Sax, 'Animals in folklore', in L. Kalof (ed.), *Oxford Handbook of Animal Studies*, Oxford: Oxford University Press, 2017, 456–474.
25 Aristotle, *Politics*, Indianapolis IN: Hackett, 1998 [c.325 BCE], 2–5.
26 Sax, *Imaginary Animals*, 95–129.
27 R. Descartes, *Discourse on Method and the Meditations*, New York: Penguin, 1968 [1637], 142–149.
28 H. Ritvo, 'Animal consciousness: some historical perspective', *American Zoologist* 40, 6 (2000): 847–852, 850.
29 H.W. Janson, *Apes and Ape Lore, in the Middle Ages and Renaissance*, London: Warburg Institute, University of London, 1952, 9.
30 L. Lorenzi, *Devils in Art: Florence, From the Middle Ages to the Renaissance*, Florence: Centro Di, second edition, 2006, 130.
31 P. Tompkins, *Monkeys in Art*, New York: M.T.Tain/Scala Books, 1994, 28–29.
32 Janson, *Apes and Ape Lore*, 30.
33 K. Walker-Meikle, *Medieval Pets*, Woodbridge: Boydell Press, 2012, 13–14.
34 Tompkins, *Monkeys in Art*, 33–37.
35 Kalof, *Looking at Animals*, 64. Walker-Meikle, *Medieval Pets*, 14.
36 Tompkins, *Monkeys in Art*, 30.
37 Tompkina, *Monkeys in Art*, plate XVI.
38 Janson, *Apes and Ape Lore*, plate XIXa, 128. Note that Janson misreads the direction of Eve's gaze and mistakenly thinks she is pointing to the monkey couple.
39 J. Guillaud and M. Guillaud, *Altdorfer and Fantastic Realism in German Art*, New York: Rizzoli, 1985, 35–36.
40 L. Impelluso, *La Natura e i suoi Simboli*, Milan: Mondadori Electra, 2004, 193.
41 For a discussion of the apparent contradictions in contemporary attitudes towards animals, see: H. Herzog, *Some We Love, Some We Hate, Some We Eat: Why It's So Hard to Think Straight about Animals*, New York: HarperCollins, 2010.
42 J. Marks, *What it Means to be 98% Chimpanzee: Apes, People, and Their Genes*, Los Angeles CA: University of California Press, 2002, 5–17.
43 Marks, *What it Means to be 98% Chimpanzee*.
44 To check this observation, on 8–10 June 2015, I counted the number of simians in pictures of Noah's Ark that had been placed online by the following museums: the Metropolitan Museum of Art (New York), the National Gallery of Art (Washington DC), the Boston Museum of Fine Arts, the Rijksmuseum (Amsterdam), the Louvre (Paris), and the Tate Gallery (London). In pictures showing the animals in Noah's Ark before 1600, I found 51 without simians and only one with them.
45 Janson, *Apes and Ape Lore*, 94–97.
46 Janson, *Apes and Ape Lore*, 134–135.
47 H. Sachs, 'Ursprung der affen', *Hans Sachsens Augewählte Werke*, I, 1940 [c.1530], 166–171, 168–171.
48 J. Swift, *Gulliver's Travels*, New York: Barnes & Noble, 2003 [1735], 307–308.
49 L. Boia, *Entre l'Ange et la Bête: Le Mythe de l'Homme Différent de l'Antiquité à Nos Jours*, Paris: Plon, 1995, 127–130.
50 L.P. Curtis, *Apes and Angels: The Irishman in Victorian Caricature*, second edition, Washington DC: Smithsonian, 1971, 29.
51 B. Sax, *Animals in the Third Reich*, second edition, Providence RI: Yogh & Thorn, 2013, 37–46.

52 Tompkins, *Monkeys in Art*, 60–80.
53 Tompkins, *Monkeys in Art*, 60–79.
54 I have personally collected illustrations from books of natural history, mostly from the latter nineteenth century, in which a simian couple resembling Adam and Eve takes on all of these forms.
55 R. Corbey, *The Metaphysics of Apes: Negotiating the Animal–Human Boundary*, Cambridge: Cambridge University Press, 2005, 47.
56 D.J. Haraway, *Primate Visions: Gender, Race, and Nature in the World of Modern Science*, New York: Routledge, 1989, 9.
57 For a biography of Nim Chimpsky, see: E. Hess, *Nim Chimpsky: The Chimp Who Would Be Human*, New York: Bantam/Dell, 2008.
58 Though the ambitions have been drastically scaled back since the 1970s, researchers continue to experiment with teaching human language to apes. The consensus among scientists is that their ability to comprehend grammar is very limited. For a review of this research, see: C.D.L. Wynne and M.A.R. Udell, *Animal Cognition: Evolution, Behavior and Cognition*, second edition, New York: Palgrave Macmillan, 2013, 277–291.
59 Sax, *Animals in the Third Reich*, 39.
60 R. Preece, 'Thoughts out of season on the history of animal ethics', *Society and Animals*, 15, 4 (2007): 365–378, 371–376.
61 Sax, *Imaginary Animals*, 73–74.
62 The model used to enhance the status of human beings in relation to other animals was the 'great chain of being', which goes back at least to Plato, in which all living things from plants to archangels were ranked in an ascending order of spirituality. As the ideas of Darwin gained acceptance, this was interpreted in a temporal way as a status determined by the degree of evolutionary progress toward perfection. For a detailed discussion of this process, see: A.O. Lovejoy, *The Great Chain of Being*, Cambridge MA: Harvard University Press, 1984.
63 E.J. Larson, *Evolution: The Remarkable History of a Scientific Theory*, New York: The Modern Library, 2004, 97–100.
64 Newkirk, *Spectacle*, 46.
65 For a discussion of 'anthropological anxiety', see V. Richter, *Literature After Darwin: Human Beasts in Western Fiction 1859–1939*, New York: Palgrave Macmillan, 2011, 8.
66 L. Winner, 'Resistance is futile: the posthuman condition and its advocates', in H.W. Baillie and T.K. Casey (eds.), *Is Human Nature Obsolete? Genetics, Bioengineering, and the Future of the Human Condition*, Cambridge MA: MIT Press, 2005, 385–411, 394–395.
67 N. Chomsky, *Language and Mind*, third edition, Cambridge: Cambridge University Press, 2006, 88–101.
68 G. Pico della Mirandola, *Oration on the Dignity of Man*, Washington DC: Gateway, 2012 [1486], 13.

References

Aristotle, *Politics*, Indianapolis IN: Hackett, 1998.
Blunt, W. *The Ark in the Park: The Zoo in the Nineteenth Century*, London: Hamish Hamilton/ Tyron Gallery, 1976.
Boia, L. *Entre l'Ange et la Bête: Le Mythe de l'Homme Différent de l'Antiquité à Nos Jours*, Paris: Plon, 1995.
Bradford, P.V. and H. Blume, *Ota: The Pygmy in the Zoo*, New York: St. Martin's Press, 1992.
Chomsky, N. *Language and Mind*, third edition, Cambridge: Cambridge University Press, 2006.

Corbey, R. *The Metaphysics of Apes: Negotiating the Animal–Human Boundary*, Cambridge: Cambridge University Press, 2005.
Curtis, L.P. *Apes and Angels: The Irishman in Victorian Caricature*, second edition, Washington DC: Smithsonian, 1971.
Descartes, R. *Discourse on Method and the Meditations*, New York: Penguin, 1968.
Descola, P. *Beyond Nature and Culture*, Chicago IL: University of Chicago Press, 2013.
Fudge, E. *Perceiving Animals: Humans and Beasts in Early Modern English Culture*, Chicago IL: University of Illinois Press, 2000.
Guillaud, J. and Guillaud, M. *Altdorfer and Fantastic Realism in German Art*, New York: Rizzoli, 1985.
Hancocks, D. 'Zoo animals as entertainment exhibitions', in R. Malamud (ed.), *A Cultural History of Animals in the Modern Age*, Oxford: Berg, 2011, 95–118.
Haraway, D.J. *Primate Visions: Gender, Race, and Nature in the World of Modern Science*, New York: Routledge, 1989.
Herzog, H. *Some We Love, Some We Hate, Some We Eat: Why It's So Hard to Think Straight about Animals*, New York: HarperCollins, 2010.
Hess, E. *Nim Chimpsky: The Chimp Who Would Be Human*, New York: Bantam/Dell, 2008.
Impelluso, L. *La Natura e i suoi Simboli*, Milan: Mondadori Electra, 2004, 193.
Janson, H.W. *Apes and Ape Lore, in the Middle Ages and Renaissance*, London: Warburg Institute, University of London, 1952.
Jonge, E.D. 'An alternative to anthropocentrism: deep ecology and the metaphysical turn', in R. Boddice (ed.), *Anthropocentrism: Humans, Animals, Environments*, London: Berg, 2011, 307–320.
Kalof, L. *Looking at Animals in Human History*, London: Reaktion, 2007.
Larson, E.J. *Evolution: The Remarkable History of a Scientific Theory*, New York: The Modern Library, 2004.
Latour, B. *We Have Never Been Modern*, trans. C. Porter, Cambridge MA: Harvard University Press, 1993.
Lorenzi, L. *Devils in Art: Florence, From the Middle Ages to the Renaissance*, second edition, Florence: Centro Di, 2006.
Lovejoy, A.O. *The Great Chain of Being*, Cambridge MA: Harvard University Press, 1984.
Marks, J. *What it Means to be 98% Chimpanzee: Apes, People, and Their Genes*, Los Angeles CA: University of California Press, 2002.
Menninger, K.A. 'Totemic aspects of contemporary attitudes towards animals', in G.B. Wilbur and W. Munsterberger (eds.), *Psychoanalysis and Culture*, New York: International Universities Press, 1951, 42–74.
Milligan, T. 'Speciesism as a variety of anthropocentrism', in R. Boddice (ed.), *Anthropocentrism: Humans, Animals, Environments*, London: Berg, 2011, 223–243.
Newkirk, P. *Spectacle: The Astonishing Life of Ota Benga*, New York: HarperCollins, 2015.
Pico della Mirandola, G. *Oration on the Dignity of Man*, Washington DC: Gateway, 2012 [1486].
Preece, R. 'Thoughts out of season on the history of animal ethics', *Society and Animals* 15, 4 (2007): 365–378.
Richter, V. *Literature After Darwin: Human Beasts in Western Fiction 1859–1939*, New York: Palgrave Macmillan, 2011.
Ritvo, H. *The Animal Estate: The English and Other Creatures in Victorian England*, Cambridge MA: Harvard University Press, 1989.
Ritvo, H. 'Animal consciousness: some historical perspective', *American Zoologist* 40, 6 (2000): 847–852.
Rybot, D. *It Began Before Noah*, London: Michael Joseph, 1972.

Sachs, H. 'Ursprung der affen', *Hans Sachsens Augewählte Werke*, I, 1940 [c.1530], 166–171.
Sax, B. *The Frog King: Occidental Fables, Fairy Tales, and Anecdotes of Animals*, New York: Pace University Press, 1990.
Sax, B. *Animals in the Third Reich*, second edition, Providence RI: Yogh & Thorn, 2013.
Sax, B. *Imaginary Animals: The Monstrous, the Wondrous and the Human*, London: Reaktion Books, 2013.
Sax, 'Animals in folklore', in L. Kalof (ed.), *Oxford Handbook of Animal Studies*, Oxford: Oxford University Press, 2017, 456–474.
Silverman, E.J. 'Anthropocentrism and the medieval problem of religious language' in R. Boddice (ed.), *Anthropocentrism: Humans, Animals, Environments*, London: Berg, 2011, 117–138.
Swift, J. *Gulliver's Travels*, New York: Barnes & Noble, 2003 [1735].
Tompkins, P. *Monkeys in Art*, New York: M.T.Tain/Scala Books, 1994, 28–29.
Walker-Meikle, K. *Medieval Pets*, Woodbridge: Boydell Press, 2012, 13–14.
Winner, L. 'Resistance is futile: the posthuman condition and its advocates', in H.W. Baillie and T.K.Casey (eds.), *Is Human Nature Obsolete? Genetics, Bioengineering, and the Future of the Human Condition*, Cambridge MA: MIT Press, 2005, 385–411, 394–395.
Wynne, C.D.L. and Udell, M.A.R. *Animal Cognition: Evolution, Behavior and Cognition*, second edition, New York: Palgrave Macmillan, 2013.

13
EXHIBITING ANIMALS
Zoos, menageries and circuses

Helen Cowie

Introduction

Exotic animals have long fascinated human beings. For thousands of years they have been collected and exhibited in menageries and zoological gardens. They have been paraded, studied and trained to perform, functioning by turns as symbols of monarchical or imperial power, items of trade, subjects for scientific enquiry and sources of entertainment.[1]

In the twenty-first century, zoos and menageries are often the focus of criticism. Zoos justify their continued existence by stressing their contributions to animal conservation and public education. Animal welfare organisations contest these claims, suggesting that keeping animals in captivity is cruel and that zoos in fact contribute little to the survival of endangered species. Conditions for animals in travelling circuses are generally assumed to be even worse, with various undercover investigations revealing the abuse of animals in training. In Britain there was a public outcry when video footage was released showing an elephant named Anne being brutally beaten by her keeper at Bobby Roberts Circus, intensifying calls for a ban on the use of wild animals in circuses.[2] These ongoing debates about the current status of exotic animal exhibitions have shaped the study of zoos and menageries in the past, influencing the kinds of histories that have been written about them.

Why study the history of exotic animal collections, and what kinds of questions have historians asked about zoos? Until relatively recently, most zoo histories were institutional biographies, often written by zoo professionals. These works charted the development of particular zoos or circuses and tended to tell a story of gradual progress over time, with larger enclosures and improved architecture leading to better conditions for captive animals.[3] In more recent years, critical studies of zoos have appeared, challenging the Whiggish narrative of these earlier histories. Some of these are explicitly anti-zoo in their approach, influenced by the growing animal rights movement.[4] Others are less overtly political, posing new questions about zoological institutions and situating them within broader historical fields, from the history of empire to the history of leisure.[5] The zoo has thus become a prism through which to study wider aspects of human culture, attracting the attention of historians of empire, social and cultural historians and historians of science.

In what follows, I outline some of the most important historical approaches to the study of zoos and menageries and situate these within the wider history of animals. I begin by exploring the role of zoos as symbols of power and sources of knowledge, before going on to consider the particular place of zoos within broader debates over animal welfare. The chapter concludes with a discussion of animal agency, and the specific ways in which zoo animals might inform this debate.

Power

A recurrent theme in the history of zoos and menageries has been the relationship between exotic animals and different forms of power. Historians have seen zoos as symbols, on the one hand, of human control over the natural world, and, on the other, of control over other humans, be they European subjects or colonial peoples.[6] Though the form and content of menageries has changed over time, these functions have remained to the fore, mediating interactions with exotic animals. As Randy Malamud observes, 'Founding and operating a zoo involves both real and metaphorical appropriative control of the earth: of nature, land and habitat, and of animals taken from natural habitats, subjugated and recontextualized in a way that upholds the captors' self-serving ideologies'.[7]

In the medieval and early modern periods, exotic animals often functioned as diplomatic currency. Embodying the novel and the rare, they were exchanged between monarchs as symbols of deference or allegiance, serving as valued gifts alongside spices, perfumes and precious metals. In 1235, for instance, the Holy Roman Emperor, Frederick II, presented Henry III of England with three leopards for his Tower of London menagerie.[8] In 1515, the Sultan of Cambay gifted a rhinoceros to the Governor of Goa, Afonso de Albuquerque, which he in turn presented to Manuel I of Portugal.[9] The association of these animals with distant and little-known places contributed heavily to their attraction, while the sheer difficulty of transporting them alive to Europe further enhanced their appeal. An elephant sent to Charles III of Spain by the Governor of the Philippines in 1773 required a daily ration of '85 quartillos of water, 24 pounds of rice, 6 pounds of sugar, 2 rations of wine, 2 and a half ordinary rations of bread and 4 servings of bananas' during its six-month voyage to Cádiz – a diet few but royalty could have afforded.[10]

If the ability to acquire such coveted species attested to the power of monarchs and nobles, their potency was further underlined by the settings in which they showcased their living possessions. As evidence of their control over the natural world – and, by extension, their subjects – some princes used their exotic animals in grandiose processions or deployed them in bloody baits for the entertainment of their courts. James I of England, for example, organised fights between the lions in the Tower of London and several English mastiffs.[11] Manuel I ordered his newly arrived rhino to be pitted against an elephant in Lisbon's Terreiro do Paço to test out the long-held belief that the two species were enemies.[12] As the seventeenth century wore on, such visceral displays of power became less common, and well-stocked menageries came to form part of the theatre of power for ambitious European monarchs. The novel semi-circular layout of Louis XIV's large menagerie at Versailles permitted the viewer to survey all of the animals at once from a central tower, showcasing the power and glory of the Sun King.[13]

The early nineteenth century witnessed a shift in focus from monarchical to national power. This shift began in 1793, when French revolutionaries transferred the surviving animals from Louis XVI's menagerie at Versailles to a new national menagerie in the Paris Jardin des Plantes. It was consolidated in 1828 with the establishment of the Gardens of the Zoological Society of London (the future London Zoo) and the creation of a large number of municipal zoos in cities such as Dublin (1831), Bristol (1835), Berlin (1844), Marseilles (1854), Budapest (1865) and Philadelphia (1874).[14] Accessible to the general public (though not without restrictions), zoos acted as symbols of national potency and commercial strength, and often competed with one another for the most novel and coveted animals. They also functioned as expressions of civic pride, forging close links with local communities. In 1914 the *Boston Post* ran a campaign to raise money to buy three ex-circus elephants for the recently opened Franklin Zoo, appealing specifically to the city's children for donations.[15]

At the same time as zoological gardens were appearing across Europe and North America, we also see the emergence of the first travelling menageries – the forerunners of the modern circus. Though primarily commercial enterprises, prioritising entertainment over education, menageries merit attention as the places where most people probably got their first glimpse of exotic beasts (Figure 13.1). Writing in 1858, the *Bristol Mercury* remarked that

> even in these days, although Bristol and a handful of the leading towns can boast of their Zoological Gardens, there are scores of communities, many of them large communities, who would never see a lion, an elephant or a rhinoceros if these menageries were driven off the road.[16]

Where zoos emphasised the 'civilisation' of wild animals under human control, menageries were more explicitly geared towards sensation, appealing to a voyeuristic desire for cheap thrills and playing up the ferocity of their animals. Historians have started to pay increasing attention to travelling animal shows, using guidebooks, handbills and contemporary newspaper reports to reconstruct their itineraries, contents and reception.[17]

Though different in emphasis, both zoos and menageries have been perceived by historians as emblems of imperial power, and key sites for transmitting the achievements of empire to domestic populations.[18] On the one hand, many of the animals exhibited in nineteenth-century zoos had been acquired through the actions of diplomats, soldiers and merchants overseas. A Bactrian camel displayed at Dublin Zoological Garden in 1856, for example, was taken 'in the flank search after the battle of Alma' in the Crimean War, and presented to the Zoo by Dr William Carte, 'having served with the British army until the close of the war'.[19] On the other hand, by gathering hundreds of different species in a single locale, zoos made empire tangible to metropolitan audiences, enabling spectators to visualise distant colonial

Figure 13.1 Robertson's Royal Menagerie, 9 The Strand, c.1820.
Courtesy State Library of New South Wales – ML 1354.

settings and to make an association between certain animals and specific agents of empire or theatres of imperial action. Writing in 1885, the *Glasgow Herald* speculated that 'the two camels' in Bostock's Menagerie, then visiting the city, 'will give the youthful portion of our citizens some idea of the chargers on which the camel corps in the Soudan are mounted' – a reference to General Gordon's ill-fated campaign against the Mahdi.[20] The exotic histories of these animals added to their symbolic value, converting them into living embodiments of empire and vehicles for imperial propaganda. The fact that many animals were exhibited against a backdrop of oriental architecture added yet further to their exoticism, associating exotic species with humans in distant lands.[21]

While empire has dominated the history of zoological attractions, some more recent scholarship has challenged this focus, suggesting that the relationship between zoos and imperial culture needs nuancing. Firstly, there is the question of the contents of zoological exhibitions, which did not necessarily emanate purely from colonial possessions. London Zoo, for instance, contained many South American animals – notably a giant anteater in 1853 – yet South America was never formally colonised by Britain.[22] What was being exhibited was therefore, a fascination with a generic 'exotic', rather than an explicit evocation of empire – at least in some cases. Another perhaps more significant issue is how far the imperial message was really absorbed by those who visited zoos. Empire undoubtedly featured heavily in the propaganda for zoos and menageries, but it is possible that many people visited zoos to feed the bears or ride on the elephant, without giving too much thought to these broader representations of power.[23] Even when they did, the conclusions they drew could be complex and troubling and did not necessarily reaffirm imperial potency; the exhibition of a 'white' elephant, Toung Taloung at London Zoo in 1884, for instance, 'seemed to challenge fixed categories of racial distinction and white superiority' by suggesting that whiteness was not immutable.[24] The relationship between zoos and empire thus requires more careful probing, particularly in relation to popular imperialism and visitor reception.

The days of empire are now over, and zoos no longer function as overt symbols of monarchical, national or imperial power. This does not mean, however, that power-relations are absent from the modern zoo. On the contrary, they are central to its management practices, shaping both how animals are perceived by the visiting public and how they exist on a day-to-day basis. Firstly, as scholars such as Randy Malamud have argued, zoo animals can be seen as participating (involuntarily) in a global consumer culture, in which zoos encourage the visiting public 'to savor its participation in the thriving Western commercial culture of the late twentieth century'.[25] Animals are converted into commodities which can be marketed and consumed. The most iconic or appealing among them appear on fridge magnets, postcards and soft toys, gracing the shelves of zoo gift shops. In 1968, London Zoo's new polar bear cub Pipaluk generated a range of bear-themed souvenirs, including 'a comic strip, two toys, a book of coloured photographs and cut-out activity books' (Figure 13.2).[26]

Secondly, modern zoos exercise a form of stewardship over their animals which Irus Braverman describes as 'pastoral power'. This stewardship extends beyond zoo inmates to their counterparts in the wild and forms part of a wider drive to protect and conserve endangered species. It entails close control and surveillance of zoo animals and involves what Braverman identifies as 'seven interrelated technologies of animal governance; naturalizing, classifying, seeing, naming, registering, regulating and ... collectively reproducing zoo animals'.[27] While zoo professionals perceive these activities as necessary and benign, they nonetheless constitute a form of power over animals, who are microchipped, filmed, transferred to other zoos and contracepted in order to regulate their reproduction. Power thus remains central to the modern zoo, even if its outward expressions and meanings have changed.

Knowledge

Another important function of the zoo has been as a venue for the production and dissemination of knowledge. Like the museum, the laboratory or the botanical garden, the menagerie has provided a space for the study of the natural world, and also, in some instances, for its control and exploitation. How effectively it has fulfilled this role, however, remains subject to debate.

Firstly, zoos and menageries have provided a place for scholars to study exotic animals and learn about their anatomy and physiology. When the first hippopotamus arrived at London Zoo in 1850, comparative anatomist Richard Owen scrutinised the young pachyderm closely, noting his 'short and small milk tusks', 'prominent eyes' and 'glistening' skin.[28] Six years later, Yorkshire naturalist Charles Waterton 'passed two hours in company with [Mrs Wombwell's] chimpanzee at Scarborough, deducing from the fact that it walked on 'the knuckles of the toes' that it was an arboreal animal.[29] Studying animal behaviour in zoos has always had limitations, given the unnatural habits induced by prolonged confinement, but exotic animal collections have nonetheless provided sites for various forms of zoological research,

Figure 13.2 Keeper Sam Morton weighs the young Pipaluk, from *Pipaluk, 'The Little One'*, Amsterdam: Lutterworth Press, 1968.

Author's collection.

from species classification to debates over evolution.[30] Perhaps more importantly, scholars have enhanced their knowledge of animal anatomy by dissecting dead menagerie inmates, of which there was always a steady supply. In 1681, for instance, Joseph Guichard Duverney dissected an African elephant from Louis XIV's menagerie, learning more about the animal's skin, trunk and skeleton.[31]

In the nineteenth century, zoological gardens contributed to another branch of contemporary science: the acclimatisation of exotic animals. Seen as a way of appropriating 'useful' species for consumption or aesthetic pleasure, acclimatisation constituted the central mission of a number of zoological institutions and was closely linked to wider economic ambitions. In France, an acclimatisation garden was established in the Bois de Boulogne in 1860, with the specific aim of breeding exotic animals.[32] In Britain, acclimatisation was part of the original remit of the Zoological

Society of London, whose founder, Sir Stamford Raffles, prioritised 'the introduction of new varieties, breeds and races of animals, for the purpose of domestication, or for stocking our farmyards, woods, pleasure gardens and wastes'.[33] The aim of acclimatisation was to find new species that could be ridden, shorn or eaten, enhancing a nation's economic prospects. Prime candidates for the process included the alpaca, valued for its silky wool, and the South African eland, said to taste like veal with 'a *soupçon* of the pheasant flavour'.[34]

More recently, the rise of environmentalism from the 1960s has seen the emphasis of most Western zoos shift from acclimatisation to conservation. Modern zoos have established breeding programmes to preserve endangered species and international stud books have been created to facilitate the exchange of animals for mating purposes. Zoo animals also act as ambassadors for their counterparts in the wild and occasionally assist directly in *in situ* conservation projects. In 1989, for instance, an African elephant in Whipsnade Zoo tested out a satellite transmitter collar which would later be used to monitor wild elephants in Kenya's Tsavo National Park.[35] While these contributions are important, serious questions remain over the contribution of zoos towards conservation. Is there any value in breeding animals who will probably never be reintroduced to the wild? Have zoos tended to prioritise the breeding of attractive and popular animals (such as the panda), over less cuddly species such as reptiles and amphibians? Would artificially bred animals survive in the wild, even if they were released, and what should happen to surplus animals, whose genetics make them unsuitable for breeding? There was widespread outrage in 2014 when Copenhagen Zoo announced that a healthy male giraffe named Marius was to be shot and publicly fed to the institution's lions, but culling zoo animals is, in fact, common practice in Northern European zoos and considered necessary to prevent inbreeding or overcrowding.[36] Zoos' genuine value as conservation centres is thus open to question, and seen by some as insufficient justification for their continued existence.

A final way in which zoos and menageries have sought to contribute to knowledge is through public education. In the nineteenth century, this focused primarily on conveying the names, origins and distinguishing features of exotic animals, information transmitted through guidebooks and reinforced by the layout of many zoological gardens, which reflected the latest thinking in classification.[37] Today, by contrast, the conservation message generally takes centre stage, with signage and guidebooks typically highlighting the endangered status of many of their animals and the measures being taken to protect them. Education is one of the key ways in which zoos have differentiated themselves from menageries and circuses, and remains central to their ethos. As with conservation, however, there are significant question marks over the zoos' effectiveness as educators, and a constant tension between education and entertainment. Observing the behaviour of twentieth-century zoo visitors, for instance, Mullan and Marvin argue that

> unless there is some particular activity in a cage or enclosure, or unless the animal is a special favourite, it seems that, for the majority of people, watching consists of merely registering that they have seen something as they quickly move past it.[38]

Writing over a century earlier, one Victorian commentator complained of the 'vapid curiosity' and 'stupid wonder' exhibited by some of his fellow zoo-goers, suggesting a similar lack of engagement with the animals on display.[39] Exotic animal collections appear, throughout history, to have been visited primarily for recreation, and there is limited evidence that those who visit zoos today have a better knowledge of animals than those who do not.[40] Nonetheless, zoos have provided opportunities for various forms of human–animal interactions, from feeding buns to the bears to stroking a llama, and their supporters have argued that these kinds of sensory interactions generate both interest in, and empathy for, animals.[41] Public reception of menageries is a particularly fruitful area of research for historians of animals, though one often complicated by the paucity and class biases of surviving sources.

Animal welfare

Zoos, menageries and circuses have also been studied from an animal welfare perspective. As sites where multiple wild animals are held captive, and, in some instances, forcibly trained to perform, menageries present a number of distinct concerns when it comes to animal cruelty. Institutional zoo histories tend to present a narrative of gradual improvement in welfare, culminating in the carefully designed, naturalistic enclosures of the modern zoo. While there are elements of truth to this argument, such a narrative is overly simplistic and conceals both the shortcomings of the present and the achievements of earlier generations. Moreover, as Nigel Rothfels has argued, it is questionable whether humans or animals have benefited most from shifting modes of display. Have these 'improvements' been introduced to make the animals happy or, as Rothfels suggests, to make human viewers believe that they are happy?[42]

Welfare concerns in relation to zoos and circuses date back to at least the early nineteenth century and have typically centred on two key issues: physical violence towards exotic animals and inappropriate living conditions. The former, often connected to training and performance, was most prevalent in some of the earliest critiques of zoos and, in particular, travelling menageries. The latter, though a constant source of criticism, became more prominent in the twentieth century, as the needs and behaviours of different species began to be better understood. Less often criticised, but nonetheless a major concern, have been the impact of the exotic animal trade, and the hidden cruelty inflicted on animals out of public view.

In the nineteenth century, the most vocal critics of zoos and menageries focused on the physical abuse of their inmates, a phenomenon that was sadly all too common in contemporary shows. In 1825 the *Liverpool Mercury* condemned menagerist George Wombwell for staging a fight between his docile lion, Nero, and six bull dogs.[43] In 1870 the RSPCA's secretary John Colam brought charges against a German named Otto Herman for 'striking the paws' of a 'blind and emaciated bear' with a stick.[44] In 1874, magistrates in Nottingham fined showmen John Day and T. Rayner 21 shillings each for making an elephant travel with a swollen foot, while in 1888 the Society secured convictions for 'beating, kicking, stabbing' a monkey and a dromedary.[45] The emphasis in all of these cases was on the physical pain inflicted upon the animals in question, either through baiting or excessive labour. The Nottingham elephant was described as enduring protracted suffering that 'amounted to positive torture' – language reminiscent of contemporary anti-vivisection campaigns.[46]

While the abuses inflicted on menagerie inmates differed little from assaults on more common animals, they did raise some specific issues. Firstly, there were questions as to the legal status of exotic species. According to the Animal Cruelty Act of 1835, it was forbidden to mistreat 'any horse, mare, gelding, bull, ox, cow, heifer, steer and pig or any other domestic animal'.[47] This left the status of zoo and menagerie inmates unclear, for though they were confined, they could hardly be considered domestic. The problems posed by this legal lacuna were clearly illustrated in 1874, when the RSPCA attempted to prosecute keeper Frederick Hewitt for making hyenas jump through a burning hoop. The prosecution, keen to secure a conviction, argued that the hyenas 'might now legally be regarded as domestic animals' as 'they were deprived of their freedom, shut in from their usual mode of life, and dependent entirely upon their owner and keeper for their food'. The defence, however, contended that 'such animals as tigers and hyenas were never contemplated within the act', and that 'naturalists say that it is impossible to tame a hyena'. Though convinced that cruelty had taken place, the magistrate reluctantly agreed with the defence and dismissed the case, concluding that 'if you asked anybody who understood the English language, and who was not a lawyer, what was a domestic animal, the answer would not include a lion, or a panther, or a hyena'.[48] The abuse of exotic animals thus raised important questions about how different animals should be classified, and what exactly was meant by 'domestication'.[49]

A second issue surrounding the physical abuse of exotic animals was that it was often a very public affair. This not only increased the likelihood of complaints, but elicited wider concerns about the effect that witnessing such cruelty was likely to have upon human spectators. The Warwick lion fight was seen as encouraging depravity among those who saw it, with one newspaper describing the incident as symptomatic of 'that ferocious and unchristian spirit which appears to be alarmingly on the increase in this country'.[50] Later in the century, the RSPCA campaigned vociferously (though unsuccessfully) against another, more insidious abuse – the feeding of live prey to the snakes at London Zoo. In an article in the Society's monthly magazine, *The Animal World*, an opponent of the practice recited horror stories of 'screaming' frogs, 'squeaking' guinea pigs and suffocating pigeons, all victims of the snakes' voracity. As well as dwelling on the time it took for the prey animals to expire, the author devoted particular attention to the reactions of the large crowds who gathered to watch the spectacle, evidently horrified that some spectators appeared to enjoy it. One visitor 'counted twenty-six women, thirteen girls, twelve boys and thirty men' among the viewers and recorded 'the eagerness of the women to indulge their morbid curiosity at the cages where [a] duck and pigeon . . . were being killed'. Another described how, while 'many of the spectators turned away overcome', many others 'seemed to gloat over the sufferings [of a duck] and tried by waving their hats and handkerchiefs to drive [its] still unhurt [companion] within the other python's reach to satisfy their still unquenched thirst for sanguinary exhibitions'. Indeed, they 'seemed to revel in a downright morbid curiosity in the same manner that they would witness the execution of a fellow-man, or a bull fight'.[51] As this last comment makes clear, contemporaries drew a direct correlation between cruelty to animals and potential cruelty to humans, deprecating the more lurid exhibitions of the menagerie – or even, in this case, of the otherwise respectable London Zoo.

If physical (and public) abuse has generated the most dramatic headlines, living conditions have presented a more chronic concern for zoos and menageries. Though less obviously cruel than direct violence, claustrophobic cages, poor feeding regimes and sickly animals have all tainted the viewing experience, giving rise to calls for change. In 1776, for instance, a man wrote to *The Public Advertiser* to protest at the mistreatment of two 'poor elephants', who were housed in 'a miserable, old, ruinous Hovel' and appeared 'to be in the last Stage of Consumption'.[52] In 1878, meanwhile, a correspondent in *The Animal World* expressed his sorrow for a seal in an Edinburgh aquarium who 'had not water enough to half cover his body' and was forced to live in a 'fancy grotto, lit by gas [and] played to by horrid pianos'.[53] Improvements to enclosures in the first half of the twentieth century went some way towards addressing these issues, but campaigners in the 1960s and 70s were still complaining about empty, sterile cages and inadequate animal husbandry. Writing in 1976, Peter Batten described the dire conditions in many dilapidated US zoos, where anteaters bruised their knuckles on concrete floors (Figure 13.3), big cats paced incessantly in cramped cages and sea lions grew fungus on their bodies in dirty, non-saline water.[54]

While Batten requested improvements to living conditions rather than the abolition of zoos, other twentieth-century critics have gone further, suggesting that

Figure 13.3 An anteater paces on an unsuitable concrete surface, Audubon Zoo, New Orleans, 1952. *The Times Picayune* 1 October 1952. Photographer O.J. Valeton.

Author's collection.

captivity per se is a cause of suffering. The contributors to *The Great Ape Project*, for example, assert that humans' closest living relatives, the chimpanzee, orang-utan and gorilla, should enjoy several fundamental rights currently extended only to humans, among these, the right 'not to be arbitrarily deprived of their liberty'.[55] Jeffrey Masson and Susan McCarthy contend similarly that 'No cage is big enough for a polar bear or a cougar' and ask whether 'freedom to choose [is not] inextricably tied into the very notion of what it means to be happy?'[56] For these writers, freedom is a moral right, and not even the best zoos can ever fully replicate the native environments of their inmates. Such claims are supported by recent research in the field of animal behaviour science, which suggests that certain species at least fare badly in zoos and live shorter lives than their counterparts in the wild; zoo-born Asian elephants, for instance, live for an average of 18.9 years, while their counterparts born in Burmese timber camps (themselves not ideal conditions) live for an average of 41.7 years.[57] While defenders of zoos tend to distinguish between good zoos and bad zoos, therefore, animal liberationists regard all zoos as cruel and call for their closure.

The mistreatment of animals in zoos and menageries was very visible, and, consequently, often criticised. Less frequently discussed, but equally (if not more) devastating, have been the cruelties perpetrated by the wild animal trade. In the nineteenth century – and indeed, well into the twentieth – many animals perished for every one that made it to the zoo, with animal catchers routinely killing mothers to secure their young and many captive animals succumbing to accident, trauma or disease during the long journey to Europe or America. The baby hippo Obaysch, for instance, was only taken after his mother had been 'mortally wounded'.[58] In 1882, meanwhile, an account of the collection of 'elephants, giraffes, ostriches, lions, hippopotami, apes and baboons' for New York dealer Charles Reiche stated that 'plenty of animals were killed' in Abyssinia, 'while the young ones were captured' and 'carried in cages on the backs of camels' to the Red Sea port of Suakin.[59] The continual losses sustained by wild populations not only entailed considerable cruelty, but threatened the very survival of particular species, many of which were already targeted by big game hunters and commercial killers. Because they were not immediately visible to metropolitan viewers, however, these losses were easily concealed, eliciting little comment. Indeed, even when descriptions of deaths were published, as in the above cases, they were often reported in a neutral, matter-of-fact manner and rarely explicitly condemned; the article on Charles Reiche, for example, appeared in the RSPCA's monthly magazine, not, as one might expect, as an instance of cruelty, but simply as an entertaining vignette.

Also largely ignored by the public, because generally unseen, has been the cruelty that occurs behind the scenes at zoos and menageries. Visible cruelty has often provoked strong responses, particularly animal baiting, unsuitable living conditions or, in earlier centuries, the feeding of live prey. Behind-the-scenes abuse, however, has caused less of an outcry, and has tended to be tolerated or excused. When, in 1886, an elephant known as 'Aston Jumbo' was subjected to 'severe castigation' by digging hooks into her ears and trunk, there were few protests, for the punishment happened while the menagerie was closed.[60] Conversely, when the gorilla Harambe was shot dead at Cincinnati Zoo in 2016 after a young boy climbed into his enclosure, there was widespread sorrow and anger.[61] Though these differing reactions may be attributed in part to the different social contexts in which they took place, a clear distinction can nonetheless be drawn between public and private forms of cruelty, with the former attracting more attention than the latter. Indeed, this public/private distinction is particularly notable in modern zoos, where sickly animals are generally screened from public view, and pain in all forms carefully concealed.[62]

Animal agency

A growing concern in Animal Studies is the issue of animal agency. This issue is perhaps particularly visible within an exhibition context, where animals interact on a regular basis with humans in a highly visible setting and are sometimes trained to perform. In the final part of this chapter, I explore the question of animal agency as it relates to zoos, menageries and circuses. I concentrate on three case studies: the celebrity animal, the deviant animal and the performing animal.

Celebrity animals exhibited agency insofar as their fame brought them to public notice. Repeated interactions with iconic beasts at the menagerie or the zoo often fostered a sense of intimacy and rapport which sometimes created the illusion of genuine friendship. This gave way, on the one hand, to intense anthropomorphism, but also to a sense that the animals themselves were active participants in these interactions and capable of human actions and emotions. Writing shortly after the famous elephant Chunee was killed in 1826, for instance, one contemporary recounted, in mournful verse, how he would frequently visit the elephant and offer him food: 'And many an apple to thy den I've brought, / And many a nod of thanks received from you'.[63] Some sixty-five years later, following the death of another popular favourite, the chimpanzee Sally at London Zoo, a writer for the RSPCA's monthly magazine expatiated on her very human qualities, even going so far as to speculate on whether she possessed a soul:

> It is not safe or scientific any longer to affirm that animals have no souls ... Sally had learned to love, as nobody could doubt who saw her shamble out from her straw when her keeper appeared, and greet him with a hideous but obviously affectionate kiss. She had also learned the great lesson of self-control, which many human beings never attain at all. If she had a passion, it was ... for sliced apples; but when her keeper laid the most tempting tit-bits upon her cage-rail she would wait with an absolute patience and obedience until he had notified her that she was at liberty to devour the delicious morsels.[64]

Famous animals were thus imputed with quasi-human manners, feelings and moral impulses and could, in turn, be sincerely mourned when they died – something that rarely happened with less high profile zoo inmates.

A particularly illuminating instance of the ways in which fame could confer agency is the case of Jumbo the African elephant. Acquired by London Zoo from the Jardin des Plantes in 1865, Jumbo remained at the zoo for another seventeen years and forged a close bond with the British public. When Jumbo was sold to the American showman P.T. Barnum in 1882 his projected departure elicited a wave of protest from his admirers, who deluged the Zoological Society with angry letters, signed petitions for his retention at the Zoo and inundated the elephant himself with gifts of 'oysters, wedding cake and champagne'.[65] While the public response to Jumbo's departure was in many ways hysterical and overblown, a notable feature of the arguments made in the elephant's defence is the degree to which some of those individuals accorded Jumbo an active role on the saga of his expatriation and presented him as a conscious actor in the drama, capable of resistance, comprehension and emotional suffering.[66] Jumbo's refusal to enter the box in which he was to be transported to the docks, for instance, was interpreted as evidence of the elephant's patriotism and loyalty to his British supporters (Figure 13.4). The elephant's apparent awareness of his own fate, meanwhile, was noted by several visitors, who ascribed to the animal the very human emotions of loss and sadness. A group of ladies visiting the elephant house in the weeks leading up to Jumbo's removal even claimed that they 'detected grief upon [Jumbo's] very countenance, and thought it wonderful that the animal should seem to have the gift of fore-knowledge as to its doom' (though it turned out they were in fact looking at the Asian elephant and not at Jumbo!).[67] Jumbo was thus conceived as a wise, faithful and wilful animal who, though ultimately forced to bow to human control, succeeded at least in delaying his departure for several weeks.

Figure 13.4 'Attempt to remove Jumbo, the great elephant, from the Zoological Gardens', *Illustrated London News*, 25 February 1882, 200.

Author's collection.

One letter, addressed directly to Jumbo, encouraged the elephant to 'Hold out bravely, old fellow! Don't budge an inch! Every child wants you to stay, and will bless you for your courage as he grows up'.[68]

While fame thus earned some zoo animals a place in the hearts of the public, it is questionable to what degree they exerted genuine agency. Fame may have made people look at particular creatures more closely than they would otherwise have done, but we should note that what was being celebrated about those animals was frequently their fulfilment of a particular moral purpose or their ability to further contemporary human concerns. Often, for example, certain animals were seen to embody desirable human qualities, such as fidelity, intelligence or gratitude, and were consequently praised for their subservience rather than their independence. This is especially evident in the eulogy to Sally, which above all admired her 'self-control' and affection for her keeper and marvelled at 'her extraordinary intellectual and moral evolution at one remove only from the ethics and comprehension of the jungle'.[69] What was being praised here was clearly not Sally's animality, but her 'apeing' of human behaviour, and, in that sense, her assimilation into human (specifically Western) society.

A second reason why we should be cautious in assessing the link between agency and fame is that the latter was often fleeting. A few beasts like Jumbo achieved lasting celebrity, but others were in the public eye for only a short time before they were supplanted by newer, more unusual zoological stars. Newly imported exotic beasts lost their wonder after a season in the spotlight, while cute cubs lost their appeal when they entered adolescence. An article in *The Times* in 1968 advised the latest sensation, the newborn polar bear, Pipaluk, to enjoy his summer of fame, for 'before he knows where he is he will be a 1.600lb white bear with a broad head and a bad temper, frightening the children with his teeth'.[70] Celebrity was thus only temporary and when this faded, so did agency and interest. Moreover, the animals themselves had no control over this process; their fame was constructed by humans for humans and often served to obscure the experiences of other, less famous animals. As Susan Nance remarks of Jumbo, 'His life, lived in public, and the resulting celebrity status . . . actually distracted consumers from the issue of declining wild animal populations', for while people cried and protested at the sufferings of this individual elephant they turned a blind eye to the wholesale slaughter of wild African elephants for their ivory.[71]

If the agency of 'celebrity' animals was thus somewhat questionable, perhaps a more authentic expression of agency is offered by our second category: the deviant animal. While many zoo and menagerie inmates endured their captivity without visible opposition, a sizeable minority actively resisted their incarceration, either by escaping or by attacking members of the public (usually following provocation). In 1835 a tiger in Wombwell's menagerie mauled a man named John Newbolt, who 'had the audacity to take hold of [the] animal's ear'.[72] More recently, we have the cases of Tyke the elephant, who escaped from a circus in Honolulu in 1994 after killing her keeper, and the orca, Tilikum, who drowned his trainer, Dawn Brancheau during a performance at Sea World, Orlando in 2010.[73] Assessing the significance of such behaviour, some historians have interpreted escapes and attacks not as random acts of aggression, but as conscious responses to oppression, explicitly equating their resistance with that of other subjugated groups. Jason Hribal, perhaps the strongest advocate of this position, asserts that

> These animals ... are rebelling with knowledge and purpose. They have a conception of freedom and a desire for it. They have agency.[74]

Jeffrey St Clair, writing in the foreword to Hribral's book, declares, likewise, that 'Tilikum is the Nat Turner of the captives of Sea', likening the whale to the African-American slave who led a violent rebellion against his white masters in 1831.[75]

Whether or not we agree with this view, it is certainly the case that deviant animals have often been described in highly anthropomorphised terms and written about in language that suggests a level of conscious action and rational decision-making. In that sense, Hribal's humanising accounts of animal resistance have their precursors at least as far back as the nineteenth century. Take the case of an elephant named Jim, who escaped from George Sanger's circus in 1893 and went on a four-and-a-half hour rampage through north London. Recounting the drama, a report in *The Animal World* described how Jim, the 'monster bull elephant' had broken away from his keeper while walking down St Anne's Road and begun a destructive march through the city, breaking into the stable of a fishmonger, 'refreshing himself with a drink of water' in a river and marching through the grounds of Upper Clapton Cricket Club, where he lifted a 'stout iron gate from its hinges'. While the text of the report clearly played up some of Jim's exploits for entertainment purposes, there is also a clear sense that the elephant was acting with rationality and not simply engaged in random vandalism. Reflecting on the cause of Jim's actions, for instance, the author observed that 'the elephant had evidently ideas of his own, and from the peculiar manner in which he looked about he was evidently making for some place only known to himself'. This theory was apparently proven correct when the elephant ended his journey 'on the St Loys estate, near Bruce Grove Station, where, it is said, he was encamped with other elephants some years ago'.[76] So in this instance the elephant was seen as acting with intentionality, heading for a specific location that had historic meaning for him.

Deviant animals (deviant, at least, in human eyes) therefore drew attention to their agency in vivid and memorable ways, and seemingly did have the power to shape the course of their own lives, or even potentially the lives of their fellow captives. Attacks and escapes could expose abuse or unsuitable conditions and sometimes force changes in the ways in which animals were treated. They could also earn particular animals a degree of notoriety, especially in the nineteenth century, when showmen often capitalised on the media attention surrounding a break-out or death to attract voyeuristic spectators to their menageries. A lion named Jim, whose 'remarkable ... career' resulted in the deaths of 'one man and thirteen different animals', was hailed as 'A Hero with a History', receiving a lengthy newspaper obituary following his own death in 1875.[77]

While we can perhaps see zoo animals as resisting oppression when they escaped or killed human associates, the effectiveness of such resistance might well be questioned, for aggressors and escapees were (and are) more likely to die in a hail of bullets than to secure their freedom. Nineteenth-century menagerists might have kept some transgressors alive as a source of ghoulish publicity, but many others have been destroyed, either shot in the street, like Tyke, or subjected to more macabre human forms of retribution like the elephant Topsy, who was electrocuted in 1903 after she killed three different handlers (a spectacle captured on film by the executioner, Thomas Edison).[78] Those animals that survived, moreover, rather than being freed, were often confined to isolation and assigned epithets such as 'wild', 'savage' or 'barbarous', which had the effect of relegating their acts of resistance to unthinking brutality, the product of instinct rather than reason. Of the lion Jim, for example, it was said that 'his savage nature [was] apparent even in his last moments', and that 'his ferocity made him a great attraction'.[79] While famous animals like Sally won praise and recognition through renouncing their animal natures, therefore, reprobates like Jim exerted agency at the cost of their perceived humanity, and, often, of their lives. As with celebrity animals, moreover, we are reliant on human accounts when studying animal actions in the past, so what we are really learning about are human *perceptions* of animal agency, rather than animal agency per se – though the former is, in itself, a worthy topic of study.

What about our final category: performing animals? Here we are looking at a different relationship between humans and animals, one (usually) of inter-species collaboration rather than conflict. From the inception of menageries in the late eighteenth century, exotic captives have been taught to perform tricks, from leaping through hoops to firing pistols. The range and complexity of these performances increased significantly from the 1890s, with the rise of the circus, and training methods grew more sophisticated. Lions have been coaxed onto pedestals, bears trained to ride bicycles and elephants to dance ballet. In 1879 the Westminster Aquarium advertised the feats of a sea lion called Toby, who fired a rifle, smoked a pipe and strummed a banjo.[80] While cruelty was (and is) often present in the training regimes of performing animals, teaching wild beasts to do tricks also entailed a high level of intimacy between the animal and its trainer and a substantial degree of interspecies communication. Persuasion and patience were crucial attributes of a successful tamer, who could not simply bludgeon his charges into submission, but had to work closely and repeatedly with his pupil to perfect a particular act. As Peta Tait has shown, moreover, trainers needed to be able to accurately read the body language of their animals and even to interpret their emotions, forging a close bond with the creatures they worked with.[81]

A couple of examples from the early twentieth century demonstrate this close relationship between keeper and animal. Firstly, we have the testimony of a lion tamer, Frank Bostock. Writing in 1903, in a manual on how to train wild animals, Bostock emphasised the key attributes of a successful trainer, who must be sober, agile, brave and in possession of an excellent 'knowledge of animal nature'. This last quality was crucial, for 'upon the trainer's knowledge of the idiosyncrasies of his charges depends his success, and very often his life'.[82] Bostock insisted that different animals, even of the same species, learned differently, for 'each is a study, alone and complete in itself, and each animal has its distinct individuality'.[83] He claimed, furthermore, that some of his animals actively enjoyed performing, citing the case of a young brown bear, trained to climb a ladder and unfurl the American flag, who was 'so proud . . . of his accomplishment that whenever anyone is looking on, he will go through the whole performance by himself, evidently simply for the pleasure of doing it'.⁸⁴ Bostock had a vested interest in relating such examples, for he was writing at a time when wild beast taming was being criticised by humanitarians on the grounds of cruelty (he pointed out, in one chapter, that he never used hot irons to subdue dangerous animals, because 'it is an extremely cruel expedient, and seldom effectual as a remedy for the attacks of wild beasts').⁸⁵ Biased as he may have been, however, the tamer clearly understood the animals he trained, and, without romanticising them, saw them as equal partners in the performing enterprise. Training thus required a close, if exploitative, relationship between human and non-human animals, in which the latter were viewed as individuals and exerted a degree of agency over their performances.

Our second example comes from an *Animal Care Journal* produced by keepers at the BelleVue Zoo, Manchester between 1908 and 1913. Written by hand, this interesting document describes the lives, and (all too often) the deaths of the various inmates of the zoo during this period, detailing the food they were given, their habits and mating attempts and the illnesses from which they suffered. Though intended

Figure 13.5 'A tame ocelot', W.S. Berridge, 'The wooing of the wild', *The Animal World* Volume II (New Series), January 1907, 230–232.

Author's collection.

primarily as a record of events, the contents of the book go beyond mere practicalities and clearly reveal the keepers' affection for their animals, as well as their curiosity about their abilities. One entry, for instance, states that 'the tapir can show quite a glorious smile when tickled in the ear – and he will lie down to be scratched for long enough'. Another reads: 'The Giraffe's knee seems stiffer. I worked it for some time, apparently to the Giraffe's pleasure, as he put his head down to caress me'. A third entry records how one keeper, Woodward, 'taught one of the 5 sea lions to balance the ball – process: keep rubbing it on and about the nose; pat him for a successful effort and fish occasionally for a transcendent improvement'.[86] Here we again see animals being treated as emotionally intelligent individuals who interact closely with their keepers. It is notable, moreover, how often the authors of the care book describe their charges in highly anthropomorphic language, endowing them with distinctly human qualities; the orang-utan is 'too tubby to my mind', the elephant moves about 'nervously and vindictively' and the giraffe is 'an importunate beggar'.[87]

As these examples illustrate, training exotic animals, or even just caring for them, could engender a close cross-species relationship that most humans do not experience. Zoo and menagerie keepers might sometimes have abused the animals they looked after, but many also developed genuine affection for their charges and exhibited curiosity as to their mental and physical abilities (Figure 13.5). More than anyone else, keepers knew their animals' diet, habits and routines, and could tell when they were sick, anxious or angry. While some may have remained detached from the creatures they worked with, others forged a close bond with their animals, viewing them as capable of human-like desires and emotions. Those who knew exotic animals best were thus often those most likely to accord them agency, and drawing on their accounts may offer new insights for historians of zoos and menageries.

Conclusion

Humans have exhibited exotic animals for thousands of years. Over that time, royal menageries have evolved into national zoos, bare cages into landscape immersion, and former plunderers of the natural world into self-styled hubs of conservation. At the same time, however, some things have remained the same. Entertainment, education, knowledge and power – in varying proportions – have undergirded animal exhibition from the Roman Empire to the present day, and questions regarding animal welfare have been raised since at least the eighteenth century. Despite a growing emphasis on conservation, the majority of zoos today exhibit the same iconic specimens that were coveted in the nineteenth century and the majority of zoo visitors come primarily for recreation. As the animal rights movement gains ground and animal behavioural science advances, the future of zoos is coming increasingly into question.

Whatever our views on the ethics of modern zoos, studying their history can be enlightening. Zoological collections have functioned as a window onto royal and imperial display, civic pride and shifting social dynamics, attracting the attention of historians of leisure, empire and science. As places where people went explicitly to see and (often) feed, ride or touch animals, they are also an excellent site for the study of human–animal relationships in the past. While earlier studies have focused predominantly on the most famous zoological institutions – notably London Zoo – increased attention is now being paid to provincial zoos, touring menageries and circuses, broadening our understanding of the geographies and social dynamics of exotic animal exhibition. Historians are also looking more closely at issues such as visitor reception, keeper–animal interaction and animal agency, moving beyond the symbolic resonances of zoos to uncover the experiences of real animals and the people who went to see them.

Notes

1 For a synopsis of the zoo's changing form and meaning in different societies see R.J. Hoage and W.A. Deiss, *New Worlds, New Animals: From Menagerie to Zoological Park in the Nineteenth Century*, Baltimore MD: Johns Hopkins University Press, 1996.
2 'Circus owner found guilty of mistreating elephant', *The Telegraph*, 23 November 2012. The use of animals in circuses has to date been banned in Austria, Bolivia, Bosnia and Herzegovina, Colombia, Costa Rica, Croatia, Cyprus, El Salvador, Greece, Israel, Malta, Mexico, The Netherlands, Paraguay, Peru, Singapore and Slovenia.
3 See, for example, J. Barrington-Johnson, *The Story of London Zoo*, London: Robert Hale, 2005.
4 For a critical take on zoos, see R. Malamud, *Reading Zoos: Representations of Animals in Captivity*, New York: New York University Press, 1998; and 'Display, performance and sport' in M. DeMello, *Animals and Society: An Introduction to Human–Animal Studies*, New York: Columbia University Press, 2012, 99–125.
5 See, for example, E. Baratay and E. Hardouin-Fugier, *Zoo: A History of Zoological Gardens in the West*, London: Reaktion Books, 2002; N. Rothfels, *Savages and Beasts: The Birth of the Modern Zoo*, Baltimore MD: Johns Hopkins University Press, 2002; and E. Hanson, *Animal Attractions: Nature on Display in American Zoos*, Princeton NJ: Princeton University Press, 2002.
6 See 'Exotic captives' in H. Ritvo, *The Animal Estate: The English and Other Creatures in the Victorian Age*, Cambridge MA: Harvard University Press, 1987, 205–242; R. Acampora, 'Extinction by exhibition: looking at and in the zoo', *Research in Human Ecology* 5, 1 (1998), 1–4; and K. Anderson, 'Culture and nature at the Adelaide Zoo: at the frontiers of "human" geography', *Transactions of the Institute of British Geographers*, 20, 3 (1995): 275-294.
7 Malamud, *Reading Zoos*, 64.
8 C. Grigson, *Menagerie: The History of Exotic Animals in England*, Oxford: Oxford University Press, 2016, 1.
9 J. Pimentel, *The Rhinoceros and the Megatherium: An Essay in Natural History*, Cambridge MA: Harvard University Press, 2017, 21.
10 'Noticia del elefante remitido de Manila para el Rey nuestro Señor en la fragata nombrada Venus, que regresó de Philipinas en 22 de Julio de este año, según una papeleta remitida de Cádiz', in *Descripción del Elefante, de su Alimento, Costumbres, Enemigos e Instinto*, Madrid: Imprenta de Andrés Ramírez, 1773, 31.
11 Grigson, *Menagerie*, 16–17.
12 Pimentel, *The Rhinoceros*, 45–50.
13 See 'The Royal Menagerie', in L. Robbins, *Elephant Slaves and Pampered Parrots: Exotic Animals in Eighteenth-Century Paris*, Baltimore MD: Johns Hopkins University Press, 2002, 37–67. For a discussion of menageries in contemporary Britain, see C. Plumb, *The Georgian Menagerie*, London: IB Tauris, 2015.

14 Baratay and Hardouin-Fugier, *Zoo*, 80–81 and 99.
15 Hanson, *Animal Attractions*, 61–67. Lisa Uddin has traced connections between zoo improvement and urban redevelopment in the 1960s and 70s, while Andrew Flack has shown how Bristol Zoo has developed close ties to the local community since its foundation in 1836. Helen Cowie has examined the relationship between zoological collections, urban improvement and civic identity in early nineteenth-century Britain. See L. Uddin, *Zoo Renewal: White Flight and the Animal Ghetto*, Minneapolis MN: University of Minnesota Press, 2015; A. Flack, *The Natures of the Beasts: An Animal History of Bristol Zoo Gardens since 1835* (PhD Dissertation, University of Bristol, 2013); and H. Cowie, "An attractive and improving place of resort": zoo, community and civic pride in nineteenth-century Britain, *Social and Cultural History* 12, 3 (2015): 365–384.
16 'The Lions in a Fix', *Bristol Mercury*, 30 January 1858.
17 See, for example, S. Nance, *Entertaining Elephants: Animal Agency and the Business of the American Circus*, Baltimore MD: Johns Hopkins University Press, 2013, and H. Cowie, *Exhibiting Animals in Nineteenth-Century Britain: Empathy, Education, Entertainment*, Basingstoke: Palgrave Macmillan, 2014.
18 See, for example: See Ritvo, 'Exotic captives'; R. Jones, '"The sight of creatures strange to our clime": London Zoo and the consumption of the exotic', *Journal of Victorian Culture* 2, 1 (1997): 1–26; and T. Ito, *London Zoo and the Victorians, 1828–1859*, Woodbridge: Boydell and Brewer, 2014.
19 'Crimea', *Belfast Newsletter*, 27 October 1856.
20 'Bostock's Menagerie', *Glasgow Herald*, 13 February 1885.
21 The elephant house at Berlin Zoo, for instance, was designed to resemble a Hindu temple. B. Mullan and G. Marvin, *Zoo Culture*, Chicago IL: University of Illinois Press, 1987, 48–49.
22 'Zoological Society of London', *The Times*, 7 October 1853; Mullan and Marvin, *Zoo Culture*, 49–50.
23 B. Porter, *The Absent-Minded Imperialists: What the British Really Thought about Empire*. Oxford: Oxford University Press, 2004, 88. Ann Colley argues similarly that 'the gathering, arranging, transporting and labelling of skins from foreign territories' represented not British power, but, 'the messiness of empire': see A. Colley, *Animal Skins in Victorian Britain: Zoos, Collections, Portraits and Maps*, Farnham: Ashgate, 2015, 4.
24 S. Amato, *Beastly Possessions: Animals in Victorian Consumer Culture*, Toronto: University of Toronto Press, 2015, 60–61.
25 Malamud, *Reading Zoos*, 92.
26 'Pipaluk awaits his Debut', *The Times*, 11 March 1968.
27 I. Braverman, *Zooland: The Institution of Captivity*, Stanford CA: Stanford University Press, 2013, 187–188.
28 'The hippopotamus at the Zoological Gardens', *The Times*, 6 June 1850.
29 'Wombwell's No. 1 and Royal Monster Menagerie', *Preston Guardian*, 12 January, 1856.
30 For a discussion of the different forms of knowledge in play at the zoo, see O. Hochadel, 'Watching exotic animals next door: "scientific" observations at the zoo (ca. 1870–1910)', *Science in Context* 24, 2 (2011): 183–214.
31 A. Guerrini, *The Courtiers' Anatomists: Animals and Humans in Louis XIV's Paris*, Chicago IL: Chicago University Press, 2015, 202–204.
32 M. Osborne, *Nature, the Exotic and the Science of French Colonialism*, Bloomington IN: Indiana University Press, 1994, 11.
33 T. Allen, *A Guide to the Zoological Gardens and Museum*, London: Cowie and Strange, 1829, 5.
34 W. Walton, *A Memoir addressed to Proprietors of Mountain and other Waste Lands and Agriculturalists of the United Kingdom, on the Naturalisation of the Alpaca*, London: Smith, Elder and Co., 1841; *Essex Standard*, 2 February 1859.

35 'London Zoo will track elephants by satellite', *The Times*, 12 September 1989.
36 'Why did Copenhagen Zoo decide to kill Marius the giraffe?', *The Guardian*, 9 February 2014. A recent BBC documentary reported that between 3,000 and 5,000 healthy animals are culled in European zoos every year. BBC, *Horizon: Should we Close our Zoos?*, first broadcast 17 April 2016. American Zoos use contraception rather than culling to control unwanted breeding. See Braverman, *Zooland*, 174–177.
37 H. Kean, *Animal Rights: Political and Social Change in Britain since 1800*, London: Reaktion Books, 1998, 44–46.
38 Mullan and Marvin, *Zoo Culture*, 133.
39 'Natural History', *Morning Chronicle*, 4 September 1849.
40 S. Kellert, *Kinship to Mastery: Biophilia in Human Evolution and Development*, Washington DC: Island Press, 1997, 99.
41 See, for example, 'Education in zoos' in S. Bostock, *Zoos and Animal Rights: The Ethics of Keeping Animals*, London: Routledge, 1993, 168–176.
42 Rothfels, *Savages and Beasts*, 201–202.
43 'Fight between Mr Wombwell's lions and six bull dogs', *Liverpool Mercury*, 29 July 1825.
44 'Cruelty to ferae naturae', *The Animal World*, December 1870, 40.
45 'Cruelty to an elephant', *Nottinghamshire Guardian*, 27 November, 1874; *The Animal World*, August 1888, 116.
46 'Cruelty to an elephant', *Nottinghamshire Guardian*, 27 November, 1874.
47 Great Britain Parliament, *Cruelty to Animals Act* (1835) [5 & 6 William IV c. 59].
48 'Singular Charge of Cruelty in a Menagerie', *Leeds Mercury*, 5 December 1874.
49 Only in 1900 were 'wild' and 'captive' animals formally protected by British law, and only in 1925 was a law passed specifically to regulate the treatment of performing animals. See Great Britain Parliament, *Wild Animals in Captivity Protection Act* (1900) [63 & 64 Victoria c. 33]; and Great Britain Parliament, *Performing Animals (Regulation) Act* (1925), [15 & 16 c.5].
50 'Fight between Mr Wombwell's lions and six bull dogs', *Liverpool Mercury*, 29 July 1825.
51 'Serpents and serpent feeding III', *The Animal World*, April 1881, 49–52.
52 'To the printer of the *Public Advertiser*', *Public Advertiser*, 16 February 1776.
53 'Seals in a Scotch aquarium', *The Animal World*, December 1878, 183.
54 'Animal Husbandry' in P. Batten, *Living Trophies*, New York: Thomas Y. Crowell Company, 1976, 39–72.
55 P. Cavalieri and P. Singer, *The Great Ape Project: Equality Beyond Humanity*, New York: St Martin's Press, 1993, 4.
56 J. Masson and S. McCarthy, *When Elephants Weep: The Emotional Lives of Animals*, London: Vintage: 1996, 147.
57 R. Clubb *et al.*, 'Compromised survivorship in zoo elephants', *Science* 322, 5908 (2008), 1649. For a discussion of how different species fare in a zoo environment, see G. Mason, 'Species differences in responses to captivity: stress, welfare and the comparative method', *Trends in Ecology and Evolution* 25, 12 (2010): 713–721.
58 'The hippopotamus in the Zoological Gardens', *Glasgow Herald*, 10 June 1850.
59 'Traffic in wild animals', *The Animal World*, July 1882, 103.
60 'A fight with an elephant at Birmingham', *North-Eastern Daily Gazette*, 6 May 1886.
61 'Family of boy who entered gorilla enclosure under investigation', *The Guardian*, 31 May 2016.
62 Malamud, *Reading Zoos*, 179.
63 'Chuny the elephant', *The Mirror of Literature, Amusement and Fashion*, 22 April 1826, 249.
64 'Sally the bald chimpanzee', *The Animal World*, November 1891, 164–165. For a discussion of the parallel rise of pet cemeteries in this period, see 'A place for the animal dead: animal souls, pet cemeteries and the heavenly home' in P. Howell, *At Home and*

Astray: The Domestic Dog in Victorian Britain, Charlottesville VA: University of Virginia University Press, 2015, 125–149.

65 'Jumbo', *The Animal World*, March 1884, 34.
66 On the public reaction to the sale of Jumbo, see Cowie, *Exhibiting Animals*, 142–153; and 'Jumbo: sentient animal celebrity' in S. Nance, *Animal Modernity: Jumbo the Elephant and the Human Dilemma*, New York: Palgrave Macmillan, 2015, 9–39.
67 'Jumbo', *Daily News*, 6 March 1882.
68 'Jumbo', *The Animal World*, March 1884, 34.
69 'Sally the bald chimpanzee', *The Animal World*, November 1891, 164–165.
70 'Pipaluk awaits his debut', *The Times*, 11 March 1968.
71 Nance, *Animal Modernity*, 84.
72 'Serious accident', *Caledonian Mercury*, 28 April 1836.
73 J. Hribal, *Fear of the Animal Planet: The Hidden History of Animal Resistance*, Oakland CA: AK Press, 2010, 55–61, 149–153. In March 2016 Sea World announced that it was ending the breeding of orca whales at its parks, a response, in part, to growing public pressure: see 'Sea World decides to stop killer whale breeding programme', *The Guardian*, 17 March 2016.
74 Hribal, *Fear of the Animal Planet*, 26.
75 Hribal, *Fear of the Animal Planet*, 18.
76 'The extraordinary freak of an elephant', *The Animal World*, October 1893, 159.
77 'A hero with a history', *Dundee Courier*, 20 April 1875.
78 On the execution of Topsy and other elephants, see A.L. Wood, '"Killing the elephant": murderous beasts and the thrill of retribution, 1885–1930', *The Journal of the Gilded Age and Progressive Era* 11, 3 (2012): 405–444.
79 'A hero with a History', *Dundee Courier*, 20 April 1875.
80 'The performing seal at the Royal Aquarium', *Illustrated London News*, 26 July 1879.
81 P. Tait, *Wild and Dangerous Performances: Animals, Emotions, Circus*, Basingstoke: Palgrave Macmillan, 2012. On the inter-species bonds forged through training and familiarity, see also L. Birke and J. Hockenhull, 'Journeys together: horses and humans in partnership', *Society & Animals* 23, 1 (2015): 81–100.
82 F. Bostock, *The Training of Wild Animals*, New York: The Century Co., 1903, 214.
83 Bostock, *Training of Wild Animals*, 193.
84 Bostock, *Training of Wild Animals*, 160.
85 Bostock, *Training of Wild Animals*, 162.
86 *Animal Care Journal*, Belle Vue Gardens, Jennison Collection, Chetham's Library, Manchester, F.5.04, 27 July 1910; 28 December 1912; and 22 March 1910.
87 *Animal Care Journal*, 9 July 1909; 2 June 1912; and 25 September 1910.

Bibliography

Acampora, R. 'Extinction by exhibition: looking at and in the zoo', *Research in Human Ecology* 5, 1 (1998): 1–4.

Allen, T. *A Guide to the Zoological Gardens and Museum*, London: Cowie and Strange, 1829.

Amato, S. *Beastly Possessions: Animals in Victorian Consumer Culture*, Toronto: University of Toronto Press, 2015.

Anderson, K. 'Culture and nature at the Adelaide Zoo: at the frontiers of "human" geography', *Transactions of the Institute of British Geographers* 20, 3 (1995): 275–294.

Animal Care Journal, Belle Vue Gardens, Jennison Collection, Chetham's Library, Manchester, F.5.04.

Baratay, E. and Hardouin-Fugier, E. *Zoo: A History of Zoological Gardens in the West*, London: Reaktion Books, 2002.

Barrington-Johnson, J. *The Story of London Zoo*, London: Robert Hale, 2005.
Batten, P. *Living Trophies*, New York: Thomas Y. Crowell Company, 1976.
Birke, L. and Hockenhull, J. 'Journeys together: horses and humans in partnership', *Society & Animals* 23, 1 (2015): 81–100.
Bostock, F. *The Training of Wild Animals*, New York: The Century Co., 1903.
Bostock, S. *Zoos and Animal Rights: The Ethics of Keeping Animals*, London: Routledge, 1993.
Braverman, I. *Zooland: The Institution of Captivity*, Stanford CA: Stanford University Press, 2013.
Cavalieri, P. and Singer, P. *The Great Ape Project: Equality Beyond Humanity*, New York: St Martin's Press, 1993.
Clubb, R., Rowcliffe, M., Lee, P., Mar, K.U., Moss, C., and Mason, G.J. 'Compromised survivorship in zoo elephants', *Science* 322, 5908 (2008): 1649.
Colley, A. *Animal Skins in Victorian Britain: Zoos, Collections, Portraits and Maps*, Farnham: Ashgate, 2015, 4.
Cowie, H., *Exhibiting Animals in Nineteenth-Century Britain: Empathy, Education, Entertainment*, Basingstoke: Palgrave Macmillan, 2014.
Cowie, H. '"An attractive and improving place of resort": zoo, community and civic pride in nineteenth-century Britain', *Social and Cultural History* 12, 3 (2015): 365–384.
DeMello, M. *Animals and Society: An Introduction to Human–Animal Studies*, New York: Columbia University Press, 2012.
Flack, A. *The Natures of the Beasts: An Animal History of Bristol Zoo Gardens since 1835*, PhD dissertation, University of Bristol, 2013.
Grigson, C. *Menagerie: The History of Exotic Animals in England*, Oxford: Oxford University Press, 2016.
Guerrini, A. *The Courtiers' Anatomists: Animals and Humans in Louis XIV's Paris*, Chicago IL: Chicago University Press, 2015.
Hanson, E. *Animal Attractions: Nature on Display in American Zoos*, Princeton NJ: Princeton University Press, 2002.
Hoage, R.J. and Deiss, W.A. *New Worlds, New Animals: From Menagerie to Zoological Park in the Nineteenth Century*, Baltimore MD: Johns Hopkins University Press, 1996.
Hochadel, O. 'Watching exotic animals next door: "scientific" observations at the zoo (ca. 1870–1910)', *Science in Context* 24, 2 (2011): 183–214.
Howell, P. *At Home and Astray: The Domestic Dog in Victorian Britain*, Charlottesville VA: University of Virginia University Press, 2015.
Hribal, J. *Fear of the Animal Planet: The Hidden History of Animal Resistance*, Oakland CA: AK Press, 2010.
Ito, T. *London Zoo and the Victorians, 1828–1859*, Woodbridge: Boydell and Brewer, 2014.
Jones, R. '"The sight of creatures strange to our clime": London Zoo and the consumption of the exotic', *Journal of Victorian Culture* 2, 1 (1997): 1–26.
Kean, H. *Animal Rights: Political and Social Change in Britain since 1800*, London: Reaktion Books, 1998.
Kellert, S. *Kinship to Mastery: Biophilia in Human Evolution and Development*, Washington DC: Island Press, 1997.
Malamud, R. *Reading Zoos: Representations of Animals in Captivity*, New York: New York University Press, 1998.
Mason, G. 'Species differences in responses to captivity: stress, welfare and the comparative method', *Trends in Ecology and Evolution* 25, 12 (2010): 713–721.
Masson, J. and McCarthy, S. *When Elephants Weep: The Emotional Lives of Animals*, London: Vintage, 1996.
Mullan, B. and Marvin, G. *Zoo Culture*, Chicago IL: University of Illinois Press, 1987.

Nance, S. *Entertaining Elephants: Animal Agency and the Business of the American Circus*, Baltimore MD: Johns Hopkins University Press, 2013.

Nance, S. *Animal Modernity: Jumbo the Elephant and the Human Dilemma*, New York: Palgrave Macmillan, 2015.

Osborne, M. *Nature, the Exotic and the Science of French Colonialism*, Bloomington IN: Indiana University Press, 1994.

Pimentel, J. *The Rhinoceros and the Megatherium: An Essay in Natural History*, Cambridge MA: Harvard University Press, 2017.

Plumb, C. *The Georgian Menagerie*, London: IB Tauris, 2015.

Porter, B. *The Absent-Minded Imperialists: What the British Really Thought about Empire*, Oxford: Oxford University Press, 2004.

Ritvo, H. *The Animal Estate: The English and Other Creatures in the Victorian Age*, Cambridge MA: Harvard University Press, 1987.

Robbins, L. *Elephant Slaves and Pampered Parrots: Exotic Animals in Eighteenth-Century Paris*, Baltimore MD: Johns Hopkins University Press, 2002.

Rothfels, N. *Savages and Beasts: The Birth of the Modern Zoo*, Baltimore MD: Johns Hopkins University Press, 2002.

Tait, P. *Wild and Dangerous Performances: Animals, Emotions, Circus*, Basingstoke: Palgrave Macmillan, 2012.

Uddin, L. *Zoo Renewal: White Flight and the Animal Ghetto*, Minneapolis MN: University of Minnesota Press, 2015.

Walton, W. *A Memoir Addressed to Proprietors of Mountain and Other Waste Lands and Agriculturalists of the United Kingdom, on the Naturalisation of the Alpaca*, London: Smith, Elder and Co., 1841.

Wood, A.L. '"Killing the elephant": murderous beasts and the thrill of retribution, 1885–1930', *The Journal of the Gilded Age and Progressive Era* 11, 3 (2012): 405–444.

14

TOPOLOGIES OF TENDERNESS AND VIOLENCE

Human–animal relations in Georgian England

Carl Griffin

Introduction

First shown at the Royal Academy in 1853, William Holman Hunt's Pre-Raphaelite oil-on-canvas masterpiece *Our English Coasts* (Figure 14.1) depicts a flock of sheep perched perilously close to the edge of the cliffs at Fairlight Glen, Sussex. Notwithstanding that it was commissioned by Charles Theobald Maud on having been impressed by Hunt's representation of sheep in his 1851 painting *The Hireling Shepherd*, the sheep are at once the figurative stars of *Our English Coasts* and yet absent. It was read as a satire of the supposedly defenceless English coastline against a feared invasion from despotic, expansionist Napoleon III, the sheep visual metaphors for feebleness, English lambs to the French slaughter. The original frame also bore the inscription 'The Lost Sheep', and when exhibited in Paris in 1855 the painting was retitled *Strayed Sheep*, both explicit biblical allusions. Other critics saw not metaphor, nor sheep, but were wowed by Hunt's treatment of light. As Ruskin saw it, 'for the first time in the history of art [it depicted], the absolutely faithful balances of colour and shade by which actual sunlight might be transposed'.[1]

Whatever Maud's admiration of Hunt's way with sheep on canvas, we can read Hunt's most famous work as mirroring conventional historical tellings of the place of sheep – and most other animals – in late eighteenth- and nineteenth-century England: implicitly everywhere and entwined in all things, and yet at best marginal and at worst entirely written out of our histories. If ploughs and cows were once the marker of agrarian histories, the cows (and other ungulates, equines, poultry, fowl, cats, dogs, and 'vermin') tended to be written as things on which capital operated, no more and no less than the ploughs (and other inanimate things). If this is to paint with a broad brush – Edith Whetham's 1977 essay on pedigree livestock notes for instance the different values attached to breeds by different cattle and sheep societies – the point still holds.[2] It is also ironic that the shift in the early 1990s towards more

Figure 14.1 William Holman Hunt, 'Our English Coasts' ('Strayed Sheep'), 1852, Tate Gallery, London.

Courtesy Tate Gallery, London.

culturally informed, *Annales*-style approaches, typified and led by the Cambridge University Press journal *Rural History*, tended, albeit unconsciously, to overlook animals altogether.[3] None of this is to say that such approaches deliberately intended to confer that animals were automata, mere fleshy machines on which the human will operated. Rather, past writings of the rural reflect established and pervasive trends of intellectual purification that have the humanities and social sciences in opposition to the natural and life sciences, the one writing culture the other nature.[4]

As with Hunt's *Our English Coasts*, animals have both been present by proxy but in other ways absent in studies of our rural pasts. And yet, the fact that Hunt chose to paint sheep and shepherding scenes speaks not only to the symbolic potency of pastoralism in English cultural politics and national identity but also to the literal fact that rural life was not reducible to the social but rather was co-constituted by the animal. Cattle, pigs and sheep, amongst other livestock, alongside working animals such as dogs, horses and oxen were at once workers' charges, companions and co-workers, while wild animals provided both income, sustenance, sport and pleasure.[5]

It is the contention of this chapter that 'being with' takes many forms. When species meet (to use Donna Haraway's formula), the companionships that follow do not stop at faithful friend, beautiful beast, but extend to an infinite web in which are folded love, affection, indifference and violent enmity.[6] Drawing on foundational work in the animal studies movement, cultural and historical geography, and in environmental history, as well as some more recent work in rural history that has been attentive to more-than-human histories, this chapter explores the different contours of 'being with' in our histories.[7] Given that animals only exist in the archive by virtue of human interventions and representations – whether in the form of documents, the zooarchaeological record, paintings, prose or preservation – any such study is necessarily reliant on, and therefore limited by, the happenstance of record. Even, as Pearson and Weismantel have suggested, to 'move beyond' the conventional archive and to 'draw upon techniques derived from ethnography, oral history, [and] literary studies' is still to be in thrall to human interpretations and framings.[8] But it is not the intention of this chapter to write a history of animals in rural England on their own terms. Rather, alert to archival framings and limitations, it considers the ways in which being with was expressed through both violence and its linguistic antonym, tenderness. The frame is eighteenth- and early nineteenth-century rural England, the context in which, as Harriet Ritvo has stated, rapid capitalist and social change was enacting new forms of human–animal.[9] In this, it draws upon both Haraway's inspiring work on the comings together between humans and dogs, as well as Sarah Whatmore's conception of complex, intertwined more-than-human worlds as fluid and relational, hence the 'topology' metaphor.[10] Before analysing these topologies of tenderness and violence, the chapter begins with a brief consideration of existing understandings of how rural human–animal relations have hitherto been written and represented.

Being with

As Phil Howell has asserted, the history of changing human attitudes to animals (and their welfare) is often writ in spatial terms, and in particular in relation to theories of spatial proximity.[11] Until recently our understanding was as follows. As J. Carter Wood has put it, the pervasive belief in early modern England was that violence and 'visible "cruelty"' was a 'generally assumed part of daily life' and 'shared among all social ranks'. Parallel to the decline in violent crime, and especially homicide, changing attitudes in the early nineteenth century to cruelty against animals reflected a culture of rising 'civility' and 'respectability'.[12] Further, animals became more removed from everyday life for an increasing proportion of the population living in towns and cities. This was not only a process of material separation but also, as John Berger has argued, one of cultural separation, as animals became present symbolically in representations rather than the flesh.[13] Being apart, being distanced, with animals increasingly enclosed – in oil on canvas, in cages in zoos, or in the parlour as domestic trophies – was a necessary spatial precondition for the emergence of new middle-class sensibilities towards animals. Livestock were banished to the canvas, wild animals either removed as vermin or placed in cages as specimens of scientific and cultural curiosity, and domestic pets were those that were left as the proper object of affection and care. This shifting sensibility extended, though in a distinctly modulated way, to working animals who should not be subjected to the brutal impulses of the brutish working class.[14]

The idea that by the early nineteenth century English cities were neatly purified, excluding nature as culture's other, is wide of the mark though. Not only were English towns home to large numbers of domestic pets – with all the problems and dedicated spaces that their existence necessitated, but working animals and livestock also helped to inscribe urban space and urban social relations. Pig-keeping remained an important practice of poor urban residents, something bolstered in places such as Manchester by Irish migrants but also by butchers and 'porkers' keeping large herds of pigs on small plots of land to help meet rising demand for pork from growing urban populations. Even in London as late as 1850 there were thought to be some 3,000 pigs in North Kensington alone, these fed on the food waste of the affluent residents in neighbouring districts of the capital.[15] Poultry-keeping was also common, not just on a small domestic scale but also in the practice of keeping chickens in vast lofts.[16] Such dedicated spaces and technologies for the keeping of animals, and the rendering of them as food, as Richie Nimmo notes, brought humans and animals together in the city but were also expressions of the way in which ideas of purification were developed and materially expressed.[17]

Persistences of 'being with' animals and animality in urban England into the early nineteenth century speak to the importance of *proximity*, as opposed to distance, in changing popular conceptions of animal welfare. Indeed, to Rob Boddice it was the making of England as an urban nation with 'animals and humans [brought] closer, on a grand scale, than they had been before' that was central to the emergence of new ways of thinking about human–animal relations and, relatedly, firing activism against animal cruelty.[18] Boddice's claims echo the earlier analysis by Keith Thomas in his genre-defining 1983 book *Man and the Natural World*, specifically, that the philosophical roots of changing human–animal relations could be found much earlier but that rapid urbanisation helped to develop the political conditions for animal activism. Thomas's analysis, in turn, mirrored those made by Dix Harwood in his pioneering but now obscure *Love for Animals and How it Developed in Great Britain*, first published in 1928.[19]

If by the late eighteenth century, English travellers, by way of asserting English cultural and moral superiority, frequently expressed their surprise and distaste at how animals in other European countries were treated, England was no paragon of saintly virtue in its treatment of animals.[20] Bull-baiting, cock- and dog-fighting, and hunting all rested upon human, and specifically male, amusement and glee in animal suffering and the sport of being denied life. As the famed naturalist the Reverend Gilbert White of Selborne noted of Woolmer and Alice Holt forests in the late eighteenth century, it was a rite of passage for local boys to chase and hunt the deer in the forest, a marker of masculinity, of becoming a man, and this notwithstanding that deer-stealing was a felony.[21] But in such acts there was also wonder at the strength and guile of the brute creation, and in cock- and dog-fighting a degree of perverse admiration for the level of bloody desperation that cocks and dogs showed in their self-defence. There is no escaping though that there were 'stylised and formal' methods of torment. And, in turn, they were mirrored by the 'informal' modes of cruelty practised in children's games and given cultural currency in nursery rhymes.[22] Whatever the rising tide of philosophical and physiological understanding of animal suffering and animal activism, for large parts of the population the abuse of animals was a key cultural form in Hanoverian England.

What of rural England? What of those places where the rhythms of everyday life were most strongly linked to animal lives? In some ways Thomas's superb book represented, at least at first, a cul-de-sac in our understandings of 'human attitudes' to flora and fauna. So wide-ranging and detailed, and so absolutely different in terms of focus and argument to prevailing trends in the historiography of early modern England, it was easy to admire Thomas's study but not to attempt a follow-up. As Malcolm Chase noted in 1992, while Thomas's book 'radically changed perceptions of the relationship between humankind and nature in past time', '[British] historical scholarship has remained largely impervious to "green" issues'.[23] Indeed, there are striking parallels between the development and status of environmental histories and animal histories in British academe. Notwithstanding the pioneering work of British historical geographers on biophysical landscape change (note, such studies did not use the term environment in the context later used by environmental historians) and representational politics of landscape, it was not until the turn of the current century that environmental history gained real intellectual traction amongst UK scholars.[24] If work on environmental histories of rural England has subsequently assumed a higher profile – this best attested by the large number of sessions with an explicitly rural focus at the 'environments'-themed 79th Anglo American Conference of Historians and that 'Landscape and Environment' was one of the recent major research programmes of the Arts and Humanities Research Council – work on human–animal relations in the English countryside remains little studied.[25]

This is not to say that the rural has not figured strongly in works on philosophical and theological conceptions of what separated humans and animals, for example Erica Fudge's superb study of early modern England, or in otherwise urban-centric analyses of the 'rise' of human concerns with animal welfare in the modern age.[26] Studies of poaching and hunting remain shibboleths of rural history, though outside of Emma Griffin's culturally nuanced studies, explicit concerns with the relationship between animals and humans have not figured.[27] The critical post-*Man and the Natural World* exception to this rule is Ritvo's *The Animal Estate*, which while not a history of the countryside per se offered several suggestive and richly detailed accounts of differing ways in which animals were immersed in complex cultural worlds in Victorian Britain.[28] An honourable mention must also be made to Stephen Caunce's oral history of the 'horselads' of the Wolds and Holderness in East Yorkshire, though it focuses only on horses – and in one particular context – not the wider relationship between humans and animals.[29]

Yet despite the rise of environmental history and the parallel rise of the animal studies movement – of which important historical works include Fudge's and Howell's aforementioned studies, as well as influential work by James Serpell – considerations of being-with and the hybridity of nature and culture in rural Britain are few.[30] Cultural geographers David Matless and Hayden Lorimer, drawing on these influences as well as wider intellectual currents in the social sciences and post-structuralist philosophy, have also considered different ways in which humans and animals come together in making rural worlds, albeit focused on the recent past.[31] Yet as Lorimer has noted, there is much to be gained even for those interested in the present to gain from 'revisiting . . . unlikely rural pasts'.[32]

If 'traditional' agrarian histories and *Annales*-style rural histories alike had long since failed to place animal–human relations centre stage, in the past decade the situation has started to change. Recent studies in the journal *Rural History* have included analyses of the cultures of hunting and poaching, changing ways in which animal welfare is represented, and the role of animals in recreation and sport.[33] The rest of this chapter seeks to extend these understandings through the dual focus of violence and tenderness. First, it explores the ways in which agrarian capital framed the relationship between rural residents and animals. Second, it looks at the ways in which co-existence ('getting by') shaped animal–human relations. Third, and finally, it looks at expressions of love, affection and attachment between animals and their humans.

'Rubbing down': capital and status

'Barons of Beef': not a hipster restaurant, but the first chapter in Ritvo's *The Animal Estate*. While agrarian historians had previously considered the late eighteenth and early nineteenth century craze for improved livestock, Ritvo's chapter places the mania for improvement into its wider cultural and socio-political context. To Ritvo, early nineteenth-century English society viewed animals, distinct from the way in which their laws viewed animals, as something other than just property.[34] If all animals were understood as being goods (or conversely as being antithetical to property, vermin), relationships with, and attitudes towards, animals were shaped by a range of sentiments that were not limited to political economy. Ritvo starts her analysis with the example of the Durham Ox. It had 'no special skills' while in appearance 'it resembled other shorthorned cattle', but on one day alone in 1802, admission fees to see the beast in London totalled £97. Nor was that day a one-off. Starting in 1801 it toured England and Scotland for six years, 'drawing crowds of admirers' wherever it went. This was a huge, fat beast of impressive breeding, a prize-specimen that captured not only the agriculturalists' imagination but also that of the public. It was a trophy, a testament to improvement rather than just a fat ox. If the value of the Durham Ox increased dramatically, this reflected its bovine celebrity and crowd pulling-power rather than its breed value. But after failing to recover from an injury to its hip on alighting from its specially constructed, four horse-drawn carriage at Oxford in early 1807, it was slaughtered. The ox's reported dead weight of '30 score per quarter' (1,200 kg) was undoubtedly freakishly prodigious, but its flesh, hide and bone entered the very same circuits of rendering and consumption as other cows. Here was an animal that at once was inscribed in circuits of capital, though these were decidedly more-than-agricultural, and yet whose complex animal–human relations – value, pride, awe, sentiment, status, identity, improvement – transcended being mere fleshy capital.[35]

In bovine terms, the case of the Durham Ox is arguably unusual, for most cattle were neither famed and feted nor primped and preened. And yet, the example demonstrates the ways in which even the most lumpen of livestock assumed multiple meanings and attachments. Prize cattle were only a few inches in height and girth and a few stones distanced from the typical denizens of the farmyard and field. As Michael Quinn notes, the development of breed standards, or specifically what the cow in the yard and field should *look* like, in the nineteenth century was in large part facilitated by the circulation of representations (and even bodies) of beasts like the Durham Ox, the idealised becoming the yardstick. The production of such representations also became a defining feature of British painting, and not just for the drawing rooms of grandees. John Boultbee's painting of the Durham Ox – one of several of that famous animal – was produced as a print that became a lucrative bestseller. While prints were not accessible to all, it is telling that public houses were often named after either generic animals of the countryside (whether agrarian such as the Red Cow or the Bull's Head, or of the hunt, such as the White Hart or Red Fox) or famed animals. The Durham Ox remains immortalised in countless pub names (and subsequently represented in their pub signs) throughout England.

The Durham Ox was both magnificent and, because it was relatably of the field, yard, market, and slaughterhouse, mundane. Indeed, it is in this decidedly mundane essence that the most interesting facet of all prize animals was manifest: people, whether urban dweller or rural worker, related to livestock. This was in part because of the obvious link to subsistence and consuming pleasures, and of political connotations – not least in relation to the patriotic dish of roast beef, that great culinary totem of English identity – but it also spoke to a profound sense of connection through the shared spaces of everyday life. By working with them, by being seen (and thus being not just a symbol but also being part of the material fabric of being and the living landscape), through inhabiting and shaping shared spaces, and the sense of one's destiny being conjoined with the other, livestock meant more than just capital.[36]

Racehorses arguably provide a more obvious example of the ways in which animals transcended being fleshy capital. If cows becoming status symbols helped to develop a significant artistic sub-genre – the Kent artist Thomas Sidney Cooper becoming known as 'Cow Cooper' as a result of his expertise in painting bovine beauties – equine paintings were, and continue as, a genre in their own right.[37] This was emphatically attested to not only by the fame of the most prolific 'horse artist' George Stubbs but also by the 2012 British Museum exhibition 'The horse from Arabia to Royal Ascot'.[38] If crowds flocked to see the Durham Ox because of its vast size, the patronage of horse racing was decidedly more aristocratic, most individuals connecting not with the horse per se but rather with the spectacle of racing, both materially and increasingly at a distance through sports reports and the emergent sporting press.[39] And yet, because of the shared love of racing, (successful) racehorses assumed a level of status that did not simply reflect their sporting value but rather their celebrity and repute. The example of one of Stubbs' best-known paintings perfectly exemplifies this dynamic. A bay colt foaled at John Hutchinson's North Yorkshire stables in 1792, Hambletonian (named after the local Hambleton Hills) proved a hugely successful racehorse. Passing through the hands of several owners, on 25 March 1799 it took part in what became a famous two-horse race at Newmarket. Beyond the drama of the race – Hambletonian won by a neck having supposedly covered 21 feet in the final stride to the line – the fact that owner Sir Henry Vane-Tempest had wagered 3,000 guineas on the result ensured notoriety. Henry duly commissioned Stubbs to record Hambletonian's victory on canvas. The painting (*Hambletonian, Rubbing Down*, Figure 14.2) depicted an exhausted Hambletonian (minus the wounds inflicted during the race) being held by Henry's groom, and being tenderly and affectionately rubbed down by a stable boy. That the race was recorded speaks more about the stake placed, and the wish to revel in the reflected glory, than the equine feat. But the actual painting is more complex in portraying animal–human relations. It speaks only of patronage in that it exists, and through depicting the care of the stable hand tending selflessly to the clearly distressed

Figure 14.2 George Stubbs, 'Hambletonian, Rubbing Down', 1799–1800, Mount Stewart Collection, County Down.

Courtesy National Trust.

Hambletonian, it tells of a world where the relationship between worker and animal could transcend capital.[40]

More-than-capital value was also invested in animals other than horses and cattle. As is well established, hunting animals was an ancient way in which status was performed, claimed and earned in rural England. The same was also true for the consumption of certain animals of the chase and freshwater fish.[41] Sheep could also become symbols of status and thus not reducible just to the logic of capital. Certain livestock breeds could imply a certain social status on the estate or farmer. Thus while in the early nineteenth century the keeping of regional livestock breeds was the norm, the development of new and improved breeds fed a demand amongst 'gentleman' farmers to not only experiment and 'improve' their farms but also stock their paddocks with the latest, most fashionable breeds. As Gavin Bowie has noted of the Southdown breed, 'owning a flock of Southdowns implied a certain social status'; a paper in the *Journal of the Royal Agricultural Society of England* on the farming of Hampshire reported that Southdown sheep were 'in favour with gentlemen farming their own estates, for the finer quality of the mutton'.[42] Similarly, agricultural commentator William Marshall asserted that Leicester sheep were not suited to the farms of Norfolk but 'may not be unfitted to "the paddocks of a gentleman"'.[43]

As with the Durham Ox, Hambletonian and gentlemen farmers' Southdowns, all animals when enrolled as capital required human labour: to feed, to protect, to care for. Purely in terms of the wage-labour nexus, this relationship was defined by the bargain struck between employer and employee. Rural workers and other people's animals were thereby locked in a decidedly uneven relationship: the one cared for;

the other the hired care. From the mid-eighteenth century, farmworkers' wages were, in real terms, in long-term decline, while, especially in the period before 1815, farmers' incomes were rising. Their contrasting fortunes engendered tension and fed a rising tide of protest.[44] Given the symbolic importance of forms of property as capital in the relationship, these protests often took the form of incendiarism and malicious attacks on buildings, dead-stock and livestock. Though not as frequently practised as arson, malicious attacks on animals ('animal maiming') were an important weapon of the weak. Indeed, that so many cases of animal maiming were motivated by revenge against an (ex)employer – or as in the case of a Lincolnshire labourer found guilty of maiming three mares in revenge for the owner having dismissed his mother and sister from his service – it made sense to symbolically attack the capital of the malefactor.[45] Of course, many farmworkers were familiar with working with animals and therefore knew how to handle and therefore hurt them, from the administering of poisons, to the docking of tails, the cutting-off of ears and genitals, to practices mimetic of butchery.[46]

Acts of animal maiming often went beyond such seemingly straightforward motivations. The case of the poisoning of 198 sheep in the Wiltshire parish of Berwick St. James belonging to 'gentleman farmer' Erlysman Charles Pinkney in January 1848 is instructive. Labourer James Blanchard had been dismissed in 1840 from Pinkney's employment, on which occasion Blanchard threatened 'to do for' Pinkney. The threat was not carried out, but when he was refused work with Pinkney in July 1847 later he again said he would have to shoot the farmer and poison his sheep. On being challenged by Pinkney's steward, the labourer countered: 'If I live, and you live, you will see; there will be mutton enough for many'. Duly arrested and only freed when he apologised to Pinkney, it later transpired that while in custody he confessed to a fellow inmate that when released he would poison hundreds of sheep. After the poisoning, Blanchard was again arrested and committed to trial. The evidence only being circumstantial, Blanchard was subsequently acquitted at the Wiltshire Assizes. This, then, was quite different from most acts of animal maiming which tended to target one or two mammals. This mass killing was not just about targeting Pinkney where it hurt, in his account book, but also through the bloodletting attacking his body by proxy – and here the repeated *threats* against his person are critical – and it makes a profound statement about the role of animals in rural England. Animals were not to make money for the rich but to provide food for the poor, to give 'mutton enough for many'.[47]

'Pretty piggy': getting by

Haraway's delineation of the situations in which species meet offers an extraordinary range of the ways in which human and animal (and especially dog) lives are intertwined, from the co-constituted spaces of the home, laboratory and sportsfield as well as in terms of food, breed book, film and technoculture. While all of Haraway's analyses are rooted in the understanding of 'being with', whether materially or virtually, ranging from the tender to the violent, what does not figure are the ways in which animals are employed to act against humans. The obvious example, and one that played out in powerful ways in rural England, was that of dogs set to guard property. Of course, such dogs were so enrolled to guard against the actions of the poor, and in this way became symbols of class oppression. Guard dogs belonging to the clergy were particularly subject to attacks by animal maimers. Two Hampshire clergymen had their Newfoundland dogs – not naturally aggressive but large and intimidating and easily trained to guard property – maimed in Hampshire in the 1820s. While that belonging to the Reverend Richards at Newport on the Isle of Wight survived being shot, Bramshott clergyman, the Reverend Monkhouse's died from being poisoned. So fond was Monkhouse of his dog that he even satirically left the assailant a shilling in his will.[48] Domestic pets acting to defend their territory against intruders could also be so treated. In August 1817 a 'house dog' of farmer Phillman of Nunton (Wiltshire) had its throat cut after it started barking at three would-be burglars.[49]

Such attacks on dogs were not just motivated by malice against the dog – the result of fear, and the fear of being found on the premises – but also against the avarice and pride of the owner. Guard dogs not only 'defended' property but also defended status and policed class difference. To keep a dog was a privilege allowed only to those above the status of rural workers. That dogs featured in so many portraits of the nobility and gentry, and were even the *subject* of many paintings, profoundly attests not just the strong attachments of many rural elites to their dogs but also the social cache attached to canines. If Mr. and Mrs. Andrews, the subjects of the famous eponymous painting by Thomas Gainsborough (c.1750), were allowed an 'obedient hound at heel and the promise of good shooting ahead' the poor were not.[50] As the rulers of rural England saw it, the only animals the poor were allowed to keep were those they might turn onto the common – if they were lucky enough to live somewhere that had not been subject to enclosure – or keep in their gardens and yards.[51] The function of animals in the domestic spaces of the poor was to provide flesh and milk rather than companionship or to hunt. In cultural hegemonic terms, dogs were absolutely off-limits. This is not to say that rural workers did not keep dogs (and ferrets) to go poaching with, and perhaps as company, but otherwise to keep a dog was to be held in constant suspicion – and surveillance – as a lawbreaker. The proliferation of so-called game acts in eighteenth-century England placed ever-greater restrictions on the use of dogs, with the Black Act of 1723 empowering magistrates to seize and kill the dogs of poachers. As E.P. Thompson notes: 'No power provoked fiercer resentment than this. A good greyhound or lurcher was a substantial investment . . . and its training – no less than that of an expert sheep-dog – may have occupied months'. And when such powers were used by magistrates, the killing of the dog often sparked an act of protest or revenge. When a greyhound belonging to Buckinghamshire labourer William Cooke was seized in 1727, 'he threatened that unless the dog was returned within a fortnight, he would come, with twenty or thirty companions, cut down the pales of a gentleman's park and drive out the deer'. The threat was carried out.[52]

The ownership of dogs by the rural poor was also a social policy battleground and used to justify the non-payment of poor relief. For instance, the vestry of Preston Candover (Hampshire) resolved in May 1827 that those who kept dogs would from then on be refused relief. Thatcham (Berkshire) vestry went further, dictating two years previously that not only those with dogs, with the exception of shepherds, but those who kept pigs and cows would likewise in future be denied any support from the parish.[53] Of course, such policy pronouncements in part rested on the suspicion that dog ownership was evidence of poaching rather than working for a living, in other words not being subject to the strictures of agrarian capitalism. But in practical terms they also spoke to the belief that if someone could afford to keep a dog they could also afford to feed themselves and had no need for relief. When a Southampton 'out pauper' – someone 'settled' to a parish and thus able to claim poor relief from that parish but resident elsewhere – had her weekly relief stopped because she owned a dog, she promptly killed the animal and carried it to a meeting of the Southampton 'Court of Guardians' so that her relief could be reinstated.[54] Such resentments about dog ownership were even a discourse in the Swing quasi-insurrection of 1830. In late October 1830, a highly mobile gang of Swing activists led by a politicised London shoemaker called Robert Price, called on genteel Charlotte Stacey at Stockbury (Kent). In the group's parley with Stacey, Price, amongst other critiques and demands, angrily stated that: 'I understand you keep a great dog to bark at beggars'.[55]

It is important to note though that it was not always the way in which dogs were socially enrolled that made canines the subject of attack. William Butler, a 'considerable paper-maker', and William Coglan were tried at the Berkshire Assizes in July 1789 on a civil charge of having shot a mastiff belonging to Elizabeth Banks of Thatcham. During the previous summer, Butler had 'undeservedly taken an antipathy against the dog' and had 'flung stones at it at different times' and declared that 'he would take an early opportunity of destroying the dog'. Then on returning from a shoot on 23 December 1788, Butler and Coglan made good the threat by shooting the dog in the throat. Supposedly, so they argued in their defence, the dog was 'ferocious', but could not attest this on oath. Instead, the court heard, the mastiff was 'quite an inoffensive animal'. The case was found in Banks' favour, and Butler and Coglan ordered to pay her costs and £20 in damages. This was no case of an impoverished labourer attacking a rich man's dog but an act born of a yet more complex set of relations, an inability to get by with, an antipathy not to animals per se but a bitter aversion to some animals' being and character. Indeed, this was no simple case of cruelty – as in the case of two dogs killed in the marketplace at nearby Reading earlier that year by having oil of vitriol thrown on them – in which the dog is a thing for the amusement of the perpetrator, but rather an act of anti-conviviality.[56]

Pigs were enrolled in a no less complex set of relations than dogs. The history of the use of 'pig' as a term of personal insult goes back to at least the mid-sixteenth century, the allusion being to unpleasantness, unattractiveness, and greediness. Infamously, in his response to the French Revolution of 1789, Edmund Burke referred to the populace at large as the 'swinish multitude', though English Jacobins were quick to reappropriate Burke's porcine pejorative into a pennant of popular pride. By the beginning of the nineteenth century 'pig' was also being used pejoratively to refer to Bow Street Runners, those London police officers sent into the provinces to investigate crimes. The use of the word swine had an even longer history as a term of abuse, it being used since the time of Chaucer as a reference to degraded habits.[57] If the precise genesis of these uses is open to conjecture, the allusion made to those living in dirty, close conditions is obvious.[58] These long-standing popular understandings carried through into perceptions of those poor members of society who lived closely with pigs. As Bob Malcolmson and Stephanos Mastoris note, the pig was closely associated with Irish migrants, a group racially framed and represented in terms of bestial characteristics and manners. The Irish migrant in England, according to Fredrick Engels, 'builds a pig-sty against the house wall as he did at home [in rural Ireland], and if he is prevented from doing this, he lets the pig sleep in the room with himself'. Notwithstanding that the 'domestic' pig was kept to be fattened, slaughtered and eaten, Irish migrants, so Engels continued, still ate, slept and played with their pigs. Their pigs were truly companion animals, but companion animals that were always destined to be killed and consumed.[59]

While Engels in his investigation of rapidly growing Manchester in the early 1840s considered the pig to be a companion, and problem, of the Irish, living with pigs (and other livestock) was not confined to immigrants. Nor was it a recent phenomenon. The practice of living in the same quarters with one's animals goes back to the point at which animals were first domesticated, some 15,000 years ago, though animals were probably first admitted into human spaces somewhere between 60,000 and 125,000 years ago. As Tim Ingold has put it, in these ways animals became 'domestic familiars'.[60] Such human–animal cohabitation arrangements persisted in a variety of contexts: from the byre-dwellings of Cumbria and parts of south-west England, to the shared human-dog-lamb space of the mobile shepherd's hut, and in other similar spaces in systems of transhumance. It was also true of the forced proximity of the peasants' or labourers' domestic space which was often shared with pigs and cattle.[61] In this, pigs were especially important in rural England, given that for the rural poor so much was tied up in their being, both economically and socially. In areas with remnant commons and wastes, pig-keeping was especially important, pigs being the only animal to get by on the poorest of soils.[62] For rural radical and self-styled friend of the rural poor, William Cobbett, the pig was the 'national animal', the pig promoting 'peace, goodwill, and happiness in a way that nothing else could'. This revered status was not simply a function of porcine culinary versatility or hogs' ability to convert waste into flesh and fat but also a reflection of the metaphysical awe in which pigs were held. If a 'couple of flitches of bacon' were worth 'fifty thousand methodist sermons and religious tracts', alive pigs were 'great softeners of the temper and promoters of domestic harmony. They are a blessing'. The cottage pig-keeper's discourse would start, so Cobbett claimed all 'rural philosophers' knew, with 'd–d hog' but soon ran to 'pretty piggy' as the hog made itself part of domestic life, becoming a porcine member of the wider family. More than any other animal in rural England, pigs truly assumed a position as, after Whatmore and Thorne, 'strange persons'. As such, the day of porcicide was thus at once a fleshy harvest yet also a day of, as Ian Dyck has put it, 'nervous anticipation'.[63] The infamous pig-killing scene in Thomas Hardy's *Jude the Obscure* depicts a day of misgivings, anxiety, fear, argument, guilt, anguish and tears.[64]

'Neighbours and playmates': tenderness

As one might expect with an animal that became a part of the family, until the day of unbearable angst, pigs could be shown a considerable amount of tenderness. According to Engels, the children of piggy families 'play with it, ride upon it, roll in the dirt with it'.⁶⁵ As Flora Thompson recalled in *Lark Rise to Candleford*, the poor family's pig would become the subject of wider affection too: 'Men callers on Sunday afternoons came, not to see the [human] family, but the pig, and would lounge with its owner against the pigsty door for an hour, scratching the piggy's back'. That 'callers' visited and paid attention to the pig was in part predicated on the understanding that when slaughtered there would be a 'pig feast', calling by way of getting an invitation. The affection and tenderness shown to the pig was real enough; it just assumed a (to us) paradoxical position juxtaposing love and the inevitable final act of violence, the giving up of meat itself an act of paradoxical love.⁶⁶

This conjunction between tenderness and violence played out in a variety of contexts involving attacks on animals by those employed to look after them. In many cases of animal maiming it was the very person engaged in their care that was found to be, or suspected of being, the culprit. In May 1830, a boy was charged with thrusting a whip down the throat of his employer's horse at Basingstoke (Hampshire), an act the local press described as a 'wanton act of barbarity'. The practice of cutting the manes and tails of horses was also common. No doubt some such acts were theft, the culprits selling the valuable hair, but many other acts were deliberate inversions of the care normally shown to the animal. It was an act of revenge against masters and mistresses, well-groomed manes and tails the work of greatest care and tenderness but also the most obvious visual symbol of the pride invested by the rulers of rural England in their animals.⁶⁷ The inversion was not just practised against horses but also against other animals of the field and yard too. Sussex shepherd Rollason was arrested in the summer of 1849 on suspicion of cutting the throats and otherwise mutilating six lambs belonging to his master, farmer Akers of Hellingly. A 'diabolical' letter received by Akers subsequently confirmed that the motive was revenge, 'rejoic[ing]' in the act and threatening 'further harm by setting fire to the premises'.⁶⁸ In an even more blood-curdling act, a 10-year-old boy employed to look after the lambs on a farm at Idmiston (Wiltshire) confessed to killing twenty-one lambs with an iron bar. Three weeks previously his master had struck him, the boy's revenge being the striking of the lambs in his care.⁶⁹

The line between care and affection and cruelty and violence was arguably most profoundly expressed in the relationship between rural workers and wild animals. If Cobbett claimed that only toads and adders came second to the hatred labourers had for rich, self-aggrandising farmers, other wild animals provided not only food (through poaching) and sport for the rural poor but also enchantment.⁷⁰ The poems of 'peasant poet' John Clare are not only replete with references to the natural world; arguably, the fact of his being at one with the wider creation (as he saw it) defined his oeuvre. This went far beyond the work of the romantic poets in that Clare both demonstrated a far greater understanding of the natural world, and wrote of it from the perspective of his everyday life working in the Northamptonshire countryside. Yet, as David Perkins has noted, even the 'nature poet' Clare wrote 'stock celebrations' of hunting.⁷¹ W.H. Hudson's semi-fictional autobiography *A Shepherd's Life* also vividly relates the apparently contradictory positions of rural workers in relation to wild animals. In Hudson's account, shepherd Caleb Bawcombe (thought to represent real-life James Lawes) was reported as being so enchanted 'with the pretty sight of all these little foxes, neighbours and playmates' that he spent evening after evening with them, sitting for 'an hour or longer watching them'. Caleb later took the tenant farmer, whose land the foxes' burrows were on, to the spot. He too 'enjoyed the sight' but was determined to get rid of the foxes 'in the usual way exploding a small quantity of gunpowder in the burrows'.[72]

The strongest bond was between that of 'horselads' – agricultural workers employed to tend to and work with working horses – and their equine charges. If, as Hudson related, farmers were decidedly unsentimental when horses came to the end of their working lives, 'worn out' horses being sold to the hunt and fed to the hounds, those that worked most closely with them developed deep, affective engagements.[73] Such relations were reciprocal. John Lawrence in an 1802 treatise on the *Moral Duties of Man Towards the Brute Creation* noted that humans and horses alike showed affection to one another, while, as Keith Thomas detailed, Gervase Markham in his 1644 guide to horse care asserted that horses felt love, hatred, sorrow and joy, something they showed to their humans.[74] Getting at the way in which those who worked most closely with horses felt about their equine charges is harder for the simple reason that such horselads had no great reason to record their feelings. As Katherine and Melanie Giles' analysis of graffiti in extant nineteenth-century farm buildings in the Yorkshire Wolds attests, however, some lads thought enough of their animal charges to represent them in graffiti.[75]

Our most detailed understanding of the relationship comes from Caunce's oral histories of East Yorkshire horselads. While Caunce's study relates to experiences in the first half of the twentieth century, the horse–human relations detailed essentially remained unaltered from the turn of the nineteenth century. Several aspects are particularly striking. There was a decisive geography as to who was responsible for cleaning and grooming the farm's horses. In the Vale of York it was the job of the waggoner, the most senior member of the horse team, whereas elsewhere in the East Riding it was the job of a lad who would feed, clean and groom up to four horses.[76] It was the acts of feeding and grooming, so Caunce's respondents related, that built up a close relation and partnership between horse and human, something that 'was essential if the work was to be done without a struggle'. The bond was further deepened by the competition between the lads as to who could turn out the glossiest and fattest horses, while during the winter when the horses were kept in the stables the lads responsible would often spend their spare time with them taking advantage of the heat they gave off.[77] Not only was this all considered to be the work of men, but there was even a gendered hierarchy based on strength: the strongest lads would care for the stallions, the less powerful lads the geldings and the mares. Not too surprisingly, the horselads – this colloquial name in itself a reference to the men becoming horsey – tended to anthropomorphise their equine co-workers. '[Y]ou used to get some nice horses, a nice type of horse . . . When I was at Ruston Parva we had twin sisters, by – talk about them moving! They used to go overfast for me!'[78] Of course, the practice of breaking a horse was to make it not only yield to command but also to make it attentive to human being and presence, it was to make the horse more human. Certainly, there was a strong sense that Caunce's respondents believed that the horses became emotionally attached to their lads – and in return 'most horselads were very fond of their teams and to be severed from them . . . was a wrench'.[79]

Conclusion

Together, the foregoing cases do not constitute *the* history of human–animal relations in rural England. Elsewhere, in other places and times, no doubt other dynamics pertained. But the examples speak to a set of important humanimal dynamics and the ways in which not only were animals central to all ways of being in rural England but also fundamentally shaped rural worlds. Central to these unfurling topologies, the relations constantly changing over time and according to spatial contexts, was the profound connection between, on the one hand, love and affection, and on the other hand, violence. We know that some animals were thought to be fair game for hunting, killing and torture, Cobbett's adders and toads amongst them, and normalised and given cultural sanction in nursery rhymes and the many forms of highly stylised forms of violence (hunting; cockfighting). The passage of 'Humanity' Martin's Act (3 Geo. IV c. 71) in 1822 – the first dedicated legislation anywhere in the world that specifically prohibited cruelty to animals in consideration of their suffering – speaks to both the persistence of a culture of violence against animals as well as a stiffening of resolve to reform such attitudes. And even then we should not read too much into the passage of Martin's Act, for it only related to cattle, horses and sheep. It was not until the 1835 Cruelty to Animals Act (5 & 6 Will. 4, c. 59) that protection was also offered to dogs, goats and sheep, and bear-baiting and cockfighting were prohibited throughout England and Wales.[80]

Hitherto the emphasis on the emergence of new conceptions of animal rights and changing attitudes towards animal cruelty have tended to mask the ways in which companionship and interspecies affection, even something approaching love, were important in determining relations between humans and animals in rural England. It is clear that in a variety of contexts humans and animals came together in ways that were determined not just by the workings of capital or the logics of domestication and captivity but by care and respect. It is telling that some acts of violence – for instance the cutting of hair or the maiming of lambs – were parodies and bitter satires of care, tenderness towards animals positioned as the other of human suffering. As 'being with' took many forms, so tenderness and violence should not be understood as being diametrically opposed. After all, the cottagers' hog was at once pretty piggy and future food, it was never just a pet or just flesh. Gentlemen's horses were sold to the hunt, walked into the woods, shot, and the skin removed before being devoured by the hounds. Even the famed and feted Durham Ox ended up nourishing human bodies.

To return to Hunt's *Our English Coasts*. Beyond (re)thinking through human–animal relations in eighteenth- and early nineteenth-century rural England, this chapter also serves as a plea to economic and social historians to put animals back in their place (and into their studies). The animal studies movement, allied to work in cultural studies and cognate disciplines, has transformed the role of animals in academic study, while work by intellectual and urban historians (and historical geographers) has begun to critically engage with animals as something more than just fleshy things. To acknowledge, then, that animals are important in studying rural pasts is a start. To think of animals as more than numbers on inventories and rolls, as there but not there, as more than things that simply existed in fields and yards while the real stuff of (purely) human life went on, requires a far greater shift in how we conceptualise the rural and how we do history. The moments, the cases, examined in this chapter offer one possible way of writing such a new more-than-human rural history.

Notes

1 William Holman Hunt, *Our English Coasts* ('Strayed Sheep'), 1852: Tate Gallery, London. See: www.tate.org.uk/art/artworks/hunt-our-english-coasts-1852-strayed-sheep-n05665, last accessed 23 March 2017; E. Prettlejohn, *The Art of the Pre-Raphaelites*, London: Tate Publishing, 2000, 177–178; L. Parris (ed.), *The Pre-Raphaelites*, exhibition catalogue, London: Tate Gallery Publications, 1984, 108. Tellingly, *The Hireling Shepherd* was received in similar ways, critics commenting not on the sheep but taking offence at the 'flushed and rubicund' shepherd in suggestive repose with a flame-haired country girl: *Athenaeum*, 22 May 1853, 581–583. That the precise setting of Hunt's later painting was at a place in Fairlight Glen known as The Lover's Seat might be a reference to the controversial themes of *The Hireling Shepherd* or a simple coincidence.
2 E.H. Whetham, 'The trade in pedigree livestock 1850–1910', *Agricultural History Review* 27, 1 (1979): 47–50. For the classic exposition of this approach see J.D. Chambers and G.E. Mingay, *The Agricultural Revolution, 1750–1880*, London: Batsford, 1966.
3 L. Bellamy, K.D.M. Snell and T. Williamson, 'Rural history: the prospect before us', *Rural History* 1, 1 (1990): 1–4.
4 On the outcome of such acts of intellectual purification see S. Whatmore, *Hybrid Geographies: Natures, Cultures, Spaces*, London: Sage, 2002, ch.1.
5 C.J. Griffin, '"Some inhuman wretch": animal maiming and the ambivalent relationship between rural workers and animals', *Rural History* 25, 2 (2014): 133–160.
6 See D.J. Haraway, *When Species Meet*, Minneapolis MN: Minnesota University Press, 2008.
7 I deliberately use the term movement for, as Nigel Rothfels notes, such scholarship is 'embedded in ethics and activism', thus constituting something with shared aims and objectives which transcends the academy and seeks political and cultural change: N. Rothfels, 'Foreword', in J. Costlow and A. Nelson (eds.), *Other Animals: Beyond the Human in Russian Culture and History*, Pittsburgh PA: University of Pittsburgh Press, 2010, x.
8 S.J. Pearson and M. Weismantel, 'Does "the animal" exist? Toward a theory of social life with animals', in D. Brantz (ed.) *Beastly Natures: Animals, Humans, and the Study of History*, Charlottesville VA: University of Virginia Press, 2010, 17–37, 22.
9 H. Ritvo, *The Animal Estate: The English and Other Creatures in the Victorian Age*, Cambridge MA: Harvard University Press, 1987.
10 Haraway, *When Species Meet*; Whatmore, *Hybrid Geographies*; S. Whatmore and L. Thorne, 'Wild(er)ness: reconfiguring the geographies of wildlife', *Transactions of the Institute of British Geographers* 23, 4 (1988): 435–454.
11 P. Howell, *At Home and Astray: The Domestic Dog in Victorian Britain*, Charlottesville VA: University of Virginia Press, 2015, introduction.
12 J.C. Wood, *Violence and Crime in Nineteenth-Century England: The Shadow of our Refinement*, London: Routledge, 2004, 28.
13 J. Berger, *Why Look At Animals?*, London: Penguin, 2009, cited in Howell, *At Home and Astray*, 187.
14 On these dynamics see: H. Buller and C. Morris, 'Farm animal welfare: a new repertoire of nature–society relations or modernism re-embedded?', *Sociologia Ruralis* 43, 3 (2003): 216–237; M. Watts, 'Afterword: enclosure', in C. Philo and C. Wilbert (eds.), *Animal Spaces, Beastly Places: New Geographies of Human–Animal Relations*, London: Routledge, 2000, 292–304.

15 R. Scola, *Feeding the Victorian City: The Food Supply of Manchester, 1770–1870*, Manchester: Manchester University Press, 1992, 38–39; R. Malcolmson and S. Mastoris, *The English Pig: A History*, London: Hambledon, 2001, 43.
16 B. Short, '"The art and craft of chicken cramming": poultry in the Weald of Sussex 1850–1950', *Agricultural History Review* 30, 1 (1982): 17–30.
17 R. Nimmo, *Milk, Modernity and the Making of the Human: Purifying the Social*, London: Routledge, 2010. Also see: P. Atkins (ed.), *Animal Cities: Beastly Urban Histories*, Farnham: Ashgate, 2012.
18 R. Boddice, *History of Attitudes and Behaviours Towards Animals in Eighteenth- and Nineteenth-Century Britain: Anthropocentrism and the Emergence of Animals*, Lewiston NY: Edward Mellen Press, 2008, 84.
19 K. Thomas, *Man and the Natural World: Changing Attitudes in England 1500–1800*, London: Penguin, 1983; D. Harwood, *Love for Animals and How it Developed in Great Britain*, New York NY: Columbia University Press, 1928.
20 Thomas, *Man and the Natural World*, 143.
21 G. White, *The Natural History of Selborne*, ed. A. Secord, Oxford: Oxford University Press, 2013, 18.
22 Thomas, *Man and the Natural World*, 147, 150–160.
23 On the reception of Thomas's study see: M. Chase, 'Can history be green? A prognosis', *Rural History* 3, 2 (1992): 243–254, 248.
24 For instance see: H.C. Darby, *The Draining of the Fens*, Cambridge: Cambridge University Press, 1940; M. Williams, *Drainage of the Somerset Levels*, Cambridge: Cambridge University Press, 1970; D. Cosgrove and S. Daniels (eds.), *The Iconography of Landscape: Essays on the Symbolic Representation, Design and Use of Past Environments*, Cambridge: Cambridge University Press, 1988.
25 Anglo-American Conference Programme, www.history.ac.uk/aac2010/schedule; the Landscape and Environment Programme, 2006–2012, www.landscape.ac.uk/landscape/index.aspx, both last accessed 23 May 2016.
26 E. Fudge, *Brutal Reasoning: Animals, Rationality and Humanity in Early Modern England*, Ithaca NY: Cornell University Press, 2006; J. Turner, *Reckoning with the Beast: Animals, Pain, and Humanity in the Victorian Mind*, Baltimore MD: Johns Hopkins University Press, 1980; H. Kean, *Animal Rights: Political and Social Change in Britain Since 1800*, London: Reaktion, 1998. For important US parallels see: D. Beers, *For the Prevention of Cruelty: The History and Legacy of Animal Rights Activism in the United States*, Athens OH: Ohio University Press, 2006.
27 E. Griffin, *Blood Sport: A History of Hunting in Britain*, New Haven CT: Yale University Press, 2007; E. Griffin, *England's Revelry: A History of Popular Sports and Pastimes, 1660–1800*, Oxford: Oxford University Press, 2005. On excellent recent studies of poaching but that do not frame their analyses in terms of human–animal relations see: H. Osborne and M. Winstanley, 'Rural and urban poaching in Victorian England', *Rural History* 17, 2 (2006): 187–212; H. Osborne, '"Unwomanly practices": poaching crime, gender and the female offender in nineteenth-century Britain', *Rural History* 27, 2 (2016): 149–168.
28 Ritvo, *The Animal Estate*, (passim).
29 S. Caunce, *Amongst Farm Horses: The Horselads of East Yorkshire*, Stroud: Alan Sutton, 1991.
30 Fudge, *Brutal Reasoning*; P. Howell, 'Flush and the *banditti*: dog-stealing in Victorian London', in C. Philo and C. Wilbert (eds.), *Animal Spaces, Beastly Places: New Geographies of Human–Animal Relations*, London: Routledge, 2000, 35–55; Howell, *At Home and Astray*; J. Serpell, *In the Company of Animals: A Study of Human–Animal Relationships*, Cambridge: Cambridge University Press, 1996.

31 D. Matless, 'Versions of animal–human: Broadland, 1945–70', in C. Philo and C. Wilbert (eds.), *Animal Spaces, Beastly Places: New Geographies of Human–Animal Relations*, London: Routledge, 2000, 115–140; H. Lorimer, 'Herding memories of humans and animals', *Environment and Planning D: Society and Space* 24, 4 (2006): 497–518. For ways in which ideas of nature and culture have been critically reworked in cultural geography see: Whatmore, *Hybrid Geographies*; Whatmore and Thorne, 'Wild(er)ness'.
32 Lorimer, 'Herding memories', 517.
33 Griffin, 'Some inhuman wretch', 135.
34 Ritvo, *The Animal Estate*, 2.
35 *Jackson's Oxford Journal*, 18 April 1807; *Derby Mercury*, 30 April 1807.
36 M. Quinn, 'Corpulent cattle and milk machines: nature, art and the ideal type', *Society & Animals* 1, 2 (1993): 145–157; B. Rogers, *Beef and Liberty*, London: Vintage, 2004; R.S. Metcalfe, *Meat, Commerce and the City: The London Food Market, 1800–1855*, London: Pickering and Chatto, 2012.
37 On Cooper see: S. Sartin, *Thomas Sidney Cooper, C.V.O., R.A., 1803–1902*, Leigh-on-Sea: F. Lewis, 1976.
38 R. Blake, *George Stubbs and the Wide Creation: Animals, People and Places in the Life of George Stubbs, 1724–1806*, London: Chatto and Windus, 2005; 'The Horse: from Arabia to Royal Ascot', available at www.britishmuseum.org/whats_on/past_exhibitions/2012/the_horse.aspx, last accessed 8 June 2016.
39 On this, see A. Harvey's excellent *The Beginnings of a Commercial Sporting Culture in Britain, 1793–1850*, London: Ashgate, 2004.
40 See www.nationaltrustcollections.org.uk/object/1220985, last accessed 23 March 2017.
41 Griffin, *Blood Sport (passim)*; M. De Belin, *From the Deer to the Fox: the Hunting Transition and the Landscape, 1600–1850*, Hatfield: University of Hertfordshire Press, 2013; N.J. Sykes, 'The impact of the Normans on hunting practices in England', in C.M. Woolgar, D. Serjeantson and T. Waldron (eds.), *Food in Medieval England: History and Archaeology*, Oxford: Oxford University Press, 2005, 162–175; N.J. Sykes, 'The dynamics of status symbols: wildfowl exploitation in England, AD 410–1550', *Archaeological Journal* 161, 1 (2004): 82–105; C.M. Woolgar, *The Culture of Food in England, 1200–1500*, New Haven CT: Yale University Press, 2016.
42 G.G.S. Bowie, 'New sheep for old – changes in sheep farming in Hampshire, 1792–1879', *Agricultural History Review* 35, 1 (1987): 15–24, 17. On the development of Southdown sheep see: S. Farrant, 'John Ellman of Glynde in Sussex', *Agricultural History Review* 26, 2 (1978): 77–88.
43 S.W. Martins, 'From black-face to white-face – an aspect of the agricultural revolution in Norfolk', *Agricultural History Review* 41, 1 (1993): 20–30, 20.
44 On these dynamics see: C.J. Griffin, *Protest, Politics and Work in Rural England, 1700–1850*, Basingstoke: Palgrave, 2014, especially ch. 2; R. Wells, 'Social protest, class, conflict, and consciousness in the English countryside, 1700–1880', in R. Wells and M. Reed (eds.), *Class, Conflict and Protest in the English Countryside, 1700–1880*, London: Frank Cass, 121–214.
45 *Leeds Intelligencer*, 15 August 1808.
46 J.E. Archer, '"A fiendish outrage"? A study of animal maiming in East Anglia: 1830–1870', *Agricultural History Review* 33, 2 (1985): 147–157; Griffin, 'Some inhuman wretch', 133–160.
47 *Hampshire Advertiser*, 20 May and 19 August 1848; *Hampshire Telegraph*, 19 August 1848.
48 *Hampshire Advertiser*, 1 December 1827; *Portsmouth, Portsea & Gosport Herald*, 21 November 1830.
49 *Salisbury and Winchester Journal*, 11 August 1817.

50 Thomas Gainsborough, Mr. and Mrs. Andrews, c.1750, National Gallery, London: see www.nationalgallery.org.uk/paintings/thomas-gainsborough-mr-and-mrs-andrews, last accessed 23 March 2017; H. Prince, 'Art and agrarian change, 1710–1815', in D. Cosgrove and S. Daniels (eds), *The Iconography of Landscape: Essays on the Symbolic Representation, Design and Use of Past Environments*, Cambridge: Cambridge University Press, 1988, 98–118, 103.

51 On these dynamics see J. Neeson, *Commoners: Common Right, Enclosure and Social Change in England, 1700–1820*, Cambridge: Cambridge University Press, 1993, especially ch.1.

52 E.P. Thompson, *Whigs and Hunters: The Origins of the Black Act*, London: Penguin, 1977, 63 and n.3.

53 Hampshire County Record Office, 49M69 PV1, Preston Candover Vestry Minute, 11 May 1827; Berkshire County Record Office, D/P130/8/1, Thatcham Vestry Minute, 28 February 1825.

54 *Southampton Herald*, 31 May 1824.

55 Centre for Kentish Studies, Q/SBw/124/9, Deposition of Charlotte Stacey, Stockbury, 19 November 1830.

56 *Reading Mercury*, 12 May 1788 and 27 July 1789. On the idea of interspecies conviviality see: S. Hinchliffe and S. Whatmore, 'Living cities: towards a politics of conviviality', *Science as Culture* 15, 2 (2006): 123–138.

57 swine, n. OED Online, Oxford University Press. www.oed.com/view/Entry/195871?redirectedFrom=swine, last accessed 13 June 2016; M. Davis, 'The British Jacobins: folk devils in the age of counter-revolution?', in D. Lemmings and C. Walker (eds), *Moral Panics, the Media and the Law in Early Modern England*, Basingstoke: Palgrave, 2009, 221–244, 237.

58 Malcolmson and Mastoris, *The English Pig*, xiii.

59 Malcolmson and Mastoris, *The English Pig*, 42–43. On British conceptions of the Irish rural poor see: D. Nally, *Human Encumbrances: Political Violence and the Great Irish Famine*, Notre Dame IN: University of Notre Dame Press, 2011, especially ch. 5.

60 A. Sabloff, *Reordering the Natural World: Humans and Animals in the City*, Toronto: University of Toronto Press, 2001, 54; T. Ingold, *What is an Animal?* London: Routledge, 1994, 1.

61 J. Thirsk, *The Agrarian History of England and Wales, Volume 4, 1500–1640, Part 2*, Cambridge: Cambridge University Press, 1967, 710–711; J. McDonnel, 'The role of transhumance in northern England', *Northern History*, 24, 1 (1988): 1–17.

62 Malcolmson and Mastoris, *The English Pig*, 45.

63 W. Cobbett, *Cottage Economy*, London: C. Clement, 1822, 112; *Cobbett's Weekly Political Register*, 13 October 1827; Whatmore and Thorne, 'Wild(er)ness', 451; I. Dyck, *William Cobbett and Rural Popular Culture*, Cambridge: Cambridge University Press, 1993, 115–116.

64 T. Hardy, *Jude the Obscure,* London: Penguin, 1998 [1895], 64.

65 Cited in Malcolmson and Mastoris, *The English Pig*, 43.

66 F. Thompson, *Lark Rise to Candleford: A Trilogy*, Boston MA: Nonpareil, 2009 [1939], 11–13.

67 *Southampton Mercury*, 1 May 1830. On the cutting of tails and manes see: Archer, 'A fiendish outrage?', 150.

68 *Sussex Agricultural Express*, 18 August and 1 September 1849; *Sussex Advertiser*, 21 August 1849.

69 *Salisbury and Winchester Journal*, 14 June and 16 August 1824; *Southampton County Chronicle*, 19 June 1824.

70 *Cobbett's Weekly Political Register*, 11 September 1824.

71 J. Bate, *John Clare: A Biography*, New York NY: Farrar Straus and Giroux, 2003; D. Perkins, *Romanticism and Animal Rights*, Cambridge: Cambridge University Press, 2003, 75.

72 W. Hudson, *The Illustrated Shepherd's Life*, London: Bodley Head, 1987 [1910], 81.

73 Hudson, *The Illustrated Shepherd's Life*, 84.
74 J. Lawrence, *A Philosophical and Practical Treatise on Horses and on the Moral Duties of Man Towards the Brute Creation*, Volume 1, London: H.D. Symonds, 1802; Thomas, *Man and the Natural World*, 101.
75 K. Giles and M. Giles, 'Signs of the times: nineteenth–twentieth century graffiti in the farms of the Yorkshire Wolds', in J. Oliver and T. Neal (eds.), *Wild Signs: Graffiti in Archaeology and History*, Studies in Contemporary and Historical Archaeology 6 (British Archaeological Reports), Oxford, 2010, 47–59.
76 Caunce, *Amongst Farm Horses*, 48.
77 Caunce, *Amongst Farm Horses*, 96, 97.
78 Caunce, *Amongst Farm Horses*, 124.
79 Caunce, *Amongst Farm Horses*, 48.
80 Kean, *Animal Rights*, 33–35; C. Sherry, *Animal Rights: A Reference Handbook*, Santa Barbara CA: ABC-Clio, 2009, 110.

Bibliography

Archer, J.E. '"A fiendish outrage"? A study of animal maiming in East Anglia: 1830–1870', *Agricultural History Review* 33, 2 (1985): 147–157.
Atkins, P. (ed.), *Animal Cities: Beastly Urban Histories*, Farnham: Ashgate, 2012.
Bate, J. *John Clare: A Biography*, New York NY: Farrar Straus and Giroux, 2003.
Beers, D. *For the Prevention of Cruelty: The History and Legacy of Animal Rights Activism in the United States*, Athens OH: Ohio University Press, 2006.
Bellamy, L., Snell, K.D.M., and Williamson, T. 'Rural history: the prospect before us', *Rural History* 1, 1 (1990): 1–4.
Berger, J. *Why Look At Animals?* London: Penguin, 2009.
Blake, R. *George Stubbs and the Wide Creation: Animals, People and Places in the Life of George Stubbs, 1724–1806*, London: Chatto and Windus, 2005.
Boddice, R. *History of Attitudes and Behaviours Towards Animals in Eighteenth- and Nineteenth-Century Britain: Anthropocentrism and the Emergence of Animals*, Lewiston NY: Edward Mellen Press, 2008, 84.
Bowie, G.G.S. 'New sheep for old – changes in sheep farming in Hampshire, 1792–1879', *Agricultural History Review* 35, 1 (1987): 15–24.
Buller, H. and Morris, C. 'Farm animal welfare: a new repertoire of nature–society relations or modernism re-embedded?', *Sociologia Ruralis* 43, 3 (2003): 216–237.
Caunce, S. *Amongst Farm Horses: The Horselads of East Yorkshire*, Stroud: Alan Sutton, 1991.
Chambers, J.D. and Mingay, G.E. *The Agricultural Revolution, 1750–1880*, London: Batsford, 1966.
Chase, M. 'Can history be green? A prognosis', *Rural History* 3, 2 (1992): 243–254.
Cobbett, W. *Cottage Economy*, London: C. Clement, 1822.
Cosgrove, D. and Daniels, S. (eds.), *The Iconography of Landscape: Essays on the Symbolic Representation, Design and Use of Past Environments*, Cambridge: Cambridge University Press, 1988.
Darby, H.C. *The Draining of the Fens*, Cambridge: Cambridge University Press, 1940.
Davis, M. 'The British Jacobins: folk devils in the age of counter-revolution?', in D. Lemmings and C. Walker (eds.), *Moral Panics, the Media and the Law in Early Modern England*, Basingstoke: Palgrave, 2009, 221–244, 237.
De Belin, M. *From the Deer to the Fox: the Hunting Transition and the Landscape, 1600–1850*, Hatfield: University of Hertfordshire Press, 2013.
Dyck, I. *William Cobbett and Rural Popular Culture*, Cambridge: Cambridge University Press, 1993, 115–116.

Farrant, S. 'John Ellman of Glynde in Sussex', *Agricultural History Review* 26, 2 (1978): 77–88.

Fudge, E. *Brutal Reasoning: Animals, Rationality and Humanity in Early Modern England*, Ithaca NY: Cornell University Press, 2006.

Giles, K. and Giles, M. 'Signs of the times: nineteenth–twentieth century graffiti in the farms of the Yorkshire Wolds', in J. Oliver and T. Neal (eds.), *Wild Signs: Graffiti in Archaeology and History*, Studies in Contemporary and Historical Archaeology 6 (British Archaeological Reports), Oxford, 2010, 47–59.

Griffin, C.J. '"Some inhuman wretch": animal maiming and the ambivalent relationship between rural workers and animals', *Rural History* 25, 2 (2014): 133–160.

Griffin, C.J. *Protest, Politics and Work in Rural England, 1700–1850*, Basingstoke: Palgrave, 2014.

Griffin, E. *England's Revelry: A History of Popular Sports and Pastimes, 1660–1800*, Oxford: Oxford University Press, 2005.

Griffin, E. *Blood Sport: A History of Hunting in Britain*, New Haven CT: Yale University Press, 2007.

Haraway, D.J. *When Species Meet*, Minneapolis MN: University of Minnesota Press, 2008.

Hardy, T. *Jude the Obscure*, London: Penguin, 1998 [1895].

Harvey, A. *The Beginnings of a Commercial Sporting Culture in Britain, 1793–1850*, London: Ashgate, 2004.

Harwood, D. *Love for Animals and How It Developed in Great Britain*, New York NY: Columbia University Press, 1928.

Hinchliffe, S. and Whatmore, S. 'Living cities: towards a politics of conviviality', *Science as Culture* 15, 2 (2006): 123–138.

Howell, P. 'Flush and the *banditti*: dog-stealing in Victorian London', in C. Philo and C. Wilbert (eds.), *Animal Spaces, Beastly Places: New Geographies of Human-Animal Relations*, London: Routledge, 2000, 35–55.

Howell, H. *At Home and Astray: The Domestic Dog in Victorian Britain*, Charlottesville VA: University of Virginia Press, 2015.

Hudson, W. *The Illustrated Shepherd's Life*, London: Bodley Head, 1987 [1910].

Ingold, T. *What is an Animal?* London: Routledge, 1994.

Kean, H. *Animal Rights: Political and Social Change in Britain Since 1800*, London: Reaktion, 1998.

Lawrence, J. *A Philosophical and Practical Treatise on Horses and on the Moral Duties of Man Towards the Brute Creation*, Volume 1, London: H.D. Symonds, 1802.

Lorimer, H. 'Herding memories of humans and animals', *Environment and Planning D: Society and Space* 24, 4 (2006): 497–518.

McDonnel, J. 'The role of transhumance in northern England', *Northern History* 24, 1 (1988): 1–17.

Malcolmson, R. and Mastoris, S. *The English Pig: A History*, London: Hambledon, 2001.

Martins, S.W. 'From black-face to white-face – an aspect of the agricultural revolution in Norfolk', *Agricultural History Review* 41, 1 (1993): 20–30.

Matless, D. 'Versions of animal–human: Broadland, 1945–70', in C. Philo and C. Wilbert (eds.), *Animal Spaces, Beastly Places: New Geographies of Human-Animal Relations*, London: Routledge, 2000, 115–140.

Metcalfe, R.S. *Meat, Commerce and the City: The London Food Market, 1800–1855*, London: Pickering and Chatto, 2012.

Nally, D. *Human Encumbrances: Political Violence and the Great Irish Famine*, Notre Dame IN: University of Notre Dame Press, 2011.

Neeson, J. *Commoners: Common Right, Enclosure and Social Change in England, 1700–1820*, Cambridge: Cambridge University Press, 1993.

Nimmo, R. *Milk, Modernity and the Making of the Human: Purifying the Social*, London: Routledge, 2010.

Osborne, H. and Winstanley, M. 'Rural and urban poaching in Victorian England', *Rural History* 17, 2 (2006): 187–212.

Osborne, H. '"Unwomanly practices": poaching crime, gender and the female offender in nineteenth-century Britain', *Rural History* 27, 2 (2016): 149–168.

Parris, L. (ed.) *The Pre-Raphaelites*, exhibition catalogue, London: Tate Gallery Publications, 1984.

Pearson, S.J. and Weismantel, M. 'Does "the animal" exist? Toward a theory of social life with animals', in D. Brantz (ed.), *Beastly Natures: Animals, Humans, and the Study of History*, Charlottesville VA: University of Virginia Press, 2010, 17–37.

Perkins, D. *Romanticism and Animal Rights*, Cambridge: Cambridge University Press, 2003.

Prettlejohn, E. *The Art of the Pre-Raphaelites*, London: Tate Publishing, 2000.

Prince, H. 'Art and agrarian change, 1710–1815', in D. Cosgrove and S. Daniels (eds.), *The Iconography of Landscape: Essays on the Symbolic Representation, Design and Use of Past Environments*, Cambridge: Cambridge University Press, 1988, 98–118.

Quinn, M. 'Corpulent cattle and milk machines: nature, art and the ideal type', *Society & Animals* 1, 2 (1993): 145–157.

Ritvo, H. *The Animal Estate: The English and Other Creatures in the Victorian Age*, Cambridge MA: Harvard University Press, 1987.

Rogers, B. *Beef and Liberty*, London: Vintage, 2004.

Rothfels, N. 'Foreword', in J. Costlow and A. Nelson (eds.), *Other Animals: Beyond the Human in Russian Culture and History*, Pittsburgh PA: University of Pittsburgh Press, 2010.

Sabloff, A. *Reordering the Natural World: Humans and Animals in the City*, Toronto: University of Toronto Press, 2001.

Sartin, S. *Thomas Sidney Cooper, C.V.O., R.A., 1803–1902*, Leigh-on-Sea: F. Lewis, 1976.

Scola, R. *Feeding the Victorian City: The Food Supply of Manchester, 1770–1870*, Manchester: Manchester University Press, 1992.

Serpell, J. *In the Company of Animals: A Study of Human-Animal Relationships*, Cambridge: Cambridge University Press, 1996.

Sherry, C. *Animal Rights: A Reference Handbook*, Santa Barbara CA: ABC-Clio, 2009.

Short, B. '"The art and craft of chicken cramming": poultry in the Weald of Sussex 1850–1950', *Agricultural History Review* 30, 1 (1982): 17–30.

Sykes, N.J. 'The dynamics of status symbols: wildfowl exploitation in England, AD 410–1550', *Archaeological Journal* 161, 1 (2004): 82–105.

Sykes, N.J. 'The impact of the Normans on hunting practices in England', in C.M. Woolgar, D. Serjeantson and T. Waldron (eds.), *Food in Medieval England: History and Archaeology*, Oxford: Oxford University Press, 2005, 162–175.

Thirsk, J. *The Agrarian History of England and Wales, Volume 4, 1500–1640, Part 2*, Cambridge: Cambridge University Press, 1967.

Thomas, K. *Man and the Natural World: Changing Attitudes in England 1500–1800*, London: Penguin, 1983.

Thompson, E.P. *Whigs and Hunters: The Origins of the Black Act*, London: Penguin, 1977.

Thompson, F. *Lark Rise to Candleford: A Trilogy*, Boston MA: Nonpareil, 2009 [1939].

Turner, J. *Reckoning with the Beast: Animals, Pain, and Humanity in the Victorian Mind*, Baltimore MD: Johns Hopkins University Press, 1980.

Watts, M. 'Afterword: enclosure', in C. Philo and C. Wilbert (eds.), *Animal Spaces, Beastly Places: New Geographies of Human-Animal Relations*, London: Routledge, 2000, 292–304.

Wells, R. 'Social protest, class, conflict, and consciousness in the English countryside, 1700–1880', in R. Wells and M. Reed (eds.), *Class, Conflict and Protest in the English Countryside, 1700–1880*, London: Frank Cass, 121–214.

Whatmore, S. *Hybrid Geographies: Natures, Cultures, Spaces*, London: Sage, 2002.

Whatmore, S. and L. Thorne, 'Wild(er)ness: reconfiguring the geographies of wildlife', *Transactions of the Institute of British Geographers* 23, 4 (1988): 435–454.

Whetham, E.H. 'The trade in pedigree livestock 1850–1910', *Agricultural History Review* 27, 1 (1979): 47–50.

White, G. *The Natural History of Selborne*, ed. A. Secord, Oxford: Oxford University Press, 2013.

Williams, M. *Drainage of the Somerset Levels*, Cambridge: Cambridge University Press, 1970.

Wood, J.C. *Violence and Crime in Nineteenth-Century England: The Shadow of our Refinement*, London: Routledge, 2004.

Woolgar, C.M. *The Culture of Food in England, 1200–1500*, New Haven CT: Yale University Press, 2016.

15
THE HISTORY OF EMOTIONAL ATTACHMENT TO ANIMALS

Ingrid H. Tague

Introduction

It may seem that humans' emotional attachment to animals needs no explanation and has no history. Evidence of human affection for animals is widespread and goes far back in time, and the potential benefits to humans of emotional connections to animals, especially through pet-keeping, are now widely recognised. A variety of studies have shown that even short-term contact with companion animals can reduce stress, and there is evidence that pets and therapy animals can provide a wide array of emotional and psychological benefits.[1] Such studies usually take for granted the existence of strong attachments between humans and animals. From another point of view, however, the depth of such attachments is surprising. Many scholars perceive contemporary affection for animals as rooted in problems or failings of contemporary society, or at least as the result of the specific conditions of industrialisation. Thus they consistently identify the nineteenth century as the moment when modern pet-keeping, with its emphasis on affection and companionship between species, first arose. In this view, pet-keeping might provide social bonds that are lacking between humans in industrial society, or a sense of connection to nature for those living in urban environments.[2]

One problem with this argument is that there is evidence of pet-keeping both long before the nineteenth century and in many non-industrialised cultures today.[3] Scholars seeking to understand the near-universality of pet-keeping have taken different approaches from those who focus on the benefits of the practice. For instance, Yi-Fu Tuan suggests that pet-keeping is a result of the innate human desire to dominate other living beings.[4] From another perspective, pet-keeping is an 'evolutionary problem' since pets use resources without contributing to their owners' material survival. Thus John Archer argues that pets are 'social parasites' who (unconsciously) manipulate humans, benefiting from humans' desire to nurture and from the fact that 'mammalian pets also possess certain human-like behavioural features, notably their emotional reactions'.[5] In this view, emotional attachment to animals is a problem to be explained, but the answer is rooted in evolutionary biology.

What is lost in the attempt to find a universal explanation for humans' emotional bonds with animals is the connection between human–animal relationships and their broader social context. The attempt to explore the nature of that connection, however, immediately raises a number of methodological problems, particularly because emotions have traditionally been seen as reflecting an individual's inner self. Indeed, one of the great challenges faced by historians is the gap between our desire to fully understand the experiences and feelings of people in the past and the access we have to those feelings and experiences. Inevitably, our understanding is a mediated one; we rely on texts, images, and material goods to put together a picture of the past. We may dream of the lost diary in which someone pours out her soul, explaining exactly why she did what she did, but we know that diaries are shaped by generic conventions, and that the very notion that diaries are intended to be private repositories for one's true feelings is specific to time and place. Even if a writer fully believed that he or she was providing a complete, unvarnished representation of the reasons for a particular action, scholars have long known that individuals might not be fully aware of their own motives, much less the broader social forces that constrain behaviours and viewpoints.

Exploring the role of emotions in history seems only to add to the complexity. We might understand strategic or geopolitical considerations that led a king to decide to make war, for instance, but it seems impossible to know what he really *felt* about that decision. Even if he expressed rage against his enemies, we could not know if his statements were mere rhetoric intended for a public audience rather than an expression of his true emotions. These questions have prompted the development of research specifically into the history of emotions. Rather than seeking to understand what individuals in the past 'really' felt, historians of emotions focus on emotions as aspects of social and cultural life. They trace changes in emotional practices over time: which expressions of emotions were considered appropriate, which feelings were seen as 'good' or 'bad', and how emotions were physically expressed.[6] This work has fostered increasingly nuanced understanding of emotions, attuned to their many social functions. Scholars have also drawn on psychology and neuroscience to try to distinguish historically-specific aspects of emotions from those 'hard-wired' in all humans.[7] Results of these efforts have been mixed, and historians have yet to reach consensus regarding methodology and conceptual approaches. Yet by identifying emotions as worthy objects of historical study, they have opened the door to seeing the history of emotional attachments to animals not merely in terms of changing functional relationships between humans and non-humans but also in terms of changing emotional experiences and norms.

Even if we might be able to grasp human motives, however, applying these ideas to animals might seem to create an insurmountable obstacle. We are distanced not merely in time and space but in species. If it seems impossible to understand fully the thoughts and feelings of humans in the past, how could we ever begin to understand how animals perceive their relationships with us? In Thomas Nagel's well-known formulation, how can we know what it is like to be a bat?[8] One response might be that it is unclear whether the difficulty is more insurmountable in the case of animals than it is in the case of humans. To the extent that we can assume continuity between past and present, we might be able to assume the same continuity between species. For instance, it is now widely acknowledged that animals experience emotions, though there is debate about the sophistication and complexity of these emotions: some scientists distinguish between 'basic, inborn' or primary emotions such as fear or anger, and 'more complex' secondary emotions, which require higher order brain function and are 'processed in the brain' through conscious thought.[9] For pet owners, animal emotions may seem to be self-evident. A 2008 survey of pet owners found that 87% of respondents believed that their dogs felt sadness, 74% guilt, and 81% jealousy.[10]

Nevertheless, there remains a critical barrier between humans and animals: we cannot (yet) use language to communicate with animals about their emotions as we can with humans. Despite recent advances, it is still extremely difficult to measure emotions in other species – do we see emotions in dogs and primates primarily because their behaviour and facial expressions closely match our own? It is possible, as Clive Wynne and Monique Udell suggest, that 'our ratings of the emotional lives of animals may be biased in ways that do not correspond well with the cognitive capabilities of different species'. We run the risk of 'paint[ing] a picture of animal emotion and personality in ways that we understand but that actually prevent us from conceptualizing the rich diversity of experience that could exist among other species than our own'.[11] Attempts to determine experimentally if animals have a 'theory of mind' – if they can understand that another creature will have a distinct point of view and imagine that other individual's point of view – have been mixed, without conclusive evidence of animals behaving in a way that definitively indicates a theory of mind.[12] This difficulty is important because so many emotions rely at least to some extent upon an understanding of another individual's state of mind (an issue that, as we will see, became particularly pressing in early modern thinking about human–animal relationships). As the ethologist Marc Bekoff notes, much of our understanding of animal emotions ultimately relies upon our observations of their behaviour and reasoning from analogy: we understand behaviour to indicate grief or joy or guilt because the behaviour is similar to the behaviour humans engage in when experiencing those emotions.[13] Yet our confidence in being able to read animal emotions can get us in trouble. A well-known study, for instance, found that dog owners confidently read 'guilt' in their dogs' faces and behaviour when told that their dogs had misbehaved, even when the dogs had not in fact done so. The dogs were simply responding to their owners' cues.[14]

Even though the temporal distance between our historical subjects and ourselves adds to the complexity of understanding emotions in the past, historians have access to humans' own statements about their feelings. Not so in the case of animals. I do not doubt that animals experience emotions, but we do not have access to their understanding of their emotional experiences as we do to humans' understanding. Moreover, we must recognise that the possibility of reciprocal emotional bonds and even the existence of animal emotions were issues very much open to debate in the early modern period. We can, I think, better understand how human emotions and human perceptions of animal emotions changed over time than how animals perceived their changing relationships with humans, much less how animal emotions themselves changed over time.

In this chapter, then, I will focus on how human perceptions of these relationships evolved, especially in Britain. An examination of the history of emotional attachments to animals reveals that changing attitudes towards human–animal bonds were rooted most strongly in early modern debates about animals' ability to experience complex, social emotions. These debates paved the way for an acceptance of deep and complex emotional ties to animals. Long seen as helpful if often disposable servants to humans, animals came to be perceived as potential friends and even family members as their ability to share human-like emotions were increasingly acknowledged. These shifts were, in turn, rooted in transformations in the understanding of human emotions and their relation to reason. The development of the culture of sensibility had the unintended effect of admitting at least some animals into the moral realm, enabling them to participate as equals in emotional relationships with humans. This chapter will focus in particular on ideas about dogs, the species most critical to these changing perceptions. I will trace some of the key shifts in thinking about animals' emotional capacities and the ways that dogs were used to exemplify those capacities.

The Christian tradition

The Christian tradition offered a specific view of the relationship between 'man' and 'nature'. According to the dominant reading of the Bible that was handed down to the early modern period, God had granted Adam dominion over the natural world, including all the animals in creation.[15] The mission of dominion was often represented in images of Adam naming the animals – the act of naming signifying both knowledge and ownership.

Yet this dominion was usually presented as stewardship. Man was God's representative on earth, and mankind's role was to act as steward for God's creation. Early modern Europeans understood this idea of stewardship quite literally, seeing a parallel between this role and the role of the steward on a landed estate. Stewardship granted authority, but it also entailed responsibility for good management. In this view, humans, like stewards, have enormous authority but also have a responsibility to leave the world in as good or better condition than they were first given it. This notion of stewardship extended easily to humans' relationship to animals, especially since ensuring the well-being of the animals on a landed estate was a critical part of the steward's responsibility. A good steward ensured the ongoing health of the animals in his care; all humans, similarly, were responsible for the care of the animals God had entrusted to them. A 1713 essay by Alexander Pope reflected this common vision: 'the more entirely the Inferior Creation is submitted to our Power, the more answerable we should seem for our Mismanagement of it'.[16]

A related metaphor presented animals as servants to humans. Early modern thinkers largely agreed that animals were made for human benefit; they literally existed *for* humans, but in return, humans had a responsibility not to abuse that power, just as a good master would not abuse his servants. A master might punish servants who misbehaved, but he also had a paternal responsibility towards them, including caring for them when they were ill and ensuring that they had adequate food and shelter. Similarly, humans were responsible for caring for the animals who served them. Just as masters and mistresses could develop warm, affectionate relationships with their servants in recognition of the good service provided, so, too, was it legitimate for humans to care about those animals who served them. A typical essay from the

Spectator, for instance, praised the recurring character Sir Roger de Coverley, a country gentleman, for his loyalty to his servants. They had all grown old with him, from his 'grey-headed' butler to 'the old House-dog, and . . . a grey Pad that is kept in the Stable with great Care and Tenderness out of regard to his past Services, tho' he has been useless for several Years'.[17] At the same time, however, it was important to maintain the appropriate hierarchy between animals and humans, just as it was between master and servant. Affection must not be allowed to overcome the positions of authority and subordination in relations between class or species. This model of animals as servants dictated a very specific, and very limited, form of human–animal attachment. True friendship was possible only between equals. It would be equally preposterous to suggest that either butler or horse could achieve that status.

The Cartesian animal automaton

During the early modern period, this traditional view came into question from two very different perspectives. One famous challenge came from the work of René Descartes.[18] Descartes argued that animals differ utterly from humans; humans are not merely superior to all animals, but occupy a distinct role in God's creation. While a human will always be identifiable as a human, he suggested, the same could not be said of an animal:

> if there were such machines having the organs and outward shape of a monkey or any other irrational animal, we would have no means of knowing that they were not of exactly the same nature as these animals, whereas, if any such machines resembled us in body and imitated our actions insofar as this was practically possible, we should still have two very certain means of recognising that they were not, for all that, real human beings.[19]

First, the human-machines would be incapable of language, and second, the human-machines would inevitably fail to do all the things humans can do, 'by which we would discover that they did not act consciously, but only because their organs were disposed in a certain way'.[20]

Language and reason were thus the key characteristics that distinguished humans from animals. Although animals have the same speech organs as humans and can imitate human speech, he argued, they are never capable of communicating original thoughts, which even mutes and mentally disabled humans can do.

> This shows not only that animals have less reason than man, but that they have none at all. For it is clear that we need very little reason in order to be able to speak; and . . . it is unbelievable that the most perfect monkey or parrot of their species should not be able to speak as well as the most stupid child, or at least a child with a disturbed brain, unless their soul were of a wholly different nature to ours.[21]

By this logic, all animal behaviours, no matter how they resembled human behaviours or emotions, stemmed not from the animal's will but from mere instinct;

they were automatic responses triggered by the animal's bodily functions. Descartes' followers famously asserted that what seems to be a dog's yelp of pain is nothing more than such an automatic response, and cannot be understood as pain in the same sense that a human would have.[22] Despite his departure from the model of animal as servant, however, Descartes' understanding of animals was just as rooted in his Christian devotion as his forebears' was; the radical difference he perceived between humans and animals emerged from his belief that human reason was a result of humans' unique possession of an immortal soul. All animals, he argued, had a merely material existence. Such souls as they had existed only to grant them life, whereas God's great gift of an immortal soul was given to mankind alone.[23]

Descartes' views have come to be seen as marking a radical break in the history of human–animal relations.[24] Once animals were perceived as mere machines, humans no longer had a moral responsibility towards them, any more than humans had a moral responsibility towards a clock. If what appeared to be pain and fear were mere automatic responses, then practices such as vivisection were completely legitimate. Moreover, the Cartesian understanding of humans and animals opened the way to seeing humans as utterly separate from the natural world. All of nature, including all animals, could come to be seen as mere tools for human use, to be used and discarded in whatever way humans saw fit. Animals became disposable.

Yet despite the tendency today to see Descartes as marking a watershed moment in the history of human–animal relations, his ideas did not come to represent a hegemonic understanding of animals. They were controversial from the outset, generating as much criticism as praise.[25] For some, simple observation of animals was enough to demonstrate that they were not machines, and the claim that animal behaviours indicating fear, pleasure, or other emotional responses were not the same as similar behaviours in humans seemed ludicrous on its face. Appealing as the idea of the animal automaton might have been to some individuals eager to proclaim human uniqueness, it was never universally accepted, and by the eighteenth century Descartes was most often cited as a straw man to be debunked.

Montaigne's critique of human pride

If Descartes' understanding of animals released humans from moral obligation and created an impassable gap between humanity and all other living creatures, another way of thinking about animals also called into question the traditional Christian view of human–animal relations, but with the opposite effect. This viewpoint, which came to dominate by the second half of the eighteenth century, emphasised similarities rather than differences between humans and other species. But it was not entirely new at that time. The best-known argument for the capabilities of animals came from Michel de Montaigne in the sixteenth century. In his 'Apology for Raymond Sebond', Montaigne called into question humanity's vaunted superiority over the natural world.[26] He suggested that man's claims to pre-eminence were rooted in knowledge of his actual weakness: 'he equals himself with God, attributes to himself divine characteristics, picks himself out and separates himself from the horde of other creatures'. But, according to Montaigne, humans have no real way of properly judging animal capacity. In his famous expression, 'When I play with my cat, who knows if I am not a pastime to her more than she is to me?'[27]

To suggest that animals were inferior because they lacked language was foolish, Montaigne said:

> This defect that hinders communication between them and us, why is it not just as much ours as theirs? It is a matter of guesswork whose fault it is that we do not understand one another; for we do not understand them any more than they do us.[28]

But animals 'understand each other, not only those of the same species, but also those of different species'.[29] So much human communication does not rely on speech – all humans communicate through physical behaviour and eye contact as well as speech – that animals' inability to speak should not be used as evidence that they lack human understanding.[30] Elsewhere, he suggests that humans *can* communicate with animals. 'They certainly speak to us, and we to them. In how many ways do we not speak to our dogs? And they answer us'.[31] Animal behaviours even indicate reason, he argued, as in the construction of beehives or birds' nests.[32] Thus,

> there is no apparent reason to judge that the beasts do by natural and obligatory instinct the same things that we do by our choice and cleverness. We must infer from like results like faculties, and consequently confess that this same reason, this same method that we have for working, is also that of the animals.[33]

Importantly, Montaigne also emphasised animal capacity to experience emotions. 'As for friendship, theirs is without comparison more alive and more constant than that of men'.[34] To back up this assertion, he cited stories of dogs mourning their dead masters and horses becoming so attached to one another that they could not travel separately.[35] 'Animals, like us, exercise choice in their amours . . . . They are not exempt from our jealousies, or from extreme and irreconcilable envy'.[36] Animals are more loyal than humans, he argued, giving examples of dogs avenging their masters' murderers and chasing after thieves.[37] And for his example of beastly gratitude, he recounted at length the story of the fugitive Roman slave who pulled a thorn from a lion's paw and was rewarded when the animal later spared his life in gladiatorial combat.[38]

Montaigne's interest in this essay was less in animals, however, than in humans. His discussion of animal capabilities was primarily aimed at puncturing man's complacency. In this he was echoing a long line of thinkers and philosophers, a fact evident in his heavy use of classical examples to showcase animal achievements.[39] But by refusing to acknowledge a clear distinction between humans and beasts, and by insisting that they shared a capacity for emotions in particular, Montaigne opened the way for others with a much greater interest in animal capabilities to reflect upon the relationship between human and non-human species. Critically, Montaigne's presentation of animal emotions emphasised animal agency, as well as the capacity for communication within and between species. Animals' emotions led to specific forms of behaviour, in Montaigne's view: horses chose to travel together, dogs' loyalty led them to decide to pursue thieves, and the lion made a decision to spare the gladiator's life. Emotion, communication, and action were mutually reinforcing, creating a network that would become critically important for later thinkers.

Sensibility and morality in the eighteenth century

If the Christian tradition came under increasing pressure in the sixteenth and seventeenth centuries, the eighteenth century saw the emergence of a radically new vision of animal emotions and thus human–animal relationships. One major reason for changes in thinking about animals was changing thinking about human capabilities and morality. Following Aristotelian thinking, human reason had long been seen as the crucial factor keeping emotions or 'passions' in check. In the Christian context, humans were inherently sinful, and the capacity for reason (along with Christian faith) was seen as an essential way for humans to keep their sinful natures under control. Reason helped to discipline nature; in fact, it was God's gift to humans to enable them to discipline themselves.[40] Possession of reason was the characteristic that distinguished humans from beasts; to allow one's passions to dominate was thus literally to engage in beastly behaviour.

In this view, reason was the critical characteristic distinguishing humans from animals, even for those who did not accept the Cartesian argument for the animal automaton. Animals might engage in behaviour that was similar to human behaviour, but because it sprang from instinct rather than reason, it was of an entirely different quality. Joseph Addison made a typical case when he argued that animals cared for their young only as long as the young depended upon them; nor was this care reciprocated from infant animals towards their parents. It was not true affection that guided this behaviour, then, but mere instinct.[41] Addison's distinction between reason and instinct did not go as far as Descartes' total rejection of animal sentience, but it nevertheless presented reason as elevating humans far above the animal world. Unlike Descartes, he acknowledged animal agency, but when it came to emotions, Addison's animals were as mechanical as Descartes'.

Over the course of the eighteenth century, however, this highly restricted view of animal capacities was challenged, at the same time that the role of reason in maintaining virtuous behaviour came into question. Thinkers increasingly emphasised the similarities between human and animal capabilities, with some even suggesting that animals have reason. Some of this work thus built upon Montaigne's comparisons of human and non-human agency. At the same time, animals' ability to form close emotional ties with each other and with humans came to be seen as much more significant than their capacity for reason (or lack thereof). Critically, thinkers began to ascribe to animals increasingly sophisticated emotions. These more complex emotions depended on communication and 'sympathy' – an ability to understand and respond to another individual's point of view.[42] In other words, they were fundamentally social. They were also seen as dependent upon a sense of morality.[43] And, finally, these social emotions were seen as engaged not only within but across species boundaries.

These transformations would not have been possible without shifts in attitudes towards the relationship between reason and emotion, particularly as they related to the promotion of moral behaviour. The concept of 'emotional communities', developed by Barbara Rosenwein, is helpful here. Emotional communities are 'groups in which people adhere to the same norms of emotional expression and value – or devalue – the same or related emotions. More than one emotional community may exist – indeed normally does exist – contemporaneously, and these communities may change over time. Some come to the fore to dominate our sources, then recede in importance'.[44] Emotional communities 'expect, encourage, tolerate, and deplore' varying 'modes of emotional expression'.[45] Eighteenth-century discussions of animals can be read in the context of the development of a new 'emotional community', built around the culture of sensibility.[46]

Historians and literary scholars have traced the emergence of a culture of sensibility in the later eighteenth century, marked by an emphasis on the expression of feeling and a connection to the natural world.[47] As Ildiko Csengei notes, 'Definitions [of sensibility] abound, though the concept is generally agreed to imply a belief in natural goodness, benevolence and compassion, and it is often associated with a cult of feeling, melancholy, distress and refined emotionalism'. Csengei also helpfully draws attention to the ways in which sensibility was manifested through bodily experiences: 'Blushing, fainting, swooning, crying, handholding, mute gestures, palpitations of the heart' all appear as familiar behaviours in the literature of sensibility.[48] These experiences were important in part because they represented one guarantee that the feelings expressed were genuine; weeping or swooning was supposed to be an irresistible bodily response, not one subject to the intellect or conscious decision. Emotions could be 'read' in the body, offering unmediated access to an individual's true feelings and beliefs. Of course, one accusation lodged against the cult of sensibility was that it offered exactly the opposite: rather than a transparent, unmediated presentation of genuine feeling, it encouraged its adherents to overwrought, self-conscious displays of hypocrisy. But by privileging physically demonstrative displays of emotion, the culture of sensibility opened the way for admission of animals into the emotional world of humans.[49]

These changes were in turn connected to the development of new theories of natural morality. Increasingly during the eighteenth century, thinkers argued that morality emerges out of innate human feelings: humans have a natural tendency to be attracted towards the good and repelled by evil. As William Reddy argues, the eighteenth century saw 'a remarkable consensus among the educated elite about the centrality of natural sentiment to virtue'.[50] This idea explicitly connected virtue and emotion; rather than relying on reason to subdue the passions and uphold correct behaviour, it implied that emotions could lead directly to morality. It also offered the possibility of effacing status differences. In theory, at least, all humans had equal access to moral sentiments; while it was possible to train oneself to act on those sentiments, they were not the special purview of a privileged elite. Indeed, famous sentimental works such as Samuel Richardson's *Pamela* and Jean-Jacques Rousseau's *Emile* contrasted the innate morality of simple country folk to the corruption of the courtly elite. In this context, it became possible to extend ideas of moral sentiments to non-human animals as well, despite their lack of reason.

Sympathy and animal emotions

An early exponent of the role of 'the passions' rather than reason in shaping human experience was David Hume. As Tobias Menely argues, Hume's concept of sympathy, central to his vision of human nature, transcends species boundaries: 'Though the sympathetic communication of passions is the constitutive principle of human social life, the very wellspring of culture and justice, it is in Hume's view by no means a uniquely human trait'.[51] Hume points out that we are affected by the suffering of creatures we do not know as well as those with whom we have an existing affectionate relationship; even the cries of pain of an animal we cannot see affect us.[52] In this view, feeling precedes language and even self-knowledge; we know how we feel and who we are because we identify similarities between our feelings and those of other creatures. 'Identity and knowledge begin in our essentially creaturely capacity to "receive by communication" the passions of others'.[53] Hume thus effectively reversed the priority of individual reason and socially communicated passions (shared across species); it was the latter, not the former, that mattered most.

In his *Treatise of Human Nature* (1739–1740), Hume deliberately constructed a view of animals that emphasised their similarities to humans. Anatomists used dissections of animals to understand human anatomy on the grounds that the physical resemblance must imply a similar function; it only made sense, he argued, to do the same for the workings of human and animal minds.[54] Humans have 'superior knowledge and understanding', so 'animals have little or no sense of virtue or vice; they quickly lose sight of the relations of blood; and are incapable of that of right and property'. But there are many other passions that do not stem from such sophisticated concepts, and animals are perfectly capable of experiencing those passions.[55] Moreover, he argued, animals could experience inter-species emotional relationships, especially in the case of domesticated animals. For instance, 'A dog naturally loves a man above his own species, and very commonly meets with a return of affection'.[56]

As we have seen, Hume excluded animals from morality – they have 'no sense of virtue or vice' – but later thinkers took his ideas much further. Advocates for the humane treatment of animals also emphasised trans-species communication. For them, this sympathetic communication was the key evidence in the case against cruelty. A few years after Hume published his *Treatise*, the cleric John Hildrop dismissed as absurd Descartes' vision of animal automatons, arguing that everyone intuitively grasps that animals have 'understanding':

> this it is that guides us in the education of our Dogs and Horses, to train them up by Correction and Discipline to the several Offices for which they are intended, and the Services which we expect to receive from them. This it is that directs us to caress and reward them when they do well, and to correct and punish them, when they are vicious and disobedient. Did we consider them as meer [sic] Machines, as Creatures that had no Sense, Understanding, or Reflection; this Conduct would be as absurd and ridiculous, as

it would be to caress and reward your Clock or your Watch for going well, or correct and punish them with a Whip or Cudgel for going wrong.[57]

Critically, just as Hume explained animal emotions with an example of attachment to humans, so Hildrop appealed to his readers' experience of human–animal cooperation for his evidence. We know that animals have understanding, he argued, because when we act as if they do, they respond in the way we expect. Animal emotions were not confined in his view merely to fear and joy; rather, animals were capable of emotional ties that depended on inter-species communication.

A more expansive view of animal abilities was not confined to those with an agenda aimed at improving their condition. William Smellie was among many naturalists whose observations of animals led them, like Hildrop, to dismiss the Cartesian argument. Smellie claimed that Descartes was self-evidently wrong:

> Though no animal is endowed with mental powers equal to those of man, yet there is not a faculty of the human mind, but evident marks of its existence are to be found in particular animals. Senses, memory, imagination, the principle of imitation, curiosity, cunning, ingenuity, devotion, or respect for superiors, gratitude, are all discoverable in the brute creation.[58]

He noted that as far as the ability to communicate went, 'Infants are exactly in the same condition with brutes'. They communicate through gestures and inarticulate noises, which are intelligible to those who care for them.[59] Like Hume, Smellie also suggested that domesticated animals could experience emotional attachments to their masters: a domesticated dog had 'a warm attachment, and a perpetual desire of pleasing . . . the dog not only receives instruction with rapidity, but accommodates his behaviour and deportment to the manners and habits of those who command him'.[60]

Eighteenth-century views of animal agency thus relied heavily on perceptions of animal emotions. The critical argument against Descartes was the appeal to humans' experience that animals could clearly communicate their emotions both within and across species. By the end of the century, the absence of reason in animals ceased to be an area of concern or a sign of animal inferiority; instead, animal capacity for emotions came to be seen as the critical feature that connected humans to animals.[61] Moreover, emotional attachment to animals was increasingly legitimised through an appeal to the reciprocal nature of that attachment. Both humans and animals could share in the social emotions; moral sentiments were innate not only in humans but in animals. By the time Ebenezer Sibly compiled his *Magazine of Natural History* at the end of the eighteenth century, he was able to present as the great benefit of studying natural history its effects on human sympathy for animals. Seeing animals, from horses to insects, taking pleasure in their own existence, humans would come to seek other species' happiness: 'Thus an equal and extensive benevolence is called forth into exertion; and having felt a common interest in the gratifications of inferior beings; we shall be no longer indifferent to their sufferings, or become wantonly instrumental in producing them'.[62] Care for animals was no longer simply the responsibility of a good steward of God's creation; it was a moral obligation in recognition of humans' and animals' shared sentiments.

Dogs as emotional exemplars

What mattered most to thinkers by the late eighteenth century was not just that animals could experience emotions; it was the potential for an explicitly moral aspect to animal emotions, as the guarantor of genuine communication and reciprocal attachment between humans and animals.[63] And the most important animal in these discussions was the dog. Hume, Hildrop, and Smellie all used dogs to exemplify animal abilities, and they were not unusual in doing so. Again and again, when writers considered animal emotions, they turned to dogs, recognising the unique interspecies bond that had been created over centuries of intimacy and cohabitation. There were good reasons for this. Humans communicate much more effectively with dogs than with any other species; dogs, for instance, understand that a human pointing at an object is meant to draw the dog's attention to that object, while even chimpanzees, our close relatives, do not.[64] Dogs thus proved to be both familiar and fertile sources for those seeking to explore the potential depth of emotional ties between humans and animals. If the ability to form a sympathetic communication paved the way for animals and humans to form true friendship, the dog seemed to be the prime candidate for such a relationship.

One of the most influential eighteenth-century presentations of the human–dog bond came from French naturalist the Comte de Buffon. Buffon unapologetically engaged in moral evaluations of the animals he discussed in his *Natural History*, and his presentation of individual species often focused on their relationships with humans. The dog thus attracted special attention. Yet Buffon was not entirely consistent in his discussion of canine emotional capacity. When discussing animal 'passions' generally, as he did in his 'Dissertation on the Nature of Animals', he was primarily concerned 'to distinguish clearly the passions peculiar to man from those which are common to him and the brutes'.[65] Animals were indeed capable of a variety of emotions, he believed, and he pointed to the dog as the animal with the greatest sense of emotional attachment. 'Can any thing exceed the attachment of a dog to his master?' he asked.

> With what fidelity does the dog attend, follow, and protect his master! With what anxiety does he seek his caresses! ... In a word, what agitation and chagrin does the dog discover when his master is absent; and what excess of joy on his return! In all these expressions, is it possible to mistake the genuine characters of friendship? Are these characters equally strong and energetic, even in the human species?

Yet, Buffon stressed, this was not true friendship; it was only an attachment 'the same with that of a lady for her goldfinch, of a child for its toy'. Buffon thus distinguished between basic emotions, available to both humans and animals, and more sophisticated ones that even dogs could not access. True friendship could only take place through 'the power of reflection', which in turn relied on the uniquely human gift of reason.[66]

But in his specific chapter on 'The Dog', Buffon took a very different view, arguing that dogs were capable of returning the affection of humans in a way that no other animal could. Some animals might be grateful for the food and shelter offered them by humans, he argued, but the dog alone was capable of true friendship with a human. He began his discussion of dogs in his *Natural History* with the comment that we admire most humans' internal qualities – in other words, sentiment – rather than external appearance. Accordingly,

> we are induced to think, that the chief excellence of an animal consists also of internal qualities. By these he differs from an automaton, rises above the vegetable tribes, and approaches the human species. It is sentiment which ennobles, governs, and gives activity to all his organs and propensities. Hence the perfection of an animal depends on sentiment alone .... The dog ... possesses every internal excellence which can attract the regard of man.[67]

The domesticated dog is capable of 'the softer sentiments of attachment, and the desire of pleasing. ... Without being endowed, like man, with the faculty of thinking, his feelings are extremely delicate, and he has more fidelity and steadiness in his affection'.[68] Buffon's conflicted presentation of canine affection stemmed from the different agendas in his work. When considering what made humans unique, he presented an unbridgeable chasm between humans and all other animals, represented by the uniquely human gift of reason. Yet when he focused on the dog alone, he allowed himself to acknowledge the depth of canine–human emotional communication that he witnessed in his own experiences.

By the late eighteenth century, this conflict had largely resolved itself. If human reason remained a special gift from God, the absence of reason no longer seemed enough to deny dogs feelings as complex as those of their human counterparts. And the best demonstration of canine emotion was through the bonds of friendship between a dog and its owner. The popular 1798 children's story *Keeper's Travels in Search of His Master* shows how deeply entrenched this vision of human–animal relationships had become by the end of the century. In one scene, a girl is told why dogs are superior to other animals. 'The understanding of dogs', says a wise magistrate, 'surpasses that of all other animals, except man and the elephant.' Canine 'superiority' is due 'to their sensibility. This makes them susceptible of affection, and capable of attachment. Nature has given them this disposition, which is improved by a constant society with man'.[69] The excellence of animals, in this view, stems from the possibility of communicating sentiments across species, a process dependent on cross-species social interactions. Canine moral sentiments are created by and made visible through their 'constant society with man'.[70] Samuel Jackson Pratt, a popular sentimental writer, similarly devoted many pages to the praise of dogs. Like others, he admired in particular

> the love, friendship, and other domestic affections of the canine for the human race. I believe, that there is in the constitution of their nature, a something that attracts them to man even more than to each other; at least, that we have their social feelings more firmly and fondly than their own species.[71]

Pratt prided himself on his sensibility, which he saw as most demonstrated in his kind treatment of animals. Nor was he alone in connecting emotional ties to dogs with a call for more humane behaviour.[72] Thomas Young, in his 1798 *Essay on Humanity to Animals*, also pointed to human–dog relationships to justify his viewpoint. Noting that humans who abuse animals are often seen as likely to be unkind to fellow humans, Young argued that this was a reasonable response:

> Betwixt a man and his horse, or dog, or other animal which is familiar to him, many cords of affection will always intervene (unless the source of sympathy be dried up in his soul) differing in degree, probably far more than in kind, from those which tie the hearts of friends together. If then he wilfully and violently rend these asunder, and pass almost in an instant from a state of friendship with his dumb companion, to the extreme of cruelty, is it not with reason that the world draws unfavourable conclusions respecting his humanity towards his own species?[73]

Shared moral sentiments enable friendship; a violation of human–animal friendship in turn implies a more general moral failure. Young focused on dogs 'because I think that there are few animals treated with greater cruelty, and scarce any towards which cruelty appears more cruel'.[74] He continued,

> Of all animals the Dog shews the greatest attachment and fidelity to Man . . . . The dog is also, perhaps, the most docile and sagacious of animals; he knows his master best, remembers him longest, understands his language and his looks the most perfectly, and feels most sensibly his kindness or his displeasure.[75]

Like many other writers, Young included copious examples of individual dogs' friendship and loyalty to humans. The strongest argument for kindness to animals, it seemed, was based on affection formed out of mutual sympathy, and no animal more clearly demonstrated the ties of mutual affection than the dog.

Conclusion

The recognition of dogs as capable of experiencing complex social emotions had lasting consequences. Although the culture of sensibility experienced a backlash that severely diminished its utility as the basis for more humanitarian behaviour, it had already created the conditions that would come to make pet-keeping a central feature of modern life.[76] The vision of a reciprocal, morally grounded relationship between humans and animals paved the way for the modern perception of pets as part of the family. This view of pets relied on a recognition of animal agency and on a perception of reciprocal affection between animals and humans. The nineteenth century saw the increasing bifurcation of animals into two distinct categories: there were pets, and then there were all other animals, who continued to be viewed in terms of the service they rendered their human masters through labour or the provision of food. Although it was possible to develop emotional attachments to the latter group, particularly horses, they were not usually identified as part of the family. Critically, they did not inhabit the physical space of the home. As has often been pointed out, nineteenth-century society relied on an opposition between domestic and public life. Domestic life was often conceived in terms of an entirely separate space, a sanctuary from the pressures of the public world. Although scholars have questioned the existence of gendered 'separate spheres' and pointed out the instability and porousness of the boundaries of public and private life, the concept of such a distinction remained important in the period, no matter how rarely it might have been achieved in practice.[77] In this context, pets could come to serve as significant indicators of domesticity by virtue of sharing the space of the home. Just as women were often constructed as domestic, private, and unproductive, serving society through the companionship and emotional support they offered, so, too, were pets distinguished from those animals who engaged in (public) labour.[78] Women, children, and pets became critical markers of a fully domestic life. In this context, as Philip Howell has argued, a dog without a home was in some sense not a proper dog at all.[79]

Transformations in the understanding of human–animal emotional relationships also helped pave the way for Charles Darwin's *The Expression of the Emotions in Man and Animals* (1872). Darwin drew heavily on examples from his own children and his pets, especially his dogs, for evidence to support his ideas.[80] Doing so was only possible because Darwin accepted that similar behaviours in humans and animals implied similar emotional states. More recently, scientists studying both animals and humans have demonstrated similarities in physiological responses between humans and animals that support a notion of shared emotions across species. Such views have clear ethical implications. The more science suggests that animals not only feel pleasure and pain but have access to richer and subtler emotional experiences, the more difficult it becomes to justify animal experimentation, factory farming, and other actions that cause animal suffering. Claims for human uniqueness, which form the basis of many justifications for these actions, become increasingly unsustainable. Jeremy Bentham's famous question 'Can they suffer?' may be expanded to include other questions: Can they grieve for family and friends? Do emotional ties with other animals matter to them? Can they anticipate the future with pleasure or anxiety?[81] The more the answers to these questions seem to be affirmative, the more difficult it is to outline a definition of human uniqueness that excludes most non-human animals.

If we cannot determine what makes humans unique, then what does that do to the study of history? Must we find a way to include animals as full members of the historical narrative, just as we have done for other excluded groups such as women, the poor, and racial and ethnic minorities? The history of emotional attachment to animals makes this issue particularly pressing. On the one hand, it seems that for more than two centuries we have accepted that humans and animals can form attachments that are meaningful to both species and that represent sophisticated and nuanced emotions. Contemporary science supports this view and has increasingly questioned attempts to distinguish unique human emotional capabilities. On the other hand, no animal has left a record of its own view of these relationships.

And this, I think, is where we come to an impasse. If the history of human emotions presents a challenge as we struggle to determine which aspects of emotions are constant across time and which are culturally determined, the challenge is immeasurably greater with animals. We may feel some confidence in our belief that when we talk about 'love' or 'grief' with someone from our own time and culture, we are talking about more or less the same thing. But if emotional communities among humans can change over time, is it possible to talk to an emotional community of animals? If we could, what would that look like? Are animals part of the emotional communities of the humans with whom they consort? Do wild animals have emotional communities? What would be the norms and conventions that guide those communities? If we seek to integrate animals fully into human history, and if we are committed – as I am – to the idea that emotions are culturally constructed as well as innate and that their meanings and practices change over time, then we must grapple with the question of how to develop a history of animals that incorporates these ideas as well. I come at the history of human–animal relations from the standpoint of a traditional cultural historian rather than as someone steeped in animal studies, so it may be that I am simply ill-suited to answer these questions. But it is not at all clear to me how to do so.

Notes

1 For an overview of the literature, see D.H. Wells, 'The effects of animals on human health and well-being', *Journal of Social Issues* 65, 3 (2009): 523–543. Despite the widespread belief (especially among pet owners themselves) that emotional attachment to pets is beneficial to human health, the evidence is mixed. See, for instance, H. Herzog, 'The impact of pets on human health and psychological well-being: fact, fiction, or hypothesis?' *Current Directions in Psychological Science* 20, 4 (2011): 236–239; J. Serpell, *In the Company of Animals: A Study of Human–Animal Relationships*, Oxford: Basil Blackwell, 1986, 89–143.

2 K. Kete, *The Beast in the Boudoir: Petkeeping in Nineteenth-Century Paris*, Berkeley CA: University of California Press, 1994, especially ch. 2; H. Ritvo, 'The emergence of modern pet-keeping', in A.N. Rowan (ed.), *Animals and People Sharing the World*, Hanover NH: University Press of New England, 1988, 13–31; H. Ritvo, *The Animal Estate: The English and Other Creatures in the Victorian Age*, Cambridge MA: Harvard University Press, 1987; K.C. Grier, *Pets in America: A History*, Chapel Hill NC: University of North Carolina Press, 2006; A. Franklin, *Animals and Modern Cultures: A Sociology of Human–Animal Relations in Modernity*, Los Angeles CA: Sage, 1999; Y.-F. Tuan, *Dominance and Affection: The Making of Pets*, New Haven CT: Yale University Press, 1984, 111–112. For a critique of many of these readings, see E. Fudge, *Pets*, Stocksfield: Acumen, 2008, 17–23.

3 K. Walker-Meikle, *Medieval Pets*, Woodbridge: Boydell Press, 2012; L. Bodson, 'Motivations for pet-keeping in ancient Greece and Rome: a preliminary survey', in A.L. Podberscek, E.S. Paul, and J.A. Serpell (eds.), *Companion Animals and Us: Exploring the Relationships Between People and Pets*, Cambridge: Cambridge University Press, 2000, 27–41; J.A. Serpell, 'Pet-keeping in non-western societies: some popular misconceptions', in *Animals and People Sharing the World*.

4 Tuan, *Dominance and Affection*.

5 J. Archer, 'Why do people love their pets?', *Evolution and Human Behavior* 18, 4 (1997): 237–259, 254.

6 For an overview of the development of this scholarship, see B.H. Rosenwein, 'Worrying about emotions in history', *American Historical Review* 107, 3 (2002): 821–845.

7 Notable examples include W.M. Reddy, *The Navigation of Feeling: A Framework for the History of Emotions*, Cambridge: Cambridge University Press, 2001; B.H. Rosenwein, *Emotional Communities in the Early Middle Ages*, Ithaca NY: Cornell University Press, 2006; J. Plamper, *The History of Emotions: An Introduction*, trans. K. Tribe, Oxford: Oxford University Press, 2015.

8 T. Nagel, 'What is it like to be a bat?', *The Philosophical Review* 83, 4 (1974): 435–450.
9 See M. Bekoff, *The Emotional Lives of Animals*, Novato CA: New World Library, 2007, 7–8. This argument draws on the claim of some psychologists – most famously Paul Ekman – that there are a small number of 'basic' emotions universal to all humans. For a forceful critique of Ekman, see Plamper, *History of Emotions*, 147–163.
10 Cited in C.D.L. Wynne and M.A.R. Udell, *Animal Cognition: Evolution, Behavior and Cognition*, second edition, New York: Palgrave Macmillan, 2013, 306.
11 Wynne and Udell, *Animal Cognition*, 306.
12 Wynne and Udell, *Animal Cognition*, 171–198.
13 Bekoff, *Emotional Lives of Animals*, ch. 2, especially 36–37.
14 J. Hecht, A. Miklósi, and M. Gácsi, 'Behavioral assessment and owner perceptions of behaviors associated with guilt in dogs', *Applied Animal Behaviour Science* 139, 1–2 (2012): 134–142.
15 See K. Thomas, *Man and the Natural World: Changing Attitudes in England, 1500–1800*, Oxford: Oxford University Press, 1983, 17–25, for a succinct explanation. For a different reading of the Christian tradition that emphasises animals' place in a trans-species moral and political system, see L. Shannon, *The Accommodated Animal: Cosmopolity in Shakespearean Locales*, Chicago IL: University of Chicago Press, 2013.
16 A. Pope, *The Guardian* 61, 21 May 1713, in J.C. Stephens (ed.), *The Guardian*, Lexington KY: University Press of Kentucky, 2015, 233.
17 J. Addison, *The Spectator* 106, 2 July 1711, in D.F. Bond (ed.), *The Spectator*, 5 volumes, Oxford: Clarendon Press, 1965, volume 1, 439.
18 For an extended discussion of Cartesian ideas, see E. Fudge, *Brutal Reasoning: Animals, Rationality, and Humanity in Early Modern England*, Ithaca NY: Cornell University Press, 2006, ch. 6, especially 154–159.
19 R. Descartes, *A Discourse on the Method of Correctly Conducting One's Reason and Seeking Truth in the Sciences*, trans. I. Maclean, Oxford: Oxford University Press, 2006 [first published 1637], 46.
20 Descartes, *Discourse on Method*, 46–47.
21 Descartes, *Discourse on Method*, 47.
22 Thomas, *Man and the Natural World*, 33–35.
23 Descartes, *Discourse on Method*, 48–49. On the related Renaissance tradition of the 'organic soul' as opposed to the 'intellectual soul', which was unique to humans, see K. Park, 'The organic soul', in C.B. Schmitt, Q. Skinner, E. Kessler, and J. Kraye (eds.), *The Cambridge History of Renaissance Philosophy*, Cambridge: Cambridge University Press, 1988, 464–484.
24 See, for example, Shannon, *Accommodated Animal*. A classic statement is J. Berger, 'Why Look at Animals?' in *About Looking*, New York: Vintage, 1991 [first published 1980], 3–28.
25 See Thomas, *Man and the Natural World*, 35; Fudge, *Brutal Reasoning*, 162–169; R. Preece, *Brute Souls, Happy Beasts, and Evolution: The Historical Status of Animals*, Vancouver: UBC Press, 2005, 146–152; R. Preece, 'Thoughts out of season on the history of animal ethics', *Society & Animals* 15, 4 (2007): 370–371.
26 For an explicit contrast between Montaigne and Descartes, see Shannon, *Accommodated Animal*, 11–17. Montaigne is also a key figure in Shannon's work as a whole.
27 M. de Montaigne, 'Apology for Raymond Sebond', in *The Complete Works of Montaigne: Essays, Travel Journal, Letters*, trans. D.M. Frame, Stanford CA: Stanford University Press, 1958, 331.
28 Montaigne, 'Apology', 331.
29 Montaigne, 'Apology', 331.
30 Montaigne, 'Apology', 332.
31 Montaigne, 'Apology', 335.

32 Montaigne, 'Apology', 332–333.
33 Montaigne, 'Apology', 336–337.
34 Montaigne, 'Apology', 346.
35 Montaigne, 'Apology', 346.
36 Montaigne, 'Apology', 346.
37 Montaigne, 'Apology', 350.
38 Montaigne, 'Apology', 350–351.
39 On Montaigne and the tradition of 'theriophily', which praised the virtue of animals, see G. Boas, *The Happy Beast in French Thought of the Seventeenth Century*, New York: Octagon Books, 1966 [first published 1933]; N. Wolloch, 'Animals in Enlightenment historiography', *Huntington Library Quarterly* 75, 1 (2012): 53–68, 53–54. Erica Fudge also notes that Montaigne's reference to playing with his cat roots his philosophy in lived experience and reinforces his philosophical stance of radical scepticism: see Fudge, *Pets*, 78–82.
40 Fudge, *Brutal Reasoning*, 8–13.
41 J. Addison, *The Spectator* 120, 18 July 1711, in Bond, *The Spectator*, volume 1, 489–493.
42 The new emotions ascribed to animals parallel the idea of primary or basic versus secondary or higher-order, culturally influenced emotions. Earlier thinkers were willing to consider that animals might experience very simple 'passions' such as joy or fear, while later thinkers expanded these ideas.
43 On animal morality – the literal sense of 'fair play' – as a critical aspect of animal emotions, see Bekoff, *Emotional Lives of Animals*, ch. 4. On the difference between ethics (accessible only to humans) and morality (understood by humans and animals), see 88–89.
44 Rosenwein, *Emotional Communities*, 2.
45 Rosenwein, 'Worrying About Emotions', 842.
46 It is important to remember that, as Rosenwein emphasises, emotional communities are not monolithic or hegemonic. Here I am tracing the emergence and influence of a particular emotional community, not arguing that it formed an 'emotional regime', in William Reddy's formulation. Although Reddy convincingly argues for the significance of sensibility to late eighteenth-century culture, his claim for its function as a 'regime' that inhibited the formation of alternative forms of emotional expression is, I think, overstated.
47 For important discussions of sentiment and sensibility in the eighteenth century, see J. Mullan, *Sentiment and Sociability: The Language of Feeling in the Eighteenth Century*, Oxford: Clarendon Press, 1988; G.J. Barker-Benfield, *The Culture of Sensibility: Sex and Society in Eighteenth-Century Britain*, Chicago IL: University of Chicago Press, 1992; M. Ellis, *The Politics of Sensibility: Race, Gender and Commerce in the Sentimental Novel*, Cambridge: Cambridge University Press, 1996.
48 I. Csengei, *Sympathy, Sensibility and the Literature of Feeling in the Eighteenth Century*, New York: Palgrave Macmillan, 2012, 5.
49 For a reading of the impact of sensibility on human–animal relations that stresses its ethical significance, see T. Menely, *The Animal Claim: Sensibility and the Creaturely Voice*, Chicago IL: University of Chicago Press, 2015.
50 Reddy, *Navigation of Feeling*, 161. Reddy provides a useful summary of the spread of these ideas in England and France: 154–161. See also Csengei, *Sympathy, Sensibility and the Literature of Feeling*, 32–39.
51 Menely, *Animal Claim*, 60.
52 Menely, *Animal Claim*, 61–62.
53 Menely, *Animal Claim*, 63.
54 D. Hume, *A Treatise of Human Nature*, D.F. Norton and M.J. Norton (eds.), Oxford: Oxford University Press, 2000 (first published 1738–1740), Book 2, Part 1, Section 12, 211–212. For an extended discussion of Hume's views on the analogy between human

and animal passions, see J. Spencer, '"Love and hatred are common to the whole sensitive creation": animal feeling in the century before Darwin', *Clio Medica* 93, (2013): 30–32.
55 Hume, *Treatise of Human Nature*, 212–213.
56 Hume, *Treatise of Human Nature*, 255.
57 J. Hildrop, *Free Thoughts Upon the Brute-Creation: Or, An Examination of Father Bougeant's Philosophical Amusement, &c. In Two Letters to a Lady*, 2 volumes, London: R. Minors, 1742–1743, volume 1, 6–7.
58 W. Smellie, *The Philosophy of Natural History*, 2 volumes, Dublin: William Porter, 1790, volume 1, 247.
59 Smellie, *Philosophy of Natural History*, volume 1, 248–249.
60 Smellie, *Philosophy of Natural History*, volume 2, 313–314.
61 For a reading of change over time that emphasises the shift away from the debate over animal souls, see Spencer, 'Love and hatred'. For a critical reading of late eighteenth-century ideas about understanding animal emotions, see R. Nash, 'Joy and pity: reading animal bodies in late eighteenth-century culture', *Eighteenth Century: Theory & Interpretation* 52, 1 (2011): 47–62.
62 E. Sibly, *Magazine of Natural History. Comprehending the Whole Science of Animals, Plants, and Minerals; Divided into Distinct Parts, the Characters Separately Described, and Systematically Arranged*, 14 volumes, London: Printed for the Proprietor, 1794, volume 1, iii–iv.
63 See Menely, *Animal Claim*, especially 30–35, on the concept of sensibility as reliant on non-verbal or pre-verbal communication.
64 H. Herzog, *Some We Love, Some We Hate, Some We Eat: Why It's So Hard to Think Straight About Animals*, New York: HarperCollins, 2010, 109–110. For an alternative view of this issue, see Wynne and Udell, *Animal Cognition*, 183–185, who point out that differences may be more related to dogs' lifelong socialisation to humans than to inherent species difference.
65 G.-L. Leclerc, Count de Buffon, *Natural History, General and Particular, by the Count de Buffon, Translated into English*, trans. W. Smellie, second edition, 9 volumes, London: W. Strahan and T. Cadell, 1785, volume 3, 271.
66 Buffon, *Natural History*, volume 3, 276–278.
67 Buffon, *Natural History*, volume 4, 2.
68 Buffon, *Natural History*, volume 4, 3.
69 E.A. Kendall, *Keeper's Travels in Search of His Master*, London: E. Newbery, 1798, 65–67.
70 Fittingly, the eponymous canine hero of the story finds himself torn between his desire to stay with the family that rescued him after he was shot and his desire to return home to his original master.
71 S.J. Pratt, *Gleanings in England; Descriptive of the Countenance, Mind and Character of the Country*, third edition, 3 volumes, London: T.N. Longman and O. Rees, 1801, volume 2, 338.
72 For a careful analysis of the role of sensibility in supporting new ways of thinking about human treatment of animals, see Menely, *Animal Claim*.
73 T. Young, *An Essay on Humanity to Animals*, London: T. Cadell, Jun. and W. Davies, 1798, 37–38.
74 Young, *Humanity to Animals*, 152.
75 Young, *Humanity to Animals*, 152–153.
76 On the backlash, see Menely, *Animal Claim*, 182–201.
77 For an extended critique of 'separate spheres' in English historiography, see A. Vickery, 'Golden age to separate spheres? A review of the categories and chronology of English women's history', *Historical Journal* 36, 2 (1993): 383–414. On the importance of domestic space in Victorian thinking, see P. Howell, *At Home and Astray: The Domestic Dog in Victorian Britain*, Charlottesville VA: University of Virginia Press, 2015, especially 14–20.

78 While pet-keeping was gendered in earlier periods, the strongly positive associations between women, domesticity, and pets in the nineteenth century marked a departure from earlier representations. See I.H. Tague, *Animal Companions: Pets and Social Change in Eighteenth-Century Britain*, University Park PA: Pennsylvania State University Press, 2015, ch. 3.

79 Howell, *At Home and Astray*.

80 Plamper, *History of Emotions*, 170–171.

81 'The question is not, Can they reason? nor, Can they talk? but, Can they suffer?' J. Bentham, *An Introduction to the Principles of Morals and Legislation*, Oxford: Clarendon Press, 1907 [first published 1789], 311n.

Bibliography

Archer, J. 'Why do people love their pets?', *Evolution and Human Behavior* 18, 4 (1997): 237–259.

Barker-Benfield, G.J. *The Culture of Sensibility: Sex and Society in Eighteenth-Century Britain*, Chicago IL: University of Chicago Press, 1992.

Bekoff, M. *The Emotional Lives of Animals*, Novato CA: New World Library, 2007.

Bentham, J. *An Introduction to the Principles of Morals and Legislation*, Oxford: Clarendon Press, 1907.

Berger, J. 'Why Look at Animals?' in *About Looking*, New York: Vintage, 1991, 3–28.

Boas, G. *The Happy Beast in French Thought of the Seventeenth Century*, New York: Octagon Books, 1966.

Bodson, L. 'Motivations for pet-keeping in ancient Greece and Rome: a preliminary survey', in A.L. Podberscek, E.S. Paul, and J.A. Serpell (eds.), *Companion Animals and Us: Exploring the Relationships Between People and Pets*, Cambridge: Cambridge University Press, 2000.

Bond, D.F. (ed.), *The Spectator*, 5 volumes, Oxford: Clarendon Press, 1965.

Csengei, I. *Sympathy, Sensibility and the Literature of Feeling in the Eighteenth Century*, New York: Palgrave Macmillan, 2012.

Descartes, R. *A Discourse on the Method of Correctly Conducting One's Reason and Seeking Truth in the Sciences*, trans. I. Maclean, Oxford: Oxford University Press, 2006.

Ellis, M. *The Politics of Sensibility: Race, Gender and Commerce in the Sentimental Novel*, Cambridge: Cambridge University Press, 1996.

Franklin, A. *Animals and Modern Cultures: A Sociology of Human–Animal Relations in Modernity*, Los Angeles CA: Sage, 1999.

Fudge, E. *Brutal Reasoning: Animals, Rationality, and Humanity in Early Modern England*, Ithaca NY: Cornell University Press, 2006.

Fudge, E. *Pets*, Stocksfield: Acumen, 2008.

Grier, K.C. *Pets in America: A History*, Chapel Hill NC: University of North Carolina Press, 2006.

Hecht, J., Miklósi, A., and Gácsi, M. 'Behavioral assessment and owner perceptions of behaviors associated with guilt in dogs', *Applied Animal Behaviour Science* 139, 1–2 (2012): 134–142.

Herzog, H. *Some We Love, Some We Hate, Some We Eat: Why It's So Hard to Think Straight About Animals*, New York: HarperCollins, 2010.

Herzog, H. 'The impact of pets on human health and psychological well-being: fact, fiction, or hypothesis?', *Current Directions in Psychological Science* 20, 4 (2011): 236–239.

Hildrop, J. *Free Thoughts Upon the Brute-Creation: Or, An Examination of Father Bougeant's Philosophical Amusement, &c. In Two Letters to a Lady*, 2 volumes, London: R. Minors, 1742-1743.

Howell, P. *At Home and Astray: The Domestic Dog in Victorian Britain*, Charlottesville VA: University of Virginia Press, 2015.

Hume, D. *A Treatise of Human Nature*, D.F. Norton and M.J. Norton (eds.), Oxford: Oxford University Press, 2000.

Kendall, E.A. *Keeper's Travels in Search of His Master*, London: E. Newbery, 1798.

Kete, K. *The Beast in the Boudoir: Petkeeping in Nineteenth-Century Paris*, Berkeley CA: University of California Press, 1994.

Leclerc, G.-L., Count de Buffon, *Natural History, General and Particular, by the Count de Buffon, Translated into English*, trans. W. Smellie, second edition, 9 volumes, London: W. Strahan and T. Cadell, 1785.

Menely, T. *The Animal Claim: Sensibility and the Creaturely Voice*, Chicago IL: University of Chicago Press, 2015.

Montaigne, M., *The Complete Works of Montaigne: Essays, Travel Journal, Letters*, trans. D.M. Frame, Stanford CA: Stanford University Press, 1958.

Mullan, J. *Sentiment and Sociability: The Language of Feeling in the Eighteenth Century*, Oxford: Clarendon Press, 1988.

Nagel, T. 'What is it like to be a bat?' *The Philosophical Review* 83, 4 (1974): 435–450.

Nash, R. 'Joy and pity: reading animal bodies in late eighteenth-century culture', *Eighteenth Century: Theory & Interpretation* 52, 1 (2011): 47–62.

Park, K. 'The organic soul', in C.B. Schmitt, Q. Skinner, E. Kessler, and J. Kraye (eds.), *The Cambridge History of Renaissance Philosophy*, Cambridge: Cambridge University Press, 1988, 464–484.

Plamper, J. *The History of Emotions: An Introduction*, trans. K. Tribe, Oxford: Oxford University Press, 2015.

Pope, A. *The Guardian* 61, 21 May 1713, in J.C. Stephens (ed.), *The Guardian*, Lexington KY: University Press of Kentucky, 2015, 233.

Pratt, S.J. *Gleanings in England; Descriptive of the Countenance, Mind and Character of the Country*, third edition, 3 volumes, London: T.N. Longman and O. Rees, 1801.

Preece, R. *Brute Souls, Happy Beasts, and Evolution: The Historical Status of Animals*, Vancouver: UBC Press, 2005.

Preece, R. 'Thoughts out of season on the history of animal ethics', *Society & Animals* 15, 4 (2007): 370–371.

Reddy, W.M. *The Navigation of Feeling: A Framework for the History of Emotions*, Cambridge: Cambridge University Press, 2001.

Ritvo, H. *The Animal Estate: The English and Other Creatures in the Victorian Age*, Cambridge MA: Harvard University Press, 1987.

Ritvo, H. 'The emergence of modern pet-keeping', in A.N. Rowan (ed.), *Animals and People Sharing the World*, Hanover NH: University Press of New England, 1988, 13–31.

Rosenwein, B.H. 'Worrying about emotions in history', *American Historical Review* 107, 3 (2002): 821–845.

Rosenwein, B.H. *Emotional Communities in the Early Middle Ages*, Ithaca NY: Cornell University Press, 2006.

Serpell, J. *In the Company of Animals: A Study of Human–Animal Relationships*, Oxford: Basil Blackwell, 1986.

Serpell, J.A. 'Pet-keeping in non-western societies: some popular misconceptions', in A.N. Rowan (ed.) *Animals and People Sharing the World*, Hanover NH: University Press of New England, 1988, 33–52.

Shannon, L. *The Accommodated Animal: Cosmopolity in Shakespearean Locales*, Chicago IL: University of Chicago Press, 2013.

Sibly, E. *Magazine of Natural History. Comprehending the Whole Science of Animals, Plants, and Minerals; Divided into Distinct Parts, the Characters Separately Described, and Systematically Arranged*, 14 volumes, London: Printed for the Proprietor, 1794.

Smellie, W. *The Philosophy of Natural History*, 2 volumes, Dublin: William Porter, 1790.

Spencer, J. '"Love and hatred are common to the whole sensitive creation": animal feeling in the century before Darwin', *Clio Medica* 93, (2013): 30–32.

Tague, I.H. *Animal Companions: Pets and Social Change in Eighteenth-Century Britain*, University Park PA: Pennsylvania State University Press, 2015.

Thomas, K. *Man and the Natural World: Changing Attitudes in England, 1500–1800*, Oxford: Oxford University Press, 1983.

Tuan, Y.-F. *Dominance and Affection: The Making of Pets*, New Haven CT: Yale University Press, 1984.

Vickery, A. 'Golden age to separate spheres? A review of the categories and chronology of English women's history', *Historical Journal* 36, 2 (1993): 383–414.

Walker-Meikle, K. *Medieval Pets*, Woodbridge: Boydell Press, 2012.

Wells, D.H. 'The effects of animals on human health and well-being', *Journal of Social Issues* 65, 3 (2009): 523–543.

Wolloch, N. 'Animals in Enlightenment historiography', *Huntington Library Quarterly* 75, 1 (2012): 53–68.

Wynne, C.D.L. and Udell, M.A.R. *Animal Cognition: Evolution, Behavior and Cognition*, second edition, New York: Palgrave Macmillan, 2013.

Young, T. *An Essay on Humanity to Animals*, London: T. Cadell, Jun. and W. Davies, 1798.

16

SURVIVING TWENTIETH-CENTURY MODERNITY

Birdsong and emotions in Britain[1]

Michael Guida

George Orwell's *Nineteen Eighty-Four* is a good place to start. The rats of Room 101 stay vivid in the mind, but there are other creatures that Orwell places carefully within the story. The possibility of a release from the oppression of 'the Party' comes when Julia and Winston Smith celebrate their defiance with a trip to the countryside. Julia had discovered a clearing in the woods on a community hike where she could safely meet men like Winston. When they arrive at the sunny clearing, Winston cannot relax though. He wonders if there are microphones hidden among the trees. He despises his false teeth and varicose veins and the 'sooty dust of London in the pores of his skin'.[2] Yet the awkwardness of their encounter among the saplings evaporates in the presence of a thrush that alights on a bough close to them and begins to pour forth a torrent of song.

> In the afternoon hush the volume of sound was startling. Winston and Julia clung together, fascinated. The music went on and on, minute after minute, with astonishing variations, never once repeating itself, almost as if the bird were deliberately showing off its virtuosity [...] For whom, for what, was that bird singing? No mate, no rival was watching it. What made it sit at the edge of the lonely wood and pour its music into nothingness? [...] But by degrees the flood of music drove all speculations out of his mind. It was as though it were a kind of liquid stuff that poured all over him and got mixed up with the sunlight that filtered through the leaves. He stopped thinking and merely felt.[3]

Orwell shaped his story in London amid the random terror of everyday life during the Second World War. By so carefully placing a bird in ecstatic song at the heart of his love scene, he demonstrated how deeply birdsong had entered the modern imagination as a tonic for world-weary nerves and as the antithesis of tyranny. Birdsong was a spur to freedom because it had ensured that the blow against 'the Party' could be fully enacted. For Winston, the song of the thrush had washed away his anxieties and, with the sunlight, restored him. Now, love-making could proceed in the woods.

Yet, Winston had been bothered by the thrush's effusive performance. In the absence of a mate or territorial rival, why was this bird singing? Was it singing for its own pleasure? And, if so, could this pleasure be contagious or communicated to human listeners? This chapter will consider such questions and others to explore the relationship between human and bird emotions under the pressures of twentieth-century change.

The resounding presence of birds in people's lives has for millennia been amplified by potent cultural and political symbolism, constructed, layered and exchanged.[4] These meanings should not, and probably never can, be separated from more immediate emotional and intellectual responses to the direct encounter with a bird and its song. However, to understand the place of birdlife in human lives the historian must consider the feature of sentimentality embedded so often in writings about birds and their song, but not necessarily to discount it because this kind of expression does itself reveal something about how the human feels in the modern world.[5] In the last hundred years or so, an interest in birds has been often construed as something 'weedy, romantic and somehow un-modern', a pursuit best left to children, poets and naturalists.[6] But it is sentiment, more than the sentimental, that this chapter will investigate, with an emphasis on lived experience, while the metaphorical riches of birds and their song will be in constant attendance.

In seeking to understand the ways in which birdsong has been part of British emotional life especially in times of stress, there will be a focus here on the aftermath of the First World War, its psychic fall-out and prevailing moods. These somewhat intangible historical elements will be uncovered through an analysis of early radio broadcasting under the control of the BBC's public service ideals in the 1920s, and of Home Front mindsets and morale during the Second World War, perceived within BBC radio and popular books about birds. In this period, 1919–1945, the tensions between notions of national identity and urban experience, the challenge of new communication technologies in the public realm and the social crisis of warfare will come to the fore. BBC broadcasting philosophy, programming and public opinion are employed as central source materials because they reflect a reasonably wide spectrum of cultural activity where emotional life can be detected. By no means serving everyone, broadcasting did to some extent mediate 'common-sense knowledge' and 'the practical experience and the everyday pleasure' of British society.[7] The BBC was, as well, a domain that took to broadcasting both live and recorded birdsong from 1924, and it also provided a forum for discussion about it.

In addition, the accounts of contemporary zoologists and naturalists will be considered. These expert scientific perspectives are interesting because their primary aim is to know *why* birds sing, to elucidate the biological purpose of song, and in attempting to answer this, scientists reveal the emotional lives birds may have themselves and the implications for human listeners. In essence then, this chapter explores human emotional responses to birdsong, while also considering accounts of bird emotions, and what interactions can take place when the two meet. In doing this, I hope to illuminate the place of birdsong in British national life, what it stood for, and how it was used – put to work – to soften the intensities of modern life.

The field of the history of emotions draws the attention of the historian away from conscious actions and rational decisions that preoccupy them, to redirect it towards the possible role of factors such as fear, anxiety, melancholy, love and happiness in shaping history. It is a field that Jan Plamper has recently reviewed and he has emphasised the virtues of thinking historically about emotions, not simply thinking about emotions in history.[8] While animals have not featured distinctly within the domain of the history of emotions, they of course are part of social, cultural and political history into which the scholars William Reddy, Barbara Rosenwein and Peter Stearns have aimed to integrate the category of emotion.[9] The *Annales* school historian Lucien Febvre, who is a foundational thinker in the history of emotions, asserted in 1938 that without histories of love, death, hate, fear and cruelty '*there will be no history possible*', the urgency of his tone stemming from the rise of Fascism.[10] Animal–human relations have generated feelings that are often a crucial counterbalance to the chiefly negative emotions Febvre prescribed for historical enquiry.

In the last decade, Joanna Bourke, Mark Jackson and Richard Overy have made significant studies of the character of fear, stress and anxiety in twentieth-century history seen from cultural, medical and political viewpoints.[11] Overy's work, for example, attempts the difficult excavation of contemporary popular reactions, to yield the moods at play in Britain between the wars. This chapter looks at fear, stress and anxiety as characteristic of the first half of the twentieth century and they form the emotional context for an analysis of the reception and place of birdsong in human lives.

The study of birds has to date been largely the concern of biologists and naturalists who seek to know the structure, function and behaviour of birds, or poets who have done the same (as perhaps the first birdwatchers) to find 'unlimited and unequalled reflections of their own world'.[12] However, there are important social and cultural histories of birds, notably written by Mark Cocker and Richard Mabey, which I look to for their scrupulous attention to the life of birds and their honesty in describing the innermost world of the observer.[13] The history of birdwatching, the figure of the naturalist and the practice of natural history of the late-modern period have had some attention from scholars.[14] In recent years, academic historians have steered clear of birds, although Tim Birkhead and Nigel Rothfels are notable exceptions.[15] David Rothenberg has produced the only non-technical monograph dedicated to birdsong and his philosophical and musical approach takes emotions into account.[16]

I have taken a distinctive social and political context in which technological innovations of mass communication and industrialised warfare impinge on the emotional status of Britons. Paying special attention to sound allows a different kind of history to be written where the senses are foremost. What I argue is that as the keynote of British nature, birdsong was used to secure a vision of a hopeful and enriching future in the face of new technological disruptions and warfare. In 1924 the song of the nightingale became part of the foundation of public service broadcasting, a broadcasting that could move the soul, not just inform and educate. The live voice of a nightingale on the wireless confirmed myths of the bird and of the Romantic rural, but it introduced a new kind of magic to the medium of radio, too. Scientific studies of birdsong in the interwar period largely agreed that exuberance in song was indicative of the presence of emotions. In these studies, by Walter Garstang, Julian Huxley and Max Nicholson, there were intimations that if birds sang in happiness, the mood in the air may be passed on to people. In the Second World War, I explore the Home Front birdsong broadcasts of Ludwig Koch and argue that they provided an emotional sustenance, distinct from speech or music on the radio, by bolstering ideals of citizenship and providing a patriotic model of the fortitude and continuity of nature in times of conflict.

'Emotionalism is revealed' when a BBC nightingale sings

When John Reith took on the role of General Manager to establish the BBC in late 1922, with a handful of other men, his aim was to shape broadcasting to be part of the permanent and essential 'machinery of civilization' bringing 'the best of everything into the greatest number of homes'.[17] The state of civilisation was in question in the years after the Armistice, a period Richard Overy has called 'the morbid age', a time of psychic fragility when so much was unspeakable, in human language at least. A mood of anxiety and pessimism drew strength from a number of shifts in social and intellectual life, not least that the violence of the First World War had undone a centuries-long civilising process.[18]

Prior to the formation of the BBC, the culture of wireless radio revolved around the potential of an enchanted technology that allowed sounds, like spirits, to move invisibly and almost instantaneously through the air.[19] During and after the war, wireless communication became a vehicle for telepathic dialogue with sons lost in the war, a possibility that apprehended the hopes of many.[20] At the same time, the flood of radio waves pulsing through buildings and bodies together with the rush of voices carried by those waves into people's homes raised questions about what this new medium might be doing to human thought and health. Nevertheless, in the early 1920s a 'broadcasting craze' was in motion, which some registered as another ubiquitous modern noise.[21] Yet, Reith wanted to see that 'any and all' Britons could 'gain access' to the world of politics and culture, which did indeed require ubiquitous reach across the nation.[22] In early 1924, one wireless magazine journalist had delighted in the thought that 'the time is at hand when no place in forest, mountain or moor shall be too isolated to be linked with the life that is throbbing in the metropolis'.[23] Reith was sensitive to these tensions, of the need to give everyone the chance to listen to the riches of national broadcasting, but at the same time he wanted to demonstrate that broadcasting had at its core an enlightening, even spiritual, purpose. It would not be enough to flood homes with the best classical and popular music and educative talks.

Reith had in fact been planning with his engineering team since late 1923 the possibility of transmitting a live broadcast from a Surrey garden of a duet between a nightingale and the cellist Beatrice Harrison.[24] She was a friend of Edward Elgar and an expert with his cello repertoire. Harrison had found that when she was practising in her leafy garden a nightingale would appear and sing with her: 'the voice of the bird followed me in thirds!' she wrote in her diary.[25] While this was to be the first live BBC broadcast from an outdoor location, outside of London, for Reith it needed to have more purpose and substance than a technical feat or publicity stunt. Reith felt this was a chance to show the listening public, the critics and his sponsors that broadcasting could surprise and enchant, rising above the everyday.

In May 1924, the bird in song with Harrison playing *Londonderry Air* was transmitted across Britain at a quarter to eleven on a Monday evening and then on several more occasions that month. The broadcasts were a sensation, perhaps a million people listening-in late at night. Harrison received 50,000 letters from listeners in Britain and beyond.[26] An analysis of the few surviving letters written by men, women, the young and the elderly, many from beyond the range of the nightingale in the North of England and Scotland, makes it clear that for most the bird was the star.[27] R.M. Monk from Bramhall in Cheshire said this: 'I wonder do you know what it means to dwellers in the commercial north to enjoy for a few moments the pleasure of the nightingale's song – if you do, then all your efforts are rewarded'. A man in Godalming wrote to tell Harrison that from the loudspeaker in his garden the broadcast nightingale provoked another to sing along. W.J. Daully had also been enthralled:

> Will you please accept the very grateful thanks of a Liverpool postman and his mother for the great joy that you were instrumental in bringing to their ears last night [. . .] Liverpool well for one day forgot tragedy, politics, cricket and horse racing.

It seems that the stresses of humdrum life had been swept away by a shy small brown bird known only for the mythic beauty of its voice, now witnessed through a domestic radio loudspeaker. From national and regional press reports it is plain that some could hear little on their rudimentary crystal sets and headphones. Others felt that broadcasting was powerless to communicate the 'exquisite richness and wonderful variety' of the song which could only really work its charms on the listener in a 'moonlit glade'.[28] Yet, the *idea* of the most loved and mysterious of all bird voices penetrating the darkened rooms of homes around the country held its own transportive powers for many.

These feelings had come from the actuality of the nightingale in song, however poor the mediated reproduction. But they were underpinned by deep-rooted stories about the bird in folklore and poetry, where its song was vivid.[29] The Romantic poets had affirmed the song as the sound of joy, yet the bird's association with the night lent a mystery which Richard Mabey has said helped 'make their song the equivalent of a psychologist's ink-blot test, capable of carrying all kinds of meaning [. . .]'.[30] The song of a blackbird, however cherished, could not have moved listeners in quite the same way. In 1924, at the time of the broadcasts, the nightingale's notes were still fresh in the minds of soldiers who had returned from Belgium and France and prominent in the writing and poetry of the conflict. The morning song of the lark and the evening notes of the nightingale had provided comforting evidence that 'ecstasy was still an active motif in the universe', Paul Fussell has argued.[31] Also in 1924, Stanley Baldwin's extraordinary speech claiming that 'England is the country, and the country is England' evoking the idyll of 'the corncrake on a dewy morning, the sound of the scythe against the whetstone' was in the air at the same moment.[32]

Reith was thrilled by the public response and he had his own theories about what had happened with the nightingale broadcasts. He wrote in the *Radio Times*, a few weeks after the broadcasts, that the nightingale 'has swept the country [. . .] with a wave of something akin to emotionalism and the glamour of romance had flashed across the prosaic round of many a life'.[33] Reith's use of the word 'emotionalism' is curious and powerful, usually meaning during this period a tendency towards a state of hysteria or nervous agitation. It was not a frame of mind Reith would have wanted to create with his broadcasting as a matter of course, but he was clearly taken by the feelings that broadcasting could rouse. The effect of all of this on Reith's vision for public service broadcasting is quite striking in his 1924 manifesto *Broadcast Over Britain* where he spells out the connections between nature and broadcasting. Written reflecting on the first 18 months of broadcasting, this passage comes from a chapter Reith named 'In Touch with the Infinite':

> Among the great paradoxes of life come the companionship of solitude and the voice of silence. To men and women confined in the narrow streets of the great cities shall be brought many of the voices of Nature, calling them to the enjoyment of her myriad delights. There is some peculiar quality about certain sounds, since they may not be incompatible with the conditions of silence. Already we have broadcast a voice which few have opportunity of hearing for themselves. The song of the nightingale has been heard all over the country, on highland moors and in the tenements of great towns. Milton has said that when the nightingale sang, silence was pleased. So in the song of the nightingale we have broadcast something of the silence which all of us in this busy world unconsciously crave and urgently need.[34]

Reith has said a great deal here. He finds that of all the thousands of hours of programming that the BBC had sent out to the nation, the nightingale broadcast had very special meanings. In everyday terms, birdsong and other sounds of the natural world were a tonic to weary urbanites in a way that radio music and voices could never be. An editorial in *The Times* was reminded by the broadcast that a good many 'are not over-keen on listening night after night to ephemeralities' of the human voice and human music. 'May we not say, wirelessly speaking, when the human voice has ceased by excessive repetition to charm, that the proper study of mankind is henceforth to be birds?'[35] There is a jaded misanthropy here but also an insistence that birdlife had a timeless and universal quality that humans might do well to contemplate if they wanted to progress.

Fundamentally, though, there was one quality that the nightingale's song encapsulated for Reith – its association with silence. Listeners had not recognised a literal need for silence on the wireless and their letters had not spoken of one perceived when they heard the nightingale. However, for Reith the nightingale song *felt* like a silent pause for reflection and contemplation, an absence of the man-made that allowed space for the infinite to speak.[36] It was as though birds while not silent themselves 'somehow inhabited the spaces of silence', as Sara Maitland has observed recently.[37] This idea is apparent in the Armistice remembrance rituals, which had raised the significance of silence in civic life and yet it was noticed that 'the bickering of sparrows, the crisp rustle of falling leaves, the creasing of pigeon wings' had made their appearance and been granted a place in this sacred silence.[38]

Reith was anxious that the rarefied mood created in 'the broadcasting of silence' was not allowed to dissipate too quickly. The feelings that had poured forth from those who heard the nightingale were actually a precious disruption to the humdrum preoccupations with 'the review of sundry divorce and murder cases now proceeding;

to the traffic problems of London, and to the threatened collapse of various bridges'.[39] Reith explained:

> There are times when the traditional stolidity of our race gives way. The barriers of reserve are broken. Latent and normally disciplined emotionalism is revealed. For a little while a measure of sentimentality is unashamed. Then, of course, 'better feelings' assert themselves. Cultured restraint, tempered with a measure of cynicism, holds sway again. The trivial weakness of the moment is forgotten; equilibrium is restored.[40]

Reith was not simply endorsing a recourse from the urban to the convenience of the pastoral idyll of the imagination that the nightingale might evoke. He was suggesting that the song gave humans a valuable way to cope with modern life. Modernity could be *managed*, not rejected, if people would allow themselves to feel nature's presence in their lives.

Surprisingly, then, the nightingale broadcasts played a distinct part in the definition of public service broadcasting, a broadcasting that could point human hearts towards a higher realm, catering to people's unconscious needs, not simply their compulsions and routines. Even a mediated nightingale could do this, Reith had discovered. The 'best of everything' that Reith had promised would have to include the songs of British birds. None of this was planned, it is important to note – there were 'no sealed orders' as Reith put it when he took charge of the BBC.[41] Reith had found that the response to the nightingale transmissions had refined his thinking about broadcasting's purpose, and that his own inner world needed the solace that the bird in song had unexpectedly brought.[42] In fact, Reith went further in his vision of broadcasting to postulate that listening to the radio would connect public minds to the stillness, harmony and order of the cosmos, through the movement of electromagnetic waves across the ether.[43] Radio broadcasting could connect nature's microcosms, of which humans and animals were part, to the macrocosm. The nightingale broadcasts should be seen as part of this grander philosophy of what broadcasting might do for humanity.

The live transmission of the song of a Surrey nightingale became a permanent part of the BBC's persona, airing for several nights every May for the next 12 years until Beatrice Harrison moved house.[44] Then a bird would sing alone annually until 1942, when the microphones picked up a British bombing raid in progress and the transmission had to be aborted.[45] During the Second World War, the broadcasting of the duet between Harrison and a nightingale was re-enacted, this time during a German bombing raid, in the propaganda film *The Demi-Paradise*. Starring Laurence Olivier, the film demonstrated that the strength of Britain's traditions, not least the eccentric ones, and the belief in duty and service, would win the war.[46] Reith's commitment to the yearly cycle of nightingale song in May lent a seasonal pattern of renewal to broadcasting itself. The song took its place alongside many other cultural treasures that Reith saw as bringing unity and civilisation to Britain and its territories. It could dispel fears that the BBC was at risk of standardising thought and taste in its mass address. When the song was transmitted it was as if the broadcaster had fallen silent to allow listeners to reflect and fill in the gaps themselves.[47] The song of the nightingale helped to make broadcasting morally edifying to Reith and transcendent to his public.

The science and sentiment of song

Next I want to shift from the public perceptions and philosophical connotations of the nightingale's song to the interwar scientific efforts to understand why birds sang. In doing this, a more animal-centred approach will be taken. While zoologists, naturalists and ornithologists were chiefly concerned with exploring the function of birdsong, such an approach often left these investigators dissatisfied with their explanations and something of birdsong unaccounted for. Part of what emerges is an inability for the scientists considered here to fully account for the exuberance they observed in birdsong that exceeded anticipated biological needs. Functionally, song was understood as an instinctive survival behaviour that was central to genes being passed on and new generations being secured. Yet, birds also seemed to sing for fun. Investigators glimpsed a possible emotional world of birds through their song outputs. Moreover, the possibility that bird emotions articulated through song could be passed on to humans was raised. The ideas of three scientists will be surveyed.

Walter Garstang, the Professor of Zoology at the University of Leeds, published an unusual little book on 'the natural history of birdsong' in 1922. In *Songs of the Birds* Garstang admitted straight away that he had fallen 'in love' with his 'models' and could not content himself with a 'purely scientific account of their performances'.[48] In his 'interpretation of bird-music' he tried several techniques to analyse birdsong: he wrote poems to capture the personality of different species; used musical notation to attempt to document timbre, resonance and rhythm; and he drew up sets of mnemonics to express bird vocalisation sounds. In this last respect, Garstang followed *the* bird poet, John Clare, in an effort to document what birds were saying and singing.[49] The results of Garstang's lark 'heralding the dawn' looked like this (and I give just the first four lines of nine):

Swee! Swee! Swee! Swee!
Zwée-o! Zwée-o! Zwée-o! Zwée-o!
Sís-is-is-Swée! Sís-is-is-Swée!
Joo! Joo! Joo! Joo![50]

Garstang's poems, music and mnemonic phrases were published in the *Yorkshire Weekly Post* and *The Times* in 1919.[51] However, they were not popular with ornithologists. A reviewer in *British Birds* found that popular phrases such as 'A little bit of bread and no cheese' and the best birdsong poems such a Shelley's 'Skylark' served the 'genius of birdsong' better.[52] This reviewer from the leading scientific bird journal was not saying that these popular forms of expressing birdsong were accurate, but that they captured the essence of the song more faithfully, and this was more valuable. This is a surprising response as scientific identification was becoming central to birdwatching during this period. Identifying a bird by its song was always difficult but that a syllabic transcription for documentation and study purposes was rejected in favour of poetry and rhythmic aides-memoires is indicative of what was thought to be needed to represent birdsong properly.

Garstang did however strike a chord with his ideas about birds' own emotions.[53] Birdsong, he argued, was an expression 'of an emotional state, a prolonged, if periodic, elevation of the spirit'.[54] Moreover, he explained that birds had 'considerable spells of leisure, which they freely devote to elevating forms of recreation' and this leisure time had given birds the opportunity to develop their own aesthetic sense.[55] If birdsong was to be understood, these creatures must be assumed to be 'sound-lovers, who cultivate the pursuit of sound-combinations as an art'.[56] In other words, Garstang rejected the idea that song was chiefly instinctive and automatic. Rather, birds were sonic artists whose creativity was driven by emotional energy.

If Garstang's theories about the emotions and aesthetic judgement of birds were novel to ornithologists in the 1920s, they were not completely original, as Charles Darwin had identified in birds both emotions and 'a taste for the beautiful' in *The Descent of Man* first published in 1871.[57] Darwin had observed male song as a way to attract females, but also as a clear expression of a range of emotions 'such as distress, fear, anger, triumph, or mere happiness'.[58] Garstang went further though when he said that beyond attracting a mate, song contained the 'whole joy of life at its climax of achievement and well-being'.[59] This notion of a 'climax of achievement' suggests evolutionary struggle followed by triumph. He continued to develop this unusual idea when he wrote that 'earth's primal songs' had always been 'the outcome of individual achievements and success under simple if inexorable conditions'.[60] The song of the bird conveyed joy but there was a deeper biological celebration of survival and perpetuation at work too, one that stretched back to a time before humans had evolved. Song arose from and signalled a sexual energy that would ensure continuity of life, perhaps even beyond human life on earth. Birdsong, Garstang felt, was a song of survival.

Julian Huxley, based at King's College in London in the mid-1920s, was another Professor of Zoology. His deep interest in ornithology was reflected in his work to get amateur and 'professional' birdwatchers to collaborate to advance biology. He would not go as far as Garstang in endorsing an aesthetic sense in birds but did think that birdsong was not limited solely to territorial and reproductive functions. 'Song', he wrote, 'is simply an outlet, and a pleasurable one'. A bird, he added, 'will continue to sing in all moments of excitement or exaltation, non-sexual as well as sexual'.[61] In the late 1930s, Huxley made a pioneering study of animal language, with the sound recordist Ludwig Koch who is discussed later in this chapter. Though this was a biological study, he explained, he did not want to 'deny the psychological basis of animal sounds'. He declared that a 'deliberate sound will almost always have an emotional reason'.[62] A bird would sing 'because it wants to, because it feels like singing; and it feels like singing because it is brimming over with energy, because it is angry, or because it is happy'. He wrote that he was in agreement with the ordinary man or woman whom he thought would say that birds sang 'because they feel happy, or excited, or full of life'.[63] Huxley was an influential public intellectual in the 1930s, the secretary of the Zoological Society of London and a familiar voice hosting science series on the radio. What is important here is not so much that Huxley confirms birds may have emotions but that experts and many others believed birds sang because they were happy. This belief seems to lead to the possibility that such bird emotions expressed through song will move human emotions too. Huxley does not say it, but the implication is that birds in song are likely to make people happy.

Perhaps the most important scientist to consider is Max Nicholson, the leading ornithologist of the 1920s and 30s who published widely about birds and established the British Trust for Ornithology. His views are emblematic of the difficulties encountered when studying birdsong. As for emotions, Nicholson was very clear about birds: 'They are all temperament and emotion, not brains as we are'.[64] But the shower of avian feelings that propelled birdsong put the expert, as much as any other listener, at risk of sentimentalising, Nicholson warned. He advised listeners to train the ear by building up their knowledge of birdsong to avoid 'false emotions or beliefs which might hinder a true appreciation'.[65] Well aware of the seductions of birdsong, Nicholson could do little to resist it himself, however refined his knowledge became. In 1931 he declared that his devotion to birds was 'something near a religion, and after all its externals have been inventoried the essence stays incommunicable'.[66] While scientific pursuit may fail to fully grasp the complexities of birdsong, all humans could *feel* what was special, Nicholson seemed to acknowledge. He, like Garstang, had fallen in love with his subjects. 'These voices of nature have a magic power and vitality', Nicholson admitted.[67]

All three scientists, in their own ways, found birds to be emotional beings and this explained their song. If birds were all emotion and no thought, as Nicholson believed, and song was the manifestation of this pure emotion, no wonder these investigators could be confounded by their own emotional responses. The high spirits of their singing subjects were difficult to interpret, but highly contagious. In the final section to follow, the broader resonance of these ideas, beyond scientific circles, will become apparent. Garstang's belief that birdsong was an emblem of 'individual achievements and success' emerging under trying conditions has added meaning during the Home Front crisis of the Second World War. That birds sang in celebration of life, driven by reproductive energy and simple emotional happiness, becomes useful when themes that might strengthen national morale take on political priority. Even Garstang's suggestions that bird music was a result of artistic temperament begins to gain currency during wartime when models of refined and civilised behaviour are in short supply and nature can be conceived of as an anchor of hope.

Emotional survival on the Home Front when garden birds sing

The picture of a 'People's War', offered by Angus Calder's account of the Second World War, brought the battle into the factory and the front room to reveal an unknown many participating in an all-encompassing conflict.[68] This version of total war involved not only humans but animals, as Hilda Kean has reminded us, with both positive and negative effects in their interactions.[69] By returning to radio listening, now on the Home Front, and examining the popular books published about birds during the conflict, I will explore how the pressures of everyday life were ameliorated by familiar British birds and their song. I will argue that radio broadcasts of recorded birdsong provided an emotional sustenance, quite distinct from the BBC staples of talk and music, by bolstering ideals of citizenship and providing a patriotic model of nature's fortitude and continuity in times of conflict. Book publishing about birds flourished during the war and took care to position birdlife and its preservation within the sphere of conflict. Birds would help Britain win the war and their recruitment could be seen as extending the notion of a purely 'People's War'.

The radio broadcasts in question began in 1941, after a period of intense German bombing raids in London, Birmingham, Liverpool, Plymouth and elsewhere. They stemmed from the passions of Ludwig Koch, a German Jew seeking refuge in Britain, who had been working with Nicholson and Huxley since 1936 to record British birds in song onto gramophone discs.[70] Koch was an expert in nature sound recording and had no doubt heard Carl Reich's recordings of the songs of his captive blackbird, sprosser, thrush and nightingale.[71] But Koch's mission was to capture the songs of 'wild' birds in order to hear their authentic voices, and his painstaking efforts in the southern counties of England assembled a unique collection of the familiar fluttering life that many knew and loved: the blackbird, song thrush, chaffinch, great tit, robin, wren, hedge sparrow, turtle dove and wood pigeon. There were more unusual treats as well in the green woodpecker, willow warbler, white throat, plus the iconic sounds of the cuckoo and nightingale.[72] A reviewer of Koch's first British gramophone record collection was enchanted, writing in the BBC's high-brow magazine *The Listener*, 'they offer a new vista of delight and knowledge to everyman [. . .] they are worth a dozen of the music everyone knows. They are worth twelve hundred cage-birds [. . .] Any person of sensibility really must have these records'.[73] These recordings formed the basis of Koch's BBC radio broadcasts throughout the war.

Two weeks before the evacuation of allied forces from the beaches of Dunkirk in 1940, a letter from Koch appeared in *The Times*. Koch encouraged readers to find comfort in the beauty of birdsong:

> War or no war, bird life is going on and even the armed power of the three dictators cannot prevent it. I would like to advise everybody in a position to do so, to relax his nerves, in listening to the songs, now so beautiful, of the British birds.[74]

Koch was convinced that the timeless sounds of nature would lift national spirits as they did his own. Of one of his first recording projects for the BBC Koch wrote this:

> I was allowed to make all kinds of recordings. I visited a number of factories to explore unusual noises, but amid the din of machinery I longed for the sounds of nature, and persuaded my superiors that this was the right moment to show the enemy, by recording all kinds of farm animals, that even bombing could not entirely shatter the natural peace of this island.[75]

The farm animal recordings do not seem to have been aired, but one 5-minute piece from 1942 called 'Early Morning on a Hampshire Farm' shows how Koch had imagined bringing a bucolic pastoral sound-world into the front room of fretful Britons.[76] There was a place for such a portrait, because part of the defining purpose of the war was to defend a way of life, not a King-and-country ideal, but a life of natural peacefulness on an island of green lanes and meadows.[77]

Koch was given regular slots on the radio in 1941 and continued broadcasting throughout the war on *Children's Hour*, *Country Magazine*, and with a series of 5–15 minute solo shows. According to the *Radio Times*, Koch and his recordings appeared on air on thirty-two occasions during the war, most of which featured birdsong.

Both *Children's Hour* and *Country Magazine* had the ears of many millions of listeners.[78] *Children's Hour* was listened to every day by under-16s, but it was very popular with adults too, acting as a daily point of contact between displaced family and friends.[79] The status of Koch's birdsong broadcasts was indicated by their inclusion in Christmas Eve programming in 1941, when *Children's Hour* comprised a piece from Koch called 'Listen to Our Song-Birds in Winter', followed by 'Visit to the Church of the Nativity in Bethlehem' and, finally, prayers.[80] His solo programmes from 1943 to 1945 had names such as 'The Nuthatch Sings in February' in which Koch played recordings and talked about birds in his extraordinary lilting German accent.

From his postbag, Koch found that his birdsong programmes had piqued interest across Britain: 'But among my listeners there are obviously a great number of adepts, men and women of all ages, and of all classes of society'.[81] The attraction of birdsong appeared to be classless in a way that tastes for music and other entertainment were not. Julian Huxley was of the same mind. Not only did birds 'give more pleasure and interest to humanity [. . .] than all the other groups of the animal kingdom taken together', they also made 'an obvious appeal to the layman, however uninstructed'.[82] In 1944, the *Western Times* told of Miss Wyness who gave a talk about British birds, using Koch's gramophone discs, at her Women's Institute meeting in Dolton village hall, Devon.[83] This kind of gathering may have reflected the wartime boom in the enjoyment and close study of birds by amateur enthusiasts. If Koch was talking to a broad church of bird lovers though, many of them lived in urban centres. Dora Read in west London in 1943 found that hearing birdsong on the radio could rejuvenate factory workers: 'Many thanks for letting us hear the wonderful birdsong, full of hope and peace to come. Millions of us, used to rambling before the war, are now in factories doing war work. Let us hear more of Ludwig Koch's birds!'[84] In addition to this kind of response, we know that throughout the war the BBC gave Koch longer programmes and his reputation rose. The broadcasting historian Sean Street has said that by the late 1940s Koch was a household name.[85]

To be able to assess how Koch's birdsong programmes might have helped to relieve worried minds on the Home Front, it is useful to sketch out some of the daily emotional tensions at play. Though the official predictions of mass air-raid neurosis failed to materialise, civilian morale was certainly undermined. Calder found ample evidence of 'widespread fear and paranoia bordering on panic' in 1940.[86] 'The British were bombed and they endured it' as he put it, yet 40,000 people died in the Blitz.[87] People carried on with their jobs and family lives while doctors reported 'weeping, or trembling and incoherent speech' and depression manifest as 'lethargy, retreat from social activities'.[88] Blackouts put the nerves on edge in anxious anticipation.[89] In light of all of this, one can suggest the evolution of a new acuity in listening-out for danger, for information and for relief. Findings from the social research organisation Mass-Observation revealed that 'fear seems to be linked above all with *noise*'. One report found, 'It is the siren or the whistle or the explosion or the drone – these are the things that terrify. Fear seems to come to us most of all through our sense of hearing'.[90]

In this heightened state of listening, tuning in to the radio was a popular daily ritual as it had long been, yet now as an 'instrument of war' the BBC Home Service had become crucial to creating a sense of unity and securing morale.[91] The broadcasting of popular music was essential to well-being and could console in ways that listening to news about the progress of the war could not.[92] Koch's broadcasts can be seen as part of quite explicit patriotic celebrations of rural heritage. *Country Magazine* was launched in 1942 and it was accompanied by *The Countryman in Wartime* and *Your Garden in Wartime*. Another programme, *The Land We Defend* pictured Britain as one vast and pretty village populated by lovers of nature and countryside.[93] However, Koch's programmes did more than refer to ideals of a romanticised pastoral southern 'England' of the past.[94] Birds and their song had a common place in most lives, including urban experiences. Birdlife was part and parcel of the crisis, and birdsong was a sensory pleasure that might be encountered from the window, street, garden, park, allotment or bombsite. There could be direct emotional contact with birds, who were carrying on as humans had to. Birds were not a symbol of rolling green landscape, the one that recruitment posters had employed in both wars, so much as a vibrant and present reality.[95]

Koch was by no means the only enthusiast for birds and their song who was active and vocal during the Second World War. Books about birds were published quite consciously in the midst of war. One small Pelican paperback placed great emphasis on the belief that paying attention to birds could improve the lives of ordinary people.[96] The ornithologist James Fisher's book was called simply *Watching Birds*. Writing just after the Battle of Britain, in November 1940, he placed birds at the centre of the conflict:

> Some people might consider an apology necessary for the appearance of a book about birds at a time when Britain is fighting for its own and many other lives. I make no such apology . . . Birds are part of the heritage we are fighting for. After this war ordinary people are going to have a better time than they have had; they are going to get about more . . . many will get the opportunity hitherto sought in vain, of watching wild creatures and making discoveries about them. It is for these men and women, and not the privileged few to whom ornithology has been an indulgence, that I have written this little book.[97]

Fisher offered the book to the public because he felt the study of birds concerned those 'who meet each other in the street', but he underlined that his was a book of 'science' not 'aesthetics'.[98] It is indeed a serious work covering anatomy, migration, habitats, territory and courtship, with technical illustrations and charts and no photography. Still, Fisher's book went on to sell over 3 million copies and is credited for enthusing a whole generation of the public into an appreciation of birds.[99] Perhaps to have this book, without getting too involved in the detail, allowed the owner to possess something of the nation's bird heritage and its consolations.

David Lack's *The Life of the Robin* was also written for a lay public as well as an ornithological readership. Published in 1943, it became a much-loved book, starting with a chapter on song, closely followed by another about fighting.[100] Lack relished the robin's war-like temperament and its use of song as a weapon. 'Not only does the song of the robin serve as a warning prelude to a fight, but robins actually sing while fighting [. . .]'.[101] In contrast with the current conflict, Lack pointed out in his preface, 'the robin is so inhuman as to achieve its victories without bloodshed'.[102] The grace of birds in war is also a theme of A.L. Turnbull's celebratory book *Bird Music,* published in the same year as Lack's work on the robin. He identifies the sensitivity of certain birds to distant gunfire as if to emphasise their sophistication, and pays special honour to the skylark, forever a trench-bird soaring above the mess of men:

> his bright bird-spirit, drawing inspiration from the wide universe which he surveys beneath him and from the glittering vault above, is rendering a tribute of song-homage to his Maker and is getting as near to Him as he can to offer it.[103]

Both Turnbull and Lack had pointed to the conduct of birds as a model for human society.

These books helped people to become more knowledgeable about British birds, a task that had for some time been associated with becoming a better citizen. Turnbull was founder and birdmaster of the London Boys' Bird Club, which was active between 1928 and 1940, and his book provided a checklist of what boys should know. At the beginning of the century, Lieutenant General Robert Baden-Powell's *Scouting for Boys: A Handbook for Instruction in Good Citizenship* had made the case for knowing about nature. 'There are 117 different kinds of birds in Great Britain', he wrote, urging 'the good scout' to get to 'know by sight and sound' as many of them as possible.[104] Two decades later, Julian Huxley was also encouraging people to be more contented citizens by getting to know birdlife and, by extension, their nation. 'To go on a country walk and see and hear different kinds of wild birds is thus to the bird-watcher rather like running across a number of familiar neighbours, local characters, or old acquaintances'.[105] One became part of the community of nature by immersing oneself in it and taking an interest. Birdsong itself was an 'expression' of the nation, Huxley said: 'The yellow-hammer's song seems the best possible expression of hot country roads in July, [. . .] the robin's song of peaceful autumnal melancholy as the leaves fall in a sun which has lost its warming power'.[106] Such hot or melancholy moods may well have been evoked by listening to, and getting to know, birdsong on the radio at home when getting out and about during wartime was limited. Through Koch's programmes, one might speculate that a small and pleasurable ceremony of wireless citizenship was enacted, social and national identity given strength. It is unclear what the BBC thought Koch's programmes were doing to listeners, but if an educative purpose was envisioned, there was equally one of emotional relief, both of which would contribute to morale.

Patriotism, but also scientific interests, were at play when British birds were declared the best singers. Koch had demonstrated on air in 1944 during *The Song Thrush is Silent in August* 'the great superiority of the British over the German song-thrush whom I also know well.' He played first his German recording, then his British one, asking the listener to make up their own mind.[107] His refugee status in the safety of Britain may well have influenced how he heard British birds, but he was not the only one who held such views. Seasoned ornithologists such as Max Nicholson had made similar claims in the 1930s, asserting that in no other country was birdsong as powerful, varied and pleasing as in England. The fact that so many resident species were 'good songsters', common to gardens and familiar to ordinary people made 'England a paradise for bird-song'.[108] There was national pride in this announcement, but if England really had the best singers, with the most refined aesthetic sense, then the intense emotions of joy that song was surely signalling might be communicated to the nation, putting them at an advantage.

One further kind of patriotic spirit, reflected in the short-lived 'Keep Calm and Carry On' poster campaign, was observed in the behaviour of birds. The Ministry of Information's slogan had drawn its inspiration from public and private discourse during the First World War.[109] The aim of the injunction was to encourage wartime resilience, particularly qualities of fortitude, on the Home Front. So it was in birds, too, that a kind of Blitz-spirit was recognised, embodied in their vocal performances amid the noise and chaos of conflict. Such apparent endurance seemed to provide inspiration and hope that birdlife, and therefore human life, would prevail. Birds had inherited a reputation for fortitude from their conduct in the First World War. At that time, they were often depicted as tiny angels rising above the decimated landscapes described in letters, poems and paintings from France and Belgium. There was much comfort to be had in witnessing a bird apparently singing out in defiance of the guns at the Front.[110] In a daylight raid of a London suburb in July 1917, observers saw 'pigeons, sparrows, and starlings moving quite unconcernedly about the roads barely a hundred yards from where shrapnel was bursting, while thrushes sang on and off throughout the raid period'.[111] In the Second World War, there was conflicting evidence of this behaviour – while Ludwig Koch boasted that 'a Spitfire's drone would not scare a nightingale', the naturalist Richard Fitter reported that 'one result of the "fly blitz" of 1944 was to drive many of the woodpigeons from the London parks'.[112] These reports may well have defined differences between species in their tolerance to noise. Nightingales were often said to be stimulated into song by noise. In any event, Fitter's 1945 New Naturalist book called *London's Natural History* can be seen as a hymn to London's wildlife as robust and regenerative, rising out of the bombsites.

In popular culture, the nightingale was an evergreen motif of romantic mystery that became part of the everyday in the 1940s' song 'A Nightingale Sang in Berkeley Square'. Vera Lynn popularised the unashamedly escapist song at the height of the Blitz. Nightingales have never been urban birds and are unlikely to have appeared in London's Mayfair. No matter, the tune was about the paradox of song in the midst of strife. We hear that the city is under blackout, and as two lovers 'kissed and said "goodnight"'in the square, they are sure a nightingale sings just for them.[113]

Conclusion

During the first half of the twentieth century, there was much to attract the human-in-crisis to stories of the survival and continuity of wildlife. If birds could sing on and even thrive under the threat of war, so might humans. Such optimism united the world of birds and humans because they could both become part of a vision of future hope. In fact, for some who had studied them closely, birds were considered to be part of civilisation alongside humans. Huxley in 1930 had argued that in a rapidly mechanising world, birds 'have a place in civilization as well as in wild nature'.[114] Nicholson, commenting about the eternal presence of birdsong in wartime, had this to say:

> We may be uncertain whether London and Paris and Berlin will be reduced to heaps of ruins by the misuse of scientific weapons in the interests of mutual destruction, but we can be sure that in any case nightingales will sing in Surrey every May, and golden orioles will still flute with civilized perfection in German and French spinneys, regardless of human barbarism or of human achievements.[115]

Birds of all nations, Nicholson has said here, could be relied upon to carry forward civilisation, however unreliable human affairs proved to be. Nicholson saw birds as ambassadors for the perfection of nature's laws. Evidence for the rarefied sensibilities of birds was obvious to many in their songs, aesthetic achievements that musicians aspired to match. In some way, then, birds could be seen to be superior to humans – they flew above human chaos, their moral and aesthetic senses pure, their communication honest and heartfelt.

John Reith had sensed this superiority of birds when he witnessed the response to his first live broadcast of the nightingale with Beatrice Harrison. The nightingale's song had touched listeners in ways that no one had expected and the response gave Reith the confidence to associate BBC broadcasting with a higher calling, 'the infinite' he called it, represented by the nightingale's song. On reflection, for Reith, the bird became part of broadcasting's 'machinery of civilization', a somewhat jarring mix of the pastoral stirred into the modern. Beginning in 2013, a 90-second programme called *Tweet of the Day*, featuring the songs of almost 250 British birds and their role in society, continued the idea that birdsong is required for human emotional survival. Going out just before the first 6 a.m. news programme of the day, the producer explained that these brief broadcasts had 'created a vital refuge where we could experience joy and delight in a troubled world'.[116]

From all this it seems clear that birdsong must be part of the history of human emotions, but this can only fully come into view if emotions become firmly part of social, cultural and political history. The French historian Lucien Febvre made many intriguing observations, one of which is especially apt here. This is the idea that emotions are contagious between individuals and groups of people. Emotions, Febvre argued in his 1941 essay on sensibility and history, 'very quickly acquire the power to set in train in all those concerned, by means of a sort of imitative contagion, the emotional complex that corresponds to the event which happened to and was felt by a single individual [. . .]'.[117] Cross-species contagion would seem to be equally possible. The scientists, Garstang, Huxley and Nicholson, concurred that they had been deeply affected in their dealings with birdsong. And if Ludwig Koch wanted his radio programmes during the Second World War to do anything, it was to disseminate the pleasure and joy he had experienced in his dealings with birds. When humans have witnessed birdsong, they have heard silence, music, sexual vitality, resilience, freedom, peace and much else. The complex sounds that birds make have been overheard by humans, listened to, interpreted and installed as part of modern emotional vocabulary.

Notes

1 Thanks to Samantha Blake and Kate O'Brien at the BBC Written Archives' Centre, Caversham, and to the following colleagues who reviewed a draft of this material: Sarah Angliss, David Hendy, Russell Moul, Geoff Sample.
2 G. Orwell, *Nineteen Eighty-Four*, London: Penguin, 2013 [first edition Secker and Warburg, 1949], 137.
3 Orwell, *Nineteen Eighty-Four*, 143.
4 J. Mynott, *Birdscapes: Birds in Our Imagination and Experience*, Princeton NJ: Princeton University Press, 2009, 188–189, 273–281; M. Cocker, *Birds and People*, London: Jonathan Cape, 2013. For a wider discussion of animal symbolism in human cognitive and expressive behaviour, see E.A. Lawrence, *Hunting the Wren: Transformation of Bird to Symbol: A Study in Human–Animal Relationships*, Knoxville TN: University of Tennessee Press, 1997, 1–13.
5 The problems, pleasures and necessities of deploying metaphorical language and the dangers of anthropomorphism are discussed in Mynott, *Birdscapes*, 291–296.
6 S. Armitage and T. Dee, *The Poetry of Birds*, London: Penguin, 2009, xxi.
7 P. Scannell and D. Cardiff, *A Social History of Broadcasting*, Oxford: Blackwell, 1991, xi.
8 J. Plamper, *The History of Emotions. An Introduction*. Oxford: Oxford University Press, 2015.
9 J. Plamper, 'The history of emotions: an interview with William Reddy, Barbara Rosenwein, and Peter Stearns', *History and Theory* 49, 2 (2010): 237–265.
10 L. Febvre, 'Sensibility and history: how to reconstitute the emotional life of the past', in P. Burke (ed.), *A New Kind of History: From the Writings of Lucien Febvre*, trans. K. Folca, London: Routledge & Kegan Paul, 1973, 24, emphasis in original. Plamper, *The History of Emotions. An Introduction*, 42.
11 J. Bourke, *Fear: A Cultural History*, London: Virago, 2005; M. Jackson, *The Age of Stress: Science and the Search for Stability*, Oxford: Oxford University Press, 2013; R. Overy. *The Morbid Age: Britain Between the Wars*, London: Allen Lane, 2009.
12 Armitage and Dee, *The Poetry of Birds*, 285.
13 M. Cocker and R. Mabey, *Birds Britannica*, London: Chatto & Windus, 2005; M. Cocker, *Crow Country*, London: Vintage, 2008; R. Mabey, *Whistling in the Dark: In Pursuit of the Nightingale*, London: Sinclair-Stevenson, 1993; R. Mabey, *Nature Cure*, London: Vintage, 2005.
14 For example, S. Moss, *A Bird in the Bush: A Social History of Birdwatching*, London: Aurum Press, 2004. D.E. Allen, *The Naturalist in Britain: A Social History*, second edition, Princeton NJ: Princeton University Press, 1994; N. Jardine, J.A. Secord, and E.C. Spary (eds.), *Cultures of Natural History*, Cambridge: Cambridge University Press, 1996.
15 A useful scientific history of birdsong makes up a chapter in T. Birkhead, *The Wisdom of Birds*, New York: Bloomsbury, 2008, 239–273. For a brief analysis of nineteenth-century canary-keeping, see N. Rothfels, 'How the caged bird sings: animals and entertainment', in K. Kete (ed.), *The Cultural History of Animals in the Age of Empire*, Oxford: Berg, 2007, 95–112.
16 D. Rothenberg, *Why Birds Sing*, London: Penguin, 2006.
17 J.C.W. Reith, *Into the Wind*, London: Hodder & Stoughton, 1949, 103; J.C.W. Reith, *Broadcast Over Britain*, London: Hodder & Stoughton, 1924, 147.
18 R. Overy, *The Morbid Age*. On the social impact of shell shock see, J. Winter, 'Shell shock', in J. Winter (ed.), *The Cambridge History of the First World War, Volume III: Civil Society*, Cambridge: Cambridge University Press, 2014, 310–333, 330–332.
19 D. Hendy, 'The Great War and British broadcasting: emotional life in the creation of the BBC', *New Formations* 82 (2014): 77–88.

20 S.J. Douglas, *Listening in: Radio and the American Imagination*, Minneapolis MN: University of Minnesota Press, 2004, 40–46.
21 The 'broadcasting craze' was already causing stress and nervous anxiety for some in the first year of the BBC's operations. See for example, Letter, *John O' London's Weekly*, 11 August 1923, 625.
22 Reith, *Broadcast*, 16.
23 John O'London, 'The lure and fear of broadcasting', *John O'London's Weekly*, 15 March 1924, 105.
24 A. Burrows, 'Broadcasting the nightingale', *Radio Times*, 14 December 1923, 428.
25 P. Cleveland-Peck, *The Cello and the Nightingales: An Autobiography of Beatrice Harrison*, London: John Murray, 1985, 128–129.
26 Cleveland-Peck, *The Cello and the Nightingales*, 133. There were just over a million licence holders at the end of 1924, but there could be several listening at once and an unknown group of unlicensed listeners too: see A. Briggs, *The History of Broadcasting in the United Kingdom. Volume I: Birth of Broadcasting*, Oxford: Oxford University Press, 1961, 17.
27 Letters and cards from 1924–1927, Royal College of Music, London, Harrison Sisters' Collection, box 224.
28 'A word for the nightingale', *Birmingham Daily Mail*, 24 May 1924.
29 The nightingale's reputation as the foremost songster was both Europe-wide and ancient. See Cocker, *Birds Britannica*, 340–341. The bird has a greater presence in poetry in the English language than probably any other species according to Armitage, *The Poetry of Birds*, 312.
30 Cocker, *Birds Britannica*, 342; Mabey, *Whistling in the Dark*, 14.
31 P. Fussell, *The Great War and Modern Memory*, New York: Oxford University Press, 1977, 241–242.
32 S. Baldwin, 'Speech to the annual dinner of the Royal Society of St George', 6 May 1924, quoted in J. Giles and T. Middleton (eds.), *Writing Englishness: An Introductory Sourcebook*, London: Routledge, 1995, 101.
33 J.C.W. Reith, 'The broadcasting of silence', *Radio Times*, 6 June 1924: 437–438.
34 Reith, *Broadcast*, 221.
35 Editorial, 'Broadcasting birds', *The Times*, 21 May 1924, 15.
36 Reith was a religious man with a faith in 'common-sense Christian ethics' as an essential part of citizenship and culture, and a conviction that it was his moral duty with broadcasting to promote them. See T. Avery, *Radio Modernism: Literature, Ethics, and the BBC, 1922–1938*, London: Routledge, 2006, 16.
37 S. Maitland, *A Book of Silence*, London: Granta, 2008, 160.
38 J. Winter, 'Thinking about silence', in E. Ben-Ze'ev, R. Genie and J. Winter (eds.), *Shadows of War: A Social History of Silence in the Twentieth Century*, Cambridge: Cambridge University Press, 2010, 3–31; H.H. Thompson, *Radio Times*, 8 November 1935, 7, quoted in A. Gregory, *The Silence of Memory. Armistice Day 1919–1946*, Oxford: Berg, 1994, 135.
39 Reith, 'The broadcasting of silence', 347.
40 Reith, 'The broadcasting of silence', 347.
41 Reith, *Broadcast*, 23.
42 David Hendy has suggested that the BBC of the 1920s can be thought of as an institution shaped by 'systems of feeling', as much as by rational policy-making. See Hendy, 'The Great War and British broadcasting', 84.
43 Reith, *Broadcast*, 221–224.
44 Mabey, *Whistling in the Dark*, 103.

45 Report from Sam Bonner, BBC Archives, 1924, British Library catalogue number C653/3.
46 *The Demi-Paradise*, 1943, A. Asquith (director).
47 Kate Lacey has discussed the place of silence in broadcasting and the nightingale broadcast in this context. See K. Lacey, *Listening Publics: The Politics and Experience of Listening in the Media Age*, Cambridge: Polity, 2013, 80–84.
48 W. Garstang. *Songs of the Birds*, London: John Lane, 1922, 12.
49 J. Clare, 'Progress of rhyme' in E. Robinson, D. Powell and T. Paulin (eds.), *John Clare: Major Works*, Oxford: Oxford University Press, 2008, 153–160.
50 Garstang, *Songs of the Birds*, 49.
51 Garstang, *Songs of the Birds*, 47. 'The tree pipit's wing song. An English Interpretation', *The Times*, 8 May 1919, 17.
52 H.G.A., 'Review', *British Birds*, 1 August 1922, 89.
53 H.G.A., 'Review', 89; 'Some books of the week', *The Spectator*, 21 July 1919, 22.
54 H.G.A., 'Review', 22.
55 H.G.A., 'Review', 14–15.
56 H.G.A., 'Review', 17.
57 Darwin, quoted in Rothenberg, *Why Birds Sing*, 34.
58 Rothenberg, *Why Birds Sing*, 36. At this time, Max Nicholson refuted the popular idea that birds sang for reproductive reasons, insisting that it was primarily for establishing and keeping territory. See E.M. Nicholson, *How Birds Live*, London: Williams and Norgate, 1927, 39–47.
59 Garstang, *Songs of the Birds*, 24.
60 Garstang, *Songs of the Birds*, 41.
61 J. Huxley, 'Bird-watching and biological science (part 1)', *Auk* 33 (1916), 156.
62 J. Huxley and L. Koch, *Animal Language*, London: Country Life, 1938, 10.
63 Huxley and Koch, *Animal Language*, 10.
64 Nicholson, *How Birds Live*, 94.
65 E.M. Nicholson and L. Koch, *Songs of Wild Birds*, London: H.F. & G. Witherby, 1951 [first edition, 1936], 185.
66 E.M. Nicholson, *The Art of Birdwatching: A Practical Guide to Field Observation*, London: H.F. & G. Witherby, 1931, 213.
67 Nicholson and Koch, *Songs of Wild Birds*, 185.
68 A. Calder, *The People's War: Britain 1939–1945*, London: Pimlico, 1992.
69 H. Kean, 'The dog and cat massacre of September 1939 and the People's War', *European Review of History* 22, 5 (2015): 741–756. See also J. Gardiner, *The Animals' War: Animals in Wartime from the First World War to the Present Day*, London: Portrait, 2006.
70 L. Koch, *Memoirs of a Birdman*, London: Phoenix House, 1955, 35–50. See also J. Burton, 'Ludwig Koch – master of nature's music', *Wildlife Sound* 2, (1974): 4–8, available at www.wildlife-sound.org/journal/archive/koch.html, last accessed 22 March 2017; J. Burton, 'The BBC Natural History Unit wildlife sound library 1948–1988', *Wildlife Sound* 12, (2012): 19–27.
71 As early as 1911, the HMV catalogue listed in the Whistling section a 'unique bird record', which was Carl Reich's caged nightingale: *The Gramophone Company Record Catalogue*, February to July, 1911, 67. The 1914 catalogue listed all four birds: *His Master's Voice Catalogue of Records*, 1914, 139.
72 Koch, *Memoirs of a Birdman*, 26.
73 'Book chronicle', *The Listener*, 4 November 1936, 877.
74 L. Koch, 'A blackbird mimic', *The Times*, 13 May 1940, 4.
75 Koch, *Memoirs of a Birdman*, 70–71.

76 Ludwig Koch sound pictures, 'Early morning on a Hampshire farm', April 1942. British Library, gramophone record 1LL0003863.
77 See for example J.B. Priestley's popular *Postscripts* broadcasts, published as J.B. Priestley, *Postscripts*, London: Heinemann, 1940.
78 *Country Magazine* was conceived as a wartime programme, which by 1946 had an audience of almost 7 million listeners. BBC Written Archive, N2/25 North Region, Country Magazine, memorandum from John Polworth, 8 March 1946. The fortnightly programme closed with one of Koch's sound-pictures of the countryside. Koch, *Memoirs of a Birdman*, 71.
79 S. Nicholas, *The Echo of War: Home Front Propaganda and the Wartime BBC, 1939–45*, Manchester: Manchester University Press, 1996, 45.
80 BBC Home Service listing, *Radio Times*, 19 December 1941, 14.
81 Koch, *Memoirs of a Birdman*, 179.
82 Nicholson and Koch, *Songs of Wild Birds*, xiii.
83 'From towns and villages in West Country', *Western Times*, 6 October 1944, 5.
84 Letter, 'Tweet-Tweet', *Radio Times*, 19 February 1943, 210.
85 Sean Street argues that Koch was as well-known to the public after the war as David Attenborough is today. See BBC Radio 4, 'Archive pioneers', *Ludwig Koch and the Music of Nature*, 15 April 2009, available at www.bbc.co.uk/archive/archive_pioneers/6505.shtml, last accessed 30 September 2016.
86 E. Jones, R. Woolven, B. Durodie and S. Wessely, 'Civilian morale during the Second World War: response to air raids re-examined', *Social History of Medicine* 17, 3 (2004): 463–479; A. Calder, *The Myth of the Blitz*, London: Pimlico, 1992, 109.
87 Calder, *The Myth of the Blitz*, 218.
88 E. Glover, *International Journal of Psychoanalysis*, 23 (1942): 17–37, quoted in B. Shephard, *A War of Nerves*, London: Jonathan Cape, 2000, 179.
89 Bourke, *Fear*, 229. T. Harrisson and C. Madge, *War Begins at Home*, London: Chatto & Windus, 1940, 201.
90 Mass Observation, 'Cars and sirens', Report 27 August 1940, MO 371, quoted in P. Adey, 'The private life of an air raid', in D. Bissell and G. Fuller (eds.), *Stillness in a Mobile World*, Abingdon: Routledge, 2011, 129, emphasis in the original.
91 Nicholas, *The Echo of War*, 2.
92 See for example, C. Baade, *Victory Through Harmony: The BBC and Popular Music in World War II*, New York: Oxford University Press, 2012.
93 Nicholas, *The Echo of War*, 233. These programmes also reflected the interwar enthusiasm for communing with the outdoors by hiking, camping and motoring.
94 The idea of the rural was usually associated with England, rather than Britain, but the relationship is complex. See A. Howkins, 'The discovery of rural England', in R. Colls and P. Dodd (eds.), *Englishness: Politics and Culture 1880–1920*, London: Bloomsbury, 2014, 85–111.
95 In the First World War the Parliamentary Recruiting Committee used idyllic rural imagery of a southern English landscape in its 1915 campaign. Posters asked Isn't This Worth Fighting For? Frank Newbould's September 1942 recruitment poster campaign *Your Britain, Fight for It Now* depicted pastures and leafy villages too.
96 J. Fisher, *Watching Birds*, London: Penguin, revised edition, 1946. Fisher claimed that he knew of all kinds of people who were interested in birds: 'a late Prime Minister, a Secretary of State, a charwoman, two policemen, two kings, one ex-king, five Communists, four Labour, one Liberal, and three Conservative Members of Parliament, the chairman of a County Council, several farm labourers . . . at least forty-six school masters, and an engine-driver'.

97 Fisher, *Watching Birds*, 11.
98 Fisher, *Watching Birds*, 14.
99 Moss, *A Bird in the Bush*, 168.
100 D. Lack, *The Life of the Robin*, fifth edition, London: Pallas Athene, 2015 [first edition H.F. Witherby, 1943].
101 Lack, *The Life of the Robin*, 29.
102 Lack, *The Life of the Robin*, 1.
103 Lack, *The Life of the Robin*, 29, 32–33.
104 R. Baden-Powell, *Scouting for Boys: A Handbook for Instruction in Good Citizenship*, Mineola NY: Dover, 2007 [first edition Horace Cox, 1908], 127.
105 J. Huxley, *Bird-Watching and Bird Behaviour*, London: Chatto & Windus, 1930, 5.
106 Huxley, *Bird-Watching*, 7.
107 L. Koch script, 'The song thrush is silent in August', 18 September 1944, BBC Written Archive.
108 Nicholson and Koch, *Songs of Wild Birds*, 26.
109 L. Mugglestone, 'Rethinking the birth of an expression: keeping calm and "carrying on" in World War One', 2 August 2016, available at https://wordsinwartime.wordpress.com, last accessed 23 September 2016. Some evidence suggests that the posters were never displayed at all.
110 Fussell, *Great War*, 242.
111 R.S.R. Fitter, *London's Natural History*, London: Collins, 1945, 230.
112 'Starman's diary', *The Star*, 8 April 1943.
113 Fitter, *London's Natural History*, 229; E. Maschwitz and M. Sherwin, *A Nightingale Sang in Berkeley Square*, London: Peter Maurice Music, 1940. Richard Mabey has written an excellent account of the meanings of the nightingale and its song: see Mabey, *Whistling in the Dark*.
114 Huxley, *Bird-Watching*, 116.
115 Nicholson and Koch, *Songs of Wild Birds*, 183.
116 B. Westwood and S. Moss, *Tweet of the Day. A Year of Britain's Birds*, London: Saltyard, 2014, 4.
117 Febvre, 'Sensibility and history', 14.

Bibliography

Adey, P. 'The private life of an air raid', in D. Bissell and G. Fuller (eds.), *Stillness in a Mobile World*, Abingdon: Routledge, 2011, 127–138.

Allen, D.E. *The Naturalist in Britain: A Social History*, second edition, Princeton NJ: Princeton University Press, 1994.

Armitage, S. and Dee, T. *The Poetry of Birds*, London: Penguin, 2009.

Avery, T. *Radio Modernism: Literature, Ethics, and the BBC, 1922–1938*, London: Routledge, 2006.

Baade, C. *Victory Through Harmony: The BBC and Popular Music in World War II*, New York: Oxford University Press, 2012.

Baden-Powell, R. *Scouting for Boys: A Handbook for Instruction in Good Citizenship*, Mineola NY: Dover, 2007.

Birkhead, T. *The Wisdom of Birds*, New York: Bloomsbury, 2008.

Bourke, J. *Fear: A Cultural History*, London: Virago, 2005.

Briggs, A. *The History of Broadcasting in the United Kingdom. Volume I: Birth of Broadcasting*, Oxford: Oxford University Press, 1961.

Burrows, A. 'Broadcasting the nightingale', *Radio Times*, 14 December 1923, 428.

Burton, J. 'Ludwig Koch – master of nature's music', *Wildlife Sound* 2, (1974): 4–8, available at www.wildlife-sound.org/journal/archive/koch.html, last accessed 22 March 2017.

Burton, J. 'The BBC Natural History Unit wildlife sound library 1948–1988', *Wildlife Sound* 12, (2012): 19–27.

Calder, A. *The Myth of the Blitz*, London: Pimlico, 1992.

Calder, A. *The People's War: Britain 1939–1945*, London: Pimlico, 1992.

Cleveland-Peck, P. *The Cello and the Nightingales: An Autobiography of Beatrice Harrison*, London: John Murray, 1985.

Cocker, M. *Crow Country*, London: Vintage, 2008.

Cocker, M. *Birds and People*, London: Jonathan Cape, 2013.

Cocker, M. and Mabey, R. *Birds Britannica*, London: Chatto & Windus, 2005.

Douglas, S.J. *Listening in: Radio and the American Imagination*, Minneapolis MN: University of Minnesota Press, 2004.

Febvre, L. 'Sensibility and history: how to reconstitute the emotional life of the past', in P. Burke (ed.), *A New Kind of History: From the Writings of Lucien Febvre*, trans. K. Folca, London: Routledge & Kegan Paul, 1973, 12–26.

Fisher, J. *Watching Birds*, London: Penguin, revised edition, 1946.

Fitter, R.S.R. *London's Natural History*, London: Collins, 1945.

Fussell, P. *The Great War and Modern Memory*, New York: Oxford University Press, 1977.

Gardiner, J. *The Animals' War: Animals in Wartime from the First World War to the Present Day*, London: Portrait, 2006.

Garstang. W. *Songs of the Birds*, London: John Lane, 1922.

Giles, J. and Middleton, T. (eds.), *Writing Englishness: An Introductory Sourcebook*, London: Routledge, 1995.

Gramophone Company Record Catalogue, February to July, 1911.

Gregory, A. *The Silence of Memory. Armistice Day 1919–1946*, Oxford: Berg, 1994.

Harrisson, T. and Madge, C. *War Begins at Home*, London: Chatto & Windus, 1940.

Hendy, D. 'The Great War and British broadcasting: emotional life in the creation of the BBC', *New Formations* 82, (2014): 82–99.

His Master's Voice Catalogue of Records, 1914.

Howkins, A. 'The discovery of rural England', in R. Colls and P. Dodd (eds.), *Englishness: Politics and Culture 1880–1920*, London: Bloomsbury, 2014, 85–111.

Huxley, J. 'Bird-watching and biological science (part 1)', *Auk* 33, (1916), 142–161.

Huxley, J. *Bird-Watching and Bird Behaviour*, London: Chatto & Windus, 1930.

Huxley, J. and Koch, L. *Animal Language*, London: Country Life, 1938.

Jackson, M. *The Age of Stress: Science and the Search for Stability*, Oxford: Oxford University Press, 2013.

Jardine, N., Secord, J.A., and Spary E.C. (eds.) *Cultures of Natural History*, Cambridge: Cambridge University Press, 1996.

John O' London's Weekly, 11 August 1923, 625.

John O'London, 'The lure and fear of broadcasting', *John O'London's Weekly*, 15 March 1924, 105.

Jones, E., Woolven, R., Durodie, B., and Wessely, S. 'Civilian morale during the Second World War: response to air raids re-examined', *Social History of Medicine* 17, 3 (2004): 463–479.

Kean, H. 'The dog and cat massacre of September 1939 and the People's War', *European Review of History* 22, 5 (2015): 741–756.

Koch, L. 'A blackbird mimic', *The Times*, 13 May 1940, 4.

Koch, K. *Memoirs of a Birdman*, London: Phoenix House, 1955.

Lacey, K. *Listening Publics: The Politics and Experience of Listening in the Media Age*, Cambridge: Polity, 2013.

Lack, D. *The Life of the Robin*, fifth edition, London: Pallas Athene, 2015.
Lawrence, E.A. *Hunting the Wren: Transformation of Bird to Symbol: A Study in Human–Animal Relationships*, Knoxville TN: University of Tennessee Press, 1997.
Mabey, R. *Whistling in the Dark: In Pursuit of the Nightingale*, London: Sinclair-Stevenson, 1993.
Mabey, R. *Nature Cure*, London: Vintage, 2005.
Maitland, S. *A Book of Silence*, London: Granta, 2008.
Maschwitz, E. and Sherwin, M. *A Nightingale Sang in Berkeley Square*, London: Peter Maurice Music, 1940.
Moss, S. *A Bird in the Bush: A Social History of Birdwatching*, London: Aurum Press, 2004.
Mugglestone, L. 'Rethinking the birth of an expression: keeping calm and "carrying on" in World War One', 2 August 2016, available at https://wordsinwartime.wordpress.com, last accessed 23 September 2016.
Mynott, J. *Birdscapes: Birds in Our Imagination and Experience*, Princeton NJ: Princeton University Press, 2009.
Nicholas, S. *The Echo of War: Home Front Propaganda and the Wartime BBC, 1939–45*, Manchester: Manchester University Press, 1996.
Nicholson, E.M. *How Birds Live*, London: Williams and Norgate, 1927.
Nicholson, E.M. *The Art of Birdwatching: A Practical Guide to Field Observation*, London: H.F. & G. Witherby, 1931.
Nicholson, E.M. and Koch, L. *Songs of Wild Birds*, London: H.F. & G. Witherby, 1951.
Orwell, G. *Nineteen Eighty-Four*, London: Penguin, 2013.
Overy, R. *The Morbid Age: Britain Between the Wars*, London: Allen Lane, 2009.
Plamper, J. 'The history of emotions: an interview with William Reddy, Barbara Rosenwein, and Peter Stearns', *History and Theory* 49, 2 (2010): 237–265.
Plamper, J. *The History of Emotions. An Introduction*. Oxford: Oxford University Press, 2015.
Priestley, J.B. *Postscripts*, London: Heinemann, 1940.
Reith, J.C.W. *Broadcast Over Britain*, London: Hodder & Stoughton, 1924.
Reith, J.C.W. 'The broadcasting of silence', *Radio Times*, 6 June 1924: 437–438.
Reith, J.C.W. *Into the Wind*, London: Hodder & Stoughton, 1949.
Robinson, E., Powell, D., and Paulin, T. (eds.), *John Clare: Major Works*, Oxford: Oxford University Press, 2008.
Rothenberg, D. *Why Birds Sing*, London: Penguin, 2006.
Rothfels, N. 'How the caged bird sings: animals and entertainment', in K. Kete (ed.), *The Cultural History of Animals in the Age of Empire*, Oxford: Berg, 2007, 95–112.
Scannell, P. and Cardiff, D. *A Social History of Broadcasting*, Oxford: Blackwell, 1991.
Shephard, B. *A War of Nerves*, London: Jonathan Cape, 2000.
Street, S. 'Archive pioneers', *Ludwig Koch and the Music of Nature*, BBC Radio 4, 15 April 2009, available at www.bbc.co.uk/archive/archive_pioneers/6505.shtml, last accessed 30 September 2016.
Westwood, B. and Moss, S. *Tweet of the Day. A Year of Britain's Birds*, London: Saltyard, 2014.
Winter, J. 'Thinking about silence', in E. Ben-Ze'ev, R. Genie and J. Winter (eds.), *Shadows of War: A Social History of Silence in the Twentieth Century*, Cambridge: Cambridge University Press, 2010, 3–31.
Winter, J. 'Shell shock', in J. Winter (ed.), *The Cambridge History of the First World War, Volume III: Civil Society*, Cambridge: Cambridge University Press, 2014, 310–333.

PART III

Themes and provocations

17
BREEDING AND BREED

Neil Pemberton, Julie-Marie Strange and Michael Worboys

Introduction

With respect to animals, the word breeding is both a verb and a noun. The verb refers to their reproduction and is used for both wild and domesticated species. The noun refers to animals *with* breeding in the sense of pedigree heritage and selection for specific properties that has produced the division of many working, farm, fancy and pet species into 'breeds'. These are animals that have been actively created by livestock producers, fanciers and other breeders to suit to human requirements for companionship, food, sport, work, fancy and other purposes. However, modern breeds are much more, especially in livestock and dogs, which have been bred to meet specific standards of shape, size, colour and other external features, and are presumed to have a superior inheritance given by their ancestral lineage from purebred stock. Both uses of the term have been applied to humans: the verb in a mostly derogatory manner to the lower classes, especially those with large families who have been said to 'breed like animals'; while the noun, perhaps perversely, was used for upper-class individuals who came from 'good families' or 'good stock', where the presumed quality of biological inheritance mirrored the quantity of inherited wealth.

The founder of eugenics, Francis Galton, pondered in 1864:

> If a twentieth part of the cost and pains were spent in measures for the improvement of the human race that is spent on the improvement of the breed of horses and cattle, what a galaxy of genius might we not create! We might introduce prophets and high priests of civilization into the world, as surely as we can propagate idiots by mating *crétins*. Men and women of the present day are, to those we might hope to bring into existence, what the pariah dogs of the streets of an Eastern town are to our own highly-bred varieties.[1]

It was twenty years before he developed these ideas into the 'science' of eugenics and not until the early twentieth century that this became a movement and the differential birth rate of different social classes and races became political issues. However, there was a close connection between ideas, though not the practices, of animal breeding with human reproduction. There were taboos against marriage to close relatives, which in animals was termed inbreeding, and fears about miscegenation, which had parallels with ideas of the weaknesses of animal hybrids.

In this chapter we discuss the history of the breeding of domesticated animals and how this practice produced varieties of animals with 'breeding', and that since the late-eighteenth century have been termed 'breeds'. We do not consider the long history of domestication in animal–human relations, which archaeologists date back 20,000 or so years, but begin instead in the eighteenth century, when the principles of selective breeding were first systematised.[2] Moreover, over the past two hundred years the degree to which animals have been altered and the speed of change has increased greatly, and this is not without consequences for animal health and well-being as 'breed populations' have become more uniform genetically and their characteristics more finely graded. Historians agree that the pioneer of 'scientific' breeding was Robert Bakewell, a farmer from Leicestershire in England, whose ideas for improving sheep, horses and cattle were widely publicised and taken up across Europe and North America.[3] Historians have questioned his status as the founder of modern livestock breeding and now point to a longer time frame of selective breeding and to the work of other eighteenth-century improving farmers, many of them obscure.[4] We consider the evolution of ideas on selective breeding through the nineteenth century and end with an assessment of the impact of the ideas of Gregor Mendel and the science of genetics in the twentieth century. From the eighteenth century, breeders have continually claimed to be making their enterprise 'scientific', yet at the same time, and with equal fervour, they have asserted that it was also an 'art' that relied upon tacit and incommunicable knowledge. This ambivalence runs through the history of breeding to the present day. The notion of 'breeds' was first developed with livestock and then transferred to thoroughbred horses, poultry and pigeons, and then to domestic dogs and cats. Breed embodied contemporary assumptions about heredity that are captured in terms such as 'purebred', 'bloodline', 'pedigree', 'inbred' and 'mongrel'. However, there is also something modern about the term. The physical form of breeds as standardised, uniform animals, broken down into points or parts, was in many ways analogous with industrial invention, design, standardisation and manufacture.

Historians of agriculture and science have discussed breeding most, though there is a growing body of work, principally by literature scholars concerned with the twentieth and twenty-first centuries, on the meanings and uses of inheritance, mostly about humans, but also exploring animal analogies.[5] Historians of science have been particularly interested in the ideas of the nature and consequences of inheritance in the work of Charles Darwin and Gregor Mendel.[6] Darwin, because of the importance of 'artificial selection' in the articulation of his theory of natural selection and his authoring of the two-volume work *The Variation of Animals and Plants under Domestication* published in 1868.[7] Mendel, because his plant-breeding studies were central to the establishment of genetics in the first decade of the twentieth century and there is now a substantial literature on its applications in breeding new plant varieties.[8] What little work there is on post-Mendelian animal breeding indicates that the impact of genetics was mixed.[9] There are many reasons for this, and the biological ones are important: the inheritance of specific characteristics in mammals is complex and does not reduce readily to simple genetic laws as in plants, while practically the lengths of their gestation and time to adulthood gives a further level of complication. In the twentieth century, the most important innovation in animal breeding was the increased reliance on artificial insemination with certain livestock and poultry, a practice that, of course, has had consequences for genetic diversity.[10]

The seminal work in the history science on animal breeding before Mendel is by Vitezslav Orel and Roger Wood on sheep breeding, which has revealed the depth and breadth of interest in animal breeding amongst central European zoologists and livestock breeders from the early nineteenth century.[11] Interestingly, this was influenced by Bakewell's work and in turn was an indirect influence on Mendel. Also seminal is Harriet Ritvo's *The Animal Estate* and her many essays on animals, which although largely on the nineteenth century, have shaped scholarship in other periods. Their work is now complemented by several monographs by Margaret E. Derry, which are interdisciplinary and span the period from the eighteenth to the twenty-first century.[12] She combines histories of science, livestock, professional and amateur breeding, and the economic history of commercial and fancy breeds with strong narratives and insightful analyses. Derry has shown the importance of continuities in genetics from the biometrician tradition, the early twentieth-century alternative to Mendelism, which stressed continuities in inheritance, rather than the discontinuities that Mendelians focused upon, and analysed these mathematically.[13]

In agricultural history, there are relatively few studies of livestock farming compared with the production of arable crops, such as corn, wheat and maize. Unfortunately, there is no equivalent for later centuries of Nicholas Russell's excellent study of heredity and animal breeding in early modern England.[14] For later centuries, agricultural historians have studied particular breeds, but their focus has tended to be on the livestock economy and the outcomes of selective breeding, not the inputs.[15] There are histories of specific breeds of livestock, often written by breeders themselves, which are rich sources of information and insight into breeding practices.[16] The best work in literary scholarship is typified by Jenny Davidson's *Breeding: A Partial History of the Eighteenth Century*.[17] She shows that in discourses of the period, breeding was 'an umbrella term that can refer to nature or nurture, generation, pregnancy, hereditary resemblance, manners, moral character, social identity, or all of the above' and that resonated across species in a predominantly agricultural economy and when pets were becoming more common.

Much of the Animal Studies literature has criticised the subordination of animals and the material effects of the institutions and practices belonging to the social and commercial world of breeding and, in doing so, has argued for different and, in their view, more ethical ways of living with animals.[18] It is interesting, therefore, that there is relatively little work on the invention of 'breed' as a way of thinking about animals, and of physically remaking animals to standards dictated by a range of factors. However, there are two recent exceptions. Martin Wallen's history of foxhounds, which adopts an Animal Studies approach and *The Invention of the Modern Dog: Breed and Blood in Victorian Britain* by the authors of this chapter.[19]

Breeding animals

The breeding of domesticated animal varieties over the past 20,000 years has been both unintentional and deliberate. The unintentional creation of varieties occurred due to the geographical isolation of different human populations and the adaptation of their animals to different environments and uses. Had such isolation been for longer and been stricter, it is likely that the differences between domesticated varieties would have widened and they would have become distinct species. Biologists call this process speciation and typically it takes much longer, hundreds of thousands, if not millions, of years, than the 20,000 years of domestication. Thus, despite the often huge differences in the size and form of dogs, for example, with the Great Dane and Chihuahua, they remain the same species and can interbreed, though in the case cited that would require artificial insemination and Caesarean delivery. The essence of Darwin's theory of evolution by natural selection was that species could change (transmutation), but that the process was gradual and occurred over an extended period of time. Two ideas that he was arguing against were: first, the religious view that species were God's creations and fixed; and second, the views, associated with the French natural historian Jean-Baptiste Lamarck (1744–1829), that species could change quite quickly by the inheritance of acquired characteristics.[20] Darwin wrote extensively on inheritance to explain how the features that 'nature selected' were passed on from generation to generation, though his ideas have not been discussed to the same extent as his main evolutionary theory, because they never gained the same support and were soon superseded.

Lamarck was a follower of Georges-Louis Leclerc, Comte de Buffon, who dominated eighteenth-century French natural history. Buffon argued that the fixity of species was demonstrated by the infertility of hybrids, which was congruent with the view that all animals (and plants) were God's Creation and directly or indirectly fitted the purposes of humanity. However, the century was also the high point of the Enlightenment, which emphasised the power of environmental forces (*climat*), of nurture over nature, and the possibilities of improvement. These ideas were influential in the French Revolution, which challenged inherited power and property and sought the reordering of society. However, in science, medicine and animal breeding there was a growing recognition of one limiting factor on change and improvement in the natural world – inherited, often fixed, features. In the nineteenth century this became known as 'heredity', but earlier was most commonly referred to as the influence of blood or seed. In the humoral model of the animal body, eggs and semen were formed from the blood, hence, it carried properties of the parents to their offspring. Orel and Wood have argued that the first scientific discourses on the influence of blood as a hereditary material were about the inheritance of diseases and abnormalities, which raised questions about the perfectibility of nature. More importantly for animal breeding, Orel and Wood argue that 'scientific' selective breeding began with efforts to avoid such defects rather than improve features in both medicine and the livestock economy.[21]

The inheritance and expression of abnormalities raised questions about accepted ideas of reproduction and generation. In animals there were two main ideas: offspring were preformed in the female and the process of growth was initiated by sexual intercourse or semen; or that the development of generative material in the female was started and shaped by semen. In both models, reflecting ideas that can be traced to Aristotle, the role of the female was passive and the male active, though mothers influenced their offspring during gestation and feeding. Another tradition, associated with Hippocrates and Galen saw generation coming from the mingling of female and male semen, with equal though different contributions, indirectly, from the blood of both parents. The physical and mental similarities between parents and the children had long been recognised in the truism that 'like begat like', but there were no clear patterns. In humans, there was sometimes a striking resemblance to one parent, sometimes to a grandparent or other relation, and sometimes to no one. The same was observed in animals, and, in dogs and cats, seen in the variety within the same litter and explained by the influence of the environment on offspring before birth and throughout life. Some natural philosophers puzzled over these matters, but without a concept of heredity they focused on environmental factors, which they could measure and alter, and worked around the serendipity of 'blood'.

Breeding livestock

The great change of views on inheritance came not from science or medicine, but from sheep breeders, first, with responses to the introduction of the Merino sheep from Spain into northern Europe, and second, with the work of Robert Bakewell and his improved New Leicester breed. Merino wool was highly valued because of its fine properties and many attempts had been made to establish the sheep outside of Spain, but these had failed seemingly due to climate.[22] However, in the eighteenth century there was more success and this raised doubts about the overriding influence of climate, suggesting that 'blood' (nature) was as important as climate (nurture). Bakewell also recognised the importance of 'blood' and sought to improve sheep by selective breeding between sheep with the desired qualities. He used cross-breeding between varieties, and breeding between closely related animals: *inbreeding* if between very close relations and *line breeding* if between more distant relations, often between generations.

Bakewell's aim was to create sheep that grew quickly and produced more meat and better Merino-type wool. He travelled around the country buying animals with the right qualities for breeding, recording in detail pedigrees, weight gain, meat quality, and the ability of parents to pass on qualities to their offspring – progeny testing. He wanted not just outstanding individuals – the goal in thoroughbred horse breeding, but consistency and uniformity across the populations of the types he produced. For these qualities he popularised the term 'breed'. Bakewell was initially successful with his New Leicester or Dishley sheep, but also sought to improve longhorn cattle and horses.[23] His principles were used by other breeders, notably Charles and Robert Colling, to create the shorthorn breed, which became important in English farming and was exported to America. In 1822 a public herd book was published, which encouraged breeding by pure bloodlines, indicated by pedigree, as well as by utility, indicated by conformation and potency.[24]

Bakewell had relied first on out-crossing with sheep from other countries, but once he had achieved his goal he switched to inbreeding. The turn to inbreeding was controversial amongst breeders as it was associated with deterioration and the converse of, so-called, hybrid vigour. There were obvious links to social mores and rules. Marriages between two very close relatives were taboo in most human societies, though given the size of most settlements and limited movement, marriages to relatives, such as first and second cousins, were not uncommon. In Europe, marriage to very close relatives was prohibited by the main religions. There were cultural reasons for these strictures, but they were also based on biology, as in some such marriages the children were weak or suffered from disabilities. Animal breeders carried over the strictures and also had the experience that inbreeding produced weaker stock. Bakewell claimed the opposite; that inbreeding consolidated and locked in desirable traits. He also argued that the contribution of both parents was equal, though the contribution of the father was easy to assess. In sheep, a ram could be 'progeny tested' with many of the ewes in a single season, whereas a ewe could be 'progeny tested' with only a single ram each season.

Bakewell's ideas were spread by the success of his breeds in sales and the demand for rams to hire across the country and in the writings of the influential agricultural campaigner and reformer Arthur Young.[25] In 1809, Sir John Saunders Sebright published a pamphlet on *The Art of Improving the Breeds of Domestic Animals*, which reasserted the dangers of inbreeding as it consolidated both good and bad points. He argued that enthusiasts had exaggerated the value of both inbreeding and cross-breeding and that the true 'art' of breeding was in selection. Unsurprisingly, Darwin used Sebright's ideas in his discussion of artificial selection and particularly his view that 'the weak and the unhealthy do not live to propagate their infirmities'.[26] Sebright's experience was that mating the best male and female rarely produced the best progeny, but rather it was the selection of the individuals that 'nicked' to produce the best. Thoroughbred horse breeders had long practised such matches, seeking the best combination of the light, fast, often nervous Arabian stallions with solid English mares that had 'substance'. Sebright also argued that breeders should not only judge by appearances, but also interrogate pedigrees and the qualities that 'have prevailed in the race from which they are descended, as they will always show themselves, sooner or later, in the progeny'.[27] In some domesticated animals this information would be found in pedigrees, which were kept privately. There had only been a public stud book for racehorses, published through the Jockey Club since 1791, but this was initially about identity and avoiding fraud rather than a resource of hereditary history. The ideal breeder's gaze, however, was to look at an animal's past, as evidenced in its pedigree; its present, as seen in its physical appearance; and its future as revealed in progeny testing.

The principles articulated by Sebright and others in the early nineteenth century were taken up by the breeders of 'fancy' animals, those bred for showing as much as, if not more than, for commercial purposes. The two were not exclusive, as Ritvo has shown in her discussion of pedigree bulls.[28] Fancy breeding as such was first developed with poultry; indeed, the Sebright Bantam was one of the first such breeds. The breeding of other small domestic animals and pigeons followed, with fancy breeding clubs and exhibitions growing rapidly after mid-century, a development favoured by the growth of leisure, the vogue for exhibitions and the rise of competitive sports.

Breeding and breed

The breeding of dogs, both sporting and non-sporting, attracted the largest number of breeders and the biggest audience at exhibitions. Consequently, it is through dogs that the principles and practice of animal breeding in the second half of the nineteenth century is best followed.

Breeding dogs

The most popular and influential book on dogs in the third quarter of the century was *The Dog* by John Henry Walsh, who published under the pseudonym 'Stonehenge'. The chapter on breeding remained unaltered from the first edition in 1859 to the fourth in 1879.[29] He set out six axioms that bring together the wisdom of practical breeders and some insights from science. Walsh had qualified as a doctor and was an early editor of what became the *British Medical Journal*. His 'facts' are worth quoting in full:

1. The male and female each furnish their quota towards the original germ of the offspring; but the female over and above this nourishes it till it is born, and, consequently, may be supposed to have more influence upon its formation than the male.
2. Natural conformation is transmitted by both parents as a general law, and likewise any acquired or accidental variation. It may therefore be said that, on both sides, 'like produces like'.
3. In proportion to the purity of the breed will it be transmitted unchanged to the offspring. Thus a greyhound bitch of pure blood put to a mongrel will produce puppies more nearly resembling her shape than that of the father.
4. Breeding in-and-in is not injurious to the dog, as may be proved both from theory and practice; indeed it appears, on the contrary, to be very advantageous in many well-marked instances of the greyhound, which have of late years appeared in public.
5. As every dog is a compound animal, made up of a sire and dam, and also their sires and dams, &c, so, unless there is much breeding in-and-in, it may be said that it is impossible to foretell with absolute certainty what particular result will be elicited.
6. The first impregnation appears to produce some effect upon the next and subsequent ones. It is therefore necessary to take care that the effect of the cross in question is not neutralised by a prior and bad impregnation. This fact has been so fully established by Sir John Sebright and others that it is needless to go into its proofs.[30]

Walsh was clear that the bitch was most important and valuable to the breeder, not only because she carried and suckled her progeny, but economically as she 'usually continues to be the property of the breeder, while the sire can be changed each time she breeds'.[31] By contrast, for the scientist interested in the principles of breeding, the male was more valuable as the results of an individual's mating with many females could be observed and repeated over many generations.[32]

The importance of knowing bloodlines was evident in that grandsires and granddams also have an influence; indeed, Walsh pointed out that often features of the seventh generation back on the dam's side could show in puppies. Walsh followed most breeders in stating that inheritance showed both the blending of characteristics and 'dominance':

> There is a remarkable fact ... which is that there is a tendency in the produce to a separation between the different strains of which it is produced, so that a puppy composed of four equal proportions of breed represented by A, B, C, and D, will not represent them all in equal proportions, but will resemble one much more than the others.[33]

This phenomenon was also evident 'in relation to the next step backwards, when there are eight progenitors', where it was termed 'throwing back'.[34] On inbreeding he observed that,

> Like many other practices essentially good, in-breeding has been grossly abused; owners of a good kennel having become bigoted to their own strain, and, from keeping to it exclusively, having at length reduced their dogs to a state of idiotcy (sic) and delicacy of constitution which has rendered them quite useless.[35]

The value of breeding in-and-in lay in concentrating 'blood' to give a 'pure breed', dogs that were most likely to pass on their features. Walsh recognised, accepted and, to an extent, recommended crossing, even detailing where breeders were to go for particular characteristics:

> Thus, speed is typified in the greyhound, courage in the bulldog, and nose or scenting power in the bloodhound; for hunting purposes, the pointer or setter, when required in conjunction with setting and the spaniel or terrier, for finding or 'questing' both fur and feather. Lastly, sagacity is displayed in the poodle, Newfoundland, and terrier, chiefly because they are the constant associates of man.[36]

This listing shows that Walsh's interests were primarily sporting, though he also was clear that crossing readily altered size and form; for example, greyhound crosses had lightened the 'heavy form of the bulldog'.[37]

On questions of 'blood' and its 'purity', dog breeders looked to a pamphlet published in 1874 by William Tegetmeier, the doyen of fancy poultry breeders, and Dr William Whytehead Boulton, a general practitioner from Beverley in Yorkshire, who bred Cocker Spaniels.[38] Boulton had produced a kennel of jet-black spaniels that bred true to colour 'generation after generation'.[39] Black spaniels, later renamed Field Spaniels, had become the dominant type of spaniel at dog shows; however, their dark colour made them unsuitable for the field where they were hard to spot. As the creations of dog shows, their status was much debated; sometimes they were considered a strain and sometimes a 'breed', though critics regarded them as 'mongrels'. Vero Shaw quoted a leading breeder, a Mr Jacobs, on the question:

> Much has been written and said on the purity of the breed, deprecating the means I have adopted to produce them as calculated to alter a presumed type, and frequent missiles have been hurled at me and my dogs from behind the hedge. But where is the purebred Black Spaniel so much talked about? Proof of the existence of the purebred one (if ever there was one) has not been forthcoming; like most other sporting dogs, they are the result of different crosses.
>
> We may keep to one strain for many years, and, in time, call them a distinct breed, but what is the result?
>
> To preserve that strain we must continually breed in-and-in to one family, until we get them difficult to rear, weedy, and devoid of sense, when they become useless for the purpose they are required. Therefore breeders have to resort to the crossing with another family, which may be of a different type or colour; by doing so you raise a great 'hubbub' and cry that your dogs are not pure. In spite of these cries I followed my own dictation; my great aim was to improve the breed of Spaniels.[40]

Jacobs concluded that he was still seeking 'improvement' and that while he had produced dogs that 'eclipse everything I have yet seen', he was still to reach 'the standard I have marked out for my beacon'.[41]

Breeders sought and claimed to have purebred animals because they assumed inbreeding gave prepotency, that is, it was more likely and happened more consistently that the parents' features would be reproduced in their offspring. Such dogs and bitches had higher sale and stud values, especially if the breeder was trustworthy on a dog's pedigree. However, there seemed to be no justification in science for the notion of 'pure bred', especially if one followed Darwin and his work on the domestication of animals and plants. Tegetmeier was Darwin's most influential populariser with breeders and in his *The Poultry Book*, published in 1867; he used rabbits as an example:

> [I]n the strictest scientific sense of the word, no particular variety of rabbit can be said to be a pure breed, as, like all others, it is descended from the wild original. In the same manner, we may deny the applicability of the term pure breed to the variety of any domesticated animal, even if, as in the case of the dog or sheep, we do not know the original from which they descended.[42]

Tegetmeier was drawing upon the distinction, vital to Darwin and his followers, between species and varieties: breeding between species was impossible or produced sterile hybrids, whereas breeding between varieties was possible because they were all the same species and descended, relatively recently in evolutionary time, from common ancestors. Biologically, any claim to be 'pure bred' was 'only comparatively true', and meant a variety had been reared for a number of years or generations without a cross with any other variety.

Scientists and breeders were not always at odds. They were for instance fascinated alike by 'antecedent impressions', or what would later be 'telegony'.[43] In 1879, Hugh Dalziel observed in his book *British Dogs* that it is,

> one of the most strange and remarkable facts, as it is one of the least understood in connection with breeding, that the union of a bitch for the first time with a dog by which she conceives frequently exerts an influence on subsequent litters.[44]

A common metaphor was the womb was 'stained' and that the taint wore off with each pregnancy. The phenomenon had been widely discussed by scientists since the 1820s and the Earl of Morton's report that one of his mares, having previously borne a foal from an experimental cross with a quagga – a type of zebra that became extinct in the 1880s – produced foals with 'a striking resemblance to the quagga', when subsequently mated with a black Arabian horse.[45] Telegony was also assumed to occur in humans.[46] Thus, a mother with a first-born illegitimate child would not have only suffered moral and social condemnation, but also would have had to endure a 'biological punishment', deterring any future husband as his children would 'inherit' the features of a likely disreputable man who had fathered the first child.[47] In Thomas Hardy's *Tess of the D'Urbervilles* (1891), Angel Clare is mortified on his wedding night when he learns that his bride, Tess Durbyfield, had borne a child after being raped by his nemesis Alec d'Urberville.[48] He then dwells on the fact that his wife is tainted and any offspring from their union would in some way be marked by Alec.

Another form of the inheritance of acquired characteristics reported by breeders was maternal-mediated impressions during pregnancy. This might be features taken from 'uterine brothers and sisters in the litter', which was particularly troublesome if 'the carelessness of servants' had given bitches the 'the slightest chance [to] steal away in search of a mate of her own selection'.[49] Breeders also held the view that physical and mental experiences during pregnancy, particularly traumas, would mark the foetus. Doctors held such views for humans and there was common folklore, which involved trying measures to counter the effect and repair the disability or mark.[50] Some authorities looked beyond trauma to the influence of her surroundings on a pregnant female, citing the perhaps extreme case of the 'celebrated breeder of black polled cattle [who] had his premises and fences tarred, with the express object of assisting Nature in keeping the colour of his stock as deep as possible'.[51] All this meant that breeders tried to ensure that their pregnant bitches were well fed and kept in quiet, comfortable surroundings.

Breeders continued to report instances of telegony in dogs and other species throughout the nineteenth century.[52] Scientists and veterinarians were increasingly sceptical; indeed, the term itself was invented in the 1890s by August Weismann, a founder of modern genetics, only to dismiss it, observing that it 'has never been known to occur.[53] For biologists, the Penicuik Experiments, conducted by the Glasgow University biologist James Cossar Ewart in 1894–95, conclusively disproved any effects from previous matings on any progeny.[54] Ewart's twin aims had been to test the notion of telegony and to produce a horse-zebra hybrid suitable for draught work in South Africa.

There is a link between the work of Robert Bakewell and the development of genetics, albeit indirect. Wood and Orel have shown that Bakewell's ideas were taken up in Brno in Moravia and applied to establish Merino sheep in the region.[55] The local community of farmers and scientists, the most influential being Ferdinand Geisslern, investigated how traits, sometimes very distinct, were passed on from parents and sometimes grandparents, and developed what they termed 'genetic laws' to capture patterns.[56] They worked on both animals and plants, and especially with the latter studied hybrids. Their work was part of a much wider interest amongst scientists in Central Europe in inheritance, which had links with plant and animal breeders. What was the connection to Mendel? The head of the monastery that Mendel joined in 1843 was Abbot Cyrill F. Napp, a member of this community, whose major interest was – 'What is inherited and why?'[57]

Breed

As we have seen, the term breed was first used for purebred livestock and commercial poultry, then sporting and fancy animals and finally with companion animals. Breed was a category for differentiating animals that was typical of a wider eighteenth-century project of classification and invention of taxonomies, which, for example, saw humans divided into races, tribes, classes, peoples, etc.[58] However, the context of its invention and association with domesticated animals in farming, transport, sport, fancy and companionship gave it particular uses and meanings. Breed signalled that the bodies and characters of domestic animals were remade by breeders in four ways:

(i) Breeds were defined by, and bred to, a physical or conformation standard, with this defined by subdividing their body into points (Figure 17.1).
(ii) Within a breed population, there was a drive to achieve greater uniformity of conformation and the previous normal distribution of size, colour, etc. diminished, or all but disappeared.
(iii) Breeds were made more distinct from each other, with a tendency to develop exaggerated points to demarcate the differences between breeds. Previously the physical forms of domesticated animals had existed on a continuum; with breeds they became segmented with gaps between, sometimes occupied by inferior cross-breeds or mongrels.
(iv) The goal of having a standardised, uniform population co-existed with that of improving and hence changing its form to better meet economic demands or the ideals of fancy breeders.

An example of the difficulties involved comes from the fact that historians of livestock have struggled with the origins of the history of types of cattle and sheep. In part, this is because of the dearth of written sources and the ambiguities of pictorial representations were coloured, metaphorically and literally by contemporary conventions of representation and technologies of reproduction. However, it is also because many historians have inappropriately used the Bakewellian notion of breed for earlier centuries. Nicholas Russell, in his book *Like Engend'ring Like*, records

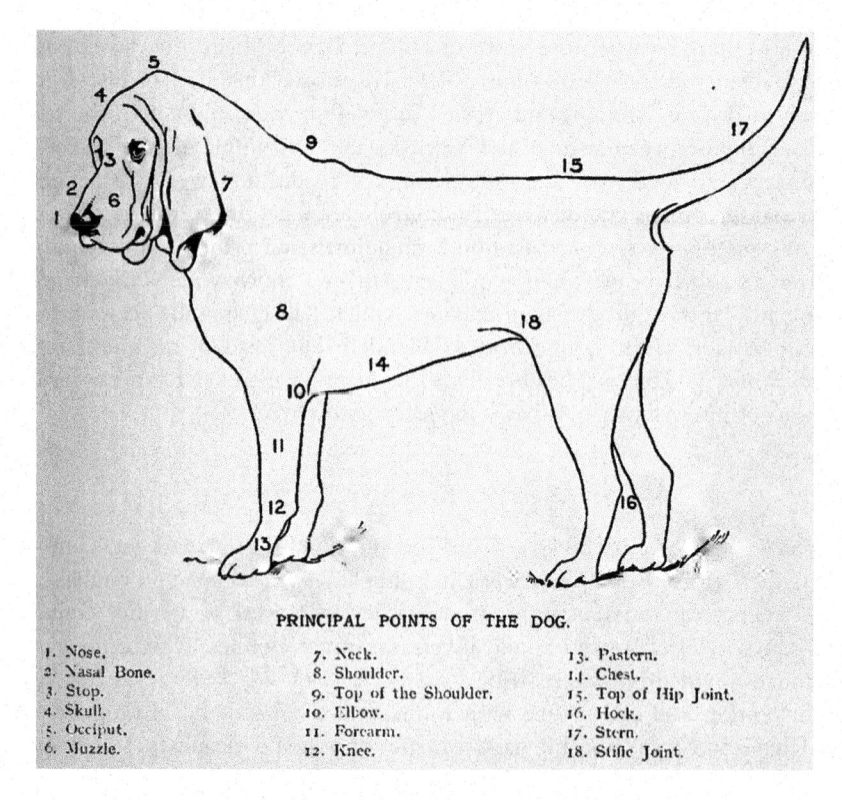

Figure 17.1 Principal points of the dog.
Collection of Michael Worboys.

how with most named types, there was variation in colour and markings, while size and shape were widespread with little uniformity. In describing sheep types in the eighteenth century, he muses that:

> It may be that the concept of "breed" in the twentieth-century sense of a group of domestic animals sharing a large number of common morphological features by virtue of genetic homogeneity, is wholly inapplicable to the regional forms outlined here.[59]

He goes on to observe, citing a survey of European primitive breeds, that,

> Even when modern relict breeds under primitive management remain isolated, the management and selection pressures working on them seem to favour the survival of diverse morphologies rather than tending towards similarity of appearance.[60]

For the late seventeenth century, Russell offers a classification of sheep in seven groups, defined by size, face colour, horns and fleece type, which he links loosely to regions and topography, but concludes that from the mid-eighteenth century this was 'dramatically altered' by the spread of Bakewell's New Leicester, and counterparts such as the Southdown, developed by farmers in Sussex.[61]

Sheep

However, Bakewell remains important for us as the inventor of the modern notion of breed, which John R. Walton has characterised as 'an ingenious marketing and publicity mechanism'.[62] Walton spells out how this worked for breeders:

> Certain identifiable physical characteristics were imprinted in animals of a particular strain, and prospective purchasers were then encouraged to associate those markers with some attribute or attributes of productivity which, it was claimed, such animals also possessed: rapid weight gain, larger size, high food conversion rates, better distribution of meat, heavier milk yields and so on. The success of a breed depended to some extent on the visual impact of the chosen marker or trademark, and the ease of its transmission from one generation to the next, to some extent on the degree to which the claims made for the breed's performance were thought to be valid.[63]

In other words, breeds were 'brands'. Bakewell's New Leicester was claimed to be a better value product, where its name and design differentiated it from its competitors. Brands were also a form of intellectual property and something more. Those who acquired or bred from the New Leicester were buying into good blood and associating with an improving ideology. Ritvo makes a similar point with regard to the prize bulls, which represented for aristocratic elites their contribution to improving farming and a metaphor for their elite position based on genealogy and visible power.[64] Distinctive physical features also were important in differentiating between breeds and were made into signs of value.

Bakewell kept his best ewes and hired out his rams, thereby controlling his material and intellectual property. This practice had a triple benefit: protection of the breed; income from fees for service; and feedback, as he insisted on inspecting the offspring of his stud animals to test their potency. The latter became known as progeny testing.[65]

Horses and cattle

The designation of types of working horses into breeds occurred at the same time as livestock, but in two contexts – farming and horse racing. Robert Bakewell developed his own new eponymous horse – the Bakewell Black, retrospectively seen as an early Shire horse.[66] Horses were mostly bred and classified by the work they undertook, hence, as well as for farm work certain types were bred for hunting, the army and transportation. The nearest to a breed in the eighteenth century was the thoroughbred racehorse, which was defined, not by conformation, but by lineage.[67] Racehorses in England had been improved in the late seventeenth and early eighteenth centuries by the importation of stallions from Arabia. The aim of breeders was to combine the lightness and speed of the Arabian, plus their assumed propensity to pass on these characteristics, with the strength of English mares, to produce a horse that was fast and had stamina. Three stallions, imported into England from the Middle East in the late seventeenth and eighteenth centuries, still remain foundational in racehorse breeding. They were the Byerley Turk, acquired by Captain Robert Byerley as his war horse in the 1680s before becoming a stud stallion; the Godolphin Arabian, foaled in Yemen and imported to England in 1729 by Edward Coke; and the Darley Arabian, bought in Aleppo in 1704 by Thomas Darley.[68] Recent studies of the genomes of thoroughbred racehorses have revealed that 95% of the quarter of a million stallions worldwide can be traced back to the Darley Arabian and 'ten founder females account for 72% of maternal lineages'.[69] The 'thorough' in thoroughbred meant, and still means, that a horse's inheritance is confined to bloodlines from limited, foundation stallions and to a lesser extent mares. This restriction was formalised in 1913 when entry was limited to the progeny of horses already accepted in earlier volumes.[70]

The belief that horses with Arabian or Turk heredity had superior powers of speed and that these were passed on to their progeny, meant that their descendants were sought after as stud animals. It was not lineage alone that counted; this was cross-referenced and combined with performance testing, both in races and at stud with their progeny. The importance of lineage was institutionalised in 1793 with the publication of the first volume of the General Stud Book, which was a public registry of the pedigrees of best thoroughbreds, while also serving as a resource for validating claims made by breeders about the identity of an individual horse.[71] Previously, stud books had been kept privately and the contemporary assumption was that openness would deter fraud. There was a default conformation standard for thoroughbreds which was set by them all being bred for the same purpose in the same conditions – turf racing. In addition, there was a high degree of close breeding that necessarily followed from the limited number of bloodlines. The designation and development of the horse breeds in general was not made until the second half of the nineteenth century. For example, the English Cart Horse Society was founded in 1876, around the same time as those for Clydesdale, Suffolk Punch and the Shire were established.[72]

Cattle breeders did not adopt formal registration and public stud books until the mid-nineteenth century, which signalled attempts to better standardise the animals they produced and to have their features recognised as breeds.[73] The Royal Jersey Agricultural and Horticultural Society, established in 1833, forbade the importation of cattle from France, allowing only improvement with cattle from England. The following year scales of points were agreed for bulls, heifers and calves, on the assumption that competitions for show prizes would improve the breed. A Herd Book recording pedigrees was only started in 1878, and then by the English Jersey Cattle Society, which along with conformation competitions organised butter testing.[74] The first Herd Book placed a significant emphasis on the importance of breed standards:

> The history of the Jersey cow points a moral which cannot be overlooked, "Beauty and utility should be combined". Although always noted for her dairy properties, it was not until the show ring points (which were indicative of good dairy cattle) were drawn up, and some approach to uniformity of

aim arrived at among breeders, that the increased demand arose for Jerseys from other countries, with a consequent increase in their value.[75]

In fact, the first Herd Book for cattle was for Herefords, published in 1846, though a society to promote the breed was not formed until 1878.[76] In 1886 the Book was 'closed', that is, only calves born to sires and dams previously entered in the book would be accepted as true Herefords. This textual practice was designed to ensure the purity of the breed and also meant a degree of inbreeding. The Aberdeen Angus First Herd Book was established in 1862 and the Aberdeen Angus Society in 1879.[77]

Poultry

The next domesticated species to be cast as breeds were poultry and pigeons. New types of poultry were created and imported to meet the economic demands of eggs and meat production and the aesthetic tastes of the fancy breeder.[78] The most popular imports were the Spanish, Cochin (China), Hamburg, Poland and Malay, and the most developed native type was the Dorking. Sir John Saunders Sebright, who was a politician and animal breeder, popularised the ideas of Robert Bakewell and produced small chickens, known as bantams.[79] He established the Sebright Bantam Club in 1810 to promote his creations, on the model of the Dishley Society, which met first in public houses and was associated with the working-class bird fancy and then to Gray's Inn Coffee House in London (Figure 17.2).[80]

Figure 17.2 Fancy poultry.
Collection of Michael Worboys.

Poultry owning, breeding and showing had been popular across social classes since the late eighteenth century, but took off in the 'hen fever' that gripped Europe and North America in the mid-nineteenth century. Consequently, there was an increase in the number and size of poultry shows and the proliferation of fancy breeds. At the Manchester Poultry Show in January 1855, the judges were instructed not to reward size and weight, but to look for 'high condition, beauty of plumage and purity of race'.[81] The tension between breeding for utility and fancy came into the open in 1885, when the leading surgeon and specialist in urology Henry Thompson, announced that he had sold his large poultry collection because his high-bred birds laid poor quality eggs.[82] He complained that the British bred for 'feather', while in France poultry was bred for meat and eggs, calling for 'the prize feather system to be swept away'.[83] He was soon joined by Tegetmeier, who wrote 'I do not hesitate to affirm . . . that no breed of fowls has been taken in hand by the fancier that has not seriously depreciated as a useful variety of poultry'.[84] In their defence, breeders argued that fancy points were a marker of pure breeding and that features such as heavy plumage had originally been linked to utility, in this particular case providing protection from the winter weather to ensure all-year-round laying. Tegetmeier's critique, which was seen as perverse as he had been the nation's principal show judge for half-a-century, was turned to advantage by breeders. They conceded some of the points on specific breeds, but generally argued that Tegetmeier was out of date: breeds had been improved and fancy points were being revised.

Many varieties of fancy pigeon had been bred for centuries, but in the eighteenth century breeding and exhibiting was institutionalised in clubs and societies.[85] Over many centuries and across the world, many and remarkably different physical forms of the rock dove (*Columbia livia*) had been produced and at shows birds were judged on their form, colour and beauty. In his *The Complete Pigeon Fancier*, published in 1790, Daniel Girton gave descriptions of 28 'species': Powters, Carriers, Horsemen, Dragoons, Croppers, Powting-Horsemen, Uplopers, Fantails, Chinese Pigeon, Lace ditto, Tumblers, Runts, Spots, Laughters, Trumpeters, Jacobines, Capuchins, Nuns, Shakers, Helmets, Ruffs, Finnikins, Turners Barbs, Mahomets, Turbits, Owls, Smiters and others.[86] In nineteenth-century England, exhibitions were regulated by two societies, the National Columbarian Society and the Philoperisteron Society. The latter pioneered a numerical system for judging birds, where the different points were weighted and scored, with the cumulative score settling which was the best bird.[87] This Gradgrindian attempt to objectify the definition and appreciation of breed did not catch on; nonetheless, it demonstrates how fine-grained the differentiation of breeds had become by the mid-nineteenth century.

Dogs

Martin Wallen has argued that 'the foxhound was the first modern dog to be recognized as a breed', pointing to the breeding practices of Robert Bakewell's neighbour Hugo Meynell, who developed hounds that had 'fine noses' and were 'stout runners'.[88] However, Wallen goes on to argue that:

Meynell and the others did not set out to create a 'breed', they plainly intended to create an improved hound that would serve a single purpose they valued within the institutional framework that cast animals as resources. Instead of adapting their activities to available hounds, they created a distinctly modern hound that facilitated their sport.[89]

In practice this meant foxhounds were bred to suit local geographies and it was not until the spread of the railway from the mid-nineteenth century, which allowed the easier movement of hounds for breeding and sport, that a singular breed was established. The development of dog shows from the 1860s was decisive in this process, encouraging breeding to ideals, which led to the creation of a more standardised and uniform foxhound population across the country.

The impact of dog shows and the drive for standardisation is well illustrated by the physical and cultural remodelling of the bulldog. In 1874 a group of men met in the Blue Post, a pub just off Oxford Street in London, to found the Bulldog Club. A club of the same name had been formed in 1864, but only lasted three years. The new initiative was prompted by concerns that certain dog breeders were trying to make the English bulldog larger, by cross-breeding with the Spanish bulldog, thus, the purity and very Englishness of the national dog was under threat.

However, their aim was not actually one of preservation, as there was no agreement on the ideal type due to the fact that many different types of dog had been used in bull baiting. Indeed, the types mostly spoken and written about had been in terms of character and ability – courage, boldness, resolution, pluck, tenacity – and only secondarily in relation to physical form. William Youatt in his book on *The Dog* in 1845, placed the bulldog at the head of an 'inferior and brutal division', which though it had a characteristic 'thick head, turned-up nose, and thick pendulous lips' was principally portrayed in terms of 'ferocity', 'fury' and 'obstinacy'. In his influential book *The Dog in Health and Disease* published in 1859, John Henry Walsh began his account of the bulldog by quoting Cuvier on the size of its brain and lack of 'sagacity', and then emphasised 'two remarkable features': 'firstly, they always make their attack on the head; and, secondly, they do not bite and let go their hold, retain it in the most tenacious manner'.[90] The illustrations that accompanied Youatt's and Walsh's descriptions (Figures 17.3 and 17.4) show a dog with a short snout, but not the flat face and without the protruding lower jaw that later Victorians emphasised. The characteristic legs and stance are evident, however, but this may have been selected for the tavern-based dog fancy of ratting and showing that developed after the banning of bear-baiting.

By 1875 when the new Bulldog Club set its standards, the development of dog shows and breeders, exhibitors, judges and commercial interests that supported it had defined dog breeds almost exclusively in terms of their physical form – size, colour, shape, coat, bodily proportions, etc. The new bulldog standard was typical in delineating 17 physical points against which individual dogs could be scored by judges in dog shows. The Bulldog Club also began a Stud Book, which recorded detailed measurements of the features of every dog along with its pedigrees back to its great,

Figure 17.3 'The bull-dog'. From W. Youatt, *The Dog*, London: Society for the Diffusion of Useful Knowledge, 1845, 151.

Collection of Michael Worboys.

" Top,"* a pure Bulldog, the property of C. Stockdale, Esq., Shepherd's Bush.

Figure 17.4 '"Top", a pure bulldog'. From Stonehenge [John Henry Walsh], *The Dog*, third edition, London: Longmans, Green, 1879.

Collection of Michael Worboys.

great grand sires and dams. Pedigrees were used to show that ancestors had been from 'good stock' and usually prizewinners, which meant closely or inbred, or what was termed 'pure bred'. Both the points and the stud book were controversial. Some, mostly older, fanciers warned against 'fixed types' and judging animals by their lineage; they argued that market demand was for dogs of character and ability, not fancy dogs of the same standardised conformation, from the same stock. The aficionados of the Club maintained that conformation was a reliable indicator of character and ability, and needed to be preserved by close breeding. There were also quarrels within the Club about who should judge at dog shows and whether it was best to decide the top dog on points alone, or to consider the overall 'look' and movement of the animal. Personal rivalries and economic interests in new social networks and institutions of a dog fancy fed such disputes, reformed from its early nineteenth-century association with blood sports and crime.

The standard points agreed by the Club were apportioned numerical scores, where 'perfection' would achieve 100 marks, distributed thus: 10 to 'general appearance', 15 to the skull and 5 each to another fifteen points.[91] In this process, and building on changes wrought through dog shows, the bulldog had been remodelled, most noticeably with a new head that had features imagined to have been essential to hang onto a bull's head. The most important were drooping jowls (dewlaps) and a protruding lower jaw, to grip the bull's soft under-chin, and a flat face, to allow breathing during the physical exertion of holding on (Figure 17.5).

BULLDOG.
Capt. G. E. A. Holdworth's SIR ANTHONY. Sire, Crib, by Duke II., out of Rush; Dam, Meg, by Old King Dick, out of Old Nell.

Figure 17.5 Captain Holdsworth's Sir Anthony, bulldog.
Collection of Michael Worboys.

The aim of producing a larger dog was also predicated on assumptions about the weight that could wear down a bull, but it was not just physique, the standard also called for dogs that convey 'an impression of determination, strength and activity, similar to that suggested by the appearance of a thickset Ayrshire or Highland bull'.[92] The fate of the bulldog typified what happened to all types of dog and saw the creation of new standards based on conformation rather than actual utility.

By the end of the nineteenth century the word breed was used for the different forms of livestock and domesticated animals. Its adoption in the nineteenth century and extension into the twentieth was more than a matter of words. Its usage signalled major changes in the physical form of individual animals and populations, as those categorised as breeds became more uniform in look and had less genetic variation. The preferred physical form of each breed had been and continued to be a subject for negotiation, but the agreed forms objectified and reified breed standards to such an extent that they appeared 'natural'. Within communities of breeders and more widely across cultures, breeds were essentialised, an important part of which was an imagined, presentist history where it, or some primitive form of it, had existed for centuries, if not longer. For example, one line of descent claimed for the English Mastiff was from the bitch of Sir Piers Legh, which accompanied him to the Battle of Agincourt in 1415.[93] Legh was wounded and was guarded by his faithful bitch, but he eventually died. His body was returned, accompanied by his bitch, to be buried at the family estate at Lyme Hall in Cheshire. The bitch became the foundation 'blood' of what became known as Lyme Hall Mastiffs and it was claimed that the family maintained its bloodline through to the nineteenth century when formal standards for the breed were proposed. Few nineteenth-century fanciers accepted the story and, playing with aristocrat stereotypes, suggested that there must have been below-stairs matings and, if the Legh story were accepted, then there would have been inbreeding and degeneration.

The pedigree breeds of dog proliferated in the latter half of the nineteenth century, with many types of dog reinvented and newly produced as 'breeds'. Some dogs, notably the Irish Wolfhound, were seemingly manufactured, the term contemporaries used, entirely from cross-breeding different kinds of dog. The emergence in the latter half of the nineteenth century of the dog show as an event distinct from agricultural shows and that measured and promoted particular 'standards' of dog breeds is testimony to public interest and investment in the notion of 'breed'. Before 'breed' there had been a range of size, shapes and colour within a variety, and there were no well-defined boundaries between varieties; they shaded into one another at the margin. After *breed*, each breed was a distinctive, ideal type that conformed to a standard, and there was uniformity within the breed population. Thus, marginal forms disappeared and their place was occupied by cross-breeds, which have become very popular in the twenty-first century. The very name – cross-breed, which has displaced mongrel, confirms the dominance of breed in modern thinking about dogs. This can be seen in recent surveys, which showed that, in 2013: 64% of British dog owners reported that their dog was a pedigree breed; 31% a cross-breed; 2% designer cross-breed and 3% 'not sure'.[94] The category 'No breed' was not an option.

Conclusion

Animal breeding in the twentieth and early twenty-first centuries showed continuities and discontinuities with early times. The tension between 'art' and 'science' persisted, but Derry has shown that this varied between different species and contexts, and over time, and was often more rhetorical than real.[95] Breeding 'science' was dramatically changed by the development of genetics, principally based on Mendelian principles, but its impact was uneven, due, as noted already, both to the complexity of animal inheritance and to the different cultures and goals of breeders. This conclusion has been endorsed by Bert Theunissen's work on animal breeding in the Netherlands.[96] Nevertheless, the alternative model supported by biometricians retained some influence in population genetics. Geneticists in this specialism charted statistical variations in different crossings, and became important from the mid-century with the advent of factory farming and the freezing of semen, allowing the global dissemination of an individual's heredity. Arguably, the most radical change in the twentieth century was the industrialising of breeding, for example in the mass production of chickens for egg-laying and rearing for meat. In both industries, where special breed companies and agencies were created, artificial insemination was used to spread the influence, qualitatively and quantitatively, of 'genetically superior cockerels'.[97] The superiority of both cockerels and brood hens has been measured by ever more sophisticated forms of 'progeny testing', which determines market prices and the subsequent selection of breed stock. In these circumstances, the breeder and rearer of the chicks are different people and may never meet.[98] The opposite remains the case with cattle and sheep, where typically breeders who are also farmers select sires and mothers, on both their physical form and their pedigree. Sheep breeding also continues to be practised on the farm, though the possibility of the end of breeding was signalled in 1996, with the cloning of Dolly.[99]

By the end of the nineteenth century most domesticated animals had been differentiated physically and culturally into breeds, and in the twentieth century became ever more opaque as species. Wild animal species are recognisable because individuals look alike: for example, urban foxes are all of a similar size, colour and shape. Dogs, however, which are similarly sized and distantly related, have been bred in all sizes, colours and shapes. We can only speculate what size, colour and shape *Canis lupus familiaris* was before it was subject to 'artificial selection', or what it might become if no longer bred selectively. Humans have wrought the greatest differences in size and shape with dogs, but the horses, cows, sheep and many species of birds have been similarly remade. We now only know these species as divided into breeds, a category that has been essentialised and naturalised.

Notes

1 F. Galton, 'Hereditary character and talent', *MacMillan's Magazine*, 2 (1864): 157–166, 165–166.

2 J. Clutton-Brock, *A Natural History of Domesticated Mammals*, London: Natural History Museum, 1999.

3 D.L. Wykes, 'Robert Bakewell (1725–95) of Dishley: farmer and livestock improver', *Agricultural History Review*, 52, 1 (2004): 38–55; J. Humphreys, 'Bakewell, Robert

(1725–1795)', revised G.E. Mingay (ed.), *Oxford Dictionary of National Biography*, Oxford: Oxford University Press, 2004, available at www.oxforddnb.com/view/article/1146, last accessed 15 June 2016.

4 R.J. Moore-Colyer, 'Sheep', G.E. Mingay (ed.), *The Agrarian History of England and Wales*, Volume 6, Cambridge: Cambridge University Press, 1989, 315–316 and 338–343.

5 P. Armstrong, *What Animals Mean in the Fiction of Modernity*, London: Routledge, 2008.

6 P.J. Bowler, *Evolution: The History of an Idea*, Berkeley CA: University of California Press, 1988; R.C. Olby, *Origins of Mendelism*, Chicago IL: University of Chicago Press, 1985.

7 C. Darwin, *The Variation of Animals and Plants under Domestication*, London: John Murray, 1868; J.A. Secord, 'Nature's fancy: Charles Darwin and the breeding of pigeons', *Isis* 72, 2 (1981): 162–186.

8 J. Harwood, 'Did Mendelism transform plant breeding? Genetic theory and breeding practice, 1900–1945', in D. Phillips and S. Kingsland (eds.), *New Perspectives on the History of Life Sciences and Agriculture*, Cham, Switzerland: Springer, 2015, 40, 345–370; B. Charnley, 'Agricultural science, plant breeding and the emergence of a Mendelian system in Britain, 1880–1930', PhD thesis, University of Leeds, 2011; J. Harwood, *Europe's Green Revolution and its Successors: The Rise and Fall of Peasant-Friendly Plant Breeding*, Abingdon: Routledge, 2012; H. Curry, *Evolution Made to Order: Plant Breeding and Technological Innovation in Twentieth-Century America*, Chicago IL: University of Chicago Press, 2016; P. Palladino, 'Wizards and devotees: on the Mendelian theory of inheritance and the professionalization of agricultural science in Great Britain and the United States, 1880–1930', *History of Science* 32, 4 (1994): 409–444.

9 B. Theunissen, 'Breeding for nobility or for production? Cultures of dairy cattle breeding in the Netherlands, 1945–1995', *Isis* 103, 2 (2012): 278–309.

10 S. White, 'From globalized pig breeds to capitalist pigs: a study in animal cultures and evolutionary history', *Environmental History*, 16, 1 (2011): 94–120.

11 V. Orel and R.J. Wood, 'Scientific animal breeding in Moravia before and after the rediscovery of Mendel's theory', *Quarterly Review of Biology*, 75, 2 (2000): 149–157, 152; R.J. Wood and V. Orel, *Genetic Prehistory in Selective Breeding: A Prelude to Mendel*, Oxford: Oxford University Press, 2001.

12 M.E. Derry, *Bred for Perfection: Shorthorn Cattle, Collies, and Arabian Horses since 1800*, Baltimore MD: Johns Hopkins University Press, 2003; M.E. Derry, *Horses in Society: A Story of Animal Breeding and Marketing Culture, 1800–1920*, Toronto: University of Toronto Press, 2006; M.E. Derry, *Art and Science in Breeding: Creating Better Chickens*, Toronto: University of Toronto Press, 2014; M.E. Derry, *Masterminding Nature: The Breeding of Animals, 1750–2010*, Toronto: University of Toronto Press, 2015.

13 Derry, *Masterminding Nature*, 35–43, 178–180.

14 N. Russell, *Like Engend'ring Like: Heredity and Animal Breeding in Early Modern England*, Cambridge: Cambridge University Press, 1986.

15 R. Trow-Smith, *A History of British Livestock Husbandry to 1700*, London: Routledge and Kegan Paul, 1957; J.G Hall and J. Clutton-Brock, *Two Hundred Years of British Livestock Farming*, London: Natural History Museum, 1989; M.L. Ryder, 'The history of sheep breeds in Britain', *Agricultural History Review* 12, 1 (1964): 1–12; J.R. Walton, 'Pedigree and the national cattle herd, c. 1750–1950', *Agricultural History Review* 34, 2 (1986): 149–170; J.R. Walton, 'Pedigree and productivity in the British and North American cattle kingdoms before 1930', *Journal of Historical Geography* 25, 4 (1999): 441–462.

16 J. Sinclair, *History of Shorthorn Cattle*, London: Vinton & Company, 1907; J. MacDonald and J. Sinclair, *History of Hereford Cattle*, London: Vinton & Company, 1909; J. MacDonald and J. Sinclair, *History of Aberdeen-Angus Cattle*, London: Vinton & Company, 1910.

17 J. Davidson, *Breeding: A Partial History of the Eighteenth Century*, New York: Columbia University Press, 2009, 2.
18 M. Brandow, *A Matter of Breeding: A Biting History of Pedigree Dogs and How the Quest for Status Has Harmed Man's Best Friend*. Boston: Beacon Press, 2015.
19 M. Wallen, 'Foxhounds, curs, and the dawn of breeding: the discourse of modern human–canine relations', *Cultural Critique* 79, 1 (2011): 125–151. M. Worboys, J-M. Strange, and N. Pemberton, *The Invention of the Modern Dog: Breed and Blood in Victorian Britain*, Baltimore MD: Johns Hopkins University Press, 2018.
20 C. Lehleiter, *Romanticism, Origins, and the History of Heredity*, Lanham MA: Bucknell University Press, 2014, 67–68.
21 Wood and Orel, *Genetic Prehistory*, 61–76.
22 Wood and Orel, *Genetic Prehistory*, 12–32, 124–187.
23 Trow-Smith *British Livestock*, 59–68.
24 Derry, *Bred for Perfection*, 18–21.
25 Derry, *Bred for Perfection*, 3.
26 J. Sebright, *The Art of Improving the Breeds of Domestic Animals*, London: John Harding, 1809, 379; Also see B. Theunissen, 'Darwin and his pigeons: the analogy between artificial and natural selection revisited', *Journal of the History of Biology* 45, 2 (2012): 179–212.
27 J. Sebright, 'On the art of improving the breed of domestic animals in a letter to Joseph Banks, K.B. by Sir John Saunders Sebright, Bart, M.P.', quoted in *Archives of Useful Knowledge* 1 (1811): 374–375.
28 Ritvo, *Animal Estate*, 45–81.
29 Stonehenge, *The Dog*, London: Longman, Green, Longman, and Roberts, 1859, 171–198; and Stonehenge, *The Dog*, third edition, 1879, London: Longmans, Green, 251–274.
30 Stonehenge, *The Dog*, 1859, 175.
31 Stonehenge, *The Dog*, 1859, 172.
32 Derry, *Masterminding Nature*, 18.
33 Stonehenge, *The Dog*, 1859, 172–173.
34 Stonehenge, *The Dog*, 1859, 173.
35 Stonehenge, *The Dog*, 1859, 188.
36 Stonehenge, *The Dog*, 1859, 185.
37 Stonehenge, *The Dog*, 1859, 179.
38 W.B. Tegetmeier and W.W. Boulton, *Breeding for Colour and the Physiology of Breeding*, privately printed, 1874.
39 W.D. Drury, *British Dogs: Their Points, Selection, and Show Preparation*. London: L. Upcott Gill, 1903, 315.
40 V. Shaw, *The Illustrated Book of the Dog*, London: Cassel, Petter, Galpin & Co., 1881, 445.
41 Shaw, *The Illustrated Book of the Dog*, 445.
42 W.B. Tegetmeier, *The Poultry Book: Comprising the Breeding and Management of Profitable and Ornamental Poultry*, London: George Routledge and Sons, 1867, 65.
43 R.W. Burkhardt, 'Closing the door on Lord Morton's mare: the rise and fall of telegony', *Studies in the History of Biology*, 3 (1979): 1–21.
44 H. Dalziel, *British Dogs, their Varieties, History, Characteristics, Breeding, Management and Exhibition*, London: 'The Bazaar Office', 1879, 461.
45 E.O. Morton, 'A communication of a singular fact in natural history', *Philosophical Transactions of the Royal Society of London* 111 (1821): 20–22; J. Endersby, *A Guinea Pig's History of Biology*, London: Random House, 2007, 17–23.
46 C. Sengoopta, *Otto Weininger: Sex, Science, and Self in Imperial Vienna*, Chicago IL: Chicago University Press, 131–137.

47 M. Carlson, 'Ibsen, Strindberg, and telegony', *PMLA* 100, 5 (1985): 774–782; R. Lewinsohn, *A History of Sexual Customs*, London: Longman Green, 1958, 204–206.
48 S. Kern, *A Cultural History of Causality: Science, Murder Novels, and Systems of Thought*, Princeton NJ: Princeton University Press, 2004, 47–48.
49 Shaw, *Illustrated Book of the Dog*, 461.
50 R.J. Lee, 'Maternal impressions', *British Medical Journal* 1, 736 (1875): 167–169; J. Clapperton, 'Maternal impressions,' *British Medical Journal* 1, 736 (1875): 169–170.
51 Shaw, *Illustrated Book of the Dog*, 525.
52 'Este', 'The influence of the first or previous sire', *Kennel Gazette*, (November 1890): 265–267; H. Ritvo, 'The animal connection', in J.J. Sheehan and M. Sosna (eds.), *The Boundaries of Humanity: Humans, Animals, Machines*, Berkeley CA: University of California Press, 1991, 76–80.
53 A. Weismann, *Germ-Plasm: A Theory of Heredity*, London: Walter Scott Ltd, 1893, 383–386; R.J. Wood, 'The sheep breeders' view of heredity (1723–1843)', in H-J. Rheinberger and S. Müller-Wille (eds.), *A Cultural History of Heredity, Volume II, 18th and 19th Centuries*, Chicago IL: University of Chicago Press, 2007, 21–46.
54 J.C. Ewart, *The Penycuik Experiments*, London: A. & C. Black, 1899; F.H.A.M. 'James Cossar Ewart. 1851–1933', *Obituary Notices of Fellows of the Royal Society* 1, 3 (1934): 189–195. H. Ritvo, *The Platypus and the Mermaid*, Cambridge MA: Harvard University Press, 1997, 110–111. In 1895, W.B. Tegetmeier wrote a book entitled *Horses, Asses, Zebras, Mules and Mule Breeding*, London: Horace Cox, 1895, which engaged with Ewart's work. See also: D. Barnaby (ed.), *Letters to Mr Tegetmeier: from J. Cossar Ewart and Others to the Editor of the Field at the Turn of the Nineteenth Century*, Timperley: ZSGM Publications, 2004.
55 Wood and Orel, *Genetic Prehistory of Selective Breeding*.
56 Orel and Wood, 'Scientific animal breeding in Moravia', 152.
57 Orel and Wood, 'Scientific animal breeding in Moravia', 152–156.
58 J. Pickstone, *Ways of Knowing: A New History of Science, Technology and Medicine*, Manchester: Manchester University Press, 2000; N. Hudson, 'From "nation" to "race": the origin of Racial classification in eighteenth-century thought', *Eighteenth-Century Studies* 29, 3 (1996): 247–264.
59 Russell, *Like Engend'ring Like*, 160–161.
60 Russell, *Like Engend'ring Like*, 161. Russell's source, which uses an essentialist and ahistorical notion of breed is M.L. Ryder, 'A survey of European primitive breeds of sheep', *Annales de Génétique et de Sélection Animale* 13, 4 (1981): 381–418. Also see Ryder, 'The history of sheep breeds in Britain', and M.L. Ryder, 'The history of sheep breeds in Britain *(continued)*', *Agricultural History Review* 12, 2 (1964), 65–82. In the first part of the article, Ryder tellingly concludes: 'Not until the end of the eighteenth century did agricultural writers begin to give definite descriptions of different breeds. This was unfortunately just after many breeds had been changed. . .' (7).
61 Trow-Smith, *British Livestock Husbandry*.
62 Walton, 'Pedigree and the national cattle herd', 152.
63 Walton, 'Pedigree and the national cattle herd', 152.
64 Ritvo, *Animal Estate*, 45–81.
65 Derry, *Masterminding Nature*, 6–7, 17–24.
66 K. Chivers, *The Shire Horse: A History of the Breed, the Society and the Men*, London: J.A. Allen, 1976, 47–57, 554–556.
67 D. Landry, *Noble Brutes: How Eastern Horses Transformed English Culture*, Baltimore MD: Johns Hopkins University Press, 2009.
68 R. Cassidy, *The Sport of Kings: Kinship, Class and Thoroughbred Breeding* in Newmarket, Cambridge: Cambridge University Press, 2002, 9.

69 E.P. Cunningham *et al.*, 'Microsatellite diversity, pedigree relatedness and the contributions of founder lineages to thoroughbred horses', *Animal Genetics*, 32, 6 (2001): 360–364.
70 The closure of the book was enacted by the so-called 'Jersey Act' to prevent the entry of American-bred thoroughbreds. It was abandoned in 1949.
71 *The General Stud Book Containing Pedigrees of English Race Horses, &c. &c. from the Earliest Accounts to the Year 1840*, London: Charles and James Watherby, 1840; Derry, *Bred for Perfection*, 4–5.
72 Chivers, *Shire Horse*, 111–145. Derry, *Bred for Perfection*, 55 et seq.
73 W. Youatt, *Cattle: Their Breeds, Management and Diseases*, London: Society for the Diffusion of Useful Knowledge, 1834.
74 H.G. Shepard, *One Hundred Years of the Royal Jersey Agricultural and Horticultural Society 1833–1933*, Jersey: J.T. Bigwood, 1934.
75 *Jersey Cattle: Their Feeding and Management*, London: Vinton & Co, 1898, 8.
76 Macdonald and Sinclair, *History of Hereford Cattle*, 137. This 1909 edition was a revision by James Sinclair of an earlier edition of 1886.
77 H.M. Briggs and D.M. Briggs, *Modern Breeds of Livestock*, fourth edition, London: Macmillan, 1980.
78 'See 'Food committee', *Journal of the Royal Society of Arts* 16, 811 (1867): 519–522.
79 D.R. Fisher, 'Sebright, Sir John Saunders, seventh baronet (1767–1846)', *Oxford Dictionary of National Biography*, Oxford: Oxford University Press, 2004; online edition, Jan 2008, available at www.oxforddnb.com/view/article/24997, last accessed 17 June 2016.
80 L. Wright, *The Illustrated Book of Poultry*, London: Cassell, Petter & Galpin, 1898, 467–471.
81 'Exhibition of Poultry in Manchester', *Manchester Courier*, 6 January 1855, 10.
82 Z. Cope, *The Versatile Victorian: Being the Life of Sir Henry Thompson Bt. 1820–1904*, London: Harvey and Blythe, 1951.
83 Wright, *Illustrated Book of Poultry*, 177.
84 W.B. Tegetmeier, *Poultry for the Table and Market versus Fancy Fowls*, London: Horace Cox, 1892.
85 J.C. Lyell, *Fancy Pigeons*, London: 'The Bazaar Office', 1881, 30.
86 D. Girton, *The New and Complete Pigeon Fancier*, London: Alexander Hogg, 1790.
87 Cited in Stonehenge, *Dogs of the British Islands*, London: Horace Cox, 1867, 266–267.
88 Wallen, 'Foxhounds', 137.
89 Wallen, 'Foxhounds', 137.
90 W. Youatt, *The Dog*, London: Society for the Diffusion of Useful Knowledge, 1845, 132.
91 Dalziel, *British Dogs*, 93.
92 Dalziel, *British Dogs*, 87.
93 B. Baxter and D. Blaxter, *The Complete Mastiff*, Letchworth: Ringpress, 1993.
94 See Statista, 'Share of dog owners in the United Kingdom (UK) in 2011 and 2013, by breed type', www.statista.com/statistics/299516/dog-owners-in-the-united-kingdom-uk-by-breed/, last accessed 24 August 2016.
95 Derry, *Masterminding*, 10–11.
96 Derry, *Masterminding*, 192; B. Theunissen, 'Breeding without Mendelism: theory and practice of dairy cattle breeding in the Netherlands 1900–1950', *Journal of the History of Biology* 41, 4 (2008): 637–676.
97 T. Getachew, 'A review of artificial insemination in poultry', *World's Veterinary Journal*, 2016, 6, 1 (2016), 25–33, 25.
98 Derry, *Masterminding*, 179–183.
99 M. Garcia-Sancho, 'Animal breeding in the age of biotechnology: the investigative pathway behind the cloning of Dolly the sheep', *History and Philosophy of the Life Sciences*, 37, 3 (2015): 282–304.

Bibliography

Armstrong, P. *What Animals Mean in the Fiction of Modernity*, London: Routledge, 2008.

Barnaby, D. (ed.) *Letters to Mr Tegetmeier: from J. Cossar Ewart and Others to the Editor of the Field at the Turn of the Nineteenth Century*, Timperley: ZSGM Publications, 2004.

Baxter, B. and Blaxter, D. *The Complete Mastiff*, Letchworth: Ringpress, 1993.

Bowler, P.J. *Evolution: The History of an Idea*, Berkeley CA: University of California Press 1988.

Brandow, M. *A Matter of Breeding: A Biting History of Pedigree Dogs and How the Quest for Status Has Harmed Man's Best Friend*. Boston: Beacon Press, 2015.

Briggs, H.M. and Briggs, D.M. *Modern Breeds of Livestock*, fourth edition, London: Macmillan, 1980.

Burkhardt, R.W. 'Closing the door on Lord Morton's mare: the rise and fall of telegony', *Studies in the History of Biology*, 3 (1979): 1–21.

Carlson, M. 'Ibsen, Strindberg, and telegony', *PMLA* 100, 5 (1985): 774–782.

Cassidy, R. *The Sport of Kings: Kinship, Class and Thoroughbred Breeding in Newmarket*, Cambridge: Cambridge University Press, 2002.

Charnley, B. 'Agricultural science, plant breeding and the emergence of a Mendelian system in Britain, 1880–1930', PhD thesis, University of Leeds, 2011.

Chivers, K. *The Shire Horse: A History of the Breed, the Society and the Men*, London: J.A. Allen, 1976.

Clapperton, J. 'Maternal impressions', *British Medical Journal* 1, 736 (1875): 169–170.

Clutton-Brock, J. *A Natural History of Domesticated Mammals*, London: Natural History Museum, 1999.

Cope, Z. *The Versatile Victorian: Being the Life of Sir Henry Thompson Bt. 1820–1904*, London: Harvey and Blythe, 1951.

Cunningham, E.P., Dooley, J. J., Splan, R.K., and Bradley, D.G. 'Microsatellite diversity, pedigree relatedness and the contributions of founder lineages to thoroughbred horses', *Animal Genetics*, 32, 6 (2001): 360–364.

Curry, H. *Evolution Made to Order: Plant Breeding and Technological Innovation in Twentieth-Century America*, Chicago IL: University of Chicago Press, 2016.

Dalziel, H. *British Dogs, their Varieties, History, Characteristics, Breeding, Management and Exhibition*, London: 'The Bazaar Office', 1879.

Darwin, C. *The Variation of Animals and Plants under Domestication*, London: John Murray, 1868.

Davidson, J. *Breeding: A Partial History of the Eighteenth Century*, New York: Columbia University Press, 2009, 2.

Derry, M.E. *Bred for Perfection: Shorthorn Cattle, Collies, and Arabian Horses since 1800*, Baltimore MD: Johns Hopkins University Press, 2003.

Derry, M.E. *Horses in Society: A Story of Animal Breeding and Marketing Culture, 1800–1920*, Toronto: University of Toronto Press, 2006.

Derry, M.E. *Art and Science in Breeding: Creating Better Chickens*, Toronto: University of Toronto Press, 2014.

Derry, M.E. *Masterminding Nature: The Breeding of Animals, 1750–2010*, Toronto: University of Toronto Press, 2015.

Drury, W.D. *British Dogs: Their Points, Selection, and Show Preparation*. London: L. Upcott Gill, 1903, 315.

Endersby, J. *A Guinea Pig's History of Biology*, London: Random House, 2007.

Ewart, J.C. *The Penycuik Experiments*, London: A. & C. Black, 1899.

F.H.A.M. 'James Cossar Ewart. 1851–1933', *Obituary Notices of Fellows of the Royal Society* 1, 3 (1934): 189–195.

Fisher, D.R. 'Sebright, Sir John Saunders, seventh baronet (1767–1846)', in *Oxford Dictionary of National Biography*, Oxford: Oxford University Press, 2004.

Galton, F. 'Hereditary character and talent', *MacMillan's Magazine*, 2 (1864): 157–166, 165–166.

Garcia-Sancho, M. 'Animal breeding in the age of biotechnology: the investigative pathway behind the cloning of Dolly the sheep', *History and Philosophy of the Life Sciences*, 37, 3 (2015): 282–304.

General Stud Book Containing Pedigrees of English Race Horses, &c. &c. from the Earliest Accounts to the Year 1840, London: Charles and James Watherby, 1840.

Getachew, T. 'A review of artificial insemination in poultry', *World's Veterinary Journal*, 2016, 6, 1 (2016), 25–33.

Girton, D. *The New and Complete Pigeon Fancier*, London: Alexander Hogg, 1790.

Hall, J.G. and Clutton-Brock, J. *Two Hundred Years of British Livestock Farming*, London: Natural History Museum, 1989.

Harwood, J. *Europe's Green Revolution and its Successors: The Rise and Fall of Peasant-Friendly Plant Breeding*, Abingdon: Routledge, 2012.

Harwood, J. 'Did Mendelism transform plant breeding? Genetic theory and breeding practice, 1900–1945', in D. Phillips and S. Kingsland (eds.), *New Perspectives on the History of Life Sciences and Agriculture*, Cham, Switzerland: Springer, 2015, 40, 345–370.

Hudson, N. 'From "nation" to "race": the origin of racial classification in eighteenth-century thought', *Eighteenth-Century Studies* 29, 3 (1996): 247–264.

Humphreys, J. 'Bakewell, Robert (1725–1795)', in revised G.E. Mingay (ed.), *Oxford Dictionary of National Biography*, Oxford: Oxford University Press, 2004.

Jersey Cattle: Their Feeding and Management, London: Vinton & Co, 1898, 8.

Kern, S. *A Cultural History of Causality: Science, Murder Novels, and Systems of Thought*, Princeton NJ: Princeton University Press, 2004.

Landry, D. *Noble Brutes: How Eastern Horses Transformed English Culture*, Baltimore MD: Johns Hopkins University Press, 2009.

Lee, R.J. 'Maternal impressions', *British Medical Journal* 1, 736 (1875): 167–169.

Lehleiter, C. *Romanticism, Origins, and the History of Heredity*, Lanham MA: Bucknell University Press, 2014, 67–68.

Lewinsohn, R. *A History of Sexual Customs*, London: Longman Green, 1958.

Lyell, J.C. *Fancy Pigeons*, London: 'The Bazaar Office', 1881, 30.

MacDonald, J. and Sinclair, J. *History of Hereford Cattle*, London: Vinton & Company, 1909.

MacDonald, J. and Sinclair, J. *History of Aberdeen-Angus Cattle*, London: Vinton & Company, 1910.

Moore-Colyer, R.J. 'Sheep', G.E. Mingay (ed.), *The Agrarian History of England and Wales*, Volume 6, Cambridge: Cambridge University Press, 1989, 315–316, 338–343.

Morton, E.O. 'A communication of a singular fact in natural history', *Philosophical Transactions of the Royal Society of London* 111 (1821): 20–22.

Olby, R.C. *Origins of Mendelism*, Chicago IL: University of Chicago Press, 1985.

Orel, V. and Wood, R.J. 'Scientific animal breeding in Moravia before and after the rediscovery of Mendel's theory', *Quarterly Review of Biology*, 75, 2 (2000): 149–157.

Palladino, P. 'Wizards and devotees: on the Mendelian theory of inheritance and the professionalization of agricultural science in Great Britain and the United States, 1880–1930', *History of Science* 32, 4 (1994): 409–444.

Pickstone, J. *Ways of Knowing: A New History of Science, Technology and Medicine*, Manchester: Manchester University Press, 2000.

Ritvo, H. 'The animal connection', in J.J. Sheehan and M. Sosna (eds.), *The Boundaries of Humanity: Humans, Animals, Machines*, Berkeley CA: University of California Press, 1991, 76–80.

Ritvo, H. *The Platypus and the Mermaid*, Cambridge MA: Harvard University Press, 1997.
Russell, N. *Like Engend'ring Like: Heredity and Animal Breeding in Early Modern England*, Cambridge: Cambridge University Press, 1986.
Ryder, M.L. 'The history of sheep breeds in Britain', *Agricultural History Review* 12, 1 (1964): 1–12.
Ryder, M.L. 'The history of sheep breeds in Britain (*continued*)', *Agricultural History Review* 12, 2 (1964): 65–82.
Ryder, M.L. 'A survey of European primitive breeds of sheep', *Annales de Génétique et de Sélection Animale* 13, 4 (1981): 381–418.
Sebright, J. *The Art of Improving the Breeds of Domestic Animals*, London: John Harding, 1809.
Secord, J.A. 'Nature's fancy: Charles Darwin and the breeding of pigeons', *Isis* 72, 2 (1981): 162–186.
Sengoopta, C. *Otto Weininger: Sex, Science, and Self in Imperial Vienna*, Chicago IL: Chicago University Press.
Shaw, V. *The Illustrated Book of the Dog*, London: Cassel, Petter, Galpin & Co., 1881.
Shepard, H.G. *One Hundred Years of the Royal Jersey Agricultural and Horticultural Society 1833–1933*, Jersey: J.T. Bigwood, 1934.
Sinclair, J. *History of Shorthorn Cattle*, London: Vinton & Company, 1907.
Stonehenge, *The Dog*, London: Longman, Green, Longman, and Roberts, 1859.
Stonehenge, *Dogs of the British Islands*, London: Horace Cox, 1867.
Stonehenge, *The Dog*, third edition, London: Longmans, Green, 1879.
Tegetmeier, W.B. *The Poultry Book: Comprising the Breeding and Management of Profitable and Ornamental Poultry*, London: George Routledge and Sons, 1867.
Tegetmeier, W.B. and Boulton, W.W. *Breeding for Colour and the Physiology of Breeding*, privately printed, 1874.
Tegetmeier, W.B. *Poultry for the Table and Market versus Fancy Fowls*, London: Horace Cox, 1892.
Tegetmeier, W.B. *Horses, Asses, Zebras, Mules and Mule Breeding*, London: Horace Cox, 1895.
Theunissen, B. 'Breeding without Mendelism: theory and practice of dairy cattle breeding in the Netherlands 1900–1950', *Journal of the History of Biology* 41, 4 (2008): 637–676.
Theunissen, B. 'Breeding for nobility or for production? Cultures of dairy cattle breeding in the Netherlands, 1945–1995', *Isis* 103, 2 (2012): 278–309.
Theunissen, B. 'Darwin and his pigeons: the analogy between artificial and natural selection revisited', *Journal of the History of Biology* 45, 2 (2012): 179–212.
Trow-Smith, R. *A History of British Livestock Husbandry to 1700*, London: Routledge and Kegan Paul, 1957.
Wallen, M. 'Foxhounds, curs, and the dawn of breeding: the discourse of modern human–canine relations', *Cultural Critique* 79, 1 (2011): 125–151.
Walton, J.R. 'Pedigree and the national cattle herd, c. 1750–1950', *Agricultural History Review* 34, 2 (1986): 149–170.
Walton, J.R. 'Pedigree and productivity in the British and North American cattle kingdoms before 1930', *Journal of Historical Geography* 25, 4 (1999): 441–462.
Weismann, A. *Germ-plasm: A Theory of Heredity*, London: Walter Scott Ltd, 1893.
White, S. 'From globalized pig breeds to capitalist pigs: a study in animal cultures and evolutionary history', *Environmental History*, 16, 1 (2011): 94–120.
Wood, R.J. 'The sheep breeders' view of heredity (1723–1843)', in H-J. Rheinberger and S. Müller-Wille (eds.), *A Cultural History of Heredity, Volume II, 18th and 19th Centuries*, Chicago IL: University of Chicago Press, 2007, 21–46.
Wood, R.J. and Orel, V. *Genetic Prehistory in Selective Breeding: A Prelude to Mendel*, Oxford: Oxford University Press, 2001.

Worboys, M. Strange, J-M. and Pemberton, N. *The Invention of the Modern Dog: Breed and Blood in Victorian Britain*, Baltimore MD: Johns Hopkins University Press, 2018.

Wright, L. *The Illustrated Book of Poultry*, London: Cassell, Petter & Galpin, 1898.

Wykes, D.L. 'Robert Bakewell (1725–95) of Dishley: farmer and livestock improver, *Agricultural History Review*, 52, 1 (2004): 38–55.

Youatt, W. *Cattle: Their Breeds, Management and Diseases*, London: Society for the Diffusion of Useful Knowledge, 1834.

Youatt, W. *The Dog*, London: Society for the Diffusion of Useful Knowledge, 1845.

18

ANIMALS IN AND AT WAR

Gervase Phillips

Introduction: what might historians of war learn from Homer?

Standing aside from the fray, Achilles' steeds wept,
as they had since they realised their charioteer
had been hurled to the dust at Hector's murderous hands.
Automedon, strong son of Diores, lashed them
again and again with the whirling whip,
sometimes coaxing them softly, or else swearing threats.
But they refused to return to Helle's strand
and the ships, or to follow the Achaeans into battle.
Standing stock-still, like a monument over the tomb
of a lord or lady, they held their place beside the matchless chariot,
arching their heads to the ground, whilst their mourning tears fell,
longing for the driver who would never return.
                    Homer The Iliad, XVII, ff 426[1]

Thus, as Achilles raged over the death of Patroclus before the gates of Troy, his horses grieved for their slain charioteer. That these horses should mourn so and, even under the lash, refuse in their grief to return to the fray, might strike historians of war as a simple poetic conceit. It would be uncomfortable for them, perhaps, to acknowledge here that the poet might have got closer than they to an idea that many biologists and ethologists now hold true: *animals experience conscious and richly emotional lives*. In 1637 the French philosopher René Descartes confidently asserted that '[animals] have no reason at all . . . it is nature which acts in them according to the disposition of their organs, just as a clock, which is only composed of weights and wheels is able to tell the hours and measure the time . . .'[2] He was wrong. Animals are not mere beast-machines, automatons without mind or agency beyond the unconscious dictates of instinct. They think and feel. They have characters, preferences and they exercise choice, through which they shape events unfolding around them. This makes their mental world, their physical experiences and their relationships with people proper subjects for historical inquiry, not merely as objects of human dominion but as agents of historical processes in their own right. We cannot now ignore the animal. History wilfully shorn of its animal actors is a pusillanimous endeavour; as the medievalist Mark Gregory Pegg has reminded us, 'past worlds (and all their messiness, grandeur, and cruelty) can be understood only if evoked as fully as possible. No half measures, no middies'.[3] This imperative might be particularly strong for historians of war, for without acknowledging the presence and the suffering of animals is any account of war really complete?

The significance of animals to the conduct of war: an overview

Yet even the simple questions of the *extent* and the *significance* of animal involvement in war has not always been appreciated by historians. For most European and Asian polities up until the middle of the twentieth century, the ability to wage war successfully was dependent upon access to an adequate supply of animals either as mounts or for draught purposes. This was especially true for societies whose military prowess was based upon fielding cavalry armies. Consider, for example, the fate of the great nomadic empires: so expansive, so militarily powerful and so short-lived. Rudi Paul Lindner has argued that the Huns, once they had moved out of the rich grassland environment of the Steppes and settled west of the Carpathians around 410 CE, could no longer feed their massive herds of horses. Military defeat followed soon after. A similar fate, Linder suggests, befell the Avars, the Hungarians, the Mongols, and the Ottomans, none of whom could carry their horse-borne campaigns of conquest further west than the Carpathians. Thus was Europe's destiny decided by a question of horse fodder.[4]

Such questions have not, however, only affected the cavalry armies of nomadic peoples but also of more settled polities. The effectiveness of medieval armies was ultimately determined by both access to a good supply of horses and by the ability to care for them on campaign. For his successful invasion of England in 1066, William Duke of Normandy had to convey between 2,000 and 3,000 horses across the channel.[5] Similarly, Simon Digby has argued that the Muslim invaders who established the Delhi Sultanate in India in the thirteenth century owed their battlefield successes over far larger Hindu armies to their efficient supply of war horses and elephants. He goes on to suggest that it was a sharp decline in the supply of war-elephants beginning in the late fourteenth century that ultimately signalled the Sultanate's eclipse.[6] During the British civil wars of 1639–1651, horse supply remained a vital determinate of victory or defeat. Both Royalist and Parliamentary commanders were preoccupied by the pressing need to secure enough animals, for the war's appetite for horseflesh was prodigious. At Oxford in May 1643 it was recorded that 144 horses were required to move just 20 pieces of the king's artillery.[7] Remounts for the cavalry were equally important. Infantry formations of pike and shot were, numerically, the most significant elements of seventeenth-century European armies; the proportion of foot soldiers to horsemen was typically between two and five to one. Yet armies that lacked that mounted component courted disaster. Irish Confederate forces could, at best, field one mounted trooper for every ten infantrymen. With the exception of their victory at Benburb (1646), they were defeated in every set-piece engagement they fought because 'enemy cavalry succeeded in breaking up their infantry formations'.[8]

The lesson was clear. As Charles V, Duke of Lorraine, one of the most successful generals of the seventeenth century, asserted: 'there is not an Enterprise of Hazard and Difficulty where the Horse is not concerned; by their means Designs are compassed, facilitated, and expedited'.[9] The invention of rail and steam did not change that lesson either; the question of horse supply would prove decisive during the American Civil War (1861–1865). The rival armies struggled both to procure sufficient remounts and draught animals and to keep alive those they had in service. Perhaps a million horses and mules succumbed to exhaustion, overloading, malnutrition, disease and injury during the conflict. As Charles Ramsdell demonstrated, for the southern Confederacy the horse supply crisis ultimately became existential. The great horse-breeding regions of the upper south, Kentucky, Missouri, much of Tennessee and trans-Allegheny Virginia, were under Federal control by mid-1862, cutting off the South's supply of remounts. General Robert E. Lee, commander of the Army of Northern Virginia, had to pace the tempo of his campaigns according to the condition of his poorly maintained, malnourished and overburdened horses and mules. Yet the challenges facing his mounted units were crippling, in some cases quite literally: in July 1864, Brigadier-General Gideon Pillow noted one cavalry brigade that needed 1,600 horseshoes, 'very many of the horses' feet being worn to the quick and utterly unable to travel'.[10] By the autumn of that year, Lee had no choice but to fight a static war in the trenches around Petersburg. When his foot-sore human soldiers attempted to extricate themselves from the siege lines, they were intercepted by Union General Philip Sheridan's Cavalry Corps and trapped at Appomattox.[11]

The particular significance of the horse to the conduct of war is well illustrated by considering the impact of its introduction into regions where it had hitherto been rare or unknown. In sub-Saharan Africa, climatic conditions and disease were long obstacles to both breeding and maintaining sizeable stocks of horses. Before the fifteenth century only a relatively small number (hardy little ponies for the most part) were present, in regions such as Dongola in the modern Sudan. It was only in the late medieval period that Islamic imperialism, and its consequent fuelling of the trans-Saharan slave trade, introduced larger breeds, more sophisticated tack and knowledge of caring for horses in challenging environments. This, in turn, allowed for the creation of cavalry armies that established a military dominance on the savannah, catalysing the growth of new politically centralised empires, such as Mali. L.A. Webb, for example, wrote of a 'cavalry revolution' in fifteenth-century Senegambia in which the horse and slave trades became intertwined in the 'desert-edge political economy'. States such as Mali sent their horse-mobile armies raiding widely for slaves, who were then traded across the Sahara in return for high-quality North African horses. Yet, well into the twentieth century, environmental factors always checked the growth of herds south of the Sahara and attempts to maintain a large national stock may have become so prohibitively expensive that in some instances they actually hindered state formation. Robin Law noted, for example, that even in the Oyo Empire, which boasted a large cavalry arm by the sixteenth century, the cost of importing and maintaining the national herd proved such a burden that it probably retarded the development of a strong, central authority.[12]

Given that the stakes for societies at war have proved so high it should come as no surprise that the requirements of breeding and maintaining key livestock herds (principally horses but also, in Africa and Asia, elephants and camels) have thus shaped national economies, fostered the growth of bureaucracies and administrative structures (catalysing the development of central governments) and determined individual status within rigidly stratified social hierarchies.[13] Nor should it be assumed that this strong relationship between the mobilisation of animals for war and the shaping of political, economic and socio-cultural destinies was principally a feature of the pre-modern world. It had just as much effect upon the industrialised and urbanised societies of the late nineteenth and twentieth centuries. The industrial revolution, the growth of cities and the transformation of everyday lives by mechanical means were all accompanied by a significant increase in the number of animals upon which societies and economies relied.[14] The same appetite for horsepower exhibited by industrial economies and manufacturing cities was evident in the demands of modern, so-called 'machine-age', warfare too.

Indeed, the number of animals mobilised for military purposes reached its peak in the first half of the twentieth century. In November 1918, at the close of the First World War, the British Empire counted 791,696 draught and riding animals with its armies in all theatres: 510,000 horses; 225,311 mules; 36,834 camels; 8,425 bullocks; 11,028 donkeys and 100,000 carrier pigeons (not to mention gas-detecting canaries and messenger and sentry dogs, whose precise numbers were not recorded).[15] And, notwithstanding interwar 'mechanisation', the Second World War actually saw a yet greater mobilisation of animals. R.L. DiNardo has noted that 'the basic means of transport in the German army was well-known to Alexander, Hannibal, Caesar, Gustavus, Marlborough, Frederick and Napoleon: namely, the horse'. When Hitler's forces invaded the Soviet Union in June 1941 during Operation Barbarossa, they were logistically dependent upon the 750,000 horses that hauled the artillery, supply wagons, field kitchens and ambulances that accompanied them. As the scale of the war grew, so did their demand for beasts of burden. By early 1945, the *Wehrmacht* deployed some 1,198,724 horses (a further 1,500,000 had, by then, died in their service).[16]

Alongside the mobilisation of draught animals, the number of cavalry units deployed in combat also increased over the course of the conflict. In September 1939, the German army counted just 18 cavalry regiments in its order of battle (each with an authorised strength of 1,440 troopers). Yet over the course of the next six years the Third Reich expanded its mounted arm and ultimately deployed no less than eight full cavalry divisions, each with a nominal strength of 11,000–15,000 troopers (only one of these, the 1st Cavalry Division, was mechanised, becoming the 24th Panzer Division in late 1941).[17] The German cavalry arm was, however, dwarfed by its Soviet counterpart. Over the course of the war the Red Army deployed as many as 50 cavalry divisions. Horse-mounted units proved able to traverse terrain impassable to other arms, such as the Pripet marshes, and were capable of operating in environmental conditions, such as deep snow or mud, that would render motor vehicles immobile. During the strategically defensive battles of 1941–42, Soviet cavalry frequently took the tactical offensive, passing through weakly held sectors of the German front line and striking deep into enemy-occupied territory. Lieutenant

General Pavel Belov's 1st Guard Cavalry Corps spent the period 20 December 1941 to 26 June 1942 severing lines of communication, overrunning depots and command centres and activating partisan units in the German rear while 'self-provisioning' off the land. Seven German divisions, including Panzer and motorised formations, failed to run him to ground.[18]

Only after World War II was it feasible for most militaries even to contemplate waging war without animals. The Soviets considered both the threats posed by nuclear weapons and a possible contest with NATO armoured forces on a densely held and relatively narrow central European front and concluded that there were unlikely to be any future opportunities for a latter-day Pavel Belov. They finally demobilised their cavalry formations at around the same time as the US army retired its last draught mules in 1956.[19] Yet, although animals were no longer a *sine qua non* of waging war, in areas with poorly developed infrastructures, where difficult terrain prevented the use of motorised transport and armoured vehicles, they continued to be deployed. In the final and most bitterly contested stages of the Greek Civil War (1946–49), the Greek National Army attacked communist forces in their mountain strongholds. There, the 4,000 mules that bore their munitions, rations and pack artillery and evacuated their wounded proved to be of far more use than the 8,000 trucks supplied by the US government. Horse-mobile units have been widely used in other post-war counter-insurgencies and the wars of decolonisation, including by the French in Algeria (1956–62), the Portuguese in Angola and Mozambique (1966–74) and the South Africans in South West Africa (1978–89). The British army continued to employ camels, particularly for the transportation of radio equipment, in Arabia into the mid-1960s. Similarly the elephant, exploited for military purposes for over 3,000 years, remained on active duty in jungle warfare in the Indochina and Vietnam wars (1946–1975), where they helped supply insurgents of the National Liberation Front and soldiers of the Vietnam People's Army fighting in South Vietnam.[20]

From 'drums and trumpets' to suffering and trauma: animals and the historiography of war

It would not have been possible to write even this, of necessity brief and selective, account of animals and warfare had not authors such as Robin Law, Simon Digby, R.L. DiNardo and Charles Ramsdell placed animals at the heart of their research. It is less clear, however, that historians of warfare more broadly have taken sufficient note of their studies. After all, military historians do not have a reputation for being especially 'inclusive' in their methodology. Their choice of topic area, often dismissed as 'drums and trumpets' history, has not been one held in high regard by colleagues working in other fields. As John A. Lynn, a superb scholar of early modern France and its armies, observed,

> military history has never been a popular specialty among academics; on the contrary, it has always been something of a pariah in U.S. universities. We used to be condemned because we were believed to be politically right-wing, morally corrupt, or just plain dumb ...[21]

Yet this attitude was never wholly fair. Indeed, long before the 'new social history' of the 1960s opened the eyes of most scholars to the necessity of recovering the experiences of the historically voiceless, some military historians had already placed ordinary combatants front and centre in their work. It is a tradition that those seeking to integrate animals into their work might usefully invoke. In the interwar years, for example, Ella Lonn and Bessie Martin had explored the subject of desertion by soldiers during the American Civil War, revealing both its scale and its underpinning motivations. They dismissed the assumption that desertion was a simple matter of cowardice. They demonstrated that deserters were often making a purposeful and politically informed choice. In the case of former Confederates, they chose to succour their starving families rather than fight on to protect the right of wealthy planters to hold slaves. Furthermore, although they were but common soldiers, deserters made a difference to the outcome of the war. For the South, mass desertion was ultimately a significant contributory factor in Confederate defeat.[22] In short, Lonn and Martin had illustrated how deserters demonstrated what later generations of historians would characterise as 'agency'. This can be defined as the ability of historical actors to act independently, regardless of the structural constraints (such as class) of the society in which they lived, and their consequent capacity to shape the outcome of events unfolding around them.

There was more such work to come. In the aftermath of World War II, and drawing on contemporary psychological studies of combat veterans, Bell Irvin Wiley published two volumes in which he recreated the physical and ideological worlds of 'Johnny Reb' and 'Billy Yank', the common soldiers of North and South during the American Civil War.[23] Like Lonn and Martin before him, Wiley can thus be seen as foreshadowing many of the concerns of 'the new social history' that transformed the wider discipline in the 1960s and 1970s by focussing attention on the lives and agency of women, the poor, the enslaved and the colonised. Yet Wiley, Lonn and Martin had all benefitted from the wealth of first-hand testimony, diaries, letters and autobiographical accounts that Civil War soldiers had left to posterity. The 'new social historians' were, in many instances, seeking to recover the mentalities of the illiterate and the disempowered, who had left no such direct testimony. To meet this problem of sources, historians borrowed theoretical approaches from other disciplines, notably the social sciences; they reconstructed inner intentions and attitudes from actions and behaviours and they read the documentary records produced by the powerful closely and critically enough to recover the voices of the dispossessed reflected therein, 'muffled but not mute', as one able practitioner, Gunja SenGupta, has commented.[24]

There were academic military historians who took note of these developments. John Keegan's study of the battles of Agincourt, Waterloo and the Somme from the perspective of the weary, frightened, blood-spattered men who fought them, is often seen as a seminal work but the trend was driven by more than one scholar.[25] In France, for example, André Corvisier pioneered a sociological approach to the study of European militaries, his work serving as an exemplar of what was sometimes termed 'the new military history' or the 'war and society' school.[26] There was however an important distinction; while historians such as Keegan put the experience of combat at the heart of their work, the 'new military historians', while lavishing attention on such topics as recruitment, conditions of service, officer–man relations and the role of the military in state formation, ignored battle altogether. A broader synthesis would emerge. The most highly regarded academic military history written from the late 1970s onwards tended to combine an emphasis on the social structures of armed services, and the motivation and experiences of combatants alongside the traditional fare of military history: studies of campaigns and leadership, logistics, weapons and tactics. The best examples of such work began to devote appropriate attention to the animal component of armies. Rhoads Murphey's study of early modern Ottoman warfare offered a forensic discussion of troop movement, transport and the provisioning of armies on campaign. This included consideration of the nutritional requirements of draught animals, of their load capacities and of the economics of their hire or purchase. Similarly Jos Gommans explored how war horses, elephants, dromedaries and oxen allowed the Mughal army to function as 'a well-lubricated moving capital, smoothly facilitated by a huge network of enterprising hauliers and bankers, and integrating the empire on its way'.[27]

Animals are thus finding their place in military history. Yet they largely figure as passive objects of human dominion. The historiographical tradition forged by Lonn, Martin, Wiley and Keegan, of foregrounding the lived experience and agency of common soldiers in accounts of war, has only tentatively begun to explore the possibility of embracing the animal experience as well. Methodologically, as Sandra Swart has observed in her seminal study of horses during the Second South African War, the tools of writing such history have now been well-established by the 'new social history' for, as has been noted, this 'offered ways of discussing the oppressed and the silenced, a category that surely now we must acknowledge includes animals'.[28] By drawing on ethology to understand animal behaviour and the sensory world they inhabit, by interpreting volition and intentionality through animal action and by critical reading of 'elite' (in this case human) testimony, historians of war may also hear the 'voice' of animals, 'muffled but not mute'. A compelling incentive to attempt this approach has arisen from the recent trend to meet head-on the charge that historians of war sanitise their subject matter. Joanna Bourke, for instance, has suggested that military commentators have traditionally 'glossed over' or even 'denied' that 'human slaughter was at the heart of military strategy and practice'. Thus, some scholars have chosen now to foreground the emotional, physical and psychological costs of war (loss, trauma, pain, suffering, killing and mutilation) in their studies.[29] Yet those costs have not been confined to humans; animals have suffered in conflicts too.

'Mutinous dogs'? Animals, agency and emotion

The evidence is not hard to find. In some instances, compassion has moved soldiers to record the plight of animals in war. 'Poor brutes!' wrote Charles Francis Adams, Jr to his mother in 1863 during the American Civil War, of the suffering horses in his federal cavalry regiment,

> ...with withers swollen to three times their natural size [and] volcanic running sores pouring matter down each side ... How it would astonish and terrify you and all others at home with your sleek well-fed animals, to see the weak,

gaunt, rough animals, with each rib visible and the hip-bones starting through the flesh, on which these 'dashing cavalry raids' were executed. It would knock the romance out of you.[30]

One may infer much, too, about equine suffering from the bureaucratic record-keeping of modern militaries, as in this response to a questionnaire issued to remount British officers during the Second South African War, December 1900:

> It is absolutely impossible to water and feed the animals in the South African cattle trucks without detraining them. This is only possible once every twelve hours ... The uncertainty of the traffic caused by continued breakages of the line has often resulted in horses being left longer than twelve hours without water...[31]

It should be acknowledged that, as with human soldiers, such ill-treatment might well provoke a response: recalcitrance, lack of co-operation, even violence. Through recourse to such behaviours, animals could actually influence their treatment. During the Second World War, John Eslick was responsible for training both sled dogs and their drivers for the Arctic search and rescue units that retrieved crashed airmen in environmental conditions that defied any other form of transport. Eslick gave his new human recruits a very clear directive on their arrival: 'Don't ever take the whip out of its bag with my dogs ... my dogs don't work with a whip'. Yet some always ignored him. After one set out on his first night run, Eslick remained at the camp. After a quarter of an hour, the team returned, minus their driver. Eslick recalled, 'here comes Nunako [the lead dog], bells ringing, he's just as happy as could be, he looked like he was smiling ... [the]sled was over, everything on it was lost off'. Eslick ordered the team to lie down, righted the sled and waited;

> in a few minutes the recruit trotted up, panting for breath, and admitted popping the whip just once, where-upon the lead dog had turned the team around and headed for home, overturning the sled and spilling the driver as he went.

This neatly executed canine mutiny had taught the recruit the lesson he had failed to heed from his human instructor.[32]

Animal agency was not only apparent in resistance but also in co-operation. Historical sources frequently yield valuable observations of animal behaviours that are powerfully suggestive of how they understood the tasks that were required of them, related them to past experiences and made appropriate, autonomous decisions accordingly. A British observer at the training establishment for Austrian 'kriegshunds' in 1893 noted that, under fire, the dogs learned to run 'zigzag' and 'develop a marvellous talent for taking advantage of every cover, running through high grass and using the safe side of roads and fallen trees'.[33] Similarly, H.S. Lloyd, a British military dog trainer of World War II, wrote of the tracker dogs he had worked with while pursuing escaped prisoners of war:

> it was interesting to see how frequently really well-trained experienced dogs would divert from the trail to explore any likely hiding place a fugitive

might make for and after investigation return to the line as though he had not checked at all.[34]

To talk of 'decision-making' by dogs tracking escaped POWs or of 'mutinous' sled dogs, is to openly acknowledge emotional states in animals akin to those in humans and to recognise their potential for agency. This might strike contemporary historians as a rather startling suggestion in a work of scholarship. Yet it is in many ways simply a revival of what was once conventional academic wisdom. A little over a century ago, the most respectable of scientists held and expressed such views quite freely. Charles Darwin asserted his belief that animals, alongside humankind, experienced joy and sorrow, dejection and excitement, fear, shame and pride. He viewed the emotions as evolved mechanisms which promoted positive social bonding, and thus reproductive success, in species that lived in groups. For Darwin, variations in the cognitive and emotional capacities between species were differences of degree but not of kind.[35] His beliefs were neither whimsy nor a reflection of Victorian sentimentality. They were based upon the same methodology of observation of animal and human physical and behavioural characteristics that had revealed the mechanism of evolution itself. He confidently asserted that 'there is no fundamental difference between man and the higher mammals in their mental faculties' before going on to note that 'the fact that lower animals are excited by the same emotions as ourselves is so well established, that it will not be necessary to weary the reader by many details'.[36]

Such enlightened attitudes survived into the twentieth century among many of those who worked with, and cared for, living animals. For example, Arthur Croxton Smith, a leading British authority on dog training and breeding, was always ready to ascribe emotional states such as 'happiness' to his charges.[37] Similarly Lieutenant-General F. Fitzwygram, author of a highly technical study of horses and stabling, confidently asserted

> that the higher class of animals suffer from pain quite acutely as man is, I think, quite susceptible of proof. That their diseases are much the same, assume the same types, and require the same treatment as those of man, is known to every Veterinarian ... We believe the pain to be the same. We can hardly doubt but that the desire of the animal to get well is the same as in man.[38]

Yet all too often, the generations of scientists who followed Darwin were of a more sceptical cast of mind. Darwin's pioneering work on evolution they embraced; his belief in animals' capacity for joy and sorrow they disdained. The writhing, howling animal on the vivisectionist's table may have seemed to be experiencing a state analogous to human suffering but this could not be proved and could thus be dismissed as unscientific and sentimental anthropomorphism. Writing in the 1970s, the experimental psychologist Robert Lubow once offered his readers an apologetic explanation for using the phrase 'eager expectation' in reference to the behaviour of a dog he had been training for military service in Vietnam; he only used the phrase as 'a simple shorthand to describe the fact that typically the dog will salivate profusely [while waiting to be fed]'. Normally, he reassured his audience, 'such phrases have no place in the vocabulary of a behaviourist' for 'they attribute to the animal a feeling derived from the experiences of humans. There is no possible way to determine whether the animal is indeed experiencing this feeling'. And thus the mere possibility that they do experience such feelings could apparently be safely disregarded. For Lubow, Darwin's argument from analogy with humans concerning animal emotions was 'a pathetic fallacy . . . Does an angry cloud feel anything, let alone share a feeling with its human observer. Of course not'.[39]

Yet this view itself was a 'pathetic fallacy', a straw man if ever there was one. Clouds have not evolved central nervous systems and one has never been observed to howl, writhe, or even 'salivate profusely' while being experimented upon. And, of course, there is now very powerful evidence from neuroscience and biology that we *can* determine that animals experience feelings analogous to those experienced by humans, just as Darwin asserted. Much of the architecture of the mammalian brain and the neurochemicals that we know are associated with emotions are shared between humans, closely related primates, dogs and other species. Some older (from an evolutionary perspective) brain structures, such as the limbic systems and the amygdale, that we also know are important in shaping emotional responses, are shared across an even greater range of living creatures (including humans, whose brains, and consequently characters, have their reptilian features). And we are achieving yet more revealing insights into how these biological structures function with regard to emotions. For example, that special class of brain cells known as mirror neurons 'that fire when an animal [or a human] sees or hears an action and when the animal carries out the same action on its own' appear to be the key to understanding cognitive empathy and indicate that other animals besides humans may have (to some degree) a theory of mind.[40]

Such knowledge *ought* to have some effect upon how historians write about animals. Perhaps we should take what we might term a neo-Darwinist approach and be confident in attributing consciousness and emotional states to the animals we write about, to draw comfortably on analogies with human behaviour and on what we now know about the complex cognitive capabilities of animals, to offer not only a greater, more complete account of the past but a more empathic and compassionate one too.

Human and dog in war: a case study in co-belligerency

Writing animals into the history of warfare thus demands a careful balance between demonstrating *how* they were deployed and attempting to, as Sandra Swart puts it, 'engage with their lives', as conscious and emotional beings, whose joys and suffering should be of concern. Let us consider what such a history might look like by considering the history of the dog in war.

The antiquity of the relationship between humans and dogs is well appreciated but its origins are mysterious. Traditionally, and predictably, historians and pre-historians have assumed that humans were the principal actors in the story of domestication. They had, it was supposed, tamed wild canids (perhaps picking up an orphaned wolf cub from a litter) and, over successive generations of selective breeding, created a creature that was smaller and more biddable. This anthropocentric account is almost certainly too simplistic. Human predation may have produced enough surplus food to lead canids *to choose* proximity to their camps and hunting parties to facilitate scavenging. With their superior sense of smell, they may then have taken over the task of orienting the human/canid group in the environment and locating prey. This in turn might have allowed for selective changes in human facial (nasal and oral) structures for more skilled production of speech. In biological terms, the two species may thus have 'co-evolved'.[41]

War, too, was part of this story. Those hunter-gatherers who first made their lives alongside dogs also engaged in frequent organised conflict with rival groups of humans. The idea, once orthodoxy among anthropologists, that warfare was a comparatively recent 'invention' in human history, linked to the switch to agriculture and the rise of states, has now largely been abandoned.[42] The frequency and deadly earnestness with which hunter-gathers pursued organised conflict with their neighbours and rivals has been established by scholars such as Lawrence Keeley, Steven LeBlanc, Jean Guilane and Jean Zammit. Indeed some anthropologists and primatologists, strongly influenced by evolutionary psychology and the putative evidence for warfare among chimpanzees, conclude that bellicosity is inherent in our nature; we were warlike even before we were fully human.[43] The dog was, in all likelihood, a co-belligerent species from the very beginnings of her relationship with us. We lack, of course, unequivocal prehistoric testimony on this point. Yet it is a safe inference, for we know that modern hunter-gatherer, nomadic and semi-sedentary societies, highly mobile and unable to avail themselves of strong walls and often with livestock to defend from both human and animal predators, have depended upon their faithful dogs as sentries and guardians. John C. Ewers, an American ethnologist who spent 35 years studying the Native Americans of the Great Plains, recalled that two of his Blackfoot informants, who had participated in the endemic horse-stealing expeditions of the late nineteenth century, told him that they 'relied heavily upon their dogs to bark and wake them if enemy raiders entered the camp at night'.[44]

The partnership was never an equal one. Human dominance is manifested in how selective breeding has both profoundly altered the morphology of dogs and enhanced, or suppressed, particular behavioural characteristics. Thus dogs with very specialist skill sets took their place within human communities: trackers of scent who led hunters in pursuit of quarry; pointers who visually communicated the location of prey to humans; retrievers, to recover the bodies of slain prey. Others demonstrated their remarkable capacity for such complex tasks as herding and guarding sheep and cattle. The latter function requires a dog who is 'attentive, trustworthy and protective with its livestock' and, in transhumant communities, able to work unsupervised when necessary.[45]

Other, darker, behaviours may have been enhanced by selective breeding too. Some ancient and medieval sources suggest that dogs characterised by their aggression and ferocity accompanied human warriors into combat. The Greek historian Zonarus wrote that during the Roman colonisation of Sardinia (231 BCE) Marcus Pomponius had 'sent for keen-scented dogs' to track the elusive Sardinians and the herds upon which they depended.[46] For later periods, those suggestions give way more frequently to explicit testimony. The pioneering Bolognese naturalist Ulisse Aldrovandi (1522–1605) wrote of 'dogs that defend mankind in the course of private, and also public, conflicts . . .' who would 'be an enemy to everybody but his master; so much so that he will not allow himself to be stroked even by those who know him best'. Besides giving a strong indication of the very close personal ties of loyalty and affection that dogs developed with individual humans, Aldrovandi's evidence describes how canine bodyguards had to be trained to their duties, in much the same way as human soldiers are trained to theirs:

> accordingly some man or other is fitted out with a coat of thick skin, which the dogs will not be able to bite through, as a sort of dummy; the dog is then spurred upon this man, upon which the man in skins runs away and then allows himself to be caught and, falling on the ground in front of the dog to be bitten . . .[47]

The late medieval/early modern war dog was thus trained not simply to aggression in defence of a person or a place but to combine that ferocity with the eager pursuit and destruction of a fleeing, hiding, or even captured, enemy. Like the Romans before him in Sardinia, Jean de Bethancourt, who conquered the Canary Isles for Castile in 1402 CE, is alleged to have unleashed hunting dogs against the indigenous people, the Guanches. Alive to scent and acute of hearing, hunting dogs could detect their presence before they sprung ambushes and, thrilled by the pursuit, could track them as they fled. Combat thus took on the qualities of the chase and Bethancourt's soldiers 'took dogs with them as if they were going sporting down the island'.[48] The peculiar horror associated with this campaign, though, is the development of *aperrear*, in which hunting dogs did not merely track their victims but were deliberately set upon them. This abhorrent practice became a feature of the pacification of the Canaries over the course of the next hundred years. And it would travel to the New World in the ships of the *conquistadors*.[49]

The Dominican friar Bartolomé de Las Casas (1484–1566) was an outraged critic of the cruelties his compatriots inflicted upon Native Americans. He penned vivid descriptions of the use of dogs as instruments of warfare, torture and execution: 'the Spanish train their fierce dogs to attack, kill and tear to pieces the Indians'.[50] Notwithstanding de Las Casas's tireless efforts to shame his countrymen into abandoning such barbarities, they became a characteristic and recurrent feature of colonialism and racial warfare in the Americas. Historians such as John Campbell and Sara Johnson have graphically chronicled how these practices became instruments of the policing of both indigenous populations and of enslaved Africans, over the next three centuries. In the event of insurrection, or during assaults on isolated maroon colonies (communities of runaway slaves, established in inhospitable areas such as the highlands of Jamaica or the everglades of Florida), the bloodhound became a savage and effective instrument of white hegemony. The Cuban bloodhound, in particular, was widely exported to slave-holding regimes across the Americas and was employed by the French against rebellious slaves during the Haitian Revolution (1791–1803), by the British in the Second Maroon War in Jamaica (1795–1796) and by the Americans during the Second Seminole War in Florida (1835–1842).[51]

It was only the collapse of American regimes based upon racial slavery over the course of the nineteenth century that brought an end to this use of dogs in war. Yet modern militaries were even then beginning to take a renewed interest in the potential of dogs to meet a number of challenges they foresaw encountering on the battlefields of the industrial age. Some of the roles were traditional. The Russians made use of sentry dogs from the Crimean War (1853–1856) onwards; the French employed them in their colonial campaigns in Africa and Asia. In Germany, by the 1890s, dogs were also being used as messengers, addressing one of the fundamental problems of early twentieth-century warfare: how to maintain communications on the expanding battlefield, where infantry formations were dispersed and hidden from modern firepower. Continental armies were also experimenting with dogs for light draught work (such as hauling the new machine guns) and for locating the wounded. Although often officially encouraged, most of these developments were still rather unsystematic. In the French army, for example, in 1914, seven or eight infantry regiments mustered dogs but there was no properly organised training school.[52]

The First World War would change all that. By 1917, about 50,000 were serving with the German, French and British armies in the field. The commandant of the British War Dog School, Edwin H. Richardson, has left a full account of the service of military dogs during the conflict. Dogs could maintain battlefield communications in devastated terrain, under conditions of heavy fire and in poor weather that, together, would defeat modern communication technologies, human runners or carrier pigeons. In 1917, 'Keeper' (handler) Nicolson reported from the infamous Ypres Salient, 'the first time I sent [the dogs] forward Jim . . . did record time; the journey he did used to take a man one hour and 10 mins . . . and Jim did it in 22 mins, through barbed wire entanglements and a large number of batteries. . .' The dogs coped remarkably well with the worst that modern warfare could inflict upon them: 'the night before last we had a very nasty attack of gas and my dogs' helmets were not available, so they had to stand bare-faced and took no harm. I think they will stand much better than man'. Jim, a 3-year-old retriever-spaniel cross, regularly carried messages up to distances of four and a half miles, at 'three or four times the speed of a runner'. On many occasions the dogs were not merely the quickest means of communication, they were the only means of communication, and their presence thus saved lives: 'I may say that Swankie's bitch Creamy helped the 3rd Londoners from being cut off on the right of Villers Bretonneux', wrote Keeper Reid of fighting during the German Spring Offensive of 1918. 'She and Tweed kept the battalion in touch with Brigade Hdqtrs. There was no way of getting a message through only by runner or a dog and the dog kept the way open'.[53]

For Richardson, and for many of the keepers who served alongside these dogs in the field, their service was a reminder of their intelligence and adaptability and of the qualities they exhibited as distinct personalities. One messenger, a collie called Roman, struck those who served with him as 'a curious character, rather self-centred and fond of taking his time on the journey, but imbued with a strong understanding always of the absolute necessity of making his way homewards'. Richardson believed that such dogs had their own conception of 'duty', evident in their 'uneasiness at stopping at any point *en route*'. The dogs were also observed to learn independently from their experiences in combat. Keeper Taylor recorded watching one dog making a run: 'I could see that Major was actually dodging the shells. He took a wide sweep from where the first shell fell, and kept working out further'. And for some of the dogs, just as for human soldiers, the stress proved too much. 'Poor Maggie was shell-shocked,' lamented the keeper of one dog who had died near Hill 60 in the Ypres Salient in early 1918. While she had lived though, he noted, she had beaten the runner every time and never made a mistake.[54] This evidence for strong ties of comradeship between dog and handler should come as no surprise. Indeed, for Richardson, the correct relationship between the two was the key to their success: 'complete confidence and affection must exist between dogs and keeper, and the man whose only idea of control is by coercion and fear is quite useless'.[55]

The precise significance of this close affective relationship was demonstrated again during World War II when, in addition to their established duties, military dogs were committed to a new task: mine detection. How exactly, whether by olfactory stimuli, visual cues or some other means, dogs were able to detect mines was not wholly clear at the time and there were significant doubts about their reliability. Their handlers, though, displayed the highest levels of trust in them. As Henry Summers Lloyd, the chief trainer of the British War Dog School, commented

> mine detecting was a dual job, the handler having to use his expert knowledge in probing likely spots, but the dogs gave confidence to the men following on and helped to increase the speed at which the ground could be traversed.[56]

Yet post-war, there would still be a contentious debate about their abilities. It was a debate that, as Robert Kirk has demonstrated, did not concern the mere utility of dogs as a tool of war, but pointed emphatically to the significance of their subjective capacity for emotion and their agency as members of a collaborative mine-detection partnership.[57]

Kirk has drawn attention to two contrasting scientific investigations of mine-detector dogs that were undertaken after the war. One of these, beginning in 1951, was conducted by the British anatomist Solly Zuckerman. This was characteristic of contemporary behavioural science. Its principal researcher rejected anecdotal evidence and assumed that animals were merely flesh and blood automatons. The investigation was, thus, hamstrung from the beginning. For example, since for Zuckerman a mine-detector dog was essentially a tool, it should be reliable when issued to any handler as and when needed, in the same manner as a rifle or wireless set. Consequently, when worked with handlers they did not know, and who did not know them, the dogs proved unreliable in detecting mines. Zuckerman continued to insist that dogs could not be trusted as mine detectors as late as the Falklands War of 1982. (The British army itself had redeployed its mine dogs to troubled Palestine after World War II where they had again proved a success and thus it had maintained its military dog programme, notwithstanding the doubters).

The second scientific investigation was undertaken by an American parapsychologist, Joseph Rhine. With the question of how exactly dogs detected buried explosives still unanswered, Rhine was investigating the possibility that they employed some form of extrasensory perception. Conscious of the scepticism that such a hypothesis might invite, Rhine was particularly rigorous and methodical in his approach. He carefully controlled against the presence of tactile and visual clues to the location of mines and of the possibility of unconscious communication between dog and handler. Yet his fundamental assumptions were different from Zuckerman's. His emphasis on extrasensory perception, of necessity, assumed dogs to be 'knowing subjects' who existed in a world of emotion and of knowledge, memory and decision-making. Anthropomorphism was part of his methodology and he was therefore far more open to ethology and the observations of those who had worked with dogs than the British behaviourist. He concluded that dogs could detect mines reliably. For Rhine, the effective handler–dog team was a partnership based upon a strong affective bond between its individual members and a subjective shared understanding of their environment.[58] Soldiers already knew this. Writing of patrol dogs in World War II, Lloyd had noted that

> it quickly became apparent that the temperament of both man and dog must be studied and the combination made on this alone. Dogs who were utter failures with one type of handler were in the hands of another just as conspicuously successful.[59]

It was, in short, essentially a question of comradeship.

Yet if modern war forged bonds of comradeship between some canine and human soldiers, the human capacity for a callous disregard of faithful friends was grimly evident too. The most infamous example was the Soviets' use of dogs as anti-tank weapons. In the aftermath of the German invasion in 1941, the Red Army trained dogs to run under tanks with explosive charges strapped to their backs that would then detonate. According to some reports, the Russian army continued to train canines for this role until the mid-1990s.[60] Less well known is that the American military contemplated a similar scheme. During fighting in the Pacific theatre, American forces had suffered severe casualties when confronted by Japanese pillboxes and fortified bunker complexes. In November 1943 the New Development Division, a research and development unit, began training dogs to run into bunkers with satchels full of explosives, detonated by a timer, attached to their backs. Problems immediately surfaced during training; dogs would turn around when released and return to their handlers. Nor could they reliably be trained to distinguish between a Japanese bunker still in enemy hands and one captured and occupied by American troops. There was also a palpable moral unease about the whole endeavour and a sense that the American public would be outraged if they learned of the project. Rather revealingly, the dogs destined for battlefield sacrifice were referred to as 'demolition wolves' in official documents. The wolf was a creature so demonised in American popular culture that presumably it was felt that this thin cover might make the ugly venture palatable to the public.[61]

Soldiering on: animals in contemporary warfare

Mercifully, the US army terminated its 'demolition wolves' project in December 1943. Yet this desire to turn living creatures into weapons has been a frighteningly recurrent impulse. In 1989, Israeli army units in Lebanon deployed dogs laden with explosives to follow Palestinian insurgents into underground bunkers, where the charges were remotely detonated.[62] Science has only expanded these dark possibilities, as evidenced by programmes for using sea mammals for military purposes. Not only dolphins, porpoises and sea lions but also orcas, belugas and pilot whales, have been used for the same kind of tasks dogs have been expected to perform (detection and recovery of objects and guarding installations) but at sea, rather than on land. Experiments had actually begun during the First World War, when the British Royal Navy unsuccessfully attempted to train sea lions (and seagulls!) to locate German submarines.[63] These efforts were revived in the 1960s. It was the extraordinary sensory and physical capabilities of marine mammals, alongside a capacity for behaviour modification, which drew military attention. It has clearly also been felt to be very important to deny the sophisticated intelligence and peculiarly marked capacity for exhibiting emotion possessed by these animals; instead they are described as 'self-propelled marine vehicle[s], or platform[s]; with a built-in sonar sensor system suitable for detecting and classifying targets; and carrying an on-board computer . . . capable of being programmed for complex performance'.[64]

However, the full scope of how these 'programmable marine platforms' have been utilised remains a subject of speculation because, regrettably, they remain on active duty and their activities are thus classified. There have, however, been some very disturbing suggestions. According to the American journalist David Morrison, a team of dolphins was deployed to South Vietnam to guard the US fleet against saboteurs in 1971. Similarly, he asserted that navy dolphins were transported to the Persian Gulf in 1987 to detect Iranian mines and guard against enemy frogmen attempting to attack a floating command post. Considerable controversy surrounds the question of what exactly these dolphins have been trained to do should they encounter saboteurs: 'In 1976 testimony before the Senate Select Committee on Intelligence, Michael Greenwood, a veteran of the Navy dolphin project, asserted that dolphins assigned to the "swimmer nullification" programme were equipped with carbon dioxide-filled syringes with which to kill intruders'. The navy denied such suggestions, but they have frequently resurfaced (and it is reported that the Soviets trained dolphins in a similar manner, which were later sold to the Iranians).[65] Morrison also made allegations of systematic mistreatment of, and poor standards of care for, animals in the US programme and noted that it had become the focus of animal rights activism. Certainly a great deal of the secrecy that continues to surround the military use of sea mammals reflects, as Morrison observed, 'the fear of exciting public opposition to its efforts, opposition sparked by the great affinity that so many humans feel for these engaging creatures'.[66]

Well into the twentieth-first century, US dolphins continue to serve in the Persian Gulf. They are not the only animals for whom war continues. Horses are still used operationally by a number of modern armies. Both the German and Austrian militaries maintain pack animal units for use in mountains simply because horses and mules can reach locations inaccessible to wheeled or tracked vehicles and where helicopters cannot land. During peace-keeping operations in Kosovo in 2002–2004, German troops purchased ponies locally to resupply outposts in terrain and weather conditions that defeated other forms of transport. At the same time, another NATO unit in Kosovo, the British army's Royal Scots Dragoon Guards, borrowed horses from local farmers and rode mounted patrols in the more remote areas under their responsibility. The same conditions apply in Afghanistan, where both tribal warriors and US Special forces actually ride into battle on horseback.[67] In Myanmar, elephants are serving as draught animals for the Karen National Liberation Army in its struggle against government forces.[68]

Dogs remain the most widely used animal employed in current warfare. In particular, their remarkable ability to detect hidden or buried explosives (by scent as we now understand) has proved indispensable in meeting the threat from mines and improvised explosive devices both during military operations in Iraq and Afghanistan and in post-war humanitarian efforts to clear munitions from former battlefields.[69] Dogs, however, are not the only species being employed in this task. The Apopo Foundation (a Belgian NGO based in Mozambique) has developed successful mine-detection programmes using the African giant pouched rat, to return hitherto lethally contaminated ground to local communities across Africa and Asia.[70] Another animal with a sense of smell as potent as that of dog or rat is the honeybee. They can also be trained quickly, simply by adding the target chemical to their syrup feed. This then forms a powerful association and bees (tracked by laser-based radar) will be drawn to that chemical signature when released to conduct their natural foraging behaviour. Experiments in the early 2000s suggested an impressive degree of accuracy in locating mines, minimal risk of actually triggering the devices, and with bees available in greater numbers, and at lower cost, than dogs. By 2007, bees were being used successfully for detecting mines left over from the 1992–1995 war in former Yugoslavia.[71] Thus, while the era of mass mobilisation of animals for the purposes of war may be over, the subject of animals in and at war remains current, if understudied.

Conclusions: writing animals into the history of war

Two principal suggestions have been made here. First, that the crucial significance of animals to the conduct of war, from prehistory to the present day, has been largely neglected in conventional historiography. Recently, however, those historians whose work is an effective synthesis of traditional campaign history and the more sociological concerns of the 'war and society' school, such as Jos Gommans and Rhoads Murphey, have made important strides in acknowledging and exploring the animal presence in military institutions. More now need to follow their example, but few, surely, would be wary of this approach. Perhaps more controversial, however, is the second suggestion: historians of war should write of animals not as Cartesian automatons, but rather, they should embrace a neo-Darwinian methodology, treating animals such as dogs and horses as knowing subjects (that is to say, as historical agents capable of emotional states analogous to those of humans and possessed of a meaningful understanding of their own actions). Contemporary advances in biology and ethology have justified such an approach, while exposing the intellectual poverty of behaviourism, whose baleful influence historians should be encouraged to reject. Novel as this suggestion is, there are already historians whose work demonstrates the essential viability of such a methodology, notably Sandra Swart. The current scholarly emphasis on the emotional and physiological costs of war adds further weight to this suggestion. If acknowledgment of such costs is essential to a full evocation of the historical reality of war then – 'no half measures, no middies' – our accounts must reckon not merely on the presence of animals but upon their suffering too.

Notes

1 Freely translated by Philip Howell, with the invaluable advice of Nigel Spivey and Christopher Whitton.
2 R. Descartes, 'Discourse on the method of rightly conducting the reason and seeking for truth in the sciences', trans. E.S. Haldane and G.R.T. Ross, in E.S. Haldane and G.R.T. Ross (eds.), *The Philosophical Works of Descartes*, Volume 1, Cambridge: Cambridge University Press, 1967, 117.
3 M.G. Pegg, *A Most Holy War: The Albigensian Crusade and the Battle for Christendom*, Oxford: Oxford University Press, 2007, xii.
4 R.P. Lindner, 'Nomadism, horses and Huns', *Past and Present* 92 (1981): 3–19. For a challenge to this thesis, see C. Barnes, 'Rehorsing the Huns', *War & Society* 34, 1 (2015): 1–22.
5 B.S. Bachrach, 'On the origins of William the Conqueror's horse transports', *Technology and Culture* 26, 3 (1985): 505–531.
6 S. Digby, *War-Horse and Elephant in the Dehli Sultanate: A Study of Military Supplies*, Oxford: Orient Monographs, 1971, 20–26, 50–51.
7 P. Edwards, 'The supply of horses to the Parliamentarian and Royalist armies in the English Civil War', *Historical Research* 68, 165 (1995): 49–66.
8 P. Edwards, *Horse and Man in Early Modern England*, London: Hambledon Continuum, 2007, 176. See also G. Robinson, 'Horse supply and the development of the New Model Army, 1642–1646', *War in History* 15, 2 (2008): 121–140.
9 Charles V, Duke of Lorraine, *Political and Military Maxims*, London, 1699, 148.
10 *The War of the Rebellion: A Compilation of the Official Records of the Union and Confederate Armies*, Series I, 39, Pt. 2, Washington DC: US War Department, 1880–1901, 689–690.
11 C.W. Ramsdell, 'General Robert E. Lee's horse supply, 1862–1865,' *The American Historical Review* 35, 4 (1930): 758–777. See also S. Jones, 'The influence of horse supply upon field artillery in the American Civil War,' *The Journal of Military History* 74, 2 (2010): 357–377.
12 L.A. Webb, 'The horse and slave trade between the western Sahara and Senegambia', *The Journal of African History* 34, 2 (1993): 221–246; R. Law, *The Horse in West African History*, Oxford: Oxford University Press, 1980. See also I. Elbl, 'The horse in fifteenth-century Senegambia', *The International Journal of African Historical Studies* 24, 1 (1991): 85–110.
13 For the shaping of a national economy to meet the needs of animal supply, see D. Roche, 'Les chevaux de la republique: l'enquette de l'an III', *Revue d'Histoire Moderne & Contemporaine* 55, 4 (2008): 82–121. For the management of horse supply as a factor in the growth of central government and shaping of political systems, see S.A.M. Adshead, 'Horse administration under the Ch'ing: an introduction', *Papers on Far Eastern History* 17, (1978): 71–79; for the relationship between animals whose primary function was war and human social status, see A. Ayton, *Knights and Warhorses: Military Service and the English Aristocracy under Edward III*, Woodbridge: Boydell, 1994.
14 See A.N. Greene, *Horses at Work: Harnessing Power in Industrial America*, Cambridge MA: Harvard University Press, 2008; F.M.L. Thompson, *Victorian England: The Horse Drawn Society: An Inaugural Lecture*, Bedford College, 1970.
15 *Statistics of the Military Effort of the British Empire during the Great War, 1914–1920*, London: HMSO, 1922, 878. D. Haig, 'Final despatch, 21 March 1919', in J.H. Boraston (ed.), *Sir Douglas Haig's Despatches, December 1915–April 1919*, London: J.M. Dent, 1979, 334. See also J. Singleton, 'Britain's military use of horses 1914–1918', *Past and Present* 139 (1993): 178–203.
16 R.L. DiNardo and A. Bay, 'Horse-drawn transport in the German army', *Journal of Contemporary History* 23, 1 (1988): 129–143, 129; R.L. DiNardo, *Mechanized Juggernaut or Military Anachronism: Horses and the German Army of WWII*, Mechanicsberg PA: Stackpole, 2008, 39.

17 For the German cavalry of World War II see D. Dorondo, *Riders of the Apocalypse: German Cavalry and Modern Warfare, 1870–1945*, Annapolis MD: Naval Institute Press, 2012.
18 F. Halder, diary entry, 17 June 1942: *War Journal of Franz Halder* 7, 328, available at http://cgsc.contentdm.oclc.org/cdm/singleitem/collection/p4013coll8/id/3974/rec/3, last accessed 18 June 2016.
19 E.M. Essin, *Shavetails and Bell Sharps: The History of the US Army Mule*, Lincoln NE: University of Nebraska Press, 1997, 189–202.
20 J.P. Cann, *Counterinsurgency in Africa: The Portuguese Way of War 1961–1974*, St Petersburg FL: Hailer, 1997, 138–140; P. Durand, 'La cavalerie à cheval pendant la guerre d'Algerie, 1956–1962: survivance ou resurrection?', *Guerres Mondiales et Conflits Contemporains* 225, 1 (2007): 81–91; A. Harfield, *Pigeon to Packhorse: The Illustrated Story of Animals in Army Communication*, Chippenham: Picton, 1989, 63–64; J.M. Kistler, *War Elephants*, Lincoln NE: University of Nebraska Press, 2007, 234; R. Thompson, 'When Greek meets Greek . . .' in R. Thompson (ed.), *War in Peace: An Analysis of Warfare from 1945 to the Present Day*, London: Orbis, 1981, 20.
21 J.A. Lynn, 'The embattled future of academic military history', *The Journal of Military History* 61, 4 (1997): 777–789.
22 E. Lonn, *Desertion During the Civil War*, New York: The Century Company, 1928; B. Martin, *A Rich Man's War, A Poor Man's Fight: Desertion of Alabama Troops from the Confederate Army*, New York: P.S. King, 1932.
23 B.I. Wiley, *The Life of Johnny Reb: The Common Soldier of the Confederacy*, Indianapolis IN: Bobbs Merrill, 1943; B.I. Wiley, *The Life of Billy Yank: The Common Soldier of the Union*, Indianapolis IN: Bobbs Merrill, 1952.
24 G. SenGupta, *From Slavery to Poverty: The Racial Origins of Welfare in New York, 1840–1918*, New York: New York University Press, 2009, 19.
25 J. Keegan, *The Face of Battle*, London: Jonathan Cape, 1976.
26 A. Corvisier, *Armies and Societies in Europe, 1494–1789*, trans. A.T. Siddall, Bloomington IN: Indiana University Press, 1979.
27 R. Murphey, *Ottoman Warfare 1500–1700*, London: UCL Press, 1999, 65–83; J. Gommans, *Mughal Warfare*, London: Routledge, 2002, 111–132.
28 S. Swart, ' "The world the horses made": A South African case study of writing animals into social history', *International Review of Social History* 55, 2 (2010): 241–263.
29 J. Bourke, *An Intimate History of Killing*, London: Granta, 1999, 2. See E.T. Dean, *Shook over Hell: Post-Traumatic Stress, Vietnam, and the Civil War*, Cambridge MA: Harvard University Press, 1999; D.G. Faust, *This Republic of Suffering: Death and the American Civil War*, New York: Random House, 2009.
30 W.C. Ford (ed.), *A Cycle of Adams Letters, 1861–1865*, Volume 2, New York: Houghton Mifflin, 1920, 5.
31 W. Birkbeck, 'Replies to questions in regard to remounts', in *Army (Remounts): Reports, Statistical Tables and Telegrams Received from South Africa, June, 1899, to January 22nd 1902*, London: HMSO, 1902, 19.
32 K. Fischer, 'Training sled dogs at Camp Rimini, 1942–1944', *Montana: The Magazine of Western History* 34 (1984): 10–19, 17.
33 'Dogs of war', *Manchester Times* 24 November 1893, 5.
34 H.S. Lloyd, 'The dog in war', in B. Vesey-Fitzgerald (ed.), *The Book of the Dog*, London: Nicolson & Watson, 1948, 177–194, 192.
35 C. Darwin, *The Expression of the Emotions in Man and Animals*, London: John Murray, 1904, 12.
36 C. Darwin, *The Descent of Man and Selection in Relation to Sex*, London: John Murray, 1871, 35–40.

37 A.C. Smith, *Everyman's Book of the Dog*, London: Hodder & Stoughton, 1910, 161.
38 F. Fitzwygram, *Horses and Stables*, London: Longmans, Green & Co., 1901, 518–519.
39 R. Lubow, *The War Animals: The Training and Use of Animals as Weapons of War*, New York: Doubleday, 1977, 135–136.
40 M. Bekoff, *The Emotional Lives of Animals*, Novato CA: New World, 2007, 31–33, 128–129.
41 A. Mikósi, *Dog: Behaviour, Evolution and Cognition*, Oxford: Oxford University Press, 2009, 95–131; J. Clutton-Brock, 'Origins of the dog: domestication and early history', in J. Serpell (ed.), *The Domestic Dog: Its Evolution, Behaviour and Interactions with People*, Cambridge: Cambridge University Press, 2008, 7–20, 10–11.
42 M. Mead, 'Warfare is only an invention – not a biological necessity', *Asia* 40 (1940): 402–405.
43 J. Guillaine and J. Zammit, *The Origins of War: Violence in Prehistory*, Oxford: Blackwell, 2005; L. Keeley, *War before Civilization: The Myth of the Peaceful Savage*, Oxford: Oxford University Press, 1996; S. LeBlanc, *Constant Battles: Why we Fight*, New York: St Martin's Press, 2004. For an example of biological determinism concerning human propensity to violence, see R. Wrangham and D. Peterson, *Demonic Males: Apes and the Origins of Human Violence*, New York: Houghton Mifflin, 1996.
44 J.C. Ewers, *The Horse in Blackfoot Indian Culture*, Washington DC: Smithsonian Institute Press, 1955, 207–208.
45 R. Coppinger and R. Schneider, 'Evolution of working dogs', in J. Serpell (ed.), *The Domestic Dog: Its Evolution, Behaviour and Interactions with People*, Cambridge: Cambridge University Press, 2008, 27–31.
46 Quoted in S.L. Dyson, *The Creation of the Roman Frontier*, Princeton NJ: Princeton University Press, 1985, 250.
47 Quoted in M.G. Lemish, *War Dogs: Canines in Combat*, London: Brasseys, 1996, 3.
48 P. Bontier and J. Le Verrier, *The Canarian or the Conquest and Conversion of the Canary Islands by Messire Jean de Bethancouurt*, trans. R.H. Major, London: Hakluyt Society, 1872, 149–150.
49 D. Karunanithy, *Dogs of War*, London: Yarak, 2008, 97–102.
50 B. de Las Casas, *The Devastation of the Indies: A Brief Account*, trans. H. Briffault, Baltimore MD: Johns Hopkins University Press, 1992, 127.
51 J. Campbell, 'The Seminoles, the "Bloodhound War" and abolitionism, 1796–1865', *Journal of Southern History* 72, 2 (2006): 259–302. S.E. Johnson, '"You should give them blacks to eat": waging inter-American wars of torture and terror', *American Quarterly* 61, 1 (2009): 65–92.
52 'The army despatch dog', *Edinburgh Evening News*, 30 June 1890, 3; 'The use of dogs in war,' *The Graphic*, 9 December 1893, Issue 1254, 723–725.
53 E.H. Richardson, *British War Dogs*, London: Skeffington, 1920, 86–88, 96.
54 Richardson, *British War Dogs*, 90–91, 122–123.
55 Richardson, *British War Dogs*, 65.
56 Lloyd, 'The dog in war', 189.
57 R.G.W. Kirk, 'In dogs we trust? Intersubjectivity, response-able relations, and the making of mine detector dogs', *Journal of the History of the Behavioural Sciences* 50, 1 (2014): 1–36.
58 Kirk, 'In dogs we trust?', 24–30.
59 Lloyd, 'The dog in war', 187.
60 Lemish, *War Dogs*, xi, 249.
61 Lemish, *War Dogs*, 88–91.
62 Lemish, *War Dogs*, 249.
63 D.A.H. Wilson, 'Sea lions, greasepaint and the U-boat threat: Admiralty scientists turn to the music hall in 1916', *Notes and Records of the Royal Society of London* 55, 3 (2001):

425–455. For the attempt to encourage seagulls to flock above submarines, thereby revealing their location, see B.F. Skinner, 'Pigeons in a pelican', *American Psychologist* 15, 1 (1960): 28–37, 28.
64 Quoted in D.C. Morrison, 'Marine mammals join the Navy', *Science* 242, 4885 (1988): 1503–1504.
65 S. Walker, 'Ukraine demanding return of combat dolphins from Russia,' *The Guardian Online*, 6 July 2014, available at www.theguardian.com/world/shortcuts/2014/jul/06/ukraine-combat-dolphins-russia-give-back, last accessed 23 April 2016.
66 Morrison, 'Marine mammals join the Navy', 1504.
67 Dorondo, *Riders of the Apocalypse*, 238–239. M. Blikaas, 'Proud KFOR mounted patrol', available at www.nato.int/kfor/chronicle/2000/nr_000803.htm, last accessed 8 July 2016; R.Y. Pelton, 'Afghan war eyewitness,' *National Geographic.com*, available at http://news.nationalgeographic.com/news/2002/02/0215_020215_peltoninterview.html, last accessed 28 April 2016.
68 Kistler, *War Elephants*, 234.
69 I.G. McClean (ed.), *Mine Detection Dogs: Training, Operations and Odour Detection*, 2003, available at www.gichd.org/fileadmin/GICHD-resources/rec-documents/MDD.pdf, last accessed 8 July 2016; Geneva International Centre for Humanitarian Demining [GICHD], *Training of Mine Detection Dogs in Bosnia and Herzegovina*, 2004, available at www.gichd.org/fileadmin/GICHD-resources/rec-documents/Training_of_MDD.pdf, last accessed 8 July 2016.
70 Apopo Foundation, 'Mine Action', available at www.apopo.org/en/mine-action/projects, last accessed 8 July 2016.
71 E. Gerstner, 'Lasers, landmines and honeybees', *Nature Physics*, 2005, available at www.nature.com/nphys/journal/vaop/nprelaunch/full/nphys103.html, last accessed 9 July 2016; J.J. Bromenshenk et al., 'Can honey bees assist in area reduction and landmine detection?' *Research Development and Technology in Mine Action* 7, 3 (2003), available at www.jmu.edu/cisr/journal/7.3/focus/bromenshenk/bromenshenk.htm, last accessed 9 July 2016. O. Solon, 'Honeybees trained to sniff out landmines in Croatia', *Wired*, 20 May 2013, available at www.wired.co.uk/article/landmine-bees, last accessed 9 July 2016.

References

Adshead, S.A.M. 'Horse administration under the Ch'ing: an introduction', *Papers on Far Eastern History* 17 (1978): 71–79.
Apopo Foundation, 'Mine Action', available at www.apopo.org/en/mine-action/projects, last accessed 8 July 2016.
Ayton, A. *Knights and Warhorses: Military Service and the English Aristocracy under Edward III*, Woodbridge: Boydell, 1994.
Bachrach, B.S. 'On the origins of William the Conqueror's horse transports', *Technology and Culture* 26, 3 (1985): 505–531.
Barnes, C. 'Rehorsing the Huns' *War & Society* 34, 1 (2015): 1–22.
Bekoff, M. *The Emotional Lives of Animals*, Novato CA: New World, 2007.
Blikaas, M. 'Proud KFOR mounted patrol', available at www.nato.int/kfor/chronicle/2000/nr_000803.htm, last accessed 8 July 2016.
Birkbeck, B. 'Replies to questions in regard to remounts', in *Army (Remounts): Reports, Statistical Tables and Telegrams Received from South Africa, June, 1899, to January 22nd 1902*, London: HMSO, 1902.
Bontier, P. and Le Verrier, J. *The Canarian or the Conquest and Conversion of the Canary Islands by Messire Jean de Bethancouurt*, trans. R.H. Major, London: Hakluyt Society, 1872.

Boraston, J.H. (ed.), *Sir Douglas Haig's Despatches, December 1915–April 1919*, London: J.M. Dent, 1979.

Bourke, J. *An Intimate History of Killing*, London: Granta, 1999.

Bromenshenk J., Henderson, C., Seccomb, R., Rice, S., Etter, R., Bender, S., Rodacy, P., Shaw, J., Seldomridge, N., Spangler, L., and Wilson, J. 'Can honey bees assist in area reduction and landmine detection?', *Research Development and Technology in Mine Action* 7, 3 (2003), available at www.jmu.edu/cisr/journal/7.3/focus/bromenshenk/bromenshenk. htm, last accessed 9 July 2016.

Campbell, J. 'The Seminoles, the "Bloodhound War" and abolitionism, 1796–1865', *Journal of Southern History* 72, 2 (2006): 259–302.

Cann, J.P. *Counterinsurgency in Africa: The Portuguese Way of War 1961–1974*, St Petersburg FL: Hailer, 1997.

Charles V, Duke of Lorraine, *Political and Military Maxims*, London, 1699.

Clutton-Brock, J. 'Origins of the dog: domestication and early history', in J. Serpell (ed.), *The Domestic Dog: Its Evolution, Behaviour and Interactions with People*, Cambridge: Cambridge University Press, 2008, 7–20.

Coppinger, R. and Schneider, R. 'Evolution of working dogs', in J. Serpell (ed.), *The Domestic Dog: Its Evolution, Behaviour and Interactions with People*, Cambridge: Cambridge University Press, 2008, 27–31.

Corvisier, A. *Armies and Societies in Europe, 1494–1789*, trans. A.T. Siddall, Bloomington IN: Indiana University Press, 1979.

Darwin, C. *The Descent of Man and Selection in Relation to Sex*, London: John Murray, 1871.

Darwin, C. *The Expression of the Emotions in Man and Animals*, London: John Murray, 1904.

Dean, E.T. *Shook over Hell: Post-Traumatic Stress, Vietnam, and the Civil War*, Cambridge MA: Harvard University Press, 1999.

Descartes, R. 'Discourse on the method of rightly conducting the reason and seeking for truth in the sciences' in *The Philosophical Works of Descartes*, trans. E.S. Haldane and G.R.T. Ross, in E.S. Haldane and G.R.T. Ross (eds.), Volume 1, Cambridge: Cambridge University Press, 1967.

Digby, S. *War-Horse and Elephant in the Dehli Sultanate: A Study of Military Supplies*, Oxford: Orient Monographs, 1971.

DiNardo, R.L. *Mechanized Juggernaut or Military Anachronism: Horses and the German Army of WWII*, Mechanicsberg PA: Stackpole, 2008, 39.

DiNardo, R.L. and Bay, A. 'Horse-drawn transport in the German army', *Journal of Contemporary History* 23, 1 (1988): 129–143.

'Dogs of war', *Manchester Times*, 24 November 1893, 5.

Dorondo, D. *Riders of the Apocalypse: German Cavalry and Modern Warfare, 1870–1945*, Annapolis MD: Naval Institute Press, 2012.

Durand, P. 'La cavalerie à cheval pendant la guerre d'Algerie, 1956–1962: survivance ou resurrection?', *Guerres Mondiales et Conflits Contemporains* 225, 1 (2007): 81–91.

Dyson, S.L. *The Creation of the Roman Frontier*, Princeton NJ: Princeton University Press, 1985.

Edwards, P. 'The supply of horses to the Parliamentarian and Royalist armies in the English Civil War', *Historical Research* 68, 165 (1995): 49–66.

Edwards, P. *Horse and Man in Early Modern England*, London: Hambledon Continuum, 2007.

Elbl, I. 'The horse in fifteenth-century Senegambia', *The International Journal of African Historical Studies* 24, 1 (1991): 85–110.

Essin, E.M. *Shavetails and Bell Sharps: The History of the US Army Mule*, Lincoln NE: University of Nebraska Press, 1997.

Ewers, J.C. *The Horse in Blackfoot Indian Culture*, Washington DC: Smithsonian Institute Press, 1955.

Faust, D.G. *This Republic of Suffering: Death and the American Civil War*, New York: Random House, 2009.

Fischer, K. 'Training sled dogs at Camp Rimini, 1942–1944', *Montana: The Magazine of Western History* 34 (1984): 10–19.

Fitzwygram, F. *Horses and Stables*, London: Longmans, Green & Co., 1901, 518–519.

Ford, W.C. (ed.), *A Cycle of Adams Letters, 1861–1865*, Volume 2, New York: Houghton Mifflin, 1920.

Geneva International Centre for Humanitarian Demining [GICHD], *Training of Mine Detection Dogs in Bosnia and Herzegovina*, 2004, available at www.gichd.org/fileadmin/GICHD-resources/rec-documents/Training_of_MDD.pdf, last accessed 8 July 2016.

Gerstner, E. 'Lasers, landmines and honeybees', *Nature Physics*, 2005, available at www.nature.com/nphys/journal/vaop/nprelaunch/full/nphys103.html, last accessed 9 July 2016.

Gommans, J. *Mughal Warfare*, London: Routledge, 2002.

Greene, A.N. *Horses at Work: Harnessing Power in Industrial America*, Cambridge MA: Harvard University Press, 2008.

Guillaine, J. and Zammit, J. *The Origins of War: Violence in Prehistory*, Oxford: Blackwell, 2005.

Halder, F. *War Journal of Franz Halder* 7, 328, available at http://cgsc.contentdm.oclc.org/cdm/singleitem/collection/p4013coll8/id/3974/rec/3, last accessed 18 June 2016.

Harfield, A. *Pigeon to Packhorse: The Illustrated Story of Animals in Army Communication*, Chippenham: Picton, 1989.

Johnson, S.E. '"You should give them blacks to eat": waging inter-American wars of torture and terror', *American Quarterly* 61, 1 (2009): 65–92.

Jones, S. 'The influence of horse supply upon field artillery in the American Civil War', *The Journal of Military History* 74, 2 (2010): 357–377.

Karunanithy, D. *Dogs of War*, London: Yarak, 2008, 97–102.

Keegan, J. *The Face of Battle*, London: Jonathan Cape, 1976.

Keeley, L. *War before Civilization: The Myth of the Peaceful Savage*, Oxford: Oxford University Press, 1996.

Kirk, R.G.W. 'In dogs we trust? Intersubjectivity, response-able relations, and the making of mine detector dogs', *Journal of the History of the Behavioural Sciences* 50, 1 (2014): 1–36.

Kistler, J.M. *War Elephants*, Lincoln NE: University of Nebraska Press, 2007.

Las Casas, B.D. *The Devastation of the Indies: A Brief Account*, trans. H. Briffault, Baltimore MD: Johns Hopkins University Press, 1992.

Law, R. *The Horse in West African History*, Oxford: Oxford University Press, 1980.

LeBlanc, S. *Constant Battles: Why we Fight*, New York: St Martin's Press, 2004.

Lemish, M.G. *War Dogs: Canines in Combat*, London: Brasseys, 1996.

Lindner, R.P. 'Nomadism, horses and Huns', *Past and Present* 92 (1981): 3–19.

Lloyd, H.S. 'The dog in war', in B. Vesey-Fitzgerald (ed.), *The Book of the Dog*, London: Nicolson & Watson, 1948, 177–194.

Lonn, E. *Desertion During the Civil War*, New York: The Century Company, 1928.

Lubow, R. *The War Animals: The Training and Use of Animals as Weapons of War*, New York: Doubleday, 1977.

Lynn, J.A. 'The embattled future of academic military history', *The Journal of Military History* 61, 4 (1997): 777–789.

Martin, B. *A Rich Man's War, A Poor Man's Fight: Desertion of Alabama Troops from the Confederate Army*, New York: P.S. King, 1932.

McClean, I.G. (ed.) *Mine Detection Dogs: Training, Operations and Odour Detection*, 2003, available at www.gichd.org/fileadmin/GICHD-resources/rec-documents/MDD.pdf, last accessed 8 July 2016.

Mead, M. 'Warfare is only an invention – not a biological necessity', *Asia* 40 (1940): 402–405.

Mikósi, A. *Dog: Behaviour, Evolution and Cognition*, Oxford: Oxford University Press, 2009.

Morrison, D.C. 'Marine mammals join the Navy', *Science* 242, 4885 (1988): 1503–1504.

Murphey, R. *Ottoman Warfare 1500–1700*, London: UCL Press, 1999.

Pegg, M.G. *A Most Holy War: The Albigensian Crusade and the Battle for Christendom*, Oxford: Oxford University Press, 2007.

Pelton, R.Y. 'Afghan war eyewitness', *National Geographic.com*, available at http://news.nationalgeographic.com/news/2002/02/0215_020215_peltoninterview.html, last accessed 28 April 2016.

Ramsdell, C.W. 'General Robert E. Lee's horse supply, 1862–1865', *The American Historical Review* 35, 4 (1930): 758–777.

Richardson, E.H. *British War Dogs*, London: Skeffington, 1920.

Robinson, G. 'Horse supply and the development of the New Model Army, 1642–1646', *War in History* 15, 2 (2008): 121–140.

Roche, D. 'Les chevaux de la republique: l'enquette de l'an III,' *Revue d'Histoire Moderne & Contemporaine* 55, 4 (2008): 82–121.

SenGupta, G. *From Slavery to Poverty: The Racial Origins of Welfare in New York, 1840–1918*, New York: New York University Press, 2009.

Singleton, J. 'Britain's military use of horses 1914–1918', *Past and Present* 139 (1993): 178–203.

Skinner, B.F. 'Pigeons in a pelican', *American Psychologist* 15, 1 (1960): 28–37.

Smith, A.C. *Everyman's Book of the Dog*, London: Hodder & Stoughton, 1910.

Solon, O. 'Honeybees trained to sniff out landmines in Croatia', *Wired*, 20 May 2013, available at www.wired.co.uk/article/landmine-bees, last accessed 9 July 2016.

Statistics of the Military Effort of the British Empire during the Great War, 1914–1920, London: HMSO, 1922.

Swart, S. '"The world the horses made": a South African case study of writing animals into social history', *International Review of Social History* 55, 2 (2010): 241–263.

The War of the Rebellion: A Compilation of the Official Records of the Union and Confederate Armies, Series I, 39, Pt. 2, Washington: US War Department, 1880–1901.

Thompson, F.M.L. *Victorian England: The Horse Drawn Society: An Inaugural Lecture*, Bedford College, 1970.

Thompson, R. 'When Greek meets Greek . . .' in R. Thompson (ed.), *War in Peace: An Analysis of Warfare from 1945 to the Present Day*, London: Orbis, 1981.

Walker, S. 'Ukraine demanding return of combat dolphins from Russia', *The Guardian Online*, 6 July 2014, available at www.theguardian.com/world/shortcuts/2014/jul/06/ukraine-combat-dolphins-russia-give-back, last accessed 23 April 2016.

Webb, L.A. 'The horse and slave trade between the western Sahara and Senegambia', *The Journal of African History* 34, 2 (1993): 221–246.

Wiley, B.I. *The Life of Johnny Reb: The Common Soldier of the Confederacy*, Indianapolis IN: Bobbs Merrill, 1943.

Wiley, B.I. *The Life of Billy Yank: The Common Soldier of the Union*, Indianapolis IN: Bobbs Merrill, 1952.

Wilson, D.A.H. 'Sea lions, greasepaint and the U-boat threat: admiralty scientists turn to the music hall in 1916', *Notes and Records of the Royal Society of London* 55, 3 (2001): 425–455.

Wrangham, R. and Peterson, D. *Demonic Males: Apes and the Origins of Human Violence*, New York: Houghton Mifflin, 1996.

19
HUNTING AND ANIMAL–HUMAN HISTORY

Philip Howell

Introduction

The antiquity and ubiquity of hunting is everywhere acknowledged. If killing animals is our predominant mode of engagement with nonhuman others, hunting is surely our oldest and most enduring relationship, 'the dominant occupation of ancestral people for the greater part of their existence on earth'.[1] Those who detest hunting and see it as exemplary of human exploitation of other animals, as an atavistic pursuit with no place in the modern world, will cavil at the idea of a *relationship* between hunter and prey, and will very likely miss or play down its enduring *historical* significance as a result. Those on the other hand who hold hunting to embody the highest and most honourable rapport with nonhuman animals and the natural world, and who see hunting as authorised by nature as much as legitimated by tradition, run the risk of portraying the hunt as so ancient and universal a practice that it seems to stand outside human history altogether. For the historian neither standpoint is of any help, but it is worth noting these extremes and pointing out right from the start that any history of hunting is going to be contentious. As the zooarchaeologist Naomi Sykes notes, our attitude to wild animals, and their deaths by human hands, says a lot about us, about our respective cultures and convictions.[2] The history of hunting speaks to who we were, but also to who 'we' believe we are.

Given this situation it is also best to state the argument here as straightforwardly as I can, which is simply that hunting does indeed always imply a relationship between nonhuman and human animal, however asymmetrical or unreciprocated, whatever else we feel about the ethics or morality of hunting (that is, by whom it is pursued, in what ways, and for what reasons). At the same time we need to insist that hunting belongs to history, in the face of all attempts to naturalise it and erase its historicity and specificity. Given that hunting is undertaken for so many reasons – for food and other necessities, for the eradication of predators or pests, for commercial profit, social performance or political propaganda, or simply for 'sport' – it is also sensible here to insist on hunting's *histories* in the plural. The purpose of writing this chapter is to assert the historical importance of hunting and the relationship it produces between humans and other animals, but at the same time its protean nature, since it takes so many different forms in different circumstances – from the most practical exigencies to the most leisured of princely luxuries, with or without the sanction of society, the animal quarry alternately portrayed as the noblest game or the basest vermin. It is invidious to pretend that hunting can be reduced to a single meaning, good or bad; and only the most partisan can pretend that the hunting scenes depicted on the cave walls of Lascaux are continuous with, say, the social media profiles of today's trophy hunters.[3] Erasing the 'great flexibility' built into what for want of any better word we call 'hunting' is no more of an option than seeing it as 'the oldest expression of our genetic nature' and denying its historical significance altogether.[4]

Hunting hypotheses

We should nevertheless note the enduring association between meat-eating, big game hunting, and our human evolution, if only to highlight the problems in arguing that hunting belongs to nature rather than to history. Let us start then with the 'hunting hypothesis', the notion that human evolution drastically speeded up with the transition from herbivorous or omnivorous scavenger to confirmed carnivore, not only in terms of the benefits of a meat-rich diet but more importantly as the stimulus to both bigger brains and higher intelligence and the sophisticated, complex social organisation that hunting for large game seems to demand.[5] The argument goes that prehumans left the African forests for the savannah some 2 or 3 million years ago, developed the taste for meat, and began the long journey to modern humanity.[6] The most modern versions of the 'hunting hypothesis' assert, in the portentous but predictable journalistic shorthand, that 'hunting makes us human'.[7] This portrait of 'Man the Hunter' (aka the 'Hunting Ape' or 'Killer Ape' theory), has been subject to decades of criticism, but the hunting hypothesis refuses to die, and it is regularly invoked, not least by those concerned to defend hunting. Here for example is the hunting advocate and antagonist of animal rights activists Ward M. Clark, praising the hunt as not only natural but 'part of our heritage as human beings':

> Hunting is indeed what makes us human; hunting is what led humans to cooperate, to plan, to anticipate, to form society. The first great turning point in Mankind's development was when two unrelated families found they could hunt large animals by working together, and so be more efficient at obtaining high-quality food; thus was the first tribe born. Hunting has made us what we are.[8]

Such pro-hunting apologia are common enough, and would need little comment in an academic overview save for the paradoxical placing of hunting as simultaneously entirely natural and fully human, a point to which we want to return. So when the likes of Clark argue that 'Man is and has long been a terminal predator, as marvellously equipped for hunting by our intellect as a lion is by his claws and fangs, as a wolf is by his swift legs and pack instinct', the divide between humans and animals seems briefly to dissolve, only to reappear in the argument that there is something special about *human* predators, namely the role that hunting played in the cultural and social evolution of human beings.[9]

The general argument has a long lineage, but in its most familiar form is the product of the anatomist Raymond Dart and the physical anthropologist Sherwood Washburn in the 1950s, subsequently popularised by the science writer Robert Ardrey in the 1960s and 1970s. Ardrey's *The Hunting Hypothesis* appeared in 1975, the culminating volume in his bestselling series on 'The Nature of Man', taking in the African origins of humanity, the social evolutionary significance of aggression, territoriality, hierarchy and inequality – before arriving specifically at the history of hunting. As the academic and popular enthusiasm for his work at the time is hard to recapture, it is worth nodding to Stanley Kubrick's *2001: A Space Odyssey* (1968), in which Ardrey's ideas were given cinematic immortality. In the 'Dawn of Man' prologue, the awakening insight of the single ape/ape-man/man-ape (he is named 'Moon-Watcher' in the Arthur C. Clarke novel) propels these proto-humans from fearful, huddled herbivores to aggressive predators, and from primate to 'man', the very start of the journey that will take humanity to the nearer planets and the furthest stars, and an unforeseeable evolutionary destiny.[10] It is a sequence justly famous for command of cinematic narrative, so much so that Kubrick is able to encapsulate the complex notion that hunting predates humanity and at the same time represents humans' escape route from nature and necessity. In miniature, it reproduces Ardrey's then-controversial argument for human beings' animal inheritance and the biological and social chasm that separates us from our animal cousins, if not from nature itself. In Ardrey's words, hunting conferred upon humans momentous and irrevocable consequences, making the human being a truly 'cultural animal', though this very path-dependence makes humans 'biological prisoners of cultural advances'.[11]

It is worth underscoring the paradoxical *pas de deux* of 'culture' and 'nature' essayed by Ardrey, here and in his symphonic 'Nature of Man' series as a whole, if only to avoid subsequent misrepresentation: not only the use and abuse of the 'hunting hypothesis' by pro-hunting groups, who see only 'nature', but also by many opponents of the hunting hypothesis, who see only 'culture'. It is easy enough to portray the likes of the amateur or armchair anthropologist Ardrey as apologists for the absolute identity of morality and evolutionary biology. Critics will cite the positive spin that Ardrey seems to place on this history of violence, his plea for a view of the human as a 'risen ape' rather than a 'fallen angel' falling on deaf ears. Critics have played up the most misanthropic aspects of the hunting hypothesis, its familiar strains of 'Paradise Lost'. A bald account of the 'hunting hypothesis' pits human *against* animal, culture *against* nature – as summarised by the evolutionary anthropologist Matt Cartmill in his influential commentary on the nature and meaning of hunting:

> the central propositions of the hunting hypothesis – that hunting and its selection pressures had made men and women out of our apelike ancestors, instilled a taste for violence in them, estranged them from the animal kingdom, and excluded them from the order of nature – became familiar themes of the national culture, and the picture of Homo sapiens as a mentally

unbalanced predator threatening an otherwise harmonious natural realm became so pervasive that it ceased to provoke comment.[12]

The implications for sexual and gender relations have been particularly obvious to critics of the hypothesis's misogyny as well as misanthropy. Feminist anthropologists have been especially keen to demolish the myth of 'Man the hunter', because of its apparent naturalisation of gender dualisms and hierarchies in 'the male-centred hunting story', as Donna Haraway puts it.[13] Star billing is reserved for aggressive alpha-male protagonists, females of all species being reduced to a secondary, subordinate, stay-at-home 'Woman the Gatherer' role. Some have argued, very vehemently, against the assumptions of this masculinist narrative, promoting the countervailing claims of foraging for hominid adaptation (the so-called 'gathering hypothesis'), or forwarding the participation of women in hunting game, small or large, or by rejecting the opposition between 'hunting' and 'gathering' upon which such a straightforward sexual division of labour rests.[14] But it is perhaps the importance attached to 'culture' *over* 'nature' that deserves comment. For many critics of the hunting hypothesis, many feminists amongst them, the history of hunting needs to be taken away from 'nature'. The most extensive and extreme critique has come from Donna Haraway, who has consistently sought to expose the proximate cultural determinants of these supposedly scientific and objective views of hunting, apes and humans, men and women.[15] For Haraway, such evolutionary narratives are a form of 'imaginary history' – critiquing here not merely the speculative 'just-so stories' familiar from the worst kind of evolutionary biology or sociobiology, but any suggestion that such scientism has a privileged access to empirical reality. There is a great deal of worth in scepticism of this kind – we might recall that Raymond Dart based his early conclusions on australopithecine bone shards, whose fragmentary and ambiguous nature did not prevent him from spinning a story of ape-to-human evolution that sounds to us now more like something out of the zombie carnage of AMC's *The Walking Dead* than sober science, picturing our ancestors in prose as lividly purple as a day-old bruise:

> Confirmed killers: carnivorous creatures that seized living quarries by violence, battered them to death, tore apart their broken bodies, dismembered them limb from limb, slaking their ravenous thirst with the hot blood of the victims and greedily devouring living writhing flesh.[16]

All the same, to reduce every such foray into the 'deep history' of hunting as no more than inventive fictions, with nothing much to tell us apart from the political circumstances of their elaboration and dissemination, seems like throwing in the towel without a blow being landed. We run the risk of capitulating to those who reject evolution or natural selection *tout court*, or to those, such as the pro-hunting advocates cited earlier, who cherry-pick from the academic literature, use selective quotation or straw man rhetoric to score their partisan points, or simply draw unwarranted inferences, confusing is with ought, then with now – for of course even if we swallowed the hunting hypothesis whole, that hardly represents a decisive justification of, say, the 'Paleo' diet, meat-eating (or for that matter cannibalism):

nothing here makes meat-eating 'natural' in this sense.[17] Even the biological anthropologist Craig Britton Stanford notes that:

> Important aspects of the behaviour of some higher primates – hunting and meat sharing and the social and cognitive skills that enable these behaviors – are shared evolved traits with humans and point to the origins of human intelligence. This does not mean that there is an instinctive desire to hunt on the part of all modern humans; only a small percentage of people in industrialized countries have ever hunted for anything that's alive.[18]

Hunting histories

The hunting hypothesis continues to be extraordinarily influential. Some of the earlier contentions and reasoning have been dropped in quiet embarrassment, others revised in the light of further evidence and innovations in interpretation, but the significance for early humans of meat provided by hunters is still regularly asserted.[19] Recent work in the field has rowed back on the competing claims of 'scavenging', whilst the significance of 'hunting' for prehistoric peoples has been reinstated in popular scientific journalism.[20] The problem for historians is not so much the intricacies of these debates, however, for which I can claim no expertise, but rather that the focus has been so much on the very remotest *antiquity*, something that inevitably lends hunting a consistency of purpose and meaning that can only be misleading. For the unwary, hunting can appear continuous from the 'dawn of Man' to the present day, speciously linking hunting as a means of survival to hunting as mere 'lifestyle'. One could cite any number of examples, but here, for fun, is the prominent Paleo-enthusiast Mark Sisson, replying to a hunting enthusiast on his prominent fitness blog, name-checking as he does so his creation 'Grok', the poster-boy for his 'Primal Blueprint':

> I'll admit – I'm no hunter. I don't own a gun or a bow and arrow. I buy my (admittedly local, organic, and sustainable) meat. But the question Chuck poses is a fascinating one. Truly, what's more Primal, more Grok-like, than stalking a wild animal for its meat? Poised over your prey, heart pounding, waiting for the perfect time to strike . . . the very idea feels raw, visceral, and utterly Primal. Pure. Man versus animal. Wit against brawn.[21]

It would take a more charitable temperament than I possess not to smirk at these sophistries, but it is evident how the 'hunting hypothesis' and the scientific search for human evolution can be bastardised into such hopeless histories. In point of fact, killing does not seem to come so naturally, and wild animal killing – or at least the evidence for it – has been sometimes more, and sometimes less common, rather than a constant, 'primal' pursuit. Moreover, the meaning of eating meat, and we may add the meaning of the hunt for game, is always 'dynamic, varied, multifaceted and context dependent'.[22] The histories of hunting are so complex that they defy even the most expert summarisers, and I restrict myself in what follows to noting only the most prominent themes in the literature, with no claim to comprehensiveness or evenness of coverage.

These caveats aside, we should, like the most enthusiastic ascetics, put the demands of the stomach firmly in their place. It is eminently possible, for both popular and academic accounts of hunting and meat-eating, to miss the fact that, like meat-eating, hunting is about pleasure and power as much as it is about protein.[23] John Speth has asked, for instance, in a deliberately counter-intuitive questioning of the perceived evolutionary advantages of hunting for large game (as opposed to hunting/scavenging for smaller game, or the herbivorous foraging that provided the vast bulk of ancient human diets), why our ancestors hunted at all.[24] For if meat from large animal prey was not so critical and energy-efficient a part of the early human diet as has sometimes been supposed, then we may reasonably ask what it was for. Speth's answer, along with others who have supported the various 'show off' or 'signalling' models for hunting, is that the practice has as much to do with men's social status as their families' or communities' sustenance.[25] This view is not canonical, but perhaps we can say, as cautiously as we can, that hunting in prehistory was a social and political pursuit as well as a source of meat and other resources for survival. And the more-than-subsistence significance of hunting must be more important still in the era of domestication, agriculture, and recorded history. As Thomas Allsen has put it, 'with successful domestication of plants and animals, the economic importance of hunting steadily decreases while its political significance steadily increases'.[26] This does not mean that hunting for game was negligible, or increasingly so; hunting for food, as well as for commercial profit, remains very significant in human history, and we might even link it to the 'accumulation by appropriation' upon which capitalist modernity depends.[27] Nor is this meant to suggest that what Allsen calls 'political hunting' and 'economic hunting' are quite so easy to differentiate. What it does indicate is that we should not let the significance of hunting for subsistence or survival, extending down to the indigenous and ancestral peoples of our own day, outweigh the long history of hunting as a cultural and political pursuit.[28]

The stress on hunting as *spectacle*, as a 'social and political drama', is hardly surprising, particularly if we place our focus on the elites, for whom, from the earliest days, the political importance of hunting predominates. J. Donald Hughes writes for instance that 'Hunting for its own sake as a sport, or in order to collect trophies and boast of one's own proficiency and success, is a pastime that probably developed soon after humankind began to live in urban conditions'.[29] Going back to the earliest literature, we know from the likes of Gilgamesh and Linear B, that hunting had acquired a special symbolic significance in the archaic world, where the importance of hunting for gods and heroes, kings and nobles is everywhere attested. For the elites, hunting, or at least a significant part of it, was a display of virtue and prowess and a training for warfare, a potent form of propaganda and a performance of politics in its own right.[30] It is necessary to stress at this point that the culture of hunting was the product and support for a pre-eminently male and masculine world. Hunting as the exercise and performance of power invariably meant male privilege and authority. I write this with more than usual tentativeness, as the contribution of women as hunters is easy to overlook, but setting aside the mythic hunters of the ancient world, the sisters of Atalanta and Artemis whose mythic transgressions perhaps only served to underscore the power of the male hunter, hunting for game in the ancient world was a male pursuit.[31] The further back in history we go, with all due respect to the likely invisibility of woman-as-hunter, parity between the sexes is even less obvious. Hunting played an unmistakable role in the construction of male gender identities in ancient Greece, for instance, with no equivalent at all for the adolescent or mature female. The language of the hunt was also freighted with sexual connotations ('venery') that point up the differences accorded to boys and girls, men and women; the enduring metaphoric equivalence of hunting and sexual pursuit by men underlines hunting's role in reproducing and not merely reflecting social norms.[32] Despite the greater contribution of women to the world of hunting in different times and places, hunting in history is disproportionately a male and a masculine pastime.[33]

As already noted, the popularity and legitimacy of hunting seems to have waxed and waned. The Romans, to take a well-known instance, seem by contrast to earlier and later societies, to exhibit little distinctive enthusiasm for hunting, even if its exotic and demotic appeal is obvious in the mock hunts of the arenas. Notable, for instance, is a critique and condemnation of the hunt's extravagance.[34] But even in this context of suspicion, Roman hunting still appears as 'an important device which demonstrated elite identity and social power within the landscape', in the words of the zooarchaeologist Martyn Allen, though immediately before asking what is surely the wrong question: 'was it really *hunting*, or merely hollow demonstrations by the wealthy few?'[35] The only sensible response is that we cannot define hunting merely by such utilitarian concerns as how much meat actually made it to the dining table: hunting has long been about power and authority, and even when a hunted animal is placed 'on the table', in virtually all societies it has typically been divided and distributed to different people according to complex criteria of desert and distinction. It is injudicious to trace too neat demarcations, but some have seen a waning of the communal spiritual reverence for the wilderness and a replacement by elite patterns of hunting in the coming of the Roman world, and the supposed Roman indifference to the hunt must be matched by an awareness of aristocratic celebrations of hunting evident at least in the late Roman period, as for instance in the mid- to late-fourth century Sevso 'Hunting Plate', probably from what is now western Hungary.[36] Long before this, animals such as lions and boars were portrayed as the proper quarry of kings, emperors, and heroes, and at least by the late Roman period, hunting was praised as part of the tutelage of leaders.

From the end of the Roman power to the long middle ages, and all the way to the *ancien régimes* in Europe, if we can once more be forgiven a Western focus, we return to a world (if indeed we ever left it) where hunting was symbolically central to the exercise of authority as well as the elite status. In the spiritual realm, notably with the legend of Saint Eustache, Christianity found a rapprochement and indeed perhaps an enthusiastic reciprocity with the culture of the hunt, whilst in the temporal, the rulers of medieval Europe seem to have rediscovered and reinvigorated the ritual significance of the ancient, pan-Eurasian royal hunt. In England, for instance, the Norman regime may mark an aristocratic takeover of hunting (as Walter Scott's *Ivanhoe* suggests), even if the process must have had a more complex genealogy. Naomi Sykes notes that the distribution of venison was from late Saxon times if not earlier increasingly restricted to the elite, suggesting that hunting had become 'less a performance of group identity and more a display of royal or thegnly power'.[37] The Conquest did not replace a commensal and democratic Saxon culture with Norman elitism at a stroke. What the Normans do seem to have achieved was an unprecedented transformation of the hunting landscape and the environment, bringing in novel quarry, a refinement of techniques (such as the use of the horse, hound, and hawk, and the introduction of '*par force*' hunting, the running to exhaustion of a singular quarry), and, most importantly of all, the formalisation of legal restrictions on access to the large game animals that became royal or aristocratic prerogatives: deer, boar, swans, herons, and the like. Without denying their contribution to the diet of the nobles, we have to underline the importance of hunting to the social and political differentiation of the elite: 'Increasingly formalized and restrictive sport hunting and legal game conservation measures thus formed part of a complex marking differential access by elites to resources needed for their own maintenance and display'.[38] In one respect at least, medieval hunting was somewhat less exclusive, for by the early middle ages in Europe, there were more women involved in hunting – and especially in hawking – even if the ritual re-enactment of male domination is readily apparent.[39] In the high middle ages hunting became a remarkably stylised pastime, celebrated and codified in the manuals and treatises that separate the age of Charlemagne and the Franks from that of the French and the Capets. However enthusiastic as hunters these sovereigns and their courts were, the later texts' precise and specialist vocabulary provide the most obvious indication of hunting's courtly and elitist nature: 'taught and learnt as a system of precise language', the 'phrases of the field' acted as 'a semi-magical key to knowledge'.[40] The proper quarry for a noble were the 'beasts of venery' (the hare, hart, wolf and boar for instance) as opposed to the beasts of the chase (the buck, doe, fox, marten and roe deer), whilst 'vermin' such as the otter or the badger could be left to the peasants. As Anne Rooney emphasises, these differences have little to do with any inherent utility, nuisance or threat; these conventions simply serve to differentiate those who know how and what and when to hunt, and those who do not.[41]

The codification of hunting produces its antipode quite naturally: illegal hunting, or 'poaching', the kind of crimes that the Norman Forest Laws and their successors were intended to extirpate. Later Game Laws in Britain followed the long-standing aim of restricting the best hunting to the elite, criminalising hunting without a sufficient estate, hunting at night or in disguise, breaking into enclosed parkland, or being caught in possession of hunting instruments or hounds, with the most draconian punishments held in reserve for malefactors. Read with the interests of the common sort in mind, we have to acknowledge that the latter shared with the elite the passion for hunting, enjoyed its various pleasures, including the close contact with the natural world – and perhaps even more so the personal freedom it afforded. So we should not see even the hunting practices of the peasant as a matter of mere subsistence, of survival alone.[42] Richard Almond is surely right to argue that in the middle ages in Europe hunting was central to the lives of all, exhibiting what he represents as a universal desire to hunt; Naomi Sykes, putting it in characteristically breezy fashion, asserts that by the mid-twelfth century in Europe hunting was the pop culture of the time.[43] The love of poaching speaks to the fact that 'country folk relished hunting, coursing, and fishing as much as their social superiors'.[44] Since the elites also hunted with servants and tenants, there could emerge a powerful set of hunting interests linking the high with the low: this is one of the reasons why cross-class rural alliances have been part of the history of hunting, with the common man, and countryside communities, conscripted in the shared economic and social and political interests of the hunt as well as the shared enthusiasm for hunting and its freedoms.

The advent and elaboration of 'poaching' therefore attests to an enduring and widely shared love of hunting (and fishing), at the same time as it indicates the elites' attempts to put such indiscriminate enjoyments in their place. In countries like England there may well have been, for many centuries, a certain sympathy generated between the classes by a shared interest in hunting, underwritten by its masculine bravado: some have argued that the influence and example of the 'gentleman poacher' came to an end only in the eighteenth century, at which point poaching does seem to have completed its descent into criminality.[45] It will not do to reduce hunting's history to a stand-off between rich hunters and poor poachers, then, even if the unmistakable accents of class warfare can eventually be heard. In early modern England, complex alliances were evident, not simply the agonistic relationship of lord and peasant, and the same might be said of other cultures of poaching. At the same time, it is equally easy to romanticise and remove this complexity, indulging in this instance a characteristic feature of the English ideology, the supposed love of 'sport' that unites the interests of the classes, up to the most recent times. The political valorisation of hunting for all was increasingly suspect from at least the Game Laws of the fourteenth century, following as they did hard on the heels of the Peasants' Revolt, transforming this most universal of sports straightforwardly into a crime.[46] The association of hunting with sedition would last long into the modern age, and has not disappeared yet. So elite hunting privileges are in many places matched by the struggle of social subordinates to maintain their traditional rights.

This is particularly obvious when racial and imperial or colonial power is added to the mix. It is an unavoidable irony that the same elites who pursued and valued the pleasures of the hunt were those whose mass destruction of hunter-gatherer societies was such an unmistakable aspect of colonial history.[47] Richard Wilk writes, of Belize, that 'The hunt brought men together in sociable groups, emphasized colonial racial boundaries, and dramatically symbolized the dominion of white men over the landscapes which the Empire had conquered and controlled'.[48] In British North America, First Nations peoples might be conscripted in the commercial hunting of animals – and in the more mutually organised 'middle ground' of the fur trade their skills were well valued, but they would, in time, lose cultural autonomy and independence.[49] But hunting never had a chance of bringing colonists and colonised together; Virginia DeJohn Anderson's brilliant history of animals in early modern America points out in passing that 'The hierarchical underpinnings of English-style hunting . . . diminished its usefulness as a bridge to Indian culture'.[50] Even for settlers, the distance between the elites and the others was starkly laid out. In the American South, for instance, an 'English' style of hunting was preserved by the planters, similarly gentrified and harshly restrictive, but it collided with the pursuits of different communities with different visions, derived as they were from the activities of indigenous peoples, commercial hunters, slaves and free blacks, and white settlers, all of whom, for different reasons, championed the right to hunt.[51] We can note this community of interests, a universal right to hunt that goes back to the settling of America, without any pretence that these added up to a unified hunting *bloc*, a kind of incipient hunting lobby, let alone one that would come to be aligned with, say, the concerns of the NRA or the GOP.[52] It is too easy, from either a pro-hunting or anti-hunting perspective, to miss the changing place of hunting in American history.[53] The ideological commitments of American sport hunting – America's enduring 'hunting myth' – came much later, paradoxically when native big game was in decline.[54] And the American sport hunter was in any event wholly differentiated from the backwoodsman and the commercial hunter.[55] For sportsmen (and women), 'sport' meant a code of honour that draws distinctions between good hunters and bad. Even the undoubted contribution of sport hunting to American wildlife conservation needs to be tempered by an awareness of the process by which settlers were transformed into outlaws and enemies of nature in precisely the same period.[56] The lesson for historians is that we need to attend to proximate struggles rather than be beguiled by contemporary cultural politics.

Similar themes can be observed in other colonial and colonised societies, such as those of the British imperial world, where the lesson about the primacy of politics needs particular emphasis. There is now a very large literature indeed on the 'intimate connection between hunting and imperialism', albeit from a slow start.[57] John Mackenzie's pioneering 1997 work, *The Empire of Nature*, made the case for hunting's significance to the British Empire, including its contribution to imperial ecological management, but it needs to be supplemented now not only by an awareness of imperial hunting's dependence on native knowledge and expertise and labour, its specific gender cultures, and the ramifying tragedies of imperial ecology, as well as by the parallel development of practices such as the 'princely ecology' of hunting in the Indian princely states.[58] We can see here that to an impressive degree the concerns of the ancient royal hunt were transposed to the modern age of empire, as 'pageants of colonial power', a 'theatre of the powerless and the powerful, the wild and the tamed, and the "civilized" and the "uncivilized"', as an ideal tableau of dominance and power.[59] Hunting and field sports appear in this new guise as a preparation for imperial duty, the killing of wildlife as a form of moral instruction, with women, for all their attempts to kick against the pricks, necessarily placed as 'outsiders' in this ethos of imperial masculinity.[60] All the same, colonial big-game hunting was a notably 'invented tradition', neither continuous with English ancestors nor with indigenous traditions. To some degree game hunters imported to the colonies part of what Mackenzie describes as a British hunting cult, but they also had to improvise, drawing all too selectively from native hunts as they did so, and at the same time reliant on native collaboration.[61] British imperial hunts were designed to supplement and supplant the displays of local rulers, to dominate alike the natural environment and colonial societies, even as they had to rely on local knowledge and expertise in order to do so.[62] Most importantly, no one has made a stronger case for the significance of hunting for colonial history than Edward Steinhart, whose *Black Poachers, White Hunters* considers the grafting of aristocratic hunting and the elimination of Kenyan hunting, including the use of horses and dogs, their transmogrification into 'poachers' – a transformation completed by modern conservationism and postcolonial politics.[63] There is much more to be said about poaching, and indeed about its commercial networks, but such struggles over the legitimacy of hunting have involved, for almost all of history, the question of *who* should hunt rather than whether one should hunt at all. Contemporary debates about, say, bush meat or trophy hunting, only serve to confirm the truth of this dictum. It is enough to note that the restrictions that codify 'legitimate' hunting are at least a thousand years old, and provide a link between the social snobbery of a vanished age and the seemingly objective science of contemporary conservation.

In this all too brief sketch, uneven and idiosyncratic as it must be, what strikes us are both the evident continuities, such as the stress on the construction of masculinities, the importance of spectacle and power, and the struggles over the limiting of hunting privileges, but also the changing nature of hunting and its connections with modernity. There are many reasons for associating hunting with modernity rather than with primal antiquity, and much of what we now associate with hunting is not at all sanctioned by the ages. If hunting for sport is 'a cultural, not a natural, activity', for instance, it is of very recent vintage.[64] Fox hunting in England (for instance) can be traced back to the sixteenth or the seventeenth centuries, perhaps earlier, depending on whom one wishes to believe, and whether we focus on hunting with hounds or with the formation of 'hunts' – but its heyday certainly came in the nineteenth century, the enthusiasts of the new 'national sport' being the urbanised middle-classes rather than their social superiors, many of these women.[65] Fox hunting was central to the vision of a settled society, writes Raymond Carr, but the theme of his history of English hunts is that of *embourgeoisement*, the ability of this supposedly timeless pursuit to repeatedly recruit hunt followers and supporters.[66] 'It had all the appearance of something entirely new or newly wrought', so Adrian Franklin critically remarks, albeit with the previously despised fox as a sadly inedible stand-in for the deer or stag or hare.[67] Contemporary enthusiasts such as the philosopher Roger Scruton appeal to an imaginary tradition, but they ignore the fact that the things that made fox hunting possible in the nineteenth are far less viable in the twentieth and twenty-first centuries.[68] Moreover, if fox hunting should be historically situated, for all its high status, so too should be its shadowy cousin, poaching. We can argue that poaching was similarly transformed by the opportunities opened up by an industrialising Britain – so much so that 'steam age poachers' seem to have forced landowners to move to more and more distant estates, the sporting preserves of northern England and highland Scotland, for instance, or even abroad.[69]

Hunting's natures

Reflecting on the continuities and transformations of hunting also sharply qualifies our understanding of the hunt as a mediation between the worlds of 'culture' and 'nature'. In this vein, the anthropologist Matt Cartmill has influentially argued that the hunter stands *between* the world of the human and that of the wild – 'Because hunting takes place at the boundary between the human domain and the wilderness, the hunter stands with one foot on each side of the boundary, and swears no perpetual allegiance to either side' – though he is at pains to argue that this is not because of nature's implacable dictates but rather as a result of culture's endless permutations.[70] The problem with such a view (and it is much cited and circulated) is that the worlds of nature and culture are here utterly opposed, in what seems merely the turning of evolutionary biology's naturalism on its head. Defining hunting as 'the deliberate, direct, violent killing of unrestrained wild animals', Cartmill could hardly put this opposition more starkly or vehemently:

> The hunt is thus by definition an armed confrontation between humanness and wildness, between culture and nature. Because it involves confrontational, premeditated, and violent killing, it represents something like a war waged by humanity against the wilderness.[71]

Cartmill's excellent account, however, which does so much to return hunting to culture, and which explicitly considers the aesthetic models associated with arguments for the hunting hypothesis, is strangely blind to its own myths and memes, amongst which we surely have to put this purported alienation of 'man' from nature.[72] Indeed, in the trope of 'war' he advances so cavalierly, Cartmill only reproduces the supposed 'enmity' between hunter and hunted essayed by 'Man the Hunter' enthusiasts Sherwood Washburn and C.S. Lancaster, or for that matter even the hunter-poet Ortega y Gasset's romantic image of 'man' as a 'fugitive' from nature.[73] Cartmill's lauded analysis, however critical and indispensable, cannot stand as a definition or a description of hunting, then or now. Perhaps only the 'collective cultural animus' against feared top predators such as the wolf really reflect this 'war' against an animal portrayed as the 'enemy' of human society.[74] The idea of a 'war' between hunter and prey is appealing in one sense to anti-hunting sensibilities – but neither historically nor anthropologically does this portrayal stand any serious scrutiny. Cartmill himself is at considerable pains to argue that hunting's advocates have simultaneously accepted, sometimes regretted, the violence involved in killing animals, the expulsion from paradise that this necessity seems to legislate, whilst insisting, without any perplexing contradiction, that hunting brings them closer to fellow animals and to nature. The idea that hunting is a matter of culture *opposed* to nature is in the end just as *culturally* overdetermined as the idea that hunting is a fact of nature. Worse, it ignores the changing historical relationship between hunters and the various animals they hunt.

Despite Cartmill's familiar and sturdily workable definition, for instance, it is not at all obvious that hunting always and everywhere means the pursuit of 'wild' animals. In today's world, of course, we might reasonably be sceptical about the idea that the chased animal is meaningfully wild. In contemporary Britain at least, much game is carefully preserved for hunters and shooting parties: foxes are not only provided with artificial earths, but caged, fed and watered until released for hunting, whilst pheasants are hatched in incubators, raised in factory conditions in sheds, moved to woodland pens, before being released to be shot; and so on.[75] Further afield, we might reflect on lions in southern Africa being raised for the business of so-called 'canned' hunting; trophy hunting in general is a by-product and financial lifeline for 'wildlife' conservation, with the knock-on effect of calling into question again what and where the 'wild' actually is.[76] It might seem anachronistic to cite such phenomena, but of course preserving and providing quarry has long been the business of the hunt. In the ancient world, exotic animals were imported specifically in order to be pursued, in the arenas or in the 'paradise parks' and preserves of princes. Parks were established as far back as Roman times, with at that time exotic fallow deer, *dama dama*, taking the place of wild, native quarry.[77] A case can be made, says Geoffrey Kron, for the accreditation of the classical and Hellenistic Greeks for 'game-farming' in particular, as well as animal husbandry in general.[78] In the later middle ages in Europe, according to Joyce Salisbury, stags and does were domesticated enough to provide milk and venison without the necessity of hunting; such deer 'lived on the border between wild and domesticated'.[79] In the deer parks that sprang up all over Europe from the twelfth century onwards, these semi-exotic fallow deer were nothing less than farmed for sport or convenience, in a predecessor of today's 'canned' hunts. They were also *property*, not simply wild game.

Preserving game was hardly an historical aberration or modern innovation, then. From the point at which hunting becomes a preserve of the aristocracy, game management is installed as its essential accompaniment, the avoidance of overhunting being almost impossible to separate from the prosecution or persecution of illicit hunters. 'Most hunting harks backwards and stands bluntly opposed to the march of progress', writes the historian of British hunting Emma Griffin, but it 'is not a timeless, peasant tradition, but an endless, and often artificial, attempt to protect huntable "wild" animals in an ever more cultivatable land'.[80] The long association of the aristocratic estates with nature and wildlife conservation, the familiar claim to stewardship and environmental leadership, must be tempered with an awareness of the often brutal consequences of making sure that the right animals are killed by the right people at the right times and in the right places.[81] Most obviously, the business (and it was increasingly a business) of providing animals for sport suggests not that wildness is irrelevant to the practice and ethos of hunting – rather that such wildness has to be carefully defined, bounded by discourse and law if not by actual fences and walls.[82] Naomi Sykes argues that in England the wild becomes, with the Norman regime, associated with the nobility, and 'domestic' with the common folk, a wholly new landscape superimposed upon the earlier mental geographies associated with animals and humans and the hunt.[83] Indeed, she makes the grand claim that over the very long term, we go 'from a situation when the "wild" did not exist because it was *all* that existed, to a situation where it did not exist because humans had largely eradicated the elements that constituted the *wildeoren*' or wilderness.[84] In a completely different setting, the Quabbin reservoir and reservation in western Massachusetts and the management of deer hunts in the twentieth century, studied by Jan Dizard, the white-tailed deer who flourished as the wolves and mountain lions were driven out exhibited 'aspects of wildness', but not (for him) genuine wilderness.[85] What these examples show, crudely abstracted as they are from the history of hunting, is that wildness is constructed as much as it is found, that hunters create rather than enter the natural world. We might note here too the obvious reliance of hunters on technology, such as the sportsman's (or woman's) gun.[86] Pro-hunters can write in praise of nature in these terms:

> To be healthy and hungry in the wilds is the way of the hunter. He strips himself of society's insulating layers of artificiality and becomes a player, a predator alive on a primal level. No longer just an observer, the hunter becomes an integral, working part of nature.[87]

But it is clear that hunting's natures (again in the plural) are carefully mediated and curated. Indeed, as technology has improved, sport hunters have had to work harder to ensure that the contest with the prey animal is evenly balanced, in their terms: this is always supposed to be 'fair game', sport rather than slaughter.

What then of the claim that hunters' relationship with their prey is one of enmity, that hunting is 'an expression of human dominion' over nature?[88] In the widest perspective, without accepting the views of the hunting lobby wholesale, this is a puzzling claim. Sykes notes that 'even in periods where the prevailing worldview was one of human dominion over nature, wild animals – particularly those that were the focus of hunting – were not all perceived as inferior to people'.[89] Moreover, if there is a 'war against animals', as some have claimed, it is rather more obviously apparent in the industrial-scale of animal slaughter in the production of meat than in the activities of hunters – and indeed hunting as what Serpell calls 'a way of life' has 'almost vanished from the face of this planet'.[90] Serpell and others see the shift from hunting to farming as the real cause of a change in human relationships with other animals, and in his estimation hunters and gatherers typically, perhaps universally, do not see themselves as superior to (other) animals. Hunting may be 'the most openly "pleasurable" joy in killing animals', but the ethical difference between hunting for food and the animal–industrial complex is vast.[91] In Tim Ingold's well-known anthropological account, indigenous hunters do not think of themselves in pursuit of 'wild' animals, nor in violent pursuit, but rather attempt to draw animals into the hunters' environment, which is a space of mutuality and coexistence, of *trust*.[92] For Garry Marvin, notably, hunting's kills are passionate deaths, a form of 'wild killing', where the hunter competes with the animal, with the environment, or with himself or herself; in sport hunting this means 'an immersion into the very difficulty of bringing about an encounter with the animal and with the pleasure and satisfaction that comes from successfully overcoming these self-imposed restrictions and difficulties'.[93] For sure, hunting involves killing animals, whether or not we put the emphasis on the pursuit of the game rather than the endgame itself, or whether the hunt is 'successful'. This lends itself to the idea that hunting means domination, that the sense of connection with the quarry and game, with the natural world itself, is simply spurious. But in hunting, '"Bloodlust" and the joy of the hunt coexist with love and veneration for the hunted animal'.[94] Moreover, in characteristically complex ways, the hunter must also become partly animal.[95] In the ecology of hunting, hunters have to recognise their quarry as selves, with points of view, in order to kill them and transform them into the other: in this way, animism and objectification coexist.[96] When Miles Olson's 'compassionate hunter' 'eats the animal they have killed, it becomes part of them. A death becomes a life; the predator and prey become one and the body of the dead, in a sense, lives on'.[97] Simply put, hunting is a cultural enclave in which animal and human identities are blurred.[98] Hunting has become iconic of an immersion with the natural world, an alternative to the 'great dualist machineries' of anthropocentric logic and culture.[99]

What, then, and finally, of the role or 'agency' of nonhuman animals themselves? Barbara Ehrenreich, in her discussion of hunting and human evolution, remarks in passing that 'It is almost beyond us to think of animals as actors in their own right, following their own agendas – much less as actors which might have shaped the course of human destiny'.[100] And yet it does not take too much imagination to consider animals' lively agencies; Ehrenreich reminds us that ancient humans did so, and of course many peoples outside the West continue to do so.[101] In respect of hunting, I am thinking about the charisma of nonhuman animals themselves, the abilities and qualities, whether ascribed or actual, which justify the chase and determine the nature of the sport involved. We might also note, however, that animals are never mere targets, but have collectively and individually responded to being hunted, for instance by adapting to hunting pressures or the lack of them. What we see as 'tameness' may for instance be a product of the relaxation of hunting, as animals may lose their fear of humans in its absence.[102] Or it might be hunting that empowers 'wild' animals: thus noble quarry like tigers in colonial India, reserved for princes, responded to their 'sovereign immunity' by attacking peasants and their livelihoods.[103] Alternatively, we might consider the traumatic effects on animals, again as individuals and populations, of hunting and poaching pressures.[104] We should note, lastly, the role that nonhumans play as partners rather than prey. Thus the thirteenth-century friar Albertus Magnus wrote in his treatise on animals of hunters with dogs 'collaborating' with birds of prey to catch birds.[105] The medievalist Joyce Salisbury similarly recognises that 'the success of the hunt depended as much on the skill of dogs as on humans', and that humans and animals joined in celebration of the victorious hunt by sharing the resultant meat.[106] Now we might cavil at words like 'collaboration' or 'alliance', but animals are plainly companion species in the hunt as well as the home.[107] In more modish language, Karen Jones writes of 'the natureculture of the nineteenth-century hunt', in which the hunter's dog existed in 'a borderland space, a realm of interspecies concord in which it (literally) ran the gamut from dumb/mechanical and loyal subaltern to expert hunter in possession of a form of furry personhood'.[108] It might be going too far to counter-hypothesise that hunting with other animals made us human, but it would be well to cultivate a sense of animals' agencies, even or especially in the histories of the hunt, and their role as 'lively fellow architects of hybrid landscapes'.[109]

A comparison by way of a conclusion

Let me end not with a magisterial summary, which is both difficult and uncongenial, but with this contrast between a narrative of human authority, and this alternative sense of complex relations between humans and animals. It is easy, through the variants of the 'hunting hypothesis' to see hunting as an expression of humans' power over other animals, as (in Darwin's words) 'the most dominant animal that has ever appeared on the earth', or (in more recent assessment) 'the world's apex predator'.[110] The caves of Lascaux in southwestern France (around 17000 BCE), famous for their portrayal of hunting, including indeed some species that may have been hunted to extinction, appeal in this way to those who see hunting as ancient, timeless, continuous – not just a 'basic fact of existence' for Stone Age people, but an index of the rightness and naturalness of hunting: 'Paleolithic cave drawings of game animals and hunt scenes are rendered with a loving reverence that is still evident today, thousands of years later'.[111] But it is worth reminding ourselves that we should not blunder into reading our *present* dominion into the prehistoric past. The even older

Chauvet cave system in the limestone gorges of the river Ardèche a few hundred kilometres away tells an apparently very different story to that of human hegemony. The images at Chauvet (dating from at least 25000 BCE) do not depict hunting, but betray an equally obvious fascination with the nonhuman animals with whom the artists shared their world (bears, lions and panthers, rhinos, mammoths, bison, oxen, horses, ibex, deer, owls). Several of these animals (the lions, mammoths and rhinos) do not appear to have been hunted at this time. Some of the images are intriguingly abstract, and some animals (as at Lascaux) are hybridised with human elements. This is another 'hybrid landscape' then, 'a world in which humans were everywhere decisively outnumbered by large land animals and lived in intimate connection with them'.[112] No fully figured human is depicted, no explicit contrast between humans and hunted animals as we seem to see in Lascaux. Moreover, rather than an expression of incipient humanity that separates *us* from *them*, as suggested by the idea that these caves are a 'Sistine Chapel' of prehistory, or even (in the filmmaker Werner Herzog's misleading summation) the birthplace of 'the modern human soul', they seem only partly or provisionally a *human* space, having been hollowed out by hibernating cave bears and only subsequently inhabited and decorated by humans.[113] These bears, far bigger than their modern descendants, have even left their own traces, in their scratches and footprints. So instead of the lonely majesty of the human soul busy being born, the yawningly familiar 'dawn of man', it might be better to speak of the power of a more-than-human world where 'human-animal-landscape relationships were interdependent'.[114] If Lascaux can be made to say that hunting is ancient, and natural, and right, the Chauvet caves might serve to instruct us of the perils of simplifying either the history of hunting or the deep history in which humans and other animals are enmeshed. Instead of placing all these very different histories under the sign of *dominion*, 'human' *over* 'animal', we might reasonably suggest that these marvellous artefacts articulate the therianthropic interdependence of humans and other animals. And this might be a *nota bene* of some significance outside the cave.

Notes

1 J.D. Hughes, 'Hunting in the ancient Mediterranean world', in L. Kalof (ed.), *A Cultural History of Animals in Antiquity*, Oxford: Berg, 2007: 47–70, 51.

2 N. Sykes, *Beastly Questions: Animal Answers to Archaeological Issues*, London: Bloomsbury, 2015, 51.

3 For caves as a source of hunting information, see S. Mithen, 'Ecological interpretations of Paleolithic art', *Proceedings of the Prehistoric Society* 57, 1 (1991): 103–114.

4 T. Allsen, *The Royal Hunt in Eurasian History*, Philadelphia PA: University of Pennsylvania Press, 206, 4; T. Kerasote, *Bloodties: Nature, Culture, and the Hunt*, New York: Kodansha, 1993, xvii. It is worth pointing out here that in Britain hunting is typically held distinct from shooting or fishing or trapping, but clearly its meaning is very broad. In what follows it will be seen that I have, for purposes of manageability neglected fishing, and indeed both commercial fishing and commercial hunting.

5 An enormous literature, but see D. van Reybrouck, *From Primitives to Primates: A History of Ethnographic and Primatological Analogies in the Study of Prehistory*, Leiden: Sidestone Press, 2012. For the 'hunting hypothesis', see R.B. Lee and I. DeVore, (eds.), *Man the Hunter*, Chicago IL: Aldine Transaction, 1968. For a well-known commentary on the

abandonment of hunting and gathering as a tragedy, see J. Diamond, 'The worst mistake in the history of the human race', *Discover* 8, 5 (1987): 64–66, recapitulating in part the views of P. Shepard, *The Tender Carnivore and the Sacred Game*, New York: Scribner, 1973. If this was a 'mistake' for humans, it was a catastrophe for other animals: see Y.N. Harari, *Sapiens: A Brief History of Humankind*, London: Vintage, 2015, 109.
6 K. Wong, 'How hunting made us human', *Scientific American* 310, 4 (2014), available at www.scientificamerican.com/article/how-hunting-made-us-human/, last accessed 16 March 2017.
7 This hypothesis is venerable and can be traced back at least to Darwin's speculations on bipedalism in *The Descent of Man, and Selection in Relation to Sex*, London: John Murray, 1871.
8 W.M. Clark, 'Why hunt?', 2004, available at www.wildfowling.co.uk/magazine/whyhunt.htm, last accessed 16 March 2017. Republished as W.M. Clark, 'Hunting is a natural, ethical, and healthy undertaking', in D. Laney (ed.), *Hunting: Opposing Viewpoints in Context*, Farmington Hills MI: Greenhaven Press, 2008.
9 Clark, 'Why hunt?'
10 A.C. Clarke, *2001: A Space Odyssey*, London: Hutchinson, 1968.
11 R. Ardrey, *The Hunting Hypothesis: A Personal Inquiry Concerning the Evolutionary Nature of Man*, London: Collins, 1976, 93.
12 Cartmill, *View to a Death*, 14. See also B. Ehrenreich, *Blood Rites: Origins and History of the Passions of War*, London: Virago, 1997, 36–57.
13 D.J. Haraway, *Simians, Cyborgs, and Women: The Reinvention of Nature*, London: Free Association Books, 1991, 91.
14 See for instance: S. Slocum, 'Woman the gatherer: male bias in anthropology', in R.R. Reiter (ed.), *Toward an Anthropology of Women*, New York: Monthly Review, 1975, 36–50; M.Z. Stange, *Woman the Hunter*, Boston: Beacon Press, 1997; A. Zihlman and N. Tanner, 'Gathering and the hominid adaptation', in L. Tiger and A. Fowler (eds.), *Female Hierarchies*, Chicago IL: Beresford Book Service, 1978, 163–194.
15 D.J. Haraway, *Primate Visions: Gender, Race, and nature in the World of Modern Science*, London: Routledge, 1989.
16 R. Dart, 'The predatory transition from ape to man', *International Anthropological and Linguistic Review* 1, 4 (1953): 201–217, 209, cited by R.W. Sussman, 'Why the legend of the killer ape never dies: the enduring power of cultural beliefs to distort our view of human nature', in D.P. Fry (ed.), *War, Peace, and Human Nature: The Convergence of Evolutionary and Cultural Views*, Oxford: Oxford University Press, 2013, 101.
17 P.Y. Lee, 'Introduction: housing slaughter', in P.Y. Lee (ed.), *Meat, Modernity, and the Rise of the Slaughterhouse*, Durham NH: University of New Hampshire Press, 2008, 1–9, 3.
18 C.B. Stanford, *The Hunting Apes: Meat Eating and the Origins of Human Behavior*, Princeton NJ: Princeton University Press, 1999, 5.
19 Despite its identification as 'myth', it can still just about claim to be the 'traditional view': see J.D. Speth, *The Paleoanthropology and Archaeology of Big Game Hunting: Protein, Fat, or Politics?* New York: Springer, 2010. For some relatively recent work, see K. Milton, 'A hypothesis to explain the role of meat-eating in human evolution', *Evolutionary Anthropology* 8, 1 (1999): 11–21. See M. Domínguez-Rodrigo, 'Hunting and scavenging by early humans: the state of the debate', *Journal of World Prehistory* 16, 1 (2002): 1–54. Qualifications include the vulnerability of early humans and protohumans to being themselves hunted: as the basis for the human sacralisation of war this is discussed in Ehrenreich, *Blood Rites*, but more recent discussion can be found in D. Hart and R.W. Sussman, *Man the Hunted: Primates, Predators, and Human Evolution*, expanded edition, New York: Westview Press, 2009.

20 Speth, *Paleoanthropology and Archaeology*. See 'Meat eating behind evolutionary success of humankind, global population spread, study suggests', *Science Daily*, 12 April 2012, available at www.sciencedaily.com/releases/2012/04/120420105539.htm, last accessed 16 March 2017; R. McKie, 'Humans hunted for meat 2 million years ago', *Guardian*, 23 September 2012, available at www.theguardian.com/science/2012/sep/23/human-hunting-evolution-2million-years, last accessed 16 March 2017; J. Kluger, 'Sorry vegans – meat-eating made us human', *Time*, 9 March 2016, available at http://time.com/4252373/meat-eating-veganism-evolution/, last accessed 16 March 2017.

21 M. Sisson, 'Real primal: hunting for dinner', 4 February 2009, available at www.marksdailyapple.com/hunting-ethics/, last accessed 16 March 2016.

22 D. Grossman, *On Killing: The Psychological Cost of Learning to Kill*, revised edition, New York: Open Road, 2014; Sykes, *Beastly Questions*, 51, 162. See N. Fiddes, *Meat: A Natural Symbol*, London: Routledge, 1991.

23 Lee, 'Introduction: housing slaughter', 3: 'meat-eating in the modern world has been narrated through ideology rather than physiology'.

24 Speth, *Paleoanthropology and Archaeology*.

25 See M. Gurven and K. Hill, 'Why do men hunt? A reevaluation of "man the hunter" and the sexual division of labour', *Current Anthropology* 50, 1 (2009): 51–74.

26 Allsen, *Royal Hunt*, 2.

27 On this important theme, almost wholly neglected in this chapter, see J. Richards, *The World Hunt: An Environmental History of the Commodification of Animals*, Berkeley CA: University of California Press, 2014. For 'accumulation by appropriation', see J. Moore, *Capitalism in the Web of Life*, London: Verso, 2015.

28 Allsen, *Royal Hunt*, 274.

29 For social and political drama, see G. Marvin, 'The problem of foxes: legitimate and illegitimate killing', in J. Knight (ed.), *Natural Enemies: People–, Wildlife Conflicts in Anthropological Perspective*, London: Routledge, 2000, 189–211.

30 J.K. Anderson, *Hunting in the Ancient World*, Berkeley CA: University of California Press, 1985.

31 See M.Z. Stange, C.K. Oyster, and J.E. Sloan (eds.), *Encyclopedia of Women in Today's World*, Volume 1, Los Angeles CA: Sage, 2011; J.M. Adovasio, O. Soffer and J. Page, *The Invisible Sex: Uncovering the True Roles of Women in Prehistory*, Washington DC: Smithsonian Books, 2007.

32 J.M. Barringer, *The Hunt in Ancient Greece*, Baltimore MD: Johns Hopkins University Press, 2001.

33 Marc Boglioli notes American hunting's 'extreme gender specificity': M. Boglioli, *A Matter of Life and Death: Hunting in Contemporary Vermont*, Amherst MA: University of Massachusetts Press, 2009, 12.

34 Hughes, 'Hunting in the ancient Mediterranean world', 65–66.

35 M. Allen, 'Not just dormice – food for thought?', emphasis in the original, available at https://notjustdormice.wordpress.com/2015/01/22/hunting-in-the-roman-world-anthropology-animal-bones-and-ancient-literature/, last accessed 16 March 2016.

36 Discussed in Sykes, *Beastly Questions*, 66–68. See K.M.D. Dunbabin, *The Roman Banquet: Images of Conviviality*, Cambridge: Cambridge University Press, 2003.

37 Sykes, *Beastly Questions*, 159.

38 S. Perdikaris and J. Woollett, 'Hunting', in P.J. Crabtree (ed.), *Medieval Archaeology: An Encyclopedia*, New York: Garland, 2001, 168–170.

39 For more on medieval hawking, see: J. Cummins, *The Hound and the Hawk: The Art of Medieval Hunting*, London: Weidenfeld and Nicholson, 1988; R.S. Oggins, *The Kings and their Hawks: Falconry in Medieval England*, New Haven CT: Yale University Press, 2004.

40 A. Rooney, *Hunting in Middle English Literature*, Cambridge: Boydell Press, 1993, 15. 'Phrases of the field' comes from Walter Scott, *Ivanhoe*.
41 Rooney, *Hunting*.
42 W.P. Marvin, *Hunting Law and Ritual in Medieval English Literature*, Cambridge: D.S. Brewer, 2006, 26.
43 Sykes, *Beastly Questions*, 75.
44 R.B. Manning, *Hunters and Poachers: A Social and Cultural History of Unlawful Hunting in England, 1485–1640*, Oxford: Oxford University Press, 1993, 17.
45 See E.P. Thompson, *Whigs and Hunters: The Origin of the Black Act*, Harmondsworth: Penguin, 1990; B.A. Hanawalt, 'Men's games, King's deer: poaching in Medieval England', *Journal of Medieval and Renaissance Studies* 18, 2 (1988): 175–193.
46 Manning, *Hunters and Poachers*.
47 H. Brody, 'The hunter's view of landscape: a response to Roger Scruton', *Open Democracy*, 21 August 2002, www.opendemocracy.net/ecology-hunting/article_430.jsp, last accessed 22 October 2016.
48 R.R. Wilk, 'Colonialism and wildlife in Belize', *Belizian Studies* 27, 2 (2005): 4–12, 9, cited by D. Dominguéz, 'At the intersection of animal and area studies: fostering Latin Americanist and Caribbeanist animal studies', *Humanimalia* 8, 1 (2016), available at www.depauw.edu/humanimalia/issue%2015/dominguez-a.html, last accessed 16 March 2017.
49 On the fur trade in North America, classic references include: C. Martin, *Keepers of the Game: Indian-Animal Relationships and the Fur Trade*, Berkeley CA: University of California Press, 1982; R. White, *The Middle Ground: Indians, Empires, and Republics in the Great Lakes Region, 1650–1815*, Cambridge: Cambridge University Press, 1991, 94–141; D.J. Wishart (1992) *The Fur Trade of the American West, 1807–1840: A Geographical Synthesis*, Lincoln NE: University of Nebraska Press, 1992; E.R. Wolf, *Europe and the People Without History*, Berkeley CA: University of California Press, 1982, 158–194.
50 V.D. Anderson, *Creatures of Empire: How Domestic Animals Transformed Early America*, New York: Oxford University Press, 2004, 70. This pioneering argument can be complemented by the recent publication of A.L. Smalley, *Wild by Nature: North American Animals Confront Colonization*, Baltimore MD: Johns Hopkins University Press, 2017.
51 S.A. Marks, *Southern Hunting in Black and White: Nature, History, and Ritual in a Carolina Community*, Princeton NJ: Princeton University Press, 1991; N.W. Proctor, *Bathed in Blood: Hunting and Mastery in the Old South*, Charlottesville VA: University of Virginia Press, 2002.
52 The NRA is the National Rifle Association, the GOP is the Republican Party.
53 D.J. Herman, 'Hunting and American identity: the rise, fall, rise and fall of an American pastime', *International Journal of the History of Sport* 31, 1–2 (2014): 55–71.
54 R. Baker, *The American Hunting Myth*, New York: Vantage, 1985; C. Bergman, 'Obits for the fallen hunter: reading the decline – and death? – of hunting in America', *American Literary History* 17, 4 (2005): 818–830; J.E. Dizard, *Mortal Stakes: Hunters and Hunting in Contemporary America*, Amherst MA: University of Massachusetts Press, 2003; D.J. Herman, *Hunting and the American Imagination,* Washington DC: Smithsonian, 2002. On gender, see A.L. Smalley, '"I just like to kill things": women, men and the gender of sport hunting in the United States, 1940–1973', *Gender & History* 17, 1 (2005): 183–209, and A.L. Smalley, '"Our lady sportsmen": gender, class, and conservation in sport hunting magazines, 1873–1920', *The Journal of the Gilded Age and Progressive Era* 4, 4 (2005): 355–380.
55 Proctor, *Bathed in Blood*, discussed by Bergman, 'Obits for the fallen hunter', 822.

56 T.R. Dunlap, 'Sport hunting and conservation 1880–1920', *Environmental History Review* 12, 1 (1988): 51–60; K. Jacoby, *Crimes Against Nature: Squatters, Poachers, Thieves, and the Hidden History of Conservation*, Berkeley CA: University of California Press, 2001.

57 J.R. Ryan, '"Hunting with the camera": photography, wildlife and colonialism in Africa', in C. Philo and C. Wilbert (eds.), *Animal Spaces, Beastly Places: New Geographies of Human–Animal Relations*, London: Routledge, 2000, 206.

58 J. Mackenzie, *The Empire of Nature: Hunting, Conservation, and British Imperialism*, Manchester: Manchester University Press, 1997. See also A. Thompsell, *Hunting Africa: British Sport, African Knowledge and the Nature of Empire*, Houndmills: Palgrave Macmillan, 2015. For princely India, see the now indispensable J.E. Hughes, *Animal Kingdoms: Hunting, the Environment, and Power in the Indian Princely States*, Cambridge MA: Harvard University Press, 2012.

59 W.K. Storey, 'Big cats and imperialism: lion and tiger hunting in Kenya and Northern India, 1898–1930', *Journal of World History* 2, 2 (1991): 135–173, 165, 173.

60 On imperial masculinity see: J.A. Mangan and C. McKenzie, *Militarism, Hunting, Imperialism: 'Blooding' the Martial Male*, Abingdon: Routledge, 2010; T. Loo, 'Of moose and men: hunting for masculinities in British Columbia, 1880–1939', *Western Historical Quarterly* 32, 3 (2001): 296–319; C. Mckenzie, '"Sadly neglected": hunting and gendered identities: a study in gender construction', *International Journal of the History of Sport* 22, 4 (2005): 545–562; J. Sramek, '"Face him like a Briton": tiger hunting, imperialism, and British masculinity in colonial India, 1800–1875', *Victorian Studies* 48, 4 (2006): 659–680.

61 Storey, 'Big cats and imperialism', 170; for other differences, see A.S. Pandian, 'Predatory care: the imperial hunt in Mughal and British India', *Journal of Historical Sociology* 14, 1 (2001): 79–107.

62 J. Sramek, '"Face him like a Briton"'; Thompsell, *Hunting Africa*. For a critique of the emphasis on colonial hunting by the British, see Hughes, *Animal Kingdoms*.

63 E.I. Steinhart, *Black Poachers, White Hunters: A Social History of Hunting in Colonial Kenya*, Oxford: James Currey, 2006.

64 Grossman, *On Killing*; Bergman, 'Obit for the fallen hunter', 819.

65 I.M. Middleton, 'The origins of English fox hunting and the myth of Hugo Meynell and the Quorn', *Sport in History* 25, 1 (2005): 1–16.

66 R. Carr, *English Foxhunting: A History*, London: Weidenfeld and Nicholson, 1986, 108. For gender as well as class in what Carr terms the hunt's 'Indian Summer', see E. Munkwitz, 'Vixens of venery: women, sport, and fox-hunting in Britain, 1860–1914', *Critical Survey* 24, 1 (2012): 74–87.

67 See A. Franklin, 'On fox-hunting and angling: Norbert Elias and the "sportisation" process', *Journal of Historical Sociology* 9, 4 (1996): 432–456, 435.

68 R. Scruton, *On Hunting*, South Bend IN: St. Augustine's Press, 2001. For the cruelty debates in Britain see A.N. May, *The Fox-Hunting Controversy, 1781–2004: Class and Cruelty*, London: Routledge, 2016.

69 H. Osborne and M. Winstanley, 'Rural and urban poaching in Victorian England', *Rural History* 17, 2 (2006): 187–212.

70 Cartmill, *View to a Death*, 31.

71 Cartmill, *View to a Death*, 30.

72 Proponents of the hunting hypothesis draw constantly on these themes and mythos: see R.W. Sussman, 'The myth of man the hunter/man the killer and the evolution of human morality', *Zygon* 34, 3 (1999): 453–471.

73 J. Ortega y Gasset, *Meditations on Hunting*, trans. B.J. Smith, Belgrade MT: Wilderness Adventures Press, 1995, 101. See Stange, *Woman the Hunter*, 45.

74 For 'collective cultural animus', see I.M. Helfant, 'That savage gaze: the contested portrayal of wolves in nineteenth-century Russia' in J. Costlow and A. Nelson (eds.), *Other Animals: Beyond the Human in Russian Culture and History*, Pittsburgh PA: University of Pittsburgh Press, 2010, 64. For the war on the wolf, see also J.T. Coleman, *Vicious: Wolves and Men in America*. New Haven CT: Yale University Press 2004. For a wider cultural history see G. Marvin, *Wolf*, London: Reaktion, 2012.
75 P. Singer and J. Mason, *The Ethics of What We Eat: Why Our Food Choices Matter*, Emmaus PA: Rodale, 2006, 258.
76 A brilliant analysis is I. Braverman, *Wildlife: The Institution of Nature*, Stanford CA: Stanford University Press, 2015.
77 Sykes, *Beastly Questions*, 68: 'the Romans . . . saw it as their spiritual duty to bring the wilderness to order, investing their efforts in the paradox of domesticating the wild so that they might dwell in the manner of their gods in close proximity to, but separate from, wild animals'.
78 G. Kron, 'Animal husbandry, hunting, fishing, and fish production', in J.P. Oleson (ed.), *The Oxford Handbook of Engineering and Technology in the Classical World*, Oxford: Oxford University Press, 2008, 175–222.
79 J.E. Salisbury, *The Beast Within: Animals in the Middle Ages*, second edition, London: Routledge, 2010, 39. Compare Hughes, *Animal Kingdoms*, on Indian princely *shikargahs* in the colonial era.
80 E. Griffin, *Blood Sport: Hunting in Britain since 1066*, New Haven CT: Yale University Press, 2007, 3.
81 On some of the politics of the hunt in Britain, see A. Taylor, '"Pig-sticking princes": royal hunting, moral outrage, and the republican opposition to animal abuse in nineteenth and twentieth-century Britain', *History* 89, 293 (2004): 30–48; M. Tichelar, 'Putting animals into politics: the Labour Party and hunting in the first half of the twentieth century', *Rural History* 17, 2 (2006): 213–234.
82 See for instance the discussion in R.J. Starr, 'Silvia's deer (Vergil, *Aeneid* 7.479-502): game parks and Roman Law', *American Journal of Philology* 113, 3 (1992): 435–439.
83 Sykes, *Beastly Questions*, 72.
84 Sykes, *Beastly Questions*, 74.
85 J.E. Dizard, *Going Wild: Hunting, Animal Rights, and the Contested Meanings of Nature*, revised edition, Amherst MA: University of Massachusetts Press, 1999.
86 See M. Yardley, 'Brief history of the sporting gun', available at www.positiveshooting.com/HistoryoftheSportingGun.html, last accessed 24 November 2016. Larger issues surrounding technology are introduced in N.C. Govaroff, 'The hunter and his gun in Haute-Provence', in P. Lemonnier (ed.), *Technological Choices: Transformation in Material Cultures since the Neolithic*, Abingdon: Routledge, 1993, 227–237.
87 R. Spomer, 'Why I hunt', http://idahoptv.org/outdoors/shows/hunt/why.html. http://video.idahoptv.org/video/2316499872/, last accessed 16 August 2016.
88 Fiddes, *Meat*, 73.
89 Sykes, *Beastly Questions*, 75.
90 D.J. Wadiwel, *The War Against Animals*, Leiden: Brill, 2015; J. Serpell, *In the Company of Animals: A Study of Human–Animal Relationships*, Cambridge: Cambridge University Press, 1996, 5. Richard Bulliet portrays identification of opposition to hunting as an expression of a 'postdomesticity' in which certain Western peoples are 'far away, both physically and psychologically' from the animals they depend on: R.W. Bulliet, *Hunters, Herders and Hamburgers: The Past and Future of Human–Animal Relationships*, New York: Columbia University Press, 2005.
91 Wadiwel, *War Against Animals*, 6, n. 19.

92 T. Ingold, 'From trust to domination: an alternative history of human–animal relations', in A. Manning and J. Serpell (eds.), *Animals and Human Society: Changing Perspectives*, London: Routledge, 2002, 1–21, 12.
93 G. Marvin, 'Wild killing: contesting the animal in hunting', in The Animal Studies Group, *Killing Animals*, Urbana IL: University of Illinois Press, 2006, 10–29, 19.
94 D. Donald, 'Pangs watched in perpetuity: Sir Edwin Landseer's pictures of dying deer and the ethos of Victorian sportsmanship', in The Animal Studies Group (eds.), *Killing Animals*, Urbana IL: University of Illinois Press, 2006, 50–68, 50.
95 Marvin, 'Wild killing', 24.
96 E. Kohn, *How Forests Think: Towards an Anthropology Beyond the Human*, Berkeley CA: University of California Press, 2013.
97 M. Olson, *The Compassionate Hunter's Guidebook: Hunting from the Heart*, Gabriola Island BC: New Society Publishers, 2014, 16.
98 H. Dahles, 'Game killing and killing games: an anthropologist looking at hunting in a modern society', *Society & Animals* 1, 2 (1993): 169–184.
99 P. Descola, *The Ecology of Others*, Chicago IL: Prickly Paradigm Press, 2013, 64. For a contrary view, see J. Knight, 'The anonymity of the hunt', *Current Anthropology* 53, 3 (2012): 334–355.
100 Ehrenreich, *Blood Rites*, 47.
101 E. Hill, 'Animals as agents: hunting ritual and relational ontologies in prehistoric Alaska and Chukotka', *Cambridge Archaeological Journal* 21, 3 (2011): 407–426; K. Armstrong Oma, 'Between trust and domination: social contracts between humans and animals', *World Archaeology* 42, 2 (2010): 175–187.
102 S. Nicholls, *Paradise Found: Nature in America at the Time of Discovery*, Chicago IL: University of Chicago Press, 2009, 353–354.
103 Hughes, *Animal Kingdoms*, 8.
104 C. Siebert, 'An elephant crackup?' *New York Times*, 8 October 2006, available at www.nytimes.com/2006/10/08/magazine/08elephant.html, last accessed 16 March 2016; T.K. Ruth et al., 'Large-carnivore response to recreational big-game hunting along the Yellowstone National Park and Absaroka-Beartooth Wilderness boundary', *Wildlife Society Bulletin* 31, 4 (2003): 1150–1161.
105 B. Resl, 'Introduction: animals in culture, ca.1000–ca.1400', in B. Resl (ed.), *A Cultural History of Animals in the Medieval Age*, Oxford: Berg, 2007, 1–26, 23.
106 Salisbury, *Beast Within*, 36, 38.
107 K. Jones, 'From the field to the frontier: hounds, hunting and the canine–human alliance', in K. Nagai, K. Jones, D. Landry, M. Mattfeld, C. Rooney and C. Sleigh (eds.) *Cosmopolitan Animals*, Houndmills: Palgrave Macmillan, 2015, 167–180.
108 Jones, 'From the field to the frontier', 168.
109 I have taken these words, rather rudely out of context, from J. Lorimer and S. Whatmore, 'After the "king of beasts": Samuel Baker and the embodied historical geographies of elephant hunting in mid-nineteenth-century Ceylon', *Journal of Historical Geography* 35, 4 (2009): 668–689, 688.
110 Darwin, *Descent of Man*, 136; M. Maslin, *The Cradle of Humanity: How the Changing Landscape of Africa Made Us So Smart*, Oxford: Oxford University Press, 2017, 1.
111 Mackenzie, *Empire of Nature*, 8.
112 Ehrenreich, *Blood Rites*, 48.
113 For instance: '"Prehistoric Sistine Chapel" gets world heritage status', BBC News, 23 June 2014, available at www.bbc.co.uk/news/entertainment-arts-27978440, last accessed 17 March 2017. For Herzog's interpretation, see *Cave of Forgotten Dreams* (2010), dir. W. Herzog, and 'The birth of the modern soul', *Spiegel Online*, 16 February 2011,

www.spiegel.de/international/zeitgeist/werner-herzog-s-cave-painting-documentary-the-birth-of-the-modern-human-soul-a-745754.html.
114 Sykes, *Beastly Questions*, 159.

Bibliography

Adovasio, J.M., Soffer, O., and Page, J. *The Invisible Sex: Uncovering the True Roles of Women in Prehistory*, Washington DC: Smithsonian Books, 2007.

Allen, M. 'Not just dormice – food for thought?', emphasis in the original, available at https://notjustdormice.wordpress.com/2015/01/22/hunting-in-the-roman-world-anthropology-animal-bones-and-ancient-literature/, last accessed 16 March 2016.

Allsen, T. *The Royal Hunt in Eurasian History*, Philadelphia PA: University of Pennsylvania Press, 206.

Anderson, J.K. *Hunting in the Ancient World*, Berkeley CA: University of California Press, 1985.

Anderson, V.D. *Creatures of Empire: How Domestic Animals Transformed Early America*, New York: Oxford University Press, 2004.

Ardrey, R. *The Hunting Hypothesis: A Personal Inquiry Concerning the Evolutionary Nature of Man*, London: Collins, 1976.

Armstrong Oma, K. 'Between trust and domination: social contracts between humans and animals', *World Archaeology* 42, 2 (2010): 175–187.

Baker, R. *The American Hunting Myth*, New York: Vantage, 1985.

Barringer, J.M. *The Hunt in Ancient Greece*, Baltimore MD: Johns Hopkins University Press, 2001.

Bergman, C. 'Obits for the fallen hunter: reading the decline – and death? – of hunting in America', *American Literary History* 17, 4 (2005): 818–830.

Boglioli, M. *A Matter of Life and Death: Hunting in Contemporary Vermont*, Amherst MA: University of Massachusetts Press, 2009.

Braverman, I. *Wildlife: The Institution of Nature*, Stanford CA: Stanford University Press, 2015.

Brody, H. 'The hunter's view of landscape: a response to Roger Scruton', *Open Democracy* 21 August 2002, www.opendemocracy.net/ecology-hunting/article_430.jsp, last accessed 22 October 2016.

Bulliet, R.W. *Hunters, Herders and Hamburgers: The Past and Future of Human–Animal Relationships*, New York: Columbia University Press, 2005.

Carr, R. *English Foxhunting: A History*, London: Weidenfeld and Nicholson, 1986, 108.

Clark, W.M. 'Why hunt?', 2004, available at www.wildfowling.co.uk/magazine/whyhunt.htm, last accessed 16 March 2017. Republished as W.M. Clark, 'Hunting is a natural, ethical, and healthy undertaking', in D. Laney (ed.), *Hunting: Opposing Viewpoints in Context*, Farmington Hills MI: Greenhaven Press, 2008.

Clarke, A.C. *2001: A Space Odyssey*, London: Hutchinson, 1968.

Coleman, J.T. *Vicious: Wolves and Men in America*. New Haven CT: Yale University Press 2004.

Cummins, J. *The Hound and the Hawk: The Art of Medieval Hunting*, London: Weidenfeld and Nicholson, 1988.

Dahles, H. 'Game killing and killing games: an anthropologist looking at hunting in a modern society', *Society & Animals* 1, 2 (1993): 169–184.

Dart, R. 'The predatory transition from ape to man', *International Anthropological and Linguistic Review* 1, 4 (1953): 201–217.

Darwin, C. *The Descent of Man, and Selection in Relation to Sex*, London: John Murray, 1871.

Descola, P. *The Ecology of Others*, Chicago IL: Prickly Paradigm Press, 2013.

Diamond, J. 'The worst mistake in the history of the human race', *Discover* 8, 5 (1987): 64–66.

Dizard, J.E. *Going Wild: Hunting, Animal Rights, and the Contested Meanings of Nature*, revised edition, Amherst MA: University of Massachusetts Press, 1999.

Dizard, J.E. *Mortal Stakes: Hunters and Hunting in Contemporary America*, Amherst MA: University of Massachusetts Press, 2003.

Domínguez, D. 'At the intersection of animal and area studies: fostering Latin Americanist and Caribbeanist animal studies', *Humanimalia* 8, 1 (2016), available at www.depauw.edu/humanimalia/issue%2015/dominguez-a.html, last accessed 16 March 2017.

Domínguez-Rodrigo, M. 'Hunting and scavenging by early humans: the state of the debate', *Journal of World Prehistory* 16, 1 (2002): 1–54.

Donald, D. 'Pangs watched in perpetuity: Sir Edwin Landseer's pictures of dying deer and the ethos of Victorian sportsmanship', in The Animal Studies Group (eds.), *Killing Animals*, Urbana IL: University of Illinois Press, 2006, 50–68.

Dunbabin, K.M.D. *The Roman Banquet: Images of Conviviality*, Cambridge: Cambridge University Press, 2003.

Dunlap, T.R. 'Sport hunting and conservation 1880–1920', *Environmental History Review* 12, 1 (1988): 51–60.

Ehrenreich, B. *Blood Rites: Origins and History of the Passions of War*, London: Virago, 1997.

Fiddes, N. *Meat: A Natural Symbol*, London: Routledge, 1991.

Franklin, A. 'On fox-hunting and angling: Norbert Elias and the "sportisation" process', *Journal of Historical Sociology* 9, 4 (1996): 432–456, 435.

Govaroff, N.C. 'The hunter and his gun in Haute-Provence', in P. Lemonnier (ed.), *Technological Choices: Transformation in Material Cultures since the Neolithic*, Abingdon: Routledge, 1993, 227–237.

Griffin, E. *Blood Sport: Hunting in Britain since 1066*, New Haven CT: Yale University Press, 2007.

Grossman, D. *On Killing: The Psychological Cost of Learning to Kill*, revised edition, New York: Open Road, 2014.

Gurven, M. and Hill, K. 'Why do men hunt? A reevaluation of "man the hunter" and the sexual division of labour, *Current Anthropology* 50, 1 (2009): 51–74.

Hanawalt, B.A. 'Men's games, King's deer: poaching in Medieval England', *Journal of Medieval and Renaissance Studies* 18, 2 (1988): 175–193.

Harari, Y.N. *Sapiens: A Brief History of Humankind*, London: Vintage, 2015.

Haraway, D.J. *Primate Visions: Gender, Race, and Nature in the World of Modern Science*, London: Routledge, 1989.

Haraway, D.J. *Simians, Cyborgs, and Women: The Reinvention of Nature*, London: Free Association Books, 1991.

Hart, D. and Sussman, R.W. *Man the Hunted: Primates, Predators, and Human Evolution*, expanded edition, New York: Westview Press, 2009.

Helfant, I.M. 'That savage gaze: the contested portrayal of wolves in nineteenth-century Russia' in J. Costlow and A. Nelson (eds.), *Other Animals: Beyond the Human in Russian Culture and History*, Pittsburgh PA: University of Pittsburgh Press, 2010, 63–76.

Herman, D.J. *Hunting and the American Imagination*, Washington DC: Smithsonian, 2002.

Herman, D.J. 'Hunting and American identity: the rise, fall, rise and fall of an American pastime', *International Journal of the History of Sport* 31, 1–2 (2014): 55–71.

Hill, E. 'Animals as agents: hunting ritual and relational ontologies in prehistoric Alaska and Chukotka', *Cambridge Archaeological Journal* 21, 3 (2011): 407–426.

Hughes, J.D. 'Hunting in the ancient Mediterranean world', in L. Kalof (ed.), *A Cultural History of Animals in Antiquity*, Oxford: Berg, 2007, 47–70.

Hughes, J.E. *Animal Kingdoms: Hunting, the Environment, and Power in the Indian Princely States*, Cambridge MA: Harvard University Press, 2012.

Ingold, T. 'From trust to domination: an alternative history of human–animal relations', in A. Manning and J. Serpell (eds.), *Animals and Human Society: Changing Perspectives*, London: Routledge, 2002, 1–21, 12.

Jacoby, K. *Crimes Against Nature: Squatters, Poachers, Thieves, and the Hidden History of Conservation*, Berkeley CA: University of California Press, 2001.

Jones, K. 'From the field to the frontier: hounds, hunting and the canine–human alliance', in K. Nagai, K. Jones, D. Landry, M. Mattfeld, C. Rooney, and C. Sleigh (eds.), *Cosmopolitan Animals*, Houndmills: Palgrave Macmillan, 2015, 167–180.

Kerasote, T. *Bloodties: Nature, Culture, and the Hunt*, New York: Kodansha, 19.

Kluger, J. 'Sorry vegans – meat-eating made us human', *Time*, 9 March 2016, available at http://time.com/4252373/meat-eating-veganism-evolution/, last accessed 16 March 2017.

Kohn, E. *How Forests Think: Towards an Anthropology Beyond the Human*, Berkeley CA: University of California Press, 2013.

Knight, J. 'The anonymity of the hunt', *Current Anthropology* 53, 3 (2012): 334–355.

Kron, G. 'Animal husbandry, hunting, fishing, and fish production', in J.P. Oleson (ed.), *The Oxford Handbook of Engineering and Technology in the Classical World*, Oxford: Oxford University Press, 2008, 175–222.

Lee, P.Y. 'Introduction: housing slaughter', in P.Y. Lee (ed.), *Meat, Modernity, and the Rise of the Slaughterhouse*, Durham NH: University of New Hampshire Press, 2008, 1–9.

Lee, R.B. and DeVore, I. (eds.), *Man the Hunter*, Chicago IL: Aldine Transaction, 1968.

Loo, T. 'Of moose and men: hunting for masculinities in British Columbia, 1880–1939', *Western Historical Quarterly* 32, 3 (2001): 296–319.

Lorimer, J. and Whatmore, S. 'After the "king of beasts": Samuel Baker and the embodied historical geographies of elephant hunting in mid-nineteenth-century Ceylon', *Journal of Historical Geography* 35, 4 (2009): 668–689.

Mackenzie, J. *The Empire of Nature: Hunting, Conservation, and British Imperialism*, Manchester: Manchester University Press, 1997.

Mangan, J.A. and McKenzie, C. *Militarism, Hunting, Imperialism: 'Blooding' the Martial Male*, Abingdon: Routledge, 2010.

Manning, R.B. *Hunters and Poachers: A Social and Cultural History of Unlawful Hunting in England, 1485–1640*, Oxford: Oxford University Press, 1993.

Marks, S.A. *Southern Hunting in Black and White: Nature, History, and Ritual in a Carolina Community*, Princeton NJ: Princeton University Press, 1991.

Martin, C. *Keepers of the Game: Indian–Animal Relationships and the Fur Trade*, Berkeley CA: University of California Press, 1982.

Marvin, G. 'The problem of foxes: legitimate and illegitimate killing', in J. Knight (ed.), *Natural Enemies: People–Wildlife Conflicts in Anthropological Perspective*, London: Routledge, 2000, 189–211.

Marvin, G. 'Wild killing: contesting the animal in hunting', in The Animal Studies Group, *Killing Animals*, Urbana IL: University of Illinois Press, 2006, 10–29.

Marvin, G. *Wolf*, London: Reaktion, 2012.

Marvin, W.P. *Hunting Law and Ritual in Medieval English Literature*, Cambridge: D.S. Brewer, 2006.

Maslin, M. *The Cradle of Humanity: How the Changing Landscape of Africa Made Us So Smart*, Oxford: Oxford University Press, 2017.

May, A.N. *The Fox-Hunting Controversy, 1781–2004: Class and Cruelty*, London: Routledge, 2016.

Mckenzie, C. '"Sadly neglected": hunting and gendered identities: a study in gender construction', *International Journal of the History of Sport* 22, 4 (2005): 545–562.

McKie, R. 'Humans hunted for meat 2 million years ago', *Guardian*, 23 September 2012, available at www.theguardian.com/science/2012/sep/23/human-hunting- evolution-2million-years, last accessed 16 March 2017.

Middleton, I.M. 'The origins of English fox hunting and the myth of Hugo Meynell and the Quorn', *Sport in History* 25, 1 (2005): 1–16.

Mithen, S. 'Ecological interpretations of Paleolithic art', *Proceedings of the Prehistoric Society* 57, 1 (1991): 103–114.

Milton, K. 'A hypothesis to explain the role of meat-eating in human evolution', *Evolutionary Anthropology* 8, 1 (1999): 11–21.

Moore, J. *Capitalism in the Web of Life*, London: Verso, 2015.

Munkwitz, E. 'Vixens of venery: women, sport, and fox-hunting in Britain, 1860–1914', *Critical Survey* 24, 1 (2012): 74–87.

Nicholls, S. *Paradise Found: Nature in America at the Time of Discovery*, Chicago IL: University of Chicago Press, 2009.

Oggins, R.S. *The Kings and their Hawks: Falconry in Medieval England*, New Haven CT: Yale University Press, 2004.

Olson, M. *The Compassionate Hunter's Guidebook: Hunting from the Heart*, Gabriola Island BC: New Society Publishers, 2014, 9.

Ortega y Gasset, J. *Meditations on Hunting*, trans. B.J. Smith, Belgrade MT: Wilderness Adventures Press, 1995.

Osborne, H. and Winstanley, M. 'Rural and urban poaching in Victorian England', *Rural History* 17, 2 (2006): 187–212.

Pandian, A.S. 'Predatory care: the imperial hunt in Mughal and British India', *Journal of Historical Sociology* 14, 1 (2001): 79–107.

Perdikaris, S. and Woollett, J. 'Hunting', in P.J. Crabtree (ed.), *Medieval Archaeology: An Encyclopedia*, New York: Garland, 2001, 168–170.

Proctor, N.W. *Bathed in Blood: Hunting and Mastery in the Old South*, Charlottesville VA: University of Virginia Press, 2002.

Resl, B. 'Introduction: animals in culture, ca.1000–ca.1400', in B. Resl (ed.), *A Cultural History of Animals in the Medieval Age*, Oxford: Berg, 2007, 1–26.

Reybrouck, D.V. *From Primitives to Primates: A History of Ethnographic and Primatological Analogies in the Study of Prehistory*, Leiden: Sidestone Press, 2012.

Richards, J. *The World Hunt: An Environmental History of the Commodification of Animals*, Berkeley CA: University of California Press, 2014.

Rooney, A. *Hunting in Middle English Literature*, Cambridge: Boydell Press, 1993.

Ruth, T.K., Smith, D.W., Haroldson, M.A., Buotte, P.C., Schwartz, C.C., Quigley, H.B., Cherry, S., Murphy, K.M., Tyers, D., and Frey, K. 'Large-carnivore response to recreational big-game hunting along the Yellowstone National Park and Absaroka-Beartooth Wilderness boundary', *Wildlife Society Bulletin* 31, 4 (2003): 1150–1161.

Ryan, J.R. '"Hunting with the camera": photography, wildlife and colonialism in Africa', in C. Philo and C. Wilbert (eds.), *Animal Spaces, Beastly Places: New Geographies of Human-Animal Relations*, London: Routledge, 2000, 205–222.

Salisbury, J.E. *The Beast Within: Animals in the Middle Ages*, second edition, London: Routledge, 2010.

Scruton, R. *On Hunting*, South Bend IN: St. Augustine's Press, 2001.

Serpell, J. *In the Company of Animals: A Study of Human–Animal Relationships*, Cambridge: Cambridge University Press, 1996.

Shepard, P. *The Tender Carnivore and the Sacred Game*, New York: Scribner, 1973.

Siebert, C. 'An elephant crackup?', *New York Times*, 8 October 2006, available at www.nytimes.com/2006/10/08/magazine/08elephant.html, last accessed 16 March 2017.

Singer, P. and Mason, J. *The Ethics of What We Eat: Why Our Food Choices Matter*, Emmaus PA: Rodale, 2006, 258.

Sisson, M. 'Real primal: hunting for dinner', 4 February 2009, available at www.marksdailyapple.com/hunting-ethics/, last accessed 16 March 2017.

Slocum, S. 'Woman the gatherer: male bias in anthropology', in R.R. Reiter (ed.), *Toward an Anthropology of Women*, New York: Monthly Review, 1975, 36–50.

Smalley, A.L. '"Our lady sportsmen": gender, class, and conservation in sport hunting magazines, 1873–1920', *The Journal of the Gilded Age and Progressive Era* 4, 4 (2005): 355–380.

Smalley, A.L. '"I just like to kill things": women, men and the gender of sport hunting in the United States, 1940–1973', *Gender & History* 17, 1 (2005): 183–209.

Smalley, A.L. *Wild by Nature: North American Animals Confront Colonization*, Baltimore MD: Johns Hopkins University Press, 2017.

Speth, J.D. *The Paleoanthropology and Archaeology of Big Game Hunting: Protein, Fat, or Politics?* New York: Springer, 2010.

Spomer, R. 'Why I hunt', http://idahoptv.org/outdoors/shows/hunt/why.html. http://video.idahoptv.org/video/2316499872/, last accessed 16 August 2016.

Sramek, J. '"Face him like a Briton": tiger hunting, imperialism, and British masculinity in colonial India, 1800–1875', *Victorian Studies* 48, 4 (2006): 659–680.

Stanford, C.B. *The Hunting Apes: Meat Eating and the Origins of Human Behavior*, Princeton NJ: Princeton University Press, 1999.

Stange, M.Z. *Woman the Hunter*, Boston: Beacon Press, 1997.

Stange, M.Z., Oyster, C.K., and Sloan, J.E. (eds.), *Encyclopedia of Women in Today's World*, Volume 1, Los Angeles CA: Sage, 2011.

Starr, R.J. 'Silvia's deer (Vergil, *Aeneid* 7.479-502): game parks and Roman Law', *American Journal of Philology* 113, 3 (1992): 435–439.

Steinhart, E.I. *Black Poachers, White Hunters: A Social History of Hunting in Colonial Kenya*, Oxford: James Currey, 2006.

Storey, W.K. 'Big cats and imperialism: lion and tiger hunting in Kenya and Northern India, 1898-1930', *Journal of World History* 2, 2 (1991): 135–173.

Sussman, R.W. 'The myth of man the hunter/man the killer and the evolution of human morality', *Zygon* 34, 3 (1999): 453–471.

Sussman, R.W. 'Why the legend of the killer ape never dies: the enduring power of cultural beliefs to distort our view of human nature', in D.P. Fry (ed.), *War, Peace, and Human Nature: The Convergence of Evolutionary and Cultural Views*, Oxford: Oxford University Press, 2013, 97–111.

Sykes, N. *Beastly Questions: Animal Answers to Archaeological Issues*, London: Bloomsbury, 2015.

Taylor, A. '"Pig-sticking princes": royal hunting, moral outrage, and the republican opposition to animal abuse in nineteenth and twentieth-century Britain', *History* 89, 293 (2004): 30–48.

Tichelar, M. 'Putting animals into politics: the Labour Party and hunting in the first half of the twentieth century', *Rural History* 17, 2 (2006): 213–234.

Thompsell, A. *Hunting Africa: British Sport, African Knowledge and the Nature of Empire*, Houndmills: Palgrave Macmillan, 2015.

Thompson, E.P. *Whigs and Hunters: The Origin of the Black Act*, Harmondsworth: Penguin, 1990.

Wadiwel, D.J. *The War Against Animals*, Leiden: Brill, 2015.
White, R. *The Middle Ground: Indians, Empires, and Republics in the Great Lakes Region, 1650–1815*, Cambridge: Cambridge University Press, 1991.
Wilk, R.R. 'Colonialism and wildlife in Belize', *Belizian Studies* 27, 2 (2005): 4–12.
Wishart, D.J. *The Fur Trade of the American West, 1807–1840: A Geographical Synthesis*, Lincoln NE: University of Nebraska Press, 1992.
Wolf, E.R. *Europe and the People Without History*, Berkeley CA: University of California Press, 1982, 158–194.
Wong, K, 'How hunting made us human', *Scientific American* 310, 4 (2014), available at www.scientificamerican.com/article/how-hunting-made-us-human/, last accessed 16 March 2017.
Yardley, M. 'Brief history of the sporting gun', available at www.positiveshooting.com/HistoryoftheSportingGun.html, last accessed 24 November 2016.
Zihlman, A. and Tanner, N. 'Gathering and the hominid adaptation', in L. Tiger and A. Fowler (eds.), *Female Hierarchies*, Chicago IL: Beresford Book Service, 1978, 163–194.

20
EATING ANIMALS

Chris Otter

Introduction

Eating animals is integral to the deep history of humanity. Human bodies have evolved to eat animals as well as plants: we are heterotrophic omnivores. We produce stomach acids which break down elastin; we need vitamin B12 to live; and our intestinal morphology strongly suggests an adaptation to a higher-energy-density diet.[1] Although it is perfectly possible (and arguably ethically and ecologically desirable) to be a vegetarian, the majority of people economically able to access meat choose to eat it. Globally, well over 50 billion animals are slaughtered annually for human consumption.[2]

The human relationship with meat, then, extends far back into deep history, and is intertwined with our evolution. Eating animals could, on this evidence, rather easily be considered something natural rather than cultural, biological rather than historical. Meat-eating is, however, a complex mix of all of these things. To make a dead animal edible, it must be made into meat, which is a deeply cultural process. Noelie Vialles has defined meat as the muscular tissue of a domesticated animal, slaughtered according to specific rituals and sold commercially.[3] This definition is, however, somewhat narrow: it should be extended to include the meat of wild animals or bushmeat, which is consumed in significant quantities in the developing world. One estimate suggests that in Ghana, around 385,000 tons of wild meat was consumed during the 1990s.[4] Another cultural dimension of meat is its symbolic resonance. In most cultures, taboos define which animals can and cannot be eaten, and meat is seldom shared equally across society: its distribution is invariably inseparable from issues of power, status, and identity.

The system which farms, slaughters and processes tens of billions of animals annually is truly monumental in scale. It shapes one of the most important relationships – biologically, morally, economically, ecologically – which humans have with animals. The first part of this chapter sketches, very sweepingly, a deep history of meat-eating and identifies key moments of transition: domestication, the Columbian Exchange, early-modern selective breeding and the 'Great Acceleration' of the last 70 years.

The remainder of the chapter concentrates on the past 200 years, and focuses on four animals: cattle, pigs, chickens, and horses. En route, it shows how eating animals has been mediated through innumerable cultural frameworks and, most fatefully, by the rise of capitalism.

Eating animals from deep history to the Great Acceleration

Paleoarchaeological evidence suggests that while early hominins were predominantly plant-eating, they were opportunistic omnivores who ate insects and small animals, scavenged carcases of larger ones, and sometimes hunted.[5] The consumption of animals was transformed by the emergence of the controlled use of fire, something evident on a widespread scale by around 125000 BCE. Cooking animal flesh makes it considerably more digestible and increases the amount of energy humans derive from it. As Richard Wrangham has argued, cooking made possible a higher-energy diet, which favoured the selection of shorter intestines and bigger brains.[6] In an evolutionary sense, we really are what we eat, or more properly, we have been shaped by what our ancestors ate.

Although meat was a relatively small part of the human diet, early hominins and humans consumed a wider range of living beings than we do today. The narrowing of the number of animals commonly eaten began during the Neolithic period, beginning around 10000 BCE. The domestication of animals was protracted and complex, but it gave settled human populations a relatively reliable stream of meat, milk, dung, and muscle power. This was a prolonged and geographically dispersed process occurring across the Near East and Central, South and East Asia from 13000 BCE onwards. No large mammal was domesticated in the Americas following the extinction of megafauna there around 13000 BCE.

Domestication meant that the evolution of cattle, pigs, sheep, chickens, dogs and horses was gradually but ineluctably shaped by humans, and that this evolution in turn shaped human history. The development of agriculture, then, was an 'evolutionary revolution' which set humans and domesticated animals on a complex co-evolutionary history.[7] Such animals were captive, and their feeding and breeding subject to control by human communities.[8] 'The domesticated animal is the epoch-changing tool, realizing human intention in the flesh', notes Donna Haraway.[9] Domesticated animals developed a 'domestic phenotype' as an adaptation to their new environment, the characteristics of which include tameness, shorter limbs, reduced brain size, floppy ears and reduced sex differences. Such phenotypes are 'a form of convergent evolution that occurs in human environments and only in human environments'.[10]

Domesticated pigs, for example, have curly tails and shorter snouts: white colouring is another mark of domestication.[11] Many animals, however, were not amenable to domestication. Only non-carnivorous, placid animals that mated in captivity and had clear dominance hierarchies could be domesticated in this way. Some animals, such as cats, are self-domesticated or semi-domesticated, retaining far closer links to their wild cousins.[12]

Although artificial selection was practised and animals developed domesticated morphologies, transformation was, for centuries, extremely gradual. Livestock remained considerably smaller and slower-maturing than they are today. During the early modern period, however, two important transformations, one quantitative and one qualitative, altered the trajectory of this conjoined human–animal history. The first, quantitative, transition, was the Columbian Exchange. Although the New World lacked megafauna by the fifteenth century, its various creatures enchanted and perturbed European travellers, and complicated European natural history.[13] In addition to such complex cultural encounters there was also, of course, biological exchange. Horses, cattle, sheep, chickens, pigs and goats were brought to the New World in 1493. Ranching began in Mexico in the 1530s.[14] These animals, particularly pigs, cattle, and horses, had abundant food and no predators, so their populations mushroomed quickly.[15] Many of them ultimately went wild. By the 1840s, the great plains of Buenos Aires supported around 3 million cattle.[16] The reintroduction of megafauna to the New World would have major repercussions for the history of human meat-eating by significantly increasing global livestock populations. In 1929, the total number of world cattle was estimated at between 600 million and 620 million; there were between 680 million sheep and goats and 280–320 million pigs.[17]

The second, qualitative, transformation was the intensification of artificial selection in Europe. The experiments of Gresley, Webster, and Bakewell in eighteenth-century England significantly changed animal form. Bakewell used relentless inbreeding to develop longhorn cattle and Leicester sheep. The aim was to reduce the ratio of bone to flesh, and make the animals mature more quickly. Although neither of Bakewell's key breeds were long-term successes, his work was furthered by early nineteenth-century breeders, who developed greater intraspecies variation and developed recording techniques to monitor progress.[18] The result was quicker-maturing animals producing more meat than previously. As Darwin commented, domesticated animals were being transformed, not for their own good, but for 'man's use or fancy'.[19]

The final phase in this schematic history is the 'Great Acceleration', a term referring to the post-1945 period, in which 'every indicator of human activity underwent a sharp increase'.[20] This includes the eating of animals; economic development and rising meat consumption have become closely intertwined. As Tony Weis notes, 'the climb up the "animal protein ladder" is part and parcel of the climb up the "development ladder", meaning that western dietary habits have globalised'.[21] In China, meat consumption rose from 4 to 61 kilogrammes per capita between 1961 and 2010.[22] During this period, global meat production increased by more than three times, exceeding 230 million tonnes annually by 2000.[23] The world's livestock population grew correspondingly by a factor of 3.5, and the number killed annually rose almost eightfold.[24] The zoomass of domesticated animals now dwarfs that of wild ones: in 2000, there were around 4.3 billion large domestic animals, including 1.65 billion cattle and water buffaloes, and 900 million pigs. This amounted to around 620 million tonnes of live zoomass, ten times that of wild terrestrial animals.[25] Monogastric animals, such as pigs and chickens, whose feed conversion rates are higher than cattle's, have become particularly populous. Their livestock are more intensely farmed and rigidly controlled than polygastric livestock.[26]

As Jason Moore has argued, the past 500 years of world history has seen the relentless interpenetration of capitalism and life.[27] Livestock are, perhaps, the most obvious example of this. While livestock's economic history (and ecological reshaping) is considerably longer, the combined impact of the Columbian Exchange, intensified selective breeding, and the Great Acceleration of livestock production show how closely interconnected capitalism and the eating of animals have become. The history of capitalism is thus entwined not with nonhuman life per se, but a select group of species amenable to domestication and, later, what the creators of Dolly the Sheep called *biological control*.[28]

Cattle

The first wave of cattle improvement, then, involved global cattle exchanges and intensified selective breeding. In the early nineteenth century, cattle breeders created numerous important cattle breeds. The Shorthorn was produced by applying Bakewell's techniques to Durham and North Yorkshire cattle: a herdbook, the first for any farm animal, was founded in 1822.[29] Like Bakewell's animals, the Shorthorn was early-maturing. By 1908, 64% of British cattle were Shorthorns.[30] Following the work of Hugh Watson at Keillor, Forfarshire, from 1808, the Aberdeen Angus became a popular beef breed.[31] The Hereford, which acquired its red colour from Anglo-Saxon cattle, and its white face from Dutch ones, was fully established by the mid-nineteenth century.[32] In the twentieth century, French breeds such as the Charolais, Simmental, and Durham-Manceaux became very popular.[33] Later twentieth-century developments included so-called 'double-muscled' breeds such as the Belgian Blue, with huge hindquarters, caused by a mutation in the breed's myostatin gene and fixed through inbreeding.[34]

During the nineteenth century, these improved European breeds were exported to the New World to create premium herds through interbreeding with the descendants of cattle brought across during the original Columbian Exchange. Shorthorn bulls were imported into Argentina from 1844: other breeds followed.[35] By 1910, older herds had been largely replaced with European pedigree herds.[36] By 1925, 227,000 pedigree bulls had been imported into Argentina, most of which were British.[37] Other South American nations imported European animals: Herefords and Shorthorns were imported into Uruguay and Paraguay.[38] In more tropical Brazil, Indian Zebu cattle were imported in the twentieth century. The large-eared Indu-Brazil was produced by crossing three Zebu breeds, the Gir, Guzerat, and Nellore.[39] Brahmans crossed with Shorthorns produced the Santa Gertrudis.[40] The Great Acceleration saw global ranching intensify. In Costa Rica, one-eighth of the country was used for cattle-raising in 1950, a figure reaching one-third by 1980.[41]

In the United States, the first Shorthorn was brought over from Britain before 1800, while Aberdeen Anguses arrived around 1860.[42] In 1884, one estimate placed the number of Herefords imported into the US over the previous five years at between 3,900 and 4,000.[43] Such animals were used to improve herds across the United States. The American landscape, like that in Argentina and Brazil, was greatly affected by this transformation. Railways allowed the disaggregation of ranching, slaughter and consumption, while barbed wire imprisoned cattle in an 'Archipelago Ranch ... strewn across the plains'.[44] Cowboys and gauchos, hemmed in by fences and subjugated to the rhythms of the international meat industry, had their way of life obliterated. In Japan, an entirely new livestock industry developed following the

Meiji restoration of 1868. In pre-Meiji restoration Japan, meat was consumed in very small quantities, but in 1871 Emperor Meiji eliminated the prohibition on meat-eating in the imperial household.[45] This stimulated the importation of European breeds which were crossed with indigenous Japanese Wagyu cattle to produce, among other breeds, those responsible for Kobe beef.[46]

Kobe beef is renowned for its marbling. Marbling is not an inherent, inevitable property of animal flesh, but a characteristic produced from new, rapidly maturing breeds subjected to a calculated feeding regimen. In the mid-nineteenth century, cattle and pigs often had a thick layer of fat over lean meat, producing what were sometimes dismissed as 'monsters'.[47] When fat was dispersed throughout the meat, the result was a more tender product. Marbling could be produced by judicious breeding.[48] The tendency, in the west at least, was towards leaner meat, with fats increasingly supplied by butter and vegetable oils. Marbling was a quality of youth: 'it is only in young, well-fed animals that the fat is dispersed between the muscles fascicule to produce *marbling*'.[49] The idea that an animal should first grow, and then fatten, was replaced by that of a single process of rapid development: 'all the improved breeds rival one another in regard to the early period at which they may be fattened'.[50] The Chicago meat trade, notes the environmental historian William Cronon, accelerated and foreshortened bovine life. There would be 'no interruption to the steady accumulation of future cash in well-muscled flesh'.[51] By 1937, 72% of the British beef herd was under two years old.[52]

As cattle were more tightly incorporated into capitalist relations, their lives became almost totally controlled, managed, and telescoped. Cattle were increasingly comprehended through biological, genetic, and statistical frames of reference, even if these epistemologies merely provided a scientific veneer to continued empiricism. Inbreeding, Bakewell's modus operandi, was 'the quickest and surest method of fixing and perpetuating a desirable character or group of characters'.[53] Crosses, however, often produced stronger, larger, quicker-maturing animals.[54] The process was, or at least was often described as, brutally eugenic: 'the wise breeder uses his knife on the inferior males, and puts the inferior females in the feed lot'.[55]

Pigs

Towards the end of the eighteenth century, small, quick-maturing, light-boned pigs were imported into Europe from China and southeast Asia, and crossed with native pigs: within 50 years, most western European pigs were at least partly descended from Asiatic imports.[56] Again, the aim was to increase flesh at the expense of bone, and as with cattle, the consequence was often excessive fat, which in turn inspired critique. The desire for leaner pigs, with flecked (or marbled) bacon underpinned the later nineteenth-century rise of the Danish bacon industry. Here, native Jutish pigs were crossed with English Large Whites to produce the Danish Landrace.[57] Denmark, noted one British observer, developed a system producing 'just the kind of bacon that the English housewife likes'.[58] The Danes, another commentator claimed, had realised 'that the front portion of the pig was not of such value per pound as the middle and the rest of the carcass, sent their experts to this and other Countries, and bought up thousands of boars with small heads and jowls'.[59] Porcine life was thoroughly shaped by the dictates of capital: pigs were bred to produce 'a standard quality and an even quantity on the British market'.[60]

Such pigs were early examples of 'designer livestock': they were produced within a sophisticated industrial network and bred to generate and perpetuate certain characteristics demanded by the international market. Such selection, when augmented by genetic knowledge, allowed pigs to be further reshaped over the twentieth century. During the final quarter of the twentieth century, pork and bacon producers selected against fatness.[61] One consequence has been PSS (porcine stress syndrome) which emerged in the 1970s. The gene which produces this condition is linked to the quality of extreme leanness, but this can produce watery, soft muscle and trigger extreme stress and death.[62] Such animals, to repeat, were profoundly commodified. Profitability was measured in terms of producing more flesh from less feed in a shorter amount of time. It took 5 kilogrammes of feed to produce 1 kilogramme of pig meat in 1946, but by the 1970s, only 3.5 kilogrammes were required.[63]

Pig-raising began using enclosed feeding units to a much greater extent than cattle-raising. In Denmark, pig-rearing was integrated with butter-making: skimmed milk provided feed and processing took place in bacon factories. In Britain, there was a drift to indoor feeding in the interwar period, something becoming more pronounced in the 1950s.[64] Selecting for leanness made pigs more uncomfortable outdoors.[65] Like humans, pigs were leaving outdoor life behind; Catron's 'life cycle housing' of pigs included air conditioning and heated floors.[66] After 1945, it was discovered that piglets could be rapidly weaned if given antibiotic and vitamin-fortified food, allowing sows to be impregnated within nine weeks of giving birth, which significantly sped up porcine reproductive patterns: a sow can produce over two litters per year.[67] Meticulous calculations of optimum temperatures and cubic airspace provision for different classes of pig were carried out.[68] This also denies pigs the 'social and tactile interactions' which structure their everyday existence in open, 'natural', settings.[69] The system has reached its pinnacle in China, where half the world's pigs (around 500 million) are produced and eaten, fed with vast quantities of soybeans imported from Brazil and Argentina.[70] Brazilian soybean farming has contributed heavily to deforestation.

The industrialisation of pig-farming heralded the age of the industrialised meat product. The bacon factory, using standardised Danish pigs as its raw material, was already producing reliable, replicable meat in the early twentieth century. Technological developments such as trimmers, rollers and pressers allowed increasingly standardised, processed meat products such as pepperoni and hot dogs.[71] The first Coney Island hot dog stands opened in the 1870s.[72] Swift developed the integrated hot dog production line, using conveyor belts and emulsification of meat, in the 1940s.[73] By the 1960s, the 'Frank-o-Matic' took emulsified meat from one end and disgorged hot dogs at the other.[74] Despite Ralph Nader's description of them as 'fatfurters', they surged in popularity.[75]

Chickens

Although chicken has been consumed for millennia, it remained a relatively insignificant part of most global diets until the twentieth century. Its rise has been particularly startling in the United States, as Steve Striffler notes: 'chicken, an afterthought on American farms before World War II, has been transformed into the most studied and industrialised animal in the world'.[76] In the United States, chicken was primarily raised for home consumption before the 1920s. Labour and feed were basically free.[77] Mass-production first appeared in Delaware in the 1920s.[78] In 1925, Americans consumed around half a pound of chicken annually; by 1995, this figure was 70 pounds.[79]

This remarkable acceleration was the result of the integration of numerous technological elements which subjugated the chicken to the demands of industrial capitalism.[80] These included thermostatically regulated incubators, lights simulating daylight, and the administration of vitamin D.[81] The chicken could now spend its entire existence indoors. By 1939, the nutrient requirements of chickens were known more precisely than for any other species, resulting in the use of high-protein corn and soybean feed by the 1950s.[82] Such feeding regimes were expensive, meaning that faster growth rates and precise measurement of nutrients to animals' metabolic requirements became necessary.[83] This feed was enhanced with antibiotics and hormones such as penicillin and oxytetracycline.[84] Meanwhile, chickens were subject to more intense and detailed comprehension of genetics, inheritance and breeding than any other species.[85] Breeding via inbreeding and then cross-breeding for hybrid vigour created a 'biological lock'.[86] Hybridisation came to dominate the chicken industry, in contrast with, say, dairy farming, where true line breeding remained more common.[87] As the biochemist André Voison noted mournfully, 'the animals whose environment and genetic characters have been most upset by Man are probably poultry. As a result, they are liable to a magnificent variety of "civilisation" diseases'.[88] Chickens' agency – particularly their liberty of movement, physical strength, and capacity to resist disease – was seriously delimited and reduced.

Large corporations were heavily involved in this reconfiguration of chickens' existence. Tyson in particular is associated with the creation of vertical integration, bringing previously dissociated elements of the industry into tight connection.[89] Vertical integration was complete by the mid-1960s, with 90% of American broiler production run by large national feed companies.[90] The broiler industry, along with confined pigs, feedlot cattle and enclosed dairy cows, became the most intensive forms of livestock production on earth.[91] The acceleration of gallinaceous life has been particularly dramatic. In 1940, it took three pounds of feed to create one pound of live chicken. This figure is now below two, meaning that larger chickens can be produced more rapidly and cheaply: industrially produced chickens now live a mere 42 days. The number of chickens killed annually has risen from 6 billion in 1960 to around 50 billion today.

Vertical integration and biological and environmental control have allowed chickens, and their meat, to be more successfully branded and reshaped than other forms of meat.[92] The chicken nugget, for example, was pioneered in the early 1950s, and it was followed by the chicken-breast patty. Processing allowed unprofitable parts of chicken to be used in products, from hot dogs to pet food.[93] Tyson once produced a giblet burger to utilise superfluous gizzards: the Arkansas prison system refused to serve it to inmates.[94] In the 1980s, the consumption of processed chicken rose remarkably. Striffler concludes that, for young people, chicken is almost entirely viewed as a processed product, with little connection to a living, breathing animal.[95]

This acceleration of livestock production has had major ecological consequences. Intense chicken production creates tremendous amounts of waste, which local ecosystems often struggle to contain. In the Delmarva Peninsula, the epicentre of the American chicken industry, 1.5 billion pounds of manure must be absorbed annually.[96] The result is the accumulation of waste nitrates, and drug-resistant bacteria, in other parts of terrestrial or aquatic ecosystems, such as the northern Gulf of Mexico.[97] Other materials accumulating from animal waste include phosphorus, copper, zinc and cadmium, originating in synthetic fertilisers and animal feed.[98] Industrial livestock production is a major cause of the 'nitrogen cascade', the percolation of nitrogen through ecological systems.[99] Additionally, ruminant flatulence, fossil fuel inputs, deforestation and cultivation of feed crops all contribute to greenhouse gas emissions.[100] Livestock farming is thus a significant contributor to climate change.

The intensification of meat-eating has had enormous consequences for global land-use patterns. The inefficiencies of animal protein production have long been recognised. In 1795, for example, William Paley noted that 'a piece of ground capable of supplying animal food and sufficient for the subsistence of ten persons would sustain, at least, the double of that number with grain, roots and milk'.[101] When livestock largely consumed wastes, surpluses or foods indigestible to humans, the ecological cost was low: they were, as Simon Fairlie notes, a 'benign extravagance'.[102] However, as livestock numbers increased significantly, vast quantities of land were brought into use to feed them. In 2000, around 7% of the Earth's ice-free land was used to grow crops for direct human consumption, while 30% of ice-free land was utilised for feed and forage for animals.[103] The result is what Tony Weis calls the 'industrial grain-oilseed-livestock complex', reliant on low-biodiversity pasturage, a major threat for endangered species and subject to soil erosion and desertification.[104]

Bovine and porcine zoomass thus exploded at the expense of non-domesticated creatures. But this zoomass has itself become more homogenous. The dominance of Herefords and Danish Landraces has come at the expense of many rarer breeds whose biological capacities meshed less successfully with the demands of the capitalist livestock industry. By 2000, over 1,300 of the 6,300 breeds of domestic livestock had become extinct or were in danger of extinction.[105] British cattle breeds which have disappeared include the Alderney, Blue Albion, Caithness, Castlemartin, Glamorgan, Irish Dun, Sheeted Somerset, and Suffolk Dun.[106] Such trends have been facilitated by artificial insemination, which has channelled and controlled male geneflows, resulting in diminished effective population size. A single Holstein bull (a dairy breed), Round Oak, is thought to have fathered 2.7 million calves around the world.[107] During the Great Acceleration, the human command of livestock genetics tightened. The developed world increasingly consumed the flesh of not simply a limited number of *species*, but a limited number of *breeds of species*. This was a more intense form of domestication: *biological control*. Here, the core of animal being – DNA itself – has been overdetermined by conscious human activity.[108]

Slaughtering

Despite regular efforts to regulate slaughter and remove it from human communities, slaughter has, for much of human history, been a small-scale, familiar, even social practice. However, over the past 200 years, in the developed world at least, slaughter has become simultaneously distanced from human communities, rendered invisible, and undertaken at hitherto unimaginable scales. As urban communities expanded during industrialisation, slaughter, and particularly the sights and sounds of slaughter, became a significant problem. It was viewed as a public health menace and a gruesome spectacle incompatible with civilising society. Extricating the killing of animals from social, urban space would have profound implications for human–animal interactions.

The first significant efforts to extricate this slaughtering system from urban ecologies came in Paris, with the development of the *abattoir* system. Napoleon issued a decree in 1807 urging the construction of abattoirs, or public slaughterhouses, extending this to the whole of France in 1810 and stipulating that these structures be built outside city walls.[109] He ordered the construction of public slaughterhouses in states he conquered.[110] The abattoir was an important departure in the history of slaughter: a larger-scale, purpose-built structure designed to efficiently kill animals away from urban centres. The reforms of Haussmann furthered those of Napoleon: La Villette, Paris's giant abattoir, opened in 1867 and concentrated slaughter in a single, vast institution, the largest in Europe.[111] In Berlin, a combined cattle-market and slaughterhouse for the whole city opened in 1881: by 1910, this abattoir was processing nearly 2.5 million animals annually.[112] In 1914, Karl Ereky persuaded two Hungarian banks to support a vast industrialised pig-slaughtering enterprise: five years later, he coined the term 'biotechnology'.[113]

The vast spaces of the New World allowed slaughter to be undertaken on greater scales. In 1926, there were 17 meat factories in Argentina. They could slaughter 27,500 cattle, 50,000 sheep and 4,000 pigs daily. Swift owned four of these, and Armour three.[114] Brazil had seven refrigerated abattoirs in 1926.[115] In the United States, the combined stockyard-abattoir was memorably described by William Cronon, who notes how the creation of the 'disassembly line' enabled meticulous division of labour and introduced manifold technological elements into the slaughtering operation, such as a revolving, horizontal wheel from which dead hogs hung while they were gutted and cleaned by workers.[116] Death, like life, was accelerated. In the early 1970s, the fastest American slaughtering lines killed 179 cattle hourly: today, this has reached 400.[117]

The abattoir created and perpetuated new relationships between humans and animals. There was a specific directionality about abattoir space: the animal moved from a dirty, moist, living space to a clean cold dead-meat side, with slaughter a threshold both absolute and nebulous.[118] Killing and bleeding remained central to the act of slaughter: bleeding, noted Vialles, is critical to the distinction between corpse and meat.[119] But to maintain compatibility with civilisation, the act of killing was triply occluded. First, killing was now entirely hidden from society. Second, within the abattoir, killing was visually differentiated from non-killing activities. Third, animals themselves were kept in separate pens until they were killed, something built into slaughterhouse design: there was a guilty appreciation that animals are affected by viewing the slaughter of their fellows.[120] These multiple acts of separation and obfuscation are necessary to maintain the illusion that killing doesn't actually happen: 'from this point on, slaughtering was required to be industrial, that is to say large scale and anonymous; it must be non-violent (ideally: painless); and it must be invisible (ideally: non-existent). It must be as if it were not'.[121] Timothy Pachirat, in his haunting account of an American abattoir, describes these structures as generally inaccessible and invisible.[122]

The act of killing itself, however, changed slowly: it is a very conservative practice. Archaeological evidence suggests that, in the ancient world, slaughter involved trussing the animal, pulling its head back, and cutting the neck, probably severing the carotid artery and jugular vein.[123] These two acts – immobilisation and bleeding – remain central to slaughtering practice. A third practice – stunning – has also commonly been interposed between immobilisation and bleeding, particularly in Christian countries, and most frequently used on cattle. There is also a long tradition of allowing animals to rest before slaughter. During the later nineteenth century, the efficacy and material technology of stunning was widely debated. In western Europe, the preferred weapon was the poleaxe, used to shatter the frontal bone of the animal's skull and perforate the brain. American abattoirs used light steel mallets with long handles.[124] The poleaxe itself was regularly criticised as clumsy and cruel: 'most skilful men have sometimes been known to drive a poleaxe into a beast's eye'.[125] Numerous novel devices were created to render slaughter as instantaneous as possible. These technologies included pistols, shooting masks, electrical instruments, guillotines, pneumatic killers and gas chambers. In Britain, many local authorities enforced stunning, but only in 1934 were cattle and pigs in slaughterhouses and knackers' yards obliged to be stunned before slaughter.[126] Today, pistols, gas and electricity are all used to stun animals.

Jewish and Islamic slaughter, which forbade stunning, remained exempt from this legislation. The argument here was that the animal bled more thoroughly without stunning.[127] In the later nineteenth century, non-Christian slaughtering techniques became controversial in Europe. Numerous studies purported to demonstrate that simply bleeding an animal without prior stunning made death slower and more painful.[128] The *British Medical Journal* argued that 'the animal, passing through the stages of terror, pain, faintness, and epileptiform convulsions, has a longer period of conscious suffering'.[129] However, defenders of the practice suggested that animals retained consciousness for only three seconds.[130] Isaac Dembo, of St Petersburg's Alexandra Hospital, thought 'that a cut made with an exceedingly sharp knife is almost painless, and that particularly must this be the case in the neck, where so few sensory nerves of any size are divided'.[131] In Germany, Nazi policies led to the banning of Jewish slaughter; in Britain, it remained legal and the debate dissipated.[132]

Traditionally, various trades, such as tannery, clustered around slaughterhouses or were situated in peripheral or extra-urban zones such as the south bank of the Thames. With industrialised slaughter, a vastly expanded range of by-products could be harvested and profitably sold: 'to-day cattle, sheep, and hogs are a great deal more than food; they are the raw material for a vast range of marketable and valuable commodities'.[133] Bones were ground into bonemeal and fertiliser; intestines used for tennis rackets and surgical ligatures; hair reused as insulation or filling for pillows;

glands processed into pharmaceutical products; fats worked up into margarine, candles and soap; blood used for sugar-refining.[134] The animal slaughtered in an abattoir was not just turned into meat: its body was dispersed into innumerable consumer products. Eating meat is only one of the ways in which we consume animals.

Ambivalent animals: the case of the horse

In 2005, 4,727,829 horses were slaughtered for food worldwide, a not inconsequential figure, but vastly lower than that of dominant world livestock. Major horsemeat-producing countries include China, Mexico, Kazakhstan, Mongolia, Argentina, Italy, Brazil, and Kyrgyzstan. In the Anglophone world, however, eating horse remains taboo. When horsemeat was discovered in frozen meat products in Britain and Ireland in 2013, the resulting scandal made the front page of newspapers and generated fears about the traceability of foodstuffs across the food chain.

Horses have been eaten by humans for millennia. Collective horse hunts were undertaken in the Upper Paleolithic in present-day France.[135] Once domesticated, horses were clearly consumed as food. Archaeological evidence suggests that in the late Neolithic, horses were probably husbanded as food animals: chopped bones have been discovered at sites along with other kitchen debris.[136] However, horses were not consumed by the Greeks, Romans, or other ancient near-eastern cultures. They were banned in Leviticus, along with pigs. Pope Gregory III banned horsemeat in 732, in a letter to St Boniface. Although largely symbolic and hardly enforceable on a wide scale, this ban connected Christianity to horsemeat-avoidance. Horsemeat-consumption remained more common in Scandinavia than elsewhere in Europe; it rose, however, during famines.

During the medieval and early modern period, we see a biological bifurcation between horses and edible livestock. Horses' basic physical capacities (speed, power) combined with numerous technological breakthroughs (saddles, collar harnesses, horseshoes) to turn equines into labouring beasts, not edible ones. Medieval armies fought on horseback, not cowback. Horses were bred for strength. Cattle were increasingly bred to be eaten, with fat dispersed across the back and buttocks. This biotechnological process, combined with cultural interdiction, produced a real and ideational chasm between horses and cattle. Horses were physically different, they occupied a different place in the economy, and they attracted different meanings. In such circumstances, the horse became 'noble'.[137] Madeleine Ferrières argues that eating horsemeat in early modern France became 'unthinkable'.[138]

In France, and much of Europe, however, this 'unthinkability' disintegrated after 1800. It was a revolution in sensibility, imagination and taste. Horsemeat was legalised in Denmark (1807), Wurttemberg (1841), Bavaria (1842), Baden (1846), Hanover (1847), Bohemia (1847), Saxony (1847), Austria (1847), Belgium (1847), Switzerland (1853), Prussia (1853), Norway (1855) and Sweden (1855).[139] In France, the legalisation of the sale of horsemeat came in 1866, but the movement to promote its use began in the late eighteenth century. Several leading public health officials and scientists, including Isidore Geoffroy Saint-Hilaire and Émile Decroix, argued that the horse taboo was entirely irrational. Not eating horses, they argued, was a gigantic waste: it was also cruel to allow such animals to suffer a painful, lingering old age.[140]

Horse banquets were held to advertise the merits of the meat. In 1866, following a request by Petit, a veterinarian, a police ordinance legalised the sale of the flesh of worn-out horses.[141] Such horses had to be healthy, and killed in the presence of veterinary inspectors in specially authorised slaughterhouses. The meat had to be sold in clearly identified locations: hence the horse's head outside such establishments. The first Parisian horse-butcher's shop was opened in 1866 at 3 Place d'Italie by Théodore Antoine, a butcher who slaughtered his own horses in a Gentilly abattoir. By March 1868, there were 23 such shops in Paris.[142]

Horses were eaten in various forms, including pot-au-feu and sausage.[143] They became a significant part of the French urban working-class diet. In Paris and its environs, 48 shops sold horsemeat in 1874, but by the 1930s, this figure was over 1,200.[144] In the early twentieth century, 11.2% of French weekly meat consumption was horsemeat, a figure higher than that for bacon, pork and poultry.[145] While horses were not explicitly selected and bred for human consumption, as their working life fell, their meat became correspondingly more palatable: indeed, horses might be fattened.[146] Nonetheless, the horse never became part of French haute cuisine: horsemeat recipes did not appear in cookbooks.[147]

The revival of horsemeat was a major phenomenon in the history of animal-eating, caused by the public engagement of scientists, concern about perceived low levels of meat-consumption, the cooperation of hippophagic butchers and transformed sensibilities. This combination was not inevitable, as the history of horsemeat in the Anglophone world suggests. In 1868, the traveller Algernon Sidney Bicknell hosted a banquet at London's Langham hotel, where 150 guests were served courses almost entirely made from horsemeat, from soups to sausages and steaks. Here was the English Decroix, a hippophagic crusader determined to overcome obdurate dietary habits. He employed French chefs and French terminology, flirting with the name *chevaline* to describe the meat. He failed.[148] The meat itself was critiqued for its poor taste, especially when prepared by incompetent British chefs. In 1870, *The Daily Telegraph* described 'the apparent collapse of the hippophagic movement in England', blaming it on 'a strong reluctance on the part of the public to follow up the experiment'.[149] Horsemeat remained strongly associated in the British mind with famines, especially following the 1870–1871 siege of Paris.[150] Butchers were wary of being associated with the movement, lest they lost business.[151] Others noted that horses were simply more valuable as labour than as meat.

In such circumstances, it is unsurprising that horsemeat became associated with other, less putatively civilised cultures, such as France and Italy. 'John Bull,' argued Peter Simmons, 'wants none of your foreign kickshaws, frogs, and snails in fricassees, or sea slug, or bird's nest soup, or horse flesh steak'.[152] Britain, Europe's highest meat consumer, sated by global beef and mutton markets, had no need to eat horsemeat. Horsemeat became associated with European protectionism, poverty and cruelty, not free trade, wealth, and humanitarianism.[153] Not eating horse became a powerful marker of British identity. The same was true of the United States, which considered 'the eating of horses and dogs' to be 'a foreign custom'.[154] The number of horses slaughtered for food in the United States was extremely small: in 1902, for example, 1,624 horses were killed.[155] Although horsemeat was consumed in greater quantities in both World Wars, it never shed its taboo. One 1918 correspondent to an

American periodical stated that 'if we can't win out this war without the eating of horse flesh we had better be whipped by the Germans'.[156]

The example of horsemeat shows the difficulty and futility of disentangling the cultural from the biological, the technological, and the economic. Gustatory divergence cannot be explained simply by appealing to one of these factors alone. For a culture to decide that a particular animal is not just edible but tasty, healthy and culturally consecrated requires a complex intermeshing of durable ideas and biological reality.

Conclusion

When human populations domesticated a small group of mammals in the Neolithic, they introduced a major bifurcation into animal history: the paths of livestock and wild animals diverged. Over the past ten millennia, but more particularly in the past two centuries, the zoomass of these domesticated megafauna has soared relative to that of wild species. The boundary between edible and non-edible animals has tightened. Those animals absorbed into the human food system have had their lives subject to increasing levels of human control: spatial, sexual, technological, biological. Today, that control has become almost as close to total as possible; from birth until death, animals in confined feeding systems are entirely enveloped in a human-built environment administering all food, water and sensory stimulation, controlling conception and birth, overdetermining the balance of fat and lean in their bodies, and advancing animals to death as quickly as possible. The evolution of these animals has been directed by agricultural environments, selective breeding, technological milieux and genetic knowledge: this is evolutionary history par excellence, and its consequences include reduced effective population size, susceptibility to disease, and a wide range of behavioural and psychological abnormalities.[157]

These are some of the most asymmetrical power relationships on the planet, with palpable ontological consequences for livestock. Being a domesticated cow, pig, or chicken is now significantly different from being a wild animal. Livestock has been thoroughly invested with the power relations of capitalism and become comprehended as pure exchange value. The genetic and metabolic capacities of livestock have been manipulated to produce the most meat in the shortest time with the cheapest inputs, with the well-being of these animals distinctly less significant than their capacity to make profit: 'nature, in short, is (re)made to work harder, faster, and better'.[158] The result, most obvious in the case of chickens, is a short and profoundly unpleasant life. In such circumstances, domestication intensifies into something we can call biological control. The capacity of animals to act and exercise influence over the action of other beings is seriously circumscribed: their bodily capabilities are exploited and shaped from before birth by another species, which acts through them for its own profit. Chickens live entirely within a machinated landscape designed to extract maximum exchange value for minimum capital inputs. Cattle, while 'outside', have their mobility delimited by fences and barbed wire.[159] Other domestic animals, such as the dog and the horse, are eaten in far lower quantities. The parameters within which they exercise agency are broader: they have greater (but still limited) freedom of movement, a less rigorously controlled feeding regimen, and experience more 'natural' life expectancies. We should not, however, assume that agency was totally crushed or that biological control was total. Small acts of rebellion were possible even for the most subjugated animals. Even battery hens, whose lifeworld was reduced to the size of a cage, found ways to probe the limits of their agency. Some smashed their pellets, ate eggs, or plucked feathers. Some enjoyed flicking water out of troughs: 'it appears to give the birds some degree of pleasure to be able to hit an attendant in the eye with a blob of water, especially at egg collecting time!'[160]

Vegetarianism emerged in its current guise at precisely the moment that meat-eating was accelerating. The term 'vegetarian' was first used around 1839: earlier terms for abstainers included 'Brahmins', 'Pythagoreans', or the eaters of a 'natural diet'.[161] Vegetarianism drew attention not only to the cruelty and suffering of animals in an industrialising meat-system, but also to the increasing occlusion of this pain. With its links to eastern philosophy and religion, vegetarianism carried an explicit critique of the west and the idea that heavy meat-eating was neither inevitable nor progressive.[162] Vegetarians often recast the deep history of human carnivory as one of deviance, decline and fall. This was perhaps best expressed by Shelley, who argued that Prometheus first taught the use of animal food, which corrupted natural diets and introduced artifice and deception into human dietary practices. *Queen Mab* and *Vindication of Natural Diet* explicitly connect carnivorousness with the fall. Human depravity, he argued, began with 'unnatural habits of life', and forsaking 'the path of nature'.[163]

Vegetarianism as we know it today, then, emerged out of profound ambivalence towards, and critique of, an urbanising and industrialising world. The abattoir allowed the asymmetry of human–animal relations to unconsciously thrive. Josiah Oldfield put this clearly: 'I must confess, however, that I contemplate with a sense of deep disquietude this building up of great central places for the mechanical doing to death of my sentient fellow creatures'.[164] The triple visual occlusion of the abattoir made killing itself visible only to killers and killed, and enabled 'animal' and 'meat' to become increasingly dissociated and disconnected. The abattoir manages to maintain the fiction that there is no real connection between living animals and meat, even as livestock are increasingly withdrawn into enclosed environments. Farm animals exist 'substantially beyond the boundaries of human awareness'.[165] This fiction is then enhanced by the rise of processed meat products, such as hot dogs, pepperoni pizza, and chicken nuggets, whose connection to the living, breathing animal is phenomenologically tenuous. The *meat product* is specifically designed to dissemble its biological origins.

Finally, no discussion of meat can ignore the issue of the Anthropocene. Leaving aside issues of dating and nomenclature, it is apparent that the massive acceleration in meat-eating is inseparable from our current environmental predicament. Nitrate leaching, greenhouse gas emissions, fossil fuel use, deforestation and soil erosion are consequences of the sheer volume of livestock our agricultural systems are currently supporting. This raises a key methodological issue: scale. These ecological effects have been present throughout history and have contributed to a longer, deeper Anthropocene advanced by some authors.[166] But the industrialisation and acceleration of livestock production, and its absorption into a vast food system, has catapulted humans, and animals, into an entirely different situation. Ten thousand cows are one thing: a billion quite another. Such multiplication and accumulation has produced the temporal emergence of a new problematic: a critical threshold has been crossed. The scale of livestock farming, and the associated costs of extinction, climate change, and interference with the Earth's biogeochemical cycles, is a central component and problematic of the Anthropocene.

Meat-eating entails the digestion of the ritually slaughtered flesh of an animal specifically bred to the requirements of our taste and the market. Meat, for most people, tastes delicious. It actively affirms national, gendered and religious identities. It sustains one of the planet's largest industries and involves historically extraordinary levels of biological control over animals. It contributes directly to the planet's complex, unpredictable ecological crisis. It often takes place at great distance (geographically, phenomenologically) from the site of meat production. Meat-eating has a multiplicity of dimensions: evolutionary, biological, gustatory, cultural, economic, ecological, ethical, perceptual. The study of meat-eating should, ideally, take all of these aspects into account.

Notes

1 S. Ulijasek, N. Mann, and S. Elton, *Evolving Human Nutrition: Implications for Public Health*, Cambridge: Cambridge University Press, 2012, 12.
2 L. Gruen, *Ethics and Animals: An Introduction*, Cambridge: Cambridge University Press, 2011, 81.
3 N. Vialles, *Animal to Edible*, Cambridge: Cambridge University Press, 1994, 128–130.
4 V. Smil, *Harvesting the Biosphere: What We Have Taken From Nature*, Cambridge MA: MIT Press, 2013, 89.
5 K. Gremillion, *Ancestral Appetites: Food in Prehistory*, Cambridge: Cambridge University Press, 2011, 19.
6 R. Wrangham, *Catching Fire: How Cooking Made Us Human*, New York: Basic Books, 2009.
7 E. Russell, *Evolutionary History: Uniting History and Biology to Understand Life on Earth*, Cambridge: Cambridge University Press, 2011, 3.
8 J. Clutton-Brock, *A Natural History of Domesticated Animals*, second edition, Cambridge: Cambridge University Press, 1999, 32.
9 D. Haraway, *The Companion Species Manifesto: Dogs, People, and Significant Otherness*, Chicago IL: Prickly Paradigm Press, 2003, 27–28.
10 R. Francis, *Domesticated: Evolution in a Man-Made World*, New York: Norton, 2015, 101.
11 Francis, *Domesticated*, 118–119.
12 Francis, *Domesticated*, 74–75.
13 S. Kirsch, *What Species of Creatures: Animal Relations From the New World*, Vancouver: New Star, 2008.
14 R. Slatta, *Comparing Cowboys and Frontiers*, Norman OK: University of Oklahoma Press, 1997, 6.
15 A. Crosby, *The Columbian Exchange: Biological and Cultural Consequences of 1492*, Westport CT: Praeger, 2003, 76.
16 R. Perren, *Taste, Trade and Technology: The Development of the International Meat Industry since 1840*, Aldershot: Ashgate, 2006, 30–31.
17 A. Duckham, *Animal Industry in the British Empire: A Brief Review of the Significance, Methods, Problems, and Potentialities of the Live-Stock and Dairying Industries of the British Commonwealth*, London: Oxford University Press, 1932, 15.

18 M. Derry, *Bred For Perfection: Shorthorn Cattle, Collies, and Arabian Horses since 1800*, Baltimore MD: Johns Hopkins University Press, 2003, x.
19 C. Darwin, *On the Origin of Species by Means of Natural Selection*, J. Carroll (ed.), Orchard Park NY: Broadview Press, 2003, 113.
20 W. Steffen, J. Grinewald, P. Crutzen, and J. McNeil, 'The Anthropocene: conceptual and historical perspectives', *Philosophical Transactions of the Royal Society A* 369, 1938 (2011): 842–867, 849.
21 T. Weis, *The Ecological Hoofprint: The Global Burden of Industrial Livestock*, London: Zed Books, 2013, 71.
22 Weis, *Ecological Hoofprint*, 84.
23 V. Smil, 'Eating meat: evolution, patterns, and consequences', *Population and Development Review* 28, 4 (2002): 599–639, 628.
24 Weis, *Ecological Hoofprint*, 140.
25 Smil, 'Eating meat', 618.
26 H. Steinfeld, P. Gerber, T. Wassenaar, V. Castel, M. Rosales, and C. de Haan, *Livestock's Long Shadow: Environmental Issues and Options*, Rome: Food and Agriculture Organisation of the United Nations, 2006, 33.
27 J. Moore, *Capitalism in the Web of Life: Ecology and the Accumulation of Capital*, London: Verso, 2015.
28 I. Wilmut, K. Campbell, and C. Tudge, *The Second Creation: Dolly and the Age of Biological Control*, Cambridge MA: Harvard University Press, 2001.
29 J. Walton, 'Pedigree and productivity in the British and North American cattle kingdoms before 1930', *Journal of Historical Geography* 25, 4 (1999): 441–462, 444.
30 J. Grundy, 'The Hereford bull: his contribution to New World and domestic beef supplies', *Agricultural History Review* 50, 1 (2002): 69–88, 80.
31 J. Watson, J. Cameron, and G. Garrad, *The Cattle-Breeder's Handbook*, London: Earnest Benn, 1926, 23; A. Sanders, *A History of Aberdeen-Angus Cattle With Particular Reference to Their Introduction, Distribution and Rise to Popularity in the Field of Fine Beef Production in North America*, Chicago IL: New Breeder's Gazette, 1928, 29.
32 J. Wilson, *The Evolution of British Cattle and the Fashioning of Breeds*, London: Vinton and Company, 1909, 103.
33 R. McFall, *The World's Meat*, London: D. Appleton & Company, 1927, 199; Grundy, 'Hereford bull', 85.
34 R. Kambadur, M. Sharma, T. Smith, and J. Bass, 'Mutations in *myostatin* (*GDF8*) in double-muscled Belgian Blue and Piedmontese cattle', *Genome Research* 7, 9 (1997): 910–915.
35 Perren, *Taste*, 31.
36 Perren, *Taste*, 32–33.
37 J. Richelet, 'The Argentine meat trade', in *The Frozen and Chilled Meat Trade: A Practical Treatise by Specialists in the Meat Trade*, London: The Gresham Publishing Company Ltd, 1929, 2 Volumes, I, 195.
38 McFall, *World's Meat*, 460, 465.
39 D. Shane, *Hoofprints on the Forest: Cattle Ranching and the Destruction of Latin America's Tropical Forests*, Philadelphia PA: Institute for the Study of Human Issues, 1986, 17–18.
40 Shane, *Hoofprints on the Forest*, 18.
41 N. Myers, 'The hamburger connection: how Central America's forests became North America's hamburgers', *Ambio* 10, 1 (1981): 3–8, 6.
42 J. MacDonald, *Food From the Far West: Or, American Agriculture, with Special Reference to the Beef Production and Importation of Dead Meat from America to Great Britain*, London: William P. Nimmo, 1878, 190–191; Sanders, *History*, 136.
43 Grundy, 'Hereford bull', 76.

44 R. Netz, *Barbed Wire: An Ecology of Modernity*, Middletown CT: Wesleyan University Press, 2009, 33.
45 E. Ohnuki-Tierney, 'We eat each other's food to nourish our body: the global and the local as mutually constituent forces', in R. Grew (ed.) *Food in Global History*, Boulder CO: Westview, 1999, 240–272, 252.
46 A. Rimas and E. Fraser, *Beef: The Untold Story of How Milk, Meat, and Muscle Shaped the World*, New York: William Morrow, 2008, 201.
47 R. Thomson, *Experimental Researches on the Food of Animals, and the Fattening of Cattle. With Remarks on the Food of Man*, New York: S. Appleton & Co., 1846, 50.
48 K. MacKenzie, *Cattle and the Future of Beef-Production in England*, Cambridge: Cambridge University Press, 1919, 113–114.
49 E. Line, *The Science of Meat and the Biology of Food Animals*, Volume I, London: Meat Trades' Journal Co. Ltd, 1931, 401.
50 H. Evershed, 'The early fattening of cattle and sheep', *Journal of the Royal Agricultural Society of England*, 1890, 66.
51 W. Cronon, *Nature's Metropolis: Chicago and the Great West*, New York: Norton, 1991, 224.
52 V. Astor and B. Rowntree, *British Agriculture: The Principles of Future Policy*, London: Longmans, Green & Co., 1938, 45.
53 L. Winters, *Animal Breeding*, second edition, New York: John Wiley & Sons, Inc., 1930, 201.
54 Line, *Science of Meat* II, 155.
55 Winters, *Animal Breeding*, 331.
56 Clutton-Brock, *Natural History*, 97.
57 *Douglas's Encyclopaedia: The Standard Book of Reference for the Food Trades*, third edition, London: William Douglas & Sons, 1924, 42.
58 D. Hall, *Our Daily Bread: A Geography of Production*, London: John Murray, 1938, 47.
59 C. Fielding, *Food*, London: Hurst and Blackett, 1923, 177.
60 Winters, *Animal Breeding*, 346.
61 G. Emmans and I. Kyriazakis, 'Consequences of genetic change in farm animals on food intake and feeding behaviour', *Proceedings of the Nutrition Society* 60, 1 (2001): 115–125, 121.
62 J. Dohner, *The Encyclopedia of Historic and Endangered Livestock and Poultry Breeds*, New Haven CT: Yale University Press, 2001, 174.
63 D. Grigg, *The World Food Problem*, second edition, Oxford: Blackwell, 1993, 130.
64 A. Woods, 'Rethinking the history of modern agriculture: British pig production, c.1910–65', *Twentieth Century British History* 23, 2 (2012): 165–191, 181.
65 Dohner, *Encyclopedia*, 177.
66 M. Finlay, 'Hogs, antibiotics, and the industrial environments of postwar agriculture', in S. Shrepfer and P. Scranton (eds.), *Industrializing Organisms: Introducing Evolutionary History*, London: Routledge, 2004, 237–260, 249.
67 Finlay, 'Hogs', 246; J. Novek, 'Discipline and distancing: confined pigs in the factory farm gulag', in A. Gross and A. Vallely (eds.), *Animals and the Human Imagination: A Companion to Animal Studies*, New York: Columbia University Press, 2012, 121–151, 126.
68 G. Brent, *Housing the Pig*, Ipswich: Farming Press, 1986, 37, 46.
69 Gruen, *Ethics and Animals*, 84.
70 'Empire of the pig', *Economist*, 20 December 2014, available at www.economist.com/news/christmas-specials/21636507-chinas-insatiable-appetite-pork-symbol-countrys-rise-it-also, last accessed 17 March 2017.
71 R. Horowitz, *Putting Meat on the American Table: Taste, Technology, Transformation*, Baltimore MD: Johns Hopkins University Press, 2006, 65.
72 Horowitz, *Putting Meat on the American Table*, 80.
73 Horowitz, *Putting Meat on the American Table*, 93.

74 Horowitz, *Putting Meat on the American Table*, 95.
75 Horowitz, *Putting Meat on the American Table*, 100.
76 S. Striffler, *Chicken: The Dangerous Transformation of America's Favorite Food*, New Haven CT: Yale University Press, 2005, 5.
77 Striffler, *Chicken*, 32–33.
78 Striffler, *Chicken*, 34.
79 W. Boyd and M. Watts, 'Agro-industrial just-in-time: the chicken industry and postwar American capitalism', in D. Goodman and M. Watts (eds.), *Globalising Food: Agrarian Questions and Global Restructuring*, London: Routledge, 1997, 139–165, 139.
80 W. Boyd, 'Making meat: science, technology, and American poultry production', *Technology and Culture* 42, 4 (2001): 631–664, 633.
81 Boyd, 'Making meat', 638–640, 645.
82 Boyd, 'Making meat', 645.
83 Boyd, 'Making meat', 646.
84 Boyd, 'Making meat', 647.
85 Boyd, 'Making meat', 652–653, 656; J. Bitgood, 'The genetic map of the chicken and availability of genetically diverse stocks', in R. Etches and A. Gibbins (eds.), *Manipulation of the Avian Genome*, Boca Raton FL: CRC Press, 1993, 61–79, 61.
86 M. Derry, *Masterminding Nature: The Breeding of Animals 1750–2010*, Toronto: University of Toronto Press, 2015, 88.
87 Derry, *Masterminding Nature*, 129.
88 A. Voisin, *Soil, Grass and Cancer: Health of Animals and Men is Linked to the Mineral Balance of the Soil*, trans. C. Herriot and H. Kennedy, New York: Philosophical Library Inc., 1959, 95.
89 Striffler, *Chicken*, 39.
90 Striffler, *Chicken*, 47.
91 D. Pickering, 'World Agriculture', in C. Spedding (ed.), *Fream's Principles of Food and Agriculture*, seventeenth edition, Oxford: Blackwell, 1992, 45–93, 93.
92 Striffler, *Chicken*, 25.
93 Striffler, *Chicken*, 22.
94 Striffler, *Chicken*, 23.
95 Striffler, *Chicken*, 19.
96 Boyd, 'Making meat', 643.
97 Gruen, *Ethics and Animals*, 89.
98 V. Smil, *Should We Eat Meat? Evolution and Consequences of Modern Carnivory*, Chichester: Wiley-Blackwell, 2013, 146.
99 J. Galloway et al., 'The nitrogen cascade', *BioScience* 53, 4 (2003): 341–356.
100 Smil, *Should We Eat Meat?*, 171.
101 W. Paley, *Moral and Political Philosophy*, in *The Works of William Paley*, London: William Smith, 1838, 685.
102 S. Fairlie, *Meat: A Benign Extravagance*, White River Junction VT: Chelsea Green, 2010.
103 J. Galloway et al., 'International trade in meat: the tip of the pork chop', *Ambio* 36, 8 (2007): 622–629, 622.
104 Weis, *Ecological Hoofprint*, 8; A. Barnosky, *Dodging Extinction: Power, Food, Money, and the Future of Life on Earth*, Berkeley CA: University of California Press, 2014, 81, 88; Smil, *Should We Eat Meat?*, 145.
105 Steinfeld et al., *Livestock's Long Shadow*, 208.
106 Dohner, *Encyclopedia*, 219.
107 Dohner, *Encyclopedia*, 224.
108 For a brilliant, nuanced and non-reductive analysis of this phenomenon, see S. Franklin, *Dolly Mixtures: The Remaking of Genealogy*, Durham NC: Duke University Press, 2007.

109 S. Giedion, *Mechanization Takes Command: A Contribution to Anonymous History* [1948], New York: Norton, 1969, 210; Grantham, *Treatise*, 40–41.
110 H. Heiss, 'The German abattoir', in C. Cash (ed.), *Our Slaughter-house System: A Plea for Reform*, London: George Bell and Sons, 1907, 85–212, 87.
111 K. Claflin, 'La Villette: city of blood (1867–1914)', in P.Y. Lee (ed.), *Meat, Modernity, and the Rise of the Slaughterhouse*, Durham NH: University of New Hampshire Press, 2008, 27–45.
112 D. Brantz, 'Animal bodies, human health, and the reform of slaughterhouses in nineteenth-century Berlin', in P.Y. Lee (ed.), *Meat, Modernity, and the Rise of the Slaughterhouse*, Durham NH: University of New Hampshire Press, 2008, 71–88, 84.
113 R. Bud, *The Uses of Life: A History of Biotechnology*, Cambridge: Cambridge University Press, 1993, 32–34.
114 R. Thévenot, *A History of Refrigeration Throughout the World*, trans. J. Fidler, Paris: International Institute of Refrigeration, 1979, 241.
115 Thévenot, *A History of Refrigeration*, 241.
116 Cronon, *Nature's Metropolis*, 228–229.
117 A. Fitzgerald, 'A social history of the slaughterhouse: from inception to contemporary implications', *Human Ecology Review* 17, 1 (2010): 58–69, 62.
118 Vialles, *Animal to Edible*, 35.
119 Vialles, *Animal to Edible*, 74.
120 C. Martin, *Practical Food Inspection, Volume I – Meat Inspection*, third edition, London: H.K. Lewis & Co., 1947, 50.
121 Vialles, *Animal to Edible*, 22.
122 T. Pachirat, *Every Twelve Seconds: Industrialised Slaughter and the Politics of Sight*, New Haven CT: Yale University Press, 2011, 4.
123 D. Rixson, *The History of Meat Trading*, Nottingham: Nottingham University Press, 2000, 51.
124 G. Leighton and L. Douglas, *The Meat Industry and Meat Inspection, Volume II*, London: The Educational Book Company, 1910, 5 Volumes, 401.
125 Martin, *Practical Food Inspection*, 57.
126 R. Maxwell, *Handbook on the Law Relating to Slaughter-Houses and Unsound Food, Including the Slaughter of Animals Act, 1933, and the Public Health (Meat) Regulations, 1924*, second edition, London: The Sanitary Publishing Company, Ltd, 1934, 30.
127 Leighton and Douglas, *Meat Industry*, Volume III, 765.
128 For example, B. Richardson, 'Public slaughter-houses: a suggestion for farmers', *The New Review*, 8 (1893), 641.
129 '"Kosher" and other meat', *British Medical Journal*, 23 December 1893: 1393.
130 J. Drabble, *Textbook of Meat Inspection*, Sydney: Angus and Robertson, 1936, 131–132.
131 'The slaughtering of animals', *British Medical Journal*, 9 June 1894, 1256.
132 R. Judd, *Contested Rituals: Circumcision, Kosher Butchering, and Jewish Political Life in Germany, 1843–1933*, Cornell NY: Cornell University Press, 2007.
133 G. Putnam, *Supplying Britain's Meat*, London: George Harrap & Co., 1923, 94.
134 D. Anthony and W. Blois, *The Meat Industry: A Text-Book for Meat Traders and Others Engaged in the Various Branches of the Meat Industry*, London: Ballière, Tindall & Cox, 1931, 107, 105; *Douglas's Encyclopaedia*, 43; Leighton and Douglas, *Meat Industry*, Volume II, 636; Anthony and Blois, *Meat Industry*, 98–101; Leighton and Douglas, *Meat Industry*, Volume II, 612–616; Grantham, *Treatise*, 6–7.
135 P. Kelekna, *The Horse in Human History*, Cambridge: Cambridge University Press, 2009, 16.
136 Clutton-Brock, *Natural History*, 100.
137 K. Thomas, *Man and the Natural World: Changing Attitudes in England, 1500–1800*, Oxford: Oxford University Press, 1996, 100–102.

138 M. Ferrières, *Sacred Cow, Mad Cow: A History of Food Fears*, trans. J. Gladding, New York: Columbia University Press, 2006, 14.
139 A. Bicknell, 'Hippophagy: the horse as food for man', *Journal of the Society of Arts* XVI, 801 (27 March 1868): 352.
140 I.G. Saint-Hilaire, *Lettres sur les Substances Alimentaires et Particulièrement sur la Viande de Cheval*, Paris: Libraire de Victor Masson, 1856, 204–205.
141 P. Berthaud, *De L'Hippophagie et du Cheval de Boucherie*, Saint-Nazaire: Imprimerie Ouvrière, 1934, 16–17; 'Hippophagy', *Chambers's Encyclopaedia*, X, London: W. & R. Chambers, 1874, n.p.
142 G. Bouchet, *Le Cheval a Paris de 1850 à 1914*, Geneva: Libraire Droz, 1993, 223–224; Bicknell, 'Hippophagy'.
143 A. Husson, 'De la consommation de la viande de cheval a Paris et dans quelques villes de l'Allemagne', *Journal de la Société de statistique de Paris* 15 (1874): 274–279, 276.
144 Berthaud, *De L'Hippophagie*, 26.
145 *Cost of Living in French Towns. Report of an Enquiry by the Board of Trade into Working Class Rents, Housing and Retail Prices, Together with the Rates of Wages in Certain Occupations in the Principal French Towns of France*, London: His Majesty's Stationery Office, 1909, xix.
146 Berthaud, *De L'Hippophagie*, 35–36.
147 A. Drouard, 'Horsemeat in France: a food item that appeared during the war of 1870 and disappeared after the Second World War', in I. Zweiniger-Bargielowska, R. Duffett, and A. Drouard (eds.), *Food and War in Twentieth Century Europe*, Burlington VT: Ashgate, 2011, 233–246, 242.
148 For a more detailed account of this failure, see C. Otter, 'Hippophagy in the UK: a failed dietary revolution', *Endeavour* 35, 2–3 (2011): 80–90.
149 'Horse-Flesh', *Glasgow Herald*, 26 April 1870.
150 Husson, 'De la consommation', 276.
151 'A pair of horse-pictures', *All the Year Round* XIX, 462 (29 February 1868): 272.
152 P. Simmonds, *The Curiosities of Food, Or the Dainties and Delicacies of Different Nations Obtained from the Animal Kingdom* [1859], Berkeley CA: Ten Speed Press, 2001, 6.
153 F. Trentmann, *Free Trade Nation: Commerce, Consumption, and Civil Society in Modern Britain*, Oxford: Oxford University Press, 2008, 99.
154 M. White, 'Eating of horses non-American', *American Journal of Veterinary Medicine* XII (1918): 296.
155 G. Holmes, *Meat Supply and Surplus, With Consideration of Consumption and Exports*, Washington DC: Government Printing Office, 1907, 61.
156 R. Libby, 'Sentiment vs. health', *American Journal of Veterinary Medicine* XII (1918): 295.
157 Russell, *Evolutionary History*.
158 W. Boyd, W. Prudham, and R. Schurman, 'Industrial dynamics and the problem of nature', *Society and Natural Resources* 14, 7 (2001): 555–570, 561.
159 Netz, *Barbed Wire*, 37.
160 W. Blount, *Hen Batteries*, London: Ballière, Tindall & Cox, 1951, 185.
161 T. Morton, *Shelley and the Revolution in Taste: The Body and the Natural World*, Cambridge: Cambridge University Press, 1994, 16.
162 T. Stuart, *The Bloodless Revolution: A Cultural History of Vegetarianism from 1600 to Modern Times*, New York: Norton, 2006, 57.
163 P.B. Shelley, *A Vindication of Natural Diet*, new edition, London: F. Pitman, 1884, 9.
164 J. Oldfield, *The Evils of Butchery*, London: William Reeves, 1895, 61.
165 Novek, 'Discipline', 122.
166 W. Ruddiman, *Plows, Plagues, and Petroleum: How Humans Took Control of Climate*, Princeton NJ: Princeton University Press, 2005.

Bibliography

'A pair of horse-pictures', *All the Year Round* XIX, 462, 29 February 1868.

Anthony, D. and Blois, W. *The Meat Industry: A Text-Book for Meat Traders and Others Engaged in the Various Branches of the Meat Industry*, London: Ballière, Tindall & Cox, 1931.

Astor, V. and Rowntree, B. *British Agriculture: The Principles of Future Policy*, London: Longmans, Green & Co., 1938.

Barnosky, A. *Dodging Extinction: Power, Food, Money, and the Future of Life on Earth*, Berkeley CA: University of California Press, 2014.

Berthaud, P. *De L'Hippophagie et du Cheval de Boucherie*, Saint-Nazaire: Imprimerie Ouvrière, 1934.

Bicknell, A. 'Hippophagy: the horse as food for man', *Journal of the Society of Arts* XVI, 801, 27 March 1868.

Bitgood, J. 'The genetic map of the chicken and availability of genetically diverse stocks', in R. Etches and A. Gibbins (eds.), *Manipulation of the Avian Genome*, Boca Raton FL: CRC Press, 1993, 61–79.

Blount, W. *Hen Batteries*, London: Ballière, Tindall & Cox, 1951.

Bouchet, G. *Le Cheval a Paris de 1850 à 1914*, Geneva: Libraire Droz, 1993, 223–224.

Boyd, W. 'Making meat: science, technology, and American poultry production', *Technology and Culture* 42, 4 (2001): 631–664.

Boyd, W., Prudham, W., and Schurman, R. 'Industrial dynamics and the problem of nature', *Society and Natural Resources* 14, 7 (2001): 555–570.

Boyd, W. and Watts, M. 'Agro-industrial just-in-time: the chicken industry and postwar American capitalism', in D. Goodman and M. Watts (eds.), *Globalising Food: Agrarian Questions and Global Restructuring*, London: Routledge, 1997, 139–165.

Brantz, D. 'Animal bodies, human health, and the reform of slaughterhouses in nineteenth-century Berlin', in P.Y. Lee (ed.), *Meat, Modernity, and the Rise of the Slaughterhouse*, Durham NH: University of New Hampshire Press, 2008, 71–88.

Brent, G. *Housing the Pig*, Ipswich: Farming Press, 1986.

Bud, R. *The Uses of Life: A History of Biotechnology*, Cambridge: Cambridge University Press, 1993.

Claflin, K. 'La Villette: city of blood (1867–1914)', in P.Y. Lee (ed.), *Meat, Modernity, and the Rise of the Slaughterhouse*, Durham NH: University of New Hampshire Press, 2008, 27–45.

Clutton-Brock, J. *A Natural History of Domesticated Animals*, second edition, Cambridge: Cambridge University Press, 1999.

Cost of Living in French Towns. Report of an Enquiry by the Board of Trade into Working Class Rents, Housing and Retail Prices, Together with the Rates of Wages in Certain Occupations in the Principal French Towns of France, London: His Majesty's Stationery Office, 1909.

Cronon, W. *Nature's Metropolis: Chicago and the Great West*, New York: Norton, 1991.

Crosby, A. *The Columbian Exchange: Biological and Cultural Consequences of 1492*, Westport CT: Praeger, 2003.

Darwin, C. *On the Origin of Species by Means of Natural Selection*, J. Carroll (ed.), Orchard Park NY: Broadview Press, 2003.

Derry, M. *Bred For Perfection: Shorthorn Cattle, Collies, and Arabian Horses since 1800*, Baltimore MD, Johns Hopkins University Press, 2003.

Derry, M. *Masterminding Nature: The Breeding of Animals 1750–2010*, Toronto: University of Toronto Press, 2015.

Dohner, J. *The Encyclopedia of Historic and Endangered Livestock and Poultry Breeds*, New Haven CT: Yale University Press, 2001.

Douglas's Encyclopaedia: The Standard Book of Reference for the Food Trades, third edition, London: William Douglas & Sons, 1924.

Drabble, J. *Textbook of Meat Inspection*, Sydney: Angus and Robertson, 1936, 131–132.

Drouard, A. 'Horsemeat in France: a food item that appeared during the war of 1870 and disappeared after the Second World War', in I. Zweiniger-Bargielowska, R. Duffett, and A. Drouard (eds.), *Food and War in Twentieth Century Europe*, Burlington VT: Ashgate, 2011, 233–246.

Duckham, A. *Animal Industry in the British Empire: A Brief Review of the Significance, Methods, Problems, and Potentialities of the Live-Stock and Dairying Industries of the British Commonwealth*, London: Oxford University Press, 1932.

Emmans, G. and Kyriazakis, I. 'Consequences of genetic change in farm animals on food intake and feeding behaviour', *Proceedings of the Nutrition Society* 60, 1 (2001): 115–125.

'Empire of the pig', *Economist*, 20 December 2014.

Evershed, H. 'The early fattening of cattle and sheep', *Journal of the Royal Agricultural Society of England*, 1890.

Fairlie, S. *Meat: A Benign Extravagance*, White River Junction VT: Chelsea Green, 2010.

Ferrières, M. *Sacred Cow, Mad Cow: A History of Food Fears*, trans. J. Gladding, New York: Columbia University Press, 2006.

Fielding, C. *Food*, London: Hurst and Blackett, 1923.

Finlay, M. 'Hogs, antibiotics, and the industrial environments of postwar agriculture', in S. Shrepfer and P. Scranton (eds.), *Industrializing Organisms: Introducing Evolutionary History*, London: Routledge, 2004, 237–260.

Fitzgerald, A. 'A social history of the slaughterhouse: from inception to contemporary implications', *Human Ecology Review* 17, 1 (2010): 58–69.

Francis, R. *Domesticated: Evolution in a Man-Made World*, New York: Norton, 2015.

Franklin, S. *Dolly Mixtures: The Remaking of Genealogy*, Durham NC: Duke University Press, 2007.

Galloway, J.N., Aber, J.D., Erisman, J.W., Seitzinger, S.P., Howarth, R.W., Cowling, E.B., and Cosby, B.J. 'The nitrogen cascade', *BioScience* 53, 4 (2003): 341–356.

Galloway, J., Burke, M., Bradford, G., Naylor, R., Falcon, W., Chapagain, A., Gaskell, J., McCullough, E., Mooney, H., Oleson, K., Steinfeld, H., Wassenaar, T., and Smil, V. 'International trade in meat: the tip of the pork chop', *Ambio* 36, 8 (2007): 622–629.

Giedion, S. *Mechanization Takes Command: A Contribution to Anonymous History* [1948], New York: Norton, 1969.

Gremillion, K. *Ancestral Appetites: Food in Prehistory*, Cambridge: Cambridge University Press, 2011, 19.

Grigg, D. *The World Food Problem*, second edition, Oxford: Blackwell, 1993.

Gruen, L. *Ethics and Animals: An Introduction*, Cambridge: Cambridge University Press.

Grundy, J. 'The Hereford bull: his contribution to New World and domestic beef supplies', *Agricultural History Review* 50, 1 (2002): 69–88.

Hall, D. *Our Daily Bread: A Geography of Production*, London: John Murray, 1938.

Haraway, D. *The Companion Species Manifesto: Dogs, People, and Significant Otherness*, Chicago IL: Prickly Paradigm Press, 2003.

Heiss, H. 'The German abattoir', in C. Cash (ed.), *Our Slaughter-house System: A Plea for Reform*, London: George Bell and Sons, 1907, 85–212.

'Hippophagy', *Chambers's Encyclopaedia*, X, London: W. & R. Chambers, 1874.

Holmes, G. *Meat Supply and Surplus, With Consideration of Consumption and Exports*, Washington: Government Printing Office, 1907.

Horowitz, R. *Putting Meat on the American Table: Taste, Technology, Transformation*, Baltimore MD: Johns Hopkins University Press, 2006.

'Horse-Flesh', *Glasgow Herald*, 26 April 1870.
Husson, A. 'De la consommation de la viande de cheval a Paris et dans quelques villes de l'Allemagne', *Journal de la Société de statistique de Paris* 15 (1874): 274–279.
Judd, R. *Contested Rituals: Circumcision, Kosher Butchering, and Jewish Political Life in Germany, 1843–1933*, Cornell NY: Cornell University Press, 2007.
Kambadur, R., Sharma, M., Smith, T., and Bass, J. 'Mutations in *myostatin* (GDF8) in double-muscled Belgian Blue and Piedmontese cattle', *Genome Research* 7, 9 (1997): 910–915.
Kelekna, P. *The Horse in Human History*, Cambridge: Cambridge University Press, 2009.
Kirsch, S. *What Species of Creatures: Animal Relations From the New World*, Vancouver: New Star, 2008.
'"Kosher" and other meat', *British Medical Journal*, 23 December 1893, 1393.
Leighton, G. and Douglas, L. *The Meat Industry and Meat Inspection*, London: The Educational Book Company, 1910, 5 Volumes.
Libby, R. 'Sentiment vs. health', *American Journal of Veterinary Medicine* XII, (1918).
Line, E. *The Science of Meat and the Biology of Food Animals*, London: Meat Trades' Journal Co. Ltd, 1931.
MacDonald, J. *Food From the Far West: Or, American Agriculture, with Special Reference to the Beef Production and Importation of Dead Meat from America to Great Britain*, London: William P. Nimmo, 1878.
MacKenzie, K. *Cattle and the Future of Beef-Production in England*, Cambridge: Cambridge University Press, 1919.
Martin, C. *Practical Food Inspection, Volume I – Meat Inspection*, third edition, London: H.K. Lewis & Co., 1947.
Maxwell, R. *Handbook on the Law Relating to Slaughter-Houses and Unsound Food, Including the Slaughter of Animals Act, 1933, and the Public Health (Meat) Regulations, 1924*, second edition, London: The Sanitary Publishing Company, Ltd, 1934.
McFall, R. *The World's Meat*, London: D. Appleton and Company, 1927.
Moore, J. *Capitalism in the Web of Life: Ecology and the Accumulation of Capital*, London: Verso, 2015.
Morton, T. *Shelley and the Revolution in Taste: The Body and the Natural World*, Cambridge: Cambridge University Press, 1994.
Myers, N. 'The hamburger connection: how Central America's forests became North America's hamburgers', *Ambio* 10, 1 (1981): 3–8, 6.
Netz, R. *Barbed Wire: An Ecology of Modernity*, Middletown CT: Wesleyan University Press, 2009.
Novek, J. 'Discipline and distancing: confined pigs in the factory farm gulag', in A. Gross and A. Vallely (eds.), *Animals and the Human Imagination: A Companion to Animal Studies*, New York: Columbia University Press, 2012, 121–151.
Ohnuki-Tierney, E. 'We eat each other's food to nourish our body: the global and the local as mutually constituent forces', in R. Grew (ed.) *Food in Global History*, Boulder CO: Westview, 1999, 240–272.
Oldfield, J. *The Evils of Butchery*, London: William Reeves, 1895.
Otter, C. 'Hippophagy in the UK: a failed dietary revolution', *Endeavour*, 35, 2–3 (2011): 80–90.
Pachirat, T. *Every Twelve Seconds: Industrialized Slaughter and the Politics of Sight*, New Haven CT: Yale University Press, 2011.
Paley, W. 'Moral and Political Philosophy', in *The Works of William Paley*, London: William Smith, 1838.
Perren, R. *Taste, Trade and Technology: The Development of the International Meat Industry since 1840*, Aldershot: Ashgate, 2006.

Pickering, D. 'World Agriculture', in C. Spedding (ed.), *Fream's Principles of Food and Agriculture*, seventeenth edition, Oxford: Blackwell, 1992, 45–93.

Putnam, G. *Supplying Britain's Meat*, London: George Harrap & Co., 1923.

Richardson, B. 'Public slaughter-houses: a suggestion for farmers', *The New Review* 8 (1893).

Richelet, J. 'The Argentine meat trade', in *The Frozen and Chilled Meat Trade: A Practical Treatise by Specialists in the Meat Trade*, 2 volumes, London: The Gresham Publishing Company Ltd, 1929.

Rimas, A. and Fraser, E. *Beef: The Untold Story of How Milk, Meat, and Muscle Shaped the World*, New York: William Morrow, 2008.

Rixson, D. *The History of Meat Trading*, Nottingham: Nottingham University Press, 2000.

Ruddiman, W. *Plows, Plagues, and Petroleum: How Humans Took Control of Climate*, Princeton NJ: Princeton University Press, 2005.

Russell, E. *Evolutionary History: Uniting History and Biology to Understand Life on Earth*, Cambridge: Cambridge University Press, 2011.

Saint-Hilaire, I.G. *Lettres sur les Substances Alimentaires et Particulièrement sur la Viande de Cheval*, Paris: Libraire de Victor Masson, 1856.

Sanders, A. *A History of Aberdeen-Angus Cattle With Particular Reference to Their Introduction, Distribution and Rise to Popularity in the Field of Fine Beef Production in North America*, Chicago IL: New Breeder's Gazette, 1928.

Shane, D. *Hoofprints on the Forest: Cattle Ranching and the Destruction of Latin America's Tropical Forests*, Philadephia PA: Institute for the Study of Human Issues, 1986.

Shelley, P.B. *A Vindication of Natural Diet*, new edition, London: F. Pitman, 1884.

Simmonds, P. *The Curiosities of Food, or the Dainties and Delicacies of Different Nations Obtained from the Animal Kingdom* [1859], Berkeley CA: Ten Speed Press, 2001, 6.

Slatta, R. *Comparing Cowboys and Frontiers*, Norman OK: University of Oklahoma Press, 1997.

Smil, V. 'Eating meat: evolution, patterns, and consequences', *Population and Development Review* 28, 4 (2002): 599–639.

Smil, V. *Harvesting the Biosphere: What We Have Taken From Nature*, Cambridge MA: MIT Press, 2013.

Smil, V. *Should We Eat Meat? Evolution and Consequences of Modern Carnivory*, Chichester: Wiley-Blackwell, 2013.

Steffen, W., Grinewald, J., Crutzen, P., and McNeil, J. 'The Anthropocene: conceptual and historical perspectives', *Philosophical Transactions of the Royal Society A* 369, 1938 (2011): 842–867.

Steinfeld, H., Gerber, P., Wassenaar, T., Castel, V., Rosales, M., and de Haan, C. *Livestock's Long Shadow: Environmental Issues and Options*, Rome: Food and Agriculture Organisation of the United Nations, 2006, 33.

Striffler, S. *Chicken: The Dangerous Transformation of America's Favorite Food*, New Haven CT: Yale University Press, 2005.

Stuart, T. *The Bloodless Revolution: A Cultural History of Vegetarianism from 1600 to Modern Times*, New York: Norton, 2006.

'The slaughtering of animals', *British Medical Journal*, 9 June 1894, 1256.

Thévenot, R. *A History of Refrigeration Throughout the World*, trans. J. Fidler, Paris: International Institute of Refrigeration, 1979.

Thomas, K. *Man and the Natural World: Changing Attitudes in England, 1500–1800*, Oxford: Oxford University Press, 1996.

Thomson, R. *Experimental Researches on the Food of Animals, and the Fattening of Cattle. With Remarks on the Food of Man*, New York: S. Appleton & Co., 1846.

Trentmann, F. *Free Trade Nation: Commerce, Consumption, and Civil Society in Modern Britain*, Oxford: Oxford University Press, 2008.

Ulijasek, S., Mann, N., and Elton, S. *Evolving Human Nutrition: Implications for Public Health*, Cambridge: Cambridge University Press, 2012.

Vialles, N. *Animal to Edible*, Cambridge: Cambridge University Press, 1994.

Voisin, A. *Soil, Grass and Cancer: Health of Animals and Men is Linked to the Mineral Balance of the Soil*, trans. C. Herriot and H. Kennedy, New York: Philosophical Library Inc., 1959.

Walton, J. 'Pedigree and productivity in the British and North American cattle kingdoms before 1930', *Journal of Historical Geography* 25, 4 (1999): 441–462.

Watson, J., Cameron, J., and Garrad, G. *The Cattle-Breeder's Handbook*, London: Earnest Benn, 1926.

Weis, T. *The Ecological Hoofprint: The Global Burden of Industrial Livestock*, London: Zed Books, 2013.

White, M. 'Eating of horses non-American', *American Journal of Veterinary Medicine* XII (1918).

Wilmut, I., Campbell, K., and Tudge, C. *The Second Creation: Dolly and the Age of Biological Control*, Cambridge MA: Harvard University Press, 2001.

Wilson, J. *The Evolution of British Cattle and the Fashioning of Breeds*, London: Vinton and Company, 1909.

Winters, L. *Animal Breeding*, second edition, New York: John Wiley & Sons, Inc., 1930.

Woods, A. 'Rethinking the history of modern agriculture: British pig production, c.1910–65', *Twentieth Century British History* 23, 2 (2012): 165–191.

Wrangham, R. *Catching Fire: How Cooking Made Us Human*, New York: Basic Books, 2009.

21
ANIMALS AND VIOLENCE
Medieval humanism, 'medieval brutality', and the carnivorous vegetarianism of Margery Kempe

Karl Steel

Human domination and human reason in the middle ages

The division between humans and nonhuman animals was central to medieval European Christianity's professional thought. Many of these medieval claims have persisted long into the present, chiefly, that among forms of mortal life, only humans possess language, free will, and moral responsibility. A study of medieval thinking and practices of dividing humans from animals thus offers a chance to rethink contemporary methods of dividing humans from nonhumans, in part because the very uncanniness of medieval articulations of these divisions – belonging at once to the Middle Ages and a present that believes itself to have surpassed the medieval – may render modern humanisms equally unfamiliar.

The dominant element of medieval humanism is its being a zero sum game: the human claim to rationality accompanied a claim that among mortal life, *only* humans were rational. Practices of violence and domination were key to these claims. Augustine of Hippo (354–430), the late antique Bishop of Carthage whose voluminous writings remain foundational to the Christian intellectual tradition, neatly demonstrates how this works. Early in his *City of God,* Augustine considers the problem of the Decalogue's sixth commandment, 'thou shalt not kill'. In this section, written in the wake of the fall of Rome, Augustine delegitimises Roman suicide by claiming that human life ultimately belongs to God; almost as an aside, he argues that the rest of mortal life belongs to us. He sneers at any idea that the sixth commandment could shelter humans and animals both: why not protect flowers too, then? Augustine thinks the answer obvious: plants can be killed because they 'have no sensation', while animals, because they do not 'share the use of reason with us . . . both their life and death are subject to our needs'.[1] Proving the disassociation of animals from humans required proving both that animals lacked reason and that humans had it. Augustine had already taken up these interlinked problems forty years earlier, in his treatise *On the Free Choice of the Will.* Rather than establishing that humans possess reason (a crucial foundation for free will) by describing scenarios where this capacity was practised (for example, the many decisions necessary for writing a philosophical treatise), Augustine instead observes that while animals may sometimes get the better of humans, in the general course of things they submit to our routine domination. He observes that we therefore must have something they lack, and, with an astonishing logical leap, names this mysterious quality 'reason'.[2] In his logic, the human subordination of animals both justifies their subordination and provides the hard evidence that humans are the one form of rational worldly life. In sum, the ongoing, repeated domination of animals is the surest proof that the human exists, if the human is defined, as it often was, as the form of life that was mortal *and* rational.

Formulations like this were common throughout the Middle Ages. Perhaps the strangest belongs to the ninth-century 'Letter on the Cynocephali' by Ratramnus, Abbot of Corbie (died c. 870). When the missionary Rimbert heard rumours that a race of dog-headed people (the 'Cynocephali') lived in the far north, he sought advice from Ratramnus.[3] Ratramnus's response, no doubt based upon Corbie's well-stocked library, explained that the Cynocephali might be reasonable; although they were said to communicate by barking rather than spoken language, they nonetheless wore clothing (and therefore were modest) and lived in settled communities. Ratramnus needed one more fact to complete his argument: the Cynocephali kept livestock, and since no other species were masters of other animals, the Cynocephali must have rational souls, and therefore merit hearing the word of God.

We can witness similar productions of human difference in Christian scriptural exegesis. Faced with the legacy of Deuteronomy 25:4, which forbade farmers from muzzling oxen as they tread corn, the commentary of the apostle Paul explains that the law cannot possibly concern animals, but rather meant only that 'he that plougheth, should plough in hope; and he that thrasheth, in hope to receive fruit' (1 Corinthians 9:10).[4] Guibert of Nogent's twelfth-century treatise against Judaism reacts with even more incredulity to Deuteronomy 22:6-7, which allows eggs to be taken from the nest of a wild bird, but demands that the adult bird herself be left alone: instead of interpreting the verse, he just dismisses it altogether as patently absurd.[5] The final verse of Jonah 4:11 features God's compassion for Nineveh's population, which comprises the persons in it who 'know not how to distinguish between their right hand and their left, and many beasts'. Here, humans and animals alike receive God's consideration; they are not split by cognitive or spiritual difference, but united by their shared ignorance, possession of life, and exposure to injury. Augustine's commentary intervenes to argue that regardless of what the scripture itself says, God could take no interest in the animals in themselves ('non servat propter ipsa'), because animals were made for humans, not humans for animals. As Augustine's commentary ringingly concludes, 'quae enim spes in pecoribus?' [what hope do livestock have?].[6]

Although claims like these elevate human life in general, they also produce a category of naturally subordinate life, applicable just as readily to animals and humans both. People with intellectual impairments were typically characterised as animals, as with Henry de Bracton's assertion in his thirteenth-century legal compilation that the insane 'are not far removed from brute beasts which lack reason', and on this basis barred from inheriting or bequeathing property.[7] A medieval anti-Semitic legend developed in late medieval England held that Jews were descended from pigs, arguing implicitly than anyone who refused to eat pigs was socially equivalent to pigs; a similar charge held that Muslims refused pork because pigs had eaten their prophet while he lay helpless in an epileptic fit.[8] A late medieval French satiric poem declared that peasants might as well go on all fours and eat nothing but stubble.[9] Medieval misogyny, most vigorously promulgated by celibate male clergy, held that women were both more bodily and more irrational than men, and, like animals, required guidance and correction by more fully rational forms of life. Then, as now, the defence of human rights at the expense of the animal put most humans in peril. Humans who were thought by dominant groups to possess the full range of human capacities were far less numerous than those humans thought to have been made only to be mastered by their intellectual and emotional superiors. Rethinking the supposedly natural subordination of nonhumans to humans, and the function of this subordination in proving the presence or absence of 'reason', is therefore advantageous for the majority of both animals and humans.[10]

Rethinking the time and space of 'medieval brutality'

Given such medieval attitudes, it should be no surprise that examples of cruelty to animals in this period are easy to compile. William Fitz Stephen's thirteenth-century portrait of London lauds the city for its entertainments, which include wrestling, target-shooting, and riverboat jousting, and also spectacular fights to the death between bulls or boars and dogs.[11] The fourteenth-century Middle English poem *Cleanness* adapts Jesus's parable of the rich man's feast, so that, like a good English magnate, he proclaims the completion of preparations with a hearty 'my bulls and my boars are baited and slain' [my boles and my bores arn bayted and slayn].[12] And one early sixteenth-century English recipe meant for a convalescent begins notoriously: 'Take a red Cock that is not too olde, and beate him to death, and when he is dead, fley him and quarter him in small peeces, and bruse the bones everye one of them'.[13]

Typical modern responses to records like these do not, however, emphasise the links between medieval and modern human supremacy, but rather habitually present the people of the Middle Ages as themselves 'brutal'. 'Medieval brutality', a cliché in the general culture – as with this, from the *New York Times*: 'experts in radicalization said that understanding the process by which people fell for the medieval brutality of a religious ideology is vital to combating it' – flatters modernity by characterising the medieval as filthier, crueller, and more 'ferocious' (from the Latin *ferox*, wild animal, as 'brutal' comes from the Latin *brutus*, 'beast').[14] In this self-regard of modernity, the medieval is not just more violent than the present; in its 'savagery' (from *saeva*, 'raging'), it is more animal: closer to beasts, more intimate with them, and unthinkingly prone to what is presumed to be 'animalistic' behaviour.[15] Recall the mud-caked peasants of *Monty Python and the Holy Grail* (dir. T. Gilliam and T. Jones 1975), the lupine pagan temptress of *Marketa Lazarová*, one of František Vláčil's medieval existential tragedies (1967), or the damp, fleshy, fecal crowds in the streets and noble courts of Alexei German's unendurable 'medieval' science-fiction film, *Hard to be a God* (2013). Assumptions like these hold that the past is cruel, the present civilised;

the past superstitious, the present rational; and by extension, the past animal, bound unthinkingly to outmoded traditions and stupid, pointlessly cruel violence, while the present is human, able to master its instincts, refuse supposedly biologically hardwired hierarchies, and open itself to create a future of its own design.

Typical mappings of the human to the modern are arguments about space as well as time. Kathleen Davis observes that eighteenth- and nineteenth-century colonial administrators developed the concept of the 'superstitious feudal Middle Ages' to divide European modernity from colonies they preferred to think of as still trapped in the past (indeed, given the specifically European origins of the category 'medieval', and its insidious modern uses, it may be wisest to reserve the term only for a European historical period).[16] The same assumptions of modernity persist into the present in a 'developmental narrative', as Geraldine Heng writes, 'whose trajectory positions' the Global West as modern 'and the rest of the world as always catching up'.[17] As a result, rethinking the cultural interchangeability of the Middle Ages and the animal, particularly in characterisations of violence, is at least implicitly a way to rethink what Kathleen Davis called the 'politics of time' and the inequities they justify.

One key way to rethink such politics is simply to recognise the heterogeneity of interactions between humans and nonhumans in the Middle Ages. While cruelty to animals was certainly not uncommon, this does not mean, for example, that medieval people were more 'in touch with' or less hypocritical in their use of animals than modern people. During this period of supposed 'medieval brutality', we can witness an unease about violence against animals, whose hypocrisy would be at home within a supposedly more enlightened modernity.

Alongside the evidence of bear- and bull-baiting, we can observe, for example, that it is not just the moderns who try to conceal how humans use and use up animal life. The difference between the English words for animal (cow, pig, sheep) and the analogous French words for meat (beef, pork, mutton) has long been a favoured classroom example of class ideology. The Francophone nobility of post-conquest England got their meat cooked and served, while their Anglophone inferiors carried out the actual husbandry and inevitable killing. The laws of well-organised cities of the later Middle Ages insisted that animals be slaughtered out of sight, and that offal be sold separately and less visibly than flesh. In London, waste products were not to be discarded in the Thames between Westminster and the Tower, to keep them from being seen by sacred and secular potentates both. Notable too is the fact that medieval butchers, although not uncommonly organised into powerful civic guilds, could also be considered unruly, dangerous to civic order, and more prone than others to committing murder.[18]

Dives and Pauper, a fifteenth-century Middle English moral treatise, preserves an especially complicated account of such attitudes in its commentary on the sixth commandment. Like Augustine, it proves that the prohibition of killing does not apply 'both to men and beasts', and insists that the Latin verb *occidere* ('to kill') should be translated into English as 'manslaughter'. It nevertheless imposes one requirement: that animals be slaughtered only on those occasions 'when it is profitable to them [that is, mankind] for food or for clothing or to avoid injury from the beasts which are injurious to men'; no one should 'slay [animals] out of cruelty or for the gratification of idle desires and depravity', as humans 'should have mercy on beasts and birds and not harm them without cause and pay attention to their being God's creatures'.[19] Historians of animal rights often favourably cite this passage as an early argument in favour of animal welfare; it may be that, but it is also a demand that animals should be slaughtered for only instrumental purposes.[20] In this passage from *Dives and Pauper,* appropriate causes for killing animals are those that use up the animal's life on the way to satisfying some human practical, material need – food, clothing, or self-defence; inappropriate causes are those that treat the death of the animal as an end in itself. In other words, the sinful killing of animals occurs when their killers are insufficiently indifferent to animal death. The sin is the acknowledgement that animal life has value in itself.

For *Dives and Pauper,* proper killers work to reduce animals to utter materiality, while violent killers work on the animal's very life – its presence, its prolongation, its end. The obverse of this sin would be to slaughter humans without 'cruelty and vanity', without grief or mourning or sadistic delight. For this would be a failure to acknowledge that humans, to be human, must possess something more than what can be calculated as a 'profit'. Slaughtering humans must therefore not be simply a job, but a sin, a horror, a drive, or an irresistible pleasure. One of Poggio Bracciolini's late medieval tales speaks of a teenage serial killer who, when caught, 'fassus est se plures alios comedisse, idque se agere, quoniam sapidiores reliquis carnibus viderentur' [confessed that he had eaten many other (children), and that he had done this because they seemed tastier to him than any other flesh].[21] Though this excessive pleasure in the death and savour of humans – not uncommon in medieval accounts of anthropophagy – is a horror, the very repetition of it *as* a horror divides human life from animal life, keeping animals where they should be, conceptually reserved as mere tools for human use.

The lived experience of medieval people with animals could of course be still more complicated than this. Although university thinkers insisted that humans could have no direct charity for animals, in practice, medieval people had non-functional, affectionate relationships with animals. This should be no surprise: James Serpell established that keeping pets is not a uniquely modern or Western trait but one general to humans of whatever class, culture, or period. Records of medieval animals obviously kept not for guarding houses, capturing game, or any other obvious practical purpose, speak of domestic deer, badgers, monkeys, parrots, and squirrels. Late medieval Paris had a lively market in imported Syrian cats.[22] The fourteenth-century *Saxon Mirror,* a German law code surviving in hundreds of manuscripts, requires owners to pay compensation if their domestic dogs, wolves, deer, bears, or monkeys cause any damage.[23] The canonisation dossier of Thomas of Cantilupe includes a miracle in which he resurrected a supplicant's dormouse, trodden upon accidentally by a clumsy knight.[24]

Even apart from these supposedly 'non-functional' animals, medieval people had emotional ties to the animals they used to guard their houses, to kill other animals, and to pull things or ride on. The knights of medieval romance mourn, some to the point of madness, when their steeds are killed beneath them (for example, in the *Awyntyrs of Arthur*).[25] English hunters bent coins over the heads of ailing hawks to attract the beneficent attention of saints, and some kings even sent their sick birds on pilgrimage.[26] Finally, Walter Map tells a story about a rich man who entered his barn 'and approached each oxen in turn, shook up their fodder, running his hand along the backbone of each, approvingly and fondly, instructing each by name to eat'.[27] They worked for him; they would end their lives of labour by being slaughtered and eaten; but at least he knew them individually; and, as the story concludes, should a deer hide itself from hunters among his herd, the rich man, even in darkness, would immediately identify it, eject it, and have it put to death. These are his working animals, and ultimately his food animals, but he still loves them. The split between notions of utility and uselessness, between ends in themselves and mere tools, is here as elsewhere unsustainable. Such splits raise the demand for proving that medieval people could 'really' love animals to a degree that could scarcely be fulfilled if it were applied to any other interpersonal relation.

The common notions that medieval people were somehow more bestial than moderns, somehow 'closer to' or 'more authentic' in their dealings with animals must be resisted, rethought, and recognised as a pernicious, persistent error. First, the belief in human superiority has not yet abandoned faith in immaterial, hierarchical categories. As demonstrated in Vinciane Despret's *What Would Animals Say if We Asked the Right Questions?*, quasi-theological categories such as 'instinct' persist in contemporary thought about animals. This is the case even among scientists, serving to sequester humans from nonhumans, and justifying ongoing, cruelly useless experiments to prove 'truths' of animal behaviour – about 'natural dominance' for example – determined long before their experimental 'proof'.[28] Suspending the certainty of the uniquely human category of reason, and the abilities that supposedly accompany it, would go far towards bettering the condition of animals, and perhaps even to remapping political chronologies and geographies that 'animalise' vast swaths of the human world.

We also require a richer on-the-ground sense of lived practices and a concomitant suspension of facile notions of historical development. We can observe, for example, that while medieval Christian Europe had no organised societies for the prevention of cruelty towards animals, in practice, given its absence of both industrialised meat production and laboratory science, it was almost certainly less quantitatively cruel to nonhumans than twenty-first century industrialised democracies. This is not to claim a causal relation, even an inverse one, between these various practices, but rather to insist at least on a fuller, less straightforward mapping of the relation between intellectual history (in which Augustine and Aquinas and the other usual suspects insist that animals have no moral considerability) and the more complicated negotiations of lived experience. My next section provides an extended example of such negotiations.[29]

Margery Kempe's carnivorous vegetarianism

The following restores to the Middle Ages the cultural complexity often denied it by a modern self-satisfaction that makes the era little more than either a barbaric anticipation of modernity or its less decadent origin, or both. My subject is the fifteenth-century bourgeoise, contemplative, preacher, troublemaker, and pilgrim, the extraordinary Margery Kempe (c. 1373–after 1438). The centrepiece, through her amanuenses, is what represents itself as the first English-language autobiography.

Kempe studies have generally sought to locate her in relation to contemporary practices of late medieval spirituality; to praise her as a figure of resistance to patriarchal rationality; to understand her *Book* as a conscious effort to refashion her experience as a hagiography; and even to argue that key sections of the work, or even the whole work, are fictional.[30] Only rarely have critics attended to her long-standing refusal to eat meat and her tendency to weep sorely at the sight of animal suffering. Those that have done so have tended to understand Kempe only in relation to intrahuman practices of hospitality (as an unruly table guest who refuses the food everyone else enjoys) or they take her, like *Dives and Pauper*, as a kind of early advocate for animal rights.[31] I argue that Kempe practises what might be called a 'carnivorous vegetarianism', a practice of avoiding meat that has little to do with kindness to animals, a 'healthy diet', or the ecological motivations of many modern vegetarianisms. The overdetermined, particularly medieval logic of this dietary practice becomes clear if we suspend our certainties about human difference from animals and attend more closely to general cultural discourses of meat-eating and fleshly embodiment as well as to Kempe's own gender, age, and life experience as mother and independent woman.

Around the year 1409, Christ granted Margery Kempe his first long visionary visitation, in which he commands her to

> forsake that which you love best in this world, and that is eating of flesh. And instead of that flesh, you shall eat my flesh and my blood, which is the true body of Christ in the sacrament of the altar [forsake that thou lovyst best in this world, and that is etyng of flesch. And instede of that flesch thow schalt etyn my flesch and my blod, that is the very body of Crist in the sacrament of the awter].[32]

Despite the exertions of pilgrimage, and despite bullying from her fellow travellers, she keeps the vow for years, begrudgingly having some meat only for 'a lytyl whyle' (Chapter 26) when her confessor insists on it. Not until Christ himself intervenes, years later, does she fully 'resort ageyn to flesch mete', and only then because Christ wants her to build up her strength for another pilgrimage. Obedient on both occasions to her divine lord, she gets 'to have her fast and eat it' too.[33]

In her fifteenth-century England, Kempe's decision to forgo meat for years on end would have been unusual for a secular woman, but was otherwise perfectly orthodox.[34] Kempe could have gone much further and still remained within the church: the twelfth-century Alpais of Cudot, for example, is said to have survived for years while eating nothing but Eucharistic hosts.[35] Even had she not been fairly wealthy, meat would still not have been necessarily rare in Kempe's diet. Late fourteenth-century harvest workers in eastern and southern England would have received nearly a pound of it daily during the labouring season.[36] She would have gone without meat not because of its scarcity but for religious reasons: by the later Middle Ages, Latin Christendom required its adherents, even laypeople, to abstain from meat for nearly a third of the year, mostly during the fasting season of Lent. Monks tended to do still more, and the Carthusian order of monks, whose practice Kempe's most closely resembled, did the most of all, by requiring that their adherents keep to an entirely meatless diet.

Generally speaking, 'meat' did not include fish or animals identified as fish, nor barnacle geese and newborn rabbits.[37] Such animals were held to be not alive in the way humans and other terrestrial animals were, and therefore unlikely to stir up our lust (as Aquinas explained), or, more simply, because in Genesis 3:17–18, God cursed only the earth, and not the waters.[38] Early medieval monastic rules tended to forbid all but the sick from eating quadrupeds and sometimes even birds; later monks developed loopholes by distinguishing forbidden *carnes* (freshly cooked meat recently cut from the joint) from licit *carnea* (pre-cooked, pre-salted meat), so much so that a monk, like the twelfth-century Samson, Abbot of Bury St Edmunds, could earn high praise for eating neither.[39]

Carthusians would have none of this. After centuries of debate, even the chancellor of the University of Paris weighed in. Jean Gerson's 1401 *De non esu Carnium Carthusienses* admitted that while abstinence from meat was bad for the health, so too were mercantile voyages and nearly all other human endeavours; as a result, Carthusians could hardly be faulted for damaging their health for God, so there was no legitimate reason for their critics to charge them, as they often did, with homicide.[40] Carthusian attitudes towards meat-eating found themselves promulgated outside the cloister in works such as the enormously popular Middle English *Mirror of the Blessed Life of Jesus Christ*, a meditative guide that explains that Christ ate meat only once, at the Last Supper, where Christ's typological role as the sacrificial, sacramental Paschal lamb made eating symbolically useful.[41] Carthusian approval for Kempe's ascetic diet is also suggested by the so-called 'red ink annotator', an early sixteenth-century reader of the sole extant manuscript of Kempe's *Book*. Willing at times to delete or even rewrite passages to suit his doctrinal preferences, he leaves the margin blank when Kempe first stops eating meat, but when she takes it up again, at folio 78v, he writes 'fleysche' near the passage, and draws a box around it: it may be too much to suggest that he was disturbed by this change in Kempe's religious practices, but he certainly found her new divergence from his own vows remarkable.[42]

In Kempe's England, the common heresy was not one of not eating meat, but of eating it at the wrong times, and without due regard for its special importance. Peter of Cluny's adversarial history of Peter of Bruys provides as bold an example as one could wish for: in the twelfth century, he dined on meat that he had roasted in front of a church, on Good Friday, on a pyre of disarticulated crucifixes.[43] The early fifteenth-century heretics of Norwich – a town some 40 miles from Kempe's own King's Lynn, which she visited frequently – broke with the church with far less fanfare, by saving leftover meat to eat on fast days, or by declaring that anyone could eat fish or flesh whenever they liked, with regard only for their personal gustatory preference.[44] This studied carelessness was punished with a temporary diet of bread and water, or, in one case, bread and ale, simultaneously depriving these heretics of meat and returning them to the penitential cycle of eating imposed upon all belonging to the community of the faithful.

The heretics who had worried the church the most were the so-called Cathars, who 'shun all flesh ... but not for the same reason as monks and others living spiritually abstain from it' [Carnem omnem vitant...non ea causa qua monachi, aut alii spiritualiter viventes ab ea abstinent], as Eckbert of Shönau complained in his 1163 sermon in praise of meat-eating. Eckbert laughs at the Cathars for believing that since some vast prince of shadows ('quemdam immanem principem tenebrarum') created the material world, they should not eat meat, the most material of foods.[45] Eckbert pretends to regret that there had been no Cathar present to whisper his doctrine in Noah's ear after the flood, when God first authorised this new meaty diet. Putting aside ongoing debates about the historical existence of Cathars, it is because of stories about beliefs such as these that one late-medieval defender of Carthusian dietary restrictions explains 'unlike certain heretics, [we] hold like other Christians that all God's creatures are good', which is to say, inherently good for food.[46]

While medieval ethnographers were willing to imagine fully vegetarian, entirely peaceful cultures, kind to animal life and even all things, they deposited them in the far east, or the distant past of the classical 'Golden Age', before humans took up carnivorousness, warfare, and commerce.[47] Good Christians, even Carthusians, were supposed to want to kill and eat animals, and to recognise that God had given them animals for exactly this purpose. They were encouraged to refuse this pleasure, but they were supposed to refuse it *as* a pleasure, so that the Christian year, even for laypeople, may be understood as an elaborate management and refinement of the satisfactions of abstinence. This is how Kempe fasts: the orthodoxy of her restricted diet is marked by what Christ says to her: leave off eating what 'thou lovyst best'.

The significant strain for her own culture is Kempe's own fleshly embodiment of a simultaneous restraint and enjoyment, which linked her to animals and the incarnated Christ himself even as she materialised the culturally loaded category of 'woman'. Karma Lochrie's foundational study of Kempe argues that the 'primary human conflict' for medieval Christianity was not body against soul, but 'the life of the flesh against the life of the spirit'.[48] The body was neutral and passive, doing nothing on its own. Kempe's *Book* tends to use 'body' to represent whole things: her body as a whole, or her husband's, or Christ's, either hanging on the cross or in the form of the Eucharist. The body, neatly bordered, coherently designates an individual. But flesh was 'heaving', 'pervious', and 'heterogeneous' – neither body nor soul, but carnal and spiritual at the same time', for it was both materiality and materiality's own disturbingly autonomous disorder.[49] When Kempe awaits an Archbishop's interrogation, she 'stod stylle, tremelyng and whakyng ful sor in hir flesch wythowtyn ony erdly comfort' (Chapter 13), standing still and trembling at the same time, as if she were commingled with another, unquiet self. Like Kempe herself, flesh was a woman: as Augustine explained in his commentary on Psalm 140, 'your flesh is like your wife . . . it lusts against you like your wife' [caro tanquam coniux est . . . Concupiscit adversus te, tanquam coniux tua].[50] Flesh is sex (as in 'fleschly knowyng' [Chapter 9] or 'fleschly comownyng' [Chapter 3]). It draws us away from spirit ('fleschly affeccyon' [Chapter 28]). Flesh is meat, because Middle English vocabulary, like the Latin *carnis*, did not distinguish between 'meat' and 'flesh' (the Middle English 'mete' simply meant 'food' in general). And finally, Flesh is sometimes the edible body of Christ, recreated every time Catholic priests performed a Mass. Kempe's flesh therefore simultaneously recalled the body in its irrational motivations, its lustiness, its vulnerability and edibility, and its sublime Eucharistic incarnation.

A short poem included in a fifteenth-century Middle English Carthusian devotional anthology helps illustrate the operations of this densely tangled node of signification.

It imagines a falconer who entices a restless bird to return by showing it a hunk of 'rede flesche': so too, explains the poem, does Christ draw us back, so that we can join him on the 'cros of penaunce' through 'discrete poneyschyng of thi body'.[51] Jessica Brantley dryly remarks that 'the poem sets up a number of complex equivalences': Christ is falconer, but also meat, while the reader is a falcon who becomes both 'meat and crucified savior' through penance, which for a Carthusian means the lifelong penance of forgoing meat, which they do not do without pleasure but rather preserve it as a mastered element of the self.[52] The Carthusian poem lacks only an explicit reference to gender. Elsewhere, the same Carthusian compilation imagines a once beautiful woman beset in the grave by hectoring and hungry vermin, gradually argued into coming to terms with her edibility and putrefaction.[53] The debate's first page features an illustration of a cloaked man kneeling before a crucifix on which hangs a nearly naked Christ figure, whose white flesh bleeds redly from its every surface.[54] The manuscript's (male) readers are encouraged to identify with this suffering flesh, to be repulsed by the suffering flesh in the grave, and to recognise that this dynamic of identification and disidentification, swerving from one edible flesh to another, one divine and the other profane, is required because of their own fleshly frailty. Flesh, especially suffering flesh, runs through this Carthusian compilation in all its forms: edible, suffering, disdained, repulsive, feminised, and the stuff of redemption.

Kempe was a woman, a mother, a single woman, and an older person (in her fifties) and widow by the time she has the book written down: her culture would have made her into a figure of flesh in its danger, its filth, its concupiscence, its edibility, all that a masculinised order sought to render governable by abjecting it from itself (so that 'your flesh . . . lusts against you, like your wife').[55] Widows were considered to be sexually knowing; as in *Sir Gawain and the Green Knight*, or Chaucer's *Wife of Bath's Tale*, older women were often portrayed as repulsive.[56] Her contemporaries prefer that she either hew to these roles or be silent. Failing that, they prefer her to be a hypocrite, so she confirms the truth of what they believe her to really be. They accuse her of pushing aside a red herring at one meal in favour of a tastier, more expensive pike (Chapter 9); by calling her both a Lollard heretic (Chapter 13 and many other places) and a Jew (Chapter 52), they accuse her of disdaining their social pleasures, particularly of Christ's Eucharistic flesh; they prefer to believe she is not actually chaste but rather that she sneaks off regularly with her husband to 'woodys, grovys, er [or] valeys to usyn the lust of her bodiis' (Chapter 76). On her pilgrimages, her fellow travellers insist she eat meat, stop weeping, and keep her conversation about holiness to herself (Chapter 27). She carries on, inhabiting, refusing, and inhabited by flesh, on terms that both enact prejudicial certainties and deny them, because she is living as a woman, sometimes as a wife, and as the embodiment of worldly desire.

Similarly dense identifications operate in Kempe's identification with suffering. When Christ first orders Kempe to eat no flesh but that of his own body, he promises too that 'you shall be eaten and gnawed at by the people of the world as much as any rat gnaws on the stockfish' [Thow schalt ben etyn and knawyn of the pepul of the world as any raton knawyth the stokfysch (Chapter 5)]. Kempe twice compares herself to being meat chopped up for stew: 'If it were your will Lord, I would for your love and for the magnifying of your name be chopped as small as meat for the pot' [Yyf it wer thy wille, Lord, I wolde for thi lofe and for magnyfying of thi name ben hewyn as smal as flesch to the potte' (Chapter 57; also see Chapter 84)]. She goes without (animal) meat; she eats the (divine) meat of the Eucharist; she imagines herself as meat, chopped up, butchered, gnawed.

The most insistently public form her piety takes, her writhing and wailing, make her even more animal-like, as they cut her off from the articulate voice that was among the definitive features of rational humankind. When she first receives her white garment, a multivalent symbol of purity, she emits her strongest wails yet, so that people 'said that she howled as if she were a dog' [seyd that sche howlyd as it had ben a dogge' (Chapter 44)]. And when she sees animal suffering, she too suffers:

> If she saw a man who had a wound or a beast of whatever sort, or if a man beat a child before her or smote a horse or another beast with a whip, if she might see it or hear it, she thought that she saw our Lord be beaten or wounded in the same way that she saw the man or beast beat or wounded, whether in the field or in the town, whether alone by herself or among the people.
>
> Yf sche sey a man had a wownde er a best wheþyr it wer, er ȝyf a man bett a childe be-for hir er smet an hors er an-oþer best wyth a whippe, ȝyf sche myth sen it er heryn it, hir thowt sche saw owyr Lord be betyn er wowndyd lyk as sche saw in þe man er in þe best, as wel in the feld as in þe town, & be hir-selfe [a]lone as wel as a-mong þe pepyl. (Chapter 28)

In a superb study, Lisa Kiser enumerates several other comparisons between Christ's and animal suffering in late medieval English religious writing. She points out how Kempe's comparison differs from expected patterns (in late medieval drama, for example) by beginning with animals and then moving to Christ. From this, Kiser proposes that, in Kempe's weeping, we witness a rare, even precocious instance of both 'emotional fervor and moral disapproval' over the suffering of animals.[57]

Kempe's compassion is not, however, for animals so much as it is for injuries in general, whether animals or human. More importantly, Kempe has no interest in preventing this suffering; rather, she passionately seeks out suffering, joins with it, and renders it, whatever its form, an occasion for entanglement with the suffering of Christ. A typical scene from the *Book* has Kempe see Christ's 'precious tender body, rent and torn with scourges all over' [hys precyows tendyr body, alto rent and toryn wyth scorgys (Chapter 28)], whereupon she collapses and shouts 'with a loud voice, wonderfully turning and wresting her body every which way, stretching out her arms as if she had died' [wyth lowde voys, wondyrfully turnyng and wrestyng hir body on every syde, spredyng hir armys abrode as yyf sche schulde a deyd (Chapter 28)], or as if she were herself hung on the cross. This is empathic identification with suffering, but without any desire to end it. All the affective elements that we might think necessary for the development of animal rights, and even critical animal philosophy, are present, yet all they do is exacerbate the need to encounter suffering animals. This is not to accuse Kempe of not being 'good enough' from a modern animal-rights perspective: that would be absurd. It is rather to keep open the chance to observe the real strangeness of Kempe's animal identifications and carnivorous vegetarianism.

However much her religious ecstasies may be contextualised, even normalised through analogues in other late medieval mystics or contemplatives, her *Book* always insists on how shocking her contemporaries find her frenzied identifications. Kempe performs this identification in and through her flesh, in public. Though she does rationally dispute with professional clergy to defend herself from charges of heresy, she expresses herself most characteristically through ecstatic weeping and dog-like howling. More accurately, none of this is her performance or expression so much as it is *a* performance, *an* expression, generated impersonally through and in the flesh, in all its qualities at once as desiring, vulnerable, edible, disdained, and sacred. This performance is not wholly deliberative, not wholly human, often not linguistic, but through all this an indelibly gendered 'physical piety'.[58] I join with Myra Seaman in stressing that 'Kempe's state is supposedly beyond human, yet it remains utterly human as well: embodied, and intensely physical', which is to say, that she is also animal and divine and woman and mother and widow, and that the medium that makes all this possible, and at once so familiar and shocking to her contemporaries, is the flesh.[59]

This is one picture of medieval relations to violence against animals. If the human domination of animals, and the refusal to recognise their lives as having any value in themselves, displays itself most spectacularly in their being routinely killed and eaten by humans, then forgoing meat might seem to be a refusal of human mastery, and, with that, a refusal of the human domination of animals essential to what Agamben memorably called 'the anthropological machine'.[60] In some contexts, such as the 'Golden Age' literature alluded to above, medieval writers did characterise vegetarians this way: Alexander the Great often sneeringly calls Dindimus, king of the Brahmans, a beast, in part because Dindimus eats no meat. Margery Kempe's long-standing refusal of meat, however, is less about refusing human mastery of animals than it is about mastering the flesh by other means: not by killing and eating animals, but by taming the flesh that was simultaneously the delicious possession of animals and the unruly, pleasurable stuff that made up one's own self. Flesh was no mere object, but a way in which matter embodied desire and material disorder, material without being reducible to an *inert* materiality. Animals were fleshy; in their irrationality and savour, they were also embodiments of this problem of the flesh. Humans were fleshy too. For a human to eat animals meant dominating them, but *not* eating them also meant dominating what they represented.

This complicated picture is now very far removed from popular conceptions about 'medieval brutality' and violence against animals. Medieval philosophy and doctrine tend to provide a clear line between humans and animals, frequently proving the existence of the category of the human by appealing to the human dominance of animals. This material excludes animals from humans altogether, denying them any direct moral considerability, excluding them from the human community, and arguing, even, that the most 'charitable' use of an animal was to put it to use, through labour or butchery.[61] Among all this, lived practice could be a great deal more complicated, as could medieval philosophy too (Blaise of Parma, for example, hypothesised that, like insects, beings with rational souls could spontaneously generate from mud).[62]

The Middle Ages produced many stories of saints taking animals under their protection, of knights forming intimate partnerships with their steeds and even lions, and stories like Kempe's, about a simultaneous identification and mastery of a fleshiness shared with both humans and animals, which sought out suffering without any desire to end it.[63] Closer attention to such historical heterogeneity will not, of course, erase distinctions between the Middle Ages and the present, but it will push aside certainties about distinctions between the medieval and modern in favour of a more complicated picture, one that might take 'brutality', that quality of being bestial, as something other than violence, something other than the past, something other than what has been, or cannot be, left behind.[64]

Notes

1 Augustine of Hippo, *The City of God against the Pagans*, Book 1–13, trans. R.W. Dyson, Cambridge: Cambridge University Press, 1998, 33.
2 Augustine of Hippo, *Free Choice of the Will*, trans. T. Williams, Indianapolis IN: Hackett Publishing, 1993, 13.
3 Ratramnus of Corbie, 'Ratramnus and the dog-headed humans', in P.E. Dutton (ed. and trans.), *Carolingian Civilization: A Reader*, second edition, Peterborough ON: Broadview Press, 2004, 452–455.
4 Biblical quotations are from the Douay Rheims English translation of the Latin Vulgate.
5 J.P. Migne (ed.), *Patrologiae Cursus Completus: Series Latina*, 217 volumes, Paris, 1844, Volume 156, 524B. Throughout, translations from Migne are mine.
6 Migne, *Patrologiae Cursus Completus*, Volume 35, 2413.
7 For the Bracton and similar medieval statements, see I. Metzler, *Fools and Idiots? Intellectual Disability in the Middle Ages*, Manchester: Manchester University Press, 2016, 108, 114, 120, 154. For an important posthumanist engagement with disability and animality, M.Y. Chen, *Animacies: Biopolitics, Racial Mattering, and Queer Affect*, Durham NC: Duke University Press, 2012.
8 Examples include the Middle English accounts of the childhood of Jesus from British Library, Harley 3954 and Harley 2399, in C. Horstmann (ed.), *Sammlung altenglischer Legenden*, Heildesheim: Georg Olms, 1878; N. Daniel, *Islam and the West: The Making of an Image*, Oxford: Oneworld, 1993, 99–130.
9 A. Jubinal (ed.), *Jongleurs et trouvères; ou, choix de saluts, épîtres, rêveries et autres pièces légères des XIIIe et XIVe siècles*, Paris: J.A. Merklein, 1835, 107–109.
10 A now classic articulation of this point is the paraphrase and amplification of Gayatri Chakravorty Spivak by C. Wolfe, *Animal Rites: American Culture, the Discourse of Species, and Posthumanist Theory*, Chicago IL: University of Chicago Press, 2003, 7.
11 W. Fitz Stephen, *Norman London*, trans. F. Stenton, New York: Italica Press, 1990, 58.
12 A.C. Cawley and J.J. Anderson (eds.), *Sir Gawain and the Green Knight; Pearl; Cleanness; Patience*, London: Dent, 1991, line 55.
13 'A.W.', *A Book of Cookrye*, London: Edward Allde, 1587, image 13.
14 K. Bennhold, 'Same anger, different ideologies: radical muslim and neo-Nazi', *The New York Times*, 5 March 2015, last accessed 30 June 2016.
15 For the *Times*' most recent use of 'Medieval Savagery', see K. Davis, *Periodization and Sovereignty: How Ideas of Feudalism and Secularization Govern the Politics of Time*, Philadelphia PA: University of Pennsylvania Press, 2008, which quotes former Secretary of State John Kerry.
16 See Davis, *Periodization and Sovereignty*, and K. Davis, 'Convolutions of time: why an "early modern" period?', presented at 'Common Eras: Law, Literature, and the Rhetorics

of Commonality in Medieval and Renaissance England', Freie Universität Berlin, 19 May 2016.
17 G. Heng, 'The invention of race in the European Middle Ages 1: race studies, modernity, and the Middle Ages', *Literature Compass* 8, 5 (2011): 258–274, 264; see also C. Dinshaw, *Getting Medieval: Sexualities and Communities, Pre- and Postmodern*, Durham NC: Duke University Press, 1999, 183–206; B. Holsinger, *Neomedievalism, Neoconservatism, and the War on Terror*, Chicago IL: Prickly Paradigm Press, 2007; and C. Monagle and L. d'Arcens, '"Medieval" makes a comeback: what's going on?', *The Conversation*, 22 September 2014, last accessed 12 October 2016.
18 K. Steel, *How to Make a Human: Animals and Violence in the Middle Ages*, Columbus OH: Ohio State University Press, 2011, 207–220.
19 P.H. Barnam (ed.), *Dives and Pauper*, Volume 2, Oxford: Oxford University Press, 1976, 33.
20 The earliest such reference may be an April 1897 article by one Abbot Gasquet in *The Dublin Review*, reprinted in the anonymously edited anthology *The Church and Kindness to Animals*, 1906, 170–171. Favourable citations continue into this century.
21 P. Bracciolini, *Facetiarum*, Krakow, 1592, 109. My translation.
22 J. Serpell, 'Pet-keeping and animal domestication: a reappraisal', in J. Clutton-Brock (ed.), *The Walking Larder: Patterns of Domestication, Pastoralism, and Predation*, New York: Routledge, 1989, 10–21; K. Walker-Meikle, *Medieval Pets*, Woodbridge: Boydell Press, 2012.
23 M. Dobozy (trans.), *The Saxon Mirror: A Sachsenspiegel of the Fourteenth Century*, Philadelphia PA: University of Pennsylvania Press, 1999, 111–112.
24 Societé des Bollandistes (eds.), *Acta Sanctorum: October I*, Antwerp, 1765, 675.
25 In T. Hahn (ed.), *Sir Gawain: Eleven Romances and Tales*, Kalamazoo: Medieval Institute Publications, 1995, lines 554–555.
26 R.S. Oggins, *The Kings and Their Hawks: Falconry in Medieval England*, New Haven CT: Yale University Press, 2004, 105.
27 W. Map, *De Nugis Curialium, Courtiers' Trifles*, revised edition, ed. and trans. M.R. James, C.N.L. Brooke, and R.A.B. Mynors, Oxford: Clarendon Press, 1983, 515–516.
28 V. Despret, *What Would Animals Say if We Asked the Right Questions?*, trans. B. Buchanan, Minneapolis MN: University of Minnesota Press, 2016.
29 For Augustine and Aquinas see L. Gruen, 'The moral status of animals', in E.N. Zalta (ed.), *The Stanford Encyclopedia of Philosophy* (Fall 2014 edition), last accessed 11 October 2016.
30 The field of Kempe studies is vast. For a compelling recent example, with ample citations of the scholarly tradition, N.N. Sidhu, *Indecent Exposure: Gender, Politics, and Obscene Comedy in Middle English Literature*, Philadelphia PA: University of Pennsylvania Press, 2016, 149–187. Sidhu's claims about Kempe's fictionality should be supplemented with S. Sobecki, '"The writing of this tretys": Margery Kempe's son and the authorship of her book', *Studies in the Age of Chaucer* 37, 1 (2015): 257–283.
31 C. Mazzoni, 'Of stockfish and stew: feasting and fasting in the Book of Margery Kempe', *Food and Foodways* 10, 4 (2002): 171–182; M. Raine, '"Fals flesch": food and the embodied piety of Margery Kempe', *New Medieval Literatures* 7 (2005): 101–126; L.J. Kiser, 'Margery Kempe and the animalization of Christ: animal cruelty in late medieval England', *Studies in Philology* 106, 3 (2009): 299–315.
32 M. Kempe, *The Book of Margery Kempe*, L. Staley (ed.), Kalamazoo: Medieval Institute Publications, 1996, Chapter 5. I will cite Kempe in the body text by chapter for ease of consultation across other editions. For a modern English version, see M. Kempe, *The Book of Margery Kempe*, trans. A. Bale, Oxford: Oxford University Press, 2015.
33 S. Salih, 'Margery's bodies: piety, work, and penance', in J. Arnold and K.J. Lewis (eds.), *A Companion to The Book of Margery Kempe*, Cambridge: D.S. Brewer, 2004, 161–176, 170.

34 M.D. Bailey, 'Abstinence and reform at the council of Basil: Johannes Nider's *De abstinencia esus carnium*', *Mediaeval Studies* 59, (1997): 225–260; D.M. Bazell, '*De esu carnium*: Arnald of Villanova's defense of Carthusian abstinence', *Arxiu de Textos Catalans Antics* 14 (1995): 227–248; D.M. Bazell, 'Strife among the table-fellows: conflicting attitudes of early and medieval Christians toward the eating of meat', *Journal of the American Academy of Religion* 65, 1 (1997): 73–99.

35 C.W. Bynum, *Holy Feast and Holy Fast: The Religious Significance of Food to Medieval Women*, Berkeley CA: University of California Press, 1987.

36 C. Dyer, 'Changes in diet in the late Middle Ages: the case of harvest workers', *Agricultural History Review* 36, 1 (1988): 21–37, 28.

37 M. Van der Lugt, 'Animal légendaire et discours savant médiéval: la barnacle dans tous ses états', *Micrologus* 10, (2000): 351–393.

38 T. Aquinas, *Summa Theologica*, trans. Fathers of the English Dominican Province, New York: Benziger Brothers, 1947, 2a2ae q. 147, a. 8; see also Alcuin, *Quaestiones in Genesim*, in Migne, *Patrologiae Cursus Completus*, volume 100, 518B.

39 B.F. Harvey, *Living and Dying in England, 1100–1540: The Monastic Experience*, Oxford: Clarendon Press, 1993, 40; Jocelin of Brakelond, *Chronicle of the Abbey of Bury St Edmunds*, trans. D. Greenway and J. Sayers, New York: Oxford University Press, 1989, 36.

40 J. Fleming, 'When "meats are like medicines": Vitoria and Lessius on the role of food in the duty to preserve life', *Theological Studies* 69, 1 (2008): 99–115, 101–103.

41 N. Love, *The Mirror of the Blessed Life of Jesus Christ: A Reading Text*, M.G. Sargent (ed.), Exeter: University of Exeter Press, 2005, 51 and 377.

42 K.A.-M. Bugyis, 'Handling the Book of Margery Kempe: the corrective touches of the red ink annotator', in K. Kerby-Fulton, J.J. Thompson, and S. Baechle (eds.), *New Directions in Medieval Manuscript Studies and Reading Practices*, Notre Dame IN: University of Notre Dame Press, 2014, 138–158; British Library Additional MS 61823, f. 9r. The manuscript is viewable online through the British Library's manuscript interface.

43 Migne, *Patrologiae Cursus Completus*, volume 189, 771C–D.

44 N.P. Tanner (ed.), *Heresy Trials in the Diocese of Norwich, 1428–31*, London: Offices of the Royal Historical Society, 1977, 46.

45 Migne, *Patrologiae Cursus Completus*, volume 195, 17B, volume 195, 14C.

46 D.J. Falls, *Nicholas Love's Mirror and Late Medieval Devotio-Literary Culture: Theological Politics and Devotional Practice in Fifteenth-Century England*, New York: Routledge, 2016, 37.

47 K. Steel, 'A fourteenth-century ecology: "The Former Age" with Dindimus', in C. van Dyke (ed.), *Rethinking Chaucerian Beasts*, New York: Palgrave Macmillan, 2012, 185–199.

48 K. Lochrie, *Margery Kempe and Translations of the Flesh*, Philadelphia PA: University of Pennsylvania Press, 1991, 19.

49 Lochrie, *Margery Kempe and Translations of the Flesh*. The book often uses 'heaving'; for later two adjectives, 4 and 39.

50 Migne, *Patrologiae Cursus Completus*, volume 37, 1835; for further discussion, Lochrie, *Margery Kempe and Translations of the Flesh*, 19–20; S. Biernoff, *Sight and Embodiment in the Middle Ages*, London: Palgrave Macmillan, 2002, 26–34.

51 British Library Additional MS 61823, f. 9r. The manuscript is viewable online through the British Library's manuscript interface.

52 J. Brantley, *Reading in the Wilderness: Private Devotion and Public Performance in Late Medieval England*, Chicago IL: University of Chicago Press, 2007, 132.

53 For one discussion, E. Robertson, 'Kissing the worm: sex and gender in the afterlife and the poetic posthuman in the Late Middle English "a disputation betwyx the body and wormes"', in E.J. Burns and P. McCracken (eds.), *From Beasts to Souls: Gender and Embodiment in Medieval Europe*, Notre Dame IN: University of Notre Dame Press, 2013, 121–154.

54 British Library Additional MS 37049, f. 33r.
55 For discussion of the *Book*'s ambiguous dating of Kempe's widowhood, see T. Williams, '"As thu wer a wedow": Margery Kempe's wifehood and widowhood', *Exemplaria* 21, 4 (2009): 345–362.
56 S. Niebrzydowski (ed.) *Middle-Aged Women in the Middle Ages*, Woodbridge: DS Brewer, 2011.
57 Kiser, 'Margery Kempe and the animalization of Christ', 315. For a representative sympathetic citation from outside medieval studies, K.W. Perlo, *Kinship and Killing: The Animal in World Religions*, New York: Columbia University Press, 2009, 89.
58 Salih, *Margery's Bodies*, 162. This paragraph owes a great deal to feminist materialisms; for an excellent representative, see S. Alaimo, *Bodily Natures: Science, Environment, and The Material Self*, Bloomington IN: Indiana University Press, 2010. J. Bennett, *Vibrant Matter: A Political Ecology of Things*, Durham NC, Duke University Press, 2010, is by now a classic.
59 M.J. Seaman, 'Becoming more (than) human: affective posthumanisms, past and future', *Journal of Narrative Theory*, 37, 2 (2008): 246–275, 258.
60 A. Agamben, *The Open*, trans. K. Attell, Stanford CA: Stanford University Press, 2004, 38; for an essential critique of Agamben and animals, see D. Lacapra, *History and its Limits: Human, Animal, Violence*, Ithaca NY: Cornell University Press, 2009, 163–177.
61 T. Aquinas, *Summa Theologica*, 2a2ae, q. 25, a.3.
62 M. Van der Lugt, *Le Ver, le démon et la vierge: les théories médiévales de la génération extraordinaire: une étude sur les rapports entre théologie, philosophie naturelle et médecine*, Paris: Les Belles Lettres, 2004, 176–181.
63 For a good anthology of such stories, see D. Bell (ed.), *Wholly Animals: A Book of Beastly Tales*, Kalamazoo: Cistercian Publications, 1992.
64 For an excellent model of doing cultural history without epistemic breaks, see the opening chapters of S. Mentz, *Shipwreck Modernity: Ecologies of Globalization, 1550–1719*, Minneapolis MN: University of Minnesota Press, 2015.

Bibliography

Agamben, A. *The Open*, trans. K. Attell, Stanford CA: Stanford University Press, 2004.
Alaimo, S. *Bodily Natures: Science, Environment, and The Material Self*, Bloomington IN: Indiana University Press, 2010.
Aquinas, T. *Summa Theologica*, trans. Fathers of the English Dominican Province, New York: Benziger Brothers, 1947.
Augustine of Hippo *The City of God against the Pagans*, Book 1–13, trans. R.W. Dyson, Cambridge: Cambridge University Press, 1998.
Augustine of Hippo *Free Choice of the Will*, trans. T. Williams, Indianapolis IN: Hackett Publishing, 1993.
'A.W.' *A Book of Cookrye*, London: Edward Allde, 1587.
Bailey, M.D. 'Abstinence and reform at the council of Basil: Johannes Nider's *De Abstinencia Esus Carnium*', *Mediaeval Studies* 59, (1997): 225–260.
Barnam, P.H. (ed.) *Dives and Pauper*, Volume 2, Oxford: Oxford University Press, 1976.
Bazell, D.M. '*De Esu Carnium*: Arnald of Villanova's defense of Carthusian abstinence', *Arxiu de Textos Catalans Antics* 14, (1995): 227–248.
Bazell, D.M. 'Strife among the table-fellows: conflicting attitudes of early and medieval Christians toward the eating of meat', *Journal of the American Academy of Religion* 65, 1 (1997): 73–99.
Bell, D. (ed.) *Wholly Animals: A Book of Beastly Tales*, Kalamazoo: Cistercian Publications, 1992.

Bennett, J. *Vibrant Matter: A Political Ecology of Things*, Durham NC: Duke University Press, 2010.
Bennhold, K. 'Same anger, different ideologies: radical muslim and neo-Nazi', *The New York Times*, 5 March 2015, last accessed 30 June 2016.
Biernoff, S. *Sight and Embodiment in the Middle Ages*, London: Palgrave Macmillan, 2002.
Bracciolini, P. *Facetiarum*, Krakow, 1592.
Brantley, J. *Reading in the Wilderness: Private Devotion and Public Performance in Late Medieval England*, Chicago IL: University of Chicago Press, 2007.
British Library Additional MS 37049.
British Library Additional MS 61823.
Bugyis, K.A.-M. 'Handling the Book of Margery Kempe: the corrective touches of the red ink annotator', in K. Kerby-Fulton, J.J. Thompson, and S. Baechle (eds.), *New Directions in Medieval Manuscript Studies and Reading Practices*, Notre Dame IN: University of Notre Dame Press, 2014, 138–158.
Bynum, C.W. *Holy Feast and Holy Fast: The Religious Significance of Food to Medieval Women*, Berkeley CA: University of California Press, 1987.
Cawley, A.C. and Anderson, J.J. (eds.) *Sir Gawain and the Green Knight; Pearl; Cleanness; Patience*, London: Dent, 1991.
Chen, M.Y. *Animacies: Biopolitics, Racial Mattering, and Queer Affect*, Durham NC: Duke University Press, 2012.
Daniel, N. *Islam and the West: The Making of an Image*, Oxford: Oneworld, 1993.
Davis, K. *Periodization and Sovereignty: How Ideas of Feudalism and Secularization Govern the Politics of Time*, Philadelphia PA: University of Pennsylvania Press, 2008.
Davis, K. 'Convolutions of time: why an "early modern" period?', presented at 'Common Eras: Law, Literature, and the Rhetorics of Commonality in Medieval and Renaissance England', Freie Universität Berlin, 19 May 2016.
Despret, V. *What Would Animals Say if We Asked the Right Questions?*, trans. B. Buchanan, Minneapolis MN: University of Minnesota Press, 2016.
Dinshaw, C. *Getting Medieval: Sexualities and Communities, Pre- and Postmodern*, Durham NC: Duke University Press, 1999.
Dobozy, M. (trans.) *The Saxon Mirror: A Sachsenspiegel of the Fourteenth Century*, Philadelphia PA: University of Pennsylvania Press, 1999.
Dyer, C. 'Changes in diet in the late middle ages: the case of harvest workers', *Agricultural History Review* 36, 1 (1988): 21–37.
Falls, D.J. *Nicholas Love's Mirror and Late Medieval Devotio-Literary Culture: Theological Politics and Devotional Practice in Fifteenth-Century England*, New York: Routledge, 2016.
Fitz Stephen, W. *Norman London*, trans. F. Stenton, New York: Italica Press, 1990.
Fleming, J. 'When "meats are like medicines": Vitoria and Lessius on the role of food in the duty to preserve life', *Theological Studies* 69, 1 (2008): 99–115.
Gruen, L. 'The moral status of animals', in E.N. Zalta (ed.), *The Stanford Encyclopedia of Philosophy* (Fall 2014 edition), last accessed 11 October 2016.
Hahn, T. (ed.) *Sir Gawain: Eleven Romances and Tales*, Kalamazoo: Medieval Institute Publications, 1995.
Hard to be a God [Trudno byt' bogom], dir. A. German, 2013, Kino Lorber.
Harvey, B.F. *Living and Dying in England, 1100–1540: The Monastic Experience*, Oxford: Clarendon Press, 1993.
Heng, G. 'The invention of race in the European Middle Ages 1: race studies, modernity, and the Middle Ages', *Literature Compass* 8, 5 (2011): 258–274.
Holsinger, B. *Neomedievalism, Neoconservatism, and the War on Terror*, Chicago IL: Prickly Paradigm Press, 2007.

Horstmann, C. (ed.) *Sammlung Altenglischer Legenden*, Heildesheim: Georg Olms, 1878.
Jocelin of Brakelond *Chronicle of the Abbey of Bury St Edmunds*, trans. D. Greenway and J. Sayers, New York: Oxford University Press, 1989.
Jubinal, A. (ed.) *Jongleurs et Trouvères; Ou, Choix de Saluts, Épîtres, Rêveries et Autres Pièces Légères des XIIIe et XIVe Siècles*, Paris: J.A. Merklein, 1835.
Kempe, M. *The Book of Margery Kempe*, L. Staley (ed.), Kalamazoo: Medieval Institute Publications, 1996.
Kempe, M. *The Book of Margery Kempe*, trans. A. Bale, Oxford: Oxford University Press, 2015.
Kiser, L.J. 'Margery Kempe and the animalization of Christ: animal cruelty in late medieval England', *Studies in Philology* 106, 3 (2009): 299–315.
Lacapra, D. *History and its Limits: Human, Animal, Violence*, Ithaca NY: Cornell University Press, 2009.
Lochrie, K. *Margery Kempe and Translations of the Flesh*, Philadelphia PA: University of Pennsylvania Press, 1991.
Love, N. *The Mirror of the Blessed Life of Jesus Christ: A Reading Text*, M.G. Sargent (ed.), Exeter: University of Exeter Press, 2005.
Map, W. *De Nugis Curialium, Courtiers' Trifles*, revised edition, ed. and trans. M.R. James, C.N.L. Brooke, and R.A.B. Mynors, Oxford: Clarendon Press, 1983.
Marketa Lazarová, dir. F. Vláčil, 1967, Ústřední půjčovna filmů.
Mazzoni, C. 'Of stockfish and stew: feasting and fasting in the Book of Margery Kempe', *Food and Foodways* 10, 4 (2002): 171–182.
Mentz, S. *Shipwreck Modernity: Ecologies of Globalization, 1550–1719*, Minneapolis MN: University of Minnesota Press, 2015.
Metzler, I. *Fools and Idiots? Intellectual Disability in the Middle Ages*, Manchester: Manchester University Press, 2016.
Migne, J.P. (ed.) *Patrologiae Cursus Completus: Series Latina*, 217 volumes, Paris, 1844.
Monagle, C. and d'Arcens, L. '"Medieval" makes a comeback: what's going on?', *The Conversation*, 22 September 2014, last accessed 12 October 2016.
Monty Python and the Holy Grail, dir. T. Gilliam and T. Jones, 1975, EMI Films.
Niebrzydowski, S. (ed.) *Middle-Aged Women in the Middle Ages*, Woodbridge: DS Brewer, 2011.
Oggins, R.S. *The Kings and Their Hawks: Falconry in Medieval England*, New Haven CT: Yale University Press, 2004.
Perlo, K.W. *Kinship and Killing: The Animal in World Religions*, New York: Columbia University Press, 2009.
Raine, M. '"Fals flesch": food and the embodied piety of Margery Kempe', *New Medieval Literatures* 7 (2005): 101–126.
Ratramnus of Corbie 'Ratramnus and the dog-headed humans', in P.E. Dutton (ed. and trans.), *Carolingian Civilization: A Reader*, second edition, Peterborough ON: Broadview Press, 2004, 452–455.
Robertson, E. 'Kissing the worm: sex and gender in the afterlife and the poetic posthuman in the Late Middle English "a disputation betwyx the body and wormes"', in E.J. Burns and P. McCracken (eds.), *From Beasts to Souls: Gender and Embodiment in Medieval Europe*, Notre Dame IN: University of Notre Dame Press, 2013, 121–154.
Salih, S. 'Margery's bodies: piety, work, and penance', in J. Arnold and K.J. Lewis (eds.), *A Companion to The Book of Margery Kempe*, Cambridge: D.S. Brewer, 2004, 161–176.
Seaman, M.J. 'Becoming more (than) human: affective posthumanisms, past and future', *Journal of Narrative Theory* 37, 2 (2008): 246–275.
Serpell, J. 'Pet-keeping and animal domestication: a reappraisal', in J. Clutton-Brock (ed.), *The Walking Larder: Patterns of Domestication, Pastoralism, and Predation*, New York: Routledge, 1989, 10–21.

Sidhu, N.N. *Indecent Exposure: Gender, Politics, and Obscene Comedy in Middle English Literature*, Philadelphia PA: University of Pennsylvania Press, 2016.

Sobecki, S. '"The writing of this tretys": Margery Kempe's son and the authorship of her book', *Studies in the Age of Chaucer* 37, 1 (2015): 257–283.

Societé des Bollandistes (eds.) *Acta Sanctorum: October I*, Antwerp, 1765.

Steel, K. *How to Make a Human: Animals and Violence in the Middle Ages*, Columbus OH: Ohio State University Press, 2011.

Steel, K. 'A fourteenth-century ecology: "The Former Age" with Dindimus', in C. van Dyke (ed.), *Rethinking Chaucerian Beasts*, New York: Palgrave Macmillan, 2012, 185–199.

Tanner, N.P. (ed.) *Heresy Trials in the Diocese of Norwich, 1428–31*, London: Offices of the Royal Historical Society, 1977.

The Church and Kindness to Animals, London: Burns & Oates, 1906.

Van der Lugt, M. 'Animal légendaire et discours savant médiéval: la barnacle dans tous ses états', *Micrologus* 10, (2000): 351–393.

Van der Lugt, M. *Le Ver, le Démon et la Vierge: Les Théories Médiévales de la Génération Extraordinaire: Une Étude sur les Rapports entre Théologie, Philosophie Naturelle et Médecine*, Paris: Les Belles Lettres, 2004.

Walker-Meikle, K. *Medieval Pets*, Woodbridge: Boydell Press, 2012.

Williams, T. '"As thu wer a wedow": Margery Kempe's wifehood and widowhood', *Exemplaria* 21, 4 (2009): 345–362.

Wolfe, C. *Animal Rites: American Culture, the Discourse of Species, and Posthumanist Theory*, Chicago IL: University of Chicago Press, 2003.

Conclusions

22

THE TRIUMPH OF ANIMAL HISTORY?

Philip Howell

I

The extraordinarily rapid proliferation of historical studies of nonhuman animals in recent years is only one aspect of the much wider academic engagement with animals and animality, a phenomenon that has freed nonhuman animals from their traditional confines within 'natural history' for good and moved them to the centre of concern in any number of disciplines. The fields that have been affected are extremely diverse: Steve Best writes that this so-called 'animal turn' has 'moved throughout humanities, the fine arts, and social sciences; it has crossed into psychology, philosophy, anthropology, political science, and sociology; and it has made its mark in literature, history, cultural studies, geography, feminism, and queer theory'.[1] It is safe to say that the horse, along with all the other animals, has long since bolted – and even those who remain sceptical of the historical study of animal–human relations will probably accept that the stable doors might as well stay open now. More than that, though, we can suggest that animal–human history, specifically, is distinctly fashionable: 'one of the hot topics of historical research' in the current decade, it has been suggested.[2] One only has to look to the volume of publications, the rounds of seminars, sessions and specialist conferences, the rise of animal-centred courses and curricula in country after country.[3] We might well say, with Joshua Specht, that 'Animal history has arrived'.[4] In fact, Specht has gone further, speaking of animal history's 'triumph'.[5] This is all aligned with the direction of travel for animal studies as a whole, a journey from the margins to the centre being a familiar trope.[6] Animal–human history might be of central significance for all that, however, history being a pillar of the humanities and an education in the liberal arts, and the historical profession (arguably – the accusation is as familiar as it is unfair) more conservative than radical.[7] Which is to say that if 'animal studies' can make inroads even into the discipline of history then surely this says something about where we are in the academy as a whole.

There is an obvious danger to any triumphalism, however. Proclaiming the 'triumph of animal history' reminds us only of George W. Bush's infamous May 2003 'Mission Accomplished' speech on the deck of the USS Abraham Lincoln, marking the end of 'major combat operations' in Iraq.[8] Even without the contentious comparison, practitioners of animal–human history might prefer not to have such enthusiastic cheerleading. So whilst Specht insists that 'mainstream historians have accepted that animals are important actors', even if this was the case (and we have our doubts) the provocation that animal–human history makes to the methodological and theoretical presumptions of conventional historiography is patently obvious.[9] There is remarkably little consensus, for instance, on many of the issues raised in this volume, such as 'agency' and the animal 'archive', nor in terms of narrative synthesis. We have wanted in this *Companion* not only to produce an up-to-date guide to animal–human history, with an informed sense of this diversity, but also to explore the ongoing challenges posed by historical studies of animals and animal–human relationships. At this point, indeed, it falls to me to summarise something of the state of the field, the problems that still beset us with regard to how we *do* 'animal–human history', but also the opportunities ahead. I want here to reflect on the methods of animal–human history, first of all in response to suggestions that animal–human history is in the end not wholly compatible with an 'animal turn' that has turned decisively against anthropocentrism. For some hostile commentators, history might still be seen as too conservative and staid a discipline, too shackled to humanist pieties, to be anything more than marginal in the project of 'animal studies'. This is a position that students of animal–human history need to confront head on, and refute.

There is a second problematic aspect in any premature triumphalism, however, and that is the downside of animal history's (and animal studies') institutionalisation within the academy. I do not mean merely that with the growth of animal history comes the diversification of interests, true though this is: Erica Fudge has recently observed that many historians have contributed and are contributing to animal–human history without needing or wanting to call themselves 'animal historians'.[10] The measure of animal–human history's growing popularity is inevitably going to be the 'good and varied company' it will keep, even at the cost of a certain dilution of purpose.[11] For many commentators whose primary concerns are with the welfare or the rights of animals, however, this institutionalisation (we might borrow, though distort, Vinciane Despret's conception of 'academocentrism'), is freighted with political dangers.[12] As I will discuss in more detail below, the 'mainstreaming' of animal studies, including the rise of animal–human history, has been succeeded by a self-consciously 'critical' animal studies movement that views such academic normalisation as nothing but complicity and collaboration with anthropocentric reason and unrelenting animal exploitation. For this reason, it is necessary to say something about the responsibilities of animal–human history and its practitioners. To some extent, this concern overlaps with the first, as questions of the role and the place of theory have been an important part of this critique, but the ethical commitments involved take us further from the realm of academic practice considered in its narrowest sense. We need to fly the flag for historical work in its own right, without conceding too much ground to those who see political and academic commitments as incompatible, or detaching ourselves completely from the inevitability of ethical and political engagement.

One present danger is that the historical study of animals can be portrayed as inadmissible or even impossible from a more theoretically positioned reading of animal studies, whilst being seen as equally irrelevant (at best) from the perspective of animal advocacy. In this curious pincer movement (the respective camps hardly agree with each other, and are not natural allies), animal–human history might be regarded as more vulnerable than victorious. And this is without mentioning the political opposition from those Hegelians or neo-Hegelians who seek to claim the ends of history for human beings alone, relegating all other animals to that dim and dusty store cupboard named 'Nature'.[13] For these reasons, I turn finally to a defence of the special position of animal–human history, and a reflection on the possibilities that lie ahead.

II

It is worth underlining the fact that the institutionalisation of animal–human history does not mean that basic questions of practice and purpose have been settled: far from it. Despite Joshua Specht's suggestion that animal–human history is already a 'mature' field, it is plainly still in its infancy, and exhibiting some of the characteristic growing pains of emergent fields, such as a lack of integration within the wider discipline, the relative isolation of enthusiastic adherents, the difficulty of agreeing upon a conceptual core or even a lingua franca.[14] Rob Boddice refers, reasonably enough, to the 'amorphous' and 'disparate' nature of animal–human history, but Pascal Eitler, more punchily and provocatively, speaks of its 'freak status' within the academy.[15]

As a ready index, we might usefully compare the situation of a close cousin. Whilst accepting the challenges that environmental history still faced, Richard White (as far back as 2001) argued that it was already a mature field; more recently, Paul Sutter's similarly careful retrospective of (specifically American) environmental history declares that it is by any measure 'one of the most vital subfields within American history and one of the fastest-growing approaches to the study of the past within the larger profession'.[16] Nothing is ever so settled, for sure, and the coherence, meaning, and significance of environmental history as an interdisciplinary project remain contested – not to mention the inevitable unevenness when we consider its global situation.[17] All the same, animal–human history clearly has a long, long way to go before it reaches the security and respectability that environmental history has achieved in the last half-century: 'a broadly conceived environmental history perspective has triumphed', writes Jason Moore, using the term more convincingly here than does Specht.[18] It is telling that one of the deans of the discipline, J.R. McNeill, has referred to environmental history's potential overlap with 'animal history' in uncharacteristic but unmistakably condescending terms: 'if that is what it is', is McNeill's terse comment on the putative 'field' of animal history, firmly putting in its place a junior, perhaps even an unacknowledged, sibling.[19]

Now there is nothing absolutely distinctive or disabling about this, and indeed we could reasonably suggest that this situation is precisely what makes the 'field' (*pace* McNeill, it is one) so lively and exciting. It may well be worth preserving the 'marginal' situation of animal–human history, wearing the 'freak' status as a badge of honour, celebrating its challenges to conventional historical practice.[20] But claims of maturity or triumph would still be out of order. We can see this when we reflect on the diversity of approaches taken by the contributors to this volume. Consider the linked issues of theory and interdisciplinarity, in particular, where talk of diversity may simply mask fractures and contradictions. It is a commonplace to argue that animal–human historians should be prepared to ignore disciplinary boundaries, just as nonhuman animals do. Animal history must be 'radically interdisciplinary', writes Susan Nance.[21] Dan Vandersommers argues, more specifically, that:

> Animal history challenges us to escape the deified anthropocentrism that has undergirded the pursuit of history, a task requiring understanding in philosophy and critical theory. Animal history challenges us to be conversant with the sciences – ethology, ecology, animal welfare science, zoology, comparative psychology, veterinary medicine – to track animal agency in historical sources.[22]

In fairness, animal–human historians have been notable for taking in insights from archaeology and anthropology and my own discipline of geography, to name but three: here, the hybrid subfields of zooarcheology, anthrozoology/zooanthropology, and 'animal geography' have much to offer animal–human history, and vice versa.[23] Moreover, attention to material culture and the supplementing of traditional historical sources is increasingly practised; even the seemingly most human creations, such as literature, have been read against their superficially anthropocentric grain – as Jennifer McDonell has shown in this volume. But we need to be cautious all the same: as Sandra Swart has noted, elsewhere, claims to interdisciplinarity are more honoured in the breach than in the observance, and evidently need to be interrogated further: bluntly, the most ambitious prospects for innovation in animal–human history are likely to be overstated.[24] Methodologically, much current animal–human history is relatively conventional. Some popular histories are light, entertaining and informative but almost by definition insubstantial.[25] But more obviously academic contributions are hardly more ambitious, learned though they are.[26] There have been some urban histories, for instance, that focus on nonhuman animals, but which serve to remind the reader of their presence rather than (as sometimes claimed) returning them their 'voice'.[27] Occasionally, these approaches remind us of the feminist academic complaints against merely incorporating women into existing scholarship – namely, 'add women and stir' – though here it is nonhuman animals who are mixed in, and anthropocentrism rather than androcentrism that remains untouched.

There are compound difficulties here. It is hard enough to be expected to be equally expert with artefacts as well as archives, conversant with ethology and ethnography as well as with the interpretation of texts. But it is also true to say that, for all the efforts and exhortations, animal–human historians are rather less likely to follow the twists and turns of contemporary critical theory than their cousins in the allied social sciences. In animal studies as a whole, a deep engagement with social and critical theory is particularly striking, even if – especially if – these theoretical stances are barely compatible. This can hardly be said for much contemporary animal–human history. The comments of the editors of a recent animal urban history collection, though they are thinking specifically about Canadian environmental history, might be presumed true for much current animal–human history: 'Discussions of animal sentience, subjectivity, or agency are seldom addressed, and concepts such as actor–network theory, assemblage, or posthumanism are even more rare'.[28] Some historians will simply be more comfortable with and more committed to these theoretical conversations than others. If I can be forgiven for alluding to my own work, two reviews of my book on Victorian dogs might be considered exemplary: one reviewer recommended a much deeper discussion of theory, particularly that of Deleuze and Guattari, whilst another specifically commended me for avoiding the 'occasionally indigestible language of cultural theorists'.[29] Present and future practitioners of animal–human history will no doubt need to be aware of the diversity of audiences that accompanies the much-heralded interdisciplinarity.

We might go a lot further, however, for the terrain of critical theory is particularly uncomfortable for historians caught up in the 'animal turn'. Their efforts, however honest and humble, may be met with incomprehension or worse from the perspective of animal studies scholars interested principally in questions of theory or philosophy, and many of whom see themselves responding to movements from outside the humanities rather than from within it.[30] For some within the wider community of 'animal studies', it is not simply that animal–human historians have by and large *not* escaped the pull of anthropocentrism: it is that they *cannot*, being yoked to the supposedly foundational presumption that history is a matter for humans alone. For some critics tracing (or excavating) a schism between proponents of history and proponents of theory, the liberal humanities are precisely the problem, and what is needed is a revolutionary realignment, away from the internal dynamics of a tradition that is by definition anthropocentric to a 'posthumanist' alternative.[31] The animal studies philosopher Cary Wolfe has taken a notably antagonistic stance towards academic history, portraying it as a 'humanist' project par excellence. Wolfe writes, in a notably direct address:

> For example, just because a historian devotes attention to the topic of nonhuman animals – let's say, the awful plight of combat operations during World War I – doesn't mean that humanism and anthropocentrism aren't being maintained in his or her disciplinary practice ... even though – to return to our historian example – your concept of the discipline's *external* relations to its larger environment is posthumanist in taking seriously the existence of nonhuman subjects and the consequent compulsion to make the discipline respond to the question of nonhuman animals foisted on it by changes in the discipline's environment, your *internal* disciplinarity may remain humanist through and through.[32]

For Wolfe, conventional history, insofar as it remains merely thematic and refuses to interrogate the discourse of species difference, is incapable of meeting the challenge that posthumanism poses, let alone the scale and nature of animal suffering. 'Animal history', from this perspective, looks more or less impossible.

Returning the compliment, some historians may think that there is little to be gained with engaging with high theory – I am thinking not just of the posthuman turn, but the rise of relational theories such as actor-network theory, assemblage theory, neo-vitalism, the more-than-human, and so on.[33] This is not my view, and I will say more about the potential of these kinds of theories towards the end of these reflections, but it would be as well to accept that the theoretical programme of animal studies can be off-putting as well as uncomfortable for academic historians. It is one of those areas of difficulty that animal–human historians should prepare to face if they have not confronted it already. There is no space here to provide a full defence of an animal–human history, let alone the 'humanities' as a whole, even if I thought I was well-placed to do so. But we can suggest, at least, that the tradition of the humanities has served to trouble the status of the 'human' and the 'animal' as much as it has done to shore up these identities – not least in terms of providing a historical perspective on the emergence of 'humanity'.[34] Think of the great 'humanist' Montaigne, and his presentation of 'the *humaine condition* with all its burdens, pitfalls, and problems, with all its essential insecurity, with all the creatural bonds which confine it'.[35] Do we really have to insist that we are now long 'after' history, living in its 'ruins', in order to record this common but historically mutable 'creaturely life', 'the peculiar proximity of the human and the animal at the very point of their radical difference'?[36] History has also long engaged with traditions and disciplines for whom 'taking seriously the existence of nonhuman subjects' is a matter of course: here again I am thinking of archaeology, anthropology, geography, and so on. The supposedly moribund humanities are currently busily diversifying in endless new forms labelled 'environmental humanities', 'ecohumanities', 'geohumanities' and so on, something that calls into question the stark opposition of humanism and posthumanism, and also the argument that change can only come from *without*.[37] Lastly, we might reasonably argue that history has always been about the power of some humans over others, rather than simply a tedious monologue about 'human' privilege. The theorist Matthew Calarco rightly points out in this regard that the history of Western culture may be considered anthropocentric but not truly *speciesist*, for the reason that many human beings and groups of human beings end up excluded and exploited, the problem being the attempt to shore up the privileges of those deemed, historically, to be fully *human*.[38] It remains for historians to extend our understanding of the costs, for people as well as nonhumans, of this spurious 'humanity'.

III

This brings us on to a second area of profound disagreement, which is the responsibility of historians to the ethical and political projects associated with animal welfare or animal rights. At one level, we might argue that no such responsibility exists. Here is the anthropologist Brian Fagan, for instance, in a preface to a popular recent history of the enduring relationship between humans and animals, matter-of-factly admitting the limited lessons that (his) history supplies: 'History provides the background but, alas, no ready solutions'.[39] Though he raises the questions of human dominion and animal exploitation, Fagan limits himself to what he rather revealingly calls 'a purely historical inquiry'.[40] Now, for sure, Fagan's work is not intended as a fully footnoted scholarly treatise, but his stance is hardly unusual as far as animal–human history goes: it might even be thought of as the default position. With regard to the age-old, purgatorial suffering of nonhuman animals, we might feel that we have responsibilities as human beings, but not – or rather, not *specifically* – as historians.

There are a few who would go further and argue that animal–human history should have nothing whatsoever to do with animal advocacy, save as it exists as an historical phenomenon. Rob Boddice, for instance, has consistently warned that animal–human historians typically neglect or distort the history of human speculation about relationships with nonhuman animals precisely because they import a priori and ahistorical ethical commitments.[41] What Boddice has in mind is the now familiar team roll call of supposedly theriophile thinkers, from Theophrastus and Plutarch and Porphyry, say, down to Montaigne and Bentham and Ruskin, and beyond – the 'long line of poets, philosophers, saints, seers, writers, and intellectuals' who have advocated for animal rights, and who form (in the words of the animal theologian Andrew Linzey) a comforting 'cloud of witnesses' in our own struggles for justice for animals.[42] Boddice's response to such invariably partial histories – here he invokes his mentor Rod Preece – is a lofty paean to the virtues of 'dispassionate and critical scholarship', stating that he 'cannot reconcile the tenets of scholarship and intellectual honesty with the blind following of empty rhetoric'.[43] What we need to do instead, Boddice insists, is to understand these historical commentaries on animal–human relations in their own terms, in their own contexts, which in all ages before our own only appears to mean different *versions* of anthropocentrism, different ways of understanding what it meant to be *human*, and never truly a focus on animals as ends in themselves. Even the record of condemnation of cruelty towards animals seems in this scholarship to orbit ceaselessly around the figure of the human, so that it can apparently never be invoked in the terms of contemporary animal politics.[44] The record of animal–human history, and the complexities of human attitudes to other animals, is invoked not so much to pour cold water on contemporary animal rights causes, as to show that even the most well-intentioned ethical argument is, likely as not, *bad history*. For some others, however (I do not mean Boddice, nor Preece), this careful historicism can be repurposed straightforwardly as a weapon against the claims of the animal rights movement, this time in the insistence that bad history means *bad politics*.[45]

Now Boddice has a certain contrarian reputation – this is not quite fair – but even so many historians may sympathise with the substance of his argument, if not necessarily the tone. Few historians would be comfortable with animal–human history merely as the handmaiden to the politics of animal liberation – and I append here a reasonably representative statement of purpose with regard to what the place of historical enquiry would look like in such a politics:

> [Critical Animal Studies] Deconstructs and reconstructs the socially constructed binary oppositions between human and nonhuman animals, a move basic to mainstream animal studies, but also looks to illuminate related dichotomies between culture and nature, civilization and wilderness and other dominator hierarchies to emphasize the historical limits placed upon humanity, nonhuman animals, cultural/political norms, and the liberation of nature as part of a transformative project that seeks to transcend these limits towards greater freedom and ecological harmony.[46]

For self-consciously critical scholar-activists, the institutionalisation of animal studies as a whole is precisely what needs to be combatted; for the likes of Steve Best, promoting the 'animal standpoint', mainstream animal studies has merely been 'defanged, declawed, and neutered by the academic-industrial complex'.[47] An alternative 'Critical Animal Studies' has more than animal–human history in its sights, obviously, and it should be noted that its ire and fire are directed more at the 'contradictory ideas and deliberate obfuscation' of 'postmodern' sophists than at the lowly empiricists who toil in history's vineyards.[48] For these critics, 'theory for theory's sake' indeed comes in for particular scorn:

> Deliberately vague and apolitical, postmodern animal studies avoids any direct commitment to animals or to serious criticism of their exploitation. Although typically presented as radical interventions, these works are characterized by obscurantist language accessible only to a tiny number of academics and offer little practical help in terms of efforts to reduce the exploitation of non-human animals and advance the cause of animal rights.[49]

More temperately, we might agree that 'posthumanism's engagement with "the animal question" does not *in and by itself* create more beneficial subject positions for animals in human society'.[50] Cary Wolfe's remark that animal studies has nothing to do, 'strictly speaking', with whether we even *like* animals, might in its own candid way be even more apposite.[51]

Now even if historians are typically less guilty of theoretical obfuscation, even if they are further from core academic respectability, the kind of animal–human history represented in this volume is still largely ground from the same academic mill so condemned by Critical Animal Studies. At best, such work can be presented as a distraction from the urgent struggles against speciesism; at worst, it is regarded as fully complicit with the human exploitation of animal others. Given the intransigence of this critique, it might, to repeat myself, be tempting to refuse all political commitments whatsoever. Boddice's Olympian detachment towards ethical commitments looks in this sense defensive and strategic as much as it is proudly principled. In his vision of animal–human history, the relationship between humans and other animals is limited to a matter of attitudes rather than behaviours, further restricted to the history of ideas or to intellectual history, finally reaching so dessicated and airless a state that no possibility of an ethical critique can ever emerge.[52] This is equally unsatisfactory. Trying to quarantine historical enquiry from what is declared by fiat to be partisan politics is surely futile – as the 'history wars' in Australia or the 'revisionist' quarrels in Ireland or debates about the record of the British Empire have taught us.[53] All research is a political act, whether we like it or not. It is hard to imagine that Boddice's strictures could be applied to the history of racism or slavery, for instance, or even to environmental history, where commonplace 'green' commitments have not attracted the same level or type of criticism: being concerned about the environment and its future does not make anyone a bad environmental historian.

In the end, animal–human historians will have to tack between these problematic positions, the invidious ideal types of the disinterested scholar and the inspired activist. Susan Nance has argued that an 'ethical purity test' for animal–human history is hardly acceptable, and I would only add that a commitment to veganism (say) would not be enough in itself by way of accreditation, given (say) the arguments of 'veganarchists' or the proponents of intersectionality who want to contest the privileges of 'white vegan men' – all of this reminding us that nonhuman animals are not the only animals who suffer, and that an animal rights movement that ignores these wider, linked forms of oppression is not above reproach.[54] Navigating these politics is never going to be easy, and I suspect that those of us who have taught animal–human history will be perfectly familiar with the difficulties of reconciling scholarship and ethical positionality (we can speak of a broader 'ecopedagogy').[55] The only reflection on teaching animal–human history I am aware of is provided by Thomas Andrews, writing of his own experiences in running a seminar course on 'Animals in America', an experiment that is sobering and inspiring in more or less equal measure.[56] He concludes:

> I hope I have helped my students see people and other animals in all sorts of new ways. Not a single student has become a political activist simply because of my course. Yet most of them now possess a much deeper understanding of the historical conditions that have given rise to animal welfare, rights, and liberation movements across the globe. They may not agree with the tactics of PETA or ALF, but my students know how animal suffering became an important issue, and they understand why many people have become so passionate about animal-related causes. If my students have not become radicalized themselves, most of them seem to have become more sympathetic toward activists most of them previously perceived as extreme, even dangerous.[57]

Perhaps, he says cautiously, it is enough 'simply to help students wake up and pay attention'.[58] Perhaps we may still dare to hope that animal–human history can contribute to a more just world, 'For, if we come to know what animals have done in the past, which human activities will we feel compelled to change in the future?'[59]

IV

I have raised these two basic questions, unavoidable for animal–human historians, concerned with the *how* of animal–human history, the practical, methodological questions, and the *why* of political or ethical purpose respectively. This still leaves the issue of *where* we go from here, and I want at this traditional point to collect some suggestions, albeit with no great claim to originality. I do not want to dwell upon issues that I think are plain enough, such as the need for animal–human history to develop in a truly global sense, and to learn from the non-Western world as it does so. At present, even non-Anglophone speakers close at hand might feel neglected in the recent emergence of animal–human history, and we clearly have an obligation towards those further afield too; the benefits of such a global conversation are also evident – this is obviously not mere charity.[60] Such an endeavour will undoubtedly require teamwork, 'the pooling of the techniques, practiced by different scholars, but all tending to throw light upon a specific subject', as the great Marc Bloch put it.[61] But important as these projects are, they are relatively uncontroversial, even platitudinous. I have in mind instead a more speculative commentary. Looking ahead – not five or ten or even twenty years ahead but further still – where might animal–human history be? What would it look like? Would we even recognise it as the same field we had in mind when we began this project? To some extent the paths that I am suggesting lead in the same direction, but there is also apparent divergence, not least in the demands that they make of animal–human historians, and implicit or explicit challenges to how we define our joint enterprise.

Firstly, we might consider the potential for integration of animal–human history with what has been called 'big history' or (not quite the same thing) 'deep history'.[62] We might suppose that it is already there, that it has always been there; other animals and the question of our animal inheritance have never been absent from accounts of past time over the *longue durée*, sometimes, it is true, as a contrastive with the rise and fall of human 'civilisations', but also more prominently in more recent 'megahistories' or 'metahistories' that exemplify E.O. Wilson's ideal of 'consilience', capable of synthesising natural science, social science, and the humanities.[63] We might imagine that animal–human histories could find a home within these ambitious narratives. But it would be difficult to see the specific purpose of animal–human history flourishing within these widescreen histories, and many historians are already wary of the simplifications involved. The purported synthesis of evolutionary biology and history is likely to be 'neither good science nor good history'.[64] True, we might expect future animal–human historians to be more conversant with the natural sciences and allied disciplines, interested and invested in a 'deep history' that extends to evolutionary time and the lessons of natural selection. We might then approach 'a co-evolutionary perspective that sees nonhuman animals as inseparably embedded in human history and as dynamic agents in their own right'.[65] But this is likely, however, to be quite distinct from the template set out by E.O. Wilson's 'consilience', not least because we need to understand evolution as natural *history* and not just natural 'science'. It has been recently pointed out that the demise of 'natural history' in the nineteenth century did not somehow surgically remove 'history' from the new sciences of nature: quite the contrary, for the triumph of natural selection installed history in the understanding of life itself:

> There are a number of ironies in the birth of biology and the attendant appearance of a new evolutionary paradigm. First, the moment at which the term 'history' disappears from the descriptor that characterizes the life sciences is the very moment at which they become genuinely historical in the modern sense. Natural history had been concerned with the manifold adaptations of static species. These species had no history. They were understood in terms of a kind of atemporal functionality. Evolutionary biology, however, assumed a long period of organic development. Creatures not only had a structure, they and their structures had a history. Thus while natural history had not been at all historical in the temporal sense, evolutionary biology was.[66]

The isolation of the humanities from the sciences that we routinely say we seek to counter is not a matter merely of the incapacities and ignorance of the former camp, but also and much more problematically of the historical emergence of the life sciences themselves. Not only the process of evolution but its theorisation belong to history rather than standing outside it as a guarantor of truth. So if an animal–human history to come is more integrated with the sciences it will not be as anyone's handmaiden. Any engagement or reconciliation of animal–human history with such big-picture 'deep history' cannot involve only the incorporation of insights from, say, zoology or ethology or animal welfare science, helpful as these may be. Sandra Swart has, for instance, blurred the genres of history and natural history in her book on horses and 'horsetory'; Jonathan Burt explains how the history of primates in primatology may be used to analyse the term 'posthuman'; and Susan Nance has skilfully incorporated ethological research into her account of the American circus elephant.[67] We might pause at this point to emphasise the need for *specificity* rather than a spuriously general account of 'animal' behaviour, thinking not just of species, but also of breeds, types, and so on. Given the sheer diversity involved, the complexity of evolutionary genealogies, and the limits of our knowledge and understanding, we might reflect on the inadequacy of terms such as 'fish' and 'birds', or even the more familiar 'dogs'.[68] Most importantly, however, the reengagement with 'science' must be a critical, historical, understanding of the status of scientific 'nature'. The example of Science and Technology Studies (STS) is an obvious resource here, and I have in mind its powerful critiques of ethology in particular.[69] There is also a rich history of the production of science, the sites in which knowledge was made, and the role of nonhuman animals themselves.[70] Animal–human history must engage with natural science, then, but also with natural history.

It follows, I think, that we might also expect future animal–human history to be more questioning of the term 'animal', and the implied separation of 'animal' from 'human'. It is not so much that the generalisation 'animal' is problematic, as I have just indicated: the '*bêtise*' or 'asinine' stupidity critiqued by Jacques Derrida.[71] It is also the fact that the term 'human' has to be understood relationally too. Pascal Eitler has expressed this problem with an excellent sense of its special significance for animal–human historians:

> [W]riting a 'symmetrical anthropology' would have serious consequences for Animal History. It would not only mean historicizing human–animal relations as being variable, but rather would also mean historicizing humans and animals themselves as products. This implies not only a specific understanding of empirical work but also of political critique.[72]

And, more succinctly:

> Animal History opens up a new perspective on humans, not only a new perspective on animals.[73]

The issue here is that we cannot assume the stability provided by a defunct nature/culture dichotomy. Eitler proposes, as an alternative to 'animal history', a 'body history', but I would prefer to use the term 'biosocial history', refusing the distinction between the 'biological' and the 'social' and promoting a general theory of evolution instead of the neo-Darwinian paradigm that animates much 'deep history'.[74] In this sense we should not assume the substantive difference between nonhuman animals and humans, nor indeed between living and inert 'things'. In place of these familiar distinctions we have instead a fully relational approach that refuses to separate humans from their 'environments' (for this reason, subsuming animal–human history within environmental history is likely to be doomed from the start), and which focuses on the bodily existence of humans and other animals (without disconnecting these bodies from one another and from the existence of plants and things and so much else). All of this is something of a mouthful, and historians might complain that we are again sitting down to dine, theory-wise, on the unpalatable or the indigestible. But all the same I suspect that future work will have to take its stand on this ground whether we like it or not: the future of animal–human history will surely be one in which the nature/culture distinction has long been left behind.

An obvious response is that we will not then have the focus on the 'animal', nor on 'history', that animates our present studies. I am reminded at this point of Bruno Latour's well-known comment (in these circles) that there were only four things wrong with his lauded 'actor-network theory', namely the words 'actor', 'network', and 'theory' . . . plus the hyphen. In a biosocial history, what would be the specific point in focusing on the relations between humans and other animals? Recognising that humans and animals – but also a whole host of other 'things' *make* history has its benefits, but it also has downsides as far as the field of animal–human history is concerned. Even in Erica Fudge's capable hands, it is hard to be enthusiastic about the potential of 'itstory'.[75] Can we still preserve a sense of historical change, even purpose, in this fashionably 'flat ontology'? In this regard, it is worth fixing, finally, on the argument that nonhuman animals have a 'history' in its most specific sense in terms of their *entanglement* with human beings, up to and including the human appropriation of 'History' as a discipline. 'An animal that has had no such confrontations with humans has no history', is how Eitler puts it.[76] This is emphatically not the same as arguing, with Ingrid Tague, that 'ultimately the study of history must be a study of humans'.[77] Rather, we need to look at the conjoined histories of humans and other animals in their specific existences. This would be to argue that 'animal history' is only ever an *animal–human history*, wherein nonhumans are bundled with human beings in historically specific sets of relations. Crucial here are those more recent conjunctures of 'modernity' and 'capitalism', with the history of the 500-year-old 'world system' a crucial referent. We might underline the opportunities of exploring animal–human history within the focus on 'historical nature' put forward by the likes of Jason Moore.[78] What Moore means by this is the ways in which such great historical transformations as global capitalism are ecological processes, not merely the predation of Nature by Capital or Culture. The dismantling of the kind of Cartesian reason that separates nature from culture on the one hand, and animal from human on the other, might well find here a powerful purpose for animal–human history in assessing the contribution of nonhuman animals to the rise of contemporary capitalism over this timescale. Nonhuman animals clearly have a major role to play in historical capitalism's dependence on 'Cheap Nature', and the 'Four Cheaps' of labour power, food, energy, and raw materials. One of the few animal–human historians to consider this at this level of generality has been Alan Mikhail, locating the changes in the modern near East within a world historical transformation of animal lives:

> Imagine what will happen when our world suddenly finds itself without the fossil fuels that make so much of our lives possible today. Cities will take a different shape; the way we communicate and move will change; how we eat will be radically altered; we will have to seek out other forms of energy to sustain the economy. What happened in Egypt at the end of the eighteenth century was just such a process – a wholesale reconfiguration of the rural world precipitated by the loss of a historic source of energy. The social, cultural, political, and special consequences of this shifting animal economy and energy regime were clearly enormous and deserve further study, both in Egypt and elsewhere. Our biases toward humans as the most important historical agents perhaps predispose us to miss some of these animal histories. We ignore them at our peril.[79]

So 'animal histories' might well be recognised within these larger narratives of 'historical nature', and perhaps more specifically within our current accumulation cycle. This would not mean dissolving animal–human history within a repurposed environmental history, but rather promises the connecting up of our specific studies with the wider historical work that animals have accomplished, up to and including the performative constitution of human beings, and of the enterprise of History itself, for our worldviews and ways of knowing are inextricably part of this historical nature. This serves inevitably to remind us that 'humans not [nonhuman] animals are writing this history', but this is not so much a methodological problem as an historical phenomenon, of the greatest importance.[80] In this sense, all history is indeed animal history.[81]

Notes

1 S. Best, 'The rise (and fall) of critical animal studies', *Liberazioni: Associazione* (2013), available at www.liberazioni.org/articoli/BestS-TheRise(and%20Fall)ofCriticalAnimalStudies.pdf, last accessed 1 March 2017. This is a revised version of S. Best, 'The rise of critical animal studies: putting theory into action and animal liberation into higher education', *Journal for Critical Animal Studies* 7, 1 (2009): 9–52.
2 B. Breen, 'Animal history: an emerging scholarly trend', 29 October 2014, available at https://daily.jstor.org/animals-in-the-archive/, last accessed 1 March 2017.
3 For history courses within Human–Animal Studies (HAS), see www.animalsandsociety.org/human-animal-studies/courses/has-courses-in-history, last accessed 1 March 2017, and H-Animal's syllabus exchange, https://networks.h-net.org/node/16560/pages/27594/h-animal-syllabus-exchange, last accessed 1 March 2017.
4 J. Specht, 'Animal history after its triumph: unexpected animals, evolutionary approaches, and the animal lens', *History Compass* 14, 7 (2016): 326–336.
5 Specht, 'Animal history after its triumph'.
6 For example, N. Taylor and R. Twine, *The Rise of Critical Animal Studies: From the Margins to the Centre*, London: Routledge, 2014; 'edging towards the mainstream' is how Harriet Ritvo expressed it before over a decade of subsequent progress: H. Ritvo, 'Animal planet', *Environmental History* 9, 2 (2004): 204–220, 205.

7 For further discussion of the humanities, see A.V. Kernan (ed.), *What's Happened to the Humanities?*, Princeton NJ: Princeton University Press, 2014; C. Emmeche, D.B. Pedersen, and F. Stjernfelt (eds.) *Mapping Frontier Research in the Humanities*, London: Bloomsbury, 2016; M.C. Nussbaum, *Not for Profit: Why Democracy Needs the Humanities*, Princeton NJ: Princeton University Press, 2016.
8 Specht, 'Animal history after its triumph'.
9 Specht, 'Animal history after its triumph', 331.
10 E. Fudge, 'What was it like to be a cow? History and animal studies', in L. Kalof (ed.), *The Oxford Handbook of Animal Studies*, Oxford: Oxford University Press, 2017, 258–278.
11 Fudge, 'What was it like to be a cow?'.
12 V. Despret, *What Might Animals Say if We Asked the Right Questions?*, Minneapolis MN: University of Minnesota Press, 2016.
13 Here is Fukuyama's gloss on Hegel's argument: 'only man is able to overcome his most basic animal instincts – chief among them his instinct for self-preservation – for the sake of higher, abstract principles and goals. According to Hegel, the desire for recognition initially drives two primordial combatants to seek to make the other "recognise" their humanness by staking their lives in a mortal battle. When the natural fear of death leads one combatant to submit, the relationship of master and slave is born. The stakes in this bloody battle at the beginning of history are not food, shelter, or security, but pure prestige. And precisely because the goal of the battle is not determined by biology, Hegel sees in it the first glimmer of human freedom': F. Fukuyama, *The End of History and the Last Man*, London: Penguin, 2012, xvi.
14 On the general academic landscape, see T. Becher and P. Trowler, *Academic Tribes and Territories: Intellectual Enquiry and the Culture of Disciplines*, second edition, Buckingham: Society for Research into Higher Education and Open University Press, 2001.
15 R. Boddice, 'The moral status of animals and the historical human cachet', *JAC* 30, 3/4 (2010): 457–489, 457, 458; P. Eitler, 'Animal history as body history: four suggestions from a genealogical perspective', *Body Politics* 2, 4 (2014): 259–274, 271, n. 36.
16 R. White, 'Environmental history: watching a historical field mature', *Pacific Historical Review* 70, 1 (2001): 103–111; P.S. Sutter, 'The world with us: the state of American environmental history', *Journal of American History* 100, 1 (2013): 94–119. See also J.R. McNeill, 'Observations on the nature and culture of environmental history', *History and Theory* 42, 4 (2003): 5–43.
17 S. Sörlin and P. Warde, 'The problem of the problem of environmental history: a re-reading of the field', *Environmental History* 12, 1 (2007): 107–130; see also D.R. Weiner (2005) 'A death-defying attempt to articulate a coherent definition of environmental history', *Environmental History* 10, 3 (2005): 404–420. An alternative prospectus for 'environmental history' is provided by J.W. Moore, *Capitalism in the Web of Life: Ecology and the Accumulation of Capital*, London: Verso, 2015.
18 Moore, *Capitalism in the Web of Life*, 39.
19 J.R. McNeill, 'Introduction' in J.R. Richards, *The World Hunt: An Environmental History of the Commodification of Animals*, Berkeley CA: University of California Press, 2014, xi–xix, xviii. For a more welcoming response, see B.L. Walker, 'Animals and the intimacy of history', *History and Theory* 52, 4 (2013): 45–67.
20 See H. Ritvo, 'On the animal turn', *Daedalus* (Fall, 2007): 118–122, 121–122: 'Within my own experience as a scholar, the study of animals has become more respectable and more popular in many disciplines of the humanities and social sciences, but it is far from the recognized core of any of them. It remains marginal in most disciplines, and (not the same thing) it is often on the borderline between disciplines. This awkward location or set of locations is, however, the source of much of its appeal and power. Its very marginality

allows the study of animals to challenge settled assumptions and relationships – to re-raise the largest issues – both within the community of scholars and in the larger society to which they and their subjects belong'.

21 S. Nance, 'Introduction', in S. Nance (ed.), *The Historical Animal*, Syracuse NY: Syracuse University Press, 2015: 1–16, 3.
22 D. Vandersommers, 'The "animal turn" in history', *AHA Today*, 3 November 2016, available at http://blog.historians.org/2016/11/animal-turn-history/, last accessed 7 March 2017.
23 See for instance N. Russell, *Social Zooarchaeology: Humans and Animals in Prehistory*, Cambridge: Cambridge University Press, 2012; M.C. Tobias and J.G. Morrison, *Anthrozoology: Embracing Coexistence in the Anthropocene*, Cham: Springer, 2017; J. Wolch and J. Emel (eds.), *Animal Geographies: Place, Politics and Identity in the Nature–Culture Borderlands*, London: Verso, 2000; C. Philo and C. Wilbert (eds.), *Animal Spaces, Beastly Places: New Geographies of Human–Animal Relations*, London: Routledge, 2000.
24 S. Swart, '"But where's the bloody horse?" Textuality and corporeality in the "animal turn"', *Journal of Literary Studies* 23, 3 (2007): 271–292, 287–288. For further critical appraisal, see A. Barry and G. Born (eds.), *Interdisciplinarity: Reconfigurations of the Social and Natural Sciences*, Abingdon: Routledge, 2013.
25 Just as a relatively random example: J. Bondeson, *The Cat Orchestra and the Elephant Butler: The Strange History of Amazing Animals*, Stroud: Tempus, 2006.
26 Again merely for example: A. Macgregor, *Animal Encounters: Human and Animal Interaction in Britain from the Norman Conquest to World War One*, London: Reaktion, 2012.
27 H. Velten, *Beastly London: A History of Animals in the City*, London: Reaktion, 2013. See also C. Plumb, *The Georgian Menagerie: Exotic Animals in Eighteenth-Century London*, London: I.B. Tauris, 2015. More ambitious and satisfying in its discussion of urban 'sorting' and 'blending' is F.L. Brown, *The City is More than Human: An Animal History of Seattle*, Seattle WA: University of Washington Press, 2016.
28 D. Ingram, C. Sethna and J. Dean, 'Introduction: *canamalia urbanis*', in J. Dean, D. Ingram, and C. Sethna (eds.), *Animal Metropolis: Histories of Human–Animal Relations in Urban Canada*, Calgary: University of Calgary Press, 2017, 1–28, 12.
29 Reviews of P. Howell, *At Home and Astray: The Domestic Dog in Victorian Britain*, Charlottesville VA: University of Virginia Press, 2015 by P. Macadré, *Journal of British Studies* 56(1): 202–204, 204, and by D.A.H. Wilson, *Anthrozoös* 29, 1 (2016): 171–172, 172.
30 C. Wolfe, 'Introduction' in C. Wolfe (ed.) *Zoontologies: The Question of the Animal*, Minneapolis MN: University of Minnesota Press, 2003, ix–xxiii.
31 C. Wolfe, 'Human, all too human: "animal studies" and the humanities', *PMLA* 124, 2 (2009): 564–575.
32 C. Wolfe, *What is Posthumanism?*, Minneapolis MN: University of Minnesota Press, 2010, 123, emphasis in original. In the previous iteration of this argument (Wolfe, 'Human, all too human', 572) history is accompanied by literary criticism in his challenge to readers to choose between humanism and posthumanism.
33 See in this volume, my own chapter, 'Animals, agency, and history'.
34 G. Goodale, *The Rhetorical Invention of Man: A History of Distinguishing Humans from Other Animals*, Lanham MD: Lexington Books, 2015.
35 E. Auerbach, *Mimesis: The Representation of Reality in Western Literature*, trans. W.R. Trask, Princeton NJ: Princeton University Press, 2013. This argument chimes with Boria Sax's commentary on Pico della Mirandola in the conclusions to his chapter in this volume.
36 E.L. Santner, *On Creaturely Life: Rilke, Benjamin, Sebald*, Chicago IL: University of Chicago Press, 2006, 12.
37 As even the partisan Rosi Braidotti points out (*The Posthuman*, Cambridge: Polity, 2013, 50), there are many 'humanisms'. For environmental, ecological and geo-humanities, see

the programmatic statements of D.B. Rose et al. 'Thinking through the environment, unsettling the humanities', *Environmental Humanities* 1, 1 (2012): 1–5; M. Dear, 'Practicing geohumanities', *GeoHumanities* 1, 1 (2015): 20–35; N. Castree, 'The Anthropocene and the environmental humanities: extending the conversation', *Environmental Humanities* 5, 1 (2014): 233–260. See also V. Plumwood, *Environmental Culture: The Ecological Crisis of Reason*, London: Routledge, 2002.

38 M. Calarco, *Thinking Through Animals: Identity, Difference, Indistinction*, Stanford CA: Stanford University Press, 2015, 26.

39 B. Fagan, *The Intimate Bond: How Animals Shaped Human History*, New York: Bloomsbury, 2015, xvii, xi.

40 Fagan, *The Intimate Bond*, xi. Similar reservations might be held about an earlier work on domestication, R.A. Caras's *A Perfect Harmony: The Intertwining Lives of Animals and Humans Throughout History*, West Lafayette IN: Purdue University Press, 1996; his conception of the 'intertwined' history of 'these two children of Earth' (19) is undermined by its peculiar title, which hardly suggests a critical stance, all this despite its author being a noted animal welfare advocate in the United States.

41 R. Boddice, *A History of Attitudes and Behaviours Toward Animals in Eighteenth- and Nineteenth-Century Britain: Anthropocentrism and the Emergence of Animals*, Lewiston NY: The Edward Mellen Press, 2008.

42 A. Linzey, 'A sense of history', *The Animals' Agenda* 20, 2 (2000): 39.

43 Boddice, 'The Moral Status of Animals', 476. See also R. Preece, *Brute Souls, Happy Beasts and Evolution: The Historical Status of Animals*, Vancouver BC: UBC Press, 2005.

44 See Boddice, *A History of Attitudes and Behaviours*.

45 See for instance: www.bedlamfarm.com/2017/01/19/animal-myths-animal-rights-animal-welfare-what-are-animals-for/, last accessed 7 March 2017.

46 www.animalliberationfront.com/Philosophy/ICAnimalStudies.htm, last accessed 7 March 2017.

47 Best, 'Rise (and fall) of critical animal studies'.

48 'Contradictory ideas and deliberate obfuscation': J. Sorensen, 'Introduction: thinking the unthinkable', in J. Sorenson (ed.), *Critical Animal Studies: Thinking the Unthinkable*, Toronto: Canadian Scholars' Press, 2014, xi–xxxiv, xvii.

49 Sorensen, 'Introduction', xix. See also Taylor and Twine, *Rise of Critical Animal Studies*, and D. McCance, *Critical Animal Studies: An Introduction*, Albany NY: SUNY Press, 2013.

50 H. Pedersen, 'Release the moths: Critical Animal Studies and the posthumanist impulse', *Culture, Theory and Critique* 52, 1 (2011): 65–81, 75, emphasis in original.

51 Wolfe, 'Human, all too human', 567.

52 An alternative approach to 'intellectual history', albeit convoluted, is provided by D. LaCapra, *History and its Limits: Human, Animal, Violence*, Ithaca NY: Cornell University Press, 2009.

53 S. Macintyre and A. Clark, *The History Wars*, Carlton VIC: Melbourne University Press, 2004; D.G. Boyce and A. O'Day (eds.), *The Making of Modern Irish History: Revisionism and the Revisionist Controversy*, London: Routledge, 2006; A. Murray, *The Imperial Controversy: Challenging the Empire Apologists*, Croydon: Manifesto Press, 2009.

54 See for instance S. Wolf, 'Beyond nonhuman animal rights: a grassroots movement in Istanbul and its alignment with other causes', *Interface* 1, 7 (2015): 40–69; N. Frambuesa, 'Intersectionality and the privilege of white vegan men', available at http://ninaframbuesa.weebly.com/ninaframbuesa/intersectionality-and-the-privilege-of-white-vegan-men, last accessed 4 March 2017.

55 R. Kahn, *Critical Pedagogy, Ecoliteracy, and Planetary Crisis: The Ecopedagogy Movement*, New York: Peter Lang, 2010.

56 T.G. Andrews, 'Contemplating animal histories: pedagogy and politics across borders', *Radical History Review* 107 (2010): 139–165, 151–152.
57 Andrews, 'Contemplating animal histories', 151–152.
58 Andrews, 'Contemplating animal histories', 152. See also C.G. Boggs, *Animalia Americana: Animal Representations and Biopolitical Subjectivity*, New York: Columbia University Press, 2013, 33.
59 Nance, *Historical Animal*, 16.
60 See for instance D. Dominguéz, 'At the intersection of animal and area studies: fostering Latin Americanist and Caribbeanist animal studies', *Humanimalia* 8, 1 (2016), available at www.depauw.edu/humanimalia/issue%2015/dominguez-a.html, last accessed 7 March 2017.
61 M. Bloch, *The Historian's Craft*, trans. P. Putnam, Manchester: Manchester University Press, 1992, 57.
62 C.S. Brown, *Big History: From the Big Bang to the Present*, New York: New Press, 2008; D. Christian, *Maps of Time: An Introduction to Big History*, Berkeley CA: University of California Press, 2004; F. Spier, *Big History and the Future of Humanity*, London, Chichester: John Wiley & Sons, 2015.
63 For such 'megahistory', consider J. Diamond, *Guns, Germs and Steel: The Fate of Human Societies*, revised edition, New York: Norton, 2005, or Y.N. Harari, *Sapiens: A Brief History of Mankind*, London: Vintage, 2011. For consilience see E.O. Wilson, *Consilience: The Unity of Knowledge*, London: Abacus, 1999.
64 P. Harrison and I. Hesketh, 'Introduction: evolution and historical explanation', *Studies in History and Philosophy of Biological and Biomedical Sciences* 58 (2016): 1–7, 6.
65 Best, 'Rise (and fall) of critical animal studies'.
66 P. Harrison, 'What was historical about natural history? Contingency and explanation in the science of living things', *Studies in History and Philosophy of Science Part C: Studies in History and Philosophy of Biological and Biomedical Sciences* 58 (2016): 8–16, 12–13.
67 Swart, '"But where's the bloody horse?"'; J. Burt, 'Invisible histories: primate bodies and the rise of posthumanism in the twentieth century', in T. Tyler and M.S. Rossini (eds.), *Animal Encounters*, Leiden: Brill, 2009, 159–170; S. Nance, *Entertaining Elephants: Animal Agency and the Business of the American Circus*, Baltimore MD: Johns Hopkins University Press, 2013.
68 See J. Balcombe, *What a Fish Knows: The Inner Lives of Our Underwater Cousins*, London: Oneworld, 2016; J. Ackerman, *The Genius of Birds: The Intelligent Life of Birds*, London: Corsair, 2016; R. Coppinger and L. Coppinger, *What is a Dog?*, Chicago IL: University of Chicago Press, 2016.
69 See for instance Despret, *What Would Animals Say*; D. Haraway, *Primate Visions: Gender, Race, and Nature in the World of Modern Science*, New York: Routledge, 1989; B. Latour, 'A well-articulated primatology: reflexions of a fellow-traveler', in S.C. Strum and L.M. Fedigan (eds.), *Primate Encounters: Models of Science, Gender, and Society*, Chicago IL: University of Chicago Press, 2000, 358–381.
70 See here, in general argument, D. Livingstone, *Putting Science in its Place: Geographies of Scientific Knowledge*, Chicago IL: University of Chicago Press, 2003, but also, as specific if diverse examples: E. Benson, *Wired Wilderness: Technologies of Tracking and the Making of Modern Wildlife*, Baltimore MD: Johns Hopkins University Press, 2010; R. De Bont, *Stations in the Field: A History of Place-based Animal Research, 1870–1930*, Chicago IL: University of Chicago Press, 2015; A. Guerrini, *The Courtiers' Anatomists: Animals and Humans in Louis XIV's Paris*, Chicago IL: Chicago University Press, 2015.
71 J. Derrida, *The Animal That Therefore I Am*, trans. D. Wills, New York: Fordham University Press, 2008.

72 Eitler, 'From animal history to body history', 272.
73 Eitler, 'From animal history to body history', 273–274.
74 T. Ingold and G. Palsson (eds.), *Biosocial Becomings: Integrating Social and Biological Anthropology*, Cambridge: Cambridge University Press, 2013.
75 Fudge, 'What was it like to be a cow?', 22.
76 Eitler, 'Animal History as Body History', 262.
77 I.H. Tague, *Animal Companions: Pets and Social Change in Eighteenth-Century Britain*, Philadelphia PA: Penn State University Press, 2015, 9.
78 Moore, *Capitalism in the Web of Life*, 48; Moore admittedly does not himself favour the term 'big history'.
79 A. Mikhail, *Under Osman's Tree: The Ottoman Empire, Egypt, and Environmental History*, Chicago IL: University of Chicago Press, 2017, 150.
80 Eitler, 'Animal history as body history', 261.
81 E. Benson, 'Animal writes: historiography, disciplinarity, and the animal trace', in L. Kalof and G.M. Montgomery (eds.), *Making Animal Meaning*, East Lansing MI: Michigan State University Press, 2011, 5.

Bibliography

Ackerman, J. *The Genius of Birds: The Intelligent Life of Birds*, London: Corsair, 2016.
Andrews, T.G. 'Contemplating animal histories: pedagogy and politics across borders', *Radical History Review* 107 (2010): 139–165.
Auerbach, A. *Mimesis: The Representation of Reality in Western Literature*, trans. W.R. Trask, Princeton NJ: Princeton University Press, 2013.
Balcombe, J. *What a Fish Knows: The Inner Lives of Our Underwater Cousins*, London: Oneworld, 2016.
Barry, A. and Born, G. (eds.) *Interdisciplinarity: Reconfigurations of the Social and Natural Sciences*, Abingdon: Routledge, 2013.
Becher, T. and Trowler, P. *Academic Tribes and Territories: Intellectual Enquiry and the Culture of Disciplines*, second edition, Buckingham: Society for Research into Higher Education and Open University Press, 2001.
Benson, E. *Wired Wilderness: Technologies of Tracking and the Making of Modern Wildlife*, Baltimore MD: Johns Hopkins University Press, 2010.
Benson, E. 'Animal writes: historiography, disciplinarity, and the animal trace', in L. Kalof and G.M. Montgomery (eds.), *Making Animal Meaning*, East Lansing MI: Michigan State University Press, 2011, 3–16.
Best, S. 'The rise (and fall) of critical animal studies', *Liberazioni: Associazione* (2013), available at www.liberazioni.org/articoli/BestS-TheRise(and%20Fall)ofCriticalAnimalStudies.pdf, last accessed 1 March 2017.
Best, S. 'The rise of critical animal studies: putting theory into action and animal liberation into higher education', *Journal for Critical Animal Studies* 7, 1 (2009): 9–52.
Bloch, M. *The Historian's Craft*, trans. P. Putnam, Manchester: Manchester University Press, 1992.
Boddice, R. *A History of Attitudes and Behaviours Toward Animals in Eighteenth- and Nineteenth-Century Britain: Anthropocentrism and the Emergence of Animals*, Lewiston NY: The Edward Mellen Press, 2008.
Boddice, R. 'The moral status of animals and the historical human cachet', *JAC* 30, 3/4 (2010): 457–489.
Boggs, C.G. *Animalia Americana: Animal Representations and Biopolitical Subjectivity*, New York: Columbia University Press, 2013.

Bondeson, J. *The Cat Orchestra and the Elephant Butler: The Strange History of Amazing Animals*, Stroud: Tempus, 2006.
Boyce, D.G. and O'Day, A. (eds.), *The Making of Modern Irish History: Revisionism and the Revisionist Controversy*, London: Routledge, 2006.
Braidotti, R. *The Posthuman*, Cambridge: Polity, 2013.
Breen, B. 'Animal history: an emerging scholarly trend', 29 October 2014, https://daily.jstor.org/animals-in-the-archive/, last accessed 1 March 2017.
Brown, C.S. *Big History: From the Big Bang to the Present*, New York: New Press, 2008.
Brown, F.L. *The City is More than Human: An Animal History of Seattle*: Seattle WA: University of Washington Press, 2016.
Burt, J. 'Invisible histories: primate bodies and the rise of posthumanism in the twentieth century', in T. Tyler and M.S. Rossini (eds.), *Animal Encounters*, Leiden: Brill, 2009, 159–170.
Calarco, M. *Thinking Through Animals: Identity, Difference, Indistinction*, Stanford CA: Stanford University Press, 2015.
Caras, R.A. *A Perfect Harmony: The Intertwining Lives of Animals and Humans Throughout History*, West Lafayette IN: Purdue University Press, 1996.
Castree, N. 'The Anthropocene and the environmental humanities: extending the conversation', *Environmental Humanities* 5, 1 (2014): 233–260.
Christian, D. *Maps of Time: An Introduction to Big History*, Berkeley CA: University of California Press, 2004.
Coppinger, R. and Coppinger, L. *What is a Dog?*, Chicago IL: University of Chicago Press, 2016.
Dear, M. 'Practicing geohumanities', *GeoHumanities* 1, 1 (2015): 20–35.
De Bont, R. *Stations in the Field: A History of Place-based Animal Research, 1870–1930*, Chicago IL: University of Chicago Press, 2015.
Derrida, J. *The Animal That Therefore I Am*, trans. D. Wills, New York: Fordham University Press, 2008.
Despret, V. *What Might Animals Say if We Asked the Right Questions?*, Minneapolis MN: University of Minnesota Press, 2016.
Diamond, J. *Guns, Germs and Steel: The Fate of Human Societies*, revised edition, New York: Norton, 2005.
Domínguez, D. 'At the intersection of animal and area studies: fostering Latin Americanist and Caribbeanist animal studies', *Humanimalia* 8, 1 (2016), available at www.depauw.edu/humanimalia/issue%2015/dominguez-a.html, last accessed 7 March 2017.
Eitler, P. 'Animal history as body history: four suggestions from a genealogical perspective', *Body Politics* 2, 4 (2014): 259–274.
Emmeche, C., Pedersen, D.B. and Stjernfelt, F. (eds.) *Mapping Frontier Research in the Humanities*, London: Bloomsbury, 2016.
Fagan, B. *The Intimate Bond: How Animals Shaped Human History*, New York: Bloomsbury, 2015.
Frambuesa, N. 'Intersectionality and the privilege of white vegan men', http://ninaframbuesa.weebly.com/ninaframbuesa/intersectionality-and-the-privilege-of-white-vegan-men, last accessed 4 March 2017.
Fudge, E. 'What was it like to be a cow? History and animal studies', in L. Kalof (ed.), *The Oxford Handbook of Animal Studies*, Oxford: Oxford University Press, 2017, 258–278.
Fukuyama, F. *The End of History and the Last Man*, London: Penguin, 2012.
Goodale, G. *The Rhetorical Invention of Man: A History of Distinguishing Humans from Other Animals*, Lanham MD: Lexington Books, 2015.
Guerrini, A. *The Courtiers' Anatomists: Animals and Humans in Louis XIV's Paris*, Chicago IL: Chicago University Press, 2015.
Harari, Y.N. *Sapiens: A Brief History of Mankind*, London: Vintage, 2011.

Haraway, D. *Primate Visions: Gender, Race, and Nature in the World of Modern Science*, New York: Routledge, 1989.

Harrison, P. 'What was historical about natural history? Contingency and explanation in the science of living things', *Studies in History and Philosophy of Science Part C: Studies in History and Philosophy of Biological and Biomedical Sciences* 58 (2016): 8–16.

Harrison, P. and Hesketh, I. 'Introduction: evolution and historical explanation', *Studies in History and Philosophy of Biological and Biomedical Sciences* 58 (2016): 1–7.

Howell, P. *At Home and Astray: The Domestic Dog in Victorian Britain*, Charlottesville VA: University of Virginia Press, 2015.

Ingold, T. and Palsson, G. (eds.), *Biosocial Becomings: Integrating Social and Biological Anthropology*, Cambridge: Cambridge University Press, 2013.

Ingram, D., Sethna, C., and Dean J. 'Introduction: *canamalia urbanis*', in J. Dean, D. Ingram, and C. Sethna (eds.), *Animal Metropolis: Histories of Human–Animal Relations in Urban Canada*, Calgary: University of Calgary Press, 2017, 1–28.

Kahn, R. *Critical Pedagogy, Ecoliteracy, and Planetary Crisis: The Ecopedagogy Movement*, New York: Peter Lang, 2010.

Kernan, A.V. (ed.), *What's Happened to the Humanities?*, Princeton NJ: Princeton University Press, 2014.

LaCapra, D. *History and its Limits: Human, Animal, Violence*, Ithaca NY: Cornell University Press, 2009.

Latour, B. 'A well-articulated primatology: reflexions of a fellow-traveler', in S.C. Strum and L.M. Fedigan (eds.), *Primate Encounters: Models of Science, Gender, and Society*, Chicago IL: Chicago University Press, 2000, 358–381.

Linzey, A. 'A sense of history', *The Animals' Agenda* 20, 2 (2000): 39.

Livingstone, D. *Putting Science in its Place: Geographies of Scientific Knowledge*, Chicago IL: University of Chicago Press, 2003.

Macgregor, A. *Animal Encounters: Human and Animal Interaction in Britain from the Norman Conquest to World War One*, London: Reaktion, 2012.

Macintyre, S. and Clark, A. *The History Wars*, Carlton VIC: Melbourne University Press, 2004.

McCance, D. *Critical Animal Studies: An Introduction*, Albany NY: SUNY Press, 2013.

McNeill, J.R. 'Observations on the nature and culture of environmental history', *History and Theory* 42, 4 (2003): 5–43.

McNeill, J.R. 'Introduction' in J.R. Richards, *The World Hunt: An Environmental History of the Commodification of Animals*, Berkeley CA: University of California Press, 2014, xi–xix.

Mikhail, A. *Under Osman's Tree: The Ottoman Empire, Egypt, and Environmental History*, Chicago IL: University of Chicago Press, 2017.

Moore, J.W. *Capitalism in the Web of Life: Ecology and the Accumulation of Capital*, London: Verso, 2015.

Murray, A. *The Imperial Controversy: Challenging the Empire Apologists*, Croydon: Manifesto Press, 2009.

Nance, S. *Entertaining Elephants: Animal Agency and the Business of the American Circus*, Baltimore MD: Johns Hopkins University Press, 2013.

Nance, S. 'Introduction', in S. Nance (ed.), *The Historical Animal*, Syracuse NY: Syracuse University Press, 2015: 1–16.

Nussbaum, M.C. *Not for Profit: Why Democracy Needs the Humanities*, Princeton NJ: Princeton University Press, 2016.

Pedersen, H. 'Release the moths: Critical Animal Studies and the posthumanist impulse', *Culture, Theory and Critique* 52, 1 (2011): 65–81.

Philo, C. and Wilbert, C. (eds.), *Animal Spaces, Beastly Places: New Geographies of Human–Animal Relations*, London: Routledge, 2000.

Plumb, C. *The Georgian Menagerie: Exotic Animals in Eighteenth-Century London*, London: I.B. Tauris, 2015.

Plumwood, V. *Environmental Culture: The Ecological Crisis of Reason*, London: Routledge, 2002.

Preece, R. *Brute Souls, Happy Beasts and Evolution: The Historical Status of Animals*, Vancouver BC: UBC Press, 2005.

Ritvo, H. 'Animal planet', *Environmental History* 9, 2 (2004): 204–220.

Ritvo, H. 'On the animal turn', *Daedalus* (Fall, 2007): 118–122, 121–122.

Rose, D.B., van Dooren, T., Chrulew, M., Cooke, S., Kearnes, M., and O'Gorman, E. 'Thinking through the environment, unsettling the humanities', *Environmental Humanities* 1, 1 (2012): 1–5.

Russell, N. *Social Zooarchaeology: Humans and Animals in Prehistory*, Cambridge: Cambridge University Press, 2012.

Santner, E.L. *On Creaturely Life: Rilke, Benjamin, Sebald*, Chicago IL: Chicago University Press, 2006, 12.

Sorensen, J. 'Introduction: thinking the unthinkable', in J. Sorenson (ed.), *Critical Animal Studies: Thinking the Unthinkable*, Toronto: Canadian Scholars' Press, 2014, xi–xxxiv.

Sörlin, S. and Warde, P. 'The problem of the problem of environmental history: a re-reading of the field', *Environmental History* 12, 1 (2007): 107–130.

Specht, J. 'Animal history after its triumph: unexpected animals, evolutionary approaches, and the animal lens', *History Compass* 14, 7 (2016): 326–336.

Spier, F. *Big History and the Future of Humanity*, London, Chichester: John Wiley & Sons, 2015.

Swart, S. '"But where's the bloody horse?" Textuality and corporeality in the "animal turn"', *Journal of Literary Studies* 23, 3 (2007): 271–292.

Sutter, P.S. 'The world with us: the state of American environmental history', *Journal of American History* 100, 1 (2013): 94–119.

Tague, I.H. *Animal Companions: Pets and Social Change in Eighteenth-Century Britain*, Philadelphia PA: Penn State University Press, 2015.

Taylor, N. and Twine, R. *The Rise of Critical Animal Studies: From the Margins to the Centre*, London: Routledge, 2014.

Tobias, M.C. and Morrison, J.G. *Anthrozoology: Embracing Coexistence in the Anthropocene*, Cham: Springer, 2017.

Vandersommers, D. 'The "animal turn" in history', *AHA Today*, 3 November 2016, available at http://blog.historians.org/2016/11/animal-turn-history/, last accessed 7 March 2017.

Velten, H. *Beastly London: A History of Animals in the City*, London: Reaktion, 2013.

Walker, B.L. 'Animals and the intimacy of history', *History and Theory* 52, 4 (2013): 45–67.

Weiner, D.R. 'A death-defying attempt to articulate a coherent definition of environmental history', *Environmental History* 10, 3 (2005): 404–420.

White, R. 'Environmental history: watching a historical field mature', *Pacific Historical Review* 70, 1 (2001): 103–111.

Wilson, E.O. *Consilience: The Unity of Knowledge*, London: Abacus, 1999.

Wolch, J. and Emel, J. (eds.), *Animal Geographies: Place, Politics and Identity in the Nature-Culture Borderlands*, London: Verso, 2000.

Wolf, S. 'Beyond nonhuman animal rights: a grassroots movement in Istanbul and its alignment with other causes', *Interface* 1, 7 (2015): 40–69.

Wolfe, C. 'Introduction' in C. Wolfe (ed.), *Zoontologies: The Question of the Animal*, Minneapolis MN: University of Minnesota Press, 2003, ix–xxiii.

Wolfe, C. 'Human, all too human: "animal studies" and the humanities', *PMLA* 124, 2 (2009): 564–575.

Wolfe, C. (2010) *What is Posthumanism?*, Minneapolis MN: University of Minnesota Press.

EPILOGUE

Harriet Ritvo

It has become commonplace to notice that the range of respectable subjects for humanistic scholarship has expanded over the last century or so. Other animals are (so far) the latest beneficiaries of this increasingly generous vision, with species thus following (as usual) in the wake of class, race, gender, and other axes of human differentiation. An analogous democratising tendency has also been manifest within the animal kingdom. Attention has transpired through the phylogenetic tree (or bush), so that scholarly scrutiny, which at first lingered on the charismatic megafauna who grace the logos of wildlife conservation societies and the equally charismatic (though smaller) domestic companions who represent humane advocacy organisations, now extends to such invertebrate fellow creatures as ants, octopi, and leeches. Or at least it does so in the most expansive reaches of multispecies ethnography and animal studies (a field that overlaps with animal history, although perhaps not as completely as the label might suggest). As the contributions to this volume show, most historians have tended to stick closer to taxonomic home, restricting their analyses to other vertebrates, other mammals, or other primates.

There are good reasons for this relatively (though far from absolutely) modest zoological reach, which reflects divergent disciplinary conventions regarding evidence and argument. But divergence does not signal indifference; as the names of subfields such as economic history and the history of technology indicate, historians routinely incorporate the insights offered and approaches offered by other disciplines. This volume demonstrates that animal–human historians are at least as open-minded as their colleagues. About a third of its chapters were contributed by scholars of geography, literary and cultural studies, and art history, and many of the chapters written by historians also engage issues raised by work in these ancillary fields or in the interdisciplinary field of animal studies. The most complex and intractable of these issues are theoretical, including the nature of agency, the consequences of representation, and the ineluctability of anthropomorphism. Such discussions tend to consider non-human animals in the abstract, so, somewhat paradoxically, the more intense they become, the less room there is for animals in the flesh. Consequently, in addition to their explicitly theoretical concerns, they implicitly broach a very pragmatic problem: how to ensure that animals themselves play a prominent role in animal history.

In a sense, of course, this concern reflects an issue inherent in the attempt to integrate non-human subjects into historical accounts that rely heavily on records written, or otherwise produced, by people (they have independent histories too, but those are usually retrieved by paleontologists and archaeozoologists); this is an extreme version of the challenges posed by attempts to retrieve the experience of humans who left relatively faint traces in the historical record. The contributions point to several possible solutions. Some, like Michael Guida's exploration of the role played by broadcast birdsong in twentieth-century Britain, offer concrete and focused examples. Others, like Liv Emma Thorsen's survey of the evidence provided by natural history museums, describe ways to expand the conventional range of historical sources. And a few, like Abigail Woods' discussion of the history of medicine, veterinary and otherwise, explicitly address the difficulty of decentring the human, even within work ostensibly focused on other animals.

The contributions also show that choices inevitably have negative as well as positive aspects; there is always at least one road not taken. The range of approaches that they illustrate is wide, but far from exhaustive. The decision to interrogate generalisations requires de-emphasis of the concrete; a focus on the richness and complexity of artistic representation can obscure the value of other kinds of sources. Animal–human history extends far beyond the North Atlantic rim, and long before the last two centuries. And interdisciplinarily inclined though they are, historians (other than historians of science and environmental historians) seem less likely to incorporate insights from science into their work, than insights from more closely allied areas. Thus Woods' essay is one of only three in this collection (the others are Robert Kirk's discussion of laboratory animals and the treatment of breeding by Neil Pemberton, Julie-Marie Strange, and Michael Worboys) to draw heavily on the non-humanistic disciplines mostly closely concerned with animals – zoology, veterinary medicine, natural history, environmental science, and agricultural science.

Such lacunae point to opportunities. At the same time that the essays collected here demonstrate the multiple disciplinary linkages of animal–human history, as well as, in their texts and their notes, the impressive work that has already been produced, they also demonstrate that many connections remain to be explored – many surfaces have only been scratched. Thus, although its historiography has become very lively and rich, the field is still opening up.

INDEX

actor–network theory 6–7, 11, 57, 62, 128–129, 148, 150, 201, 277, 525, 532; *see also* Science and Technology Studies
Adam and Eve 14, 280–291, 348; *see also* Eden, Garden of
Adams, Carol J. 232–234
Addison, Joseph 352
Adenauer, Konrad 111
Adorno, Theodor 60
Aelian (Claudius Aelianus) 290
Afghanistan 437–438
Agamben, Giorgio 510
agency: animal 5–16, 63–64, 81–91, 147–148, 159–160, 197–210, 253–254, 262–263, 299, 309–316, 351–358, 422–430, 435, 459–460, 480, 486–487, 522–524, 544; as resistance 205–207, 234–235, 311–313, 429, 487; concept of dependent agency 208, 210; in philosophy and political theory 198–201, 279, 351–352; in sociology and social theory 57–58, 199, 427; relational, networked or assembled theories of 6, 8–9, 12–13, 57–58, 60–62, 128–129, 172, 201–210, 234–235
Ahuja, Neel 35
Alberti, Samuel 177, 179
Aldrovandi, Ulisse 432–433
Alexander the Great 425, 510
Algeria 426
Allen, Martyn 452
Allsen, Thomas 451
Almond, Richard 453
Altdorfer, Erhard 281–284, 286
America, Spanish Conquest of 433; *see also* Columbian Exchange

American Civil War 424, 427, 428
anatomy, comparative 285, 302–303, 354, 379
Anderson, Perry 33
Anderson, Virginia DeJohn 454
Andrews, Thomas 529
Anglo-Saxons 452–453, 477, 502
Angola 31, 178, 285, 426
animal agriculture: dairy farming and milk consumption 153–154, 157–158, 186, 262, 331, 405–406, 458, 475, 479–481; factory farming 413, 476–481, 486–488, 504; intensive livestock farming 397–398, 405–413, 474–488; rare breeds 481
animal baiting 36, 40, 42, 54, 123, 230, 299, 305–306, 308, 325, 336, 386, 409, 452, 501–502, 545; bear-baiting 123, 230, 336, 409, 502; bull-baiting 305, 325, 409, 502; cockfighting 36, 40, 42, 230, 336; dog-fighting 305, 409
animal biographies/autobiographies 58, 203, 226, 228–229, 236–237
animal maiming 330–331, 334
animal rights 14, 19, 82, 90, 137, 152, 205, 207, 238, 253–254, 265, 277, 279, 298, 308, 315, 437, 503, 505, 509, 522–523, 526–529
animal studies 76, 78, 86, 88, 90, 121–122, 128, 197, 222–225, 234, 236, 309, 323, 336, 360, 395, 521–525, 543–544; Critical Animal Studies 205, 527–528
animal–human history: future of 529–533; overview 3–21; politics of 526–529; relation to animal studies 523–526
Animal Welfare Science (AWS) 10, 121, 130, 152, 206, 308, 524, 531

animals, cruelty and violence towards 14–15, 17–19, 35, 82, 298, 305–309, 322–337, 499–511
Ankeny, Rachel A. 133
Annales School 55–56, 323, 326, 368
Antarctica 44
anteaters 301, 307
Antebi, Laura 89
Anthropocene 487–488
anthropocentrism 6, 8, 10, 13–18, 58, 159, 197, 199–202, 204, 208–210, 225, 234–235, 254, 273–292, 431, 459, 522, 524–527
anthropology 6, 17–18, 20, 42, 127, 134, 200, 277, 432, 449, 456–457, 459, 524, 526–527, 531
anthropomorphism 13–14, 44, 225, 235–236, 273–292, 309, 312, 335, 430, 436
antivivisection movement 123–126, 132, 134–137, 149–151, 230–231, 238, 258–259, 306
ANZAC day, ANZAC spirit 79–82
apartheid 33, 43–47, 107
apes *see* primates
Appadurai, Arjun 176
aquariums 307, 313
Aquinas, Thomas 7, 277, 504, 506
archaeology 6, 87, 200, 278, 323–324, 394, 446, 452, 475, 483–484, 524, 526, 544
Archer, John 345
archives, in relation to animal–human history 4, 6, 20, 63, 88–91, 101, 111, 126–128, 171, 202, 259–260, 267, 323–324, 522, 524
Arctic 429
Ardrey, Robert 7, 33, 448
Argentina 476–477, 479, 482, 484
Aristotle 7, 57, 279, 352, 397
Arluke, Arnold 121
Armstrong, Philip 13, 235
Arnold, Matthew 237
art history 13, 251–268, 322–337, 544
art, animals and 3–4, 13, 20, 88–89, 101, 251–268, 327, 331, 544
Ashton, Paul 77
ASPCA (American Society for the Prevention of Cruelty to Animals) 36
assemblage theory 11, 201, 207–210, 525
Assmann, Jan and Aleida 101–103
Augustine of Hippo 499–500, 502, 504, 507
Australia 9, 31, 37, 41, 77, 79–83, 87–89, 183, 277, 528
Austria 108, 429, 437, 484

baboons 152, 308
bacteriology 123, 150–154
Baden-Powell, Lieutenant General Robert 380
badgers 453, 503
Baker, Steve 3, 252
Bakewell, Robert, agriculturalist and stock breeder 394–398, 403, 405, 407–408, 476, 478
Balcombe, Jonathan 78
Baldwin, Stanley 371
Baldy, captive chimpanzee, Bronx Zoo 273–278, 280, 290–291
Balfour, Clara 233
Bali 36
Ballantyne, R.M. 233
Balto, Alaskan malamute, deliverer of diptheria vaccine 79
Bandura, Albert 200
Barad, Karen 59
Barnum, P.T. 203, 222, 224, 310
Bartolomé de Las Casas 433
bats 346
Batten, Peter 307
Baumann, Oscar 108
BBC 368–369, 376–382
Bean, Charles, journalist 79
bears 31–32, 34, 37, 41, 58, 76, 88–89, 101, 107, 113, 123, 230, 301, 304–305, 313, 336, 461, 502–503; bear-baiting *see* animal baiting; *see also* polar bears
beavers 32, 37
Beer, Gillian 229
behaviourism, and animals 430, 435, 438
Bekoff, Marc 347
Belgium 371, 381
Belize 454
Bell, Charles, physiologist 124, 135, 149
Bell, Ernest, humanitarian and animal welfare campaigner 91
Bella, dog companion of poet Henrik Wergeland 172–173, 176–177, 180–181, 184
Belov, Pavel, Lieutenant-General, Russian army 426
Bender, Daniel 19
Benga, Ota, exhibited pygmy 273–278, 290–291
Bennett, Jane 201
Benson, Etienne 63
Bentham, Jeremy 230, 359, 527
Berger, John 14, 324
Berlin, Isaiah 34

Bernard, Claude, experimental physiologist 123, 135, 149
Best, Steve 200, 521, 527–528
Bethancourt, Jean de 433
Bewick, Thomas, naturalist 228
Biehler, Dawn Day 209
Billig, Michael 32
biocentrism 277
biomedicine 122, 128–130, 151–154, 477, 481
biopolitics and biopower 58, 63, 208
birds 38, 65, 100, 121, 158, 178–179, 203, 207, 226, 230, 291, 351, 356, 407–408, 413, 460, 487, 500, 503, 506, 508, 531, 544; canaries 130, 237, 425; chickens 18, 36, 157, 325, 407–408, 413, 475–476, 479–481, 486–487; ducks 306; eagles 31, 37, 58, 178; finches 240, 356, 377; hawks 453, 460, 503; kiwis 31; larks 371, 374, 380; nightingales 368, 360–362; parrots 284, 349, 503; penguins 32, 44; pheasants 457; pigeons 16–17, 80, 121, 130, 229, 306, 372, 394, 398, 407–408, 425; ravens 291; skuas 44; swans 278, 453
birdsong 16–17, 38, 367–382
birdwatching 368
Birke, Lynda 121
Birkhead, Tim 368
bison 39
black Americans 287, 433–434, 454; caricatures of 287
Black, Jeremy 86
Blaise of Parma 510
Bloch, Marc 529
Blue, Gwendolyn 63
Bluen, K-J. 43
boars 452–453, 501
Boddice, Rob 325, 523, 527–528
Boniface, St 484
Borneo 285
Bosch, Hieronymous 279
Bosnia 34
Bostock, Frank 313–314
Bostock's Menagerie 301
botanical gardens 173–174, 302
Bough, Jill 82
Boultbee, John, artist 327–378
Bourke, Joanna 369, 428
Bowie, Gavin 329
Bown, Nicola 238
boy scout movement 380
Bracciolini, Poggio 503
Bradley, Katharine Harris *see* Field, Michael
Brahmans, Brahmanism 487, 510

Braidotti, Rosi 225
Brancheau, Dawn 311
Brandt, Nick, photographer and conservationist 3–4, 20
Brandt, Willy 111
Brantley, Jessica 508
Brantz, Dorothee 5, 204
Braverman, Irus 302
Brazil 477, 479, 482, 484
breeding of animals 16–18, 32, 38–40, 64–66, 111–113, 132, 151, 182–183, 222, 230, 322, 393–413, 424–425, 474–486; captive breeding 111–113, 303–304; in Nazi Germany 38–40, 64–66; of laboratory animals 151; selective and scientific breeding 18, 38–40, 327–330, 393–413, 430–432, 474–466
Britain 12, 13, 21, 31, 40, 66, 83, 109, 136, 155–156, 175, 204, 287, 359, 423, 426, 437, 481, 484–485, 502, 504–511; affection towards animals in 322–337, 347–348; animal experimentation in 123–126, 149–154; animal welfare campaigns in 123–126, 251–268, 305–309; animals in Victorian literature 222–239; breeding of animals in 397–412, 476–479; hunting in 452–458; London 89, 123, 153, 174–175, 222, 226, 235, 251, 263–267, 300–304, 309–312, 316, 325, 327, 367, 373, 376, 381–382, 407, 485, 501–502; military dog training in 434–435; pets and petkeeping in 202, 208; political and public history in 56, 60, 77, 79–80, 88; rural violence against animals in 322–337; Scotland 34, 100, 301, 307, 327, 371, 402, 456; zoos and menageries in 174, 299–300, 305–316
British Empire 38, 425, 528
Brontë, Anne 233, 235
Brontë, Charlotte 235
Brontë, Emily 235
Brown Dog Riots, London 231
Brown, Duncan 42
Brown, Frederick 20
Brown, Laura 204
Brown, Robert 106
Browning, Elizabeth Barrett 237–239
Browning, Robert 229
Bruegel, Pieter, the Elder 279
Brueghel, Jan, the Younger 283–284
Buchan, John 233
Buckley, Arabella B. 228

Buddhism 279
Budras, Klaus-Dieter 111
Buffon, Comte de 356–357, 396
bull-baiting *see* animal baiting
Burdett-Coutts, Baroness Angela 266
Burke, Edmund 332
Burrows, Mrs E. 233, 236
Burt, Jonathan 254, 256, 531
Bush, George W. 79, 521
butchers and butchery 40–41, 231–232, 325, 330, 485, 502, 510; *see also* slaughterhouses and animal slaughter
Butler, Judith 237
Butler, Samuel 235

cabinets of curiosity 172–174
Caesar, Julius 425
Calarco, Matthew 19, 526
Calder, Angus 376, 378
Caldwell, Edmund, artist 251, 261, 263–267
Calhoun, John B. 133–134
Callinicos, Alex 199
Callon, Michel 6
camels and camelids 300, 425, 426, 428
Campbell, John 433
Canada 37, 222, 524–525
Canary Isles 433
Candelaria, Matthew 205, 209
capitalism 15, 18, 20, 324–327, 451; and animals 327, 330–332, 475–481, 486, 532
Captain Swing protests, Britain 332
Carboni, Raffaello 84
Carlyle, Jane Welsh 237–239
Carr, Raymond 456
Carroll, Lewis 226, 229, 235
Carruthers, Jane 107
Carter, Bob 62
Cartesianism 14–15, 198, 204, 279, 291, 349–350, 352, 354–355, 422, 438, 532; *see also* Descartes, René
Cartmill, Matt 448–449, 456–457
Cartwright, Lisa 253
Catron, Damon V., pig breeder 479
cats, domestic 12, 65, 100, 130, 136, 159, 203, 229, 322, 351, 394, 396, 475, 503
Caunce, Stephen 326, 335
cave paintings 278, 446, 460–461
celebrity animals 222, 309–313, 327–328
Chambers, Robert, naturalist 229
Charlemagne 453
Charles III of Spain 299
Charles V, Duke of Lorraine 424
Charles, Nicki 62

Chartism 83
Chase, Malcolm 326
Chaucer 332, 508
cheetahs 100
chickens *see* birds
chimpanzees 5, 13, 33, 273–278, 280, 285, 290–291, 302, 308–311, 313, 356, 432; *see also* primates
China 31, 183, 279, 476, 478–479, 484
Chomsky, Noam 292
Christianity 14, 18, 36, 80, 228, 234, 277, 280–286, 288–291, 322, 348–350, 352, 452, 483–484, 499–504
Cicero 279
circuses 14, 203, 206–207, 222, 224, 227, 276, 298, 300, 304–305, 309–316, 531
citizenship, and animals 32, 36, 44
Clare, John, poet 334
Clark, Ward M., hunting enthusiast 447
Clarke, Arthur C. 448
class relations 32, 36, 54–55, 83, 122, 125–126, 148, 150, 153, 183–185, 209, 231, 236–237, 305, 324, 348–349, 359, 378, 393–394, 403, 407–408, 502–503, 543; and hunting 453–456; in British rural history 324, 327–337
Clause, Bonnie Tocher 132
Clever, Iris 62
climate change 159, 481, 487
cloning of animals 413, 477, 481
Cobbe, Frances Power 124, 236
Cobbett, William 333–336
Cocker, Mark 369
cockfighting *see* animal baiting
Coke, Edward 406
Colam, John, RSPCA secretary 305
Cold War 41, 107, 426
collecting, cultures of 173–174
Colley, Ann C. 177
Colling, Charles and Robert, sheep breeders 397
colonialism 14, 36–37, 44, 54–55, 104–106, 108–110, 127, 148, 154–156, 231, 233, 262, 273, 290, 299–301, 426, 454, 460, 502; *see also* imperialism; postcolonialism
Columbian Exchange 474–477
Comaroff, Jean and John 42
companion animals *see* pets and petkeeping
Congo 31, 273
consciousness, of animals 5, 7
conservation of animals 6, 9–10, 14, 38, 43–43, 104–113, 262, 298, 302, 304, 315, 453, 455, 457, 543; rewilding 104, 112, 304

Convention concerning the Protection of World Cultural and National Heritage, 1972 101, 111
Cook, Captain James 262, 288–289
Cooper, Edith Emma *see* Field, Michael
Cooper, Thomas Sidney, artist 251, 328
Copeland, Marion 236
Corbey, Raymond 288
Corlett, Peter 80
Corvisier, André 427
Cosgrove, Dennis 108
Cosimo III de Medici 174
cosmopolitanism, and animals 8, 35
Cosslett, Tess 236
Costa Rica 477
cougars 308
Cowie, Helen 14
cows 32, 39–40, 65, 150, 153–157, 175, 203, 240, 322–323, 327–328, 332–333, 336, 393, 406–407, 413, 432, 461, 475–478, 480, 482, 486–488, 501–502, 504
Craw, Charlotte 41
crocodiles 229, 235
Cronin, Keri 13, 91, 203
Cronon, William 478, 482
Cruelty to Animals Act, 1835, Britain 306, 336
Cruelty to Animals Act, 1876, Britain 150–151
Csengei, Ildiko 353
Cuba 36, 433
cultural history 15, 56, 58, 171–177, 299, 360, 368, 382
cultural landscape 108
cultural studies 60, 336, 521, 543
Curtis, Perry 287
Cutrara, Samantha 252
Cuvier, Georges 409

Daly, Nicholas 230
Dalziel, Hugh, dog expert 402
Dana, Charles Loomis, neurologist 125
Dart, Raymond 448–449
Darwin, Charles 14, 31, 121, 158, 227–229, 234–236, 290, 359, 375, 394–398, 401, 430–431, 438, 460, 476, 532
Darwin, Erasmus 229
Daston, Lorraine 130–131, 134–136, 172, 175, 180–181, 183
Davidson, Jenny 395
Davis, Janet 36
Davis, Kathleen 502
Decroix, Émile, advocate of hippophagy 484

deep history 200, 210, 449, 474, 530–532
deer 278, 284, 325, 331, 453, 456–458, 461, 503–504
Deleuze, Gilles 201, 525
DeMello, Margo 236
Denmark 304, 478–479, 484
Derrida, Jacques 35, 57, 137, 222–223, 531
Derry, Margaret E. 395, 413
Descartes, René 14–15, 198, 279, 291, 349–350, 352, 354–355, 422, 438; *see also* Cartesianism
Descola, Philippe 277
Despret, Vinciane 61, 137, 205, 234–235, 504, 522
Dickens, Charles 226–228, 231–236
Digby, Simon 423, 426
DiNardo, R.L. 425–426
Dinzelbacher, Peter 203
disability studies 208, 237
diseases of humans 147–151, 152–157, 208, 263–267; bubonic plague 155; cowpox 247; diptheria 79; HIV/AIDS 152–153; malaria 158; smallpox 150
diseases of animals: East Coast Fever (thelleriosis) 155; foot and mouth disease 155; myxomatosis 158; rinderpest 154; Texas Fever 155; trypanosomiasis 155
diseases of zoonotic origin: anthrax 150, 153–154; BSE/CJD 11, 153–154; glanders 53; mallein 154; rabies and hydrophobia 153–154, 263–267; SARS (severe acute respiratory syndrome) 153; tuberculosis 153–154
Dizard, Jan 458
dogs 31, 44, 80, 100–101, 200, 203, 207–208, 227, 235–239, 279–280, 290, 299, 305, 322–325, 330–333, 455, 460, 475, 485–487, 501, 503, 509, 525, 531; and animal welfare campaigns 230–231, 255–259, 263–266, 305, 336; and public history 76, 82–86, 172, 176–186; dog fighting *see* animal baiting; dog shows 409–412; Dogs Act, Britain, 1906 151; dogs in war 17, 425–438; emotional attachments to 347–359; guard dogs 330–331; guide dogs 208; in experimental and veterinary medicine 124, 130, 132, 136, 149–159, 230–231; in Nazi Germany 54–56, 60, 65–66; individualised dogs 11, 79, 222–223, 238, 264–265; muzzling controversies 66, 153–154, 263–267; pedigree dog breeding 16–17, 153, 393–413
Dolly, cloned sheep 413, 477, 481

dolphins 35, 437
domestication of animals 18, 39, 56, 61, 111–112, 182–183, 207, 306; ancient domestication 111–112, 333, 394, 396, 431–432, 475, 484, 486; domestication as 'biological control' 11, 18, 477–478, 480–481, 486–488
Donald, Diana 3, 79, 255–256
Donaldson, Sue 207–208
Donovan, Josephine 234
Dorré, Gina 237
Doughty, Robin 230
Dror, Otniel 134
du Chaillu, Paul 233
Duncan, James S. 108
Durham Ox, celebrity Shorthorn bull 327–329, 336
Duverney, Joseph Guichard, anatomist 303
Dyck, Ian 333

Eckbert of Shönau, on meat-eating 506–507
eco-cosmopolitanism 8, 35
ecology 18, 108, 226, 455, 524
Eden, Garden of 14, 280–286, 288
Edison, Thomas 313
Egypt 80, 278, 280, 533
Ehrenreich, Barbara 459–460
Eisenmann, Stephen 253–254, 268
Eitler, Pascal 61, 63, 523, 531–532
Elden, Stuart 8
elephants 3, 178, 203, 206–207, 222, 224, 298–301, 303–305, 307–315, 357, 423, 425–426, 428, 531
Elgar, Edward 370
Elias, Norbert 232
Eliot, George 233
Emmett, Peter 87
emotion: emotion towards animals 10–17, 203, 225, 238, 332–337, 505–509; emotions of animals 134, 152, 158, 279, 313–315, 345–347, 351–352, 355–356, 359, 368, 374–376, 422, 430–431, 435–437, 482–483; history of emotions 15–16, 79–80, 84, 89, 133–137, 345–360, 353, 367–382, 428, 438
Engels, Friedrich 333–334
Enlightenment 11, 173, 234, 396
Enright, Kelly 206
environmental degradation 18, 105–106, 290, 481, 487–488
environmental history 5, 12, 14, 20, 78, 105, 323, 326, 523–525, 528, 532–533, 544
environmentalism 304, 326

Epstein, James 62
Ereky, Karl 482
Eslick, John, military dog trainer 429
ethics and animals 10, 19–20, 122, 129–131, 135–137, 152, 173, 230–231, 234, 279, 395, 528–529
ethology 5, 33, 121, 206–207, 209, 226, 347, 428, 436, 438, 524, 531
eugenics 65, 393–394, 478
Eureka Rebellion, Ballarat, Victoria, Australia 82–86
Eustache, St 452
Eustis, Dorothy Harrison, philanthropist and dog breeder 208
evolution and evolutionary theory 5, 7, 12, 16–17, 31–33, 61, 111–112, 121, 136, 158–159, 200, 206–207, 229, 279–292, 303, 345, 375, 396, 401, 430, 447, 460, 486–488, 530–532; and hunting 447–451, 459; and meat-eating 474–475, 488; and nationalism 32–33; and selective breeding 396, 486; ape and human evolution and anthropological anxiety 279–292; coevolutionary history 61; evolutionary biology 345, 449, 457, 530–531; evolutionary psychology 432
Ewart, James Cossar, biologist 402
Ewers, John C., ethnologist 432
Ewing, Juliana Horatia 233
exhibition, animals and 9, 11, 13–14, 80, 87–89, 171–186, 206, 222, 273–276, 290–291, 298–316, 327
exotic animal trade 305, 308
experimental animals 10, 11, 121–137, 544; drosophila fly 128–130, 132; standardisation of 132; Wistar Rat 132
experimental medicine 123–126, 147–152
extinction of species 100, 112–113, 460, 475, 488

Fagan, Brian 526
Fairlie, Simon 481
falconry 453, 460, 503, 508; see also birds
Falz-Fein, Baron 113
farming see animal agriculture
fascism 8–9, 32, 38–40, 54–57, 59, 64–66, 287, 369, 425, 483; see also Germany, Third Reich
Fasher, Harrie, artist 90
Febvre, Lucien 369, 382
feminism 125–127, 226, 233–234, 449, 521, 524
feminist history and feminist studies 78, 83, 127, 226, 234, 237, 449, 521, 524

Fenn, G.M. 233
ferrets 130, 158, 331
Ferrières, Madeleine 484
Field, Michael (Katharine Harris Bradley, with Edith Emma Cooper) 237–239
Findlen, Paula 173
Finn, Michael R. 125
fish 32, 38, 41–42, 203, 291, 329, 506, 531
Fisher, James, ornithologist 379
fishing 6, 454
Fitter, Richard, naturalist 381
Fitz Stephen, William, cleric 501
Fitzgerald, Amy 178
Fitzwygram, Frederick, Lt-General, horse expert 430
Flegel, Monica 233, 236
Flush, dog companion of Elizabeth Barrett Browning 238–239
Foster, Kate 179
Foster, Michael 149
Foucault, Michel 63, 122, 208, 231–232
Fox, Anselmo 4
foxes 34, 38, 130, 278, 334, 413, 453, 456–457
foxhunting 396, 408–409, 456
France 56, 280–281, 288, 300, 322, 406, 408, 426, 453, 501–503, 506; and military history 426–427; and World War I 371, 381–382; captive animals in 222, 300, 303, 309; cave painting sites 278, 447, 460–461; experimental medicine in 123–126, 149; horsemeat 484–485; Paris 123, 226, 231, 280–281, 322, 382, 485, 503, 506; slaughterhouses and abattoirs in 231, 482
Franklin, Adrian 456
Frederick II, Holy Roman Emperor, 'the Great' 299, 425
French, Richard D. 125–126
frogs and toads 100, 150, 151, 306, 334, 336, 485
Fudge, Erica 126, 202, 204, 254, 259, 267, 326, 522, 532
fur trade 454
Furedi, Frank 200
Fussell, Paul 371

Gainsborough, Thomas 331
Galen 397
Gallipoli campaign 76, 79–81
Galton, Francis 393
Gambia (Senegambia) 424
game laws 331, 453
game reserves 43, 104–105

Garstang, Walter, naturalist 369, 374–376, 382
Geertz, Clifford 36
Geisslern, Ferdinand, scientist 403
Gellner, Ernest 34
gender and sexuality 36, 54, 61, 122, 125–127, 148, 150, 233–238, 325, 359, 505, 543; gender studies 107; in relation to hunting 448–449, 451–456; in relation to nationalism 32, 36; medieval misogyny 501, 507–508; queer theory 233, 237, 521
genetics 16, 101, 105–106, 111, 128–129, 132, 151, 304, 394–395, 402–404, 412–413, 447, 478–481, 486, 543
geography, discipline of 8, 62, 88, 323, 326, 336, 521, 524, 526, 543
German Animal Protection Association 40
German, Alexei, film director 501
Germany 9, 38–41, 54–56, 58–60, 64–66, 101, 107–109, 149, 287, 300, 377, 382, 425, 434, 436–437, 482–486, 503; Berlin 4, 38–39, 58, 107, 300, 382, 482; Third Reich in 32, 38–40, 54–57, 59, 64–66
Gerson, Jean 506
Ghana 474
Giles, Katherine and Melanie 335
giraffes 100–101, 178, 304, 308, 315
Goa 299
goats 130, 261, 336, 476
Gombe Stream National Park, Tanzania 33
Gommans, Jos 428, 438
Goodall, Jane 33
Gordon, General Charles George 301
Göring, Hermann 39
governmentality 58, 66, 208
Grady, John 267
Grant, Robert 229
Great Ape Project 136, 308
Greece 426; ancient Greece 149, 278–280, 285, 422, 432, 451–452, 458, 484
Gregory III, Pope 484
Gregory, Kate 87
Grele, Ronald 77
Gresley, Thomas, stock breeder 476
Grey, Caroline Elizabeth 236
Greyfriars Bobby 100
Grier, Katherine 226
Griffin, Carl 14–15
Griffin, Emma 326, 458
Grzimek, Bernhard 109–111, 113
Grzimek, Michael 109
Guattari, Felix 201, 525
Guibert of Nogent 500

Guida, Michael 16, 544
Guilane, Jean 432
guinea pigs 130, 151, 306
Gustavus Adolphus of Sweden 425

Hagenbeck, Carl 112–113
Haggard, H. Rider 233
Haiti 433
Halbwachs, Maurice 101–102
Hall, Marcus 41
Hambletonian, racehorse 328–329
Hannibal 425
Hansen, Rikke 89
Harambe, captive gorilla, Cincinnati Zoo 308
Haraway, Donna 35, 59–60, 62, 127–128, 135, 184, 225, 288, 323–324, 330, 449, 475
Hardy, Thomas 235, 333, 402
Harrison, Beatrice, cellist 370–371, 373, 382
Harwood, Dix 325
Haupt, Heinz-Gerhard 56
Haussmann, Baron Georges Eugène 482
hawks *see* falconry
Heck, Heinz and Lutz, cattle breeders 38–40
Hegel, Georg Wilhelm Friedrich 199, 523
Heidegger, Martin 198
Helmreich, Stefan 225
Heng, Geraldine 502
Henning, Michelle 185
Henry de Bracton 500
Henry III of England 299
Henty, G.A. 233
Herder, Johann Gottfried von 7, 34–35, 38, 44
heredity, theories of 396–397
heritage *see* public history
Herzog, Werner 461
Hildrop, John, cleric 354–356
Hippocrates 397
hippopotamuses 11, 173–174, 302, 308
history and philosophy of science 122–123, 126–135, 299
Hitler, Adolf 40, 55, 60, 65, 425
Hobbes, Thomas 198–199
Holland, Steven Mark 81
Holtorf, Cornelius 112
Homer 17, 422
Horkheimer, Max 60
horses and equines 10, 111–113, 203, 226–227, 236–237, 286, 306, 349, 351–355, 393–394, 408, 413, 430, 432, 453, 455, 461, 475–476, 509, 531; donkeys 76, 80–82, 85, 278, 425; draught and working horses 175, 236–237, 259–260, 323, 326–327, 334–336, 405–406; horsemeat 18, 484–486; in experimental and veterinary medicine 124, 130, 148–151, 153–157; in Nazi Germany 39, 54, 56, 64–66; mules 424, 426; ponies 100; Przewalski's horse 10, 111–113; racehorses 16, 198, 328–330, 334–336, 358, 394, 397–398, 402, 405–406; war horses and cavalry horses 17, 80, 82, 89–90, 422–429, 437–438
Howell, Philip 11–12, 17–18, 66, 324, 326, 359, 525
Hribal, Jason 205, 312
Hudson, W.H. 334–335
Huffman, Brent 111
Hughes, J. Donald 451
Huisman, Michel, artist 101
human exceptionalism, doctrine of 349–351
humanism 19, 126, 197, 200, 234, 277, 292, 499, 522, 525–528; *see also* posthumanism
humanitarian movement 36, 90, 230–231, 262, 314, 358, 438, 485
humanities, and animal studies 12, 26, 76, 127, 137, 172, 180, 200, 225, 229, 253, 277, 521–522, 525–526, 530, 543–544
Hume, David 354–356
Humphreys, Jasper 43
Hungary 300, 452
Hunt, William Holman 322–323, 336
hunting 17–18, 31, 35, 55, 233, 239, 279–280, 325–326, 329, 331, 334, 336, 432–433, 446–461, 503–504; big game and trophy hunting 178, 182, 184, 230, 308, 446–447, 455–457; commercial hunting 446, 451, 454–455; hunters and hunter-gathering in prehistory 108, 110, 432, 447–450, 475, 484; poaching 39, 42–43, 325–326, 331–332, 334, 453–456, 458, 460; sport hunting 405, 451–452, 454–459; *see also* meat-eating
Hustain Nuruu Park, Mongolia 112
Huxley, Aldous 238
Huxley, Julian 369, 375, 377–378, 380–382
hyenas 306

imperialism 12–14, 54–55, 230, 233, 299–301, 315, 454; *see also* colonialism; postcolonialism
India 5, 55, 183, 233, 279, 423, 428, 455, 460
indigenous peoples 105, 110, 113, 155, 231, 233, 273–277, 285, 290, 433, 451,

454–455, 459; Native Americans 107, 432–433, 454–455
Ingold, Tim 333, 459
insects 4, 45, 128–130, 203, 209, 229, 235–236, 255, 279, 292, 351, 355, 458, 475, 510, 544; mosquitoes 225
interdisciplinarity, and animal studies 21, 226, 523–525, 543–544
International Union for Conservation of Nature 112
International Whaling Commission 35
intersectionality, and animal studies 13, 32, 529
Iran 437
Iraq 44, 521–522
Ireland 89, 287, 300, 423, 484, 528; emigration from 325, 333
Islam 40, 277, 423–424, 483, 501
Israel 436
Italy 11, 173–174, 433, 484, 485

Jackson Laboratory, Maine, USA 132–133
Jackson, Mark 369
Jacobs, T., dog breeder 401
Jamaica 433
James I of England 299
Janet, Pierre, psychologist 125
Japan 35–36, 287, 436, 477–478
Jenner, Edward, vaccination pioneer 150
Jews and Jewishness 40, 44, 65, 287, 377; *see also* Judaism
Jewson, Nicholas 122
Johnson, Sara 433
Johnson, Walter 197, 205
Jones, Karen 460
Judaism 14, 277, 286, 483, 500
Jumbo the elephant 203, 222, 224, 309–311

Kalof, Linda 178
kangaroos 32, 41
Kay, Jeanne 106
Kazakhstan 484
Kean, Hilda 9–10, 101, 126, 147, 210, 376
Keegan, John 427–428
Keeley, Lawrence 432
Kempe, Margery 19, 504–511
Kennel Club 182–183
Kenya 108–111, 304, 455
Kete, Kathleen 55, 226
Kheel, Marti 234
Kingsley, Charles 229
Kipling, Rudyard 229, 233
Kirk, Robert 10, 435, 544
Kirksey, Eben 225

Kiser, Lisa 509
Koch, Ludwig, naturalist, ornithologist 369, 375, 377–382
Koch, Robert 150, 153
Kohler, Robert 128–130, 136
Kosovo 437
Kron, Geoffrey 458
Kruger National Park, South Africa 43, 107
Kruger, Paul 107, 113
Kubrick, Stanley 448
Kuzya, Siberian tiger 31, 45
Kymlicka, Will 207–208
Kyrgystan 484

laboratories 148–152, 230–231, 258, 302, 330
laboratory animals *see* experimental animals
labour history 82–86
Lack, David, ornithologist and evolutionary biologist 379
Lamarck, Jean-Baptiste 396
Lambert, George 79
Lancaster, C.S. 457
landscape history and landscape studies 108, 326
Landseer, Edwin 3, 255–260, 265–266
language, and animals 290–292, 349, 351, 375
Lansbury, Coral 125
Latour, Bruno 57–58, 63, 128, 150, 201, 225, 277, 532
Law, Robin 424, 426
Lawrence, John 335
Lawson, Henry 79
Lazarus, Emma 205
Le Guin, Ursula K. 18
Leavis, F.R. 238
LeBlanc, Steven 432
Lederer, Susan 135
Lee, Robert E. 424
Leighton, Frederick 262
Lekan, Thomas 110
Leonelli, Sabina 133
leopards 31, 299
Leopold II, Grand Duke of Tuscany 173
Leopold, Aldo 277
Levinas, Emmanuel 237
Levine, George 224
Lewes, George Henry 226
Lien, Marianne Elisabeth 199
liminality 171–172, 181, 205, 207–209
Lindner, Rudi Paul 423
Lindsay, Walter Lauder 158
Linnaeus, Carl 14, 228, 284–285

Linzey, Andrew 527
lions 5, 31, 37, 46, 158, 299–300, 304–308, 312–313, 351, 447, 452, 457–458, 461, 511
literature, and animals 12–13, 222–239, 324, 521
Little, Clarence Cook 132
livestock 16–17, 32, 38–40, 65, 66, 148–150, 154–157, 203, 230, 306, 322–330, 393–398, 403–405, 413, 432, 476, 481, 488, 500
Lloyd, Henry Summers, military dog trainer 429–430, 435–436
Lochrie, Karma 507
Lonn, Ella 427–428
Lorenz, Konrad 33, 39, 44
Lorimer, Hayden 179, 326
Lorimer, Jamie 127
Louis XIV of France 300, 303
Lubow, Robert, experimental psychologist 430–431
Lydekker, Richard, natural historian 182–183
Lyell, Charles 229
Lynn, John A. 426

Mabey, Richard 369, 371
Macintyre, Stuart 83
Mackenzie, John 455
Magendie, Francois, experimental physiologist 123–124, 135, 149
Magnus, Albertus 460
Maimonides 277
Maitland, Sara 372
Malamud, Randy 253, 299, 302
Malcolmson, Bob 333
Mali 31, 424
Mandela, Nelson 37, 45
Mangum, Teresa 237
Manuel I of Portugal 299
Map, Walter, medieval writer 503–504
Marius, captive giraffe, Copenhagen Zoo 304
Markham, Gervase 335
Marlborough, 1st Duke of 425
Marryat, Frederick 234
Marshall, William, agriculturalist 329
Martin, Bessie 427–428
Martin, Richard 123, 230, 336
Martin's Act, 1822, Britain 230, 336
Marvin, Garry 304, 459
Marx, Karl 199
Masson, Jeffrey 308
Mastoris, Stephanos 333

material culture, in relation to animal–human history 11, 54, 62, 88–89, 128, 131–133, 148, 171–186, 201, 251–252, 254–256, 524
Matless, David 88, 326
Mattfield, Monica 203
Matthew Bible 281–282
Maud, Charles Theobald 322
McCarthy, Susan 308
McDonell, Jennifer 12–13, 524
McKenzie, Gayton, South African politician 42
McNeill, J.R. 523
McNeur, Catherine 205
meat-eating 35–36, 40–41, 66, 153–154, 157, 185–186, 232–234, 262, 304, 325, 333–334, 447–451, 459, 474–488; bushmeat 456, 474; horsemeat 484; relation to histories of hunting 17–18, 447–453, 456, 459–460; *see also* vegetarianism and abstention from meat-eating
Mechling, Jay 267
medical history 10–11, 121–123, 147–159, 544
memory collective, cultural, social 9–10, 101–103, 111
menageries 14, 280, 298–316
Mendel, Gregor 129, 394–395, 403, 413
Menely, Tobias 354
Mexico 476, 481, 484
Meynell, Hugo, foxhunting champion 408
mice 130, 132–133, 151
Michael, Mike 121
Michelet, Jules 205
Middle Ages 12, 14, 18–19, 54, 280, 288, 299, 423, 432–433, 452, 458, 484, 499–511
Midgley, Mary 238
Mikhail, Alain 532–533
military history 17, 126, 300, 422–438
Mill, John Stuart 226
Millais, John Everett 251
Miller, Daniel 186
Miller, John 233
Milton, John 372
Mirzoeff, Nicholas 253
Mitchell, W.J.T. 256
Mitchell, Timothy 225
modernity 6, 8, 13, 15–16, 18–19, 55, 105, 121, 239, 345, 368–373, 451, 456, 501–502, 511, 532
Möhring, Maren 65
Mongolia 112–113, 484

Montaigne, Michel de 15, 290, 350–352, 526–527
Monty Python and the Holy Grail 501
Moore, Jason W. 476, 523, 532
moral ecology of science 134–136
moral economy 129–130
moral sentiments and animals 353–355, 357–358, 371–372
Morgan, Mary 86
Morgan, T.H. 129
Morrison, David 437
Mozambique 43, 426
Mughal Empire 55, 428
Muir, John 277
Mullan, Bob 304
Murphey, Rhoads 428, 438
Myanmar 308, 438
Mynott, Jeremy 178–179

Nader, Ralph 479
Nagel, Thomas 346
Nance, Susan 204–209, 260, 267, 311, 524, 528, 531
Napoleon Bonaparte 89, 425, 482
Napoleon III 322
Napp, Cyrill F., abbot of Gregor Mendel's monastery 403
Nash, Catherine 105
nationalism, animals and 7–9, 31–46, 78–90, 104–105, 124, 309–310, 323, 325, 328, 333, 409, 485
national parks 9–10, 33, 43, 101, 106–111, 304
nativism, applied to animals 32–46, 58, 262
NATO 426, 437
natural history 11, 20–21, 37, 42, 121, 227–233, 263, 284, 288, 302, 306, 325, 355–357, 368–369, 374, 381, 396, 432–433, 521, 530–531, 544
natural history museums 11, 88–89, 171–181, 230
natural science 277, 530–531
nature: and hunting 456–460; Christian views of 348–349; conceptions of 12, 14–15, 17–18, 20, 127–128; nature–culture dualism and critique of 6, 9, 12, 62, 181–183, 200, 276–277, 323, 448–449, 456–457, 527, 531–532
Nazism *see* fascism
neo-vitalism 525
Nero, dog companion of Jane Welsh Carlyle 238–239
Netherlands, the 40–41, 101, 413
Neumann, Roderick P. 108–109

neuroscience 346, 431
New York Zoological Park *see* zoos
New Zealand 31, 77, 79, 235, 262–263
Nicholson, Max 369, 375–377, 380, 382
Nietzsche, Friedrich 38–39
Nigeria (Oyo Empire) 424
Nightingale, Leonard, artist 251, 261–263
Nim Chimpsky, chimpanzee 290
Nimmo, Richie 325
non-representational theory 201
Nora, Pierre 101
Norman Conquest of England 423, 452–453, 458, 502
Norway 11, 41, 175–176, 184–185, 484

Ocean Policy Research Foundation 36
octopuses 100, 291–292, 543
Okubo, Ayako 36
Oldfield, Josiah 487
Olivier, Laurence 373
Olson, Miles, hunting advocate 459
Olsson, P.O., zoologist 185
Olwig, Kenneth 41–42
One Health movement 11, 159–160
oral history 102, 156, 202, 324, 335
orangutans 41, 273, 275, 285, 308, 315
orcas 203, 311, 437
Orel, Vitezslav 395–396, 403
ornithology 375–376, 379
Ortega y Gasset 457
Orwell, George 367–368
Otter, Chris 18
otters 453
Ottoman Empire 423, 428
Ouida (Louise de la Ramé) 230, 237
Overy, Richard 369
Owen, Richard, comparative anatomist 302

Pachirat, Timothy 232, 483
Palestine 435
Paley, William 481
Palladino, Paolo 131
pandas 304
panthers 281, 306, 461
Paraguay 477
parapsychology 435–436
Parkes, Bessie Rayner 233
Pasteur, Louis 123, 150
Patchett, Merle 179
Patterson, Banjo 79
Paul Pry, dog, animal welfare icon 256–259
Paul, St 500
Pavlov, Ivan 134, 151–152
Pearson, Susan J. 202, 324

Pegg, Mark Gregory 423
Pemberton, Neil 16–17, 544
performativity theory 9, 54, 59–60, 66–67
performing animals 203, 227, 305, 313–315
Perkins, David 334
personhood, applied to animals 198–199, 203, 460
pests, animals as *see* vermin, animals considered as
Peter of Bruys 506
Peter of Cluny 506
pets and petkeeping 65, 100, 181, 208, 230, 234, 258, 288, 324, 331, 393, 395; and animal experimentation 132, 150–151; death and mourning 185, 237–239; emotional attachment to pets 14, 176–177, 183, 225–226, 345–360; individuation of companion animals 176–177, 203; medical and veterinary issues 153–159; pet industry and consumer products 175, 226, 480; scholarship on 11, 15, 148, 185, 201–202, 226, 233–234, 359, 503
phenomenology 198
Philippines 36, 299
Phillips, Gervase 17, 85
Philo, Chris 173
'Phineas, Charles', author of spoof animal history paper 197, 205
photography, and animals 3–4, 100, 135, 171, 178, 182, 222–223, 252, 255–256, 259–260, 302
physiology 123, 134, 149–152, 230, 302, 354
Pickering, Andrew 201
Pico della Mirandola, Giovanni 292
pigs 15, 18, 130, 152, 157, 203, 305, 232, 323–325, 332–336, 475–476, 478–482, 486, 501–502
Pillow, Gideon, American Civil War Brigadier 424
Pipaluk, captive polar bear, London Zoo 302–303, 311
Plamper, Jan 369
Plumwood, Val 234
Plutarch 290, 527
poaching *see* hunting
Poland 39
polar bears 32, 37, 76, 88–89, 302–303, 308, 311
Poliquin, Rachel 79, 177, 179–180, 183
politics, and animals 7–10, 31–46, 53–67; animals and political history 54–67, 368, 382; animals and political theory 57, 207

Pomponius, Marcus, Roman Consul 432
Pope, Alexander 348
Porphyry 527
porpoises 437
Porter, Roy 63
Portugal 299, 426
postcolonialism 10, 56, 104–107, 225, 233, 455
posthumanism 19, 85, 200–201, 225, 525, 528, 531; *see also* humanism
postmodernism 528
poststructuralism 326
Power, Emma 61
Pratt, Samuel Jackson 357
praxiography 9, 61
Preece, Rod 527
Premack, Ann and David 5
primates 13, 130, 135–137, 152–153, 158, 273–276, 279–281, 285, 288–292, 308, 431, 449–450, 531, 543; gibbons 292; gorillas 290, 308; monkeys 130, 135–137, 158, 279–281, 288–292, 305, 349, 503
primatology 121, 127–128, 226, 273, 432, 449, 531
Prince Edward Islands 44
property, animals and: animals as capital 15, 177, 199, 203, 327–330, 458; animals as collective or cultural property 9, 104, 129; animals as intellectual property 405
Prussia 21, 59, 484
Przewalski's horse *see* horses and equines
psychology 521; behavioural 151; comparative 226, 278, 346, 524; evolutionary 432
public history, and animals 4, 9–10, 76–91
Puerto Rico 36
Putin, Vladimir 31
Pycior, Helena 79
pygmies 13, 273–278, 291

quagga 402
Quinn, Michael 327

rabbits 38, 124, 158, 229, 401, 456, 506
rabies *see* diseases of zoonotic origin
raccoons 34
race and racism 32–34, 40–45, 55–57, 65, 122, 125–126, 148, 209, 228, 231, 233–234, 236–237, 273–276, 359, 394, 433, 454, 528, 543; relation to anthropomorphism 13–14, 286–287, 291; relation to animal breeding 17, 65, 403; whiteness and white supremacy 37, 41–45, 233, 302, 433, 454–455, 529

Index

Rader, Karen 132–133
Raffles, Sir Stamford 304
Rajamanner, Shefali 233
Rakestraw, Lawrence 104
Ramsdell, Charles 424, 426
Ramsden, Edmundo 133–134
Rangajaran, Mahesh 5–6
Ranke, Leopold von 54–56
Rasch, Halvor H., zoologist 176
Ratramnus, Abbot of Corbi 500
rats 76, 87–88, 130, 132, 151, 207, 209, 228–229, 367, 438
reason, capacity to, in relation to animals 352–353, 357, 499–500
Reddy, William 353, 369
Reich, Justin 106
Reiche, Charles, exotic animal dealer 308
reindeer 184–186
Reith, Lord John, BBC Director-General 370–373, 382
religion 228–229, 238, 288–291, 396, 484
Renaissance 11, 277, 279–284
Renan, Ernest 34
representation, animals and 8–9, 12–14, 53–54, 58–59, 63–64, 66–67, 90, 224–225, 251–268, 324, 544
reptiles 130, 275, 304, 431
Rhine, Joseph, parapsychologist 435–436
rhinoceroses 32, 42–44, 299–300, 461
Richards, I.A. 238
Richardson, Edwin H., military dog trainer 434–435
Richardson, Samuel 353
risk society 11
Ritvo, Harriet 21, 125, 228, 324, 326–327, 395, 398, 405
Robbins, Louise 19–20
Robertson, Philadelphia, Australian Red Cross 82
Rock, Melanie 63
Roman Empire 31, 54, 174, 279–280, 315, 351, 432–433, 451–452, 457, 484, 499
Romanticism and Romantic movement 11, 38–39, 44, 105, 108, 176, 334, 368–369, 371, 457
Rooney, Anne 453
Roscher, Mieke 8–9
Rose, Gillian 253
Rosenwein, Barbara 353, 369
Rothenberg, David 369
Rothfels, Nigel 171, 305, 369
Rousseau, Jean-Jacques 198, 353
Roux, Emile, bacteriologist 123

Royal Academy of Arts, Britain 251, 257, 260–263, 265, 322
Royal Humane Society, Britain 257
RSPCA (Royal Society for the Prevention of Cruelty to Animals), Australia 85
RSPCA (Royal Society for the Prevention of Cruelty to Animals), Britain 230, 251, 260–263, 265, 305–306, 308–309
Ruberg, Willemijn 62
rural crime and protest, in Britain 330–334, 454
rural history 14–17, 322–327, 332–327
Rüsen, Jörn 104–106
Ruskin, John 226, 229, 238–239, 322, 527
Russell, Edward 61
Russell, Nicholas 395, 403–405
Russia 31, 34, 41, 152, 425–426, 433, 436, 483
Rwanda 45

Sachs, Hans, folk poet 286
safaris and safari parks 14, 55, 110
Saint-Hilaire, Isidore Geoffroy, naturalist 484
Salcedo-Chourré, Tracy 107
Salisbury, Joyce 458, 460
Salisbury, Lord 45
Sally, captive chimpanzee, London Zoo 309–311, 313
Salt, Henry, humanitarian 91
Samson, Abbot of Bury St Edmunds 506
Samuel, Raphael 77, 82
Sanderson, John Burdon 149
Sandy, horse in Gallipoli campaign 80, 82
Saraiva, Tiago 8
Sardinia 432
Savi, Paolo 181
Sax, Boria 13–14
Schmitt, Cannon 229
Schongauer, Martin 279
Schuetze, Craig 225
'Schulte, Christiane', author of spoof animal history paper 197
Science and Technology Studies 6, 9–13, 57–59, 62, 128–129, 201, 210, 531
Scott, Matthew, keeper of Jumbo the elephant 203, 224
Scott, Shelly R. 198
Scott, Walter 452
Scruton, Roger 456
sea lions 41, 315, 437
Sea World, Orlando 311
seals 307
Seaman, Myra 510

Sebright, John Saunders, agriculturalist 398–399, 407
Sefton, horse, IRA victim 89
Sekula, Allan 256
Senegal (Senegambia) 424
SenGupta, Gunja 427
sentimentality and sensibility 15–16, 225, 237–239, 348, 353–358, 368, 373
Serbia 34
Serengeti national park 108–111
Serpell, James 326, 459, 503
service animals 207–208
Sewell, Anna 236–237
Sewell, William 199, 204
Shamu, captive orca 203
Sharp, dog companion of Queen Victoria 222–223
Shaw, David Gary 6, 61, 205
Shaw, Vero, dog fancier 401
sheep 38, 130, 152–153, 156–157, 184, 235, 279, 322–323, 329–330, 334–336, 394–397, 403–405, 413, 432, 481–482, 502
Shelley, Percy Bysshe 374, 487
Shepherd, J.A., artist 266
Sheridan, Philip, General 424
Shetler, J.B. 109
Sibly, Ebenezer, naturalist 355
Sidgwick, Henry 230
Simmons, Peter 485
Simpson, Jack, Gallipoli stretcher bearer 80–81
Singapore 107
Singer, Peter 3
Sisson, Mark, life style guru 450
Sjölander, David, taxidermist 178
slaughterhouses and animal slaughter 32, 40, 66, 154, 230–234, 327–328, 474, 478, 482–485, 487, 502–503; religious or 'ritual' slaughter 40, 483
slavery 36, 197, 205, 230, 236–237, 312, 424, 427, 433, 454, 528
Smellie, William, naturalist 355–356
Smith, Anthony 37
Smith, Arthur Croxton, dog trainer and breeder 430
Smith, Charles, artist 86
Smith, David 40
Smith, M.L.R. 43
Smithfield Market, London 231–234, 251
Snaebjörnsdóttir, Bryndis, artist 88–89
snakes 275–276, 280–281, 306
social history 12, 55–56, 122–126, 132, 135–136, 199, 299, 336, 368, 427–428

sociology 6, 101, 122, 127, 131–134, 200
South Africa 31, 37, 42–43, 45, 107, 153, 155, 402, 426, 428
Spain 31, 36, 299, 397, 433
Spate, Oskar 83
Specht, Joshua 521–523
speciesism 8, 234, 237–238, 526, 528
Speth, John 451
Spielmann, Marion Harry 258
Spivak, Gayatri Chakravorty 225
Spotte, Stephen H. 111
springbok 31, 37
squirrels 503
St Clair, Jeffrey 312
St Rimbert, missionary 500
Stanescu, James 237
Stanford, Craig Briton 450
Stearns, Peter 369
Steel, Karl 14, 18–19
Steinbrecher, Aline 61
Steinhart, Edward 455
Steinkrüger, Jan-Erik 9–10
Steinmetz, Willibald 56
Stephen, Leslie 226
Stevenson, Robert Louis 229
Strange, Julie-Marie 16–17, 544
Street, Sean 378
Striffler, Steve 480
Stubbs, George, artist 328–329
Stubby, WWI guard dog 79
Sturken, Marita 253
subaltern studies 56, 107, 225
Sudan 34, 301, 424
Sumeria 278
Sunter, Anne Beggs 85
Sutter, Paul 523
Swanson, Drew 197
Swart, Sandra 7–8, 44, 428, 431, 438, 524, 531
Sweden 178, 185, 484
Swift, Jonathan 286
Swinney, Geoffrey N. 89
Switzerland 152, 179, 484
Sykes, Naomi 446, 452–453, 458–459
Syria 406, 503

Taft, William Howard 276
Tague, Ingrid 15, 201–202
Tait, Peta 313
Tamen, Miguel 172
Tanner, Michael 238
Tanzania 33, 104–106, 108–111
tapirs 315

taxidermy 11, 76, 79, 88–89, 171–174, 176–184, 222, 226, 230
taxonomy 122, 173, 227–228, 284–285
Taylor, Frederick W. 132
Taylor, Nik 78
Tegetmeier, William 400–401, 408
telegony, theory of 402
Terrace, Herbert S., psychologist 290
territoriality 7–8, 33, 45
Theophrastus 527
theory of mind 347, 431
theriomorphism 44
theriophily 18
Theunissen, Bert 413
Thomas Cantilupe of Hereford, St 503
Thomas, Keith 4, 239, 325–326, 335
Thompson, E.P. 129, 331
Thompson, Flora 334
Thompson, Henry, poultry fancier 408
Thorne, Lorraine 333
Thorsen, Liv Emma 11, 544
Tiergarten, Berlin *see* zoos
Tiger, Lionel 33
tigers 31, 306, 311, 460
Tilikum, orca, Sea World 311
Tilley, Christopher 171
Todd, Kim 262
Todes, Daniel 134
Tolstoy, Leo 234
Tompkins, Ptolemy 280
toponymy 103, 106–107, 113
Topsy, captive killer elephant, electrocuted 313
Toung Taloung, captive elephant, London Zoo 301–302
Tozzetti, Giovanni Targioni, naturalist 173
Trentmann, Frank 58, 60, 62
Trotsky, Leon 34
Tsavo National Park, Kenya 304
Tsing, Anna 20, 225
Tuan, Yi-Fu 184–185, 345
Tucker, Abraham 12
Tucker, Charlotte Maria 228–229, 236
Tulp, Nicholas 285
Turkey 183
Turkle, Sherry 180
Turnbull, A.L., ornithologist 380
Turner, Nat 312

Udell, Monique 347
Ukraine 41
UNESCO 101, 108, 111
United Nations 45, 101, 108, 111
Universities Federation for Animal Welfare (UFAW) 130
Urbanik, Julie 86, 100
Uruguay 477
USA 35–36, 41–42, 44, 107, 159, 175, 197, 205–209, 226, 260, 397, 432, 458, 531; animal exhibition in 206–207, 273–276, 287, 300, 307–308, 311, 313–314; animals in food production in 477–483, 485; animals in military history in 424, 426, 435–438; Boston 300; Chicago 175, 276, 478; Cincinnati 308; Honolulu, Hawaii 311; New Orleans 307; New York 79, 175, 205, 273–275, 290, 308; Orlando 311; Philadelphia 300; political and public history in 56, 60, 77, 79, 91, 260; use of animals in experimental medicine in 132, 150, 152
USSR 34, 426, 436; *see also* Russia
utilitarianism 230

vaccination 150, 155–156, 158
Van der Watt, Lize-Marié 44
Vane-Tempest, Henry 328
vegetarianism and abstention from meat-eating 18–19, 90, 233–234, 474, 487, 504–511, 528
Verard Antoine 280–281, 284
vermin, animals considered as 32, 44–45, 65, 205, 209, 228, 262, 322, 324, 327, 446–447, 453, 508
veterinary medicine 10–11, 65–66, 147–159, 484, 524, 544
Vialles, Noelie 474, 482
Victoria, Queen 222–223, 239
Vietnam 426, 430, 437
visual methods in animal studies 3–4, 13, 251–268, 327, 332–337
vivisection 10–11, 59, 123–126, 132–137, 149–151, 230–231, 238, 258–259, 306, 350, 430
Vláčil, František 501
Voison, André, biochemist 480

Wagner, Richard 38–39
Wallace, Alfred Russell 229
Wallen, Martin 395, 408–409
walruses 178
Walsh-Smith, Joan, artist 86
Walsh, John Henry ('Stonehenge'), dog expert 399–400, 409–410
Walton, John R. 405
war, and animals 17, 18, 33, 35, 45, 65–66, 79–82, 89, 100, 207, 237, 368–382,

422–438, 484; in Algerian War of Independence 426; in Anglo-Boer War, 1899–1902 429; in Battle of Agincourt 412; in Crimean War 300, 434; in Falklands War 435; in Vietnam war 426, 430, 437; mine detection by animals 81, 435–438; *see also* World War I; World War II
Warburg, Aby 101–102
Warren, Sir Charles, Metropolitan Police Commissioner 265
Washburn, Sherwood 448, 457
water buffalo 100, 476
Waterton, Charles, naturalist 302
Watson, Hugh, cattle breeder 477
Watt, Isaac 235
Webb, L.A. 424
Webster, of Canley, animal breeder 476
Weis, Tony 476, 481
Weiskopf, Julie M. 104
Weismann, August, geneticist 402
Weismantel, Mary 202, 324
Wells, H.G. 229–230
Wergeland, Henrik, poet 176, 180
West Indies 433
whales 35, 437
Whatmore, Sarah 324, 333
Whelan, Yvonne 106
Whetham, Edith 322
White, Gilbert, naturalist 325
White, Richard 523
Wilberforce, William 230
Wilbert, Chris 173
wild animal trade *see* exotic animal trade
wilderness, conception of 20, 108, 110, 113, 452, 456–458, 527
wildness, conceptions of 18, 34, 39, 109–112, 205, 273, 276, 285–286, 313, 458–460, 501
Wiley, Bell Irvin 427–428
Wilk, Richard 454
William of Normandy, the Conqueror 423
Williams, Paul 84
Wills, W.H. 231
Wilson, E.O. 530
Wilson, Mark, artist 88–89
Wolfe, Cary 525, 528
wolves 58, 279, 431, 436, 447, 453, 457–458, 503
wombats 38
Wombwell, George 305
Wombwell's Menagerie 302, 305, 311

women's suffrage 238
Wood, J. Carter 324
Wood, Roger 395–396, 403
Woods, Abigail 10–11, 544
Worboys, Michael 16–17, 544
World War I 79–82, 88–89, 291, 368–371, 381, 425, 427, 434–435, 437, 485–486, 525
World War II 16, 35, 38–40, 65–66, 154, 157–158, 287, 367–369, 376–382, 425–427, 429, 435–436, 485
Wrangham, Richard 475
Wylie, Grace 276
Wynne, Clive 347

xenotransplantation 152

Yemen 406
Yosemite National Park 107
Youatt, William, dog expert 409–410
Young, Arthur, agriculturalist 398
Young, Thomas 358
Yugoslavia 438

Zammit, Jean 432
zebras 402
Zonarus, Greek historian 432
zoology 13, 39–40, 111, 173–174, 176, 178, 185, 226, 228, 233, 276, 301–303, 315–316, 374–375, 395, 524, 531, 543–544
zoomorphism 13–14, 273–292, 335
zoonotic diseases *see* diseases of animals; diseases of zoonotic origin
zoos 4, 13–14, 38–39, 41, 58, 101, 109, 111–113, 158, 203, 222, 230, 273–276, 280, 290–291, 298–316, 324; Audubon Zoo, New Orleans 307; BelleVue Zoo, Manchester 314; Berlin Zoo 4, 38–39, 58, 300; Bristol Zoo 300; Bronx Zoo, New York 273, 275; Brookfield Zoo, Chicago 276; Budapest Zoo 300; Cincinnati Zoo 308; Copenhagen Zoo 304; Dublin Zoo 300; Frankfurt Zoo 109; Franklin Park Zoo, Boston, 300; Jardin des Plantes, Paris 222, 300, 309; London Zoo 158, 174, 222, 300–304, 306–307, 309–311, 316, 375; Marseilles Zoo 300; Moscow Zoo 41; Munich Zoo 38; Philadelphia Zoo 300; Whipsnade Zoo 304
Zuckermann, Solly, anatomist and zoologist 435–436